Film Review
2005-2006

Film Review

2005-2006

JAMES CAMERON-WILSON

Founding father: F. Maurice Speed 1911-1998

Reynolds & Hearn Ltd
London

To Ian Paton, whose passion for the
cinema has re-ignited my own.

Acknowledgements

The author would like to express his considerable
thanks to the following, without whom this book
would have been an even greater labour of love:
Charles Bacon, Reuben Barnes, Sarah Barrett, Eva
Birthistle, Ewen Brownrigg, Joel Finler, Gwyneth,
Marcus Hearn, Tony Hillman, Wendy Lloyd, David
Miller, Scot Woodward Myers, Daniel O'Brien,
Damien O'Donnell, Carolynn Reynolds, Richard
Reynolds, Jonathan Rigby, Mansel Stimpson
(especially), Jayne Trotman, Jo Ware and
Derek Winnert.
Thank you all.

Faces of the Year and Film World Diary pictures:
Rex Features
In Memoriam pictures: The Joel Finler Collection
All other pictures © their respective distributors

First published in 2005 by
Reynolds & Hearn Ltd
61a Priory Road
Kew Gardens
Richmond
Surrey TW9 3DH

© James Cameron-Wilson 2005

A CIP catalogue record for this book
is available from the British Library.

ISBN 1 905287 01 1

Designed by James King.

Printed and bound in Great Britain by Biddles Ltd,
King's Lynn, Norfolk.

Contents

Introduction

You really mustn't believe what you read in print. Much has been made of the decline in cinema attendances this year. Yet, hand-in-hand, the cult of celebrity continues unabated. A dichotomy, no? Well, Neal Gabler in the *Los Angeles Times* observed that far more people will 'read, hear or joke' about Tom Cruise and Katie Holmes than will see *War of the Worlds* or *Batman Begins*.

True, but then cultural landmarks have always been more heard about than engaged in (try James Joyce's *Finnegan's Wake* or Stephen Hawking's *A Brief History of Time*). It's unfortunate, though, that Gabler cites *War of the Worlds* and *Batman Begins* as neglected blockbusters. In fact, *War of the Worlds* has made more money in North America than any previous Tom Cruise film (worldwide it has grossed well over $588 million). And *Batman Begins*, while an initial disappointment commercially, went on to exceed expectations. At the time of writing, it is the third highest grossing film of 2005 in the US.

True, fewer cinemagoers turned out to the multiplex in the summer of 2005 than in the previous year. And, true, Tom Cruise's obsessive courting of Katie Holmes became a global obsession. But that doesn't support Gabler's argument. He went on to remark that more people will know about the romantic entanglements of Brad Pitt and Angelina Jolie than will have seen *Mr. and Mrs. Smith*. Again, he chose the wrong film to support his case. *Mr. and Mrs. Smith* happens to be the most successful film that either Brad or Angie has made, which suggests that the gossip-mongering did no harm at all to the movie's performance.

Gabler's point is that people today seem to be more interested in the stars than in seeing their movies. Again, he's rather off the mark. As the legendary gossip columnists Hedda Hopper, Louella Parsons and Liz Smith knew only too well, their readers couldn't get enough dirt on the likes of Bette Davis, Joan Crawford or Marilyn Monroe. The difference today is that, without the major studios' imperial guard, it's harder to hide the truth. While Cruise initially denied having romantic interests in either Penélope Cruz or Katie Holmes, the long-nosed cameras of the paparazzi begged to differ. And so, eventually, the truth did out.

The thing about celebrities is that because we *do* watch their movies, they become like our friends, only on a much bigger scale. We watch them; we read about them; we dream about them. *Of course* we're interested in their private lives. The difference today is that with the increasing availability of websites, cable channels and trash mags, the stars are more prominent than ever. And as the celebrity soap operas become more visible, so does the public appetite. Which is precisely why films like *War of the Worlds*, *Batman Begins* and *Mr. and Mrs. Smith* have done so well. The summer's big turkeys – primarily *The Island* and *Stealth* – had little flagrant grist to their mills. Cinemagoers are no longer content with car chases and video games. They want personalities. Sadly, though, there are just not enough real stars to go around.

James Cameron-Wilson
August 2005

Top 20 UK Box-Office Hits
July 2004 – June 2005

1. Shrek 2
2. Star Wars: Episode III – Revenge of the Sith
3. Bridget Jones: The Edge of Reason
4. The Incredibles
5. Meet the Fockers
6. Spider-Man 2
7. Shark Tale
8. War of the Worlds
9. Hitch
10. I, Robot
11. Batman Begins
12. Lemony Snicket's A Series of Unfortunate Events
13. Ocean's Twelve
14. Robots
15. Mr. and Mrs. Smith
16. The Bourne Supremacy
17. The Hitchhiker's Guide to the Galaxy
18. The Village
19. Dodgeball: A True Underdog Story
20. The Polar Express

Shrek and Fiona celebrate their commercial success

Top 10 Box-Office Stars
Star of the Year: Will Smith

With six-and-a-half animated films in the top twenty, movie stars are finding it harder and harder to make an impression at the box-office. True, Garfield: The Movie has live performers (Breckin Meyer, Jennifer Love Hewitt), but its central figure is animated, providing Bill Murray an opportunity to hone his vocal sarcasm above and beyond those heavy-lidded eyes. Will Smith played a cleaner fish in the charmless Shark Tale, a film that, relatively, was a bigger hit in the UK than in the US. And although a cartoon, its vocal stars were afforded major billing, a phenomenon that must have Robin Williams fuming, considering what little financial and promotional recompense he got for Disney's phenomenally successful Aladdin (1992).

It's hard to measure the influence Will Smith had on the box-office of Shark Tale, but with Hitch and I, Robot also in the top ten, there's no denying that Will is our Man of the Year. Hugh Grant was placed second last year and with the astonishing success of Bridget Jones: The Edge of Reason, still retains his grip on this list. Meanwhile, Ben Stiller proved to be a potent second to Will Smith, thanks to his continuing popularity in Meet the Fockers and Dodgeball, while Ewan McGregor was omnipresent as a Jedi, robot and pigeon. Runners-up include Julia Roberts, George Clooney, Orlando Bloom, Clive Owen, Leonardo DiCaprio, Keanu Reeves, Jennifer Lopez, Tom Hanks and Colin Firth.

2. Ben Stiller
3. Ewan McGregor
4. Jim Carrey
5. Renée Zellweger
6. Hugh Grant
7. Brad Pitt
8. Matt Damon
9. Tom Cruise
10. Mike Myers

Releases of the Year

This section contains details of all the films released in Great Britain from 1 July 2004 to the end of June 2005 – the period covered by all the reference features in this book.

Leading actors are normally credited with the roles they played, followed by a summary of supporting players. Where an actor further down a cast list is of special interest then his/her role is generally credited as well.

For technical credits the normal abbreviations operate, and are as follows: Dir – for Director; Pro – for Producer; Ex Pro – for Executive Producer; Co Pro – for Co-Producer; Ass Pro – for Associate Producer; Line Pro – for Line Producer; Scr – for Screenwriter; Ph – for Cinematographer; Ed – for Editor; Pro Des – for Production Designer; and M – for composer.

Abbreviations for the names of film companies are also obvious when used, such as Fox for Twentieth Century Fox, and UIP for Universal

International Pictures. The production company (or companies) is given first, the distribution company last.

Information at the foot of each entry is presented in the following order: running time/ country of origin/year of copyright/ date of British release/British certification.

Reviewers: Charles Bacon, Ewen Brownrigg, James Cameron-Wilson, Wendy Lloyd, Scot Woodward Myers, Frances Palmer, Mansel Stimpson and Derek Winnert

Star ratings

★★★★★ **Wonderful**
★★★★ **Very good**
★★★ **Good**
★★ **Mediocre**
★ **Insulting**

Aaltra ★★

Engaged in a fracas with his neighbour Gus, Ben is given 30 minutes to get to his desk in Paris or lose his job. Deliberately obstructed by Gus (who's driving a tractor) on his way to the station, Ben misses his train. Returning home, he finds his wife being serviced by another man and decides to unleash his anger and frustration on Gus. During the ensuing scuffle, both men get caught up in the tractor's machinery and both lose the use of their legs... A grimy, bitter and ugly film shot in a grey, smudged black-and-white, *Aaltra* has to be one of the most depressing experiences of the year. From the cheerless countenance of its leading men (whose expressions never vary), to the bleak landscapes of France, Belgium and Finland, *Aaltra* is unremittingly grim. Only half way through does it become apparent that it is actually a comedy, a nod to the acerbic oeuvre of Aki Kaurismäki and Jan Bucquoy (both of whom appear in cameo roles). There may be some dour cultists who will get a chuckle out of this, but the primitive production values may put even them off. JC-W

• *M. 'Ben' Vives* Benoît Delepine, *'Gus'* Gustave Kervern, *with* Michel De Gavre, *Aaltra boss* Aki Kaurismäki, Jason Flemyng, Benoît Poelvoorde, Noël Godin, *lover* Jan Bucquoy, Pierre Carl, Robert de Houx, Isabelle Delépine, Isabelle Girard.

• *Dir* and *Screenplay* Benoît Delepine and Gustave Kervern, *Pro* Vincent Tavier, Guillaumew Malandrin and Adriana Piasek-Wanski, *Ph* Hugues Poulain, *Pro Des* Isabelle Girard, *Ed* Anne-Laure Guégan.
La Parti/Moviestream/OF2B-Gala.
93 mins. Belgium. 2004. Rel: 3 December 2004. Cert. 15.

Adam & Paul ★★★½

Dublin; today. Comedy in despair. Poetry of the gutter. Or possibly *Trainspotting* reinvented by Samuel Beckett. This is a minimalist, almost existential black comedy shot for next to nothing in one of the most miserable places on earth. When our two protagonists wake up in the middle of a field, with Adam glued to a mattress, we can feel these men's desolation. Adam and Paul are dirty, unshaven, homeless and addicted to heroin. Paul is covered in horrific sores and is biorhythmically challenged. He walks into a scooter and is always the first to be clouted by a stranger. Adam is the 'brains' of the partnership, a ghostly scarecrow resembling a Gallagher brother after a night on the town. Constantly on the scrounge for money and their next 'hit,' Adam and Paul are the unseen victims of society and their film really shows the horror of what it means to be homeless. It's not just that they're cold and hungry; they are denied their dignity, where even the act of relieving themselves becomes a monumental problem. While there's caustic humour aplenty, Mark O'Halloran's script allows no false flickers of sentimentality. Just as we warm to Adam and Paul, they mug a boy with Down's syndrome. JC-W

• *Adam* Mark O'Halloran, *Paul* Tom Murphy, *Janine* Louise Lewis, *Georgie* Gary Egan, *Marian* Deirdre Molloy, *Orla* Mary Murray, *Bulgarian man* Ion Caramitru, *Clank* Gerry Moore, *with* Paul Roe, Thomas Farrell, Ian Cregg, Anthony Morris, Ray Meade, Anita Reeves.

• *Dir* Lenny Abrahamson, *Pro* Jonny Speers, *Ex Pro* Ed Guiney and Andrew Lowe, *Screenplay* Mark O'Halloran, *Ph* James Mather, *Pro Des* Padraig O'Neill, *Ed* Isobel Stephenson, *M* Stephen Rennicks, *Costumes* Sonia Lennon, *Sound* Nikki Moss.

Speers Film/Element Films/Bord Scannán na hÉireann/
Irish Film Board-Guerilla Films.
86 mins. Ireland. 2004. Rel: 3 June 2005. Cert. 15.

Ae Fond Kiss ★★★★

Not a fist is raised nor a gun is pulled, yet the emotional
violence in this pertinent film is virtually palpable. The power
of Ken Loach's dramatic attack is that because he creates such a
naturalistic stage he can take the audience anywhere and they
will believe him. His trick is that he casts non-professionals
in parts that are close to their own characters and that he can
get decent performances out of them. Here, he has selected
part-time model and post-grad student Atta Yaqub for the lead
role of Casim, a second generation Pakistani from Glasgow.
Due to be married in seven weeks to a Pakistani cousin he
has never met, Casim falls for Roisin, a white Catholic music
teacher a few years his senior. Something between them
'clicks' and before they know it they are embroiled in an
intense relationship – before, even, Roisin knows that Casim
is engaged to someone else… Unlike other films that explore
the Pakistani community in Britain, *Ae Fond Kiss* employs
humorous observation rather than caricature to enrich its
characters, a device that reaps dramatic dividends when things
turn sour. The performances are exemplary (Eva Birthistle, a
professional actress, is a real find) and the climate of intolerance
frighteningly credible. JC-W

• *Casim Khan* Atta Yaqub, *Roisin Murphy* Eva Birthistle, *Tariq
Khan* Ahmad Riaz, *Sadia Khan* Shamshad Akhtar, *Tahara Khan*
Shabana Bakhsh, *Rukhsana Khan* Ghizala Avan, *Wee Roddie*
David McKay, *Big Roddie* Raymond Mearns, *Danny* Gary Lewis,
Hammid Shy Ramzan, *Annie* Emma Friel, *with* Karen Fraser,
John Yule, Ruth McGhie, Jacqueline Bett.

A cultural affair: Eva Birthistle
and Atta Yaqub in Ken Loach's
frighteningly credible *Ae Fond
Kiss* (from Icon)

• *Dir* Ken Loach, *Pro* Rebecca O'Brien, *Ex Pro* Ulrich Felsberg,
Screenplay Paul Laverty, *Ph* Barry Ackroyd, *Pro Des* Martin
Johnson, *Ed* Jonathan Morris, *M* George Fenton; Mozart;
'Strange Fruit' sung by Billie Holiday, *Costumes*
Carole K. Millar.

Sixteen Films/Bianca Films/Tornasol Films/Matador
Pictures/Scottish Screen/Glasgow Film Office/National
Lottery-Icon.
104 mins. UK/Italy/Germany/Spain/France. 2004.
Rel: 17 September 2004. Cert. 15.

Afterlife ★★★½

Deeply humane and with superlative acting from Lindsay
Duncan and Paula Sage in particular, this film bravely tackles
uncommercial subject matter. It focuses on the plight of a
21-year-old with Down's Syndrome (Sage) when her mother
(Duncan), who has devoted her life to her daughter, discovers
that she is dying of cancer. Equally central is the theme of
euthanasia, but here the screenplay seems dangerously unsure
of how to express itself and, indeed, of what to say. The film
suffers accordingly, but the power of Duncan's final scene is
remarkable and the acting achievement of Sage, herself a victim
of Down's syndrome, must be an inspiring example to others
in her situation. At the very least, the film should promote
passionate discussion about the issues touched on. MS

• *May* Lindsay Duncan, *Kenny* Kevin McKidd, *Roberta*
Paula Sage, *George Wilkinshaw* James Laurenson, *Ruby* Shirley
Henderson, *Lucy* Fiona Bell, *with* Anthony Strachan, Emma
D'Inverno, Eddie Marsan, Isla Blair.

• *Dir* Alison Peebles, *Pro* Catherine Aitken and Ros Borland,
Ex Pro Steve McIntyre and Angus Wilkie, *Screenplay* Andrea
Gibb, *Ph* Grant Scott Cameron, *Pro Des* Jacqueline Smith,
Ed Colin Monie, *M* Paddy Cunneen, *Costumes* Rhona Russell.

New Found Film/Scottish Television/Grampian Television/
Gabriel Films-Soda Pictures.
104 mins. Scotland. 2003. Rel: 13 August 2004. Cert. 15.

After the Sunset ★★½

A pair of jewel thieves (Brosnan and Hayek) apparently retire
to the Caribbean after one last big score. However, the FBI
agent whom they humiliated during their last job follows them
to Paradise and becomes their personal serpent, offering both
knowledge and temptation in the form of the one diamond that
'got away'… Intentionally or not, this comes off as a sequel to
The Thomas Crown Affair, with Hayek and Harrelson subbing
for Rene Russo and Denis Leary. Hayek provides ample sex
appeal but Harrelson lacks the charm and intelligence to sell
his fallen FBI agent persona. SWM

• *Max Burdett* Pierce Brosnan, *Lola Cirillo* Salma Hayek,
Stan Lloyd Woody Harrelson, *Henri Moore* Don Cheadle, *Sophie*
Naomie Harris, *Rowdy Fan* Chris Penn, *Agent Stafford* Mykelti
Williamson, *Zacharias* Obba Babatundé, *Jean-Paul* Russell
Hornsby, *Agent Kowalski* Rex Linn, *Luc* Troy Garity, *with* Rex
Linn, Michael Bowen, Shaquille O'Neal, Gianni Russo, Jeff

Garlin, Lisa Thornhill, Kate Walsh, Paul Benedict.

• *Dir* Brett Ratner, *Pro* Tripp Vinson, Jay Stern and Beau Flynn, *Ex Pro* Patrick Palmer, Toby Emmerich and Kent Alterman, *Screenplay* Paul Zbyszewski and Craig Rosenberg, from a story by Zbyszewski, *Ph* Dante Spinotti, *Pro Des* Geoffrey Kirkland, *Ed* Mark Helfrich, *M* Lalo Schifrin, *Costumes* Rita Ryack.

New Line Cinema/Firm Films/Contrafilm and Rat Entertainment-Entertainment.
97 mins. USA. 2004. Rel: 19 November 2004. Cert. 12A.

The Alamo ★

Texas; 1836. Remember *The Alamo*? Well, not this version, anyway, for this murky-looking and mostly boring movie is a totally unmemorable remake of the 1960 John Wayne movie, without any of the excitement or spectacle. It's an attempt to make a gritty, realistic 'modern' movie, but it just comes over as a dreary plod with a few unintentional giggles. Billy Bob Thornton, Jason Patric and Patrick Wilson are monotonous and uninspired as reluctant Texan heroes whose tragic fate is to try to hold out against a vast, mighty Mexican force. Just when his career started to spark up again, Dennis Quaid's inanimate and pompous performance comes close to being risible; he plays Sam Houston, the founder of Texas who finally defeated the Mexicans after The Alamo had fallen (and thus turned a famous tale of American defeat into a victory after all!). Emilio Echevarria slices the ham as Mexican dictator Santa Ana while Billy Bob's violin fiddling while The Alamo burns is a hysterical moment worthy of Monty Python. And, wow, this seems a long haul at two hours 20 minutes! DW

• *General Sam Houston* Dennis Quaid, *Davy Crockett* Billy Bob Thornton, *Colonel James 'Jim' Bowie* Jason Patric, *Lt. Col.*

William Barret Travis Patrick Wilson, *General Antonio López de Santa Anna* Emilio Echevarría, *Captain Juan Seguín* Jordi Mollà, *Sgt. William Ward* Leon Rippy, *with* Tom Davidson, Marc Blucas, Robert Prentiss, Laura Clifton, Emily Deschanel, W. Earl Brown, Tom Everett, Rance Howard, Matt O'Leary.

• *Dir* John Lee Hancock, *Pro* Mark Johnson and Ron Howard, *Ex Pro* Todd Hallowell and Philip Steuer, *Screenplay* Hancock, Leslie Bohem and Stephen Gaghan, *Ph* Dean Semler, *Pro Des* Michael Corenblith, *Ed* Eric L. Beason, *M* Carter Burwell, *Costumes* Daniel Orlandi, *Choreography* Jerry Evans, *Fiddle coach* Craig Eastman.

Touchstone Pictures/Imagine Entertainment-Buena Vista International.
137 mins. USA. 2004. Rel: 3 September 2004. Cert. 12A.

Alexander ★½

A pretty Macedonian king decides to conquer the world... Poor Alexander. Deemed great by history, he has been systematically abused by Hollywood. First there was the plonking *Alexander the Great* (1956) with Richard Burton, then Oliver Stone squandered $150 million to present him as an Irish nancy boy, while potentially the best film about him – Baz Luhrmann's version with Leonardo DiCaprio and Nicole Kidman – was abandoned. And so to Oliver Stone. An intermittently interesting director, Stone had some nice ideas here and some great ingredients, but the resultant borscht is nothing short of indigestible. Talking of borscht, the Russian accent adopted by Angelina Jolie as Olympias is indicative of the film's lack of focus. She was Greek, by Zeus. And so was Alex, so why has Colin Farrell kept his Dublin brogue, forcing poor Val Kilmer (who has already lost one eye) to brush up his Irish burr? Poor enunciation, unwieldy flashbacks (and jumps forward) and Jared Leto's Pythonesque death scene add to the utter misery and bum-

Mexican standoff: Billy Bob does Davy Crockett in John Lee Hancock's disappointing *The Alamo* (from Buena Vista International)

shifting. Shapeless, tedious, camp and above all self-indulgent and overlong, this is an utter travesty. JC-W

• *Alexander* Colin Farrell, *Olympias* Angelina Jolie, *Philip* Val Kilmer, *Hephaistion* Jared Leto, *Roxane* Rosario Dawson, *Ptolemy* Anthony Hopkins, *Aristotle* Christopher Plummer, *Cassander* Jonathan Rhys Meyers, *with* Brian Blessed, Tim Pigott-Smith, Gary Stretch, John Kavanagh, Nick Dunning, Marie Meyer, Rory McCann, Féodor Atkine, Robin Lane Fox.

• *Dir* Oliver Stone, *Pro* Thomas Schühly, Jon Kilik, Iain Smith and Moritz Borman, *Ex Pro* Paul Rassam and Matthias Deyle, *Co-Ex Pro* Gianni Nunnari and Fernando Sulichin, *Screenplay* Stone, Christopher Kyle and Laeta Kalogridis, *Ph* Rodrigo Prieto, *Pro Des* Jan Roelfs, *Ed* Tom Nordberg, Yann Herve and Alex Marquez, *M* Vangelis, *Costumes* Jenny Beavan, *Choreography* Piers Gielgud, *Historical Consultant* Robin Lane Fox.

Warner/Intermedia Films/Pathé Renn/Gordian Prods-Warner. 175 mins. France/UK/Netherlands/Germany/USA/Italy. 2004. Rel: 7 January 2005. Cert. 15.

Driving women crazy: Jude Law in the title role of Charles Shyer's obsolete *Alfie* (from UIP)

Alfie ★★

Alfie Elkins is a Cockney bounder working as a limousine driver in Manhattan, dedicating his life to the hedonistic pleasures that his salary will allow, making sure that he never gets tied to one woman for too long… What a great idea for a movie. Take Alfie, the amoral womaniser played by Michael Caine in the 1966 film of the same name, and transplant him into the 21st century. And then let him combat all the sexual tripwires of the new millennium: Aids, the morning-after pill and the shadow of Germaine Greer. What a terrific film that would make. But this isn't it. But then everything about this neon-lit, glossed-up version of Lewis Gilbert's original is smugly off-key. Far from dragging Alfie Elkins into a brave new world, the remake struggles to rebuild him from scratch in a city that has passed him by. This is retro-chic, weighed down by all the clichés that that implies. Alfie, who manipulates a woman's heartstrings like a diabolical puppeteer, flashes a killer smile that ends up shooting blanks. With 'a lighter touch' diluting the edginess of the original and a sitcom humour force-fed into the proceedings, the film is like a social dinosaur all dressed up with nowhere to go. Even sadder, it's not even funny or sexy. JC-W

• *Alfie Elkins* Jude Law, *Julie* Marisa Tomei, *Marlon* Omar Epps, *Lonette* Nia Long, *Dorie* Jane Krakowski, *Nikki* Sienna Miller, *Liz* Susan Sarandon, *with* Jeff Harding, Kevin Rahm, Max Morris, Gedde Watanabe, Jo Yang, Renée Taylor, Julienne Davis, Anastasia Griffith, Deborah Lynn-Shyer, Marjan Neshat, Finlay Robertson, Stephen Gaghan, Paul Brooke.

• *Dir* Charles Shyer, *Pro* and *Screenplay* Shyer and Elaine Pope, from the play Alfie by Bill Naughton, *Ex Pro* Diana Phillips and Sean Daniel, *Ph* Ashley Rowe, *Pro Des* Sophie Becher, *Ed* Padraic McKinely, *M* Mick Jagger, David A. Stewart and John Powell; songs performed by Mick Jagger, David A. Stewart, UnAmerican, Joss Stone, Nadirah 'Nadz' Seid, Dumstruk, Gary 'Mudbone' Cooper, The Impressions, Teddy Pendergrass, The Isley Brothers, N.E.R.D., The Beach Boys, Wyclef Jean, The Righteous Brothers, etc, *Costumes* Beatrix Aruna Pasztor.

Paramount-UIP. 105 mins. USA. 2004. Rel: 22 October 2004. Cert. 15.

Alien vs. Predator ★½

The Bitch is back and this time she's got competition. Two thousand feet beneath the surface of the Antarctic ice a 'heat bloom' has been detected and billionaire industrialist Charles Bishop Weyland wants to be the first to discover its source. Recruiting the usual mix of racially balanced scientists, archaeologists and engineers, Weyland sets off to the South Pole and is surprised to find a subterranean pyramid bearing the hallmarks of Aztec, Cambodian and Egyptian culture. But far from being a pre-Ice Age Atlantis, the enormous structure appears to be a terrestrial battleground for rival aliens… Nice idea, laughable outcome. From the moment that ice guide Sanaa Lathan is surprised by an inaudible helicopter, the film gallops through the *Jurassic Park*/*Sphere* template and refuses to recover. A combination of ostentatious sound effects, dispensable characters and dumb dialogue is one thing, but a scare-free showdown between two such horror veterans is unforgivable. FYI: Lance Henriksen played the android 'Bishop' in *Aliens* and *Alien³*. Here he plays Charles 'Bishop' Weyland. Wow. JC-W

• *Alexa Woods* Sanaa Lathan, *Sebastian De Rosa* Raoul Bova, *Charles Bishop Weyland* Lance Henriksen, *Graeme Miller* Ewen Bremner, *Maxwell Stafford* Colin Salmon, *Mark Verheiden* Tommy Flanagan, *Joe Connors* Joseph Rye, *Adele Rousseau* Agathe De La Boulaye, *with* Carsten Norgaard, Sam Troughton, Petr Jákl.

• *Dir* and *Screenplay* Paul W.S. Anderson, from a story by Anderson, Dan O'Bannon and Ronald Shusett, *Pro* John Davis, Gordon Carroll, David Giler and Walter Hill, *Ex Pro* Wyck Godfrey, Thomas M. Hammel and Mike Richardson, *Ph* David Johnson, *Pro Des* Richard Bridgland, *Ed* Alexander Berner, *M* Harald Kloser, *Costumes* Magali Guidasci, *Visual Effects* John Bruno, *Creature Effects* Alec Gillis and Tom Woodruff Jr, *Original Alien design* H.R. Giger.

Fox/Davis Entertainment/Brandywine/
Inside Track 2 LLP-Fox.
100 mins. UK/Czech Republic/Canada/Germany/USA.
2004. Rel: 22 October 2004. Cert. 15.

The Amityville Horror ★★★

'Houses don't kill people,' notes George Lutz. 'People kill people.' Therein lies the power at the heart of *The Amityville Horror* phenomenon. Following the best-seller, the 1979 movie and its three sequels, now comes the inevitable remake. Based on the 'true story' in which George and Kathy Lutz move into 112 Ocean Avenue in Amityville, Long Island – only to find the house haunted – the film works because we're made to care for the tormented family. Kathy's first husband has died and she is trying to build a new life with George, a handsome, witty and charming building contractor who's doing his level best to connect with his new wife's three kids. So, when the house starts turning these nice people against each other, we share their nightmare. As remakes go, it could've been a lot worse. Apart from the hokey prologue and some lapses in continuity, the film is well made and doesn't overplay its hand. Ryan Reynolds is an engaging presence as George, while the fleeting apparitions maintain a note of constant unease. Only Melissa George as Kathy sounds a discordant note. The actress is 28 but looks much younger, which makes it a stretch to believe she has three kids and is on her second marriage. JC-W

• *George Lutz* Ryan Reynolds, *Kathy Lutz* Melissa George, *Billy Lutz* Jesse James, *Michael Lutz* Jimmy Bennett, *Chelsea Lutz* Chloë Grace Moretz, *Lisa* Rachel Nichols, *Father Callaway* Philip Baker Hall, *Jodie Defeo* Isabel Conner, *realtor* Annabel Armour.

• *Dir* Andrew Douglas, *Pro* Michael Bay, Andrew Form and Brad Fuller, *Ex Pro* Ted Field and David Crockett, *Co-Ex Pro* Steven Whitney, Paul Mason, Randall Emmett and George Furla, *Screenplay* Scott Kosar, based on a screenplay by Sandor Stern, based on the book by Jay Anson, *Ph* Peter Lyons Collister, *Pro Des* Jennifer Williams, *Ed* Christian Wagner and Roger Barton, *M* Steve Jablonsky, *Costumes* David Robinson.

MGM/Dimension/Michael Bay/Platinum Dunes/
Radar Pictures-Fox.
89 mins. USA. 2005. Rel: 15 April 2005. Cert. 15.

Anacondas:
The Hunt for the Blood Orchid ★½

The original *Anaconda*, which was released in 1997 with Jennifer Lopez, Jon Voight and Owen Wilson, was abysmal. And this hokey follow-up is no better – although, like the first, the rainforest is an impressive co-star. Still, the premise is not all bad. Alerted to the existence of a life-enhancing orchid, a motley group of pharmaceutical goons heads to the Borneo jungle (where, incidentally, the largest snake is actually the reticulated python) to capture the *perrenium mortalis*, which only blooms once every seven years. However, the anaconda has beaten them to it, and because the snake only stops growing when it dies, the immortal properties of the *mortalis* has allowed it to develop to spectacular proportions... Why, oh *why?* The facts don't add up, the snake looks like a CGI reject and only healthy bouts of unintentional laughter can keep this one afloat. Thankfully, top-liner Johnny Messner (*Operation Delta Force 4*) sets the right tone, adopting a Clint Eastwood whisper and providing an uncanny impression of a B-movie hunk. JC-W

• *Bill Johnson* Johnny Messner, *Sam Rogers* KaDee Strickland, *Dr Jack Byron* Matthew Marsden, *Cole Burris* Eugene Byrd, *Gail Stern* Salli Richardson-Whitfield, *Dr Ben Douglas* Nicholas Gonzalez, *Tran* Karl Yune, *CEO* Dennis Arndt, *Gordon Mitchell* Morris Chestnut.

• *Dir* Dwight H. Little, *Pro* Verna Harrah, *Ex Pro* Jacobus Rose, *Screenplay* John Claflin, Daniel Zelman and Michael Miner, from a story by Hans Bauer, Jim Cash and Jack Epps Jr., based on a screenplay by Bauer, Cash, Epps and Ed Neumeier, *Ph* Stephen F. Windon, *Pro Des* Bryce Perrin, *Ed* Marcus D'Arcy and Marc Warner, *M* Nerida Tyson-Chew, *Costumes* Terry Ryan, *Visual Effects* Dale Duguid.

Screen Gems/Middle Fork-Columbia TriStar.
96 mins. USA. 2004. Rel: 12 November 2004. Cert. 12A.

Anatomy of Hell ★★

An anonymous woman in a nightclub makes a bizarre proposition to a homosexual stranger. She will pay him to watch her 'where I'm unwatchable.' Reluctantly, he agrees... Following *Romance*, *A ma Soeur* and now this, Catherine Breillat has established herself as the most challenging, confrontational and daring director working in France today. Along with *Last Tango in Paris* and *Intimacy*, Breillat's *Anatomy of Hell* is the most intimate and candid study of a sexual liaison ever captured on film. Except Mlle Breillat goes one step further. She has hired a professional porn star to play her male protagonist and is unstinting in her close-ups of genitalia and sexual action. Even so, the film is defiantly untitillating, portraying female flesh, visually and verbally, as an unsightly, repellent organism of function and suppuration. Not so much misogynistic as sexually misanthropic, this is uncomfortable viewing, sometimes thought-provoking and almost poetic in its psychological dissection. It also errs towards pretension and a profound unpleasantness. JC-W

• *the woman* Amira Casar, *the guy* Rocco Siffredi, *young girl* Carolina Lopes, *Amira Casar's body in close-up* Pauline Hunt, *narrator* Catherine Breillat.

• *Dir* and *Screenplay* Catherine Breillat, from her novel *Pornocratie*, *Pro* Jean-François Lepetit, *Ph* Yorgos Arvanitis, Guillaume Schiffman, Miguel Malheiros and Susana Gomes, *Art Dir* Pedro Sá Santos, Jean-Marie Milon, Paula Szabo and Pedro García, *Ed* Pascale Chavance and Frédéric Barbe, *Costumes* Valérie Guegan, Betty Martins, Catherine Meillan and Sanine Schlumberger

Flach Film/CB Films/Canal Plus-Tartan Films.
77 mins. France. 2003. Rel: 26 November 2004. Cert. 18.

Media moron: Will Ferrell does his shtick in Adam McKay's puerile
Anchorman: The Legend of Ron Burgundy (from UIP)

Anchorman:
The Legend of Ron Burgundy ★★

In the days before cable, people believed what they heard on
the news and the news king of San Diego in the 1970s was one
Ron Burgundy. Then a woman was hired as a fellow newscaster.
So the employees of the Channel Four newsroom had to invent
a new name ('it's anchor*man*, not anchor*lady* – it's a medical
fact!') and fan their flames of male chauvinism... Working
from his own script in collaboration with director and fellow
Saturday Night Live alumnus Adam McKay, Will Ferrell has
created a fertile character and milieu in the vain, bombastic
Ron Burgundy and his bigoted news team. Ferrell is a very
funny man and is surrounded by reliable support, but the film's
reliance on puerile slapstick and bad taste doesn't add up to
much. There are some noteworthy sequences (an enraged Jack
Black kicking Burgundy's dog off a bridge, for instance), but
more often than not the humour is obvious and downright
moronic. JC-W

• *Ron Burgundy* Will Ferrell, *Veronica Corningstone* Christina
Applegate, *Brian Fantana* Paul Rudd, *Brick Tamland* Steve
Carell, *Champ Kind* David Koechner, *Ed Harken* Fred Willard,
Garth Holliday Chris Parnell, *Helen* Kathryn Hahn, *Wes
Mantooth* Vince Vaughn, *with* Fred Armisen, Danny Trejo,
Holmes Osborne, Shira Piven, Laura Kightlinger, *custodian*
Adam McKay, Judd Apatow, Luke Wilson, *and* (uncredited)
Jack Black, Tim Robbins, Ben Stiller, Missi Pyle.

• *Dir* Adam McKay, *Pro* Judd Apatow, *Ex Pro* Shauna
Robertson and David O. Russell, *Co-Pro* David Householter,
Screenplay McKay and Will Ferrell, *Ph* Thomas Ackerman, *Pro
Des* Clayton R. Hartley, *Ed* Brent White, *M* Alex Wurman;
songs performed by Cornelius Brothers and Sister Rose, Friends
of Distinction, Neil Diamond, Bill Withers, The Isley Brothers,
Marty Robbins, Marc Ellis, Tom Jones, The Newbeats, Hall &
Oates, Kansas, etc, *Costumes* Debra McGuire.

DreamWorks/Apatow-UIP.
94 mins. USA. 2004. Rel: 10 September 2004. Cert. 12A.

Andrew & Jeremy Get Married ★★★

Andrew is 49, a former bus driver, heroin addict and convict.
He hails from Croydon, South London, enjoys clubbing and
admires films like *The Matrix*. Jeremy is two decades his senior

and is a professor and writer. He was born in India, emerged
from the closet in his fifties and loves art, poetry, ballroom
dancing and Latin versions of *Hamlet*. Jeremy and Andrew have
been a couple for five years and, in spite of their differences,
got married in May 2004. When writer-director Don Boyd
stumbled across the couple at a dinner party hosted by Hanif
Kureishi, he was struck by their contrasting personalities.
How could two men from such opposite backgrounds and with
such contradictory tastes – not to mention the age difference
– decide to spend the rest of their lives together? It is to Don
Boyd's credit that his subjects are so natural and candid for the
camera. Produced for the BBC by Charles Sturridge and the
director's own daughter Clare, the film is excellent, humanist
television. On the big screen, though, the grainy photography
and short running time suggests that this was rushed into
cinemas merely to capitalise on the new rage for fly-on-the-wall
documentaries. JC-W

• *with*: Andrew Thomas, Jeremy Trafford, Hanif Kureishi,
Jean de Paul, etc.

• *Dir* and *Screenplay*, Don Boyd, *Pro* and *Ph* Don and
Clare Boyd, *Ex Pro* Charles Sturridge and Nick Fraser,
Ed Kate Spankie.

Firstsight Films/BBC-Tartan Films.
72 mins. UK. 2004. Rel: 29 April 2005. Cert. 15.

Angel On the Right ★★

Humour doesn't always travel well and this is particularly
the case with Tajikistani humour. Supposedly a powerful and
darkly comic tale of the nature of man, solitude and religion,
Angel On the Right failed to prompt a single titter in the house.
It is a poetic fable, and boasts top-rate production values, but
its power lurks in the more obscure regions of the Tajikistani
psyche. The director's brother, Maruf Pulodzoda, plays the
central character, a strutting thug who looks like he's escaped
from a Hollywood B-movie. He's a dour, amoral lug who
returns to his Tajikistani village in the hope of selling his
mother's home to pay off his debts. His mother, a wry but
saintly figure, knows his game and pretends to be at death's
door. Her dying wish is that he coughs up the money to pay for
a decorative double gate, so that her coffin can be carried out
of the courtyard rather than be ignominiously hoisted over the
wall. It's all very pretty and wilfully ironic and will no doubt
have arty-farty types chuckling into their latte. JC-W

• *Halima* Uktamoi Miyasarova, *Hamro* Maruf Pulodzoda,
Yatim Kova Tilavpur, *the mayor* Mardonqul Qulbobo,
Savri Malohat Maqsumova.

• *Dir* and *Screenplay* Djamshed Usmonov, *Pro* Marco Müller,
Ex Pro Müller and Elise Jalladeau, *Co-Pro* Elda Guidinetti, *Ph*
Pascal Lagriffoul, *Pro Des* Maslodov Farosatshoev, *Ed* Jacques
Comets, *M* Mike Galasso, *Costumes* Marina Yakunina.

Fabrica Cinema/Rai Cinema-Tartan Films.
89 mins. Tajikistan/Italy/Switzerland/France. 2002.
Rel: 12 November 2004. Cert. 12A.

Anything Else ★

There comes a point in most people's creative trajectory when it's a good idea to change tack. Now 68, Woody Allen has been recycling the same formula for decades and it has become stale and embarrassing. Still harping on about anti-Semitism and being Jewish and dropping philosophical quotes, Allen's recipe exudes a desperate air of stasis. Jason Biggs is a joke writer in Manhattan and is having problems getting sex. Christina Ricci is his Annie Hall, a chain-smoking actress with an eating disorder. At least this time Woody doesn't attempt to get the girl, although it's still uncomfortable to hear him pontificating on masturbation. Twenty-seven years ago (in *Annie Hall*) he quipped, 'Don't knock masturbation, it's sex with somebody I love.' Here, he's masturbating in public with a very flaccid joystick. JC-W

• *David Dobel* Woody Allen, *Jerry Falk* Jason Biggs, *Paula* Stockard Channing, *Harvey* Danny DeVito, *Bob* Jimmy Fallon, *Amanda* Christina Ricci, *with* Anthony Arkin, William Hill, David Conrad, Erica Leerhsen, Adrian Grenier, Fisher Stevens, Joseph Lyle Taylor, KaDee Strickland, Diana Krall.

• *Dir* and *Screenplay* Woody Allen, *Pro* Letty Aronson, *Ex Pro* Stephen Tenenbaum, *Co-Ex Pro* Jack Rollins and Charles H. Joffe, *Co-Pro* Helen Robin, *Ph* Darius Khondji, *Pro Des* Santo Loquasto, *Ed* Alisa Lepselter, *M* various, songs performed by Billie Holiday, Ravi Shankar, Diana Krall, Wes Montgomery, Teddy Wilson, Lester Young, Moby, and Stockard Channing, *Costumes* Laura Jean Shannon.

DreamWorks/Gravier Prods/Perdido-Optimum Releasing. 108 mins. USA . 2003. Rel: 30 July 2004. Cert. 15.

Are We There Yet? ★★½

When divorced mother of two Suzanne (*The Fresh Prince of Bel-Air*'s Nia Long) has to stay in Vancouver over the New Year holiday, her new boyfriend Nick volunteers to bring her kids the 350 miles from Portland, Oregon. Precocious, rambunctious and, ultimately, precious, the tykes set out to sabotage the budding romance as surely as they sabotage the journey. Obviously part of Ice Cube's 'two pic deal', this is far more family-friendly fare than *xXx 2*. The adults end up more as window dressing so that the kids can steal the show – especially Aleisha Allen. More fun for children than parents, though that's not always a bad thing. And, yes, that *is* Nichelle Nichols as Miss Mable! SWM

• *Nick* Ice Cube, *Suzanne* Nia Long, *Marty* Jay Mohr, *voice of Satchel Paige* Tracy Morgan, *Al* M.C. Gainey, *Kevin Kingston* Philip Daniel Bolden, *Lindsey Kingston* Aleisha Allen, *with* Henry Simmons, Frank C. Turner, Sean Millington, Jerry Hardin, Nichelle Nichols.

• *Dir* Brian Levant, *Pro* Ice Cube, Matt Alvarez and Dan Kolsrud, *Ex Pro* Todd Garner and Derek Dauchy, *Screenplay* Steven Gary Banks and Claudia Grazioso and J. David Stern and David N. Weiss, *Ph* Thomas Ackerman, *Pro Des* Stephen Lineweaver, *Ed* Lawrence Jordan, *M* David Newman, *Costumes* Gersha Phillips.

Tyke talkin': Ice Cube reaches for the PG factor in Brian Levant's family-friendly *Are We There Yet?* (from Columbia Tri-Star)

Revolution Studios/Cube Vision-Columbia TriStar.
94 mins. USA. 2005. Rel: 18 February 2005. Cert. PG

Around the Bend ★½

A strait-laced banker in the throes of divorce finds his life
turned upside down with the arrival of his long-lost father. On
the run from the FBI, the latter coerces his son and grandson to
embark on a bizarre pilgrimage across the Southwest to fulfil
the last will and testament of his own father... The prospect
of Michael Caine, Christopher Walken and Josh Lucas playing
three generations of an American family is enough to put off
even the most dedicated film buff. Then one's worst misgivings
are exacerbated by a jokey music score and the addition of
Glenne Headley as a Danish nurse with an appetite for slasher
videos. Walken, who doesn't do normal, almost salvages the
scenes he's in, but Caine as a moribund American Cockney is a
terminal embarrassment. If the offbeat humour in this eccentric
road movie was to have worked at all, it should have been of a
much darker hue. JC-W

• *Turner Lair* Christopher Walken, *Jason Lair* Josh Lucas, *Henry
Lair* Michael Caine, *Katrina* Glenne Headley, *Zach Lair* Jonah
Bobo, *Sarah* Kathryn Hahn, *Walter* Norbert Weisser, *Albert's
mother* Jean Effron, *John* David Eigenberg, *with* Laurie O'Brien,
Gerry Bamman, David Marciano, and (uncredited)
Eva Blaylock.

• *Dir* and *Screenplay* Jordan Roberts, *Pro* Elliott Lewitt and
Julie Kirkham, *Ex Pro* Ronald G. Smith, *Ph* Michael Grady,
Pro Des Sarah Knowles, *Ed* Francoise Bonnot, *M* David
Baerwald; songs performed by The New Velvet Pillow
Orchestra, Jill Zadeh and Gary LeMel, Leon Russell,
Harry Nilsson, Warren Zevon, Bob Dylan, and Fleetwood Mac,
Costumes Alix Friedberg.

Warner Independent Pictures/Kirkham-Lewitt/
Sundance Institute-Warner.
83 mins. USA. 2004. Rel: 22 April 2005. Cert. 15.

Around the World in 80 Days ★★

If you can imagine a Jackie Chan film starring Steve Coogan,
directed by regular Adam Sandler helmsman Frank Coraci
and woven into a Jules Verne scenario, then you can picture
the mess that is *Around the World in 80 Days*. Chan, now 51,
has kicked his way across the Bronx, into the Wild West and
through Victorian London, so Verne's globetrotting saga seems
as apt a vehicle as any to spread the Chinaman's combative
reach. Taking enormous liberties with history (Constantinople
didn't become Istanbul until 1926, by the way), the film rides
roughshod over its literary source and turns Phileas Fogg's
French valet into a Chinese warrior. Yet, in spite of some
lacklustre fight choreography, shameful slapstick and a welter
of missed opportunities, the film is partially saved by Steve
Coogan as an amusing Fogg, while the Belgian actress Cécile de
France lends a lot of charm. There are also some neat computer
effects, although the roster of star cameos – a gimmick
borrowed from the Oscar-winning 1956 adaptation – is largely
squandered; indeed, the governor of California proves to be a
particular embarrassment. JC-W

• *Passepartout/Lau Xing* Jackie Chan, *Phileas Fogg* Steve Coogan,
Monique La Roche Cécile de France, *Lord Kelvin* Jim Broadbent,
Inspector Fix Ewen Bremner, *Colonel Kitchner* Ian McNeice,
Orville Wright Luke Wilson, *Wilbur Wright* Owen Wilson, *Queen
Victoria* Kathy Bates, *Prince Hapi* Arnold Schwarzenegger, *with*
Karen Joy Morris, Roger Hammond, David Ryall, Mark Addy,
Richard Branson, John Cleese, Will Forte, Macy Gray, Sammo
Hung, Rob Schneider, Daniel Wu.

• *Dir* Frank Coraci, *Pro* Hal Lieberman and Bill Badalato,
Ex Pro Jackie Chan, Willie Chan, Solon So, Alex Schwartz
and Thierry Potok, *Screenplay* David Titcher, David Benullo
and David Goldstein, *Ph* Phil Meheux, *Pro Des* Perry Andelin
Baker, *Ed* Tom Lewis, *M* Trevor Jones, *Costumes* Anna Sheppard,
Sound Nick Adams, *Stunt Choreography* Jackie Chan.

Walt Disney Pictures/Walden Media-Entertainment.
119 mins. UK/Germany/Ireland. 2004. Rel: 9 July 2004. Cert PG.

The Assassination of Richard Nixon ★★★★½

Of course, Richard Nixon wasn't assassinated, and more's
the pity. But many wished he had been, especially Samuel
Joseph Byck. Samuel Byck had a plan, a plan fuelled by the
humiliation of his life as a divorcee, third-rate salesman and
all-round failure. Forced by his domineering boss to memorise
Norman Vincent Peale's *The Power of Positive Thinking* and
to embrace Richard Nixon as a role model, Byck could not
reconcile himself with a man who built his reputation on lies.
Byck knew that America was a land of plenty, but plenty only
for the few, and that the cancer eating at the heart of a country
built on morals decent and true was a tumour called Richard
M. Nixon... Samuel Byck really did plan to kill Tricky Dickie,
but because he failed, his name was consigned to the rubbish
bin of history. In the wake of 9/11, it takes a brave film to
empathise with the plight of an assassin, even a failed one.
It's even braver to cast an actor like Sean Penn in the role of a
man we should respond to. Byck's story is often unbearable to
endure – his intentions are noble, his perseverance admirable,
and it's the system that let him down. With his weasel-like
countenance and flights of physical psychosis, Penn makes Byck
a sympathetic, compulsively watchable presence. JC-W

• *Samuel Joseph Byck* Sean Penn, *Bonny Simmons* Don Cheadle,
Jack Jones Jack Thompson, *Marie Byck* Naomi Watts, *Martin
Jones* Brad Henke, *Tom Ford* Nick Searcy, *Julius Byck* Michael
Wincott, *Harold Mann* Mykelti Williamson, *with* April Grace,
Jenna Milton, Eileen Ryan, Derek Greene.

• *Dir* Niels Mueller, *Pro* Alfonso Cuaron and Jorge Vergara,
Ex Pro Arnaud Duteil, Avram Butch Kaplan, Kevin Kennedy,
Frida Torresblanco, Alexander Payne and Leonardo DiCaprio,
Assoc Pro Kurt Mueller, *Line Pro* Debra Grieco, *Screenplay* Niels
Mueller and Kevin Kennedy, *Ph* Emmanuel Lubezki, *Pro Des*
Lester Cohen, *Ed* Jay Cassidy, *M* Steven Stern; Beethoven,
Costumes Aggie Guerard Rodgers

Anhelo Prods/Appian Way-Metrodome.
95 mins. USA. 2004. Rel: 8 April 2005. Cert. 15.

Assault on Precinct 13 ★★★★½

The cops are the bad guys, we're rooting for the criminals and all hell's breaking loose. It's New Year's Eve, a snow storm has descended on Detroit and crime kingpin Marion Bishop has finally been caught. There are a lot of rumours about Marion Bishop – how he took five bullets and lived; how he ripped the spine out of a man with his bare hands. Now he's in police custody and is about to rat on his colleagues-in-crime. His colleagues happen to be a whole bunch of cops and they're ready to take Bishop down – along with all the cops protecting him at Precinct 13... The original *Assault on Precinct 13*, directed by John Carpenter in 1976, was a stripped-down, visceral joyride of trauma and has become a cult classic. The remake is a thriller of a very different hue, but is a worthy successor. An unexpected, edgy and shocking prologue sets the pace and signals the arrival of a filmmaker erupting with potential. Ethan Hawke and Laurence Fishburne square off against each other with deadly, ambivalent force, while the tension refuses to let up. The violence is relentless, the stakes spectacular and the escalating frenzy genuinely gut-wrenching. JC-W

• *Jake Roenick* Ethan Hawke, *Marion Bishop* Laurence Fishburne, *Beck* John Leguizamo, *Alex Sabian* Mario Bello, *Smiley* Jeffrey 'Ja Rule' Atkins, *Iris Ferry* Drea de Matteo, *Capra* Matt Craven, *Jasper O'Shea* Brian Dennehy, *Marcus Duvall* Gabriel Byrne, *Anna* Aisha Hinds, *with* Kim Coates, Tig Fong, Dorian Harewood.

• *Dir* Jean-François Ríchet, *Pro* Pascal Caucheteux, Stephane Sperry and Jeffrey Silver, *Ex Pro* Don Carmody, Sebastien Kurt Lemercier and Joseph Kaufman, *Co-Pro* and *Screenplay* James DeMonaco, *Ph* Robert Gantz, *Pro Des* Paul Denham Austerberry, *Ed* Bill Pankow, *M* Graeme Revell, *Costumes* Vicki Graef and Georgina Yarhi, *Sound* Craig Henighan and Paula Fairfield, *Visual Effects* Dennis Berardi.

Rogue Pictures/Why Not/Liaison Films/Biscayne Pictures-Entertainment.
108 mins. USA/France. 2005. Rel: 28 January 2005. Cert. 15.

The Aviator ★★★★

As a child, Howard Hughes was warned by his mother that he was not safe, that 'they' were out to get him. It was a prophecy that haunted him throughout his life, yet he still managed to turn his father's fortune – which he inherited at 19 – into a billion-dollar empire. He also had a way with women, and dated – and bedded – the likes of Katharine Hepburn, Ava Gardner, Jean Harlow, Ginger Rogers and Lana Turner. Yet when he was not making and losing fortunes, changing aviation history (in 1938 he circled the globe in just 91 hours and nine years later built the world's biggest aircraft), he felt increasingly divorced from reality and retreated into a private hell fuelled by a fear of contamination... Leonardo DiCaprio followed a train of actors pencilled in to play Hughes – Warren Beatty, Nicolas Cage, Johnny Depp, even Jim Carrey – and is still too baby-faced (at the age of 29) to inhabit the haunted countenance of the eccentric billionaire. Indeed, with the likes of Cate Blanchett, Jude Law and Gwen Stefani embodying household icons, one is forced to suspend disbelief by its fingernails. Nonetheless, this is a colourful, compelling and accomplished portrait of one of the most flamboyant characters of the 20th century – and DiCaprio is surprisingly commanding and unhinged in the title role. There is also excellent support from Blanchett, Alda and Baldwin and the whole thing unfolds like an Axminster carpet. JC-W

• *Howard Hughes* Leonardo DiCaprio, *Katharine Hepburn* Cate Blanchett, *Ava Gardner* Kate Beckinsale, *Noah Dietrich* John C. Reilly, *Juan Trippe* Alec Baldwin, *Senator Ralph Owen Brewster* Alan Alda, *Professor Fitz* Ian Holm, *Jack Frye* Danny Huston, *Jean Harlow* Gwen Stefani, *Erroll Flynn* Jude Law, *Glenn Odekirk* Matt Ross, *Mrs Hepburn* Frances Conroy, *Johnny Meyer* Adam Scott, *Faith Domergue* Kelli Garner, *Louis B. Mayer* Stanley DeSantis, *Roland Sweet* Willem Dafoe, *Dr Hepburn* Kenneth Walsh, *Howard Hughes' mother* Amy Sloan, *with* Brent Spiner, Edward Herrmann, J.C. Mackenzie, Sam Hemmings, Rufus Wainwright, Loudon Wainwright, Francesca Scorsese, Martha Wainwright, Vincent Laresca, and (uncredited) Anne V. Coates, *voice of Martin Hughes' projectionist* Martin Scorsese.

• *Dir* Martin Scorsese, *Pro* Michael Mann, Sandy Climan, Graham King and Charles Evans Jr, *Ex Pro* Leonardo DiCaprio, Chris Brigham, Rick Yorn, Harvey Weinstein, Bob Weinstein, Rick Schwartz and Colin Vaines, *Screenplay* John Logan, *Ph* Robert Richardson, *Pro Des* Dante Ferretti, *Ed* Thelma Schoonmaker, *M* Howard Shore; J.S. Bach; songs performed by Rufus Wainwright, Vince Giordano and His Orchestra, Al Jolson, Bing Crosby, Loudon Wainwright III, Django Reinhardt, Benny Goodman and His Orchestra, Martha Wainwright, Ella Fitzgerald and the Ink Spots, Leadbelly, etc, *Costumes* Sandy Powell, *Choreography* Matthew Dickens.

Forward Pass/Appian Way/IMF/Warner/Miramax-Buena Vista International.
170 mins. USA. 2004. Rel: 26 December 2004. Cert. 12A.

AVP Alien vs. Predator

see *Alien vs. Predator*.

Baadasssss! ★★★★

In 1971, acclaimed director Melvin Van Peebles brought us the world's first ever 'blaxploitation' film with *Sweet Sweetback's Baad Asssss Song*. Some 30-odd years later, his son Mario tells the incredible (but true!) story of what it took to get that movie made. Inhabiting the role of his father, Mario recreates Melvin's struggles with studios, unions, and a societal mindset which simply resisted the entire notion of blacks controlling their own cinematic endeavours. Mario avoids any obvious sugar-coating, even of his father, as he reveals the astonishing lengths to which his pioneering parent would go to open the door for every single black filmmaker to follow. Easily one of the best movies about making movies out there. Aka *How to Get the Man's Foot Outta Your Ass*. SWM

• *Priscilla* Joy Bryant, *Bill Cosby* T.K. Carter, *Big T* Terry Crews, *Grandad* Ossie Davis, *Clyde Houston* David Alan Grier, *Sandra* Nia Long, *Jose Garcia* Paul Rodriguez, *Howard 'Howie' Kaufman* Saul Runinek, *Mario* Khleo Thomas, *Melvin Van Peebles* Mario Van Peebles, *with* Vincent Schiavelli, Karimah Westbrook, Rainn Wilson, Sally Struthers, Adam West, Glenn Plummer, Pamela Gordon, Joseph Culp, John Singleton, Mandela Van Peebles, Marley Van Peebles, Maya Van Peebles, Bill Cosby, Jose Garcia, Megan Van Peebles, and (uncredited) Melvin Van Peebles.

• *Dir* and *Pro* Mario van Peebles, *Ex Pro* Michael Mann and Jerry Offsay, *Co-Ex Pro* Tobie Haggerty, *Screenplay* Mario Van Peebles and Dennis Haggerty, *Ph* Robert Primes, *Pro Des* Alan E. Muraoka, *Ed* Anthony Miller and Nneka Goforth, *M* Tyler Bates, *Costumes* Kara Saun.

MVP Filmz/Showtime Networks-BFI.
108 mins. USA. 2003. Rel: 10 June 2005.
Cert. 15.

Bad Santa ★★★★

A bracing antidote to such slushy Yuletide offerings as *Elf* and *The Santa Claus*, Terry Zwigoff's *Bad Santa* is a *Grinch* for adults. Billy Bob Thornton takes the spirit of Ebenezer Scrooge and animates it with profanity, vomiting, butt-fucking and pissing in front of his wide-eyed charges. You ain't ever seen Father Christmas like this, kids. Billy Bob plays Willie Soke, an alcoholic, small-time safebreaker who pays for his annual booze bill by posing as a shopping mall Santa. He's aided and abetted by Marcus, a three-foot elf who's the brains in the partnership, while Willie dons the red suit and white beard. After closing time, Willie and Marcus help themselves to the mall's takings and any nick-nacks that take their fancy. But in a reverse spin on the eternal classic *Miracle on 34th Street*, a kid – a moronic, fat one in this instance – changes the way that Santa fits into his own scheme of things. Based on an idea by Ethan and Joel Coen, *Bad Santa* is very, very dark and sometimes oversteps the mark. Considering that the director's last film was the deftly sardonic *Ghost World*, his sophomore entry is a little over-egged – but it's also very, very funny. Billy Bob is unremittingly odious in the title role and is neatly undercut by the impassive ten-year-old newcomer Brett Kelly. Dedicated to the memory of John Ritter. JC-W

• *Willie Soke* Billy Bob Thornton, *Marcus* Tony Cox, *Thurman, the kid* Brett Kelly, *Sue* Lauren Graham, *Bob Chipeska* John Ritter, *Gin* Bernie Mac, *with* Ajay Naidu, Alex Borstein, Ethan Phillips, and (uncredited) *grandma* Cloris Leachman.

• *Dir* Terry Zwigoff, *Pro* John Cameron, Sarah Aubrey and Bob Weinstein, *Ex Pro* Joel Coen and Ethan Coen, *Co-Ex Pro* Harvey Weinstein and Brad Weston, *Screenplay* Glenn Ficarra and John Requa, *Ph* Jamie Anderson, *Pro Des* Sharon Seymour, *Ed* Robert Hoffman, *M* David Kitay, *Costumes* Wendy Chuck.
Dimension Films/Triptych Pictures-Buena Vista International.
91 mins. USA. 2003. Rel: 5 November 2004.
Cert. 15.

Batman Begins ★★★★★

Plagued by guilt for the murder of his parents, industrial heir Bruce Wayne embarks on a voyage of discovery that leads him to the Himalayas. There he learns the ways of the ninja and returns to Gotham City to put his new creed into practice… Batman has come a long way since the cheesy film serial of 1943. Director and co-writer Christopher Nolan not only rationalises Bruce Wayne's obsession with bats, but hoists the comic-book dynamic to a whole new level. Though saddled with an unwieldy prologue, *Batman Begins* soon enough finds its stride and explains exactly where Bruce Wayne is coming from. It's an intelligent, even plausible approach to the comic-book legend, which should gratify diehard devotees as well as winning over a whole new audience. Christian Bale is terrific as Wayne (beefed up considerably since the skeleton he played in *The Machinist*), Caine is a delight (and surprisingly moving) as the butler Alfred, while Gary Oldman is a most sympathetic and believable Gotham cop. Indeed, the casting-against-type reaps enormous dividends, while the photography is exceptionally good, the music rhapsodic and the plotting terrific. Thrilling, scary, wry and even profound, this is one blockbuster that manages to simultaneously appeal to the intellect, the gut and the funny bone. JC-W

• *Bruce Wayne/Batman* Christian Bale, *Alfred* Michael Caine, *Henri Ducard* Liam Neeson, *Rachel Dawes* Katie Holmes, *Jim Gordon* Gary Oldman, *Lucius Fox* Morgan Freeman, *Dr Jonathan Crane* Cillian Murphy, *Carmine Falcone* Tom Wilkinson, *Richard Earle* Rutger Hauer, *Ra's al Ghul* Ken Watanabe, *Thomas Wayne* Linus Roache, *Flass* Mark Boone Junior, *Martha Wayne* Sara Stewart, *Bruce Wayne aged eight* Gus Lewis, *with* Larry Holden, Gerard Murphy, Rade Sherbedgia, Emma Lockhart, John Nolan, Tamer Hassan, Vincent Wong, Patrick Nolan, Lucy Russell, Shane Rimmer, Alexandra Bastedo, John Judd, Tom Nolan.

• *Dir* Christopher Nolan, *Pro* Emma Thomas, Charles Roven and Larry Franco, *Ex Pro* Benjamin Melniker and Michael E. Uslan, *Screenplay* Nolan and David S. Goyer, based upon characters created by Bob Kane, *Ph* Wally Pfister, *Pro Des* Nathan Crowley, *Ed* Lee Smith, *M* Hans Zimmer and James Newton Howard; Mozart, *Costumes* Lindy Hemming, *Visual Effects* Janek Sirrs, Dan Glass and Tim Field.

Warner/Syncopy/Patalax III-Warner.
140 mins. USA/UK. 2005. Rel: 16 June 2005. Cert. 12A.

Beautiful Dreamer ★★★½

Sub-titled *Brian Wilson and the story of SmiLE*, this documentary feature tells the story of Brian Wilson of The Beach Boys, that famed pop group of the 1960s. However, it places its strongest emphasis on the album *SMiLE* which, although awaited with anticipation in 1967, failed to see the light of day. The fact that Wilson was eventually to resurrect his career and to complete this music for live performance in 2004 gives a natural sense of shape and drama to this documentary, which is enjoyable despite its faults. With Wilson contributing, the film's tone is absurdly and amusingly hagiographic, Wilson being seen as the Picasso of pop. But, if it would take a devout fan to find the piece beyond criticism, for the rest of us it offers a relaxing experience. MS

• *with*: Brian Wilson, Roger Daltrey, George Martin, Van Dyke Parks, Andrew Loog Oldham, Elvis Costello, Jeff Bridges, Jimmy Webb, Lou Adler, Burt Bacharach, Paul McCartney, Phil Ramone, Rob Reiner, Rufus Wainwright, Melinda Wilson, etc.

• *Dir* and *Screenplay* David Leaf, *Pro* Leaf, Richard Waltzer, John Scheinfeld and Steve Ligerman, *Ex Pro* Melinda Wilson, *Ph* James Mathers, *Ed* Peter S. Lynch II, *M* Brian Wilson.

Showtime/LSL Prods-ICA Projects.
109 mins. USA. 2004. Rel: 10 December 2004. No Cert.

Beauty Shop ★★★

Switching from *Barbershop 2* to her own franchise, Queen Latifah's character Gina Norris moves to Atlanta to work her hairstyling magic. When boss Jorge (an over-the-top Kevin Bacon) takes the credit for Gina's outrageous hair designs, she leaves with shampoo girl Alicia Silverstone to open a beauty shop of her own in the proverbial 'hood'. An eclectic blend of stylists and clientele convene to crack wise about men, women, race and hairdos with varying degrees of humour and insight. While I wish the dialogue had been a bit cleverer and more daring, I'd pay to watch Queen Latifah read a telephone book and get some good laughs while doing it. Much like going and having your hair done at your own local beauty shop, Gina's is a fine one in which to spend an hour and a half. SWM

• *Gina Norris* Queen Latifah, *Lynn* Alicia Silverstone, *Terri* Andie MacDowell, *Ms Josephine* Alfre Woodard, *Joanne* Mena Suvari, *Mrs Towner* Della Reese, *Chanel* Golden Brooks, *Paulette* Miss Laura Hayes, *Vanessa* Paige Hurd, *Willie* L'il JJ, *Rochelle* LisaRaye McCoy, *Darnelle* Keshia Knight Pulliam, *Ida* Sherri Shepherd, *Jorge Christophe* Kevin Bacon, *Joe* Djimon Hounsou, *with* Kimora Lee Simmons, Sheryl Underwood, Bryce Wilson, Adele Givens, Baby, Otis Best.

• *Dir* Bille Woodruff, *Pro* David Hoberman, Robert Teitel, George Tillman Jr, Queen Latifah and Shakim Compere, *Ex Pro* Todd Lieberman, Ice Cube and Matt Alvarez, *Co-Pro* Louise Rosner, *Assoc Pro* Otis Best, *Screenplay* Kate Lanier and Norman Vance Jr, from a story by Elizabeth Hunter, *Ph* Theo Van de Sande, *Pro Des* Jon Gary Steele, *Ed* Michael Jablow, *M* Christopher Young, *Costumes* Sharen Davis.

MGM/State Street Pictures/Mandeville Films/
Flavor Unit-Verve Pictures.
105 mins. USA. 2005. Rel: 22 April 2005.
Cert. 12A.

Be Cool ★★

Chili Palmer used to be a loan shark. But the movies suited him better. Now, tired by the pressure to turn out sequels (*Get Leo* was a hit, *Get Lost* wasn't), he's switching to the music biz. As luck would have it, he stumbles across a star-

Blowing hot and cool: Uma Thurman heats up F. Gary Gray's recycled *Be Cool* (from Fox)

in-the-making, Linda Moon, unaware that her contractual ties take in a corrupt music producer (who thinks he's black) and a posse of gangsta rappers. But it's all in a day's work for Chili… In-jokes can only be recycled for so long. Without some genuine wit, chemistry and pizazz, recycled junk like this is as fleeting as the starry-eyed wannabes churned out by the music biz. So in-jokes about Tom Hanks are exchanged for in-jokes about Snoop Dogg. Somehow, Travolta manages to rise above it all, allowing the likes of Vince Vaughn, Andre Benjamin and The Rock (as a gay bodyguard) to play the fool. And whadya know? Chili Palmer is as good a dancer as Tony Manero, Danny Zuko and Vincent Vega. And so a lukewarm copy of Travolta and Thurman's jig in *Pulp Fiction* is trotted out (to the accompaniment of The Black Eyed Peas), to remind us further that this is merely bling parading as gold. JC-W

• *Chili Palmer* John Travolta, *Edie Athens* Uma Thurman, *Raji* Vince Vaughn, *Sin LaSalle* Cedric the Entertainer, *Dabu* Andre Benjamin, *Steven Tyler* Steven Tyler, *Joe Loop* Robert Pastorelli, *Linda Moon* Christina Milian, *Hy Gordon* Paul Adelstein, *Marla* Debi Mazar, *Darryl* GregAlan Williams, *Nick Carr* Harvey Keitel, *Elliot Wilhelm* The Rock, *Martin Weir* Danny DeVito, *Tommy Athens* James Woods, *with* Wyclef Jean, Fred Durst, Sergio Mendes, Gene Simmons, The RZA, Joe Perry, Anna Nicole Smith, Anthony J. Ribustello, Steve Maye, Alex Kubik, Kimberly J. Brown, Margaret Travolta, Noelle Scaggs, Joyce Tolbert, Areosmith, The Black Eyed Peas, and (uncredited) *director* Seth Green.

• *Dir* F. Gary Gray, *Pro* Danny DeVito, Michael Shamberg and Stacey Sher, with David Nicksay, *Ex Pro* Gray, Elmore Leonard and Michael Siegel, *Screenplay* Peter Steinfeld, from the novel by Leonard, *Ph* Jeffrey L. Kimball, *Pro Des* Michael Corenblith, *Ed* Sheldon Kahn, *M* John Powell, *Costumes* Mark Bridges.

MGM/Jersey Films/Double Feature Films-Fox.
119 mins. USA. 2005. Rel: 25 March 2005. Cert. 12A.

Before Sunset ★★★★

Nine years ago Ethan Hawke and Julie Delpy starred in *Before Sunrise*, a two-handed romance in which Jesse, a 24-year-old American in Europe, talked his way into the arms and heart of Celine, a young French woman. The film ended with their promise to meet six months later in Vienna. *Before Sunset*, co-scripted by Hawke and Delpy in collaboration with their director, finds Jesse in Paris promoting the book he has written about his night of lost love. At a press conference in a bookshop, Jesse catches sight of his muse and, after exchanging pleasantries, they decide to spend Jesse's last hour in Paris together. Like the first film, *Before Sunset* is all talk but, once again, the talk is engaging, enlightening and fascinating. At first, Jesse comes off as a bit of a jerk (he punctuates every sentence with 'right' and makes dumb jokes), but gradually the erstwhile lovers peel off the layers of their small talk to reveal their real yearning. Revealing as much about Ethan Hawke and Julie Delpy as it does the motivation and truth of their characters, *Before Sunset* hits some telling notes and invites the viewer into a very personal, poignant and thought-provoking kinship. JC-W

• *Jesse Wallace* Ethan Hawke, *Celine* Julie Delpy, *with* Vernon Dobtcheff, Louise Lemoine Torres, Rodolphe Pauly, Albert Delpy.

• *Dir* Richard Linklater, *Pro* Anne Walker-McBay, *Ex Pro* John Sloss, *Co-Pro* Isabelle Coulet, *Screenplay* Linklater, Julie Delpy and Ethan Hawke, from a story by Linklater and Kim Krizan, *Ph* Lee Daniel, *Pro Des* Baptiste Glaymann, *Ed* Sandra Adair, *M* Alex Wurman, *Costumes* Thierry Deletrre.

Warner Independent Pictures/Castle Rock/Detour Film-Warner.
80 mins. USA. 2004. Rel: 23 July 2004. Cert 15.

Being Julia ★★★

London; 1938. Julia Lambert, darling of the West End stage and worshipped by the cognoscenti, is on the verge of a nervous breakdown. Then, taking a young American lover, she experiences a new lease of life… Like so many *grande dames* of the British theatre, Julia Lambert is a monster. She is childish, wilful, temperamental, manipulative, petulant, insecure and egocentric – to a staggering degree. While this sort of character may have proved a revelation when W. Somerset Maugham created her in his 1937 novel *Theatre*, it has now become a rather tedious stereotype, *darling*. Nonetheless, Annette Bening grabs the part by the horns (complete with Gertrude Lawrence accent) and rides it to a triumphant finish. She's well supported, too, by Jeremy Irons' fleshed-out stereotype of the vain, caddish

impresario, Juliet Stevenson's long-suffering, down-to-earth dresser and Michael Gambon's impassioned, straight-speaking drama coach. It's a sumptuous production besides (perhaps too much so), in which the familiar Jerome Kern standards, ritzy nightspots and lushly pastoral English countryside conspire to suffocate a sense of real life. But then maybe that's the point. JC-W

• *Julia Lambert* Annette Bening, *Michael Gosselyn* Jeremy Irons, *Lord Charles* Bruce Greenwood, *Dolly De Vries* Miriam Margolyes, *Evie* Juliet Stevenson, *Tom Fennel* Shaun Evans, *Avice Crichton* Lucy Punch, *Roger Gosselyn* Tom Sturridge, *Walter Gibbs* Maury Chaykin, *Grace Dexter* Sheila McCarthy, *Mrs Lambert* Rosemary Harris, *Aunt Carrie* Rita Tushingham, *Archie Dexter* Leigh Lawson, *Jimmy Langton* Michael Gambon, *with* Julian Richings, Mari Kiss, Max Irons, Michael Culkin, Marsha Fitzalan, Denzal Sinclaire, Bryan Burdon.

• *Dir* István Szabó, *Pro* Robert Lantos, *Ex Pro* Mark Milln, Marion Pilowsky, Donald A. Starr and Daniel J.B. Taylor, *Co-Pro* Julia Rosenberg, Mark Musselman, Sandra Cunningham and Lajos Ovari, *Screenplay* Ronald Harwood, *Ph* Lajos Koltai, *Pro Des* Luciana Arrighi, *Ed* Susan Shipton, *M* Mychael Danna, *Costumes* John Bloomfield.

Serendipity Point Films/First Choice Films/Astral media/
Telefilm Canada/Sony Pictures Classics, etc-Columbia TriStar.
104 mins. Canada/UK/Hungary/USA. 2004.
Rel: 19 November 2004. Rel: Cert. 12A.

The Best of Youth ★★★

Over a period of 37 years – from the 1960s to the present – the political and social canvas of Italy unfolds as two brothers, Nicola and Matteo, attempt to find their place in it. The former, very much the reformist, is keenly interested in the greater human picture and after travelling the world becomes a psychiatrist. His brother, the more solitary and impulsive one, decides on a career in the police force, a move that fuels his self-destructive impulses… Originally planned as a TV series, this intimate epic really tests the patience at 373 minutes. Even so, much of the action flies past, in spite of the directors' predilection for close-ups and tight, intimate scenes. The antithesis of Bertolucci's cinematic *1900* – which covered the first half of the century through the eyes of two siblings – *The Best of Youth* taxes credibility at times as Nicola and Matteo always seem to be at the centre of their country's most dramatic upheavals. Still, the film is to be commended for its refusal to succumb to sentimentality and is superbly played by Lo Cascio, Boni and the legendary Adriana Asti. Original title: *La meglio gioventù*. CB

• *Nicola Carati* Luigi Lo Cascio, *Matteo Carati* Alessio Boni, *Adriana Carati* Adriana Asti, *Giulia Monfalco* Sonia Bergamasco, *with* Fabrizio Gifuni, Maya Sansa, Valentina Carnelutti.

• *Dir* Marco Tullio Giordana, *Pro* Angelo Barbagallo, *Ex Pro* Alessandro Calosci, *Screenplay* Sandro Petraglia and Stefano Rulli, *Ph* Roberto Forza, *Art Dir* Franco Ceraolo, *Ed* Roberto

Missiroli, *Costumes* Elisabetta Montaldo.

RAI Radio Televisione Italiana/RaiCinema-Buena Vista International.
373 mins. Italy. 2003. Rel: 2 July 2004. Cert 15.

Beyond the Sea ★★★★

Kevin Spacey crooned an accomplished rendition of 'That Old Black Magic' on the soundtrack of *Midnight in the Garden of Good and Evil*. He also exhibited a masterly touch as a director with the 1996 *Albino Alligator*, a tense, nuanced heist thriller with Matt Dillon and Faye Dunaway. And so he combines both these talents as the director and star of this rousing biography of Bobby Darin. Born Walden Robert Cassotto in the Bronx in 1936, Darin – who took his stage name from the last five letters of 'Mandarin' – had a colourful childhood in spite of his rheumatic fever, a condition that doctors feared would barely see him into his mid teens. So, in a hurry to realise his dreams, Darin became a singing sensation at 22, wooed and married the movie star Sandra Dee two years later and snared an Oscar nomination (for *Captain Newman M.D.*) three years after that. And all while his hair was falling out and his heart was playing him up... Inviting comparisons with the contemporaneous *De-Lovely* (in that both films observe the subject's life through their own retrospective eyes), *Beyond the Sea* is powered by a magnificent performance from Spacey. Indeed, Spacey convinces us that, if her weren't running the Old Vic, he could well make a splash in Vegas if he so chose. JC-W

• *Bobby Darin/Walden Robert Cassotto* Kevin Spacey, *Sandra Dee* Kate Bosworth, *Steve Blauner* John Goodman, *Charlie Maffia* Bob Hoskins, *Polly Cassotto* Brenda Blethyn, *Mary* Greta Scacchi, *Nina Cassotto Maffia* Caroline Aaron, *Dick Behrke* Peter Cincotti, *little Bobby* William Ullrich, *with* Michael Byrne, Matt Rippy, Gary Whelan, Andrew Laws, David Westhead.

• *Dir* Kevin Spacey, *Pro* Spacey, Andy Paterson, Jan Fantl and Arthur E. Friedman, *Screenplay* Spacey, Lewis Colick and (uncredited) Paul Attanasio and Lorenzo Carcaterra, *Ph* Eduardo Serra, *Pro Des* Andrew Laws, *Ed* Trevor Waite, *M* Christopher Slaski, *Costumes* Ruth Myers, *Choreography* Rob Ashford, *Makeup* Peter King.

Archer Street/QI Quality International/Trigger Street/ Endgame Entertainment/Lions Gate, etc-Entertainment.
118 mins. USA/UK/Germany. 2004. Rel: 26 November 2004. Cert. 12A.

The Big Kahuna ★★★★

Three industrial lubricant salesmen spend their last evening in Wichita, Kansas. There they hope to land one big client at a party they're hosting in their hotel's hospitality suite. While the titular 'big kahuna' eludes seasoned sales vets Larry and Phil, neophyte Bob Walker inadvertently establishes a religious rapport with the man. As Bob chooses to hawk Jesus over lubricants, sparks and philosophies fly, all the while revealing the simple truth that men are wonderful creatures

indeed. Adapting his play *Hospitality Suite*, screenwriter Roger Rueff invokes salesmen characters that we've seen before but seldom with such fresh vigour and canny dialogue. Kevin Spacey's Larry embodies the efficient sales raconteur with speeches that wax both poetic and neurotic – as always, he's a joy to behold. Yet it's Danny DeVito, with his rich, subtle turn as the world-weary yet still affirming Phil, who gives the best performance of his career. SWM

• *Larry Mann* Kevin Spacey, *Phil Cooper* Danny DeVito, *Bob Walker* Peter Facinelli, *bellboy* Paul Dawson.

• *Dir* John Swanbeck, *Pro* Kevin Spacey, Elie Samaha and Andrew Stevens, *Ex Pro* Gerard Guez, *Co-Pro* Joanne Horowitz, *Line Pro* Barbara A. Hall, *Screenplay* Roger Rueff, based on his play *Hospitality Suite*, *Ph* Anastas N. Michos, *Pro Des* Kalina Ivanov, *Ed* Peggy Davis, *M* Christopher Young, *Costumes* Katherine Jane Bryant.

Franchise Pictures/Trigger Street-Redbus Film Distribution.
90 mins. USA. 1999. Rel: 15 October 2004. Cert. 15.

Birth ★★★½

New York City; the present. Shortly after accepting the marriage proposal of the steadfast, wealthy Joseph, Anna is approached by a ten-year-old boy in her Manhattan apartment. Without a trace of irony, the young stranger tells her that he is her husband, who died ten years earlier. Bizarrely, the boy seems to have an uncanny knowledge of Anna's past life and, in spite of repeated threats, refuses to back down from his apparently romantic pursuit... Some films are high-concept; this is deep-concept. The slowest mainstream Hollywood feature of the year (and the quietest), *Birth* is a sensuous and metaphysical romantic mystery that's in dire need of a shot of menace. Set in the giddy world of the rich, privileged classes of Manhattan, the film glides into the subconscious under the assured, confident direction of Britain's Jonathan Glazer (*Sexy Beast*) with more intriguing questions than it can answer. More of a fleshed-out idea than a rounded feature film, *Birth* piques and teases rather than actually engaging the emotions. However, as a big-screen experience it is quite hypnotic and superbly realised, with Nicole Kidman again commanding centre stage with an ethereal majesty. JC-W

• *Anna* Nicole Kidman, *Joseph* Danny Huston, *Eleanor* Lauren Bacall, *Clara* Anne Heche, *young Sean* Cameron Bright, *Laura* Alison Elliot, *Bob* Arliss Howard, *Clifford* Peter Stormare, *Mr Conte* Ted Levine, *Mrs Conte* Cara Seymour, *Lee* Novella Nelson, *Mrs Hill* Zoe Caldwell, *with* Michael Desautels, Milo Addica, Lisa Barnes.

• *Dir* Jonathan Glazer, *Pro* Jean-Louis Piel, Nick Morris and Lizie Gower, *Ex Pro* Kerry Orent, Mark Ordesky and Xavier Marchand, *Assoc Pro* Kate Myers, *Screenplay* Glazer, Jean-Claude Carrière and Milo Addica, *Ph* Harris Savides, *Pro Des* Kevin Thompson, *Ed* Sam Sneade and Claus Wehlisch, *M* Alexandre Desplat; Richard Wagner, *Costumes* John Dunn.

Puppy love: Nicole Kidman falls for the ultimate toy boy in Jonathan Glazer's profound, deeply provocative *Birth* (from Entertainment)

New Line Cinama/Fine Line Features/Lou Yi/ Academy-Entertainment.
100 mins. USA/UK/Germany. 2004.
Rel: 5 November 2004. Cert. 15.

Blade: Trinity ★½

Having combated a variety of evil bloodsuckers over the years, the half-human, half-vampiric Blade faces his greatest challenge yet. After years of repose in a Syrian tomb, Dracula himself is resurrected by a quartet of contemporary vampires. Impervious to the detrimental effects of sunlight and rather good at physical transformation, Dracula – or Drake, as he's known here – is now bent on colonising the world… The *Blade* franchise is all about energy and style, and first-time director and comic book author David S. Goyer certainly supplies the series' characteristic verve. However, Goyer's attempts at humour leave a lot to be desired, while Snipes has adopted a rather smug disposition that plunges the film into music video stasis. There's also a sameness about the endless fight sequences, resulting in sensorial overload and intellectual fatigue. CB

• *Blade* Wesley Snipes, *Abigail Whistler* Jessica Biel, *Hannibal King* Ryan Reynolds, *Abraham Whistler* Kris Kristofferson, *Danica Talos* Parker Posey, *Drake* Dominic Purcell, *Dr Edgar Vance* John Michael Higgins, *Cumberland* James Remar, *Bentley*

Tittle Eric Bogosian, *Hedges* Patton Oswalt, *Asher Talos* Callum Keith Rennie, *Jarko Grimwood* Triple H, *Sommerfield* Natasha Lyonne, *Chief Martin Vreede* Mark Berry.

• *Dir* and *Screenplay* David S. Goyer, based on the Marvel Comics characters created by Marv Wolfman and Gene Colman, *Pro* Peter Frankfurt, Wesley Snipes, David S. Goyer and Lynn Harris, *Ex Pro* Toby Emmerich, Stan Lee and Ari Arad, *Co-Pro* Art Schaefer, *Ph* Gabriel Beristain, *Pro Des* Chris Gorak, *Ed* Howard E. Smith and Conrad Smart, *M* Ramin Djawadi and The RZA, *Costumes* Laura Jean Shannon, *Visual Effects* Joe Bauer, *Second Unit Dir* Vic Armstrong and Edward G. Perez.

New Line Cinema/Amen Ra Films/Imaginary Forces-Entertainment.
112 mins. USA. 2004. Rel: 8 December 2004. Cert. 15.

Blueberry ★★★

Generally derided by the critics, this mythical Western does indeed collapse in its over-extended and inept final section. Until then, however, it's a fascinating oddity. Derived from French graphic novels, it carries many echoes, among them Sergio Leone's view of the Wild West, *Raiders of the Lost Ark*, the darker-toned American Westerns of the late sixties, *The Trip* and Eisenstein's *Battleship Potemkin*. Blueberry, the hero traumatised in his youth by violence that requires revenge and later brought up by Indians whose mystical beliefs he shares, is played by a stolid Vincent Cassel. The film always looks great though, and until the last scenes it has enough sense of style to be decidedly enjoyable in its own overblown way. It's not a Spike Lee joint but it is, as the credits confirm, a Jan Kounen session. MS

• *Mike Blueberry* Vincent Cassel, *Maria* Juliette Lewis, *Wally Blount* Michael Madsen, *Runi* Temuera Morrison, *Rolling Star* Ernest Borgnine, *Woodhead* Djimon Hounsou, *young Mike* Hugh O'Conor, *Sullivan* Geoffrey Lewis, *with* Nichole Hiltz, Kateri Walker, Tchéky Karyo, Eddie Izzard, Colm Meaney, Jan Kounen, Richard Jones, Val Avery.

• *Dir* Jan Kounen, *Pro* Ariel Zeïtoun and Thomas Langmann, *Screenplay* Kounen, Gérard Brach and Matt Alexander, *Ph* Tetsuo Nagata, *Pro Des* Michel Barthélemy, *Ed* Bénédicte Brunet, Joël Jacovella and Jennifer Augé, *M* Jean-Jacques Hertz and François Roy.

Thomas Langmann/Ajoz Films/UCG Images/ Crystalcreek/Ultra Films, etc-UGC Films. 124 mins. France/UK/Mexico. 2004. Rel: 23 July 2004. Cert. 15.

Blue Gate Crossing ★★★½

This gentle, appealing study of adolescents in Taipei is daringly minimal plot-wise – too much so for its own good perhaps. However, director Yee Chih-yen gets fine performances from his non-professional cast and proves himself a master of atmospheric Scope images. The central figure is a 17-year-old girl named Ke-rou who approaches a boy on the school's swimming team on behalf of her shy best friend, Yueh-chen. But the boy believes that it is Ke-rou herself who is really attracted to him and is oblivious to the fact that Ke-rou's feelings for Yueh-chen are such as to make her sensitive to the possibility of being a lesbian. No big drama ensues, but, if you can accept the minimalism, this contemplative movie is engaging and the ending in particular is quite admirably judged. MS

• *Zhang Shihao* Chen Bo-Lin, *Men Kerou* Guey Lun-Mei, *Lin Yuezhen* Liang Shui-Hui, *with* Joanna Chou, Cheng Ming-Gin.

• *Dir* and *Screenplay* Yee Chih-Yen, *Pro* Peggy Chiao Hsiung-Ping and Hsü Hsiao-Ming, *Ex Pro* Toon Wang, *Ph* Chienn Hsiang, *Art Dir* Hsia Shao-Yu, *Ed* Liao Ching-Song, *M* Chris Hou.

Arc Light Films/Ming Film Corp/Pyramide Prods-Peccadillo Pictures. 83 mins. Taiwan/France. 2001. Rel: 2 July 2004. Cert 12A.

Bombón El perro ★★★★

Having explored the vast, wind-swept plains of Patagonia with Daniel Day-Lewis in his 1989 *Eversmile, New Jersey*, director Carlos Sorín now opts for a cast of non-professionals. Adapting a scenario to fit his actors' personalities, Sorín has

fashioned a beguiling, charming tale of destiny in which an unemployed mechanic struggles to make ends meet. For 15 years Juan Villegas parked the director's car in Buenos Aires and is now a local celebrity thanks to his turn here. Virtually playing himself, Villegas radiates a suppressed optimism as fate repeatedly undermines him, his eyes sparkling beneath a visage of disconcerted bemusement. Always eager to help, Villegas is grateful for any donation and so accepts the gift of a dog in return for repairing a stranger's car. On his own merits, Villegas would have been reason enough to see this delightful film, but the dog – a handsome white Dogo Argentino – adds to the pleasure. Skilfully edited, exquisitely scored and refreshingly unsentimental, *Bombón* is a sensitive, comic hymn to the underdog, both human and canine. JC-W

• *Juan Villegas* aka 'Coco' Juan Villegas, *Walter Donado* Walter Donado, *Susana* Rosa Valsechi, *Hija de Coco* Mariela Díaz, *Claudina* Claudina Fazzini.

• *Dir* Carlos Sorín, *Pro* Oscar Kramer, *Screenplay* Sorín, Santiago Calori and Salvador Roselli, *Ph* Hugo Colace, *Art Dir* Margrita Díaz, *Ed* Mohamed Rajid, *M* Nicolás Sorín, *Costumes* Ruth Fisherman, *Sound* Abbate & Díaz.

Guacamole Films/OK Films/Wanda Vision, etc-Pathé. 98 mins. Argentina/Spain. 2004. Rel: 17 June 2005. Cert. 15.

Boogeyman ★

Tim Jensen is one frightened little boy. And, because he's only eight, he happens to believe in the Boogeyman. One night (during a raging storm), Tim's father tries to assuage Tim's fears when he is sucked into the closet and never heard of again. Fifteen years later, Tim must confront his childhood fears or face losing more of his nearest and dearest... Oooh, the Boogeyman will get you. He's in the closet. He's under the bed. The trouble is, the Boogeyman isn't real and neither is this perfunctory programmer designed to make a quick killing at the box-office for the least amount of effort. Three credited scriptwriters contributed to this cliché-bloated thread of an idea, which is stretched to 86 minutes and still feels padded. There's the predictable quota of sudden loud noises, characters who say things you only hear in silly horror films and a resolution that feels prematurely circumcised. JC-W

• *Tim Jensen* Barry Watson, *Kate* Emily Deschanel, *Franny* Skye McCole Bartusiak, *Jessica* Tory Mussett, *Tim's mother* Lucy Lawless, *Boogeyman* Andrew Glover, *Tim's father* Charles Mesure, *young Tim Jensen* Aaron Murphy, *with* Phillip Gordon, Jennifer Rucker, Scott Wills.

• *Dir* Stephen Kay, *Pro* Sam Raimi and Rob Tapert, *Ex Pro* Joe Drake, Nathan Kahane, Carsten Lorenz, Steve Hein and Gary Bryman, *Line Pro* Chloe Smith, *Screenplay* Eric Kripke, Juliet Snowden and Stiles White, *Ph* Bobby Bukowski, *Pro Des* Robert Gillies, *Ed* John Axelrad, *M* Joseph Luduca, *Costumes* Jane Holland.

Ghost House Pictures-UIP. 86 mins. USA. 2004. Rel: 4 March 2005. Cert. 15.

Crazy taxi: Matt Damon's still running in Paul Greengrass's flat-out *The Bourne Supremacy* (from UIP)

The Bourne Supremacy ★★★★

Jason Bourne doesn't know whether he's coming or going but he knows that he can handle himself. Wanted for the assassination of two American agents in Berlin, he is being hunted by the CIA, the German police, the Russians and God only knows who else. Smoked out of his Goa retreat by an unknown agent, Bourne heads for Naples where he is apprehended by CIA operatives. In minutes, he has incapacitated both his interrogator and a guard and has tapped into a private conversation with a top agent in Langley, Virginia. He may be suffering from amnesia, but he knows he didn't kill those two men in Berlin… One has to admire a man who can attack a knife-wielding opponent with a newspaper, and, in just one minute, turn a house into a bomb. But it's the ingenuity of Robert Ludlum's story that really holds the interest, in spite of this sequel's refusal to respect the quieter moments of the original film, *The Bourne Identity*. Basking in its locations of Goa, Berlin, Virginia, Moscow, London, Amsterdam, Naples and Munich, *The Bourne Supremacy* moves like an express train and displays a rare intelligence until succumbing to formula in its later stages. JC-W

• *Jason Bourne* Matt Damon, *Marie Kreutz* Franka Potente, *Ward Abbott* Brian Cox, *Nicky* Julia Stiles, *Kirill* Karl Urban, *Danny Zorn* Gabriel Mann, *Pamela Landy* Joan Allen, *Tom Cronin* Tom Gallop, *Teddy* John Bedford Lloyd, *with* Marton Csokas, Ethan Sandler, Michelle Monaghan, Karel Roden, Tomas Arana, Patrick Crowley, and (uncredited) *Alexander Conklin* Chris Cooper.

• *Dir* Paul Greengrass, *Pro* Frank Marshall, Patrick Crowley and Paul L. Sandberg, *Ex Pro* Doug Liman, Jeffrey M. Weiner and Henry Morrison, *Screenplay* Tony Gilroy, *Ph* Oliver Wood, *Pro Des* Dominic Watkins, *Ed* Christopher Rouse and Richard Pearson, *M* John Powell, *Costumes* Dinah Collin.

Universal/MP Theta prods/Kennedy/Marshall/ Ludlum Entertainment-UIP.
108 mins. USA/Germany. 2004. Rel: 13 August 2004. Cert: 12A.

Bride and Prejudice ★½

A large part of the enduring appeal of Robert Z. Leonard's 1940 adaptation of Jane Austen's *Pride and Prejudice* was the smouldering presence of Laurence Olivier's Darcy. Indeed, the popularity of the BBC's 1995 production was also largely due to the brooding intensity of Colin Firth's reading of the part. This Bollywood version, besides the wit of its title, is a travesty. Gurinder Chadha is not known for her subtle portrayals of Indian family life and here aims for an end-of-pier slapstick mentality, complete with plummeting trousers and 'funny' laughs. The director does generate an agreeable energy, but without an ounce of credibility the scenario is a house of cards. Seldom have four sisters looked less alike (presumably so that a Western audience can tell the difference between them), the lyrics are frequently embarrassing and the disembodied singing a surreal nod to *Top of the Pops*. But the film's real weakness is Martin Henderson's Darcy, a one-dimensional mannequin who just looks humiliated to be caught in a Bollywood film. JC-W

• *Lalita Bakshi* Aishwarya Rai, *Will Darcy* Martin Henderson, *Mr Bakshi* Anupam Kher, *Mrs Bakshi* Nadira Babbar, *Jaya Bakshi* Namrata Shirodkar, *Mr Wickham* Daniel Gillies, *Mr Balraj* Naveen Andrews, *Miss Bingley* Indira Varma, *Chetan Kholi* Nitin Ganatra, *Mrs Darcy* Marsha Mason, *Maya Bakshi* Meghnaa, *Lucky Bakshi* Peeya Rai Chodhuri, *with* Ashanti, Sonali Kulkarni, Alexis Bledel.

• *Dir* Gurinder Chadha, *Pro* Chadha and Deepak Nayar, *Ex Pro* Francois Ivernel, Cameron McCracken and Duncan Reid, *Line Pro* Michelle Fox, Pravesh Sahmi and Brigitte Mueller, *Screenplay* Chadha and Paul Mayeda Berges, *Ph* Santosh Sivan, *Pro Des* Nick Ellis, *Ed* Justin Krish, *M* Anu Malik and Craig Pruess, *Costumes* Ralph Holes and Eduardo Castro, *Choreography* Saroj Khan.

Pathé/UK Film Council/Kintop Pictures/Bend It Films/ Inside Track/National Lottery-Pathé.
111 mins. UK/Germany. 2004. Rel: 8 October 2004. Cert. 12A.

The Bridesmaid ★★

Working in 'sales', Philippe Tardieu is an apparently successful white-collar worker even though he stills lives with his mother and two younger sisters. When he catches the gaze of the bridesmaid 'Senta' at the wedding of his younger sister Sophie, he makes a half-hearted attempt to pick her up, a move that is unceremoniously rejected. However, later that night, Senta turns up at his house and seduces him. And, as it happens, her subsequent romantic demands are Nietzschean in the extreme... In 1995, Claude Chabrol adapted Ruth Rendell's novel *A Judgement in Stone* into the fascinating and

disturbing *La Cérémonie*. Here, he draws on Rendell again, but to much weaker effect. For a start, there is no suspense, while the central 'romance' just doesn't ring true. Part of the problem is that Benoît Magimel fails to embody the complex contradictions of his character and for much of the time seems uncomfortable both as a smooth operator in business and as a man in love. When he tells Senta that, after a brief fling in the sack, he loves her more than he has loved any woman, one cannot but scoff at his insincerity. Original title: *La Demoiselle d'honneur*. JC-W

• *Philippe Tardieu* Benoît Magimel, *Senta* Laura Smet, *Christine* Aurore Clément, *Gérard Courtois* Bernard Le Coq, *Sophie Tardieu* Solène Bouton, *Patricia Tardieu* Anna Mihalcea, *with* Eric Seigne, Michel Duchaussoy, Suzanne Flon, Thomas Chabrol.

• *Dir* Claude Chabrol, *Pro* Antonio Passalia and Patrick Godeau, *Screenplay* Claude Chabrol and Pierre Leccia, from the novel by Ruth Rendell, *Ph* Eduardo Serra, *Pro Des* Francoise Benoit-Fresco, *Ed* Monique Fardoulis, *M* Matthieu Chabrol, *Costumes* Mic Cheminal.

Alicéleo/Canal Diffusion/France 2 Cinéma/Integral Film/ Canal Plus-Cinefile.
110 mins. France/Germany/Italy. 2004. Rel: 13 May 2005. Cert. 15.

Bridget Jones: The Edge of Reason ★★

London; the present. Bridget Jones has found true happiness. She has landed a successful barrister with a fantastic bottom, her career is blossoming and all those presumptuous calories

Outré duvet: Renée Zellweger in Beeban Kidron's premeditated and predictable *Bridget Jones: The Edge of Reason* (from UIP)

no longer seem to be a problem. But then the glamorous Mark Darcy hires a sexy new secretary and Doubt and Suspicion become new enemies in Bridget's life... Not all sequels are crap. *Shrek 2* put the lie to that. Nevertheless, formulae are so often diluted in the reproduction. *The Edge of Reason* is more of the same, brimming with *faux pas*, fat jokes and love lost and won. Renée Zellweger looks porkier than ever (earning her $15m), the locations branch out to include Austria, Italy and Thailand and there's a new rival for Mark Darcy's attention. There is also the premeditated soundtrack of tired and tested hit songs, a predictable comic rhythm and a preponderance of obvious physical humour. Fans of the first film will no doubt lap this up, but the kernel of truth at the heart of the original book is repeatedly trampled by sitcom caricature. JC-W

• *Bridget Jones* Renée Zellweger, *Daniel Cleaver* Hugh Grant, *Mark Darcy* Colin Firth, *Dad* Jim Broadbent, *Mum* Gemma Jones, *Jude* Shirley Henderson, *Shazzer* Sally Phillips, *Tom* James Callis, *Richard Finch* Neil Pearson, *Rebecca* Jacinda Barrett, *Magda* Jessica Stevenson, *with* James Faulkner, Celia Imrie, Dominic McHale, Donald Douglas, Shirley Dixon, Tom Brooke, Lucy Robinson, Mark Tandy, Ian McNeice, Alex Jennings, Catherine Russell, Jeremy Paxman, Wolf Kahler, Paul Nicholls, Ting-Ting Hu, Neil Dudgeon, Peter Gordon.

• *Dir* Beeban Kidron, *Pro* Tim Bevan, Eric Fellner and Jonathan Cavendish, *Ex Pro* Debra Hayward and Liza Chasin, *Screenplay* Andrew Davies, Helen Fielding, Richard Curtis and Adam Brooks, *Ph* Adrian Biddle, *Pro Des* Gemma Jackson, *Ed* Greg Hayden, *M* Harry Gregson-Williams; songs performed by Perry Como, Renée Zellweger, Average White Band, Burt Bacharach and The Staple Singers, Will Young, Jamelia, Kylie Minogue, Joss Stone, Mary J. Blige, Robbie Williams, Jamie Cullum, Barry White, Beyoncé with Jay-Z, Rufus Wainwright with Dido, 10CC, Carly Simon, Primal Scream, The Darkness, Amy Winehouse, Minnie Riperton, Aretha Franklin, Leona Naess, Madonna, Marvin Gaye, Sting with Annie Lennox, *Costumes* Jany Temime.

Universal Pictures/StudioCanal/Miramax/Working Title/Little Bird-UIP.
107 mins. UK/USA/France. 2004. Rel: 12 November 2004. Cert. 15.

Bright Leaves ★★½
Documentary film-making that is highly personal can be very engaging and for an hour Ross McElwee's take on the tobacco industry is just that. He had always known that his great-grandfather had lost out to a rival in North Carolina who had acquired wealth and fame in the tobacco trade but only recently was he alerted to the possibility that this family history could have been the basis of *Bright Leaf*, the novel filmed in 1950. Since this theory proves incorrect McElwee's pursuit of it seems pointless and in the exceedingly boring later stages everything in his film goes on for too long, be it a humorous sequence featuring a film theorist or religious songs included for local atmosphere. But it's only fair to add that what eventually came across to me as self-important and over-indulgent has been found by many to be quirkily delightful. MS

• *with*: John McElwee, Elizabeth King, Dr Tom McElwee, David Williamson, Patricia Neal, Jack Clayton, Dooley Strange, etc.

• *Dir, Pro, Screenplay, Ph, Ed* and *Narration* Ross McElwee, *Assoc Pro* Linda Morgenstern.

Homemade Movies/WGBH/Channel 4/American Film Institute/Pinewood Foundation-ICA Projects.
107 mins. USA/UK. 2003. Rel: 8 October 2004. Cert. PG.

Broken Lizard's Club Dread
See *Club Dread*.

Brotherhood ★★★
South Korea; 1950. Lee Jin-tae is a cobbler who dotes on his younger brother, Jin-seok, a class-A student, and his widowed mother. With Jin-tae about to be married, all would seem to be copacetic with the Lee family when North Korea invades their country. With both brothers conscripted, Jin-tae realises that the only way he can protect his younger sibling is to become a decorated hero, a path that leads to his inevitable dehumanisation... Publicised as South Korea's answer to *Saving Private Ryan*, this is certainly a bloody, epic look at the folly of war. Ruthlessly gratuitous, its message is clear – war is hell and only the bonds of family are worth caring about. Manipulative and often simplistic, the film shattered box-office records in Korea, proving that with this and his 1999 *Shiri*, writer-director Kang Je-Gyu is an efficient authority on his audience. Aka: *TaeGukGi: The Brotherhood of War*. EB

• *Lee Jin-tae* Jang Dong-gun, *Young-shin* Lee Eun-ju, *Lee Jin-seok* Won Bin, *young man* Gong Hyeong-jin, *Young-guk* Go Do-hee, *mother* Lee Yeong-ran, *Yoo-jin* Cho Yoon-hee.

• *Dir* and *Screenplay* Kang Je-Gyu, *Pro* Choi Jin-wha and Kim Woo-teak, *Ex Pro* Kang Je-gyu, *Ph* Hong Gyung-pyo, *Pro Des* Shin Bo-kyung, *Ed* Park Gok-ji and Chung Jin-hee, *M* Lee Dong-jun.

Kang Je-Gyu Films-Premier Asia.
147 mins. South Korea. 2004. Rel: 3 June 2005. Cert. 15.

Brothers ★★★½
Fresh from the triumph of *Open Hearts*, Susanne Bier has, perhaps inevitably, created a successor that is overshadowed by it. Both films investigate the consequences of a sudden tragic event – here it's the supposed death of a married Major serving in Afghanistan. When his younger brother consoles his widow, a woman with two young daughters, we may think we know where the plot is going, but in fact we are to some extent being wrong-footed. Bier's tale develops into a tragedy concerning human weakness of varying kinds and it cleverly plays on audience assumptions by changing their perceptions of the two brothers as the story progresses. It's well made and well acted (Connie Nielsen returned to Denmark to do it) but unfortunately the focus is wrong. Instead of concentrating on one man's tragedy as he comes to hate himself, the movie invites more generalised sympathy and so leaves the viewer not

caring too much about the outcome. Interesting for all that. Original title: *Brodre*. MS

• *with:* Connie Nielsen, Ulrich Thomsen, Nikolaj Lie Kaas, Bent Mejding, Solbjorg Hojfeldt, Paw Henriksen, Laura Bro, Nieks Olsen, Sarah Juel Werner, Rebecca Longstrup Soltau, Lars Ranthe, Lars Hjortshoj, Andre Babikian, Lene Maria Christensen, Henrik Koefoed.

• *Dir* Susanne Bier, *Pro* Sisse Graum Jorgensen and Peter Aalbaek Jensen, *Ex Pro* Peter Garde, *Line Pro* Karen Bentzon, *Screenplay* Anders Thomas Jensen, from a story by Bier and Jensen, *Ph* Morten Soborg, *Art Dir* Viggo Bentzon, *Ed* Pernille Bech Christensen, *M* Johan Soderqvist, *Costumes* Signe Sejlund.

Zentropa Entertainments14 Aps/Two Brothers/Sigma Films/Memfis Film Intl. AB/Fjellape Film AS/ Danish Film Institute/Swedish Film Institute/Nordic Film & TV Fund-Soda Pictures.
110 mins. Denmark. 2004. Rel: 6 May 2005. Cert. 15.

Bubba Ho-Tep ★★★★

Comedy horror is fiendishly hard to do, but this one from Don Coscarelli (who
made the *Phantasm* films) is as appealing as it is strange –
and boy is it strange!
Bruce Campbell makes a funny, funny job of a dream role
as Elvis Presley. Apparently, The King is alive and well
and living in a Texas care home called Shady Rest, having
swapped identities with an Elvis impersonator before breaking
a hip in a fall. However, there is little rest at the home when
an Egyptian mummy starts killing off the old folk by sucking
out their souls… Despite his Zimmer frame and bedpan,
old Elvis decides to fight back, helped by fellow resident
Jack (the late, great Ossie Davis), who believes he is John F.
Kennedy. In his best part for ages, Campbell turns his crazy
role into a six-course banquet and this striking-looking movie
is consistently hilarious, creepy, inventive and winning. DW

• *Elvis* Bruce Campbell, *Jack* Ossie Davis, *nurse* Ella Joyce, *Callie* Heidi Marnhout, *Kemosabe* Larry Pennell, *Bubba Ho-tep* Bob Ivy, *with* Reggie Bannister, Daniel Roebuck, Harrison Young, Linda Flammer.

• *Dir* and *Screenplay* Don Coscarelli, *Pro* Don Coscarelli and Jason R. Savage, *Ex Pro* Dac Coscarelli, *Ph* Adam Janeiro, *Pro Des* Daniel Vecchione, *Ed* Donald Milne and Scott J. Gill, *M* Brian Tyler, *Costumes* Shelley Kay, *Sound* Paul Menichini, *Elvis Consultant* Tim Welch.

Silver Sphere-Anchor Bay Entertainment.
91 mins. USA. 2004. Rel: 8 October 2004. Cert. 15.

Bullet Boy ★★★½

Hackney, East London; today. Fresh out of juvenile detention, Ricky, 19, is determined to put his life straight, even if it means working at McDonald's. However, a minor traffic incident sets in motion a potentially fatal vendetta. Ricky wants to leave town, and his girlfriend is willing to go with

him, but first Ricky must help out his best friend, the volatile Wisdom. Meanwhile, Ricky's 12-year-old brother, Curtis, finds his gun… The real coup of this film is the casting of Ashley Walters, who is not only very good but brings his own personal history to the part. A rapper with the garage act So Solid Crew, Walters was sentenced to 18 months in a young offenders' institution for possessing a loaded gun. This is his public apology. While hardly broaching new narrative territory (it recalls such American films as *My New Gun* and *Sugar Hill*), *Bullet Boy* does provide a fresh perspective on modern-day London, far from the streets of Richard Curtis. If there is an inevitability to it all, then it merely reflects the cycle of violence that is becoming increasingly endemic in contemporary Britain. JC-W

• *Ricky* Ashley Walters, *Curtis* Luke Fraser, *Beverley* Clare Perkins, *Wisdom* Leon Black, *Shea* Sharea-Mounira Samuels, *Leon* Curtis Walker, *Rio* Rio Tyson, *Godfrey* Clark Lawson, *Meadow* Jadiel Vitalis.

• *Dir* Saul Dibb, *Pro* Marc Boothe and Ruth Caleb, *Ex Pro* David M. Thompson, Paul Trijbits and Paul Hamann, *Co-Pro* Michael Tait, *Assoc Pro* Abi Bach, *Screenplay* Dibb and Catherine Johnson, *Ph* Marcel Zyskind, *Pro Des* Melanie Allen, *Ed* Masahiro Hirakubo and John Mister, *M* Neil Davidge and Robert del Naja, *Costumes* James Keast.

BBC Films/UK Film Council/Portman Films/Shine/ National Lottery-Verve.
89 mins. UK. 2004. Rel: 8 April 2005. Cert. 15.

Café Lumière ★★★

Having been commissioned to make a film in Japan commemorating the birth of that country's master director Yasujiro Ozu, Hou Hsiao-Hsien opts for minimalism. He applies it to a persuasive portrait of a 23-year-old Japanese girl pregnant by an unsympathetic Taiwanese boyfriend but prepared to make her own way in life. The slow pace creates the same sense of reality that marks Ozu's work but the film unfortunately lacks his skill in making small details build up into a subtly structured whole. Without this *Café Lumière* may assert that life goes on but the last third of it just unravels. Ozu made less seem more, but there's no comparable achievement here, despite Hou's sincerity. Original title: *Kohi Jikou*. MS

• *Yoko Inoue* Yo Hitoto, *Hajime* Tadanobu Asano, *Sei* Masato Hagiwara, *Yoko's stepmother* Kimiko Yo, *Mr Inoue, Yoko's father* Nenji Kobayashi.

• *Dir* Hou Hsiao-Hsien, *Pro* Hideshi Miyajima, Liao Ching-sung, Ichiro Yamamoto and Fumiko Osaka, *Screenplay* Hou and Chu T'ien-Wen, *Ph* Lee Ping-Bing, *Pro Des* Tashiharu Aida, *Ed* Liao Ching-Sung, *M* Jiang Wen-Ye, *Costumes* Kazumi Hoshino and Yoji Yamada.

Shochiku/Asahi Shimbun/Sumimoto/Eisei Gekijo/ IMAGICA-ICA Projects.
102 mins. Japan/Taiwan. 2003. Rel: 10 June 2005. No cert.

Callas Forever ★★★

Fanny Ardant gives a splendid portrayal of the opera diva Maria Callas with strong support from Jeremy Irons as a music business entrepreneur. But the setting for this is taken not from real life but from an odd fantasy concocted by Franco Zeffirelli who offers a mini-version of *Sunset Boulevard*. We see the 53-year-old Callas attempting a kind of comeback by giving a mimed performance on film to be synchronised with her classic recording of *Carmen*. Yet, lacking both the melodramatics and wit of Wilder's film, this is all too slight, while subplots added for weight go nowhere. You do get to hear the real thing musically, but the brief extracts here count for nothing next to the Callas recordings available in the shops. MS

• *Maria Callas* Fanny Ardant, *Larry Kelly* Jeremy Irons, *Sarah Keller* Joan Plowright, *Michael* Jay Rodan, *Marco* Gabriel Garko, *with* Manuel DeBlas, Stephen Billington, Alessandro Bertolucci, Jean Dalric, Olivier Galfione, Roberto Sanchez, El Camborio, Achille Brugnini, Justino Diaz.

• *Dir* Franco Zeffirelli, *Pro* Riccardo Tozzi and Giovanella Zannoni, *Ex Pro* Marco Chimenz and Giovanni Stabilini, *Assoc Pro* Pippo Pisciotto, *Screenplay* Zeffirelli and Martin Sherman, *Ph* Ennio Guarnieri, *Pro Des* Bruno Cesari, *Ed* Sean Barton, *M* Alessio Vlad, *Costumes* Anna AnniAnni, Alberto Spiazzi and Alessandro Lai.

Medusa Film/Cattleya/Film & General Prods/Galfin/Mediapro Pictures/Alquimia Cinema-Enjoy Cinema. 108 mins. Italy/UK/France/Romania/Spain. 2002. Rel: 19 November 2004. Cert. 15.

The Cat Returns ★★★½

Coming from Studio Ghibli that gave us *Spirited Away*, this animated feature from a different director, Hiroyuki Morita, is lightweight and far more traditional in style (think Disney 50 years ago). Nevertheless, even if its short length doesn't prevent its contrived climax from seeming drawn out, this is engaging enough. It's the tale of a girl taken into the Kingdom of Cats as a reward for saving a cat from traffic but then becoming perturbed when she realises the nature of this reward: to be married off to the kingdom's cat prince. There are echoes here of *The Wizard of Oz* and *Alice In Wonderland* and it's all reasonably agreeable. If you are a cat-lover, add at least one more star to the rating. It is available both dubbed and sub-titled and I saw the latter version. Original title: *Neko no Ongaeshi*. MS

• *voices*: *Haru* Chizuru Ikewaki, *the Baron* Yoshihiko Hakamada, *Haru's mother* Kumiko Okae, *Cat King* Tetsuro Tanba (Japanese dialogue version); *Haru* Anne Hathaway, *the Baron* Cary Elwes, *Muta* Peter Boyle, *Toto* Elliott Gould, *Natoru* Andy Richter, *Cat King* Tim Curry, *Haru's mother* Kristine Sutherland, *with* René Auberjonois, Judy Geer, Kristen Bell, Andrew Bevis (English language version).

• *Dir* Hiroyuki Morita, *Project Concept* Hayao Miyazaki, *Pro* Toshio Suzuki and Nozomu Takahashi, *Assoc Pro* Takeyoshi Matsushita, Sanchiro Ujie, Koji Hoshino, Tomoo Miyagawa,

Hononori Aihara and Hideyuki Takai, *Screenplay* Reiko Yoshida, based on the work of Aoi Hiragi, English language adaptation Cindy Davis Hewitt and Donald H. Hewitt, *Art Dir* Naoya Tanaka, *Ed* Megumi Uchida, *M* Yoji Nomi, *Character Creation* Satoko Morikawa.

Tokuma Shoten/Studio Ghibli/Nippon Television Network/Buena Vista Home Entertainment-Optimum. 75 mins. Japan/USA. 2002. Rel: 27 May 2005. Cert. U.

Catwoman ★★★½

Patience Phillips is *pusi*llanimous to say the least. Forever apologising for her apparent shortcomings and unable to stand up for her basic human rights, she is murdered when she stumbles onto a terrible secret: the cosmetics giant she worked for – Hedare Beauty – is promoting a face cream with disfiguring side-effects. Resurrected by an ethereal feline of Egyptian descent, Patience awakes to find that she has acquired some cat-like tread – and a whole new attitude... Maybe in years to come *Catwoman* will be acknowledged as a key example of the purest form of comic-strip cinema. Devoid of ponderous explanation or philosophy – and thankfully free of any attempts at shoehorning realism into an artificial scenario – *Catwoman* is unsullied, unadulterated fun. And in the hands of the French visual effects supervisor Pitof (real name Jean-Christophe Comar) it is a visual treat, a photo-comic alternative reality that blends computer-generated architectural lines with a heightened palette of lustrous colour. And on top of all this is Halle Berry's heartfelt performance as the kitten-turned-minx, plus Sharon Stone to add some steely kitsch. JC-W

• *Patience Phillips* Halle Berry, *Tom Lone* Benjamin Bratt, *George Hedare* Lambert Wilson, *Laurel Hedare* Sharon Stone, *Ophelia* Frances Conroy, *Sally* Alex Borstein, *Armando* Michael Massee, *with* Byron Mann, Kim Smith, Christopher Heyerdahl, Peter Wingfield.

• *Dir* Pitof, *Pro* Denise Di Novi and Edward L. McDonnell, *Ex Pro* Michael Fottrell, Benjamin Melniker, Michael E. Uslan, Robert Kirby and Bruce Berman, *Co-Pro* Alison Greenspan, *Screenplay* John Brancato & Michael Ferris and John Rogers, from a story by Theresa Rebeck, John Brancato and Michael Ferris, based on characters created by Bob Kane, *Ph* Thierry Arbogast, *Pro Des* Bill Brzeski, *Ed* Sylvie Landra, *M* Klaus Badelt; songs performed by Hoobastank, Mis-Teeq, The Hiss, Zino and the Human Beat Box, and Natasha Schneider, *Costumes* Angus Strathie, *Visual effects* Ed Jones.

Warner/Village Roadshow/Di Novi Pictures-Warner. 104 mins. USA/Australia. 2004. Rel: 12 August 2004. Cert. 12A.

Cellular ★★★½

Suburban ubermom Jessica Martin is kidnapped by a gang of dirty cops who hope to force her husband to surrender an accidental videotape of them committing a gangland slaying. Managing to make a random call from a shattered phone, she enlists GenX ne'er-do-well Ryan to rescue her entire family as they both try to stay one step ahead of her captors via his cell phone… Despite powerhouse casting in Basinger and William H. Macy, both give fairly lacklustre performances. It's actually Chris Evans who deftly sells the story, a Good Samaritan barely managing to hang on while his world spirals out of control. SWM

• *Jessica Martin* Kim Basinger, *Ryan* Chris Evans, *Ethan* Jason Statham, *Chad* Eric Christian Olsen, *Deason* Matt McColm, *Jack Tanner* Noah Emmerich, *Mooney* William H. Macy, *with* Brendan Kelly, Eric Etebari, Caroline Aaron, Jessica Biel, Lin Shaye.

• *Dir* David R. Ellis, *Pro* Dean Devlin and Lauren Lloyd, *Ex Pro* Douglas Curtis, Toby Emmerich, Richard Brener and Keith Goldberg, *Co-Pro* Marc Roskin, *Screenplay* Chris Morgan, from a story by Larry Cohen, *Ph* Gary Capo, *Pro Des* Jaymes Hinkle, *Ed* Eric Sears, *M* John Ottman, *Costumes* Christopher Lawrence, *Sound* Hector C. Gika.

New Line Cinema/Electric Entertainment-Entertainment. 94 mins. USA/Germany. 2004. Rel: 24 September 2004. Cert. 15.

Chicken Tikka Masala ★★½

An Indian family living in Preston tries to marry off an eligible son to an Indian girl, blithely unaware that he is gay and has a boyfriend. This is Gurinder Chadha territory given a gay slant but, despite the writer of the screenplay being all of 18 years old, it's desperately unsophisticated and lacking in any cutting edge. It does possess warmth of feeling but the happy ending makes nonsense of the all-too-likely supposition that this family could never accept a son and heir who is gay. It's good to see Zohra Segal, born in 1912, on characteristic

form in a central role as the grandmother, but despite her presence this farce achieves little regardless of its good intentions. MS

• *Jimi Chopra* Chris Bisson, *Chandra P. Chopra* Saeed Jaffrey, *Vanessa* Sally Bankes, *Jack* Peter Ash, *grandmother* Zohra Segal, *Hannah* Katy Clayton, *with* Jinder Mahal, Sushil Chudasama, Louisa Eyd, Shobu Kapoor, Jamila Massey, Harish Patel, Rony Ghosh.

• *Dir* Harmage Singh Kalirai, *Pro* Sanjay Tandon and Rony Ghosh, *Ex Pro* Ajit Medtia, *Screenplay* Roopesh Parekh, from a story by Sanjay Tandon and Rony Ghosh, *Ph* Mike Muschamp, *Pro Des* Mark Leeming, *Ed* Zoran Trajkovic, *M* Pravin Manai, Jasmine Eden and Illegal Demo, *Costumes* Venkat Chennubotla.

Media Group/Seven Spice-Film Incubation Ltd. 95 mins. UK. 2004. Rel: 22 April 2005. Cert. 15.

The Choir

See *The Chorus*.

The Chorus ★★★★½

In 1949 Clément Mathieu, an unemployed music teacher, is hired as a supervisor at a school for 'difficult' boys. A ruthlessly oppressive institution, the school is ruled by the dictum of 'action – reaction', a justification for unmitigated punishment. Opposed to such draconian measures, Clément resorts to undermining the authority of his employer and decides to introduce his mutinous wards to the joy of song… The concept of *The Chorus* isn't exactly new. There are strong echoes here of *Dead Poet's Society, Mr Holland's Opus, Music*

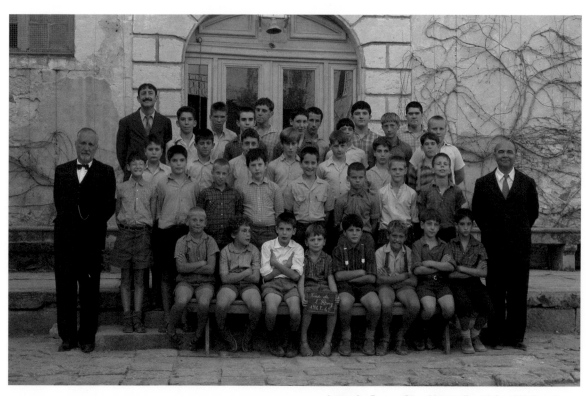

A song for Europe: Gérard Jugnot (far right) and his boys in Christophe Barratier's intensely moving *The Chorus* (from Pathé)

of the Heart and even *School of Rock*. And yet its source, Jean Dréville's 1945 *La Cage aux rossignols*, pre-dates all these films and this is an exquisite remake. Marking the directorial debut of the guitarist Christophe Barratier, the film flirts with sentimentality but, unlike *Cinema Paradiso* (with which it also shares similarities), it artfully sidesteps out-and-out schmaltz. Indeed, its odour of irony – mixed with optimism – suggests that this might have been a true story. As it is, it's a beautifully judged drama, intensely moving, elegantly crafted and impeccably acted by a superlative cast. As for the singing – well, it's the self-raising flour in a Dickensian homily. Original title: *Les Choristes*. Aka *The Choir*. JC-W

• *Clément Mathieu* Gérard Jugnot, *Rachin* François Berléand, *Chabert* Kad Merad, *Father Maxence* Jean-Paul Bonnaire, *the Countess* Carole Weiss, *Pierre Morhange* Jean-Baptiste Maunier, *Pépinot* Maxence Perrin, *Mondain* Grégory Gatignol, *the mother* Monique Ditisheim, *grown-up Pierre Morhange* Jacques Perrin, *grown-up Pépinot* Didier Flamand, *with* Philippe Du Janerand, Erick Desmarestz, Thomas Blumenthal, Simon Fargeot, Théodule Carré-Cassaigne.

• *Dir* Christophe Barratier, *Pro* Jacques Perrin, Arthur Cohn and Nicolas Mauverney, *Screenplay* Barratier and Philippe Lopes Curval, *Ph* Carlo Varini and Dominique Gentil, *Art Dir* François Chauvaud, *Ed* Yves Deschamps, *M* Bruno Coulais and Christophe Barratier, *Costumes* Françoise Guégan.

Jacques Perrin/Galatée Films/Pathé Renn/France 2 Cinéma/Canal Plus-Pathé.
96 mins. France/Switzerland/Germany. 2004.
Rel: 11 March 2005. Cert. 12A.

Christmas with the Kranks ★½
With daughter Blair away for Christmas, perennial Yuletide paragons Luther and Nora Krank decide to forego the revelry and take a Caribbean cruise. Bullied by overzealous neighbours and workmates to join in the Christmas obsession, the Kranks stick to their guns until Blair decides she's coming home for the holidays after all. Then it's full steam ahead to pull together the full festive hullabaloo for which the Kranks had hitherto been famous. It's a holiday picture painted with broad, cartoonish strokes, leaving little room for subtlety or any genuine humour. Poor Tim Allen and Jamie Lee Curtis are forced to race through this lacklustre adaptation of a John Grisham novel (!) by producer-cum-bad director Joe Roth. The disingenuous schmaltz at the end just adds more insult to injury. SWM

• *Luther Krank* Tim Allen, *Nora Krank* Jamie Lee Curtis, *Vic Frohmeyer* Dan Aykroyd, *Spike Frohmeyer* Erik Per Sullivan, *Officer Salino* Cheech Marin, *Officer Treen* Jake Busey, *Walt Scheel* M. Emmet Walsh, *Bev Scheel* Elizabeth Franz, *Mr Scanlon* Kevin Chamberlain, *Enrique DeCardenal* Rene Lavan, *Umbrella Santa/Marty* Austin Pendleton, *with* Caroline Rhea, Patrick Breen, Felicity Huffman, Arden Myrin, Julie Gonzalo, Alan King.

• *Dir* Joe Roth, *Pro* Chris Columbus, Mark Radcliffe and Michael Barnathan, *Ex Pro* Charles Newirth and Bruce A.

Block, *Co-Pro* Allegra Clegg, *Screenplay* Chris Columbus, from the novel *Skipping Christmas* by John Grisham, *Ph* Don Burgess, *Pro Des* Gareth Stover, *Ed* Nick Moore, *M* John Debney, *Costumes* Susie DeSanto.

Revolution Studios/1492 Films-Columbia TriStar.
98 mins. USA. 2004. Rel: 3 December 2004. Cert. PG.

The Chronicles of Riddick ★½
In the modestly budgeted sleeper hit *Pitch Black*, Vin Diesel's Richard B. Riddick was a bad ass. Here, he's turned into the good guy, much like Schwarzenegger's Terminator in *T2*. In the words of director David Twohy, 'This is a story not of good guys versus bad guys, but of bad guys versus *evil* guys.' Whatever. Armed with a budget of over $100m (Vin Diesel was paid $12.5m), this CGI headache is a bizarre blend of grim self-importance and corny dialogue. Diesel is the Man With No Mane, who likes to be alone but finds himself fighting a warrior race of 'half-alive, half-something else' Necromongers led by the absurdly miscast Colm Feore. The latter is intent on colonising the universe and gives the word 'ruthless' new edge as he obliterates worlds that refuse to cooperate. Along for the ride are Judi Dench as a mysterious hologram and Thandie Newton as a pantomime minx. The whole thing is wildly over-plotted, over-designed and over-baked and is barely saved by the odd good joke, such as when Riddick, having disposed of a villain with a 'tea cup', threatens two heavily-armed bad guys with a petite corned beef tin-opener. JC-W

• *Richard B. Riddick* Vin Diesel, *Dame Vaako* Thandie Newton, *Lord Vaako* Karl Urban, *Sixth Lord Marshal* Colm Feore, *Aereon* Judi Dench, *Lyra* Alexa Davalos, *The Purifier* Linus Roache, *Imam* Keith David, *The Guv* Yorick Van Wageningen, *Toombs* Nick Chinlund, *with* Mark Gibbon, Roger R. Cross, Christina Cox, Kim Hawthorne, and the voice of Kristin Lehman.

• *Dir* and *Screenplay* David Twohy, *Pro* Scott Kroopf and Vin Diesel, *Ex Pro* Ted Field, George Zakk and David Womark, *Assoc Pro* Wendy S. Williams, *Ph* Hugh Johnson, *Pro Des* Holger Gross, *Ed* Martin Hunter and Dennis Virkler, *M* Graeme Revell, *Costumes* Ellen Mirojnick and Michael Dennison, *Visual Effects* Peter Chiang.

Universal/Radar Pictures/One Race Films-UIP.
119 mins. USA. 2004. Rel: 27 August 2004.
Cert. 15.

Churchill The Hollywood Years ★★
Hitler has invaded France, King George VI doesn't know there's a war on and Winston Churchill can't wait to get into Princess Elizabeth's pants. Oh, and in this version, Churchill is an American GI played by a buffed-up Christian Slater... With Hollywood's increasing propensity for historical accuracy, the madcap antics of this burlesque do seem rather dated. Indeed, were it not for the proliferation of the f-word – not to mention 'motherfucker' – this would have looked perfectly at home in the 1970s. Still, there are a sprinkling of chuckles, more often than not at the expense of some geographical anomalies (such as Buckingham Palace Station). In its favour,

Slater and Neve Campbell keep their mugging to a minimum and Harry Enfield is a hoot as a sozzled, parsimonious and deeply ignorant George VI. JC-W

• *Winston Churchill* Christian Slater, *Princess Elizabeth/Jane Commoner* Neve Campbell, *Adolf Hitler* Antony Sher, *Eva Braun* Miranda Richardson, *King George* Harry Enfield, *Lord W'ruff* Leslie Phillips, *Baxter* Rik Mayall, *Princess Margaret* Jessica Oyelowo, *Jim Charoo* Mackenzie Crook, *Roberts* Alexander Armstrong, *Chester* Steve Pemberton, *Potter* Bob Mortimer, *Bendle* Vic Reeves, *Martin Bormann* Phil Cornwell, *Goering* Steven O'Donnell, *with* Romany Malco, James Dreyfus, Sally Phillips, Henry Goodman, Alistair McGowan.

• *Dir* and *Screenplay* Peter Richardson, *Pro* Jonathan Cavendish and Ben Swaffer, *Ex Pro* James Mitchell, François Ivernel, Cameron McCracken, Duncan Reid and Steve Christian, *Co-Pro* Dixie Linder, *Line Pro* Brian Donovan, *Ph* Cinders Forshaw, *Pro Des* Tom Burton, *Ed* John Wilson and Geoff Hoog, *M* Simon Boswell, *Costumes* James Keast.

Pathé Pictures/Sky Movies/UK Film Council/Isle of Man Film/Little Bird/Inside Track/National Lottery-Pathé. 86 mins. UK/Ireland. 2004. Rel: 3 December 2004. Cert. 15.

A Cinderella Story ★★½

It's a testament to the narrative strength of the Cinderella story that it can still provoke a lump in the throat when transported to a modern high school setting. However, *A Cinderella Story* owes as much to *You've Got M@il*, *Hamlet* and any number of high school comedies as it does to the original fairy tale. The endearing Hilary Duff plays Samantha Montgomery, a Californian innocent who viewed the San Fernando Valley as her kingdom and her widowed father as her own Prince Charming until, one day, he married the ghastly Fiona and was killed in the Northridge earthquake of 1994. In a jump to the present, Samantha has become a slave to her stepmother and two ugly stepsisters and, in spite of working all hours at Fiona's Diner, is achieving straight A's at school. Her would-be swain is one Austin Ames, football captain, president of the student body and closet poet. He, like she, is working towards a *Prince*ton scholarship and falls for Samantha in cyberspace in a college chat room… In spite of some naff slapstick, *A Cinderella Story* has good jokes, engaging characters and pushes its emotional buttons with some expertise. It's a shame, though, that Samantha's Prince Charming just doesn't seem good enough for her. JC-W

• *Sam Montgomery* Hilary Duff, *Fiona* Jennifer Coolidge, *Austin Ames* Chad Michael Murray, *Carter* Dan Byrd, *Rhonda* Regina King, *Shelby* Julie Gonzalo, *Mrs Wells* Lin Shaye, *Brianna* Madeline Zima, *Gabriella* Andrea Avery, *Bobby* Paul Rodriguez, *Sam's dad* Whip Hubley, *with* Mary Pat Gleason, Kevin Kilner, Erica Hubbard, Art La Fleur, John Billingsley.

• *Dir* Mark Rosman, *Pro* Clifford Werber, Ilyssa Goodman, Hunt Lowry and Dylan Sellers, *Ex Pro* Michael Rachmil, Peter Greene and Keith Giglio, *Co-Ex Pro* Susan Duff,

Screenplay Leigh Dunlap, *Ph* Anthony B. Richmond, *Pro Des* Charles Been, *Ed* Cara Silverman, *M* Christophe Beck; songs performed by Natalie Cole, Goo Goo Dolls, Hilary and Haylie Duff, Soul Patrol, Busted, Robert D. Palmer and Michael Duff, Cirrus, Mya, Herb Alpert, Josh Kelly, etc, *Costumes* Denise Wingate, *Choreographer* Michelle Johnston.

Warner/Clifford Werber/Dylan Sellers Prods-Warner. 95 mins. USA. 2004. Rel: 20 August 2004. Cert. PG.

Le Clan ★★★½

There is nothing clannish about the brothers featured in this dark, poetic and seriously homoerotic paean to Jean Genet. Framed by the picture-postcard scenery of the Rhône-Alpes, the film shows that knife-wielding, drug-peddling youths are not confined to the city. Here, three very different siblings try to come to terms with the death of their mother. The first chapter is dedicated to Marc, a profoundly beautiful, shaven-headed 22-year-old whose sensuous features are offset by a brutish manner. Arrogant and boorish, he shows courtesy to no one but his dog. Then there's his older brother, Christophe, who, just out of prison, has learned the power of self-control and with it forges a respectable future in a ham-salting factory. The last act focuses on Olivier, a 17-year-old introvert who may just learn from the mistakes of his siblings… With its shameless, lingering shots of naked men at the peak of their sexual energy, the film recalls Claire Denis' *Beau Travail* but reveals a much tougher motor. It's certainly well made, although its evasion of a single female form (until the last five minutes) – and a somewhat pat ending – comes off as rather glib and perfunctory. Aka *Three Dancing Slaves*. JC-W

• *Marc* Nicolas Cazalé, *Christophe* Stéphane Rideau, *Olivier* Thomas Dumerchez, *father* Bruno Lochet, *Hicham* Salim Kechiouche, *Robert* Jackie Berroyer, *teacher* Vincent Martinez, *with* Aure Atika, Nicolas Paz, Mathias Olivier, Gary Mary, Geordie Piseri-Diaz.

• *Dir* Gaël Morel, *Pro* Philippe Jacquier, *Ex Pro* Bertrand Guerry, *Screenplay* Morel and Christophe Honoré, *Ph* Jean-Max Bernard, *Art Dir* Ze Branco, *Ed* Catherine Schwartz, *M* Camille Rocailleux; `Morning Bird' performed by Sleepy Jackson.

.

Sépia Prods/Rhône-Alpes Cinéma-Peccadillo Pictures. 89 mins. France/Switzerland. 2004. Rel: 13 May 2005. Cert. 15.

Clifford's Really Big Movie ★★½

After seeing a carnival act called 'Larry's Amazing Animals' with owner Emily Elizabeth, Clifford (the Big Red Dog) worries that keeping him in food will break her father financially. So he runs off to join the carnival and enters a contest wherein the winners will receive a lifetime supply of Tummy Yummies. While they manage to win the contest, Clifford is taken away to be another girl's pet and has to be rescued by the other 'Amazing Animals' before he can make his way home. Charmingly voiced by the late John Ritter, Clifford's adventure might be a tad simplistic for an adult audience. It is, however, an affirming and enjoyable diversion for young children. And wouldn't we all secretly love to have a giant, red dog like Clifford? SWM

• voices: *Clifford the Big Red Dog* John Ritter, *Shackelford* Wayne Brady, *Emily Elizabeth* Grey DeLisle, *Jetta/Madison* Kath Soucie, *Cleo* Cree Summer, *Mr Howard/Marcus* Cam Clarke, *Dorothy* Jenna Elfman, *George Wolfsbottom* John Goodman, *T-Bone* Kel Mitchell, *Larry* Judge Reinhold, *P.T.* Ernie Hudson.

• *Dir* Robert C. Ramirez, *Pro* Deborah Forte, *Co-Pro* Martha Atwater and Jef Kaminsky, *Assoc Pro* Kathleen Zuelch, *Screenplay* Ramirez and Rhett Reese, *Art Dir* Michael Humphries, *Ed* Monte Bramer, *M* Jody Gray, *Sound* Robert Poole II, *Visual Effects* Matt Hullum and Matthew W. Johnson, *Animation* Young Gil Lee.

Warner Bros/Scholastic Entertainment/Big Red Dog Prods-Warner.
74 mins. USA. 2004. Rel: 29 April 2005. Cert. U.

Too close for comfort? Natalie Portman and Jude Law get personal in Mike Nichols' lacerating *Closer* (from Columbia TriStar)

Closer ★★★★

An English journalist and a stripper from New York catch sight of each other on a crowded London street. Distracted by the former's gaze, the latter, Alice, is knocked down by a taxi. The journalist, Dan, takes Alice to hospital and a kinship is made. Later, Alice meets Dan as he is being photographed for the jacket of his first novel, a book that she herself has inspired. Dan and the photographer, Anna, make a connection, a bond which is not lost on Alice. Anna also takes Alice's picture, which ends up in a prestigious exhibition. Later, while viewing her portrait – 'a lie,' she calls it – Alice meets Larry, Anna's boyfriend… Four characters in search of true love form the spine of this shocking romantic drama, adapted by Patrick Marber from his own stage play. While it's hard to dissociate the film from its source, the original is so powerful that its cinematic close-up acts as daunting drama. Mike Nichols, returning to the visceral, character-driven arena of his early films (*Who's Afraid of Virginia Woolf?*, *Carnal Knowledge*) has extracted naked, eviscerating performances from his name cast, with Clive Owen and Julia Roberts proving especially good. This is grown-up cinema for adults, an articulate assault on the most private aspect of human relationships.
JC-W

• *Anna Cameron* Julia Roberts, *Dan* Jude Law, *Alice Ayres/Jane Jones* Natalie Portman, *Larry* Clive Owen, *with* Nick Hobbs, Colin Stinton.

• *Dir* Mike Nichols, *Pro* Nichols, John Calley and Cary Brokaw, *Ex Pro* Scott Rudin, Celia Costas and Robert Fox, *Co-Pro* Michael Haley, *Screenplay* Patrick Marber, *Ph* Stephen Goldblatt, *Pro Des* Tim Hatley, *Ed* John Bloom and Antonia Van Drimmelen, *M* Mozart, Rossini; songs performed by Damien Rice, The Devlins, Prodigy, The Smiths, and Renée Fleming, *Costumes* Ann Roth, *Anna's photographs* Steve Pyke and Mick Lindberg.

Columbia/Inside Track-Columbia TriStar.
103 mins. USA. 2004. Rel: 14 January 2005. Cert. 15.

Cloud Cuckoo Land ★★★½

Something of a companion piece to *Afterlife* (in which the key role was brilliantly played by a young actress with Down's Syndrome), this movie tells of the dreams and aspirations of a man, Sandy Kenyon, who has cerebral palsy – as has the actor playing him. Having built up an interest in finding and restoring crashed planes on account of his grandfather (Jacobi) working in this field, Sandy shows courage and independence in going north to the Lake District to seek a long-lost aircraft for which a reward is offered. Despite sharing with *Afterlife* a character dying of cancer, this is basically a feel-good film and, as such, cannot match the depth and conviction of the other movie. Nevertheless, it is, on its own terms, able, as well as being a brave venture. And there must be special praise for the colour photography of Andy Martin. MS

• *Victor Kenyon* Derek Jacobi, *Sandy Kenyon* Steve Varden, *Lucy* Boo Pearce, *Jasmine* Jane Wall, *Vijay* Kriss Dosanjh, *Trevor* Billy Fane, *Emma* Rachel Tozer, *with* Fuman Dar, Sarah Beauvoisin, Graham Cowley, Rosalind Blessed, Josephine Myddelton.

• *Dir* Matt Dickinson, *Pro* Chris Bradley, *Line Pro* Elizabeth Boucher, *Screenplay* Dickinson and Steve Varden, *Ph* Andy Martin, *Art Dir* Ray Parry, *Ed* Rachel Meyrick, *M* Ed Poole, Artie Melvin and Andy Lagowski, *Costumes* Katrina Frith and Suzie Harmon.

Airborne Productions/Zanzibar Film Prods-Airborne Productions.
94 mins. UK. 2004. Rel: 5 November 2004 (Sheffield and Bradford). Cert. 12A.

Club Dread ★½

A poor man's riposte to *Scary Movie*, *Club Dread* is a Z-grade comedy that sends up the serial killer genre. Conceived by the comedy troupe Broken Lizard (who brought us the marginally funnier *Super Troopers*), the film is set on the hedonistic Pleasure Island, a Costa Rican resort. It is operated by one Coconut Pete, a washed-up singer whose back catalogue includes such vinyl classics as *Sea Shanties and Wet Panties*. Then, when a new load of fun-seeking morons spills onto the island to abuse their minds with drugs and alcohol, a masked killer starts hacking up the staff with a machete. On the positive side, there is an accomplished, full-bloodied score from Nathan Barr, who seems to be the only person to find the right tone. US title: *Broken Lizard's Club Dread*. JC-W

• *Coconut Pete* Bill Paxton, *Putman Livingston* Jay Chandrasekhar, *Lars* Kevin Heffernan, *Juan Castillo* Steve Lemme, *Dave* Paul Soter, *Sam* Erik Stolhanske, *Jenny* Brittany Daniel, *Hank* MC Gainey, *Yu* Lindsay Price, *Roy* Michael Weaver, *with* Nat Faxon, Samm Levine, Dan Montgomery Jr., Elena Lyons, Tanja Reichert.

• *Dir* Jay Chandrasekhar, *Pro* Richard Perello, *Ex Pro* Lance Hool and Peter E. Lengyel, *Co-Pro* Conrad Hool, *Screenplay* Broken Lizard (Chandrasekhar, Paul Soter, Erik Stolhanske, Steve Lemme and Kevin Heffernan), *Ph* Lawrence Sher, *Pro Des* Benjamin Conable, *Ed* Ryan Folsey, *M* Nathan Barr; songs performed by Bill Paxton, Lee Perry, Hardwire, Little Lenny, Dillinger, Gregory Isaacs, Bob Marley & The Wailers, Desmond Dekker & The Cherry Pies, etc, *Costumes* Melissa Bruning.

Fox Searchlight/Cataland Films/Broken Lizard-Fox. 103 mins. USA. 2004. Rel: 2 July 2004. USA. Cert. 15.

Coach Carter ★★★½

Ken Carter is not sure he wants to coach the basketball team at California's Richmond High School. Richmond is one 'tough little city' and its African-American youth are more likely to end up in jail than college. But Carter was once a student at Richmond himself and so decides to knock some sense and respect into his rebellious charges. They can't play basketball worth a shit, but they're gonna learn to love him and call him 'Sir'... Sometimes a performance can make or break a film. It's hard to imagine any actor other than Samuel L. Jackson who could have brought so much powerful credibility to the role of the real-life Ken Carter. A disciplinarian with a heart of gold, he sees basketball as a sport that serves as a metaphor for team spirit and personal improvement. Jackson is unassailable, a towering, charismatic presence you wouldn't want to mess with, but to whom you would entrust your life. The film itself is a little long, and some of the plotting a tad mechanical, but it holds the interest and manages to convey an edge of danger and reality without resorting to cheap profanity, sex or violence. JC-W

• *Coach Ken Carter* Samuel L. Jackson, *Kyra* Ashanti, *Damien Carter* Robert Ri'chard, *Kenyon Stone* Rob Brown, *Tonya* Debbi Morgan, *Timo Cruz* Rick Gonzalez, *Worm* Antwon Tanner, *Junior Battle* Nana Gbewonyo, *Jason Lyle* Channing Tatum, *Maddux* Texas Battle, *Principal Garrison* Denise Dowse, *Coach White* Mel Winkler, *Renny* Vincent Laresca, *Willa Battle* Octavia Spencer, *with* Sidney Faison, Sonya Eddy, Gwen McGee, Ausanta, Bob Costas, Ray Baker, Marc McClure, Jenny Gago, Ben Weber.

• *Dir* Thomas Carter, *Pro* Brian Robbins, Mike Tollin and David Gale, *Ex Pro* Van Toffler, Thomas Carter, Sharla Sumpter and Caitlin Scanlon, *Screenplay* Mark Schwahn and

John Gatins, *Ph* Sharone Meir, *Pro Des* Carlos Barbosa, *Ed* Peter Berger, *M* Treevor Rabin; songs performed by DMX, Red Café, Fabolous, Chingy and G.I.B., The Game, Ciara, Malik Yusef, Twista and Faith Evans, Van Hunt, Ak'Sent, CzarNok, Mack 10, St Lunatics, LeToya, Trey Songz, LL Cool J, Alicia Keys, The Main Ingredient, etc, *Costumes* Debrae K. Little, *Choreography* Dave Scott, *Basketball Coordinator* Mark Ellis, *Executive Consultants* Ken Carter and Damien Carter.

Paramount/MTV Films/Tollin/Robbins/MMDP Munich Movie Developement-UIP. 136 mins. Germany/USA. 2004. Rel: 25 February 2005. Cert. 12A.

Code 46 ★★★★

William Geld, a psychic investigator, is sent to Shanghai to uncover the fraudulent production of papelles, permits that act as a combination of passport, visa and insurance policy. Immediately recognising Maria Gonzalez as the forger, William falls for her ethereal charms and risks his career by protecting her... Few movies have presented a very plausible view of the future. *Code 46*, filmed in Shanghai, Hong Kong, Dubai and Rajasthan, blends futuristic skylines with scenes of Third World poverty to convincing effect. However, the mixing of English, Mandarin and Spanish into a generic language, along with the commonplace minutiae of genetic, technological and even psychological detail, really gives this film its stamp of authority. An intelligent sci-fi romance with a strong undercurrent of *film noir*, *Code 46* fuses elements of *1984*, *Blade Runner* and *Eternal Sunshine of the Spotless Mind*. Yet in spite of these comparisons, it inhabits a totally unique universe, a world that is at once alien and recognisable. A scenario of ideas married to a lush visual palette, *Code 46* doesn't completely work on an emotional level (some may even dismiss it as 'cold'), but it is a cerebral revelation. JC-W

• *William Geld* Tim Robbins, *Maria Gonzalez* Samantha Morton, *Sylvie* Jeanne Balibar, *Backland* Om Puri, *doctor* Essie Davis, *with* David Fahm, Kerry Shale, Nina Wadia, Benedict Wong, Nina Fog, Christopher Simpson, Mick Jones, Nina Sosanya.

• *Dir* Michael Winterbottom, *Pro* Andrew Eaton, *Ex Pro* David M. Thompson and Robert Jones, *Line Pro* Rosa Romero, *Screenplay* Frank Cottrell Boyce, *Ph* Alwin Kuchler and Marcel Zyskind, *Pro Des* Mark Tildesley, *Ed* Peter Christelis, *M* David Holmes, Steve Hilton and The Free Association; 'Warning Sign' performed by Coldplay, *Costumes* Natalie Ward, *Rain* Richard Conway

UK Film Council/United Artists/BBC Films/Revolution Films-Verve Pictures. 93 mins. UK/USA. 2003. Rel: 17 September 2004. Cert. 15.

Coffee and Cigarettes ★½

A series of brief encounters, *C&C* is an interesting idea that is severely undernourished. Inspired by a short film that Jim Jarmusch directed for TV's *Saturday Night Live*, *C&C* is nothing more than 11 vignettes comprising two or three characters, a table, coffee and cigarettes. Each table is different and the coffee ranges from espresso to mud, so it's ironic that the most arresting chapter is a meeting over tea and biscuits. This is an encounter in which the English actor Alfred Molina, a Los Angeles resident, has invited Steve Coogan to tea so as to spring a surprise. Molina is all star-struck admiration and Coogan something of a prima donna, a scenario that both actors play to comically uncomfortable effect. Shot in black-and-white and devoid of any real conversation (time to check out *My Dinner With André* again), the rest of *C&C* is a dramatic waste of talent. Smug and self-indulgent, this is celluloid ephemera for cinemagoers with too much time on their hands. JC-W

• *as themselves*: Roberto Benigni, Steven Wright, Joie Lee, Cinqué Lee, Steve Buscemi, Iggy Pop, Tom Waits, Joe Rigano, Vinny Vella, Vinny Vella Jr., Renée French, E.J. Rodriguez, Alex Descas, Isaach de Bankolé, Cate Blanchett, Meg White, Jack White, Alfred Molina, Steve Coogan, GZA, RZA, Bill Murray, Bill Rice, Taylor Mead, *as Shelly* Cate Blanchett.
• *Dir* and *Screenplay* Jim Jarmusch, *Pro* Joana Vicente and Jason Kliot, *Co-Pro* Stacey Smith and Gretchen McGowan, *Ph* Frederick Elmes, Ellen Kuras, Robby Müller and Tom DiCillo, *Pro Des* Mark Friedberg, Tom Jarmusch and Dan Bishop, *Ed* Jay Rabinowitz, Melody London, Terry Katz and Jim Jarmusch, *M* Richard Berry & The Pharoahs, Jerry Byrd, Funkadelic, Tom Waits, The Stooges, Janet Baker, Iggy Pop, etc.

Smokescreen/Asmik Ace/Bim Distribuzione/Open City Films-Tartan Films.
96 mins. USA/Japan/Italy. 2003. Rel: 22 October 2004. Cert. 15.

Collateral ★★★★½

Max Durocher is no ordinary cabbie. His interior is immaculate, his knowledge of the LA streets scientific, his perception of people uncanny and his dreams are on hold. Then, one night, he connects with a beautiful female passenger and falls foul of a second one. In fact, the latter could be the last fare of his life… You have to hand it to Tom Cruise. He will try anything: a supporting role in *Magnolia*, a cameo in *Austin Powers in Goldmember*, two years with Stanley Kubrick, an existential adaptation of a Spanish mind-trip. Now he's trying on his first villain and turns in a performance of chilling, intelligent amorality – a silver-haired assassin loaded with bullets, attitude and philosophy. A high-concept thriller with a highly polished palette, *Collateral* is a visually seductive ride that begins with some telling detail and builds into a breakneck rollercoaster of suspense. However, unlike most high-concept thrillers, this one is developed through its characters, namely a conscientious under-achiever and a ruthless professional, 'taking out the garbage.' There are also some surprising moments of humour (a delicious cameo from Irma P. Hall), poetic pauses (Max and Vincent's observation of a prowling coyote) and action set-pieces to make your heart pound. JC-W

• *Vincent* Tom Cruise, *Max Durocher* Jamie Foxx, *Annie Farrell* Jada Pinkett Smith, *Fanning* Mark Ruffalo, *Richard Weidner* Peter Berg, *Pedrosa* Bruce McGill, *Daniel* Barry Shabaka Henley,

Ida Irma P. Hall, *Felix* Javier Bardem, *young professional woman* Debi Mazar, *man at airport* Jason Statham, *with* Richard T. Jones, Emilio Rivera, Jamie McBride, Inmo, Angelo Tiffe.

• *Dir* Michael Mann, *Pro* Mann and Julie Richardson, *Ex Pro* Frank Darabont, Chuck Russell, Rob Fried and Peter Giuliano, *Screenplay* Stuart Beattie, *Ph* Dion Beebe and Paul Cameron, *Pro Des* David Wasco, *Ed* Jim Miller and Paul Rubell, *M* James Newton Howard; J.S. Bach, *Costumes* Jeffrey Kurland, *Sound* Elliott L. Koretz.

DreamWorks/Paramount-UIP.
120 mins. USA. 2004. Rel: 17 September 2004. Cert. 15.

Comme une image
See *Look at Me*.

A Common Thread ★★★★

Short on incident but wonderfully rich in characterisation, Eléonore Faucher's feature debut is centred on two French women and on the influence that each has on the other. The superb Ariane Ascaride is an embroiderer weighed down by the death of her son in a road accident; the no-less marvellous Lola Naymark is the pregnant teenager who becomes her assistant. The latter is pondering her future, having hidden her pregnancy from parents and friends alike. There are a few misjudgments here (the ending needs re-editing) and some audiences may not respond. Nevertheless, Faucher is a strikingly individual talent and the decision to use limited dialogue has resulted in a film of quite exceptionally expressive facial acting. It's a remarkable achievement. Original title: *Brodeuses*. MS

• *Claire* Lola Naymark, *Madame Melikian* Ariane Ascaride, with Thomas Laroppe, Jacky Berroyer, Marie Felix, Marina Tome, Arthur Quechen.

• *Dir* Eléonore Faucher, *Pro* Alain Benguigui and Bertrand Van Effenterre, *Screenplay* Faucher and Gaëlle Macé, *Ph* Pierre Cottereau, *Pro Des* Philippe Van Herwijnen, *Ed* Joelle Van Effenterre, *M* Michael Galasso, *Costumes* Pascaline Suty.

Sombrero Prods/Mallia Films/Canal Plus-Soda Pictures.
87 mins. France. 2004. Rel: 20 May 2005. Cert. 12A.

The Consequences of Love ★★★★½

Titta di Girolamo has lived in the same Swiss hotel for more than eight years. Aloof and punctilious, he smokes incessantly, ignores the staff (even when spoken to) and injects himself with heroin every Wednesday precisely at ten o'clock. He would appear to be waiting for something to happen, which is maybe why he keeps a gun concealed in the television in his room. Or maybe he's just plucking up the courage to speak to the barmaid he can't take his eyes off. Or perhaps he's just waiting for the advent of his 50th birthday, which is very close indeed… Stylishly photographed and gorged with anticipation, *The Consequences of Love* is a film that really creeps up on you. One might be apt to call it a little gem, something of a discovery, had it not swept the Italian Oscars, winning the David Di Donatello for best film, director, actor, cinematography and screenplay. Dominated by a remarkable performance of sustained minimalism by Toni Servillo, the film is by turns touching, shocking, mesmerising and sublime. FYI: Olivia Magnani, who plays the barmaid Sofia, is the granddaughter of the great Italian actress Anna Magnani. Original title: *Le conseguenze dell'amore*. JC-W

• *Titta di Girolamo* Toni Servillo, *Sofia* Olivia Magnani, *Valerio* Adriano Giannini, *Carlo* Raffaele Pisu, *Isabella* Angela Goodwin, *director* Diego Ribon, *waitress* Giselda Volodi, *Letizia* Giovanni Vettorazzo, *bank manager* Antonio Ballerio, *assassins* Gilberto Idonea and Gaetano Bruno, *Pippo d'Antò* Enzo Vitagliano, *mafioso* Nino d'Agata.

• *Dir* and *Screenplay* Paolo Sorrentino, *Pro* Domenico Procacci, Nicola Giuliano, Francesca Cima and Angelo Curti, *Line Pro* Viola Prestieri, Gennaro Formisano and Chiara Cordaro, *Ph* Luca Bigazzi, *Pro Des* Lino Fiorito, *Ed* Giorgiò Franchini, *M* Pasquale Catalano, *Costumes* Ortensia De Francesco.

Fandango/Indigo Film/Medusa-Artificial Eye.
104 mins. Italy. 2004. Rel: 27 May 2005. Cert. 15.

Constantine ★★½

That's Constantine, John Constantine, tormented exorcist and chain smoker. Just as he discovers that he's got terminal lung cancer (30 fags a day since 15 – go figure), JC smells a gathering of evil forces on our earthly plane. The Spear of Destiny has been discovered in Mexico and the Catholic twin of a recent suicide case wants answers, so JC starts some serious digging… So, Keanu – the Chosen One – is back saving the world from inhuman forces, just like in *The Matrix*, *The Devil's Advocate* and *Bram Stoker's Dracula*. Actually, Keanu, the hardboard Messiah, is perfect for this comic-strip adaptation – he's so strikingly anodyne, wooden and angular. The film itself starts beautifully with the ominous discovery of Destiny's dagger and a genuinely scary exorcism, both empowered by fantastic special effects. But after the appearance of a variety of grisly demons, the digital trickery eventually takes over completely, undermining the visceral thrills and resulting in a tricksy TV commercial for the anti-smoking lobby. Still, Tilda Swinton is a natty Archangel Gabriel. FYI: Keanu and Rachel Weisz were previously on the run from the forces of evil in 1996's *Chain Reaction*. JC-W

• *John Constantine* Keanu Reeves, *Angela Dodson/Isabel Dodson* Rachel Weisz, *Chas* Shia LaBeouf, *Gabriel* Tilda Swinton, *Father Hennessy* Pruitt Taylor Vince, *Midnite* Djimon Hounsou, *Balthazar* Gavin Rossdale, *Satan* Peter Stormare, *Beeman* Max Baker, *with* Jose Zuniga, Francis Guinan, Larry Cedar, April Grace.

• *Dir* Francis Lawrence, *Pro* Lauren Shuler Donner, Benjamin Melniker, Michael E. Uslan, Erwin Stoff, Lorenzo DiBonaventura and Akiva Goldsman, *Ex Pro* Gilbert Adler and Michael Aguilar, *Co-Pro* Josh McLaglen and Cherylanne Martin, *Screenplay* Kevin Brodbin and Frank Cappello, *Ph* Philippe Rousselot, *Pro Des* Naomi Shohan, *Ed* Wayne

Tattoo you: Keanu Reeves fights his outer demons in Francis Lawrence's tricksy *Constantine* (from Warner)

Wahrman, *M* Brian Tyler and Klaus Badelt, *Costumes* Louise Frogley, *Visual Effects* Michael Fink.

Warner/Village Roadshow/Donners' Company/Batfilm Productions/Weed Road Pictures/3 Arts Entertainment-Warner.
121 mins. USA. 2005. Rel: 18 March 2005. Cert. 15.

Control Room ★★★★

In contrast to the powerful and fascinating polemic that is Michael Moore's *Fahrenheit 9/11*, this feature-length documentary by Jehane Noujaim, an Arab American, encourages the audience to reach their own conclusions. Shot in Doha, Qatar, it is a study of how the media reported the Iraq war. The strongest emphasis is placed on the independent news network Al Jazeera, condemned by Donald Rumsfeld for its bias. But almost as much prominence is given to the nearby American Central Command media headquarters, centre for the world press. What emerges all too clearly is the near impossibility of balanced war reporting when propaganda through the media is part of the military strategy of both sides. The film is undoubtedly critical of Bush, but that it features an American press officer increasingly able to see things from more than one viewpoint is characteristic of this sane and sensitive documentary. MS

• *Dir* Jehane Noujaim, *Pro* Rosadel Varela and Hani Salama, *Ex Pro* Noujaim, Varela and Abdallah Schleifer, *Ph* Noujaim and Salama, *Ed* Julia Bacha, Lilah Bankier and Charles Marquardt, *M* Salama, Kinan Azmeh, Hamsy El Din, Thomas DeRenzo, etc.

Noujaim Films-ICA Projects.
84 mins. USA. 2004. Rel: 23 July 2004. No cert.

The Corporation ★★★½

Despite having been shortened for its UK release, this feature documentary remains over-long at 144 minutes, and that's all the more evident because it is not so shaped as to intensify in impact during its later stages. That said, this is a wide-ranging look at corporations with important points to make. It covers such disparate areas as the history of the institution, its increasing world-wide dominance and its limited legal responsibility together with such related issues as exploitation of foreign labour, media control and practices harmful to the environment. There's humour to lighten the tone but the film is intended to disturb and it does. Nevertheless, for all its qualities you may be thankful when the end credit finally comes up. MS

• *with*: Ira Jackson, Robert Keyes, Joe Badaracco, Noam Chomsky, Michael Moore, Sir Mark Moody-Stuart, Milton Friedman, Naomi Klein, etc. *Narrator*: Mikela J. Mikael.

• *Dir* Mark Achbar and Jennifer Abbott, *Pro* Achbar and Bart Simpson, *Ex Pro* Achbar, *Co-Pro* Cari Green, Nathan Neumer and Tom Shandel, *Screenplay* Joel Bakan, with narration written by Achbar and Harold Crooks, based on the book *The Corporation: The Pathological Pursuit of Profit and Power* by Bakan, *Ed* Abbott, *M* Leonard J. Paul, *Sound* Velcrow Ripper, *Archival research* Paula Sawadsky.

Big Picture Media Corp/Cineworks Independent Filmmakers Society, etc-Metrodome.
144 mins. Canada. 2003. Rel: 29 October 2004. Cert. PG.

Creep ★★½

London; today. On her way to a potential tryst with George Clooney, fashion executive Kate falls asleep on the platform at Charing Cross tube station. Unable to get out, she is approached by a work colleague who makes an unseemly advance. But then he is dragged onto the tracks by an unseen assailant... Practically every horror film convention is thrown into the stew of this stylish co-production – a woman alone, the dark, claustrophobia, Something Unknown, rats, gore, you name it – but still it comes up reeking different. For a start, the setting of the London Underground – previously eviscerated in *Death Line* (1972) and touched on in *Reign of Fire* (2002) – is fertile territory for any thriller. Here, first-time director Christopher Smith is perhaps too eager to cram every touchstone he can into his maiden voyage. In fact, *Creep* is at its best when it doesn't appear to be trying – particularly in its latter half and in the ironic ending. The location work – much of it shot in Germany – is particularly effective. JC-W

• *Kate* Franka Potente, *George* Vas Blackwood, *Arthur* Ken Campbell, *Guy* Jeremy Sheffield, *Jimmy* Paul Rattray, *Mandy* Kelly Scott, *Craig* Sean Harris, *with* Debora Weston, Emily Gilchrist, Craig Fackrell, Elizabeth McKechnie.

• *Dir* and *Screenplay* Christopher Smith, *Pro* Julie Baines

and Jason Newmark, *Ex Pro* Robert Jones, *Co-Pro* Martin Hagemann, Kai Künnemann and Barry Hanson, *Line Pro* Alexandra Ferguson, *Ph* Danny Cohen, *Pro Des* John Frankish, *Ed* Kate Evans, *M* The Insects, *Costumes* Phoebe de Gaye, *Make-up Design* Jan Sewell, *Make-up Effects* Mike Bates and Mike Stringer.

UK Film Council/Filmstiftung Nordhein-Westfalen/
Dan Films-Pathé.
85 mins. UK/Germany/USA. 2004. Rel: 28 January 2005. Cert. 18.

Criminal ★★½

Los Angeles; today. A seasoned conman, Richard Gaddis takes a young pretender, Rodrigo, under his wing when the latter bungles a scam at an up-market casino. Explaining that he has lost his own partner, Gaddis offers to teach Rodrigo the tricks of his trade for one day. Then they stumble onto a sting that could, potentially, make them extremely rich men. Yet, in spite of their combined skills, Fate keeps on getting in the way... Dear old Hollywood. It just can't seem to get it right. Yet another remake of a foreign-language hit, *Criminal* flounders in spite of its pedigree. With Clooney and Soderbergh as co-producers, John C. Reilly in his first lead and with a first-time director, the prognosis was promising. While it's easy to understand the appeal of the story – quite faithfully lifted from the 2001 Argentinean film *Nine Queens* – its success is undermined by the disastrous miscasting of Reilly. He isn't a bad actor – he was nominated for an Oscar for *Chicago* – but he lacks the smarm, suavity and menace that his character calls for. Instead, Gaddis comes off as a cocky buffoon, a grating presence who could no more fool a shark like Peter Mullan's Hannigan (an excellent creation) than fly. Visually, however, the film is superb, while the story more than withstands its transfer from Buenos Aires. JC-W

• *Richard Gaddis* John C. Reilly, *Rodrigo/Brian* Diego Luna, *Valerie* Maggie Gyllenhaal, *William Hannigan* Peter Mullan, *Ochoa* Zitto Kazann, *Michael* Jonathan Tucker, *waitress* Laura Ceron, *grandmother* Ellen Geer, *Frank Hill* Malik Yoba, *with* Enrico Colantoni, Brandon Keener, Deborah Van Valkenburgh, Maeve Quinlan, Brent Sexton, Jack Conley, Michael Shannon.

• *Dir* Gregory Jacobs, *Pro* Jacobs, Steven Soderbergh and George Clooney, *Ex Pro* Jennifer Fox, Ben Cosgrove, Georgia Kacandes, Todd Wagner and Mark Cuban, *Screenplay* Jacobs and Sam Lowry, *Ph* Chris Menges, *Pro Des* Philip Messina, *Ed* Steve Mirrione, *M* Alex Wurman, *Costumes* Jeffrey Kurland.

Warner Independent Pictures/2929 Entertainment/Section Eight-Warner.
87 mins. USA. 2004. Rel: 18 February 2005. Cert. 15

Cursed ★

A wolf hasn't been sighted in Southern California in over 70 years, yet it was definitely a creature of lupine appearance that caused Ellie to lose control of her vehicle on Mulholland Drive. Running to the rescue of the car they've knocked off the road, Ellie and her brother Jimmy are mauled by the very same creature. Later, they find themselves endowed with an enhanced sense of smell and an increased physical strength... The fact is, the werewolf genre is inherently silly and only the use of considerable naturalism, subtlety or satire can make it work. Considering his post-modern take on horror with *Scream*, Wes Craven plays it pretty straight with this pointless variation of the 1957 *I Was a Teenage Werewolf*. Furthermore, Christina 'Munchkin' Ricci is an odd choice as a lycanthropic heroine and the orchestra dramatically overplays its hand. Oh, and the CGI effects suck. JC-W

• *Ellie* Christina Ricci, *Jake* Joshua Jackson, *Jimmy* Jesse Eisenberg, *Joannie* Judy Greer, *himself* Scott Baio, *Bo* Milo Ventimiglia, *Brooke* Kristina Anapau, *Zela* Portia de Rossi, *Becky Morton* Shannon Elizabeth, *Jenny* Mya, *Kyle* Michael Rosenbaum, *with* Jonny Acker, Eric Ladin, Craig Kilborn, Lance Bass.

• *Dir* Wes Craven, *Pro* Kevin Williamson and Marianne Maddalena, *Ex Pro* Bob Weinstein, Harvey Weinstein, Andrew Rona and Brad Weston, *Co-Pro* Julie Plec, Jennifer Breslow, Dan Arredondo and Dixie Capp, *Co-Ex Pro* Stuart Besser and David Crockett, *Screenplay* Williamson, *Ph* Robert McLachlan, *Pro Des* Bruce Alan Miller and Chris Cornwell, *Ed* Patrick Lussier and Lisa Romaniw, *M* Marco Beltrami; songs performed by Bowling for Soup, Seven Wiser, Alkaline Trio, Dashboard Confessional, Apollo 440, The Crystal Method, Collective Soul, MBD, etc, *Costumes* Alix Friedberg, *Visual Effects* Richard R. Hoover, *Make-Up Effects* Rick Baker.

Dimension Films/Outerbanks Entertainment/Craven/ Maddalena-Buena Vista International.
96 mins. USA. 2005. Rel: 22 April 2005.
Cert. 15.

Czech Dream ★★★

This documentary feature from the Czech Republic shows the filmmakers themselves hoaxing the public by setting up a professional advertising campaign for a new supermarket which, on opening day, will prove to be nothing but a facade. As a view of how advertising functions, it is thoroughly diverting and revealing in the manner of Vance Packard's classic book *The Hidden Persuaders*. But the gullible public actually behave quite reasonably on the whole and, by the time that aged folk put themselves out to try the bargains at the new market, you feel that it's the filmmakers who are the exploiters and that their film exposes them as much as it exposes the system. For a far more potent attack on capitalism try *Mondovino*, *The Corporation* or (best and most serious of all) *Darwin's Nightmare*. Original title: *Cesky sen*. MS

• *Dir and Screenplay* Vit Klusák and Filip Remunda, *Pro* Vit Klusák, Filip Remunda and Filip Cermak, *Ph* Klusák, *Ed* Zdenek Marek, *M* Hynek Schneider.

Hypermarket Film/Studio Mirage-Soda Pictures.
90 mins. Czech Republic/UK. 2004. Rel: 24 June 2005.
Cert. 12A.

Dans ma Peau
See *In My Skin*.

Darkness ★★★½

Forty years ago in rural Spain, Albert Rua participated in an occult ritual but failed to complete it when he couldn't sacrifice his own son. Now, with his own wife and two children, a fully grown Mark returns to Spain, moving them into a beautiful but mysterious manse built atop the sacrificial ring. As Mark's mind and health deteriorate, it falls to daughter Regina to discern the truth and resolve events begun four decades earlier... Far more challenging than the usual haunted-house fare, *Darkness* lives up to its title through the astonishing cinematography of Xavi Giménez. It's oddly appropriate that child Oscar-winner Paquin shares the screen with the startling film debut of Stephan Enquist, who gives a too-genuine performance as her onscreen brother. As nihilistic as it is creepy, this is a dark film indeed. SWM

• *Regina Rua* Anna Paquin, *Maria* Lena Olin, *Mark* Iain Glen, *Albert Rua* Giancarlo Giannini, *Carlos* Fele Martínez, *Villalobos* Fermí Reixach, *Paul Rua* Stephan Enquist.

• *Dir* Jaume Balagueró, *Pro* Brian Yuzna and Julio Fernández, *Ex Pro* Julio Fernández, Carlos Fernández and Guy J. Louthan, *Co-Ex Pro* Antonia Nava, *Line Pro* Teresa Gefaell, *Screenplay* Balagueró and Fernando de Felipe, *Ph* Xavi Giménez, *Pro Des* Llorenç Miguel, *Ed* Luís D. la Madrid, *M* Carles Cases, *Costumes* Eva Arretxe.

Filmax/Dimension Films-Buena Vista International.
88 mins. Spain/USA. 2002. Rel: 18 March 2005.
Cert. 15.

Darwin's Nightmare ★★★★

The last half hour of Hubert Sauper's first documentary feature slightly loses its way, becoming a touch repetitive and containing some redundant material. For the rest, however, it's brilliant. Quietly angry and controlled like that greatest of all documentaries *Night and Fog*, Sauper's film builds up a stunning indictment of capitalism in Tanzania. It starts with information about the Nile perch, a fish that ate up others when placed in Lake Victoria in the 1960s and then became the source of the region's huge export trade. The big profits are earned at severe cost to the local people and Sauper shows this not by making personal judgments or through emotional manipulation but by allowing the facts to speak for themselves. Highly recommended. MS

• *Dir* and *Screenplay* Hubert Sauper, *Pro* Sauper, Edouard Mauriat, Antonin Svoboda, Martin Gschlacht, Barbara Albert and Hubert Toint, *Ph* Sauper, *Ed* Denise Vindevogel, *Sound* Veronika Hlavatsch.

Mille et une prods/Coop99/Saga Film-ICA Projects.
105 mins. Canada. 2004. Rel: 6 May 2005.
Cert. 15.

Dead Man's Shoes ★★★★

Over-praised by some who wrongly regard this Shane Meadows film as akin to his masterpiece *A Room for Romeo Brass* rather than to *Once Upon a Time in the Midlands*, this piece, co-authored by its admirable star Paddy Considine, is extraordinary. It begins as a kind of pastiche-cum-parody of revenge dramas just as its predecessor drew on Westerns. Here vengeance involves knocking off the guilty one by one but against a background of lower class life in the Midlands. As rough as a Warhol movie in contrast to the sheen found in many recent movies shot digitally, this uneasy mix of laughs and thrills grows increasingly serious. Ultimately it becomes a drama of guilt and redemption that really does examine the cost of wreaking vengeance. Uneven as it is in every way, it eventually resonates hauntingly. Not Meadows' best film but arguably his most remarkable. MS

• *Richard* Paddy Considine, *Sonny* Gary Stretch, *Anthony* Toby Kebbell, *Herbie* Stuart Wolfenden, *Soz* Neil Bell, *with* Paul Sadot, Seamus O'Neill, Paul Hurstfield, Jo Hartley, Emily Aston, Craig Considine, Matthew Considine, Arthur Meadows, Gill Meadows.

• *Dir* Shane Meadows, *Pro* Mark Herbert, *Ex Pro* Tessa Ross, Peter Carlton, Steve Beckett and Will Clarke, *Co-Pro* Louise Meadows, *Screenplay* Meadows and Paddy Considine, *Ph* Danny Cohen, *Art Dir* Adam Tomlinson, *Ed* Chris Wyatt, Lucas Roche and Celia Haining, M various; Arvo Pärt; songs performed by Smog, Danger Mouse and Jemini, Calexico, Adem, DJ Armchair, ABBC, Position Normal, Laurent Garnier, Richard Hawley, Aphex Twin, etc, *Costumes* Teresa Hughes.

Film Four/EMMI/Warp Films/Big Arty-Optimum Releasing.
90 mins. UK. 2004. Rel: 1 October 2004. Cert. 18.

Dear Frankie ★★★★★

Frankie Morrison is nine years old, bright as a button and deaf. He is the son of Lizzie, a suspicious, defensive young woman who barely fits in her own skin. Frankie and Lizzie are running away and at the beginning of this beautifully crafted, extraordinarily moving film they have just checked into a new apartment in Greenock, Scotland. There, they lead a humdrum life with Lizzie's chain-smoking mother and slowly adapt to the new neighbourhood. It transpires that Lizzie is running away from her abusive husband and has manufactured a fictitious, absent father for Frankie, a sailor to whom Frankie writes often (and whose letters Lizzie answers in a disguised hand). Then, due to a confusion of misinformation, the imaginary sailor docks at Greenock and Frankie expects to finally meet his 'da'… Adapted from a short script called *Natural History*, *Dear Frankie* marks the directorial debut of the stills photographer Shona Auerbach and is also the first screenplay by Andrea Gibb. Together, Auerbach and Gibb have fashioned a credible, poetic tale that resonates with poignancy without a hint of manipulation. Emily Mortimer is totally believable as Lizzie, from her uncomfortable walk to her faltering gaze, and the rest of the cast is spot-on. So is the photography, editing and music, amounting to a modern classic that touches the heart with a rare profundity. JC-W

• *Lizzie Morrison* Emily Mortimer, *the stranger* Gerard Butler, *Frankie Morrison* Jack McElhone, *Marie* Sharon Small, *Nell* Mary Riggans, *Catriona* Jayd Johnson, *Ricky Monroe, the class bully* Sean Brown, *Davey* Cal Macaninch, *with* Sophie Main, Kate Murphy, Anna Hepburn, *waitress* Andrea Gibb.

• *Dir* and *Ph* Shona Auerbach, *Pro* Caroline Wood, *Ex Pro* Stephen Evans, Angus Finney, François Ivernel, Cameron McCracken and Duncan Reid, *Co-Pro* Gillian Berrie, *Screenplay* Andrea Gibb, *Pro Des* Jennifer Kernke, *Ed* Oral Nottie Ottey,

Life without father: Emily Mortimer, Jake McElhone and Gerard Butler in Shona Auerbach's poetic, credible and poignant *Dear Frankie* (from Pathé)

M Alex Heffes; Arvo Pärt; songs performed by Clarksville, Obi, and Jesse Harris, *Costumes* Carole K. Millar.

Pathé/UK Film Council/Scottish Screen/Scorpio Films/Sigma Films/Inside Track/National Lottery-Pathé.
104 mins. UK. 2003. Rel: 14 January 2005. Cert. 12A.

De-Lovely ★★½

Rather than capturing the spirit of the effortlessly witty songwriter Cole Porter, or focusing on one chapter of his life, the film takes an ambitious guided tour through the years and the latex. Kevin Kline would have been the ideal actor to play Porter ten years ago, but at 56 he looks a tad middle-aged to be gadding about Paris picking up both sexes. Not that the Porter story isn't a fascinating one – a bisexual genius of privilege, he ended up a one-legged recluse – it's just an unwieldy canvas to tame for a two-hour film. It's unfortunate, too, that the whole thing was shot in Europe (with those cloudy skies) and that an inordinate number of British actors are asked to adopt a variety of American twangs. Thank God, then, for the songs, a number of which are highlighted in some imaginative set-pieces, while others are interpreted by a host of contemporary names of pop, rock and soul. JC-W

• *Cole Porter* Kevin Kline, *Linda Porter* Ashley Judd, *Gerald Murphy* Kevin McNally, *Monty Woolley* Allan Corduner, *Sara Murphy* Sandra Nelson, *Irving Berlin* Keith Allen, *Edward Thomas* James Wilby, *actor in 'Night and Day'* John Barrowman, *Bobby Reed* Kevin McKidd, *Gabe* Jonathan Pryce, *Louis B. Mayer* Peter Polycarpou, *Diaghilev* Peter Jessop, *with* Richard Dillane, Edward Baker-Duly, Susannah Fellows, Teddy Kempner, Natalie Cole, Elvis Costello, Sheryl Crow, Lara Fabian, Vivian Green, Mick Hucknall, Diana Krall, Lemar, Alanis Morissette, Caroline O'Connor, Robbie Williams.

• *Dir* Irwin Winkler, *Pro* Irwin Winkler, Rob Cowan and Charles Winkler, *Ex Pro* Simon Channing Williams and Gail Egan, *Line Pro* Georgina Lowe, *Screenplay* Jay Cocks, *Ph* Tony Pierce-Roberts, *Pro Des* Eve Stewart, *Ed* Julie Monroe, *M* Stephen Endelman; songs by Cole Porter, *Costumes* Janty Yates, *Choreography* Francesca Jaynes.

MGM/DeLux Prods-Fox.
125 mins. USA/Luxemburg. 2004. Rel: 1 October 2004. Cert. PG.

A Dirty Shame ★★½

When repressed, Baltimore suburb-based Sylvia Stickles (a brilliant Tracey Ullman) gets conked on the head, she turns into a sex-starved pervert and is determined to experience every form of sex imaginable. With the help of pornographic hedonist Ray-Ray (Johnny Knoxville, in all his lascivious glory), the residents of Harford Road expose their sexual underbelly to a disapproving community led by Sylvia's mother, Big Ethel. Typical of John Waters' particular oeuvre, the story is simplistic, the acting over the top, and the production values low. But it does retain the filmmaker's omnipresent determination to discuss in broad daylight (or flickering movie light) topics we'd all rather avoid but, as Waters knows, all think about. In a society where sexual freedom is constantly at war with sexual repression, not having a film like this would be a dirty shame. SWM

• *Sylvia Stickles* Tracey Ullman, *Ray-Ray Perkins* Johnny Knoxville, *Caprice Stickles* Selma Blair, *Vaughn Stickles* Chris Isaak, *Big Ethel* Suzanne Shepherd, *Marge the Neuter* Mink Stole, *Paige* Patricia Hearst, *Dora* Jackie Hoffman, *with* Wes Johnson, Susan Allenbach, Paul DeBoy, Jewel Orem, James Ransone, Alan J. Wendl, Jonas Grey, David Hasselhoff.

• *Dir* and *Screenplay* John Waters, *Pro* Christine Vachon and Ted Hope, *Ex Pro* Mark Ordesky, Mark Kaufman, Merideth Finn, John Wells and the Fisher Brothers [Danny, Jack and Joe Fisher], *Co-Pro* Anne Ruark, *Co-Ex Pro* Michael Almog and Bob Jason, *Ph* Steve Gainer, *Pro Des* Vincent Peranio, *Ed* Jeffrey Wolf, *M* George S. Clinton; songs performed by Don Gardner and Dee Dee Ford, Connie Vannett, Slim Harpo, Jody Reynolds, Johnny Burnette, Run C&W, The Chipmunks, Jerry Lee Lewis, Little Ritchie Ray, James Intved, Screamin' Jay Hawkins, Billy Lee Riley, Faye Richmonde, Earl Grant, etc, *Costumes* Van Smith.

Fine Line Features/This is That/Killer Films/City Lights Pictures-Entertainment.
88 mins. USA. 2004. Rel: 29 April 2005. Cert. 18.

Dodgeball: A True Underdog Story ★½

Peter LaFleur runs a gymnasium for losers – Average Joe's – and owes $50,000 to the bank. To avoid a hostile take-over by a glitzy rival – Globo Gym – LaFleur is persuaded against his better judgment to enter his clientele into a cut-throat contest of Dodgeball. The prize money: $50,000. The competition: the vain and bulked-up White Goodman, owner of Globo Gym… On a superficial level, it's hard to comprehend how such an obvious, moronic and familiar comedy like this could take more than $114m at the US box-office. The fifth Ben Stiller vehicle to be released in the UK in 2004 (along with *Along Came Polly*, *Starsky and Hutch*, *Our House* and *Envy*), *Dodgeball* is the worst offender not least because Stiller jettisons his trademark straight guy in favour of over-acting. His pompous over-achiever might've passed muster on a *Saturday Night Live* slot, but is wearisome dragged over a whole movie. The rest is predictable, derivative, adolescent swill. JC-W

• *Peter LaFleur* Vince Vaughn, *White Goodman* Ben Stiller, *Kate Veatch* Christine Taylor, *Patches O'Houlihan* Rip Torn, *Justin* Justin Long, *Gordon* Stephen Root, *Owen* Joel David Moore, *Dwight* Chris Williams, *Steve the Pirate* Alan Tudyk, *Fran Stalinovskovicdaviddivichski* Missi Pyle, *Me'Shell Jones* Jamal E. Duff, *Cotton McKnight* Gary Cole, *Pepper Brooks* Jason Bateman, *Amber* Julie Gonzalo, *with* Hank Azaria, Lance Armstrong, Chuck Norris, William Shatner, David Hasselhoff, Rusty Joiner, Curtis Armstrong, Tate Chalk, Amy Stiller, *Vegas homophobe* Rawson Marshall Thurber, Sik End.

• *Dir* and *Screenplay* Rawson Marshall Thurber, *Pro* Ben Stiller and Stuart Cornfeld, *Ex Pro* Mary McLaglen and Rhoades Rader, *Ph* Jerzy Zielinsky, *Pro Des* Maher Ahmad, *Ed* Alan Baumgarten and Peter Teschner, *M* Theodore Shapiro; songs performed by Infomercial, Kelis, The Donnas, Stereophonics, Chris De Burgh, Claude Jay McLin, Sugarhill Gang, Romeo Void, Jamelia, 12 Gauge and James Brown, Tom Morello, and The Bleacher Heroes, *Costumes* Carol Ramsey, *Choreography* Eartha Robinson, *Cheerleading Coordinator* Tate Chalk.

Fox/Mediastream IV/Red Hour-Fox.
92 mins. USA/Germany. 2004. Rel: 27 August 2004. Cert. 12A.

Don't Move ★★
On a very wet day a 15-year-old girl is knocked off her scooter. She is taken to the hospital, unconscious, where her father, Timoteo, works as a surgeon. As Timoteo's colleagues fight to save his daughter's life, he recalls a summer 16 years earlier when he did a terrible, uncharacteristic thing… The photography is very pretty, Penélope Cruz is anything but and the style and eccentricity triumph over any real emotional involvement. Recalling the giddy, passionate and courageous cinema of the Spanish New Wave (the film is actually a Spanish co-production), *Don't Move* is impressive in parts (Cruz is a stand-out), but ultimately fails to connect on an intimate, human level. And as this is a story of love, marriage and infidelity, the emotions should count for something. As a director, actor Sergio Castellitto (*The Starmaker*) reveals a true understanding of the cinematic flourish (he co-adapted this from his own wife's novel), but a far more engaging, excoriating and memorable exploration of marital ambivalence was Virginie Wagon's *Le Secret* (2000) (there are several thematic comparisons). Still, people will be talking about Cruz's self-sacrificing, almost masochistic performance for years to come. Original title: *Non ti muovere*. JC-W

• *Italia* Penélope Cruz, *Timoteo* Sergio Castellitto, *Elsa* Claudia Gerini, *Ada* Angela Finocchiaro, *Manlio* Marco Giallini, *Alfredo* Pietro De Silva, *Angela* Elena Perino, *with* Vittoria Piancastelli, Lina Bernardi, Gianni Musy.

• *Dir* Sergio Castellitto, *Pro* Riccardo Tozzi, Giovanni Stabilini and Marco Chimenz, *Assoc Pro* Giovannella Zannoni, *Screenplay* Castellitto and Margaret Mazzantini, *Ph* Gianfilippo Corticelli, *Pro Des* Francesco Frigeri, *Ed* Patrizio Marone, *M* Lucio Godoy, *Costumes* Isabella Rizza.

Cattleya/Medusa Film-Dogwoof Pictures.
122 mins. Italy/Spain/UK. 2004. Rel: 18 March 2005. Cert. 15.

The Door in the Floor ★★★★
The Door in the Floor is the name of a children's book by the celebrated writer and artist Theodore Cole. It also serves as a potent metaphor for the emerging hole in Cole's own life as witnessed by his new assistant, the callow and impressionable 16-year-old Eddie O'Hare. Eddie plans to be a writer himself and has read everything Cole has written, although he is drawn more towards Cole's wife, the brittle but very beautiful

Marion… Adapted from John Irving's 1998 novel *A Widow for One Year*, *The Door in the Floor* is a rich, nuanced and grown-up drama that interweaves a number of themes, including marriage, loss, emotional stasis, the creative process, betrayal and sexual awakening. Jeff Bridges totally embodies the charismatic contradictions of Cole – a Bohemian figure with a dash of Hemingway – while Kim Basinger gives a delicate, understated performance as Cole's psychologically cauterised wife. The direction and screenplay by Tod Williams are first-rate. JC-W

• *Theodore Cole* Jeff Bridges, *Marion Cole* Kim Basinger, *Eddie O'Hare* Jon Foster, *Evelyn Vaughn* Mimi Rogers, *Ruth Cole* Elle Fanning, *Alice* Bijou Phillips, *Eduardo Gomez* Louis Arcella, *with* Larry Pine, John Rothman, Harvey Loomis, Donna Murphy.

• *Dir* and *Screenplay* Tod Williams, *Pro* Michael Corrente, Ted Hope and Anne Carey, *Ex Pro* Amy J. Kaufman and Roger Marino, *Co-Pro* Marisa Polvino, *Ph* Terry Stacey, *Pro Des* Thérèse DePrez, *Ed* Affonso Gonçalves, *M* Marcelo Zarvos, *Costumes* Eric Daman, *Children's illustrations* Jeff Bridges.

Focus Features/Revere Pictures/This is That-Momentum.
110 mins. USA. 2004. Rel: 11 February 2005. Cert. 15.

Downfall ★★★
Berlin; 1945. Berlin is surrounded by Russian troops and Adolf Hitler has bunkered down in his well-appointed headquarters beneath the city's streets. As defeat appears to be increasingly inevitable, the Führer pumps his officers with fanciful notions of triumph while blaming the German people for his country's overthrow… Virtually a dramatisation of the 2002 talking head documentary *Blind Spot: Hitler's Secretary*, *Downfall* offers little new on a subject that has been filmed to death. The difference here, though, is that Hitler is not played by Richard Basehart, Alec Guinness, or even Antony Sher, but by the Zurich-born Bruno Ganz. Furthermore, this is a German version of events and shows the Führer to be every bit as mad as Hollywood suspected. Even so, it's hard to sympathise with any of the Nazis, even in the film's closing chapters when suicide becomes an epidemic. However, *Downfall* is competently made and by the end, the catalogue of death, summary amputations, suicide and histrionic tantrums combine to create a salutary history lesson. And the sequence in which Frau Goebbels methodically poisons her six young children will be hard to erase from the memory. JC-W

• *Adolf Hitler* Bruno Ganz, *Traudl Junge* Alexandra Maria Lara, *Magda Goebbels* Corinna Harfouch, *Joseph Goebbels* Ulrich Matthes, *Eva Braun* Juliane Koehler, *Albert Speer* Heino Ferch, *Professor Dr Ernst-Günther Schenck* Christian Berkel, *Hermann Fegelein* Thomas Kretschmann, *Heinrich Himmler* Ulrich Noethen, *Gerda Christian* Birgit Minichmayr, *Martin Bormann* Thomas Thieme.

• *Dir* Oliver Hirschbiegel, *Pro* and *Screenplay* Bernd Eichinger, *Ex Pro* Christine Rothe, *Ph* Rainer Klausmann, *Art Dir* Bernd Lepel, *Ed* Hans Funck, *M* Stephan Zacharias, *Costumes* Claudia Bobsin, *Sound* Stefan Busch and Nico Krebs.

Constantin Film/NDR/WDR/Degeto Film/
ORF-Momentum Pictures.
155 mins. Germany/Austria/Italy. 2004.
Rel: 1 April 2005. Cert. 15.

Dr. Rey ...
See *Merci Dr Rey*.

Duck Season ★★½
Duck Season is not a film for everyone. In fact, it's hard to imagine who would want to pay good money to see a black-and-white Mexican movie about a day in the life of two bored teenagers. Set almost entirely in one apartment, *Duck Season* opens with a series of still lives depicting urban decay. Once inside, the film grinds to a halt. Moko and Flama have been left to themselves for the day and so they drink Coke, eat potato chips and wrestle with their PlayStation. They also order a pizza. A 16-year-old neighbour, Rita, pops in to borrow their oven and attempts to bake a cake. There is much talk about hair colour, some expletives and even a kiss. Exciting, huh? Actually, first-time director Fernando Eimbcke reveals a poetic eye, a wry sense of humour and an astonishing knack for coaxing naturalistic performances from his inexperienced actors. In its own small way, *Duck Season* is quite daring and revealing, even if it's undermined by the limitations of its ambition. Original title: *Temporada de patos*. JC-W

• *Ulises* Enrique Arreola, *Moko* Diego Catano, *Flama* Daniel Miranda, *Rita* Danny Perea.

• *Dir* Fernando Eimbcke, *Pro* Christian Valdelievre, *Ex Pro* Jaime Bernardo Ramos, *Screenplay* Eimbcke, Paula Markovitch and Felipe Cazals, *Ph* Alexis Zabé, *Art Dir* Diana Quiroz, *Ed* Mariana Rodríguez, *M* Alejandro Rosso and Liquits, *Costumes* Lissi de la Concha, *Sound* Lena Esquenazi.

Cinepantera/Lulu Producciones-Optimum Releasing.
90 mins. Mexico. 2004. Rel: 11 March 2005.
Cert. 15.

Duma ★★★★
When 12-year-old Xan's father dies, his mother is forced to rent out their South African farm and move to an apartment in the city. This proves a problem for Xan's orphaned cheetah, Duma (Swahili for 'cheetah') who, no longer a cub, must be returned to the wild. But Xan dotes on his feline companion and cannot bear to see Duma go... Carroll Ballard has exhibited a gift for crafting magnificent movies from natural settings, and is a past master at directing children and especially animals, be they horse (in *The Black Stallion*), wolf (*Never Cry Wolf*) or geese (*Fly Away Home*). Here, he is on typically assured form, creating a gripping story (inspired by real events) with a delicacy and intelligence, while setting it in some awe-inspiring landscapes. As our natural world dwindles around us, films like *Duma* should be embraced by everybody (from Bob Geldof down) to reveal what a wonderful place we live in – for now. Shame on Warner Bros. for throwing this rare gem away. It was barely released. CB

• *Xan* Alexander Michaletos, *Ripkuna* Eamonn Walker, *Peter* Campbell Scott, *Kristin* Hope Davis, *Thandi* Mary Makhatho.

• *Dir* Carroll Ballard, *Pro* John Wells, Hunt Lowry, E.K. Gaylord II, Kristin Harms and Stacy Cohen, *Ex Pro* Doug Claybourne, *Co-Pro* David Wicht and Vlokkie Gordon, *Screenplay* Karen Janszen and Mark St. Germain, from a story by Janszen and Carol Flint, based on the book *How It Was with Dooms* by Carol Cawthra Hopcraft and Xan Hopcraft, *Ph* Werner Maritz, *Pro Des* Johnny Breedt, *Ed* T.M. Christopher, *M* John Debney and George Acogny, *Costumes* Jayne Forbes, *Sound* Ann Kroeber.

Warner/Gaylord Films-Warner.
100 mins. USA. 2005. Rel: 27 May 2005. Cert. U.

The Edukators ★★★★
A family returns home to find that somebody has been in their house. The alarm has been disabled, the furniture rearranged and a note left which proclaims, 'Your Days of Plenty Are Numbered.' It's a chilling opening to this novel drama, whose narrative switches from the disconcerted victims to the perpetrators of the crime. The latter are Jan and Peter, two idealistic young men dedicated to shaking up the Establishment. They don't mean any real harm to anybody but they do hope to change a constitution that systematically exploits the Third World. Then they make a terrible mistake... Director Hans Weingartner obviously has revolution on his mind. Having revealed the irresponsible *modus operandi* of his villains, he then colours in their lives so that we cannot but warm to them. Indeed, the director has said that 'I want people to come out of *The Edukators* and tap into their revolutionary zeal.' Yet he also sustains an almost constant tone of suspense as events spiral out of control – which, considering the film's length, is no mean feat. JC-W

• *Jan* Daniel Brühl, *Jule* Julia Jentsch, *Peter* Stipe Erceg, *Hardenberg* Burghart Klaussner, *landlord* Hanns Zischler, *Paolo* Claudio Caiolo.

• *Dir* Hans Weingartner, *Pro* Weingartner and Antonin Svoboda, *Line Pro* Karsten Aurich, *Screenplay* Weingartner and Katharina Held, *Ph* Matthias Schellenberg and Daniela Knapp, *Pro Des* Christian M. Goldbeck, *Ed* Dirk Oetelshoven and Andreas Wodraschke, *M* Andreas Wodraschke, *Costumes* Silvia Pernegger, *Sound* Uwe Dresch.

y3/coop99-UGC Films UK.
129 mins. Germany/Austria. 2004. Rel: 15 April 2005.
Cert. 15.

Elektra ★
Having recovered from her death at the hands of Bullseye, Elektra Natchios cuts herself off from her emotions and gets back to killing people. However, when she's contracted to wipe out a handsome widower and his 13-year-old daughter, she cannot bring herself to do it. So an invincible, supernatural quartet of Japanese assassins – collectively known as The Hand – are hired to finish the job... Whoosh!

Jenny alias *Elektra*.
(from Fox)

There goes a self-indulgent sound effect. Swoosh! There goes an ostentatious CGI creation. Clunk! There goes another line of dialogue. And Jennifer Garner was doing so well. Sure, there was the mawkish and interminable *Pearl Harbor* (with Ben Affleck) and there was the overwrought and wearisome *Daredevil* (with Ben Affleck). But there was also her Golden Globe Award, the Spielberg movie and *13 Going On 30*. Then Ms Garner started dating Ben Affleck... Pompous, self-important and stylised to a fault, *Elektra* is the most tedious superhero movie since, well, *Daredevil*. JC-W

• *Elektra Natchios* Jennifer Garner, *Stick* Terence Stamp, *Mark Miller* Goran Visnjic, *Abby Miller* Kirsten Prout, *Roshi* Cary-Hiroyuki Tagawa, *Kirigi* Will Yun Lee, *Tattoo* Chris Ackerman, *Kinkou* Edson T. Ribeiro, *Typhoid* Natassia Malthe, *McCabe* Colin Cunningham, *young Elektra* Laura Ward, *with* Bob Sapp, Hiro Kanagawa, Mark Houghton, and (uncredited) *DeMarco* Jason Isaacs.

• *Dir* Rob Bowman, *Pro* Arnon Milchan, Gary Foster and Avi Arad, *Ex Pro* Stan Lee, Mark Steven Johnson and Brent O'Connor, *Screenplay* Zak Penn, Stuart Zicherman and Raven Metzner, *Ph* Bill Roe, *Pro Des* Graeme Murray, *Ed* Kevin Stitt, *M* Christophe Beck, *Costumes* Lisa Tomczeszyn.

Fox/Regency Enterprises/Marvel Enterprises/New Regency/Horseshoe Bay-Fox.
98 mins. USA. 2005. Rel: 21 January 2005. Cert. 12A.

Ella Enchanted ★½

Once upon a time the new-born daughter of Sir Peter of Frell is given the gift of obedience (by the sassy sister and sometime fairy Lucinda Perriweather). Thus, when Ella of Frell grows up to be a full-bosomed lass, she is at the beck and call of whomsoever should bid her. Then Ella's father marries the ghastly Lady Olga, whose cruel, grabby daughters move into the family fold... After *Shrek*, any revision of the traditional fairy tale format ought to have a damn good concept. Alas, *Ella* is far from enchanting, being an adolescent jumble of slapstick, creaking pop songs and some shockingly bad acting. To date, director Tommy O'Haver has exhibited a freshness and energy (cf. *Billy's Hollywood Screen Kiss*, *Get Over It*) but belabours the wrong tone with his adaptation of Gail Carson Levine's popular novel. Very young girls may connect with the pantomimic material and swoon over Hugh Dancy (who may or may not be doing a parody of Orlando Bloom), but few others will care. Cary Elwes, who starred in the canny 1987 fairy tale *The Princess Bride*, should've known better – here he gives the worst performance of his career. JC-W

• *Ella of Frell* Anne Hathaway, *Prince Charmont* Hugh Dancy, *Sir Edgar* Cary Elwes, *Lucinda Perriweather* Vivica A. Fox, *Dame Olga* Joanna Lumley, *Mandy* Minnie Driver, *narrator* Eric Idle, *Benny, the talking encyclopaedia* Jimi Mistry, *Heston* Steve Coogan, *Hattie* Lucy Punch, *Olive* Jennifer Higham, *Sir Peter of Frell* Patrick Bergin, *Slannen of Pim* Aidan McArdle, *Brumhilda* Heidi Klum, *Nish* Jim Carter, *Areida* Parminder Nagra, *with* Donna Dent, Rory Keenan.

• *Dir* Tommy O'Haver, *Pro* Jane Startz, *Ex Pro* Su Armstrong, Bob Weinstein, Harvey Weinstein and Julie Goldstein, *Screenplay* Laurie Craig, Karen McCullah Lutz, Kirsten Smith, Jennifer Heath and Michele J. Wolff, *Ph* John de Borman, *Pro Des* Norman Garwood, *M* Nick Glennie-Smith; songs performed by Darren Hayes, Jump 5, Kelly Clarkson, Leo Sayer, Anne Hathaway, Raven, Stimulator, etc, *Costumes* Ruth Myers, *Choreography* Bruno Tonioli.

Miramax/World 2000 Entertainment-Buena Vista International.
96 mins. USA/UK/Ireland. 2004. Rel: 17 December 2004. Cert. PG.

End of the Century:
The Story of the Ramones ★★★

In contrast to the more insightful *Metallica: Some Kind of Monster*, this feature about the punk rock band The Ramones has limited appeal unless you happen to be fans of their music. This is so despite both films revealing the tensions that can arise from performing as a touring group while also containing sequences that amuse. Admittedly some of the footage here is striking (as in the portrait of record producer Phil Spector, who could make you perform at gunpoint), but much of the film stock showing The Ramones in concert is of poor quality. Furthermore, short as the songs were (this being one of the odder characteristics of The Ramones' music), the filmmakers frequently allow comments to intrude distractingly over the performances. MS

• *with*: The Ramones (Mark Bell, John Cummings, Chris Ward, Douglas Colvin, Tom Erdelyi, Jeff Hyman), Captain Sensible, Jayne County, Debbie Harry, Anthony Kiedis, Glen Matlock, Chris Stein, Arturo Vega, Joe Strummer, Rob Zombie, etc.

• *Dir, Pro* and *Ed* Michael Gramaglia and Jim Fields, *Ex Pro* Jan Rofekamp, Diana Holtzberg and Andrew Hurwitz, *Co-Pro* Rosemary Quigley, *Ph* Fields, Michael Gramaglia, David Bowles, John Gramaglia, Peter Hawkins, Robert Pascal and George Seminara, *Sound* Marshall Grupp.

Gugat Films/Magnolia Pictures-Tartan Films.
112 mins. USA. 2004. Rel: 7 January 2005.
Cert PG.

Enduring Love ★★★★

The title, taken from Ian McEwan's 1997 novel, can be interpreted in several ways. Love can, with luck, endure. And then there are those who are forced to 'endure' love. Joe Rose is a writer and lecturer who is on the brink of proposing to his live-in girlfriend, Claire, a sculptor. But a dagger of bad luck severs the fateful moment and leaves a gaping wound that begins to fester. Meanwhile, Joe finds himself at the receiving end of a love he doesn't even realise is such. The film's beginning, as in the book, has the same nauseous, discomfiting effect of witnessing an unexpected and horrible death. In the hands of director Roger Michell (*The Mother, Changing Lanes*), the event resonates throughout in a series of Proustian shockwaves. The cumulative result is sickly unnerving, as Joe and Claire lose control of their carefully ordered lives. After all, it could happen to any one of us. JC-W

• *Joe Rose* Daniel Craig, *Jed Parry* Rhys Ifans, *Claire* Samantha Morton, *Robin* Bill Nighy, *TV producer* Andrew Lincoln, *Mrs Logan* Helen McCrory, *Rachel* Susan Lynch, *professor* Corin Redgrave, *Spud* Ben Whishaw, *with* Bill Weston, Justin Salinger, Alexandra Aitken.

• *Dir* Roger Michell, *Pro* Kevin Loader, *Ex Pro* François Ivernel, Cameron McCracken, Duncan Reid and Tessa Ross, *Line Pro* Rosa Romero, *Assoc Pro* Ian McEwan, *Screenplay* Joe Penhall, *Ph* Haris Zambarloukos, *Pro Des* John-Paul Kelly, *Ed* Nic Gaster, *M* Jeremy Sams; 'Naima' performed by John Coltrane, *Costumes* Natalie Ward.

Pathé Pictures/UK Film Council/FilmFour/Inside Track/Free Range Films- Pathé.
100 mins. UK/USA. 2004. Rel: 26 November 2004. Cert. 15.

Envy ★★★

The partnership of Ben Stiller and Jack Black should be a union made in comic Heaven. With Stiller's skill for wresting humour from a panoply of reaction shots and Black's talent for supplying plenty to react to, they could be the Laurel and Hardy of the new millennium. It's strange, then, that director Barry Levinson has opted for a somewhat surreal, studied feel to this potentially hilarious black comedy. Tim

Dingham and Nick Vanderpark are best friends who work at a sandpaper factory and live next door to each other in a ghastly Californian suburb. Nick is a dreamer and is falling behind at work when one of his wild ideas – an aerosol for vaporising dog shit – takes off and makes him a multi-millionaire. To remain close to Tim, Nick transforms his bungalow into a gaudy mansion, adds a carousel and an archery range, and drives Tim to jealous distraction… There are a few good laughs in *Envy* (many supplied by Christopher Walken as yet another of his weirdoes), but the tone of the film is off-kilter. Had the escalating mess of Tim's life been rooted in some recognisable reality, then his situation would have been really painful and, thus, genuinely funny. JC-W

• *Tim Dingham* Ben Stiller, *Nick Vanderpark* Jack Black, *Debbie Dingham* Rachel Weisz, *Natalie Vanderpack* Amy Poehler, *J-Man* Christopher Walken, *with* Ariel Gade, Sam Lerner, Lily Jackson, Connor Matheus, Hector Elias, Angee Hughes, Manny Kleinmuntz, Blue Deckert, John Gavigan, Terry Bozeman, Brian Reddy, E.J. Callahan, Edith Jefferson, Tom McCleister.

• *Dir* Barry Levinson, *Pro* Levinson and Paula Weinstein, *Ex Pro* Mary McLaglen, *Co-Pro* Josh McLaglen, *Screenplay* Steve Adams, *Ph* Tim Maurice Jones, *Pro Des* Victor Kempster, *Ed* Stu Linder and Blair Daily, *M* Mark Mothersbaugh, *Costumes* Gloria Gresham.

DreamWorks/Columbia Pictures/Castle Rock/Baltimore/Spring Creek Pictures-Columbia TriStar.
99 mins. USA. 2004. Rel: 27 August 2004.
Cert 12A.

Evil ★★★★

This Swedish film was Oscar nominated and that's understandable because it's a very powerful work, excellently acted and very competently presented. Set in the 1950s, its central figure is a 16-year-old (Wilson) sent to a select boarding school where the power given to the senior students results in severe punishments and bullying. Our hero is determined to resist passively but when both his girl and his best friend are victimised he is driven to violent retaliation as the only effective answer. That's hardly a comforting outcome and the film's raw depiction of torture and humiliation leaves it open to the accusation that it's relishing what it condemns. But that doubt aside, this is a very effective work, a compelling study of a time and place that also touches on wider issues. Original title: *Ondskan*. MS

• *Erik Ponti* Andreas Wilson, *Pierre Tanguy* Henrik Lundstrom, *Otto Silverhielm* Gustaf Skarsgård, *Marja* Linda Zilliacus, *Erik's mother* Marie Richardson, *Erik's father* Johan Rabeus, *Ekengren* Kjell Bergqvist, *Tosse Berg* Magnus Roosman.

• *Dir* Mikael Håfström, *Pro* Hans Lönnerheden and Ingemar Leijonberg, *Co-Pro* Per Holst, *Screenplay* Håfström and Hans Gunnarsson, based on the novel by Jan Guillou, *Ph* Peter Mokrosinski, *Pro Des* Anna Asp, *Ed* Darek Hodor, *M* Francis Shaw, *Costumes* Kersti Vitali.

Moviola/Nordisk Film/TV4-Metrodome.
113 mins. Sweden/Denmark. 2003. Rel: 24 June 2005.
Cert. 15.

Exorcist: The Beginning ★★

In this surprisingly belated prequel to *The Exorcist* (1973),
Stellan Skarsgård is ideally cast as Father Merrin (earlier played
by Max Von Sydow), who feels he can no longer call himself a
man of God after witnessing the Nazi atrocities in WW2. He's
now an Oxford-educated archaeologist and, after arriving in
Cairo, is sent to Kenya to find a devilish relic newly unearthed
by the British. Making contact with an American priest, a
foreign doctor and an English officer, Merrin soon discovers an
ancient Evil lurking, and initially thinks the Devil himself has
entered the body of a small African boy... Despite Skarsgård's
stalwart star turn, marvellous cinematography by Vittorio
Storaro, a splendid production and sparing but decent effects,
this is a stubbornly ordinary horror film that has to get by on
competent professionalism. Director Renny Harlin does manage
some very stylish shots and provides an eerie atmosphere
and, when Satan materialises, the movie shifts up a gear for a
pounding, reasonably scary climax. DW

• *Father Lankester Merrin* Stellan Skarsgård, *Father Francis*
James D'Arcy, *Dr Sarah Novack* Izabella Scorupco, *Joseph* Remy
Sweeney, *Major Granville* Julian Wadham, *Chuma* Andrew
French, *sergeant major* Ralph Brown, *Semelier* Ben Cross, *Father
Gionetti* David Bradley, *with* Alan Ford, Israel Aduramo, Eddie Osei.

• *Dir* Renny Harlin, *Pro* James G. Robinson, *Ex Pro* Guy
McElwaine and David C. Robinson, *Co-Pro* Wayne Morris,
Screenplay Alexi Hawley, from a story by William Wisher
and Caleb Carr, based on characters created by William Peter
Blatty, *Ph* Vittorio Storaro, *Pro Des* Stefano Ortolani, *Ed* Mark
Goldblatt, *M* Trevor Rabin, *Costumes* Luke Reichle, *Special
Effects* Danilo Bollettini, *Makeup Effects* Gary Tunnicliffe, *Aramic
consultant* Professor Geoffrey Kahn.

Morgan Creek-Warner.
113 mins. USA. 2004. Rel: 29 October 2004. Cert. 15.

Facing Window ★★★½

Ferzan Özpetek's first feature *Hamam – The Turkish Bath*, still
his best film, identified him as a writer/director whose work
reflects his welcome humanity. If gay sexuality is a recurrent
theme, it is always handled within a broad canvas, and so it is
with this new film set in Rome and quite splendidly acted by
Giovanna Mezzogiorno and the late Massimo Girotti, to whom
the film is dedicated. She plays a wife and mother tempted
to leave her husband for another man; he plays an amnesiac
whose past is gradually uncovered. The film's weakness lies
in its unconvincing attempt to draw a parallel between the
choice that confronts the wife and a decision taken by the man
way back in 1943. This is a fault at the very heart of the film
but it nevertheless contains much to admire and is warmly
sympathetic. MS

• *Giovanna* Giovanna Mezzogiorno, *Davide* Massimo Girotti,
Lorenzo Raoul Bova, *Filippo* Filippo Nigro, *Emine* Serra Yilmaz,

young Davide Massimo Poggio, *Sara* Maria Grazia Bon.

• *Dir* Ferzan Özpetek, *Pro* Tilde Corsi and Gianni Romoli,
Screenplay Özpetek and Romoli, *Ph* Gianfilippo Corticelli, *Art
Dir* Andrea Crisanti, *Ed* Patrizio Marone, *M* Andrea Guerra,
Costumes Catia Dottori.

Tilde Corsi/Gianni Romoli/R&C Produzioni/Redwave
Films/Eurimages, etc- Soda Pictures.
106 mins. Italy/UK/Turkey/Portugal. 2003. Rel: 3
September 2004. Cert. 15.

Fahrenheit 9/11 ★★★★½

Adopting a satirical tone, Michael Moore opens his movie by
telling us 'This is not a dream – it really happened.' What
really happened is that George W. Bush was sworn into the
White House when more people voted for Al Gore. Moore,
director of the Oscar-winning *Bowling for Columbine* and
scribe of the best-selling *Stupid White Men*, lays out the facts
like letting off small bombs, all accompanied by a mocking
musical soundtrack. It's old news that Bush won his presidency
by fixing the votes in Florida – with the help of Katherine
Harris, Florida's secretary of state in charge of elections (and
co-chairman of Bush's presidential campaign), and Jeb Bush,
the governor of Florida (and Dubya's brother) – but it still
comes over with an indignant sting. Shuffling the facts to
his advantage, Moore kindles an incendiary attack on the
corruption, hypocrisy and greed of the Bush administration.
But even though we know we're being manipulated by
nimble propaganda, it's still compelling drama. Moore shows
photogenic children playing in the streets of Baghdad, then
cuts to the bombing of 20 March 2003. He does reveal some
astonishing statistics and goes for the solar plexus with ground-
level *vox populi*. This is documentary filmmaking of the most
gripping kind, a comedy-drama with a kick and a cause. JC-W

• *with* George W. Bush, Michael Moore, Donald Rumsfeld,
Colin Powell, Britney Spears, Congressman Jim McDermott,
Howard Lipscomb, Congressman John Tanner, etc.

• *Dir* and *Screenplay* Michael Moore, *Pro* Moore, Jim Czarnecki
and Kathleen Glynn, *Ex Pro* Harvey Weinstein, Bob Werinstein
and Agnes Mentre, *Supervising Pro* Tia Lessin, *Co-Pro* Jeff
Gibbs and Kurt Engfehr, *Ed* Engfehr, Christopher Seward and
T. Woody Richman, *M* Gibbs; Benjamin Britten, Arbo Pärt;
songs performed by The Go-Gos, Bob Golden, REM, Low Mass
Tone, The Bloodhound Gang, Jethro Tull, Bing Crosby and
The Andrews Sisters, Neil Young, John Ashcroft, etc.

Lions Gate/IFC Films/Dog Eat Dog-Optimum Releasing.
122 mins. USA. 2004. Rel: 9 July 2004. Cert 15.

Fakers ★★½

When Nick Edwards has to cough up £50,000 in a few days
to pay off a nasty, art-fan crook – or end up dead – he's lucky
enough to find a painting in an old drawing-box he's bought
for a woman. Then they can rip off several London galleries
at once, if only her artist brother can make enough copies in
time... Matthew Rhys makes a pleasantly cheery and cheeky

anti-hero in this lively, if far-fetched, low-rent British comedy caper, which kicks up enough tension and entertainment value to make it reasonably appealing and worthwhile. A promising first-time work from producer-director Richard Janes. DW

• *Nick Edwards* Matthew Rhys, *Eve Evans* Kate Ashfield, *Tony Evans* Tom Chambers, *Phil Norris* Tony Haygarth, *Foster Wright* Art Malik, *Edward Fisher* Edward Hibbert, *with* Paul Clayton, Larry Lamb, Rula Lenska, Stephen Greif, Jonathan Cecil, Timothy Bateson.

• *Dir* Richard Janes, *Pro* Janes, Claire Bee and Todd Kleparski, *Ex Pro* Rosemary Chambers, Robert Kirkland, Christopher Shepley, Fleur Hetherington and Luke G. Jones, *Screenplay* Paul Gerstenberger, *Ph* Balazs Bolygo, *Pro Des* Jason Harris, *Ed* Adam Green, *M* Kevin Sargent, *Costumes* Katie Waite.

Kleparski & Bee-Guerilla Films.
84 mins. UK. 2004. Rel: 5 November 2004.
Cert. 15.

Falcons ★★½

This contemporary drama set first in Iceland but then switching to Hamburg has the initial advantage of leading players who are perfectly cast. Keith Carradine is the ex-con and son of an Icelandic mother, a man contemplating suicide in the belief that his life has been of no value to anybody. However, on arriving in Iceland from America he encounters and helps a put-upon young woman (Margrét Vilhjálmsdóttir) who could well be a daughter he fathered on his earlier visit there. Even the first part of the tale has its unlikely moments, but, as the couple head for Germany to sell a valuable Icelandic falcon, the plotting becomes ever more absurd. Furthermore, the final scene is exceedingly sentimental, so, despite some pleasing views of Iceland, the film sinks. The players, for all their talent, cannot save it. MS

• *Simon* Keith Carradine, *Dúa* Margrét Vilhjálmsdottir, *Jóhann* Ingvar E. Sigurdsson, *Lobbi* Magnús Ólafsson, *young policeman* Fridrick Fridricksson.

• *Dir* Fridrick Thór Fridricksson, *Pro* Fridricksson, Anna Maria Karlsdóttir, Peter Rommel, Egil Ödegård, Mike Downey and Sam Taylor, *Screenplay* Fridricksson and Einar Kárason, *Ph* Harald Paalgard, *Art Dir* Árni Páll Jóhannsson, *Ed* Sigvaldi J. Kárason, *M* Hilmar Örn Hilmarsson, *Costumes* Helga I. Stefánsdóttir.

Icelandic Film Corp/Filmhuset SA/Film & Music Entertainment/Peter Rommel Prods-Tartan Films.
96 mins. Iceland/Norway/Germany/UK. 2002.
Rel: 9 July 2004. Cert 15.

Father and Son ★★

A young soldier, Alexsey, curls up on top of his father and, er, suckles him. A young woman, in period dress, talks of leaving Alexsey. He responds by saying, 'A father's love crucifies – a loving son let's himself be crucified.' Maybe the woman's new lover is Alexsey's father. The latter is certainly handsome

enough, flexing his muscles and preening like a good-looking Sylvester Stallone (it's possible). This exploration of the bond between a young father and his teenage son is a deeply personal work from Russia's greatest living director and will fly over most people's heads. The setting is changeable. Father and son listen to an antique radio, but there's a computer monitor in the son's bedroom. Everybody talks in Russian, but the movie was shot on location in Lisbon. Maybe it is all a dream. Maybe that is the point. It certainly encourages drowsiness. Original title: *Otets i syn*. JC-W

• *father* Andrey Shchetinin, *son* Alexsey Neymyshev, *Sasha* Alexander Razbash, *Fedor* Fedor Lavrov, *girl* Marina Zasukhina.

• *Dir* Alexander Sokurov, *Pro* Thomas Kufus, *Line Pro* Claudia Spiller, *Screenplay* Sergey Potepalov, *Ph* Alexander Burov, *Art Dir* Natalya Kochergina, *Ed* Sergey Ivanov, *M* Andrey Sigle, *Costumes* Bernadette Corstens, *Sound* Sergey Moshkov.

zero film/Lumen Films/Nikola Film/Mikado Film/Isabella Films, etc-Artificial Eye.
86 mins. Russia/France/Germany/Italy/Netherlands/Switzerland. 2003. Rel: 20 August 2004. Cert. PG.

Fat Slags ★

Tracy and Sandra are a pair of Falstaffian, randy and alcoholic factory workers who share accommodation at 69 Shit Street, Fulchester, northern England. On a trip to London they encounter an American tycoon suffering from transitory brain damage who decides to transform them into national celebrities. And so it comes to pass that Tracy and Sandra win the Turner prize, make a hit record and fart their way into the hearts of the great British public... Adapted from the irreverent and vivacious pages of *Viz* magazine, *Fat Slags* misses the point on every level. A decent array of TV actors look forlornly lost and the gross-out antics lack originality and wit. If there's one film that can match the embarrassment of *Sex Lives of the Potato Men*, this is it. From the director of *Kevin and Perry Go Large*. EB

• *Sandra 'San' Burke* Fiona Allen, *Tracy 'Tray' Tunstall* Sophie Thompson, *Sean Cooley* Jerry O'Connell, *Victor* Anthony Head, *Paige* Geri Halliwell, *Fidor Constantin* James Dreyfus, *sales assistant* Naomi Campbell, *Maurice, hotel receptionist* Angus Deayton, *with* Hugh Dennis, Les Dennis, Tom Goodman-Hill, Michael Greco, Ralf Little, Dolph Lundgren, Henry Miller, Steve Punt, John Thomson, Helen Lederer, Finlay Robertson, and *Kofi Annan* Don Warrington.

• *Dir* Ed Bye, *Pro* Charles Finch and Luc Roeg, *Ex Pro* Nigel Green and John Brown, *Line Pro* Richard Johns, *Screenplay* William Osborne, *Ph* John Sorapure, *Pro Des* Grenville Horner, *Ed* Mark Wybourn, *M* David A. Hughes, *Costumes* Linda Alderson.

Entertainment/Artists Independent Network-Entertainment.
75 mins. UK. 2004. Rel: 15 October 2004. Cert. 15.

Fear and Trembling ★★★★

At once comic yet inherently serious, this is a remarkably faithful adaptation of Amélie Nothomb's best-selling novella. A Belgian born in Japan, her insider's knowledge shapes this tale of a namesake working in Tokyo for a huge corporation. The company ethos portrayed so tellingly reflects Japanese society in general, including what is expected of women and pressures that prevent individuality being asserted. In the lead role Sylvie Testud is magnificent. But all of the casting is sublime and, despite reservations (a fantasy scene of confrontation with guns seems out of place, the second half lacks the freshness of the first), this is a memorable film. It incisively defines differences between east and west and criticises a system of life with deadly clarity, while showing understanding and sympathy for those condemned to practice it. MS

• *Amélie* Sylvie Testud, *Miss Fubuki* Mori Kaori Tsuji, *Mr Saito* Taro Suwa, *Mr Omochi* Bison Katayama, *Mr Tenshi* Yasunari Kondo.

• *Dir* and *Screenplay* Alain Corneau, from the novel by Amélie Nothomb, *Pro* Alain Sarde, *Ex Pro* Christine Gozlan and Kenzo Horikoshi, *Ph* Yves Angelo, *Art Dir* Philippe Taillefer and Valérie Leblanc, *Ed* Thierry Derocles, *M* JS Bach.

Les Films Alaine Sarde/France 3 Cinema/Divali Films/ Canal Plus-Cinéfrance.
106 mins. France. 2003. Rel: 27 August 2004. Cert. 12A.

15 ★★★½

It may be set in contemporary Singapore, but this film's portrait of disaffected adolescents – males of 15 or thereabouts – covers familiar ground. Stylistically, however, this is fresh, and with its visual range (jump cuts, speeded-up shots, colour changes, even animation inserts) it speaks directly to a generation brought up on music videos. For older audiences, there are echoes of Godard in written statements and hints of a gay sensibility recall Kenneth Anger. There's a disturbing emphasis on suicide and some audiences will recoil with feelings somewhere between boredom and disgust. For myself, I find Larry Clark's naturalism in such films as *kids* and *Ken Park* far more involving, but this film's approach makes it highly individual. MS

• *Shaun* Shaun Tan, *Melvin* Melvin Chen, *Vynn* Vynn Soh, *Erick* Erick Chun, *Armani* Melvin Lee, *voice-over* Royston Tan.

• *Dir* and *Screenplay* Royston Tan, *Pro* Eric Khoo and Tan Fong-cheng, *Ex Pro* Jacqueline Khoo, James Toh and Lim Ching-leong, *Co-Pro* Freddie Yeo and Mabelyn Ow, *Ph* Lim Ching-leong, *Art Dir* Daniel Lim, *Ed* Jeff Stevens, Nigel Fernandez, Darlene Lim and Azhar Ismon, *M* Yellow Box (comprised of Rennie Gomes and Jonathan Lim), *Sound* Rennie Gomes.

Zhao Wei Films/Singapore Film Commission-Peccadillo Pictures.
96 mins. Singapore. 2003. Rel: 4 February 2005. Cert. 18.

Finding Neverland ★★★½

J.M. Barrie enjoyed an enormously successful career as a dramatist, but he will forever be associated with his 1904 play *Peter Pan*. Its fruition is explored in this resonant, touching story of a man from an estranged marriage who connects with the four sons of the widowed Sylvia du Maurier, daughter of the novelist George du Maurier. Just as the boys were forced

Park master: Johnny Depp as the great J.M. Barrie - with Freddie Highmore – in Marc Foster's sublimely moving *Finding Neverland* (from Buena Vista International)

to grow up prematurely under such tragic circumstances, so Barrie brought childhood back into their lives and, in return, they provided him with the inspiration for his most successful play. As adapted from 'real events,' this is a remarkable enough story to prompt one to ask 'Did all these things really happen?' Well, yes and no – this is quite a liberal interpretation of the facts, but the essence is true enough. Considering the material – and the potential for tear-jerking – director Foster (*Monster's Ball*) provides a surprisingly muted reading, garnished with some priceless moments of magic and fantasy. FYI: Dustin Hoffman, who as theatre impresario Charles Frohman scoffs at the idea of crocodiles and pirates on stage, previously had the title role in Steven Spielberg's *Hook*. JC-W

• *James Matthew Barrie* Johnny Depp, *Sylvia Llewelyn Davies* Kate Winslet, *Mrs Emma du Maurier* Julie Christie, *Mary Ansell Barrie* Radha Mitchell, *Charles Frohman* Dustin Hoffman, *Peter Llewelyn Davies* Freddie Highmore, *Jack Llewelyn Davies* Joe Prospero, *George Llewelyn Davies* Nick Roud, *Michael Llewelyn Davies* Luke Spill, *Arthur Conan Doyle* Ian Hart, *Peter Pan* Kelly Macdonald, *Mr Jaspers, the usher* Mackenzie Crook, *Mrs Snow* Eileen Essell, *Mr Snow* Jimmy Gardner, *Nana/Mr Reilly* Angus Barnett, *with* Oliver Fox, Toby Jones, Kate Maberly, Jane Booker, Paul Whitehouse, Catherine Cusack, Nicholas Pritchard, Laura Duguid, Luciano Cusack, Serafina Cusack, Molly Whitehouse, Sophie Whitehouse.

• *Dir* Marc Foster, *Pro* Richard N. Gladstein and Nellie Bellflower, *Ex Pro* Gary Binkow, Neal Israel, Bob Weinstein, Harvey Weinstein and Michelle Sy, *Assoc Pro* Tracey Becker, *Screenplay* David Magee, based on the play *The Man Who Was Peter Pan* by Allan Knee, *Ph* Roberto Schaefer, *Pro Des* Gemma Jackson, *Ed* Matt Chesse, *M* Jan A.P. Kaczmarerk; 'Peter's Song' performed by Elton John, *Costumes* Alexandra Byrne, *Sound* Matthew Collinge.

Miramax/FilmColony-Buena Vista International. 101 mins. UK/USA. 2004. Rel: 29 October 2004. Cert. PG.

First Daughter ★★½

For as long as she can remember, Samantha Mackenzie has been a prisoner in a privileged, very large cell. The only child of the President of the United States, she is, in her own words, a victim of 'genetic limelight'. But now she's going to college and can at last live her own life and be herself. Or so she thinks… The latest entry in a sub-genre that includes *The Princess Diaries*, *The Prince & Me*, *Chasing Liberty* and the immortal *Roman Holiday* (1953), *First Daughter* is a largely mechanical and predictable offering given a severe case of the cutes. Nevertheless, its intended audience (teenage girls) should lap it up, while Katie Holmes, having proved her acting chops in *Wonder Boys* and *Pieces of April*, rises well above the material. JC-W

• *Samantha Mackenzie* Katie Holmes, *James Lamson* Marc Blucas, *Mia* Amerie, *President John Mackenzie* Michael Keaton, *Melanie Mackenzie* Margaret Colin, *Liz Pappas* Lela Rochon

Fuqua, *Agent Dylan* aka '*Motor Mouth*' Dwayne Adway, *narrator* Forest Whitaker, *with* Michael Milhoan, Barry Livingston, Damon Whitaker, Teck Holmes, Andrea Avery, Vera Wang, Joan Rivers, Melissa Rivers, Jay Leno, Sonnet Noel Whitaker.

• *Dir* Forest Whitaker, *Pro* John Davis, Mike Karz and Wyck Godfrey, *Ex Pro* Whitaker, Arnon Milchan, Jerry O'Connell and Jeffrey Downer, *Screenplay* Jessica Bendinger and Kate Kondell, from a story by O'Connell and Bendinger, *Ph* Toyomichi Kurita, *Pro Des* Alexander Hammond, *Ed* Richard Chew, *M* Michael Kamen and Blake Neely, *Costumes* Francine Jamison-Tanchuck, *Sound* Tim Chau and Nils C. Jensen.

New Regency/Davis Entertainment/Spirit Dance-Fox. 106 mins. USA. 2004. Rel: 11 February 2005. Cert. PG.

Five ★★★★

The films made by Iran's Abbas Kiarostami can be wonderful but some are tedious. This new one is his most minimalist yet, containing five sections each of which consists of a single shot (the last one, filmed at night, being a composite image taken over a period of time). Expecting the worst (and for those who cannot adjust to this kind of viewing it will be just that), I found instead that I was intrigued and held by these five contemplative views of enduring nature (the sea in particular) and of the ephemeral life on its margins (man, dogs, ducks). It deals also in visual transformations and there is welcome humour in the fourth segment. It's easiest to judge it by the first ten-minute sequence, showing a piece of wood at the mercy of the waves: the sound stresses the power of the sea, the flow of the tide gives an illusion of camera movement and the driftwood becomes symbolic of man's place in the universe. MS

• *Dir* and *Screenplay* Abbas Kiarostami, *Pro* Marin Karmitz. MK2/NHK-BFI. 74 mins. Japan/Iran. 2004. Rel: 20 May 2005. Cert. U.

Five Children and It ★★½

It is a sad fact of contemporary cinema that films which children love, their parents abhor. There are still good family films around, but the kids don't get them. Only rarely – as in the case of *Shrek 2* – does the whole family tune in (albeit on different levels). *Five Children and It* might well have been a success 25 years ago, but today is merely a modest pleasure which should engage older parents and much younger children. Like Lionel Jeffries' exquisite *The Railway Children* (1972), *Five Children and It* is an adaptation of a novel by E. Nesbit and has some charm. As the Blitz rages in London, Robert, Anthea, Jane, Cyril and their baby brother are sent to stay with their eccentric Uncle Albert in his run-down castle by the sea. Immersed in writing his magnum opus, *Difficult Sums for Children*, Albert is not thrilled at the prospect of sharing his home with five nephews and nieces but quickly sets them impossible domestic tasks. Forbidden from entering the greenhouse, the children soon discover its secret, a Parallel Universe-on-Sea where the grumpy sand fairy lives… Branagh is delightful, the child acting variable (Freddie Highmore is obviously a talent to watch) and the special effects quite effective. JC-W

• *Uncle Albert* Kenneth Branagh, *Martha* Zoë Wanamaker, *mother* Tara Fitzgerald, *father* Alex Jennings, *Robert* Freddie Highmore, *Cyril* Jonathan Bailey, *Anthea* Jessica Claridge, *Jane* Poppy Rogers, *Horace* Alexander Pownall, *Peasemarsh* John Sessions, *the voice of Psammead aka 'It'* Eddie Izzard, *Nesbit* Norman Wisdom, *sergeant* Duncan Preston.

• *Dir* John Stephenson, *Pro* Lisa Henson, Samuel Hadida and Nick Hirschkorn, *Ex Pro* Jane Barclay, Kristine Belson, Steve Christian, Victor Hadida, Sharon Harel, Robert Jones, Hannah Leader and James D. Stern, *Co-Pro* Kathy Sykes, *Screenplay* David Solomons, *Ph* Michael Brewster, *Pro Des* Roger Hall, *Ed* Michael Ellis, *M* Jane Antonia Cornish; 'Robert's Theme' sung by Sean Lennon, *Costumes* Phoebe De Gaye.

Capitol Films/UK Film Council/Isle of Man Film Commission/Endgame Entertainment/Jim Henson Co-Pathé.
Rel: 15 October 89 mins. UK/France/USA. 2004.
Rel: 15 October 2004. Cert. U.

5x2 ★★★

Marion Chabart and Gilles Ferron have come to the end of their relationship. But, as Marion walks away from her ex-husband down an anonymous hotel corridor, we cut back to the night of a fateful dinner party, and then, before that, to the day that Marion gave birth to their son, and then, before that... In cinematic terms, at least, falling in love and getting married have become commonplace, even banal. Divorce, on the other hand, wields a far more potent stick. As an examination of a

heterosexual relationship through its five stages – from first meeting to legal termination – *5x2* is gripping drama in so much as it is real and often unexpected. To up the ante, director Ozon presents his five chapters in reverse chronological order (in the tradition of Pinter's *Betrayal* and Gasper Noé's *Irréversible*). With this perspective, it's hard to believe in the couple's nuptial bliss at the end/beginning, however besottedly the actors lay it on. As such, the romantic coda is something of an anticlimax, although it allows time for ample deliberation. JC-W

• *Marion Chabart* Valéria Bruni-Tedeschi, *Gilles Ferron* Stéphane Freiss, *Valérie* Géraldine Pailhas, *Monique Chabart* Françoise Fabian, *Bernard Chabart* Michael Lonsdale, *Christophe Ferron* Antoine Chappey, *Mathieu* Marc Ruchmann, *American stranger* Jason Tavassoli.

• *Dir* François Ozon, *Pro* Olivier Delbosc and Marc Missonnier, *Ex Pro* Philippe Dugay, *Screenplay* Ozon and Emmanuèle Bernheim, *Ph* Yorick Le Saux, *Art Dir* Katia Wyszkop, *Ed* Monica Coleman, *M* Philippe Rombi, *Costumes* Pascaline Chavanne.

Fidélité/France 2 Cinéma/Roz/Canal Plus-UGC Films UK.
90 mins. France. 2004. Rel: 18 March 2005. Cert. 15.

The Flight of the Phoenix ★★★½

For Frank Towns and his co-pilot 'AJ', the evacuation of staff from a remote oil outstation is just another job. But on their departure, the plane is hit by the mother of all sandstorms and Frank is forced to crash-land his aircraft in the middle of the Gobi desert. They have enough water for 30 days, but with the radio destroyed and July being the hottest month of the year

Name that dune: Dennis Quaid and the Gobi in John Moore's accomplished and suspenseful remake, *The Flight of the Phoenix* (from Fox)

(precluding any heroic treks), there is no chance of seeking outside help... The 1965 film of the same name would seem an unlikely vehicle for a remake and Dennis Quaid an improbable replacement for James Stewart. Yet, while there's a distinctly old-fashioned air about the proceedings (and the odd corny speech), this is an accomplished and suspenseful drama in which the desert has seldom seemed more destructive or unpredictable. The opening crash is in a class right up there with *The Fugitive* and *Fearless* and Galvin's photography and the Namibian locations are a major asset. There's also a splendid exercise in menace from Giovanni Ribisi, whose transformation from nonentity to Nazi is genuinely chilling. JC-W

• *Frank Towns* Dennis Quaid, *Elliott* Giovanni Ribisi, *A.J.* Tyrese Gibson, *Kelly* Miranda Otto, *Ian* Hugh Laurie, *Rodney* Tony Curran, *Jeremy aka 'Patch'* Kirk Jones, *Sammi* Jacob Vargas, *Liddle* Scott Michael Campbell, *Rady* Kevork Malikyan, *John Davis* Jared Padalecki, *with* Paul Ditchfield, Martin 'Mako' Hindy, Bob Brown.

• *Dir* John Moore, *Pro* John Davis, William Aldrich, Wyck Godfrey and T. Alex Blum, *Ex Pro* Ric Kidney, *Screenplay* Scott Frank and Edward Burns, from the screenplay by Lukas Heller and the novel by Elleston Trevor, *Ph* Brendan Galvin, *Pro Des* Patrick Lumb, *Ed* Don Zimmerman, *M* Marco Beltrami; songs performed by Johnny Cash, James Brown, Steve Winwood, OutKast, and Massive Attack, *Costumes* George L. Little, *Dune Groomer* Marius P. Bekker.

Fox/Aldrich Group/Davis Entertainment-Fox.
112 mins. USA. 2004. Rel: 4 March 2005. Cert. 12A.

The Flower of Evil ★★½

After living in America for three years, François returns to his family in France to find that little has changed. His mother is still pursuing her political career. His father is still an unsupportive philanderer. His cousin (and step-sister) is still anxious to be his lover. And his Aunt Line is still the quiet, unassuming star around which his family orbits. Family non-secrets of incest and murder seem to be par for the course in this very matter-of-fact slice of one family's life. The story telling is so uniform, with neither highs nor lows, that it's hard to feel anything beyond neighbourly interest. Only the ethereal reminiscences of Suzanne Flon's Aunt Line lend any real charm. The music, written by director Claude Chabrol's son, seems a jarring and inappropriate afterthought. Original title: *La Fleur du mal*. SWM

• *Anne Charpin-Vasseur* Nathalie Baye, *François Charpin-Vasseur* Benoît Magimel, *Aunt Line* Suzanne Flon, *Gérard Charpin-Vasseur* Bernard LeCoq, *Michèle* Mélanie Doutey, *with* Thomas Chabrol, Henri Attal, Françoise Bertin.

• *Dir* Claude Chabrol, *Pro* Marin Karmitz, *Ex Pro* Yvon Crenn, *Screenplay* Claude Chabrol, Caroline Eliacheff and Louise L. Lambrichs, *Ph* Eduardo Serra, *Art Dir* François Benoît-Fresco, *Ed* Monique Fardoulis, *M* Matthieu Chabrol, *Costumes* Mic Cheminal.

Marin Karmitz/MK2/France 3 Cinéma/Canal Plus-Cinéfrance.
104 mins. France. 2002. Rel: 2 July 2004. Cert 15.

The Forgotten ★★★★½

What if somebody suggested that your own child had never existed? Then what if other people collaborated in the notion that you were delusional? And what if your very own spouse, backed by a psychiatrist, told you that you had never had a child? Such a dilemma faces Telly Paretta when, 14 months after her son's supposed disappearance in a plane crash, little shreds of evidence that he existed start to vanish... Six years after his last film (the intelligent, emotionally complex *Return to Paradise*), director Joseph Ruben returns to superlative form. Edging into genre territory occupied by David Fincher's *The Game* and René Clement's *The Deadly Trap* (with Faye Dunaway), *The Forgotten* is a magnificent psychological thriller that really keeps one guessing and jumping. Of course, to have an actress of the calibre of Julianne Moore on board is a definite advantage. JC-W

• *Telly Paretta* Julianne Moore, *Ash* Dominic West, *Dr Jack Munce* Gary Sinise, *Anne Pope* Alfre Woodard, *omnipresent onlooker* Linus Roache, *Jim Paretta* Anthony Edwards, *Carl Dayton* Robert Wisdom, *Eliot* Jessica Hecht, *Eileen, the accountant* Ann Dowd, *with* Christopher Kovaleski, Tim Kang, Kathryn Faughnan, J. Tucker Smith.

• *Dir* Joseph Ruben, *Pro* Bruce Cohen, Dan Jinks and Joe Roth, *Ex Pro* Steve Nicolaides and Todd Garner, *Screenplay* Gerald DiPego, *Ph* Anastas Michos, *Pro Des* Bill Groom, *Ed* Richard Francis-Bruce, *M* James Horner, *Costumes* Cindy Evans, *Sound* Dane A. Davis, *Visual effects* Carey Villegas.

Revolution Studios/Jinks/Cohen Company-Columbia TriStar.
90 mins. USA. 2004. Rel: 26 November 2004. Cert. 12A.

Friday Night Lights ★★

Odessa, West Texas; August-December 1988. The Panthers – the football team of Permian High – have something of a reputation. They've won the state championship four times and that's a helluva record to live up to. Frankly, the town of Odessa doesn't have a lot going for it, so those boys better bring home that trophy. But for coach Gary Gaines, 'being perfect' isn't just about winning... A True Story about a real town and its young athletes, *Friday Night Lights* doesn't really seem worth the effort. Director Peter Berg (er, *Welcome to the Jungle*) attempts to inject a documentary realism into the proceedings, with a lot of zooms and a desaturated colour palette. The problem is that the sketchy back-story of the characters doesn't give us anybody to root for, while Billy Bob phones in his performance. If you don't know much about American football, then all the excitement will seem quite mystifying. JC-W

• *Coach Gary Gaines* Billy Bob Thornton, *Boobie Miles* Derek Luke, *Brian Chavez* Jay Hernandez, *Mike Winchell* Lucas Black, *Charlie Billingsley* Tim McGraw, *Don Billingsley* Garrett Hedlund, *Chris Comer* Lee Thompson Young, *Ivory Christian*

Rain people: Peter Sarsgaard, Natalie Portman and Zach Braff in Braff's touching, episodic and enlightening *Garden State* (from Buena Vista International)

Lee Jackson, *with* Grover Coulson, Connie Britton, Morgan Farris, Gavin Grazer, Kenneth Plunk, Stephen Bishop.

• *Dir* Peter Berg, *Pro* Brian Grazer, *Ex Pro* James Whitaker and John Cameron, *Screenplay* Berg and David Aaron Cohen, from the book by H.G. Bissinger, *Ph* Tobias Schliessler, *Pro Des* Sharon Seymour, *Ed* David Rosenbloom, *M* Explosions in the Sky (Brian Reitzell, Justin Stanley and David Torn), *Costumes* Susan Matheson, *Stunt coordinator* Allan Graf.

Universal/Imagine Entertainment-UIP.
117 mins. USA/Germany. 2004. Rel: 13 May 2005. Cert. 12A

Garden State ★★★½

New Jersey; the present. Andrew Largeman – 'Large' to his friends – is working in a Vietnamese restaurant in Los Angeles. He's actually an actor typecast as mentally handicapped people and hasn't seen his parents in nine years. When his mother, a paraplegic, dies in the bath, 'Large' heads back to New Jersey for the funeral. There, he hooks up with his old friend Mark, now a gravedigger, and meets the beautiful Sam, a compulsive liar and epileptic... Zach Braff has secured some major talent (Natalie Portman, producer Danny DeVito) for his debut as writer and director. Best known for playing Dr John 'J.D.' Dorian on TV's *Scrubs*, Braff as filmmaker has conjured up a quirky, eccentric and original universe not a million miles away in style from the oeuvre of Jarmusch, Wes Anderson and Sofia Coppola. There are some magical deadpan moments and Braff reveals a generous hand with his actors (Portman, Holm, Leibman and several dogs). If the film doesn't grip like it might, it's because Braff's approach is decidedly gentle and whimsical and a tad episodic. But it's also very touching and at times quite enlightening. JC-W

• *Andrew 'Large' Largeman* Zach Braff, *Gideon Largeman, Andrew's father* Ian Holm, *Dr Cohen* Ron Leibman, *Diego* Method Man, *Sam* Natalie Portman, *Mark* Peter Sarsgaard, *Carol* Jean Smart, *Dave* Alex Burns, *Aunt Sylvia Largeman* Jackie Hoffman, *Jesse* Armando Riesco, *Dana* Amy Ferguson, *Tim* Jim Parsons, *Albert* Denis O'Hare, *with* Ann Dowd, Michael Weston, Trisha LaFrache, Wynter Kullman, Geoffrey Arend, Debbon Ayer.

• *Dir* and *Screenplay* Zach Braff, *Pro* Pamela Abdy, Richard Klubeck, Gary Gilbert and Dan Halstead, *Ex Pro* Danny DeVito, Michael Shamberg and Stacey Sher, *Co-Pro* Bill Brown, *Line Pro* Ann Ruark, *Ph* Lawrence Sher, *Pro Des* Judy Becker, *Ed* Myron Kerstein, *M* Chad Fischer; songs performed by Alexi Murdoch, Dante Ross, Coldplay, The Shins, Zero 7, Colin Hay, Cary Brothers, Remy Zero, Nick Drake, Thievery Corporation, Simon & Garfunkel, Iron and Wine, Frou Frou, and Bonnie Somerville, *Costumes* Michael Wilkinson.

Miramax/Fox Searchlight/Camelot Pictures/Jersey Films/
Double Feature Films-Buena Vista International.
102 mins. USA. 2003. Rel: 26 November 2004. Cert. 15

Garfield: The Movie ★

Quintessential fat-cat Garfield is none too pleased when owner Jon brings a dog home. However, when local TV host Happy Chapman kidnaps the talented canine Odie to boost his career, it's up to Garfield to rescue him... There is nothing here for adults to enjoy and even kids will likely be put off by the somewhat disturbing CGI Garfield. Breckin Meyer (as Jon Arbuckle) does the best he can with the one-note story and Jennifer Love Hewitt... well, I hope this helped her make her mortgage. Stephen Tobolowsky certainly delivers when you can't afford Nathan Lane but it's only Bill Murray (voicing Garfield) who lends any enjoyment. SWM

• *Jon Arbuckle* Breckin Meyer, *Liz Wilson* Jennifer Love Hewitt, *Happy Chapman* Stephen Tobolowsky, *Wendell* Evan Arnolds, *Christopher Mello* Mark Christopher Lawrence, *with* Eve Brent, Daamen Krall, Michael Monks. *Voice cast: Garfield* Bill Murray, *Louis* Nick Cannon, *Persnikitty* Alan Cumming, *Nermal* David Eigenberg, *Luca* Brad Garrett, *Spanky* Jimmy Kimmel, *Arlene* Debra Messing.

• *Dir* Pete Hewitt, *Pro* John Davis, *Ex Pro* Neil Machlis, *Screenplay* Joel Cohen and Alec Sokolow, based on the comic strip created by Jim Davis, *Ph* Dean Cundey, *Pro Des* Alexander Hammond, *Ed* Peter Berger, *M* Christophe Beck, *Costumes* Marie France, *Animation* Chris Bailey.

Fox/Davis Entertainment-Fox.
80 mins. USA. 2004. Rel: 30 July 2004.
Cert. U.

Godsend ★★½

Godsend tries to be many things but ends up being none. Superficially a cautionary tale about the dangers of cloning, it makes little biological sense. As a character study it starts off interesting but then its protagonists do things they really wouldn't. And as a horror film it is genuinely unsettling but then descends into stock shock tactics that are patently absurd. However, putting all these caveats aside, *Godsend* is not without its rewards. For a start, it's visually very arresting (the cut-away from the credits sequence of cellular formation to an overshot of umbrellas sets the pace) and it does open up discussion for the ethics of artificial reproduction. The absurdly good-looking Greg Kinnear and Rebecca Romijn-Stamos play an ideal couple (he's a model teacher, she's a talented photographer) that have a handsome, loving eight-year-old son. Then the unimaginable happens and Greg and Becky are offered the chance to start over again. Robert De Niro plays the good doctor who provides them with their dream, an enormous house and gainful employment, but he must wonder what he's doing in such a nondescript role. There is a genuine creepiness at play here but it winds up as dishonest intimidation. JC-W

• *Paul Duncan* Greg Kinnear, *Jessie Duncan* Rebecca Romijn-Stamos, *Richard Wells* Robert De Niro, *Adam Duncan* Cameron Bright, *Cora Williams* Janet Bailey, *with* Merwin Mondesir, Jake Simons, Elle Downs, Chris Britton, Devon Bostick.

• *Dir* Nick Hamm, *Pro* Cathy Schulman, Sean O'Keefe and Marc Butan, *Ex Pro* Todd Wagner, Mark Cuban, Jon Feltheimer, Mark Canton, Michael Paseornek, Michael Burns and Eric Kopeloff, *Screenplay* Mark Bomback, *Ph* Kramer Morgenthau, *Pro Des* Doug Kramer, *Ed* Steve Mirkovich and Niven Howie, *M* Brian Tyler, *Costumes* Suzanne McCabe.

Lions Gate/Artists Production Group-Pathé.
102 mins. USA/Canada. 2003. Rel: 2 July 2004.
Cert 15.

Goldfish Memory ★★★★

Described by a colleague as an Irish variant on *Love Actually*, this is a lightweight piece but one that achieves exactly what it sets out to do. The movie suggests that if goldfish have a short memory span so do human beings, a fact that accounts for their readiness to pursue sex and love however disillusioning their earlier experiences. Set in Dublin, this modest but agreeable piece presents itself as a comedy of love affairs, taking in a range of relationships between characters mainly in their twenties. Deliberately encompassing the love lives of gays, lesbians and bisexuals as well as heterosexuals, it puts all of them on a similar footing. The warm, sympathetic tone – this lacks the coarseness of much comedy today – is down to writer/director Liz Gill, while the location shooting is extremely pleasing. MS

• *Tom* Sean Campion, *Angie* Flora Montgomery, *Red* Keith McErlean, *Larry* Stuart Graham, *Clara* Fiona O'Shaughnessy, *Isolde* Fiona Glascott, *Kate* Justine Mitchell, *with* Peter Gaynor, Lise Hearns, Jean Butler, Britta Smith, Niall O'Brien, Laura Brennan.

• *Dir* and *Screenplay* Liz Gill, *Pro* Breda Walsh, *Ex Pro* Brendan McCarthy, *Ph* Ken Byrne, *Art Dir* Mags Linnane, *Ed* Dermot Diskin, *M* Richie Buckley.

Bord Scannán na hÉireann/Irish Film Board/Goldfish Films-Millivres Multimedia.
87 mins. Ireland/UK. 2003. Rel: 8 October 2004. Cert. 15.

Good Morning, Night ★★★

The veteran Italian filmmaker Marco Bellocchio is still best known here for *Fists in the Pocket* (1965). This new drama deals with the kidnapping in 1978 by The Red Brigade of Italy's former prime minister Aldo Moro and relies heavily on political knowledge of the period to make its impact. Roberto Herlitzka brings dignity to the role of Moro and, although told from the viewpoint of the terrorists, the film does not endorse their actions, despite being critical of church and state. Presumably we are meant to sympathise with the leading female character (Maya Sansa) who partakes in the kidnapping plot yet wavers. Her internal conflict could have made for a compelling internal drama but it is never fleshed out sufficiently. We remain observers of the events depicted, distant rather than emotionally or even intellectually involved. Original title: *Buongiorno, notte*. MS

• *Chiara* Maya Sansa, *Mariano* Luigi Lo Cascio, *Aldo Moro* Roberto Herlitzka, *Enzo* Paolo Briguglia, *Ernesto* Pier Giorgio Bellocchio, *Primo* Giovanni Calcagno.

• *Dir* and *Screenplay* Marco Bellocchio, *Pro* Marco Bellocchio and Sergio Pelone, *Ph* Pasquale Mari, *Pro Des* Marco Dentici, *Ed* Francesca Calvelli, *M* Riccardo Giagni, *Costumes* Sergio Ballo.

Filmalbatros/RAI Cinema/Sky-Artificial Eye.
106 mins. Italy. 2003. Rel: 19 November 2004.
Cert. 15.

A Good Woman ★★½

Amalfi, Italy; 1930. Notorious for sleeping with married men, New York's Mrs Erlynne causes something of a stir when she turns up at the respectable resort. Tongues wag even harder when she is seen in the company of the young, dashing and wealthy American Robert Windermere – who has only been married to the trusting Meg for two years... At least Julianne Moore and Reese Witherspoon played their Wildean heroines with English accents. This seventh big-screen adaptation of *Lady Windermere's Fan* wrenches the action out of 1890s London and transplants it to the Mediterranean in the 1930s. Sadly, this is not the cinematic move one might have hoped for, while Los Angeles' Helen Hunt is tragically miscast – she is not a convincing predator and is a tad too old. Meanwhile, Stephen Campbell Moore chucks Lord Darlington away (he's neither charming nor funny), leaving old pros like Tom Wilkinson and John Standing to mine the gold in Wilde's rich aphoristic seams. In spite of all this – along with some artless editing and inauthentic costumes – it's good to see such a terrific play, albeit one wresting its way out of a mediocre film. JC-W

• *Mrs Erlynne* Helen Hunt, *Margaret 'Meg' Windermere* Scarlett Johansson, *'Tuppy'* Tom Wilkinson, *Lord Darlington* Stephen Campbell Moore, *Robert Windermere* Mark Umbers, *Contessa Lucchino* Milena Vukotic, *Lady Plymdale* Diana Hardcastle, *Cecil* Roger Hammond, *Mrs Stutfield* Jane How, *Alessandra* Giorgia Massetti, *Dumby* John Standing.

• *Dir* Mike Barker, *Pro* Howard Himelstein, Alan Greenspan, Jonathan English and Steven Siebert, *Ex Pro* John Evangelides, Jimmy de Brabant, Michael Dounaev, Liam Badger, Duncan Hopper, Hilary Davis and Rupert Preston, *Screenplay* Himelstein, *Ph* Ben Seresin, *Pro Des* Ben Scott, *Ed* Neil Farrell, *M* Richard G. Mitchell; Puccini, Fauré, *Costumes* John Bloomfield.

Beyond Films/Magic Hour Media/Thema/Lighthouse Entertainment-Vertigo Films.
93 mins. UK/Italy/Spain. 2004. Rel: 13 May 2005. Cert. PG

Gozu ★★★½

Yakuza rookie Minami is ordered to dispose of a fellow gang member he holds in high regard. However, on the way to the appointed 'dumping ground', an emergency stop appears to perform Minami's job for him. But then the corpse goes missing. As Minami becomes more and more desperate, he encounters a lactating seductress, the ghost of his victim and a cow-headed demon called Gozu... Director Takashi Miike doesn't do genres. That is what is so exciting about his films: he bends back the borders of cinematic possibility and runs with it. Here, in the slipstream of the British releases of his *Audition* and *The Happiness of the Katakuris*, comes this surreal, disgusting, farcical and extremely gory melange of demonic styles. Of course, this is not for everyone, and Miike doesn't always pull off his shocking rabbit tricks, but *Gozu* is a true original and is wildly entertaining – if you have the stomach for it. EB

• *Minami* Hideki Sone, *female Ozaki* Kimika Yoshino, *Nosechi*

Shohei Hino, *inkeeper's sister* Keiko Tomita, *Kazu* Harumi Sone, *Ozaki* Sho Aikawa.

• *Dir* Takashi Miike, *Pro* Harumi Sone, Tsuneo Seto, Misako Saka, Shigeji Maeda and Tatsuya Mukai, *Screenplay* Sakichi Sato, *Ph* Kazunari Tanaka, *Art Dir* Akira Ishige, *Ed* Yasushi Shimamura, *M* Koji Endô.

Klockworx-Tartan Films.
127 mins. Japan. 2003. Rel: 30 July 2004. Cert. 18.

The Grudge ★½

The Ring was such a success that anything from Japan with a ghost attached to it is being automatically recycled. And so Disney remade *Dark Water* (or *Honogurai Mizu No Soko Kara*) and, perhaps more appropriately, Sony snapped up the rights to *The Grudge*. Now, *The Ring* (or *Ringu*) was a genuinely frightening movie with a fantastic concept. *The Grudge* is *The Ring* without the concept and without a story to speak of. There's a boy and girl covered in white make-up and they stare at the camera when the orchestra tells us they are going to. And that's it. OK, there's a little more to it than that: a social worker, Rika, turns up at the house of an old woman and finds a boy covered in white make-up hiding in a cupboard. This is very disturbing for her and he then pops up all over the place, killing people with his evil stare. The result is slow, episodic, repetitive, shallow, nonsensical and very, very dreary. Original title: *Ju-On*. JC-W

• *Nishina Rika* Okina Megumi, *Tokunaga Hitomi* Ito Misaki, *Toyama Izumi* Uehara Misa, *Chiharu* Ichikawa Yui, *Tokunaga Katsuya* Tsuda Kanji, *Mariko* Shibata Kayoko, *Toshio* Yuya Ozeki, *with* Kukuri Yukako, Matsuda Shuri, Tanaka Yoji.

• *Dir* and *Screenplay* Takashi Shimizu , *Pro* Taka Ichise, *Ph* Kikumura Tokusho, *Pro Des* Tokiwa Toshiharu, *Ed* Takahashi Nobuyuki, *M* Sato Shiro.

Oz/Pioneer LDC/Nikkatsu/Xanadeux-Premier Asia.
92 mins. Japan. 2003. Rel: 2 July 2004. Cert 15.

The Grudge ★½

A US social worker visits a modest Tokyo home inhabited by fellow Americans and discovers something entirely more alien... The Americanisation of the South-East Asian horror film has got out of hand. Since the clanging success of Gore Verbinski's *The Ring*, anything with a chopstick and a spectre has been bought up by the Hollywood machine. The prognosis for *The Grudge* did look promising, though. The location was to remain in Tokyo, the director was to remain the same and even the two spectral actors from the original (and *Ju-on: The Grudge 2*) were going to make an encore. Here was also a wonderful opportunity to explore the Americans at sea in an Eastern culture and perhaps to redress some of the embarrassment of Jerry Bruckheimer's *Pearl Harbor*. But no, this is just another anodyne visual accompaniment to the string section of Christopher Young's orchestra. Shimizu's original was slow, episodic and repetitive and the sequel is more of the same, while even the preternatural **Yuya Ozeki** – now 18 months older and chubbier of cheek – is no longer scary. Despite the glorious photography of an anonymous Tokyo, *The Grudge* is extraordinarily boring. JC-W

• *Karen* Sarah Michelle Gellar, *Doug* Jason Behr, *Susan* KaDee Strickland, *Jennifer* Clea DuVall, *Peter* Bill Pullman, *Emma* Grace Zabriskie, *Maria* Rosa Blasi, *Matthew* William Mapother, *Alex* Ted Raimi, *Det. Nakagawa* Ryo Ishibashi, *Yoko* Maki Yoko, *Kayako* Takako Fuji, *Toshio* Yuya Ozeki.

• *Dir* Takashi Shimizu, *Pro* Sam Raimi, Rob Tapert and Taka Ichise, *Ex Pro* Joe Drake, Nathan Kahane, Carsten Lorenz, Roy Lee and Doug Davison, *Screenplay* Stephen Susco, *Ph* Hideo Yamamoto, *Pro Des* Iwao Saito, *Ed* Jeff Betancourt, *M* Christopher Young, Costumes Shawn Holly Cookson and Miyuyki Taniguchi, *Special FX Makeup* Yûichi Matsui.

Ghost House Pictures-UIP.
91 mins. USA. 2004. Rel: 5 November 2004. Cert. 15.

Guerrilla: The Taking of Patty Hearst ★★½

The story of Patty Hearst's kidnapping was certainly an intriguing episode of the 1970s. The granddaughter of the legendary media tycoon William Randolph Hearst, Patty was just 19 when she was abducted by the Symbionese Liberation Army. And the demands of the little-known revolutionaries were certainly unusual: in exchange for the safe return of the teenage heiress, they asked their hostage's father to provide an estimated $300,000 in the form of food for California's hungry. Meanwhile, Patty Hearst set off to rob a bank with an automatic rifle… Interesting, but how relevant is all this to today? In light of the power of such recent documentaries as *Fahrenheit 9/11* and *Enron*, Robert Stone's *Guerrilla* seems a day late and a dollar short. The film's coup would seem to be the first on-camera confession from SLA founder Russ Little, who's given generous screen time even though he's not very engaging (he uses 'you know' for punctuation). So where is Patty Hearst when you need her? Appearing in movies of dubious taste directed by John Waters. JC-W

• *with*: Russ Little, Mike Bortin, Timothy Findley, Dan Grove, Ludlow Kramer, John Lester.

• *Dir* and *Pro* Robert Stone, *Ex Pro* Nick Fraser and Mark Samuels, *Co-Pro* and *Ed* Don Kleszy, *Ph* Stone, Howard Shack and Richard Neill, *M* Gary Lionelli.

Magnolia Pictures/American Experience/BBC/Court TV-Tartan Films.
89 mins. USA/UK. 2004. Rel: 3 June 2005. Cert. 12A.

Guess Who ★½

Theresa brings her boyfriend home to meet her parents. But she hasn't told them he's white… We've met the parents a number of times – now it's time to meet the aspiring son-in-law. And, guess what? He's not Sidney Poitier. A comic negative of 1967's *Guess Who's Coming to Dinner*, *Guess Who* is every bit as awful as you'd expect it to be. Ashton Kutcher fumbles around looking cute and vacuous, Bernie Mac spits

out his lines with much eye-bulging and the music tells us when to laugh. Except that there are no laughs, not even when Ashton is forced to share a bed with his future father-in-law. And, guess what? Bernie Mac snores like a trooper. JC-W

• *Percy Jones* Bernie Mac, *Simon Green* Ashton Kutcher, *Theresa Jones* Zoë Saldaña, *Marilyn Jones* Judith Scott, *with* Hal Williams, Kellee Stewart, Robert Curtis Brown, Jessica Caulfield, Kimberly Scott, Richard Lawson, J. Kenneth Campbell, Richard T. Jones.

• *Dir* Kevin Rodney Sullivan, *Pro* Jenno Topping, Erwin Stoff and Jason Goldberg, *Ex Pro* Betty Thomas, Steven Greener and Joseph M. Caracciolo, *Screenplay* David Ronn, Jay Scherick and Peter Tolan, *Ph* Karl Walter Lindenlaub, *Pro Des* Paul J. Peters, *Ed* Paul Saydor, *M* John Murphy, *Costumes* Judy Ruskin Howell.

Fox/Regency Enterprises/3 Arts/Tall trees/Katalyst Films-Fox..
105 mins. USA. 2005. Rel: 29 April 2005. 12A.

Harold + Kumar Get the Munchies… ★★½

Kumar Patel is a brilliant medical student but is more interested in getting high. His flatmate, Harold Lee, is an anally retentive workaholic in a low-level position in banking. It's Friday night and although Harold has a whole lotta work to do, they smoke some weed and decide to sate their hunger by heading off for the nearest White Castle burger joint. However, en route they are waylaid by a pair of toilet-loving babes, the world's ugliest man, a bunch of racist cops, a cheetah and a TV star … *Dude, Where's My Weed?* OK, it's corny, but this allusion does sum up this adolescent pot odyssey from the director of that Ashton Kutcher benchmark. Taken on its own terms of throwaway, Saturday night goofing off, *Harold + Kumar* has a few chuckles, but it's more interesting as a cultural watershed. This has got to be the first mainstream movie to star an Indian and a Korean, in particular in a gross-out comedy. Thankfully, neither Kal Penn nor John Cho exploit the stereotyping of their respective races and exhibit a nice understatement in their knockabout banter. Silly this may be, but it's inoffensively distasteful and almost endearing. US title: *Harold & Kumar go to White Castle.* JC-W

• *Harold Lee* John Cho, *Kumar Patel* Kal Penn, *Maria* Paula Garcès, *Neil Patrick Harris* Neil Patrick Harris, *male nurse* Ryan Reynolds, *Freakshow* Christopher Meloni, *Billy Carver* Ethan Embry, *J.D.* Robert Tinkler, *Goldstein* David Krumholtz, *Rosenberg* Eddie Kaye Thomas, *Burger Shack employee* Anthony Anderson, *Cindy Kim* Siu Ta, *Liane* Malin Akerman, *Officer Palumbo* Sandy Jobin-Bevans, *with* Bobby Lee, Kate Kelton, Brooke D'Orsay, Errol Sitahal, Shaun Majumder, Gary Archibald.

• *Dir* Danny Leiner, *Pro* Greg Shapiro and Nathan Kahane, *Ex Pro* J. David Brewington Jr and Luke Ryan, Joe Drake, Carsten Lorenz and Hanno Huth, *Screenplay* Jon Hurwitz and

Hayden Schlossberg, *Ph* Bruce Douglas Johnson, *Pro Des* Steve Rosenzweig, *Ed* Jeff Betancourt, *M* David Kitay, *Costumes* Alex Kavanagh.

Senator International/New Line Cinema/Kingsgate Prods/ Endgame Entertainment-Icon.
87 mins. USA/Canada. 2004. Rel: 4 March 2005. Cert. 15.

Head-On ★★½

This is modern German cinema at the other extreme from that represented by *Good Bye Lenin!* The filmmaker, Fatih Akin, is a German-born Turk and his story centres on two Turks, both suicidal, who marry to enable the girl to get away from her domineering, traditionally minded parents. Essentially it's a marriage in name only and the freedom these two embrace is centred on promiscuous sex and drug-taking. Acting and photography are fine and initially the film's in-your-face style has a real cutting edge. However, stylised scenes clash with brutal realism, while unlikely plot developments play as melodrama. And the notion of the couple eventually falling in love for real sounds a note of mushy sentimentality (with slow motion, wouldn't you know?). The ending should be moving but by then – how shall I put it? – well, frankly my dear, I didn't give a damn. Original title: *Gegen die Wand*. MS

• *Cahit Tomruk* Birol Unel, *Sibel Guner* Sibel Kekilli, *Maren* Catrin Striebeck, *Seref* Guven Kirac, *Selma* Meltem Cumbul, *Yilmaz Guner* Cem Akin, *Birsen Guner* Aysel Iscan, *Yunus Guner* Demir Gokgol, *Nico* Stefan Gebelhoff, *Dr Schiller* Hermann Lause, *Lukas* Adam Bousdoukos, *Ammer* Ralph Misske, *Huseyin* Mehmet Kurtulus.

• *Dir* and *Screenplay* Fatih Akin, *Pro* Ralph Schwingel and Stefan Schubert, *Co-Pro* Akin, Andreas Thiel and Mehmet Kurtulus, *Ph* Rainer Klausmann, *Pro Des* Tamo Kunz, *Ed* Andrew Bird, *M* Klaus Maeck.

Wueste/Corazon International/NDR/Arte-Soda Pictures.
121 mins. Germany. 2004. Rel: 18 February 2005. Cert. 18.

Heimat 3: A Chronicle of Endings and Beginnings ★★★★

The veteran German filmmaker Edgar Reitz, now 72, is unique in cinema history in that basically his reputation rests on the three sets of films centred on the Simon family and on the village of Schabbach. A man of strong story-telling skills, he unfolds the family's history and that of Germany in the 20th century. The original *Heimat* (11 films in total) was released in our cinemas in 1985 and covered the period from 1919 to 1982. Such major events of history were involved that what was potentially a standard family saga was transcended and became a portrait of an ordinary family in the grip of history. *Heimat 2*, side-stepping back to the period from 1960 to 1970 but comprising 13 films, was denied cinema distribution here but Artificial Eye now brings us the six features that make up *Heimat 3*. This time the period ranges from 1989 (the fall of the Berlin wall) to the dawn of the new millennium and Reitz's narrative gifts remain intact. Cleverly he presents his material

so that audiences for *Heimat 3* do not need knowledge of the earlier films – indeed, episodes 1 and 5 could almost be seen as complete in themselves. But, while aspects of the decade filter through these six films, there's no opportunity as in the original *Heimat* to show exceptional events through ordinary lives. Consequently, *Heimat 3* is essentially good quality soap opera to be relished by fans of the genre – but since *Heimat* was much more than that, my star rating has to reflect this set's lower level. Original title: *Heimat 3 – Chronik einer Zeitenwende*. MS

• *Hermann Simon* Henry Arnold, *Clarissa Lichtblau* Salome Kammer, *Ernst Simon* Michael Kausch, *Anton Simon* Matthias Kniesbeck, *Hartmut Simon* Christian Leonard, *Mara Simon* Constance Wetzel, *Lulu Simon* Nicola Schoessler, *Gunnar* Uwe Steimle, *Udo* Tom Quaas, *Tillman* Peter Schneider, *Galina* Larissa Ivleva, *Tobi* Heiko Senst, *Petra* Karen Hempel, *Reinhold* Peter Goetz, *Matko* Patrick Mayer, *Herr Boeckle* Rainer Guldener.

• *Dir* Edgar Reitz, *Pro* Robert Busch, *Screenplay* Reitz and Thomas Brussig, *Ph* Thomas Mauch (episodes 1-4), Christian Reitz (episodes 5-6), *Pro Des* Franz Bauer and Michael Fechner (episodes 1-2), Irmhild Gumm (episodes 3-6),*Ed* Susanne Harmann, *M* Nikos Mamangakis and Michael Riessler, *Costumes* Rosemarie Hettmann.

Edgar Reitz Filmproduktion, SWR, ARD, ARD Degato, ARRI Cine Technik (Germany), Recorded Picture Co.-Artificial Eye.
675 mins. Germany/UK. 2004. Rel: 6 May 2005. Cert. 15.

Hellboy ★★★

Finding the right tone for comic book characters has always proved problematic for filmmakers, but self-professed geek Guillermo del Toro (*Cronos*, *Blade II*) has found a satisfying middle-ground. Apart from a rather clunky prologue, *Hellboy* gets into its stride with the introduction of the title character, who is anything but boyish. Six-foot-five and built like a tank, he chews on cigars, has a fondness for kittens and, like a good boy, keeps his horns well filed. He's also an escapee from Hell but, thanks to the kindly ministrations of Professor Broom (John Hurt looking like Professor Calculus from the Tintin books), has opted to defend humanity on behalf of the Bureau of Paranormal Research and Defense. Largely adapted from the first *Hellboy* book *Seed of Destruction* and a later title, *The Corpse*, the film is strong on understated humour that nicely punctuates the mandatory bursts of CGI wizardry. There are monsters galore and a preposterous plot about a resurrected Rasputin recruited by the Nazis to unleash all the forces of Hades. It's good fun, though, and Hellboy himself is an enticing cross between a boastful, indestructible killing machine and an emotionally conflicted lost soul. JC-W

• *Hellboy* Ron Perlman, *Liz Sherman* Selma Blair, *Tom Manning* Jeffrey Tambor, *Professor Trevor 'Broom' Bruttenholm* John Hurt, *Grigori Rasputin* Karel Roden, *John Myers* Rupert Evans, *Sammael* Brian Steele, *Abe Sapien* Doug Jones, *with* Ladislav Beran, Bridget Hodson, Angus MacInnes, William Hoyland, Bob Sherman.

• *Dir* and *Screenplay* Guillermo del Toro, from the Dark Horse comic created by Mike Mignola, *Pro* Lawrence Gordon, Mike Richardson and Lloyd Levin, *Ex Pro* Patrick Palmer, *Co-Ex Pro* Mike Mignola, *Ph* Guillermo Navarro, *Pro Des* Stephen Scott, *Ed* Peter Amundson, *M* Marco Beltrami; songs performed by Johnny Crawford, Tom Waits, Pete Yorn, Al Green, and Vera Lynn, *Costumes* Wendy Partridge, *Sound* Steve Boeddeker, *SF/X Make-up* Rick Baker, *Visual consultant* Mignola.

Revolution Studios/Dark Horse Entertainment-Columbia TriStar.
121 mins. USA. 2004. Rel: 2 September 2004. Cert. 12A.

Hero ★★★★

In the third century BC, a warrior known only as Nameless is invited to the royal palace to receive a private audience with the king for slaying the three most dangerous opponents of Qin. Permitted to sit just ten paces from his sovereign, Nameless explains how he managed to overpower the indestructible Sky, Broken Sword and Flying Snow. He tells the king that he studied the technique of each assassin before challenging them, learning that Sky drew his swordsmanship from the rhythms of music and that Broken Sword utilised the principles of calligraphy…

Nominated for Best Foreign Language Film of 2002, Zhang Yimou's *Hero* is a mammoth undertaking, reportedly costing twice as much as *Crouching Tiger, Hidden Dragon* and taking almost two years to make. It is an astonishing achievement. Employing a fantastic use of colour, motion and texture, Zhang reveals himself to be at the peak of his pictorial powers. He has also elicited some of the best acting in Chinese cinema, crafting strong performances from his stellar cast, in particular Chen Daoming as the wise and articulate King of Qin. Incidentally, this is the third recent Chinese film to draw on the story of the assassin and the king, following Zhou Xiaowen's *The Emperor's Shadow* (1996) and Chen Kaige's *The Emperor and the Assassin* (1999). JC-W

• *Nameless* Jet Li, *Broken Sword* Tony Leung Chiu Wai, *Flying Snow* Maggie Cheung Man Yuk, *Moon* Zhang Ziyi *King of Qin* Chen Daoming, *Sky* Donnie Yen.

• *Dir* Zhang Yimou, *Pro* Zhang and Bill Kong, *Ex Pro* Dou Shou Fang and Zhang Wei Pin, *Line Pro* Philip Lee, *Screenplay* Zhang, Li Feng and Wang Bin, *Ph* Christopher Doyle, *Pro Des* Huo Tingxiao and Yi Zhenzhou, *Ed* Zhai Ru and Angie Lam, *M* Tan Dun; violin by Itzhak Perlman and Tan Dun, drumming by KODO, *Costumes* Emi Wada, *Sound* Tao Jing, *Action Dir* Tony Ching Siu Tung, *Fight choreography* Tung Wai.

Elite Group Enterprises/Miramax/Edko Films/Zhang Yimou Studio/China Film-Buena Vista International.
99 mins. Hong Kong/China/USA. 2002. Rel: 24 September 2004. Cert. 12A.

Hide and Seek ★★

David and Alison Callaway are not exactly a happy couple, but they both adore their ten-year-old daughter Emily.

Then, following an unexpected tragedy, David moves Emily to upstate New York in the hope of stabilising her. But Emily retreats further and further into herself until she befriends 'Charlie', a friend that nobody can see… Stephen King got there first, but even if this were a total original it wouldn't have much impact. The problem is nothing to do with Dariusz Wolski's glorious cinematography, nor Dakota Fanning's unforgiving performance as the unresponsive Emily, but everything to do with Robert De Niro. For a start, the 61-year-old actor is a little old to be the father of a ten-year-old (an anomaly not alluded to in the script). And even in such tragic circumstances, he is terribly charmless and unsympathetic, which doesn't give an audience much emotional traction to work with (what does the beautiful and sunny Elisabeth Shue see in him?). And, when the film finally descends into arch silliness, he's not even much fun. JC-W

• *David Callaway* Robert De Niro, *Emily Callaway* Dakota Fanning, *Katherine* Famke Janssen, *Elizabeth* Elisabeth Shue, *Alison Callaway* Amy Irving, *Sheriff Hafferty* Dylan Baker, *Laura* Melissa Leo, *Steven* Robert John Burke, *Amy* Molly Grant Kallins, *Mr Haskins* David Chandler.

• *Dir* John Polson, *Pro* Barry Josephson, *Ex Pro* Joe Caracciolo Jr, *Co-Pro* Dana Robin and John Rogers, *Screenplay* Ari Schlossberg, *Ph* Dariusz Wolski, *Pro Des* Steven Jordan, *Ed* Jeffrey Ford, *M* John Ottman, *Costumes* Aude Bronson-Howard, *Sound* Erik Aadahl.

Fox/Josephson Entertainment-Fox.
100 mins. USA. 2005. Rel: 11 February 2005. Cert. 15.

High Tension

See *Switchblade Romance*.

Highwaymen ★★½

For the past five years, Rennie Cray has cruised America's highways hunting down the hit-and-run killer of his wife. Now, with the help of the enigmatic Molly Poole, he's about to come face-to-face with their mutual enemy. Colm Feore plays the wheelchair-bound killer with chilling credibility, lending an almost cyborg-like quality to his murderous vehicle while eerily personifying the frightening power some men gain from their cars. *Highwaymen* doesn't just pit two cinematic archetypes against one another, but two iconic GM cars: the '72 Cadillac Eldorado and the '68 Barracuda. The result is a harrowing cat-and-mouse game undermined by poorly written dialogue. SWM

• *Renford 'Rennie' Cray* Jim Caviezel, *Molly Poole* Rhona Mitra, *Will Macklin* Frankie Faison, *James Fargo* Colm Feore, *Alex* Andrea Roth, *Ray Boone* Gordon Currie, Noam Jenkins, Toby Proctor, James Kee.

• *Dir* Robert Harmon, *Pro* Mike Marcus, Carroll Kemp, Brad Jenkel and Avi Lerner, *Ex Pro* Tim Van Rellim, Toby Emmerich, Lynn Harris, Dave Brewington and Trevor Short, *Screenplay* Craig Mitchell and Hans Bauer, *Ph* Rene Ohashi,

Andrea Roth in Robert Harmon's harrowing
Highwaymen (from Entertainment)

Pro Des Paul Austerberry, *Ed* Chris Peppe, *M* Mark Isham,
Costumes Luis Sequeira.

New Line Cinema/Millennium Films/Cornice
Entertainment- Entertainment.
80 mins. USA. 2003. Rel: 2 July 2004. Cert. 18.

The Hillside Strangler ★

Between 18 October 1977 and 17 February 1978, cousins
Kenneth Bianchi and Angelo Buono terrorised Los Angeles by
sexually assaulting and strangling at least 12 young women,
aged between 12 and 28. As accurate as it is ugly, *The Hillside
Strangler* chronicles these real-life events with no moral
judgment whatsoever. In fact, it doesn't even attempt to explain
why they did these things, it just shows how they did it – in
excruciating detail – as if playing out the filmmaker's own
sadistic fantasies. Despite its attention to detail, the script gives
no insight at all and the direction, while competent, is more
suited to television. SWM

• *Kenneth A. Bianchi* C. Thomas Howell, *Angelo Buono* Nicholas
Turturro, *Claire Shelton* Allison Lange, *Christina Chavez* Marisol
Padilla Sanchez, *Jenny Buono* Lin Shaye, *Felicia Walker* Aimee
Brooks, *Heather Brewer* Tricia Dickson, *with* Damon Whitaker,
Molly Brenner, Keva Hargrove, Alexa Jago, Julia Lee, Zarah
Little, Kent Masters King, Natasha Melnick, Sarah Ann Morris,
Kevin Mukherji, Laura Mulrenan, Robbie Peron, Brandin
Rackley, Ken Rosier, Jennifer Tisdale, Roz Witt, Cletus Young.

• *Dir* Chuck Parello, *Pro* Hamish McAlpine and Michael
Muscal, *Ex Pro* Michael Avery, Carol Siller and Alexa Jago, *Co-
Ex Pro* John Steinfield, *Screenplay* Parello and Stephen Johnston,
Ph John Pirozzi, *Pro Des* Gregg Gibbs, *Ed* Paul Heiman, *M*
Danny Saber and David Catching, *Costumes* Niklas J. Palm.

Tartan Films-Tartan Films.
97 mins. USA. 2004. Rel: 12 November 2004. Cert. 18.

Histoire de Marie et Julien ★★

Pretentious, *moi?* Julien meets Marie in a park. He tells her that
he was just thinking about her. She tells him that she was just
thinking about him. She then pulls out a knife. Julien wakes
from his dream to find that he is late for an appointment with
Madame X. Out on the street he bumps into Marie. He tells
her that he was just dreaming about her. She tells him that she
recently dreamed of him. Later – much later – Julien spends a
lot of time sweeping his kitchen floor. Marie tells Julien's cat
that she doesn't bleed. In bed, Julien and Marie swap sado-
masochistic sweet nothings. Soon, sometime, something has
got to happen. The substance of this studied romantic mystery
– or metaphysical puzzle – would make an excellent 30-minute
short. Unfortunately, *Histoire de Marie et Julien* is two hours
longer than that. Its outcome is also rather similar to two
relatively recent American hits. Stodgy, *moi?* JC-W

• *Marie* Emmanuelle Béart, *Julien* Jerzy Radziwilowicz,
Madame X Anne Brochet, *Adrienne* Bettina Kee, *the friend*
Nicole Garcia, *the publisher* Olivier Cruveiller, *concierge* Mathias
Jung.

• *Dir* Jacques Rivette, *Pro* Martine Marignac, *Ex Pro*
Maurice Tinchant, *Screenplay* Rivette, Christine Laurent and
Pascal Bonitzer, *Ph* William Lubtchansky, *Art Dir* Manu de
Chauvigny, *Ed* Nicole Lubtchansky, *M* `Our Day Will Come'
sung by Blossom Dearie, *Costumes* Laurence Struz.

Pierre Grise Prods/Cinemaundici/Arts France Cinéma/VM
Prods/Canal Plus/Eurimages, etc-Artificial Eye.
151 mins. France/Italy. 2003. Rel: 8 October 2004. Cert. 15.

Hitch ★★★★

Alex 'Hitch' Hitchens reckons that any guy on earth can sweep any woman off her feet – he just needs the right broom. Hitch puts his conviction into practice, grooming romantically challenged guys into fashion-savvy, smooth-talking Lotharios. He's now landed the challenge of his career – an accident-prone lump of lard who wants to date the gorgeous, world-famous millionairess Allegra Cole. Meanwhile, Hitch has fallen in love himself, but is having a hard time of turning the head of the cynical, ball-breaking reporter Sara Melas… High-concept comedies don't come flashier than this. Built around a to-die-for premise – a know-all date doctor fighting his own corner in a romantic meltdown – *Hitch* is smart, funny and even thought-provoking. And Will Smith is great company. Parlaying his effortless charm into a deliciously fine-tooled deadpan delivery, he has ascended a new plateau of comic excellence. There's also a great script, bursting with terrific one-liners and delivered with pizazz and energy. It's unfortunate, then, that Eva Mendes fails to provide any empathy as Hitch's romantic obsession. Grating and obnoxious, she's just not good enough for our principled hero. JC-W

• *Alex 'Hitch' Hitchens* Will Smith, *Sara Melas* Eva Mendes, *Albert Brennaman* Kevin James, *Allegra Cole* Amber Valletta, *Max Trundle* Adam Arkin, *Vance* Jeffrey Donovan, *Cressida* Robinne Lee, *Ben* Michael Rapaport, *Casey* Julie Ann Emery, *Pete* Matt Malloy, *with* Nathan Lee Graham, Philip Bosco, Kevin Sussman, Austin Lysy, Paula Patton, Adam LeFevre, Rain Phoenix.

• *Dir* Andy Tennant, *Pro* James Lassiter, Will Smith and Teddy Zee, *Ex Pro* Michael Tadross and Wink Mordaunt, *Screenplay* Kevin Bisch, *Ph* Andrew Dunn, *Pro Des* Jane Musky, *Ed* Troy Takaki and Tracey Wadmore-Smith, *M* George Fenton, *Costumes* Marlene Stewart.

Columbia Pictures/Overbrook Entertainment-Columbia TriStar.
118 mins. USA. 2005. Rel: 4 March 2005. Cert. 12A.

The Hitchhiker's Guide to the Galaxy ★½

The Hitchhiker's Guide to the Galaxy is, as it sounds, a *Lonely Planet* for intergalactic sightseers. So when the mild-mannered Arthur Dent escapes the annihilation of Earth, he finds it a rather useful survival manual… Tricky one, this. How do you turn Douglas Adams' zany, intergalactic radio series into a full-blown movie? There was Adams' own hugely successful novelisation and its five spin-offs, then the TV series, the stage play, computer game, audio cassettes, CD-Roms and towel. As long ago as 1982 Ivan Reitman tried to give it a go – with Dan Aykroyd as Ford Prefect – but made *Ghostbusters* instead. Terry Gilliam would have been the obvious choice to take up the baton, but 22 years after the initial sortie, the task has fallen to complete amateurs. The subject itself is so farcical that it seems ludicrous to play it for laughs, complete with 'funny' music. And then, in the madcap role of Zaphod Beeblebrox, they cast an actor hardly known for his comic dexterity – Sam Rockwell (where's Jim Carrey when you need him?). In fact, the filmmakers seem to have misjudged every step of the way, from the performances of the central quartet to the unintelligible diction to the predictable voice-over from Stephen Fry. Visually, though, it's wonderful. JC-W

• *Zaphod Beeblebrox* Sam Rockwell, *Ford Prefect* Mos Def, *Trillian* Zooey Deschanel, *Arthur Dent* Martin Freeman,

Radio flyer: Martin Freeman and Marvin are a long way from Radio 4 in Garth Jennings' wrong-footed adaptation of Douglas Adams' *The Hitchhiker's Guide to the Galaxy* (from Buena Vista)

Slartibartfast Bill Nighy, *Marvin* Warwick Davis, *Questular* Anna Chancellor, *voice of Marvin* Alan Rickman, *voice of Deep Thought* Helen Mirren, *narrator* Stephen Fry, *Humma Kavula* John Malkovich, *voice of the whale* Bill Bailey, *voice of Jeltz* Richard Griffiths, *voice of Kwaltz* Ian McNeice, *with* Su Elliott, Simon Jones, Thomas Lennon, Mark Longhurst, Kelly Macdonald, Steve Pemberton, Albie Woodington.

• *Dir* Garth Jennings, *Pro* Nick Goldsmith, Jay Roach, Jonathan Glickman, Gary Barber and Roger Birnbaum, *Ex Pro* Douglas Adams, Robbie Stamp and Derek Evans, *Screenplay* Adams and Karey Kirkpatrick, *Ph* Igor Jadue-Lillo, *Pro Des* Joel Collins, *Ed* Niven Howie, *M* Joby Talbot; songs performed by Betty Wright, Al Green, Perry Como, and Stephen Fry, *Costumes* Sammy Sheldon, *Sound* Ian Wilson, *Creature Effects* Jim Henson's Creature Shop.

Touchstone Pictures/Spyglass Entertainment/Hammer and Tongs-Buena Vista International.
108 mins. UK/USA. 2005. Rel: 28 April 2005. Cert. PG.

A Hole in My Heart ★

As his teenage son Eric does 'mostly nothing' in his bedroom, Rickard embarks on the production of a porn film in the living room. However, as Rickard has only managed to recruit two performers – Geko and Tess – he hopes that his son can operate the camera so that he himself can join in the action. But it all gets rather out of hand... A confrontational statement on the nature of pornography and damaged humanity, *A hole in my heart* tries very hard to provoke and offend. The four principals are dermatologically challenged grotesques and the narrative is all over the place, while close-ups of genital surgery pop up like periodic exclamation marks. The result is not only defiantly uncinematic (the whole thing is set in a claustrophobic flat), but is an affront to human decency. Without the means to act out real hardcore sex, the film goes beyond the bounds of actual perversion, climaxing when Geko vomits into Tess's prized open mouth. Bring back *Emmanuelle*. Original title: *Ett hål i mitt hjärta.* JC-W

• *Rickard* Thorsten Flinck, *Eric* Björn Almroth, *Tess* Sanna Bråding, *Geko* Goran Marjanovic.

• *Dir* and *Screenplay* Lukas Moodysson, *Pro* Lars Jönsson, *Assoc Pro* Anna Knochenhauer, *Ph, Art Dir* and *Costumes* Moodysson, Malin Fornander, Jesper Kurlandsky and Karel Strandlind, *Ed* Michal Leszczyowski.

Memfis Film Rights3 AB/Canal Plus-Metrodome.
97 mins. Sweden/Denmark. 2004. Rel: 14 January 2005. Cert. 18.

The Holy Girl ★★★

Considering that Lucrecia Martel's follow-up to *La ciénega* has been warmly received, its failure to fulfil its promise took me by surprise. Expertly cast and admirably acted it certainly is, especially in the key roles, with Mercedes Morán as the divorced Helena and Maria Alché as her teenage daughter Amalia. The latter may share the growing sexual preoccupations of her best

friend but she subjugates them to a sense of religious duty by seeking to find a way to save from sin a visiting doctor (Carlos Belloso), who, in addition to goosing the girl, is developing a relationship with her mother. Too often the story-telling is oblique, the plot development contrived and the eccentric compositions a tiresome self-indulgence. Eventually truths are revealed while lies complicate matters by muddying the water further, yet when the film seems headed for a climax it simply breaks off, leaving one exasperated.
Aka *The Holy Child/La niña santa.* MS

• *Helena* Mercedes Morán, *Dr Jano* Carlo Belloso, *Freddy* Alejandro Urdapilleta, *Amalia* María Alché, *Josefina* Julieta Zylberberg, *with* Monica Villa, Marta Lubos, Alejo Mango, Arturo Goetz, and *Inés* Mía Maestro.

• *Dir* and *Screenplay* Lucrecia Martel, *Pro* Lita Stantic, *Ex Pro* Pedro Almodovar, Agustin Almodovar and Esther Garcia, *Assoc Pro* Nora Kohen, Alfredo Ghirardo, Cesare Petrillo, Vieri Razzini, Tilde Corsi and Gianni Romoli, *Ph* Felix Monti, *Pro Des* Graciela Oderigo, *Ed* Santiago Ricci, *M* Andrés Gerszenzon, *Costumes* Julio César Suarez.

Lita Stantic/El Deseo/Senso Producciones/La Passionaria/ Teodora/R&C Produzion-Artificial Eye.
103 mins. Argentina/Spain/Italy/Netherlands/Switzerland. 2004. Rel: 4 February 2005. Cert. 15.

A Home at the End of the World ★★★½

Cleveland 1967, 1974; New York/Phoenix 1982. Bobby Morrow never really had much of a family but he remembers his older brother as a receptive, laidback and open-minded individual. Now in his teens, Bobby has taken on many of his brother's characteristics, presenting a persona that young Jonathan Glover finds extremely inviting. Soon Bobby is one of the family – he introduces Jonathan's mother to pot – and when the boys are reunited in New York and manhood, Bobby is equally taken by Jonathan's flatmate Clare... A character-driven drama from the 1990 novel by Michael Cunningham (who also wrote *The Hours*), *A Home...* is a subtle, reflective and life-affirming film without a shred of sentimentality. Few American actors of Colin Farrell's stature would have dared to play a hippy who snogs both his leading man and the wife of Sean Penn, but Farrell inhabits the part with tenderness and conviction (is this the same man who played the Irish psycho in *interMission?*). In fact, this is really an actor's film, with everybody on top form, tapping into the warmth, humanity and emotional integrity of a remarkable story. Great soundtrack, too. JC-W

• *Bobby Morrow, 1982* Colin Farrell, *Clare* Robin Wright Penn, *Jonathan Glover, 1982* Dallas Roberts, *Alice Glover* Sissy Spacek, *Bobby Morrow, 1967* Andrew Chalmers, *Carlton Morrow* Ryan Donowho, *Bobby Morrow, 1974* Erik Smith, *Jonathan Glover, 1974* Harris Allan, *Ned Glover* Matt Frewer, *Jonathan's co-worker* Michael Mayer, *with* Asia Vieira, Jeffrey Authors, Ron Lea, Shawn Roberts, Barna Moricz.

• *Dir* Michael Mayer, *Pro* Tom Hulce, Christine Vachon,

Katie Roumel, Pamela Koffler, John Wells, John N. Hart Jr. and Jeffrey Sharp, *Ex Pro* John Sloss and Michael Hogan, *Screenplay* Michael Cunningham, *Ph* Enrique Chediak, *Pro Des* Michael Shaw, *Ed* Lee Percy, *M* Duncan Sheik; Mozart; songs performed by Jefferson Airplane, Bob Dylan, Laura Nyro with LaBelle, Paul Simon, Steve Winwood, Yaz, Leonard Cohen, Steve Reich, Patti Smith, Dusty Springfield, The Band, Bombs Over Providence, and Mack James, *Costumes* Beth Pasternak.

Killer Films/Hart Sharp Entertainment-Warner.
97 mins. USA. 2004. Rel: 5 November 2004. Cert. 15.

Home On the Range ★★★

Reportedly one of the very last Disney 'toons to be traditionally animated, *Home On the Range* pays homage to the oeuvre of the Looney Tunes and in particular such creations as Yosemite Sam and Wile E. Coyote. While this tribute to a former age may beguile older viewers, it does emphasise a problem. Kids of the 21st century are becoming increasingly sophisticated and demanding and are unlikely to connect with the sketchy visual references of a film like this. Having said that, *Home On the Range* is a breezy confection, enhanced by a strong narrative concept and an above-average voice cast. Set in the Wild West, it blends *Babe* with *The Good, The Bad and The Ugly* as farmyard animals track down a rascally hustler. Allusions to Sergio Leone and even the recent *Spirit: Stallion of the Cimarron* abound, but it's the interaction between three dairy cows – voiced by Roseanne Barr, Judi Dench and Jennifer Tilly – that really distinguishes the film. It just shows that when it comes to pure entertainment, you can't beat decent dialogue and good actors. JC-W

• voices: *Maggie* Roseanne Barr, *Mrs Caloway* Judi Dench, *Grace* Jennifer Tilly, *Alameda Slim* Randy Quaid, *Buck* Cuba Gooding Jr, *Wesley* Steve Buscemi, *Rusty the dog* G.W. Bailey, *Junior the buffalo* Lance LeGault, *Sheriff Sam Brown* Richard Riehle, *Audrey the chicken* Estelle Harris, *Lucky Jack* Charles Haid, *Abner* Dennis Weaver, *with* Charles Dennis, Sam J. Levine, Joe Flaherty, Carole Cook, Charlie Dell, Governor Ann Richards, Patrick Warburton, Edie McClurg, Phil Proctor, John Sanford, Bruce A. Young.

• *Dir* and *Screenplay* Will Finn and John Sanford, *Pro* Alice Dewey Goldstone, *Art Dir* David Cutler, *Ed* H. Lee Peterson, *M* Alan Menken; Ennio Morricone; lyrics Glenn Slater; songs performed by k.d. lang, Randy Quaid, Bonnie Raitt, Tim McGraw, and The Beu Sisters, *Sound* Tim Chau.

Walt Disney Pictures-Buena Vista International.
76 mins. USA. 2004. Rel: 6 August 2004. Cert. U.

Hostage ★★★½

Jeff Talley used to be a cherished hostage negotiator for the LAPD – but never again. Leaving the dangerous streets of Los Angeles for a quieter life in rural California, Talley is now Chief of Police of Bristo Camino, Ventura County. Then, on a day Talley dubs 'Low-Crime Monday', three teenage troublemakers decide to steal a car belonging to the affluent Smith family. What the miscreants don't know is that Walter Smith is an accountant for the Mob. So, when they break into his house and shoot a policewoman in cold blood, all hell breaks loose… After some rather slow-burning movies of late, Bruce Willis returns with a bang in this stylish, tightly drawn thriller that steadily builds the suspense until exploding into a rather overblown finale. Bespectacled and shaven-headed, Willis cuts an endearing figure and his attempts to hold his disintegrating family together reaps emotional dividends. There are also some ingenious layers of conflicting psychological agendas (deftly adapted from the novel by Robert Crais), but it's a shame that the film is so relentlessly nasty. JC-W

• *Jeff Talley* Bruce Willis, *Walter Smith* Kevin Pollak, *Mars Krupcheck* Ben Foster, *Dennis Kelly* Jonathan Tucker, *Kevin Kelly* Marshall Allman, *Jennifer Smith* Michelle Horn, *Tommy Smith* Jimmy Bennett, *Laura Shoemaker* Tina Lifford, *watchman* Kim Coates, *Jane Talley* Serena Scott Thomas, *Wil Bechler* Robert Knepper, *Amanda Talley* Rumer Willis, *with* Ransford Doherty, Marjean Holden, Michael D. Roberts, Art LaFleur, Johnny Messner, Glenn Morshower.

• *Dir* Florent Emilio Siri, *Pro* Mark Gordon, Bob Yari, Bruce Willis and Arnold Rifkin, *Ex Pro* Andreas Thiesmeyer, Joseph Lautenschlager, Hawk Koch and David Wally, *Co-Pro* David Willis, *Assoc Pro* Susanne Bohnet, *Screenplay* Doug Richardson, *Ph* Giovanni Fiore Coltellaci, *Pro Des* Larry Fulton, *Ed* Olivier Gajan and Richard J.P. Byard, *M* Alexandre Desplat, *Costumes* Elisabetta Beraldo, *Sound* Stephen Hunter Flick and Steven Ticknor, *Acting Coach* Asia Argento.

Stratus Film Company/Miramax/Cheyenne Enterprises/ Equity Pictures-Entertainment.
113 mins. USA/Germany. 2004. Rel: 11 March 2005. Cert. 15.

Hotel Rwanda ★★★

Kigali, Rwanda; 1994. Paul Rusesabagina, manager of the up-market Hotel Des Milles Collines in the Rwandan capital, is the king of his castle. He knows his single malt Scotch and Cuban cigars and leads a life of relative luxury. And by kowtowing to the right authorities, he is both liked and admired. But when the suspicious death of the President is blamed on the Tutsi minority, Paul's magnanimity towards all creeds can only be tolerated for so long… Few can even come close to conceiving of the human tragedy of Rwanda. The statistics alone are beyond comprehension: the indiscriminate butchery of more than 800,000 men, women and children in the space of less than 100 days. Terry George, who previously brought our attention to the atrocities of Northern Ireland in his 1996 *Some Mother's Son*, again explores social iniquity through the eyes of one family. And yet he doesn't convincingly explore the dynamics of Paul's family life, any more than he excavates the complex issues at the heart of the Hutu/Tutsi conflict. This is a one-man show – and Don Cheadle is superb – but the film fails to kinetically capture the horrors of the time and too often feels like a well-intentioned TV movie. JC-W

• *Paul Rusesabagina* Don Cheadle, *Tatiana Rusesabagina* Sophie Okonedo, *Colonel Oliver* Nick Nolte, *Jack Daglish* Joaquin Phoenix, *Dube* Desmond Dube, *David* David O'Hara, *Pat Archer* Cara Seymour, *General Bizimungu* Fana Mokoena, *Fedens* Leleti Khumalo, *with* Hakeem Kae-Kazim, Tony Kgoroge, Mosa Kaiser, Neil McCarthy, and (uncredited) Jean Reno.

• *Dir* Terry George, *Pro* George and A. Kitman Ho, *Ex Pro* Hal Sadoff, Martin F. Katz, Duncan Reid, Roberfto Cicutto, Francesco Melzi D'Eril and Sam Bhembe, *Co- Pro* Bridget Pickering and Luigi Musini, *Co-Ex Pro* Keir Pearson and Nicholas Meyer, *Line Pro* Sally French, *Screenplay* George and Keir Pearson, *Ph* Robert Fraisse, *Pro Des* Tony Burrough and Johnny Breedt, *Ed* Naomi Geraghty, *M* Andrea Guerra, Rupert Gregson-Williams and Afro Celt Sound System, *Costumes* Ruy Filipe.

Lions Gate/Miracle Pictures/Seamus/Inside Track-Entertainment.
121 mins. UK/South Africa/Italy/USA. 2004. Rel: 25 February 2005. Cert. 12A.

Killing fields: Oscar nominee Sophie Okonedo in Terry George's well-meaning but surprisingly muted *Hotel Rwanda* (from Entertainment)

House of Flying Daggers ★★★★½

China; 859 AD. With unrest spreading through the land as the Tang Dynasty declines, a secret sect is established to fight the corruption of the government. Phenomenally adept at the martial arts, the movement calls itself the House of Flying Daggers. Two rural deputies, Leo and Jin, map out a plan to infiltrate the sect by following a blind prostitute, Mei, who is suspected of being the leader's daughter. However, neither had anticipated the beauty and fighting skills of this extraordinary young woman... On one level, *House of Flying Daggers* is a homage to the *wuxie* cinema of King Hu, the cinema of swordplay and chivalry. On another, it is a rich playground where action and art meet to celebrate the essence of cinema. Once again employing the full palette of colour like no other director, Zhang Yimou has created an operatic epic in which

the visual and the emotional conspire to imagine a world of human and natural extremes. Working from a solid story devised by himself, Li Feng and Wang Bin, the director has pushed the boundaries of *wuxie* to fashion a series of sequences that are truly astounding, from the ambush in the bamboo forest to the snow-blown finale. A genuine masterpiece. JC-W

• *Jin/Wind* Takeshi Kaneshiro, *Leo* Andy Lau, *Mei* Zhang Ziyi, *Yee* Song Dandan, *with* Wang Yabin, Zheng Lu, Wu Weifeng, Yan Yan, Zheng Jie.

• *Dir* Zhang Yimou, *Pro* Zhang Yimou and Bill Kong, *Ex Pro* Zhang Weiping, *Assoc Pro* Zhang Zhenyan, *Screenplay* Li Feng, Zhang Yimou and Wang Bin, *Ph* Zhao Xiaoding, *Pro Des* Huo Tingxiao, *Ed* Cheng Long, *M* Shigeru Umebayashi, *Sound* Tao Jing, *Action Dir* Tony Ching Siu-Tung.

Elite Group/Edko Films/Zhang Yimou Studio-Pathé.
118 mins. Hong Kong/China. 2004. Rel: 26 December 2004. Cert. 15.

House of the Dead ★

Why anyone would plan a giant, corporate-sponsored rave on an island called La Isla del Muerte (The Island of Death) is beyond me. But, sure enough, when a group of tawdry, privileged urbanites arrive on the island to join the party, everyone has disappeared, a retrieved video camera showing that the rave was attacked by zombies (kind of fun in its own way). The group is then steadily picked off as they're chased through the night and hole-up in an old house, with each kill 'scored' by an inexplicable and embarrassing flash from the actual arcade game... *House of the Dead* may well have been the video game that sparked pop culture's renewed interest in the zombie genre. But, where successive video game-cum-movie adaptations like *Resident Evil* have been fanned into roaring franchises, *House of the Dead* is a tragic legacy for a video game that was genuinely horrific. SWM

• *Rudy* Jonathan Cherry, *Simon* Tyron Leitso, *Salish* Clint Howard, *Alicia* Ona Grauer, *Casper* Ellie Cornell, *Greg* Will Sanderson, *Karma* Enuka Okuma, *Liberty* Kira Clavell, *Cynthia* Saloma Salomaa, *Hugh* Michael Eklund, *Castillo* David Palffy, *Captain Kirk* Jurgen Prochnow, *with* Steve Byers, Erica Durance, Birgit Stein, Jay Brazeau, Adam Harrington, Colin Lawrence, Ben Derrick, Elisabeth Rosen, Bif Naked, Penny Phang, Kris Pope, Mashiah Vaughn-Hulbert.

• *Dir* Uwe Boll, *Pro* Boll, Wolfgang Herold and Shawn Williamson, *Ex Pro* Mark A. Altman, Mark Gottwald, Dan Bates, Daniel S. Kletzky and Michael Roesch, *Assoc Pro* Max Wanko and Dan Sales, *Screenplay* Mark A. Altman and Dave Parker, based on the Sega video game, *Ph* Mathias Neumann, *Ed* David M. Richardson, *M* Reinhard Besser, *Pro Des* Tink, *Costumes* Lorraine Carson, *Makeup Effects* Bill Terazakis, *Visual Effects* Alain and Doug de Silva, Jan Stolz and Christian Haas.

Boll Kino Beteiligungs/Brightlights/Mindfire-Redbus Film Distribution.
90 mins. USA/Canada/Germany. 2003.

Model victims: Jon Abrahams, Chad Michael Murray, Elisha Cuthbert and Jared Padalecki in Jaume Collet-Serra's thrilling *House of Wax* (from Warner)

House of Wax ★★★★

Six college students are on their way from Florida to Louisiana to attend a football game. Stopping off for the night in a field, they get on the wrong side of an inquisitive stranger (whom they do not see) and in the morning the fan belt of one of their vehicles has been slashed. So, plucky Carly and boyfriend Wade stay behind to get the car fixed. And there, in a nearby town, they stumble across Trudy's 'world famous' Wax Museum. It's a profoundly eerie place made entirely from wax, from the occupants to the furniture to the brickwork... Borrowing its title from the 1953 classic starring Vincent Price, this sensational shocker pits teen slasher clichés against something entirely more inventive. Scripted by the twin brothers Chad and Carey W. Hayes, it presents a primal story of good versus evil, with Carly's self-styled evil twin Nick (a transformed Murray) coming of age as he battles genuinely evil twins in a town cut off from contemporary civilisation. Exploiting pop-cultural banality with a gratuitous striptease from Paris Hilton, the film then enters another dimension that is every bit as scary and intense as *The Texas Chain Saw Massacre*. It's also stylishly photographed and unapologetically gory, while the eye-popping climax is a thrilling original. JC-W

• *Carly Jones* Elisha Cuthbert, *Nick Jones* Chad Michael Murray, *Bo/Vincent* Brian Van Holt, *Paige Edwards* Paris Hilton, *Wade* Jared Padalecki, *Dalton Chapman* Jon Abrahams, *Blake* Robert Ri'chard, *roadkill driver* Damon Herriman, *sheriff* Andy Anderson.

• *Dir* Jaume Collet-Serra, *Pro* Joel Silver, Robert Zemeckis and Susan Levin, *Screenplay* Chad and Carey W. Hayes, from a story by Charles Belden, *Ph* Stephen Windon, *Pro*

Des Graham 'Grace' Walker, *Ed* Joel Negron, *M* John Ottman; songs performed by Deftones, Chops and Raekwon, Disturbed, The Von Bondies, Interpol, The Prodigy, Har Mar Superstar, Stutterfly, My Chemical Romance, The Stooges, bloodsimple, Marilyn Manson, Brothers Conti, Joy Division, and Dark New Day, *Costumes* Alex Alvarez and Graham Purcell, *Sound* Richard Adrian, *Visual Effects* John Breslin.

Warner/Village Roadshow/Dark Castle-Warner.
112 mins. USA/Australia. 2005. Rel: 27 May 2005.
Cert. 15.

Hukkle ★★★½

As bizarre as *Aaltra* but far more intriguing, this superbly photographed study of life in a Hungarian village offers comic quirkiness on the surface but also a disconcerting undertow. In these respects it echoes the memorable Swedish movie *Songs from the Second Floor* (2000), but it's a wholly individual piece as is proved by the total omission of dialogue. Characteristic is the use of close-ups which, when followed by a track back, are equally likely to reveal that we are looking at the flesh of a pig or at part of a bicycle. Filmmaker György Pálfi is less clear about the points he wants to make about life than the Swedish film was, but if his movie is puzzling it is also a genuine one-off with much artistic merit. MS

• *Uncle Cseklik* Ferenc Bandi, *midwife* Mrs Jozsef Racz, *police officer* Jozsef Farkas, *beekeeper* Ferenc Nagy, *beekeeper's wife* Mrs Ferenc Virag, *with* Janos F. Kovacs, Mrs Janos Nagy, Agi Margitai, Eszter Onodi, Attila Kaszas, Katalin Balatoni.

• *Dir* and *Screenplay* György Pálfi, *Pro* Csaba Bereczki and András Bohm, *Ph* Gergely Poharnok, *Set Decor* Andrea Hoffer

Nyíriné and Zsolt Kovács, *Ed* Gabor Marinkas, *M* Balázs Barna and Samu Gryllus, *Puppet master* Ivan Pohárnok.

Mokép Rt and the Academy of Dramatic and Cinematic Art/Hungarian Public Funds for Motion Picture, etc-Soda Pictures.
75 mins. Hungary. 2002. Rel: 26 November 2004. Cert 12A.

I am David ★★½

Good intentions abound in this adaptation of Anne Holm's novel for young adults, but that's not enough to prevent this film from being unconvincing and old-fashioned. The story concerns the desperate journey of a boy who escapes from a labour camp and travels through Greece and Italy, en route for Denmark and a discovery that will bring new hope into his life. It's not really fair to expect a child actor to handle convincingly a character so traumatised and, with everyone speaking English and the script being undistinguished, conviction is never attained. That's a pity because, despite having a 1950s setting, the tale is a laudable warning about a world in which conflicts and imprisonment lead to the suffering of the innocent. Entering late on, Joan Plowright at least provides a warm presence. MS

• *David* Ben Tibber, *Sophie* Joan Plowright, *Johannes* Jim Caviezel, *the man* Hristo Shopov, *Elsa* Silvia De Santis, *Giovanni* Paco Reconti, *Baker* Roberto Attias, *Roberto* Francesco De Vito, *American man* Paul Feig, *American woman* Lucy Russell, *David's mother* Maria Bonnevie, *Maria* Viola Carinci.

• *Dir* and *Screenplay* Paul Feig, from the novel by Anne Holm, *Pro* Davina Belling, Lauren Levine and Clive Parsons, *Line Pro* Andrea Borella, *Ph* Roman Osin, *Pro Des* Giovanni Natalucci, *Ed* Steven Weisberg, *M* Stewart Copeland, *Costumes* Uliva Pizzetti.

Film and General-Enjoy Cinema.
92 mins. USA. 2004. Rel: 5 November 2004. Cert. PG.

I ♥ Huckabees ★

Bumping into the same Sudanese doorman three times, the environmentalist and dismal poet Albert Markovski begins to think that there is more to life than meets the five senses. Stumbling on the business card of an Existential Detective agency, Albert engages the surreal services of Bernard and Vivian Jaffe, who tell him that they will spy on his every move. His job, Bernard tells him, is to dismantle his day-to-day reality so as to see the bigger picture… Considering the track record of director David O. Russell (*Spanking the Monkey, Flirting with Disaster, Three Kings*), I ♥ *Huckabees* is a numbing disappointment. Returning to the farcical milieu of *Flirting* (which was actually hilarious), Russell has made the fatal error of thinking that shouting, profanity and utter chaos can generate humour. The film strains so hard to be interesting and quirky that you can almost see the stretch marks, while a wonderful cast buzzes around without direction. It is unfortunate, too, that in the central role Jason Schwartzman is such an unappealing and profoundly mirthless presence. JC-W

• *Albert Markovski* Jason Schwartzman, *Caterine Vauban* Isabelle Huppert, *Bernard Jaffe* Dustin Hoffman, *Vivian Jaffe* Lily Tomlin, *Brad Stand* Jude Law, *Tommy Corn* Mark Wahlberg, *Dawn Campbell* Naomi Watts, *Angela Franco* Angela Grillo, *Darlene* Darlene Hunt, *Marty* Kevin Dunn, *Mrs Silver* Talia Shire [Jason Schwartzman's mother], *Mr Silver* Bob Gunton, *Mrs Hooten* Jean Smart, *with* Ger Duany, Benny Hernandez, Richard Appel, Tippi Hedren, Saïd Taghmaoui, Shania Twain, Jake Hoffman, and (uncredited) *Mr Hooten* Richard Jenkins.

• *Dir* David O. Russell, *Pro* Russell, Gregory Goodman and Scott Rudin, *Ex Pro* Michael Kuhn, *Co-Pro* Dara L. Weintraub, *Screenplay* Russell and Jeff Baena, *Ph* Peter Deming, *Pro Des* K.K. Barrett, *Ed* Robert K. Lambert, *M* Jon Brion; Beethoven; 'Man! I Feel Like a Woman!' sung by Shania Twain, *Costumes* Mark Bridges.

Fox Searchlight/Qwerty Films/Kanzeon/Scott Rudin/N1 European Film Produktions-Fox.
106 mins. USA/UK/Germany. 2004.
Rel: 26 November 2004. Cert. 15

In Casablanca Angels Don't Fly ★★★½

Three stories in one, this Moroccan feature, a first by Mohamed Asli as writer/director, is a heartfelt work about three individuals who, to support their families or to better their lot, have come to Casablanca. Here they earn money as employees in a restaurant. Despite elements of humour, it's a bleak work, sometimes clumsy in its transitions from tale to tale (or into flashback) and over-directed on occasion. Nevertheless, its social concern is obviously genuine and those with an interest in Moroccan life today will find it worthwhile. The players are convincing and the film gains from being created by an insider, Mohamed Asli having been born in Casablanca. MS

• *Ismail* Abdessamed Miftah El Kheir, *Saïd* Rachid El Hazmir, *Aicha* Leila El Ahyani, *Ottman* Abdelaziz Essghyr, etc.

• *Dir, Pro* and *Screenplay* Mohamed Asli, *Ex Pro* Thami Hejjaj, *Ph* Roberto Meddi, *Art Dir* Fettah Attaoui, *Ed* Raimondo Aiello, *M* Stephan Micus.

Gherardo Pagliei and Mohamed Asli/Gam Film/Dagham Film-ICA Projects.
97 mins. Morocco/Italy. 2003. Rel: 3 September 2004. Cert. PG.

The Incredibles ★★★★½

Bob Parr is so strong that he can stop a train in its tracks. Helen Parr is so flexible that she can disarm three guards simultaneously in as many rooms. Bob and Helen are truly incredible, but when an avalanche of law suits threatens to bankrupt the city they are forced into anonymous retirement. But how do two superheroes, along with three preternaturally gifted kids, adapt to domesticity? Pixar, the company behind *Toy Story, Monsters, Inc.* and *Finding Nemo*, have done it again. *The Incredibles* is as exciting and suspenseful as any superhero movie before it, but it is so much more. And while it occasionally meanders into territory previously explored by *Spy Kids* and *Thunderbirds*, it is a whopping original. It's just a great idea. What if the Caped Crusader or the Man of Steel hung up their tights, married the superheroine of their dreams and tried to settle down to the drudgery of real life? The strength of the cartoon is that it succeeds and appeals on so many levels. Visually inventive, laugh-out-loud funny and even moving (Holly Hunter is wonderful as the long-suffering Helen aka Elastigirl), *The Incredibles* has something for everyone. It is a tad too long, but this is a minor quibble. JC-W

• voices: *Bob Parr/Mr Incredible* Craig T. Nelson, *Helen Parr/Elastigirl* Holly Hunter, *Lucius Best/Frozone* Samuel L. Jackson, *Buddy Pine/Syndrome* Jason Lee, *Gilbert Huph* Wallace Shawn, *Violet Parr* Sarah Vowell, *Dashiell Parr (Dash)* Spencer Fox, *Edna 'E' Mode* Brad Bird, *Mirage* Elizabeth Peña, *Bomb Voyage* Dominique Louis, with Jean Sincere, Lou Romano, Michael Bird, Bud Luckey, Bret Parker, Kimberly Adair Clark, John Ratzenberger, Nicholas Bird, Andrew Stanton, Pamela Gaye Walker, Patrick Walker.

• *Dir* and *Screenplay* Brad Bird, *Pro* John Walker, *Ex Pro* John Lasseter and Andrew Jimenez, *Assoc Pro* Kori Rae, *Pro Des* Lou Romano, *Ed* Stephen Schaffer, *M* Michael Giacchino, *Sound* Randy Thom, *Character Design* Tony Fucile and Teddy Newton, *Supervising Animation* Fucile, Steven Clay Hunter and Alan Barillaro.

Walt Disney/Pixar Animation-Buena Vista International. 120 mins. USA. 2004. Rel: 19 November 2004. Cert. U.

Infernal Affairs II ★★★

Hong Kong; 1991-1997. When police cadet Yan's half-brother Hau inherits control of the local triad, Yan is instructed by his superior to infiltrate the gang. Meanwhile, Yan's colleague Ming, who is in fact a triad mole, is proving to be an extremely competent policeman... Filling in the temporal gap between the first film's prologue and the bulk of its action, this swift prequel takes the cyclical paradox of *Infernal Affairs* and runs with it. Indeed, this is a thinking man's action movie, loaded with allegory, visual puns and allusions to the first film, and is a bit of a mind-stretch. Broadening out the original's taut intimacy, *IAII* soars into epic grandeur, although it fails to generate the freshness of its predecessor. *Infernal Affairs III* is on the way. CB

• *Inspector Wong* Anthony Wong, *Sam* Eric Tsang, *Ngai Wing Hau* Francis Ng, *Mary, Sam's wife* Carina Lau, *SP Luk* Hu Jun, *Keung* Chapman To, *Law* Roy Cheung, *Ming* Edison Chen, *Yan* Shawn Yue.

• *Dir* Andrew Lau and Alan Mak, *Pro* Andrew Lau, *Ex Pro* John Chong Ching, Daniel Yun and Ma Baoping, *Line Pro* Ellen Chang and Lorraine Ho, *Screenplay* Alan Mak and Felix Chong, *Ph* Andrew Lau and Ng Man Ching, *Art Dir* Bill Lui, *Ed* Danny Pang and Pang Ching-Hung, *M* Chan Kwong-Wing, *Costumes* Silver Cheung, *Sound* Kinson Tsang.

Media Asia Films/Raintree Pictures/Eastern Dragon Film/

Basic Pictures-Tartan Films. 119 mins. Hong Kong. 2003. Rel: 6 August 2004. Cert. 15.

In Good Company ★★★½

The title is hardly inspiring but makes more sense once you've seen the movie. The company in question owns the venerable, top-selling *Sports America* magazine. And it is a good company. Its head of ad sales, Dan Foreman, has established a solid reputation in the business as well as the respect of his loyal staff. Then, on the day that he discovers his wife is pregnant again, he is demoted and replaced by the 26-year-old Carter Duryea. Dan's daughter, 18-year-old Alex, then gets into NYU and Dan is forced to take out a second mortgage. So he's none too pleased when Alex and his new boss start getting romantic... This is pretty 'high concept' stuff but is given a fresh spin by making the threatening whiz kid in Dan's life a human, vulnerable and really nice guy. The film looks at both sides of the men's dilemma – what's it like to replace a man who's older than your father and is your girlfriend's parent? – and it ratchets up the emotional dynamic. Indeed, these salesmen, at sea in a parallel universe, are in good company. The film is also very funny, with a sprinkling of good lines, some fine songs and first-rate performances. JC-W

• *Dan Foreman* Dennis Quaid, *Carter Duryea* Topher Grace, *Alex Foreman* Scarlett Johansson, *Ann Foreman* Marg Helgenberger, *Mortie* David Paymer, *Steckle* Clark Gregg, *Eugene Kalb* Philip Baker Hall, *Corwin* Frankie Faison, *Kimberley* Selma Blair, with Ty Burrell, Kevin Chapman, Amy Aquino, Colleen Camp, Lauren Tom, Enrique Castillo, John Cho, and (uncredited) *Teddy K* Malcolm McDowell.

• *Dir* and *Screenplay* Paul Weitz, *Pro* Paul Weitz and Chris Weitz, *Ex Pro* Rodney Liber and Andrew Miano, *Co-Pro* Kerry Kohansky, *Ph* Remi Adefarasin, *Pro Des* William Arnold, *Ed* Myron Kerstein, *M* Stephen Trask; songs performed by David Byrne, The Soundtrack of Our Lives, The Shins, Iron & Wine, Aretha Franklin, Damien Rice, Diana Krall, Steely Dan, and Peter Gabriel, *Costumes* Molly Maginnis.

Universal/Depth of Field-Entertainment. 109 mins. USA. 2004. Rel: 18 February 2005. Cert. PG.

Inheritance ★★

Having turned his back on his family's steel business in Denmark, Christoffer has moved to Stockholm with his actress wife. As she flourishes on the stage performing Shakespeare, so Christoffer is finding equal success with his restaurant nearby. Then his father commits suicide and Christoffer is pressured into taking over the company, immediately dismissing 900 members of his father's workforce... An examination of the corruption of power and the emotional pull between love and professional duty, *Inheritance* is all rather obvious and unexciting. Shot on DV, it is doggedly uncinematic yet lacks the danger and spontaneity of the Dogme films. The performances are good (Lisa Werlinder has the potential to be a major European star), but they might have fared better on the small screen. Original title: *Arven*. JC-W

• *Christoffer* Ulrich Thomsen, *Maria* Lisa Werlinder, *Annelise* Ghita Nørby, *Ulrik* Lars Brygmann, *Benedikte* Karina Skands, *Niels* Peter Steen, *Aksel* Ulf Pilgaard, *Annika* Diana Axelsen.

• *Dir* Per Fly, *Pro* Ib Tardini, *Ex Pro* Peter Aalbæk Jensen and Peter Garde, *Line Pro* Jens Arnoldus, *Screenplay* Fly, Kim Leona, Mogens Rukov and Dorte Høgh, *Ph* Harald Gunnar Paalgard, *Pro Des* Søren Gam, *Ed* Morten Giese, *M* Halfdan E., *Costumes* Stine Gudmundsen-Holmgreen.

Zentropa Entertainment6 ApS/Danish Film Institute-Swipe Films.
115 mins. Denmark/Norway/Sweden/UK. 2004.
Rel: 31 December 2004. Cert. 15.

In My Father's Den ★★★★

Jeff Prior's 'den' is a secret place. It's where he can escape the rigours of everyday life and indulge his love of books and fine wine. One day, Jeff's son, Paul, discovers the secret hideaway and takes it to his own heart. Years later, returning to New Zealand for his father's funeral, Paul finds the hideaway virtually untouched by time (save for a few cobwebs) and takes over its tenure. But unbeknownst to Paul – now a world-famous war photographer – his father's den has become home to the like-minded Celia, a local 16-year-old girl… An atmospheric, masterfully acted adaptation of Maurice Gee's 1972 novel, *In My Father's Den* is a remarkable debut for the writer-director Brad McGann. Artfully sidestepping the pitfalls of the first-time filmmaker, McGann unfolds his story in layers of sharp character studies, building a scenario that is as much a part of the rural New Zealand landscape as it is the mindset of its guarded protagonists. McGann has also paid extraordinary attention to the casting process, so that Celia really does look like the daughter of her mother and is a far cry from the photo-ready ingénues of the Hollywood mainstream. This is actually a thriller, but one that emerges from the fabric of its *dramatis personae*, rather than a series of technical effects. Only the final chapter, with its awkward cuts between time frames, stumbles into generic formula. JC-W

• *Paul Prior* Matthew MacFadyen, *Penny Prior* Miranda Otto, *Celia Steimer* Emily Barclay, *Jackie* Jodie Rimmer, *Andrew Prior* Colin Moy, *Jonathan Prior* Jimmy Keen, *teenage Paul Prior* Toby Alexander, *Jeff Prior* Matthew Chamberlain, *Ms Seager* Vicky Haughton, *teenage Jackie* Meredith Black, *Detective Farnon* Geraldine Brophy, *with* Vanessa Riddell, Mabel Burt, Saengtip Kirk, Daniel Lucas, Antony Starr, John Pace, Geoffrey Dolan, Anne Chamberlain.

• *Dir* and *Screenplay* Brad McGann, *Pro* Trevor Haysom and Dixie Linder, *Ex Pro* Jim Reeve, Steve Robbins, Paul Trijbits, Sue Bruce Smith and James Mitchell, *Ph* Stuart Drysburgh, *Pro Des* Jennifer Kernke, *Ed* Chris Plummer, *M* Simon Boswell, *Costumes* Kirsty Cameron.

New Zealand Film Commission/UK Film Council/Visionview/NZ On Air/National Lottery, etc-Optimum Releasing.
125 mins. New Zealand/UK/Ireland. 2004. Rel: 24 June 2005. Cert. 15.

In My Skin ★★★★

Esther likes her own skin, telling her boyfriend that she finds her body 'nice'. But Esther has an unusual fetish – she has taken to eating herself… In the tradition of the 'New French

Fine young cannibal: Marina de Van in her own very surreal *In My Skin* (from Tartan Films)

Extreme', *In My Skin* is characteristically disturbing and horrific but deals intelligently with a very real phenomenon. The writer-director Marina de Van takes the central role herself and is very good, exploring self-harm and auto-cannibalism with a sincerity, depth and illumination seldom found in films that are so physically visceral. At times branching off into the surreal, *In My Skin* questions our own relationship with our bodies and opens our eyes to a macabre condition that is far more complex than the pat explanations of self-hate and cries for help. Indeed, de Van takes human objectification to a whole new level. Original title: *Dans ma peau*. EB

• *Esther* Marina de Van, *Vincent* Laurent Lucas, *Sandrine* Léa Drucker, *Daniel* Thilbault de Montalembert, *female client* Dominique Reymond, *male client* Bernard Alane, *with* Marc Rioufol, Francois Lamotte, Adrien Rimoux.

• *Dir* and *Screenplay* Marina de Van, *Pro* Laurence Farenc, *Ph* Pierre Barougier, *Pro Des* Baptiste Glaymann, *Art Dir* Baptiste Glaymann, *Ed* Mike Fromentin, *M* EST (Esbjörn Svensson Tri) and Bassmati, *Costumes* Maielle Robaut, *FX Make-Up* Diminique Collandant.

Lazennec/Canal Plus-Tartan Films.
95 mins. France. 2002. Rel: 17 September 2004. Cert. 18.

Inside Deep Throat ★★½

The 1972 porno *Deep Throat* cost $25,000 to shoot and went on to gross $600 million. Its maker, Gerard Damiano, allegedly never saw a penny (thanks to the Mafia), its eponymous fellator, Linda Lovelace, was killed in a car crash and its male lead, Harry Reems, was arrested for his artistic contribution to the film and ended up an alcoholic (although, today, he has found God and real estate). More importantly, *Deep Throat* opened the way for porno chic and rearranged the goal posts of what was cinematically acceptable in mixed company... Sitting through *Inside Deep Throat* is rather like leafing through a smutty magazine you've unearthed among your father's personal effects. *Deep Throat* seems so long ago now – and has been covered by so many sensational documentaries on Channels Four and Five – that this tabloid-style film seems dated, jaded and rather desperate. Still, there is an impressive line-up of interviewees – Hugh Hefner, Larry Flynt, Norman Mailer, Camille Paglia, Gore Vidal, Dr Ruth Westheimer – and plenty of palliative humour. In fact, the

film's real joys are its incidental moments, such as the odd cutaway to Linda Lovelace's cat, Adolf Hitler, and when the truculent wife of a cinema manager interrupts his interview on camera. JC-W

• *featuring*: Peter Bart, Carl Bernstein, Tony Bill, Helen Gurley Brown, Dick Cavett, Wes Craven, Gerard Damiano, Alan Dershowitz, Larry Flynt, Al Goldstein, Hugh Hefner, Xaviera Hollander, Erica Jong, Bill Maher, Norman Mailer, Camille Paglia, Harry Reems, Georgina Spelvin, Annie Sprinkle, Gore Vidal, John Waters, Dr Ruth Westheimer, etc. *Narrator*: Dennis Hopper.

• *Dir* and *Screenplay* Fenton Bailey and Randy Barbato, *Pro* Bailey, Barbato and Brian Grazer, *Ex Pro* Kim Roth, *Co-Pro* Mona Card, *Assoc Pro* Ashley York and Sarah Brown, *Ph* David Kempner and Teodoro Maniaci, *Ed* William Grayburn and Jeremy Simmons, *M* David Steinberg.

Imagine Entertainment/HBO Documentary Films/World of Wonder-Momentum Pictures.
89 mins. USA. 2005. Rel: 10 June 2005. Cert. 18.

Inside I'm Dancing ★★★½

Films that tackle cerebral palsy face an emotional minefield. A thematically challenging subject to process, physical disability has a habit of provoking sentimentality, self-righteousness or sermonising. Happily, this fictitious account of two contrasting prisoners of the wheelchair is far from mawkish, although its narrative trajectory is predictable. It is hugely entertaining, though, thanks in large part to a star-making turn from James McAvoy (*Bollywood Queen*, *Bright Young Things*), who makes the most of a difficult part in which he can act only from the neck up. He plays Rory O'Shea, a young man with Duchenne muscular dystrophy who arrives at the Carrigmore Home for the Disabled in Dublin with a smart mouth and a whole lot of attitude. He also believes in making the most of every minute and is not afraid to mince his words. He makes an unlikely ally for the shy, proud Michael Connolly, who, suffering from cerebral palsy, has learned to conform to the rules of the home. The script is a little too neat, and the characters pre-packaged, but the film has a warmth and generous humour and makes a number of valid, imperative points. US title: *Rory O'Shea Was Here*. JC-W

• *Rory O'Shea* James McAvoy, *Michael Connolly* Steven Robertson, *Siobhán* Romola Garai, *Con O'Shea* Tom Hickey, *Fergus Connolly* Gerard McSorley, *Eileen* Brenda Fricker, *Tommy* Alan King, *Annie* Ruth McCabe, *Alice* Anna Healy, *with* Stanley Townsend, Derbhle Crotty, Donal Toolan, Tony Kenny, Michele Forbes, Conor McPherson, Adam Fergus.

• *Dir* Damien O'Donnell, *Pro* James Flynn and Juanita Wilson, *Co-Pro* Catherine Tiernan, *Screenplay* Jeffrey Caine, from a story by Christian O'Reilly, *Ph* Peter J. Robertson, *Pro Des* Tom Conroy, *Ed* Fran Parker, *M* David Julyan; Rachmaninov; songs performed by The Avalanches, Hinterland, Interference, Groove Armada, James McAvoy,

Johnny Cash, Supergrass, Gavin Friday, Dusty Springfield, Elbow, etc, *Costumes* Lorna Marie Mugan.

StudioCanal/Universal Pictures/Working Title/Bord Scannán na hÉireann/Octagon Prods, etc-Momentum. 104 mins. UK/Ireland/Germany/USA. 2004. Rel: 15 October 2004. Cert. 15.

The Interpreter ★★★½

Silvia Broome deals in listening for a living. Tobin Keller reads faces. She is an interpreter at the United Nations in New York, the daughter of a British mother and white African father. When she overhears a seditious conversation at the UN, Keller, an agent with the Secret Service, is called in to question her. He doesn't trust her face and doesn't believe her story. Then an attempt is made on her life. Who is Silvia Broome? What is she? And can Keller break through her layers of reserve? Thirty years ago Sydney Pollack directed the accomplished conspiracy thriller *Three Days of the Condor*, and after such artistic digressions as *Sabrina* and *Random Hearts*, he returns to the genre on cracking form. While *The Interpreter* slows to a dawdle on the odd occasion, for the most part it is an intelligent, scary and topical piece, with a real cinematic flair tempered by first-rate performances. Pollack, who gained unprecedented access to film within the UN for five months, makes the most of his modern canvas, as well as reproducing the fictitious nation of Matobo in South Africa. Incidentally, can it be a coincidence that Matobo happens to be the name of a historic national park in that great democracy of Zimbabwe? JC-W

Lost in translation: Nicole Kidman in Sydney Pollack's scary and topical *The Interpreter* (from UIP)

• *Silvia Broome* Nicole Kidman, *Tobin Keller* Sean Penn, *Dot Woods* Catherine Keener, *Nils Lud* Jesper Christensen, *Philippe* Yvan Attal, *Marcus Mantu* Michael Wright, *Edmund Zuwanie* Earl Cameron, *Kuman-Kuman* George Harris, *Luan* Tsai Chin, *Simon Broome* Hugo Speer, *with* Sydney Pollack, Clyde Kusatsu, Eric Keenleyside, Terry Serpico.

• *Dir* Sydney Pollack, *Pro* Tim Bevan, Eric Fellner and Kevin Misher, *Ex Pro* Pollack, Anthony Minghella and G. Mac Brown, *Co-Pro* Liza Chasin and Debra Hayward, *Screenplay* Charles Randolph, Steven Zaillian and Scott Frank from a story by Martin Stellman and Brian Ward, *Ph* Darius Khondji, *Pro Des* Jon Hutman, *Ed* William Steinkamp, *M* James Newton Howard, *Costumes* Sarah Edwards.

Universal/Working Title/Misher Films/Mirage Entertainment-UIP.
128 mins. USA/UK. 2005. Rel: 15 April 2005. Cert. 12A.

Into the Mirror ★★★★

Alone in a deserted department store, a young woman stares at herself in the mirror. As she does so, her reflection pulls out a pizza cutter from her bag and slits her throat. Other employees at the store die off quickly over the ensuing days, all murdered by their reflections. Unfortunately, the detective in charge of the case doesn't believe in ghosts… Wes Craven hit on a great idea with *A Nightmare on Elm Street*, in which his protagonists were safe so long as they stayed awake. Writer-director Kim Seong-ho has come up with an equally ingenious concept in which his characters are secure so long as they avoid their reflection. The twist is that nobody knows who the killer is and that reflective surfaces are all around us. Kim has great fun playing with the theme of the mirror, drawing on such cultural references as Jan van Eyck's *Giovanni Arnolfini and His Wife* and even the mirror script of Leonardo Da Vinci, stopping short of including Lewis Carroll. He has also fashioned a highly stylish film, a visual feast flavouring an ingenious ghost story that for once doesn't cheat the viewer. JC-W

• *Wu Young-min* Yoo Ji-tae, *Ha Hyun-su* Kim Myung-min, *Lee Ji-hyun/Lee Jung-hyun* Kim Hye-Na, *Jeon Il-sung* Ki Ju-bong, *Choi Sang-ki* Kim Myung-su, *Chief Kim Il-hwan* Jeong Eun-pyo.

• *Dir* and *Screenplay* Kim Seong-ho, *Pro* Kim Eun-young, *Ex Pro* Kang Woo-suk, *Ph* Chung han-cheol, *Pro Des* Lee Hyung-joo, *Ed* Kim Sun-min, *M* Kim Hyun-jong, Park Jung-ho and Park Yo-han, *Sound* Lee In-gyu and Lee Jae-hyuk.

Cinema Service/Keyplus Pictures/SBS, Hana Bank-Tartan Films.
113 mins. South Korea. 2003. Rel: 8 October 2004. Cert. 15.

In Your Hands ★★½

A recent graduate of theological school, Anna is appointed chaplain at the women's arm of a local prison. At about the same time, Kate is transferred to the block and immediately stirs up interest with the other inmates. Rumour has it that Kate can perform miracles… Think Bergman without the craftsmanship and you get a rough idea of the timbre of this slow, languid and disconsolate drama. Officially the 34th Dogme film, *In Your Hands* starts promisingly and boasts a few flecks of intriguing narrative, but largely it's an exercise in the art of the pregnant pause. The acting is fine – in a withdrawn, Bergmanesque way – and the premise is ripe with potential. Original title: *Forbrydelser*. JC-W

• *Anna* Ann Eleonora Jørgensen, *Kate Kristofferson* Trine Dyrholm, *Henrik* Nicolaj Kopernikus, *Marion* Sonja Richter, *Frank* Lars Ranthe, *the doctor* Henrik Prip, *Carsten* Jens Albinus, *prison warden* Kirsten Olesen, *Åse* Mette Munk Plum, *Lizzie* Benedikte Hansen.

• *Dir* Annette K. Olesen, *Pro* Ib Tardini, *Ex Pro* Peter Aalbæk Jensen, *Line Pro* Karen Bentzon, *Screenplay* Olesen and Kim Fupz Aakeson, *Ph* Bøje Lomholdt, *Ed* Molly Malene Stensgaard, *M* Jeppe Kaas.

Zentropa Entertainment/DR TV-Drama/Danske Filminstitut/Danish Film InstituteMetrodome. 100 mins. Denmark. 2003. Rel: 29 April 2005. Cert. 15.

I, Robot ★★★★½

It would seem that the cinema has had its fill of robots. Indeed, recollections of *Metropolis*, *2001*, *The Terminator*, *A.I.* and even *Bicentennial Man* cross the mind as *I, Robot* unfolds. Still, the debate on human/mechanical intelligence is a fascinating one and is given a kinetic jump-start in this fabulously accomplished adaptation of Isaac Asimov's short story collection. Will Smith plays a Chicagoan cop in the year 2035 who treasures his Converse All Stars trainers (vintage 2004) and likes machines that respond by the old-fashioned touch of a button. When it comes to robots, he's deeply cynical and throws himself into the suicide (?) case of his friend Dr. Alfred Lanning, who happened to be the chief engineer at U.S. Robotics... Neatly positioning Will Smith's throwaway humour against the awesome hardware of this $105m behemoth, *I, Robot* starts well and gathers agreeable momentum as the plot thickens. It almost makes you nostalgic for today, 'when people were killed by other people.' JC-W

• *Det. Del 'Spoon' Spooner* Will Smith, *Dr Susan Calvin* Bridget Moynahan, *Lawrence Robertson* Bruce Greenwood, *Dr Alfred J. Lanning* James Cromwell, *Lt John Bergin* Chi McBride, *Sonny* Alan Tudyk, *Farber* Shia LaBeouf, *Granny* Adrian L. Ricard, *with* Jerry Wasserman, Fiona Hogan, Nicola Crosbie, Emily Tennant.

• *Dir* Alex Proyas, *Pro* Laurence Mark, John Davis, Topher Bow and Wyck Godfrey, *Ex Pro* Will Smith, James Lassiter, Michael Shane and Anthony Romano, *Screenplay* Jeff Vintar, suggested by the book by Isaac Asimov, *Ph* Simon Duggan, *Pro Des* Patrick Tatopoulos, *Ed* Richard Learoyd, Armen Minasian and William Hoy, *M* Marco Beltrami, *Costumes* Elizabeth Keogh Palmer, *Mechanical SFX* Paul Noël, *Robot Design* Tatopoulos, *Robo Movement* Paul Mercurio.

Twentieth Century Fox/Mediastream IV/Davis Entertainment/Laurence Mark/Overbrook Films-Fox. 114 mins. USA/Germany. 2004. Rel: 6 August 2004. Cert. 12A.

The Isle ★★★½

Hyun Shik is a suicidal sadomasochist who arrives at a remote, picturesque fishing bay where he hires a yellow bathhouse to while away the last hours of his life. However, the mute, lonely beauty who ferries the fishermen to and from their 'floats' intercepts Shik's first attempt on his own life. Consumed by passion for his comely saviour, Shik takes advantage of the girl's responsiveness and almost rapes her... A story of obsessive love, indescribable sadomasochism and fishing, *The Isle* can be taken as absurdist black comedy, surreal allegory or as a romantic horror film. Regardless of such critical estimates, Kim Ki-duk's film is visually ravishing, deeply disturbing and one of a kind, not unlike Takashi Miike's *Audition*. So, depending on your taste for the visceral or aesthetic, this is a masterwork of daring vision or a handsome curiosity item. JC-W

• *Hee-Jin* Suh Jung, *Hyun Shik* Kim Yoo-suk, *Eun-a* Park Sung-hee, *Mang-chee* Jo Jae-hyeon, *middle-aged man* Jang Hang-seon.

• *Dir, Screenplay* and *Pro Des* Kim Ki-duk, *Pro* Lee Eun, *Ph* Seo-shik Hwang, *Ed* Min Hokyung, *M* Jeon Sang-yun, *Costumes* Joo Eun-jung.

Tartan Films. 89 mins. South Korea. 2000. Rel: 10 September 2004. Cert. 18.

It's All Gone Pete Tong ★★★

He's not quite as famous as David Beckham, but dance maestro Pete Tong has found his way into the Oxford English Dictionary. Here, he merely has a cameo (as himself), leaving the lead role of DJ giant Frankie Wilde to Paul Kaye. A hedonistic god of the club scene in Ibiza, Frankie certainly lives up to his surname, snorting coke off his mixer board, shagging groupies in the company of his wife and vomiting into swimming pools. Then, at the height of his record-producing frenzy, he starts to lose his hearing... Paul Kaye is a fearless actor and it is to his credit that he can turn a self-serving monster into a sympathetic character. Writer-director Michael Dowse (*Fubar*) has created a fascinating hybrid, with a style that's part *Trainspotting* and part *Kevin & Perry*, while the soundtrack of thumping rave music is chillingly complemented by Wilde's increasing deafness. Much of *Pete Tong* is unrestrained silliness and excess, but it pumps a cinematic spark into the club scene and ends on a poignant, human note. JC-W

• *Frankie Wilde* Paul Kaye, *Penelope Garcia* Beatriz Batarda, *Sonya Slowinski* Kate Macgowan, *Max Haggar* Mike Wilmot, *Jack Stoddart* Neil Maskell, *Charlize Bondo* Monica Maja, *Pete Tong* Pete Tong, *with* Ron Lloy Hugh Elliston, Dan Antopoloski, Tim Plester, Paul J. Spence, Dave Lawrence,

Tiesto, Barry Ashworth, Lol Hammond, Carl Cox, Charlie Chester, Sarah Main.

• *Dir* and *Screenplay* Michael Dowse, *Pro* Allan Niblo and James Richardson, *Ex Pro* Rupert Preston, Rob Morgan and Kim Roberts, *Assoc Pro* Pete Tong, Tony Arman Jones, Robert Blagojevic and Simon Rodgers, *Ph* Balasz Bolygo, *Pro Des* Paul Burns, *Ed* Stuart Gazzard, *M* Graham Massey, *Costumes* Ita Murray, *Sound* Michael A. McCann, Tony Gort and Michael Thomas.

Vertigo Films/True West Films/Téléfilm Canada/Movie Network, etc-Redbus Film Distributors.
92 mins. UK/Canada. 2004. Rel: 27 May 2005.
Cert. 15.

The Jacket ★★½

Jack Starks is a US Marine serving in the Persian Gulf War. After a particularly bloody conflict, he approaches a young Iraqi boy with a smile and is rewarded with a bullet in the head. Diagnosed dead, he comes round with a blink and shock-related amnesia. Twelve months later, in his native Vermont, Jack encounters a little girl and her drunken mother stranded by a broken-down snow-bound vehicle. He fixes the car but is attacked by the mother when she sees him in a spontaneous embrace with her child. Later the same day he is picked up by a young man who, when stopped by a highway patrolman, shoots the cop dead and leaves Jack alongside him. Blamed for the crime, Jack is sent to an institute for the criminally insane and becomes the victim of some highly unethical experiments in behavioural modification… The jacket of the title is a straitjacket and poor Jack Starks seems straitjacketed by a

series of most unfortunate events. The story is straight out of a comic-strip and its illogical digressions into time travel merely underscore its pulp fiction origins. Nevertheless, under the direction of former painter John Maybury (*Love is the Devil*), *The Jacket* is surprisingly gripping – with compelling turns from Brody and Knightley – until slipping into the sentimental bathos of *Heaven Can Wait*. JC-W

• *Jack Starks* Adrien Brody, *Jackie Price* Keira Knightley, *Dr Becker* Kris Kristofferson, *Dr Lorenson* Jennifer Jason Leigh, *Jean* Kelly Lynch, *stranger* Brad Renfro, *Mackenzie* Daniel Craig, *young Jackie* Laura Marano, *Dr Hopkins* Steven Mackintosh, *Damon* Brendan Coyle, *Nurse Harding* Mackenzie Phillips, *with* Jason Lewis, Richard Dillane, Kerry Shale, Angus MacInnes, Richard Durden, Colin Stinton, Fish.

• *Dir* John Maybury, *Pro* Peter Guber, George Clooney and Steven Soderbergh, *Ex Pro* Ben Cosgrove, Ori Marmur, Jennifer Fox, Peter E. Strauss, Todd Wagner, Mark Cuban, Andy Grosch, Chris Roberts and Timothy J. Nicholas, *Co-Ex Pro* Peter McAleese, *Co-Pro* Marc Rocco, Marc Frydman, Philip A. McKeon, Donald C. McKeon, Andreas Schmid and Kia Jam, *Screenplay* Massy Tadjedin, from a story by Tom Bleecker and Marc Rocco, *Ph* Peter Deming, *Pro Des* Alan Macdonald, *Ed* Emma E. Hickox, *M* Brian Eno, *Costumes* Doug Hall.

Warner Bros Pictures International/Warner Independent Pictures/Mandalay Pictures/2929 Entertainment/Rising Star/Section Eight/Scottish Screen/Glasgow Film Office-Warner.
103 mins. USA/UK/Germany. 2004.
Rel: 13 May 2005. Cert. 15.

Somewhere in time: Adrian Brody in John Maybury's odd but gripping *The Jacket* (from Warner)

Joy of Madness ★★★½

Whatever else this unique project achieves, it paints a vivid and authentic picture of Afghanistan in the wake of the Taliban's downfall. A documentary on the casting process of the Iranian film *At Five in the Afternoon*, *Joy of Madness* reveals far more than your average making-of PR job. As the 22-year-old Iranian director Samira Makhmalbaf struggles to find an Afghan woman willing to shed her burka and inhibitions to become a star, the director's younger sister records the proceedings on a digital camera. Here, then, is an immediate platform for contrast as sophisticated young women from neighbouring Iran interact with and motivate Afghani women conditioned to subjugation and anonymity. Hana Makhmalbaf herself, at 14 the youngest feature film director of all time, pushes her camera into the centre of the action to record the fear and conflict on the faces of her protagonists. Basically a home movie, *Joy of Madness* is anything but slick. But it's a fascinating, human and insightful document of a country still in social turmoil after such barbaric repression. Original title: *Lezate divanegi*. JC-W

• *with*: Agheleh Rezaei, Agheleh Farahmand, Bibigol Asef, Samira Makhmalbaf, Mohsen Makhmalbaf, etc.

• *Dir, Screenplay* and *Ph* Hana Makhmalbaf, *Pro* Mohsen Makhmalbaf, *Ed* Mastaneh Mohajer, *M* Mohammad Reza Darvishi.

Makhmalbaf Film House-Tartan Films.
73 mins. Iran. 2003. Rel: 16 July 2004. Cert U.

Ju-On

see *The Grudge*.

The Keys to the House ★★★

Fifteen years after he walked out on his disabled child, Gianni has a new wife and a newborn son. Suddenly, he has decided to take responsibility for his lost child Paolo, who has blossomed into a canny, delightful boy. But Paolo comes with some very demanding problems and Gianni is not sure he's up to the task... To all intents and purposes, the 16-year-old Andrea Rossi is the heart and only real reason to see this film. Of course, director Gianni Amelio deserves considerable credit for enabling young Rossi to flower for the camera, and Amelio knows his children – most of his films have featured young actors in substantial parts, notably the 1992 Cannes winner *The Stolen Children*. Here, his theme is the responsibility, shame and joy of being the parent of a child with muscular dystrophy. And while Kim Rossi Stuart is quite remarkable as the father attempting to bridge the gap between his guilt and nascent love for the child he abandoned, it is the younger Rossi who dominates the film, infecting its very bones with his irresistible *joie de vivre*. But without him, *The Keys to the House* would have been a very dull ride indeed. Original title: *Le chiavi di casa*. JC-W

• *Gianni* Kim Rossi Stuart, *Nicole* Charlotte Rampling, *Paolo* Andrea Rossi, *Nadine* Alla Faerovich, *Alberto* Pierfrancesco Favino.

• *Dir* Gianni Amelio, *Line Pro* Gianfranco Barbagallo, *Co-Pro* Karl Baumgartner and Bruno Pesery, *Screenplay* Amelio, Sandro Petraglia and Stefano Rulli, *Ph* Luca Bigazzi, *Pro Des* Giancarlo Basili, *Ed* Simona Paggi, *M* Franco Piersanti, *Costumes* Piero Tosi and Cristina Francioni.

RAI Cinema Achab Film/Pola Pandora Film/Arena Films/Arte France Cinema/Canal Plus-Artificial Eye.
111 mins. Italy/Germany/France. 2004. Rel: 1 April 2005. Cert. PG.

Kill Your Idols ★★★

This succinct documentary about the art-rock movement which flourished at the end of the seventies in punk rock's aftermath may well please devotees of that music. It's a neat enough assemblage of old performance footage and of recent interviews with those involved. But there's no attempt to clarify what was being attempted (some regard it as musically innovative and others as anti-music), to argue its value (if any) or to explain why some music of 2002 should be judged by what was being done 20 years earlier. It's also focused entirely on New York. But if you want to learn all about such bands as Teenage Jesus and the Jerks, this is the movie to see. MS

• *with*: Martin Rev, Lydia Lunch, Arto Lindsay, Lee Ranaldo, Thurston Moore, Jim Sclavunos, Glenn Branca, Michael Gira, Karen O., Brian McPeek, Eugene Hutz, Sergey Rjabtzev.

• *Dir, Pro, Screenplay, Ph* and *Ed* S.A. Crary, *Ex Pro* Dan Braun and Josh Braun.

Etoile Rouge Prods/ Hunger Artist Prods-ICA.
75 mins. USA. 2004. Rel: No cert.

King Arthur ★★★½

Ostensibly an authentic revision of the Arthurian myth, *King Arthur* is set in 452 AD and has our Once and Future King battling corrupt Romans, villainous Saxons and his own conscience. His band of merry men feels less like the Knights of the Round Table than a motley gang of mercenaries, especially as played by a Welsh Lancelot, a Danish Tristan, an Australian Gawain and Ray Winstone as an East End wideboy who can't remember the names of his 11 bastard children. Clive Owen also seems odd casting as the future king, bringing a North Country, boy-next-door simplicity to his role and uncomfortably matched with Keira Knightley (two decades his junior) as a Guinevere who sounds like she's playing hookey from Roedean. But, hey, this is a Jerry Bruckheimer production and it's the deafening sound effects, snarling film extras and giddy camerawork that takes centre stage in a rousing Hollywood revamp of English history. Thus, the most interesting character is Stellan Skarsgård's monosyllabic Saxon, who looks like he's strayed off a Sergio Leone western and squints accordingly. There are some terrific battle sequences (particularly one conducted on a frozen lake), a few amusing one-liners and photography you can hang on your bedroom wall. JC-W

• *Arthur* Clive Owen, *Guinevere* Keira Knightley, *Cerdic*

Arthurian legerdemain: Ioan Gruffudd, Keira Knightley and Clive Owen in Antoine Fuqua's *King Arthur* (from Buena Vista International)

Stellan Skarsgård, *Merlin* Stephen Dillane, *Bors* Ray Winstone, *Galahad* Hugh Dancy, *Cynric* Til Schweiger, *Lancelot* Ioan Gruffudd, *Gawain* Joel Edgerton, *Tristan* Mads Mikkelsen, *Dagonet* Ray Stevenson, *Jols* Sean Gilder, *Marius Honorius* Ken Stott, *Ganis* Charlie Creed-Miles, *with* Pat Kinevane, Ivano Marescotti, Lorenzo de Angelis, Bosco Hogan, David Wilmot, Clive Russell, Stephanie Putson.

• *Dir* Antoine Fuqua, *Pro* Jerry Bruckheimer, *Ex Pro* Mike Stenson, Chad Oman and Ned Dowd, *Screenplay* David Franzoni, *Ph* Slawomir Idziak, *Pro Des* Dan Weil, *Ed* Conrad Buff and Jamie Pearson, *M* Hans Zimmer; 'Tell Me Now (What You See)' sung by Moya Brennan, *Costumes* Penny Rose, *Historical consultant* John Matthews, *Sword master* Mark Ryan.

Touchstone Pictures/Jerry Bruckheimer Films-Buena Vista International.
125 mins. USA/Ireland/UK. 2004. Rel: 30 July 2004. Cert. 12A.

Kingdom of Heaven ★★

France/Jerusalem; 1184. A humble French blacksmith, Balian is mourning the death of his wife and son when his long-lost father pops up and invites him to the Holy Land. At first Balian demurs, but after killing a degenerate priest, he decides to join his father's band of Crusaders. Once in Jerusalem, Balian proves he is made of strong moral fibre and sets about making the Holy Land a better place… The greatest tragedy of this $110 million epic is that you can't tell it's directed by Ridley Scott. In spite of some spectacular vistas and a rather good battle scene near the end, it is a muddled, incomprehensible wade through war in which the characters are just colourful ciphers. Orlando Bloom, at times looking surprisingly like a young Omar Sharif, is rather one-note, while his enemies sneer and glare like comic-book villains. The best scene is the opening, in which our hero toils in an impressive reproduction of a smithy, but then we are given no time to get to know him. Suddenly, he is off to Jerusalem and we are expected to care if he lives or dies. He's obviously a rather noble fellow, but that's not enough to secure our interest – or empathy – for the next two hours or so. JC-W

• *Balian* Orlando Bloom, *Princess Sibylla* Eva Green, *Tiberias* Jeremy Irons, *Hospitaler* David Thewlis, *Reynald of Chatillon* Brendan Gleeson, *Guy de Lusignan* Marton Csokas, *Godfrey of Ibelin* Liam Neeson, *Saladin* Ghassan Massoud, *Richard Coeur de Lion* Iain Glen, *English sergeant* Kevin McKidd, *King Baldwin* Edward Norton, *priest* Michael Sheen, *Balian's wife* Nathalie Cox, *with* Philip Glenister, Nikolaj Coster-Waldau, Steven Robertson, Jon Finch, Ulrich Thomsen.

• *Dir* and *Pro* Ridley Scott, *Ex Pro* Branko Lustig, Lisa Ellzey and Terry Needham, *Co-Pro* Mark Albela, Denise O'Dell, Henning Molfenter and Thierry Potok, *Assoc Pro* Teresa Kelly and Ty Warren, *Screenplay* William Monahan, *Ph* John Mathieson, *Pro Des* Arthur Max, *Ed* Dody Dorn, *M* Harry

Gregson-Williams and Stephen Barton, *Costumes* Janty Yates, *Weapons Master* Simon Atherton.

Fox/Scott Free/Inside Track-Fox.
144 mins. UK/USA/Spain/Germany. 2005. Rel: 6 May 2005. Cert. 15.

Kings and Queen ★★½

Nora Cotterelle, 35, would seem to be a contented woman. She runs a successful art shop, is excitedly preparing for her father's birthday and is ready to settle down with a compatible mate. Conversely, the violist Ismaël Vuillard is being pursued by the IRS, appears to be plotting his own suicide and is dragged to the nuthouse against his will. One of these stories is a comedy, the other a tragedy. But which is which? *Rois et Reine* is an ungainly beast. Painted in broad, spontaneous, erratic and passionate brush strokes, it is the cinematic equivalent of a Van Gogh or even a Jackson Pollock. The story doesn't so much unfold as tumble down a staircase. Splurges of black farce merge into brutal tragedy; guns are fired; ghosts appear; time is but a splash of linseed oil. It's all quite kinetically cinematic, but the characters never fully emerge from behind their brush strokes. Original title: *Rois et Reine*. JC-W

• *Nora Cotterelle* Emmanuelle Devos, *Ismaël Vuillard* Mathieu Amalric, *Madame Vasset, the psychiatrist* Catherine Deneuve, *Louis Jenssens* Maurice Garrel, *Chloé Jenssens* Nathalie Boutefeu, *Abel Vuillard* Jean-Paul Roussillon, *Arielle* Magali Woch, *M. Mamanne, the lawyer* Hippolyte Girardot, *Elizabeth* Noémie Lvovsky, *Dr Devereux, the psychoanalyst* Elsa Wolliaston, *Elias* Valentin Lelong.

• *Dir* Arnaud Desplechin, *Pro* Pascal Caucheteux and Grégoire Sorlat, *Screenplay* Desplechin and Roger Bohbot, *Ph* Eric Gautier, *Pro Des* Dan Bevan, *Ed* Laurence Briaud, *M* Grégoire Hetzel, *Costumes* Nathalie Raoul.

Why Not Prods/France 2 Cinéma/ Rhône-Alpes Cinéma/ Canal Plus, etc-Artificial Eye.
152 mins. France. 2004. Rel: 10 June 2004. Cert. 15.

Kinsey ★★★★½

Kinsey is not a compelling film because it is about sex. It is a compelling film because it is an articulate – and entertaining – study of anthropology, ignorance, hypocrisy and sex. Alfred Kinsey is also an extraordinary figure, a man whose father was a Methodist preacher who railed against dance, music and the invention of the zip (the latter because it allowed 'easy access to moral oblivion'). An obsessive collector of gall wasps (he accumulated and indexed several hundred thousand), Kinsey was brought up in an age that felt masturbation would naturally lead to insanity, epilepsy, blindness and death. As it happens, Kinsey didn't lose his virginity until 27 (on his wedding night), and that led to disaster because of the prodigious size of his erection. Attempting to come to terms with his guilt, he embarked on a scientific study that was to reveal that only a fraction of America's national sexuality was actually sanctioned – or legally permitted – by society. Candid, provocative, informative and often quite moving (Lynn Redgrave delivers a very touching cameo), *Kinsey* is also a surprisingly funny film, celebrating the diversity of the human species while taking an unerring shot over the bows of current American Puritanism. JC-W

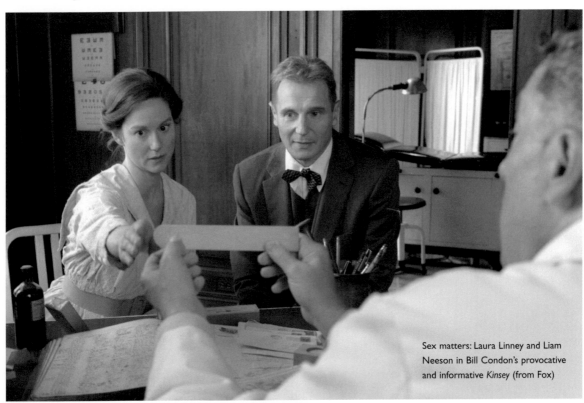

Sex matters: Laura Linney and Liam Neeson in Bill Condon's provocative and informative *Kinsey* (from Fox)

• *Alfred Kinsey* Liam Neeson, *Clara McMillen* Laura Linney, *Wardell Pomeroy* Chris O'Donnell, *Clyde Martin* Peter Sarsgaard, *Paul Gebhard* Timothy Hutton, *Alfred Seguine Kinsey* John Lithgow, *Thurman Rice* Tim Curry, *Herman Wells* Oliver Platt, *Alan Gregg* Dylan Baker, *Kenneth Bruan* William Sadler, *Huntington Hartford* John McMartin, *Sara Kinsey* Veronica Cartwright, *final interview subject* Lynn Redgrave, *with* Julianne Nicholson, Kathleen Chalfant, Heather Goldenhersh, Dagmara Dominczyk, Harley Cross, Romulus Linney, Katharine Houghton, John Epperson, Reno.

• *Dir* and *Screenplay* Bill Condon, *Pro* Gail Mutrux, *Ex Pro* Michael Kuhn, Francis Ford Coppola, Bobby Rock and Kirk D'Amico, *Ph* Frederick Elmes, *Pro Des* Richard Sherman, *Ed* Virginia Katz, *M* Carter Burwell; Chopin, Mozart, Sibelius, Bruch; songs performed by Ella Fitzgerald, Little Willie John, Daniel May, and Kacee Clanton, *Costumes* Bruce Finlayson, *Dialect coach* Deborah Hecht.

Fox Searchlight/Qwerty Films/N1 European Film Produktions/American Zoetrope/Pretty Pictures-Fox. 118 mins. USA. 2004. Rel: 4 March 2005. Cert. 15.

Koktebel ★★★★

Originally and more appropriately announced as *Roads to Koktebel*, this Russian drama is centred on a father/son relationship most convincingly and unsentimentally portrayed, but it's also a road movie. This is because we follow the duo hitch-hiking across country as the unemployed, impoverished father seeks to improve the lot of his 11-year-old son by delivering him to his aunt in Koktebel. Impeccably acted, this film is not undemanding (the long-held opening shot is a pointer) but one feels totally involved with the main characters, not least when their bond is strained by the father's amorous encounter with a woman doctor en route. Furthermore, the film blends this personal tale with a wider view of life, the people becoming figures in a landscape and pawns in the hand of fate, or even of God. This richness is less strong in the last section of the story but *Koktebel* is to my mind far superior to that other recent father/son tale from Russia, *The Return*. MS

• *father* Igor Chernevich, *boy* Gleb Puskepalis, *Kseniia Viktorovna, the doctor* Agrippina Stekhlova, *truck driver* Alexander Ilyin, *with* Vladimir Kucherenko, Yevgeni Sytyi.

• *Dir* and *Screenplay* Boris Khlebnikov and Alexei Popogrebsky, *Pro* Roman Borisevich, *Ex Pro* Andrei Murtalaziev, *Ph* Shandor Berkeshi, *Art Dir* Gennady Popov, *Ed* Ivan Lebedev, *M* Lutgardo Luga Lebad.

Cinematography Service/RF Ministry of Culture/ Roman Borisevich-Artificial Eye. 104 mins. Russia. 2003. Rel: 31 December 2004. Cert. 15.

Kontroll ★★★½

This welcome glimpse of contemporary Hungarian cinema is a prize-winning first feature from writer/director Nimrod Antil. Setting his film in the Budapest underground railway system and taking a young ticket collector as his central character, he comes up with an odd and idiosyncratic blend. There's quirky humour in the attitudes of the employees, echoes of *Rebel Without a Cause* when it comes to dangerous dares, a touch of orthodox romance and a hooded figure pushing passengers under trains. As the strong music by NEO confirms, this is a movie to appeal to young audiences especially. Furthermore there's no doubt that, viewed in isolation, the various elements are powerful and individual, but they don't exactly cohere and the film's aims remain undefined. It's very ICA, however, and just what their audience likes. MS

• *Bulcsu* Sándor Csányi, *professor* Zoltán Mucsi, *Muki* Csaba Pindroch, *Lecso* Sándor Bádar, *Tibi* Zsolt Nagy, *Bootsie* Bence Matyassy.

• *Dir* and *Screenplay* Nimrod Antal, *Pro* Tamás Hutlassa, *Ph* Gyula Pados, *Pro Des* Balazs Hujber, *Ed* Istvan Király, *M* NEO, *Costumes* Janos Breckl.

Café Film/Bonfire Film-ICA Projects. 110 mins. Hungary. 2003. Rel: 17 September 2004. Cert. 15.

Kung Fu Hustle ★★★★½

China; the 1940s. With the police in their pocket, the Axe Gang will stop at nothing to take total control of the city. But when they move in on the ghetto of Pig Sty Alley, they haven't reckoned on the kung fu skills of its ageing residents… Stephen Chow is a phenomenon. Not only does he boast sculpted cheekbones and defined musculature, but the man can write, produce and direct. Exhibiting a style reminiscent of both Sergio Leone and Quentin Tarantino – fused with a mutant gene snatched from the animator Chuck Jones – Chow has an extraordinary knack for storytelling. Combining traditional kung fu with farce and Yangtze-broad satire, he spins his tale of revenge and redemption with an inspired lunacy and inventive zeal. Musical notes turn into deadly missiles (literally), combatants plough through a series of walls at once and a gang of axe men break into a dance routine. Chow doesn't so much raise the bar as twist it round the neck of the kung fu oeuvre. Taken on its own terms, *Kung Fu Hustle* is wacky, surreal, creative, cruel, insane and exhilarating entertainment. Mandarin title: *Gong Fu*. JC-W

• *Sing* Stephen Chow, *landlord* Yuen Wah, *Beast* Leung Siu Lung, *Donut* Dong Zhi Hua, *tailor* Chiu Chi Ling, *coolie* Xing Yu, *Brother Sum* Chan Kwok Kwan, *Sing's sidekick* Lam Tze Chung, *Axe Gang advisor* Tin Kai Man, *harpist #1* Jia Kang Xi, *harpist #2* Fung Hak On, *Crocodile Gang boss* Feng Xiao Gang, *Fong* Huang Sheng Yi, *landlady* Yuen Qiu.

• *Dir* Stephen Chow, *Pro* Chow, Chui Po Chu and Jeff Lau, *Ex Pro* Bill Borden, Zhao Hai Cheng and David Hung, *Screenplay* Chow, Tsang Kan Cheong, Lola Huo and Chan Man Keung, *Ph* Poon Hang Sang, *Pro Des* Oliver Wong, *Ed* Angie Lam, *M* Raymond Wong, *Costumes* Shirley Chan, *Sound* Steven Ticknor and Paul Pirola, *Action Choreography* Yuen Wo Ping and Sammo Hung, *Visual Effects* Frankie Chung.

Ladder 49 (from Buena Vista International)

China Film/Columbia Pictures Film Production
Asia-Columbia TriStar.
98 mins. Hong Kong/China. 2004. Rel: 24 June 2005.
Cert. 15.

Ladder 49 ★★½

Baltimore; present day. Having saved a man's life in a
monstrous warehouse inferno, firefighter Jack Morrison is
swallowed up in the smoke-choked debris of the building.
As he lies there waiting to be rescued, he reflects on his
life, both professional and domestic... For all its star power
and heart-pounding scenes of conflagration, *Ladder 49* still
feels like a sentimental treatise with an agenda. *The Towering
Inferno* remains the cinema's most exciting fire-fighting epic
because it had a plot, whereas this is an episodic character
study with some really dodgy continuity. The day-to-day
detail of a fireman's life is interesting up to a point but is not
enough to sustain an audience's interest for two hours. There
was just as much human detail in *Roxanne* – in which Steve
Martin played fire chief CD Bales – and that film was also
funny and moving. *Ladder 49* – instigated after the events of
11 September 2001 – ends with a stiff upper lip and a music
video written and sung by Robbie Robertson. Enough said.
JC-W

• *Jack Morrison* Joaquin Phoenix, *Mike Kennedy* John Travolta,
Linda Morrison Jacinda Barrett, *Tommy Drake* Morris Chestnut,
Lenny Richter Robert Patrick, *Ray Gauquin* Balthazar Getty,
Keith Perez Jay Hernandez, *Dennis Gauquin* Billy Burke, *Tony
Corrigan* Tim Guinee, *with* Kevin Daniels, Kevin Chapman,
Steven Maye, Beau Russell.

• *Dir* Jay Russell, *Pro* Casey Silver, *Ex Pro* Armyan Bernstein
and Marty Ewing, *Screenplay* Lewis Colick, *Ph* James L. Carter,
Pro Des Tony Burrough, *Ed* Bud Smith and Scott Smith, *M*
William Ross; songs performed by Robbie Robertson, Bonnie
Raitt, The Black Crowes, The Breeders, Tom Petty, Ohio
Players, Sam Phillips, The Pogues, David Gray, etc, *Costumes*
Reneé Ehrlich Kalfus, *Stunt Coordinator* George Aguilar, *Fire
Consultant* Lt. Mark Yant.

Touchstone Pictures/Beacon Pictures-Buena
Vista International.
115 mins. USA. 2004. Rel: 21 January 2005. Cert. 12A.

Ladies in Lavender ★★★★

It is a truism that the best literary adaptations originate
from the short story format. Taking this notion on board,
the actor Charles Dance has chosen the eponymous tale by
William J. Locke for his directorial and screenwriting debut.
Steeping his fable in atmosphere and period detail, Dance has
summoned up a piquant plate on which to serve his dramatic
repast. And, with a mouth-watering cast at his disposal, he
has managed to simmer his narrative with some finesse. Best
friends and fellow dames, Judi Dench and Maggie Smith draw
on their instinctive shorthand with an accomplished skill
that lends considerable credibility to the proceedings. They
play Ursula and Janet Widdington, sisters who share a cliff-
top abode in Cornwall in the year 1936. Sealed off from the
outside world and to some extent protected from their own
unfulfilled past, the sisters find their lives turned upside down
when they take in a young man washed up on their beach. It
transpires that the latter is Polish – and very handsome with

it – and his presence sparks an unexpected and deep-seated jealousy. Lovingly photographed and peppered with humour, *Ladies in Lavender* is an exquisite little tale that speaks volumes about the English character, accentuating both its defects and its virtues. JC-W

• *Ursula Widdington* Judi Dench, *Janet Widdington* Maggie Smith, *Andrea Marowski* Daniel Brühl, *Dorcas* Miriam Margolyes, *Olga Danilof* Natascha McElhone, *Dr Mead* David Warner, *Jan Pendered* Freddie Jones, *Adam Penruddocke* Clive Russell, *with* Gregor Henderson-Begg, Richard Pears, Ian Marshall, Toby Jones, Geoffrey Bayldon, Timothy Bateson, Finty Williams, Jimmy Yuill, Peter Cellier, Alan Cox.

• *Dir* and *Screenplay* Charles Dance, *Pro* Nicolas Brown, Elizabeth Karlsen and Nik Powell, *Ex Pro* Dance, Robert Jones, Bill Allan and Emma Hayter, *Ph* Peter Biziou, *Pro Des* Caroline Amies, *Ed* Michael Parker, *M* Nigel Hess; Paganini, J.S. Bach, Mendelssohn, Jules Émile; violin performed by Joshua Bell, *Costumes* Barbara Kidd, *Choreography* Lindsay Dolan.

UK Film Council/Baker Street/Future Films/Scala Prods/National Lottery-Entertainment.
103 mins. UK. 2004. Rel: 12 November 2004. Cert. 12A.

The Last Horror Movie ★½

London; today. A potentially interesting idea lies at the heart of this low-budget horror film. Inspired by the mix of fiction and reality in *Blair Witch* and *Texas Chain Saw*, Julian Richards sets out to unnerve his audience by exposing the video diary of a 'real life' serial killer. To up the ante, he has his hero, Max, try to implicate the viewer in his crimes ('Are you still watching?'). This might have reaped dividends had Richards been a more skilful filmmaker and his charismatic lead actor less smug and more, well, ordinary. By the mid-way mark, *The Last Horror Movie* commits the cardinal sin of its genre – it bores. JC-W

• *Max Parry* Kevin Howarth, *assistant* Mark Stevenson, *Petra* Antonia Beamish, *Sam* Christabel Muir, *with* Jonathan Coote, Tamara Ustinov, David Redgrave.

• *Dir* Julian Richards, *Pro* Zorana Piggott, *Ex Pro* William Richards, Julian Richards and Mike Tims, *Co-Pro* Louis Melville, *Screenplay* James Handel, *Ph* Chris St John-Smith, *Pro Des* Bettina Eberhard, *Ed* Claus Wehlisch, *M* Simon Lambros, *Costumes* Jason Gill.

Prolific Films/Snakehair Prods/MTN Movies-Tartan Films.
78 mins. UK. 2003. Rel: 13 May 2005. Cert. 18.

Last Life in the Universe ★★★★

In a total reversal of style from his *Mon-rak Transistor*, Pen-ek Ratanruang comes up with a film which, despite echoing 1960s cinema, is completely original in its take on the disenchantment of lonely lives. If its emphasis on mood and atmosphere recalls Antonioni, it also incorporates some delicious black comedy. The central character is a would-be suicide who, having previously been attracted to a girl who dies following an accident, finds himself drawn to her sister.

At the same time he is being targeted by gangsters, but it's not the plot (which grows ever more complex and puzzling) that counts. The superb images provided by Christopher Doyle and direction so imaginative that you are glued to the screen make this an out-and-out triumph of style. Not for everyone, of course, but a stunning experience for those who take to this kind of thing. MS

• *Kenji* Tadanobu Asano, *Noi* Sinitta Boonyasak, *Nid* Laila Boonyasak, *Yukio* Yutaka Matsushige, *Takashi* Riki Takeuchi, *yakuza, Tajima* Takashi Miike.

• *Dir* Pen-ek Ratanaruang, *Pro* Wouter Barendrecht, Duangkamol Limcharoen and Nonzee Nimibutr, *Ex Pro* Meileen Choo, Charoen Iamphungporn, Fran Rubel Kuzui, Kaz Kuzui, Michael J. Werner and Arai Yoshikiyo, *Screenplay* Ratanaruang and Prabda Yoon, *Ph* Christopher Doyle, *Pro Des* Saksiri Chantarangsri, *Ed* Patamanadda Yukol, *M* Hualongpong Riddim and Small Room, *Costumes* Sombatsara Teerasaroch.

Bohemian Films/Fortissimo Film Sales/Cathay Asia Films-Artificial Eye.
108 mins. Thailand/Netherlands/Hong Kong/UK. 2003. Rel: 30 July 2004. Cert. 15.

The Last Victory ★★★★

Central to John Appel's feature-length documentary is the Palio, that annual horse race that famously takes place in Italy in the main square of Siena. Nevertheless, truth to tell, the heart of this film lies not in that event or in the preparations for it but in its portrait of what it can still mean to have a keen community sense. Appel concentrates on Civetta, one of the ten districts that compete in the race, and their spirited response is shown to be remarkable. But if that's a quality often lamented as something lost in the modern world, *The Last Victory* reveals also the downside. The extreme emotions engendered by the race and the hatred felt for one rival community in particular make for rewardingly disturbing viewing, even if the ending is a shade too soft. MS

• *Dir* and *Screenplay* John Appel, *Pro* Carmen Cobos, *Assoc Pro* Judith Vreriks, *Ph* Erik Van Empel, *Ed* Mario Steenbergen, *M* Wouter Van Bemmel, *Sound* Hugo Dijkstal.

Cobos Films-Metrodome.
89 mins. Netherlands/Australia/Finland/Spain. 2003. Rel: 6 August 2004. Cert. PG.

Layer Cake ★★★

Matthew Vaughn produced Guy Ritchie's *Lock, Stock and Two Smoking Barrels* and *Snatch* and knows a good recipe when he smells it. Here he's taken the same ingredients for his directorial debut and has cooked up a tasty gangster thriller – if not as fulfilling as the aforementioned. Vaughn certainly exhibits a confident, original style and has a fresh visual eye, but the stript, a convoluted affair adapted by J.J. Connolly from his own novel, ultimately lets the side down. Daniel Craig is a slick drug dealer, a man with a plan and a determination to retire early. But before he receives his golden

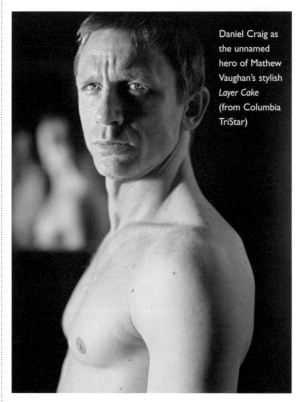

Daniel Craig as the unnamed hero of Mathew Vaughan's stylish *Layer Cake* (from Columbia TriStar)

The League of Gentlemen's Apocalypse ★½

Having enjoyed a ten-year run as the cult creations of Dyson, Gatiss, Pemberton and Shearsmith (The League of Gentlemen), the grotesque inhabitants of Royston Vasey discover that they are to be 'discontinued'. So three of their number escape into the 'real' world – Soho Square, London – to sort the scriptwriters out… A depressingly puerile gallimaufry of Lewis Carroll and *Wes Craven's New Nightmare* – with a dash of *Blackadder* – *TLOG'sA* is the scatological underbelly of *The Hitchhiker's Guide*. Like a raunchy end-of-term revue banished to the woodshed, the film is little more than a string of smutty jokes in a surreal blender. Sadly, the only decent gag is the very first one in the film. PS: The premise was previously employed in the equally dispiriting *The Adventures of Rocky and Bullwinkle*. JC-W

• *Matthew Chinnery/Hilary Briss/Mickey/Mark/Sir Nicholas Sheet-Lightning* Mark Gatiss, *Tubbs/Pauline/Herr Lipp/Steve/ Lemuel Blizzard* Steve Pemberton, *Edward/Papa Lazarou/Geoff/ Bernice/Reece/Father Halfhearte/Red Devil* Reece Shearsmith, *Jeremy Dyson* Michael Sheen, *Lindsay* Emily Woof, *King William III* Bernard Hill, *Queen Mary II* Victoria Wood, *Dr Erasmus Pea* David Warner, *with* Danielle Tilley, Alan Morrissey, Bruno Langley, Lucy Miller, Liam Cunningham, Kate O'Toole, Peter Kay, Simon Pegg, David Ryall.

• *Dir* Steve Bendelack, *Pro* Greg Brenman and Ed Guiney, *Ex Pro* Peter Bennett-Jones, Andrew Love, Jeremy Dyson, Mark Gatiss, Steve Pemberton and Reece Shearsmith, *Co-Pro* Rachel Salter, *Line Pro* Séamus McInerney, *Screenplay* Dyson, Gatiss, Pemberton and Shearsmith, *Ph* Rob Kitzmann, *Pro Des* Richard Bridgland, *Ed* Tony Cranstoun, *M* Joby Talbot, *Costumes* Yves Barre.

Universal Pictures/FilmFour/Tiger Aspect Pictures/Hell's Kitchen International/Irish Film Industry-UIP. 91 mins. UK/Ireland/USA. Rel: 3 June 2005. Cert. 15.

Lemony Snicket's A Series of Unfortunate Events ★★★½

Violet, 14, Klaus, 12, and Sunny, one, find their world turned upside down when their home and their parents are consumed by a terrible fire. But this is just the first of a series of unfortunate events in which the Baudelaire children have to draw on their ingenuity, knowledge and fearlessness in order to survive in a merciless world. Then a distant relative, the grotesque and diabolically camp actor Count Olaf, takes the children under his wing so that he can rob them of their inheritance… Carrying the torch for the Brothers Grimm, *Struwwelpeter* and Roald Dahl, Lemony Snicket's literary phenomenon is a joyfully cheerless read. And the film, narrated by Mr Snicket himself (Jude Law in silhouette), perfectly catches the tongue-in-cheek foreboding of the books. Adapting the first three titles – *The Bad Beginning*, *The Reptile Room* and *The Wide Window* – the film launches into a Victorian dystopia where cobbled streets intermingle with fax machines and the spirit of Dickens presides. Adding a grotesque note of ham, Jim Carrey has a

handshake, our hero is asked one favour – or sacrifice, if you will – by an important cog in the narcotic wheel. Then things get complicated… Vaughn and Guy Ritchie have almost invented their own genre, a flash, imaginative world in which characters talk to the camera, hit songs blast from the soundtrack and everybody says 'fuck' a lot. Vaughn adds a few flourishes of his own (he obviously watches way too many music videos), but cannot disentangle the narrative knots from his array of colourful characters and set-pieces. JC-W

• Daniel Craig, *Eddie Temple* Michael Gambon, *Clarkie* Tom Hardy, *Gene* Colm Meaney, *JD* aka *'Duke'* Jamie Foreman, *Tammy* Sienna Miller, *Jimmy Price* Kenneth Cranham, *Mr Mortimer* aka *'Morty'* George Harris, *Slavo* Marcel Iures, *Terry* Tamer Hassan, *Sidney* Ben Whishaw, *Gazza* Burn Gorman, *Slasher* Sally Hawkins, *Cody* Dexter Fletcher, *with* Steven John Shepherd, Brinley Green, Francis Magee, Garry Tubbs, Natalie Lunghi, Rab Affleck, Ivan Kaye, Jason Flemyng.

• *Dir* Matthew Vaughn, *Pro* Vaughn, Adam Bohling and David Reid, *Ex Pro* Stephen Marks, *Screenplay* J.J. Connolly, from his novel, *Ph* Ben Davis, *Pro Des* Kave Quinn, *Ed* Jon Harris, *M* Lisa Gerrard and Ilan Eshkeri; songs performed by FC Kahuna, The Cult, Scissor Sisters, Kylie Minogue, The Source and Candi Staton, XTC, Duran Duran, The Rolling Stones, Craig Armstrong, Starsailor, and Joe Cocker, *Costumes* Stephanie Collie, *Sound* Matthew Collinge.

Columbia Pictures/MARV Films-Columbia TriStar. 105 mins. UK/USA. 2004. Rel: 10 September 2004. Cert. 15.

Burnt offerings: Shelby Hoffman, Emily Browning and Liam Aiken in *Lemony Snicket's A Series of Unfortunate Events* (from UIP)

ball as Count Olaf, achieving the near impossible by being both genuinely abhorrent and very funny. The production design is also wondrous, while the one-year-old twins Kara and Shelby Hoffman – as the sardonic, razor-toothed infant Sunny – steal every scene they're in. Even so, the film is so surreal that it's hard to engage with on an emotional level, or even to feel real concern for the fate of the miserable Baudelaire orphans. JC-W

• *Count Olaf* Jim Carrey, *Lemony Snicket* Jude Law, *Klaus Baudelaire* Liam Aiken, *Violet Baudelaire* Emily Browning, *Mr Poe* Timothy Spall, *Justice Strauss* Catherine O'Hara, *Uncle Monty* Billy Connolly, *Aunt Josephine* Meryl Streep, *Sunny Baudelaire* Kara and Shelby Hoffman, *with* Cedric the Entertainer, Luis Guzmán, Jamie Harris, Jennifer Coolidge, Craig Ferguson, Jane Adams, Fred Gallo, *impressed theatregoer* Dustin Hoffman.

• *Dir* Brad Silberling, *Pro* Laurie MacDonald, Walter F. Parkes and Jim Van Wyck, *Ex Pro* Scott Rudin, Barry Sonnenfeld, Julia Pistor and Albie Hecht, *Co-Pro* Minor Childers and Scott Aversano, *Screenplay* Robert Gordon, from the *Lemony Snicket* books by Daniel Handler, *Ph* Emmanuel Lubezki, *Pro Des* Rick Heinrichs, *Ed* Michael Kahn, *M* Thomas Newman, *Costumes* Colleen Atwood, *Visual Effects* Stefen Fangmeier, *Make-Up* Kevin Yagher.

DreamWorks/Paramount/Parkes/MacDonald/
Nickelodeon Movies-UIP.
103 mins. USA. 2004. Rel: 17 December 2004. Cert. PG.

Levity ★★★★½

For 23 years Manuel Jordan has stared at the black-and-white photograph of Abner Easley pinned to the wall of his prison cell. Manuel killed Abner in a raid on a convenience store and he's never forgiven himself. Then, suddenly and unexpectedly, Manuel is released into the real world and seeks to find redemption with Abner's sister, who now has a teenage son of her own… In spite of its strong cast, *Levity* took two years to reach Britain and even then was virtually thrown away. This is a shame as it is a minor gem, a resonant character study showcasing an exquisite performance from Billy Bob Thornton. With his grey hair hanging to his shoulders and his eyes drained of emotion, he resembles a hobo poet and recalls the profound stillness of Peter Sellers' Chauncey Gardiner in *Being There*. But there is an equally intelligent turn from Holly Hunter as the damaged, unforgiving Adele Easley, while Roger Deakins' elemental photography and Ed Solomon's sparse script combine to create an unsentimental, intensely moving parable for our times. Dedicated to Pat Boone. JC-W

• *Manuel Jordan* Billy Bob Thornton, *Miles Evans* Morgan Freeman, *Adele Easley* Holly Hunter, *Sofia Mellinger* Kirsten Dunst, *Senor Aguilar* Manuel Aranguiz, *Mackie Whittaker* Dorian Harewood, *Abner Easely* Geoffrey Wigdor, *young Abner Easely* Luke Robertson, *with* Billöah Greene, Catherine Colvey, Sadiki Burke.

• *Dir* and *Screenplay* Ed Solomon, *Pro* Solomon, Richard N. Gladstein and Adam J. Merims, *Ex Pro* Morgan Freeman, Lori McCreary, Fred Schepisi, Andrew Spaulding, James Burke and Doug Mankoff, *Co-Pro* Irene Litinsky, *Ph* Roger Deakins, *Pro Des* François Seguin, *Ed* Pietro Scalia and Ned Bastille, *M* Mark Oliver Everett; songs performed by Squeak Ru, Dawn and Goldie, Johnny Hawksworth, Miles Davis, E-40, and eels, *Costumes* Marie-Sylvie Deveau.

Sony Pictures Classics/StudioCanal/FilmColony/
Revelations Entertainment/Echo Lake/Entitled
Entertainment-Redbus.
100 mins. USA/France. 2002. Rel: 19 November 2004.
Cert. 15.

The Life and Death of Peter Sellers ★★★½

The last film that Charlize Theron starred in was called
Monster. This would have made a much better title for this
new film, whose very name points up the predicaments of
the biographical format. Even more problematic is the fact
that not only is Peter Sellers such a well-known figure, he's
also a man who for many viewers died in recent memory.
How can any actor on earth be expected to inhabit a star
who was himself so chameleonic and distinctive? Geoffrey
Rush, although far too old to play Sellers in his early years, is
an extraordinary performer and is wise to aim for a physical
approximation and to focus on the spirit of the tortured artist.
Sellers is, though, a fascinating subject and director Hopkins
has mitigated the usual stumbling blocks of the biopic by
providing a stylish and surreal approach in which the events
almost unfold in the subject's own mind. This is dramatic
stuff, peppered with glamorous cameos, much humour and
a lively soundtrack. The period scenes are also exceptionally
well handled and in spite of one's worst expectations this is an
engrossing, disturbing, enlightening, shocking, courageous
and very funny film.
JC-W

• *Peter Sellers/Blake Edwards/Peg Sellers, etc* Geoffrey Rush,
Britt Ekland Charlize Theron, *Blake Edwards* John Lithgow,
Peg Sellers Miriam Margolyes, *Stanley Kubrick* Stanley Tucci,
Anne Sellers Emily Watson, *Bill Sellers* Peter Vaughan, *Sophia
Loren* Sonia Aquino, *Maurice Woodruff* Stephen Fry, *Dennis
Selinger* Henry Goodman, *Ted Levy* Peter Gevisser, *Spike
Milligan* Edward Tudor Pole, *Harry Secombe* Steve Pemberton,
David Niven Nigel Havers, *Michael Sellers, aged 3* George
Cicco, *Michael Sellers, aged 7-10 years* James Bentley, *Sarah
Sellers* Eliza Darby, *singer Ray Ellington* Lance Ellington, *Ursula
Andress* Heidi Klum, *Carlo Ponti* Joseph Long, *with* Alison
Steadman, David Robb, Mackenzie Crook, Lucy Punch, Jane
Milligan, Robert Sherman, Tope Oluwole, Osmund Bullock.

• *Dir* Stephen Hopkins, *Pro* Simon Bosanquet, *Ex Pro*
Freddy Demann, George Faber, Charles Pattinson and David
M. Thompson, *Screenplay* Christopher Markus and Stephen
McFeely, *Ph* Peter Levy, *Pro Des* Norman Garwood, *Ed*
John Smith, *M* Richard Hartley; Johann Strauss Jr.; songs
performed by Tom Jones, Lance Ellington, Peter Sellers and
Sophia Loren, Shirley Bassey, Marvin Gaye, Wilson Pickett,
The Animals, The Hollies and Peter Sellers, David Bowie,
Geoffrey Rush, The Clash, and The Kinks, *Costumes* Jill
Taylor.

BBC/HBO Films/DeMann Entertainment/Company
Pictures-Icon.
126 mins. USA/UK. 2004. Rel: 1 October 2004.
Cert. 15.

The Life Aquatic with Steve Zissou ★

When, on his last expedition, his best friend is devoured
by an unseen sea creature, renowned oceanographer and
documentarian Steve Zissou sets off to record his revenge.
With fluctuating funds, the aid of a young man who may
or may not be his son and a pushy, pregnant reporter, the
enterprise looks doomed from the start... Following the
enormous critical acclaim heaped on *The Royal Tenenbaums*, its
director had a dream. He dreamed that he could attract actors
of the calibre of Bill Murray, Owen Wilson, Cate Blanchett
and Jeff Goldblum and cast them in anything, so long as it
was 'different' and eccentric. He then dreamed that Jacques
Cousteau had become Bill Murray. With animated fish, gun-
toting pirates and a comic delivery so deadpan it's got rigor
mortis, *The Life Aquatic* is a bizarre abortion. Like a burlesque
version of Munch's *The Scream*, the film shrieks 'funny' and
lands with an inglorious thud. JC-W

• *Steve Zissou* Bill Murray, *Ned Plimpton* Owen Wilson, *Jane
Winslett-Richardson* Cate Blanchett, *Eleanor Zissou* Anjelica
Huston, *Klaus Daimler* Willem Dafoe, *Alistair Hennessey* Jeff
Goldblum, *Oseary Drakoulias* Michael Gambon, *Vladimir
Wolodarsky* Noah Taylor, *Bill Ubell* Bud Cort, *Pelé dos Santos*
Seu Jorge, *Esteban du Plantier* Seymour Cassel, *with* Robyn
Cohen, Waris Ahluwalia, Rudd Simmons, Eric Chase
Anderson, Noah Baumbach.

• *Dir* Wes Anderson, *Pro* Anderson, Barry Mendel and Scott
Rudin, *Ex Pro* Rudd Simmons, *Screenplay* Anderson and Noah
Baumbach, *Ph* Robert Yeoman, *Pro Des* Mark Friedberg,
Ed David Moritz, *M* Mark Mothersbaugh; JS Bach, Ennio
Morricone; songs performed by Seu Jorge, David Bowie, Joan
Baez, Iggy and The Stooges, Paco de Lucía, Scott Walker, The
Zombies, and Sigur Rós, *Costumes* Milena Canonero, *Naval
Advisor* Gino Ciriaci.

Touchstone Pictures/American Empirical-Buena Vista
International.
118 mins. USA. 2004. Rel: 18 February 2005. Cert.15.

Life is a Miracle ★★½

This has some of the best colour photography of the year
(it's by Michel Amathieu) and the film can be strongly
recommended to those in tune with the work of its director
and co-writer Emir Kusturica. But what a Bosnian stew it

is! This rural tale set in 1992 turns the war into a background for farce, knockabout, tragedy, song and dance, and sheer sentimentality as a married Serbian engineer falls in love with a Muslim prisoner who might be exchanged for his own son captured by the Bosnians. Kusturica keeps the pace going for the whole of the film's two and a half hours but appreciation depends entirely on having a taste (that I have never acquired) for his work. The mix attempted may seem impossible to many but something like it did work in *The Life and Extraordinary Adventures of Private Ivan Chonkin* (1994).
Original title: *Zivot Je Cudo*. MS

• *Luka* Slavko Stimac, *Sabaha* Natasa Solak, *Jadranka* Vesna Trivalic, *Milos* Vuk Kostic, *Veljo* Aleksandar Bercek, *Captain Aleksic* Stribor Kusturica, *Filipovic* Nikola Kojo, *Nada* Mirjana Karanovic, *Predsjednik* Branislave Lalevic, *Tomo* Davor Janjic, *Eso* Adnan Omerovic, *Vujan* Obrad Durovic.

• *Dir* Emir Kusturica, *Pro* Alain Sarde, Maja Kusturica and Emir Kusterica, *Ex Pro* Christine Gozlan and Pierre Edelman, *Assoc Pro* Marie-Christine Malbert, *Screenplay* Ranko Bozic and Emir Kusturica, *Ph* Michel Amathieu, *Pro Des* Milenko Jeremic, *Ed* Svetolik Mica Zajc, *M* Dejan Sparavalo and Emir Kusturica, *Costumes* Zora Popovic.

Artificial Eye.
154 mins. France/Serbia/Montenegro. Rel: 11 March 2005. Cert. 15.

Little Black Book ★★★½
Brittany Murphy gives an achingly on-target performance as Stacy Holt, the naïve associate producer for a trashy daytime talk show. After she accidentally accesses the address book of her out-of-town boyfriend's palm pilot, she sets up faux interviews with some of his exes hoping to understand why her own relationship seems to have stalled. Encouraged, empowered, and ultimately betrayed by office mate Barb (an overwrought Holly Hunter), Stacy is set up to confront not only the ex-girlfriends but her own boyfriend, Derek – all on live TV. It's a post-millennium *Working Girl* that neither aspires nor pretends to be anything else and suffers a bit because of that. Still, this is a thinking person's movie that posits the painful question: what do you do when the person with whom you're in love clearly belongs with someone else? The answer is as devastating as it is ultimately uplifting. SWM

• *Stacy Holt* Brittany Murphy, *Barb* Holly Hunter, *Kippie Kann* Kathy Bates, *Derek* Ron Livingston, *Joyce* Julianne Nicholson, *Carl* Stephen Tobolowsky, *Ira* Kevin Sussman, *Dr Rachel Keyes* Rashida Jones, *Lulu Fritz* Josie Maran, *Larry* Jason Antoon, *Mom* Sharon Lawrence, *Stacy Holt, aged 7* Katie Murphy, *with* Gavin Rosdale, Cress Williams, Dave Annable, Vivian Bang, and (uncredited) Diane Sawyer, Carly Simon.

• *Dir* Nick Hurran, *Pro* Elaine Goldsmith-Thomas, Deborah Schindler, William Sherak and Jason Shuman, *Ex Pro* Herbert W. Gains, Rachael Horowitz, Warren Zide and Craig Perry, *Assoc Pro* Lauren Kisilevsky, *Screenplay* Melissa Carter and Elisa Bell, *Ph* Theo van de Sande, *Pro Des* Bob Ziembicki, *Ed* John

Richards, *M* Christophe Beck, *Costume* Susie DeSanto.

Revolution Studios/Blue Star Pictures-Columbia TriStar. 106 mins. USA. 2004. Rel: 29 October 2004. Cert. 12A.

Lizard ★★★
Unlike most Iranian films shown here (even those that can be described as comedies), this movie is a mainstream offering – even if one that is likely to be limited to art-house screenings in this country. The engaging Parviz Parastouie plays a crook who, escaping from jail dressed as a mullah, finds himself having to live up to this disguise as he awaits forged papers that will get him over the border. It's a neat enough comic idea but over-extended here and without the imagination and wit to build effectively on this foundation. Despite being banned in Iran following protests by the Islamic clergy, its espousing of the notion that everyone has their own path to God could mean that the movie is more pro-religious than anti-religious. It's an uncertainty that is, however, all too characteristic of this flabby film. For all that, this is undeniably a genuine curiosity. MS

• *Reza Mesghali* Parviz Parastoie, *with* Rana Azadvar, Mehran Najafi, Shahrokh Forutanian, Farideh Sepah Mansour.

• *Dir* Kamal Tabrizi, *Pro* Manouchehr Mohammadi, *Screenplay* Peyman Ghassemkhani, *Ph* Hamid Khozoui-Abyaneh, *Ed* Hossein Zandbaf, *M* Moahammad Reza Aligholi, *Sound* Mohammad Sammakbashi.

Faradis Co./Farabi Cinema-ICA Projects.
115 mins. Iran. 2004. Rel: 22 April 2005. No cert.

Look at Me ★★★★
Most famous men and women have children. Yet the cinema has seldom explored the problems of the child of a celebrity. Lolita Cassard is 20, overweight and totally at the emotional mercy of her father, a celebrated writer and publisher. Brutally insensitive to his daughter's needs, Étienne Cassard is a monstrous figure cloaked in charm, erudition and material generosity. His friends and colleagues seem blinded by his self-possession and only Lolita and her young (and slim) stepmother see him for what he really is. Crippled by insecurity, Lolita finds a brief escape in her singing lessons and in the teacher, Sylvia, she so admires. Then Sylvia discovers that Lolita is the daughter of Étienne Cassard… Winner of the Best Screenplay award at the 2004 Cannes festival, *Look at Me* marks the sixth collaboration between the husband-and-wife writing team of Jean-Pierre Bacri and Agnès Jaoui, who also excel themselves in the roles of Étienne and Sylvia. Rippling with humour and insight, the film is a complex and intelligent study of identity, fame, family and the literary circle of Paris, enhanced by a sublime classical score and peerless performances. FYI: Newcomer **Marilou Berry, who plays Lolita, is herself the child of a celebrity, being the daughter of the actress-director-comedienne-writer Josiane Balasko**. Original title: *Comme une image*. JC-W

• *Étienne Cassard* Jean-Pierre Bacri, *Sylvia Miller* Agnès Jaoui, *Lolita Cassard* **Marilou Berry**, *Pierre Miller* **Laurent**

Grevill, *Karine* Virginie Desarnauts, *Sebastien* Gregoire Oestermann, *Vincent* Serge Riaboukine, *Felix* Michele Moretti, *Edith* Emma Beziaud, *with* Guillaume Huet, Julien Baumgartner, Olivier Doran.

• *Dir* Agnès Jaoui, *Pro* Jean-Philippe Andraca and Christian Bérard, *Screenplay* Jaoui and Jean-Pierre Bacri, *Ph* Stéphane Fontaine, *Pro Des* Olivier Jacquet, *Ed* François Gedigier, *M* Philippe Rombi; Mozart, Offenbach, Handel, Schubert, Monteverdi, Verdi, Beethoven, etc, *Costumes* Jackie Budin.

Les Films A4/StudioCanal/France 2 Cinéma/Lumière/ Eyescreen/Canal Plus-Pathé.
111 mins. France/Italy. 2004. Rel: 5 November 2004. Cert. 12A.

Los Angeles Plays Itself ★★★★
This highly acclaimed documentary is a remarkable undertaking: a portrait of Los Angeles as seen through the images of it in movies. It starts with the city as background and features buildings and locations chosen to suit various films, adapted where necessary. Moving on to the city as character it shows us the views of outsiders such as Jacques Deray, Antonioni and Jacques Demy, while admiring the veracity of vision in such quintessentially American movies as *Kiss Me Deadly*. When it comes to the city as subject, longer analysis is offered. The latter section separates fact from fiction in such films as *Chinatown* and *L.A. Confidential* and the whole represents the viewpoint of a filmmaker, Thom Andersen, who is a resident there. Despite lasting nearly three hours, the film does not drag, but those who positively revel in it are those for whom the film's specialist appeal is spot on. MS

• *Narrator*: Encke King.

• *Dir, Pro, Screenplay* and *Research* Thom Andersen, *Ph* Deborah Stratman, *Ed* Yoo Seung-Hyun, *Sound* Thor Moser and Craig Smith.

Burton/Floyd-ICA Projects.
169 mins. USA. 2003. Rel: 10 December 2004. No cert.

A Lot Like Love ★★
Seven years ago, Oliver Martin caught the gaze of a beautiful stranger at Los Angeles airport. Not long afterwards, on a plane heading for New York, he and she consummated their transient connection in a moment of blind lust. Over the years, Oliver and Emily meet up and have wonderful, one-off romantic reunions. Unfortunately, the timing is always wrong... For a while there Ashton Kutcher was shaping up to be the next Freddie Prinze Jr (tall, studly, celebrated squeeze, awful teen comedies). Here, though, he's beginning to show signs of an actor who may well last another two or three years. He's endearingly self-effacing, self-deprecatory and throwaway goofy. You almost want to like him. However, the real reason for seeing this lightweight *When Harry Met Sally...* is for the luminous, appealing and seductive charms of Amanda Peet, who has seldom been given her due on the big screen. Indeed,

she pumps chemistry into the scenes with her co-star (six years her junior) and the film manages for much of the time to catch the silliness, spontaneity and earnestness of young love. However, such sweetness cannot save it from a lack of sparkle, too many longueurs and an inevitable predictability. FYI: A billboard for *Raising Helen* appears four years before a marquee showing Zack Snyder's *Dawn of the Dead*, even though the former was released three months afterwards! JC-W

• *Oliver Martin* Ashton Kutcher, *Emily Friehl* Amanda Peet, *Michelle* Kathryn Hahn, *Jeeter* Kal Penn, *Gina* Ali Larter, *Ellen Geary* Taryn Manning, *Peter* Gabriel Mann, *Ben Miller* Jeremy Sisto, *Brent Friehl* James Read, *with* Aimee Garcia, Lee Garlington, Moon Bloodgood, Linda Hunt, Conrad Bluth, *upstairs neighbour* Colin Patrick Lynch, Rick Overton, Holmes Osborne.

• *Dir* Nigel Cole, *Pro* Armyan Bernstein and Kevin Messick, *Ex Pro* Charlie Lyons, Zanne Devine and Suzann Ellis, *Co-Pro* Lisa Bruce, *Screenplay* Colin Patrick Lynch, *Ph* John De Borman, *Pro Des* Tom Meyer, *Ed* Susan Littenberg, *M* Alex Wurman; songs performed by Third Eye Blind, Eagle-Eye Cherry, Smash Mouth, The Cure, Hooverphonic, Travis, Aqualung, Jet, Butch Walker, Moby, Chicago, Groove Armada, Ashton Kutcher, Ann Nalick, etc, *Costumes* Alix Friedberg.

Touchstone Pictures/Beacon Pictures-Buena Vista International.
106 mins. USA. 2005. Rel: 24 June 2005. Cert. 12A.

Love Me If You Dare ★
Echoing the infinitely superior *Ma Vie en rose* (1997), Yann Samuell's debut feature seeks to bring together humour, fantasy and serious psychological truths. His tale tells of a boy and girl who indulge in games of dare and continue this into their adult lives. Playing up crude humour in the childhood scenes and then combining that with a traumatic death that leaves a sense of guilt makes for a wholly uneasy mix. Furthermore, the infantile behaviour of the adults, far from being either whimsically charming or seriously affecting, only suggests that each of the leading characters is a suitable case for treatment. How sad that this totally misjudged work should be the one that gives star billing to Marion Cotillard who, following her supporting role in *Big Fish*, has the potential to be a delightful new star. MS

• *Julien* Guillaume Canet, *Sophie* Marion Cotillard, *Julien, aged 8* Thibault Verhaeghe, *Sophie, aged 8* Josephine Lebas Joly, *Julien's mother* Emmanuelle Grönvold, *Julien's father* Gerard Watkins, *with* Elodie Navarre, Gilles Lellouche, Julia Faure, Laetizia Venezia.

• *Dir* Yann Samuell, *Pro* Christophe Rossignon, *Ex Pro* Eve Machuel, *Co-Pro* Patrick Quinet and Stephen Quinet, *Screenplay* Samuell and Jacky Cuckier, *Ph* Antoine Roch, *Ed* Andréa Sedlackova, *Art Dir* Jean-Michel Simonet, *M* Philippe Rombi, *Costumes* Julie Mauduech.

Nord-Ouest Prods/StudioCanalStudioCanal/Artemis Prods/
France 2 Cinéma/M6 Films/Caneo Films/Media Services-
94 mins. France/Belgium. 2003. Rel: 20 August 2004. Cert. 15.

The Machinist ★★★★

Trevor Reznik hasn't slept for a year. And this is not good news
for a man who spends his days operating dangerous machinery.
At night he keeps company with a prostitute, Stevie, or just
sits at the airport making small talk with a waitress, Marie.
Gradually, the two women begin to blend into one, and
they say the same things. Then, back at his stark apartment,
Trevor finds enigmatic notes left on the door of his fridge…
In spite of high-profile roles in *American Psycho* and *Reign of
Fire*, Christian Bale remains the best-kept secret of British
cinema. Losing an incredible 63 pounds to play the shadowy
figure of Trevor Reznik, Bale establishes himself as the De
Niro of the new millennium. Yet while *The Machinist* is a
film of striking uniqueness, it wears its multiple allusions on
its sleeve. Hitchcock, Kafka, Polanski and Dostoevsky are all
referenced, composer Roque Baños appropriates the insistent
chords of Bernard Herrmann and the Brandoesque John Sharian
perpetuates the deception with a Brandoesque burr. At once
knowing and surreally inside its own head, *The Machinist* is a
hallucinogenic trip anchored by a masochistic performance from
Bale and a startling visual panache. Filmed in Spain. JC-W

• *Trevor Reznik* Christian Bale, *Stevie* Jennifer Jason Leigh,
Marie Aitana Sanchez-Gijon, *Ivan* John Sharian, *Miller* Michael
Ironside, *Mrs Shrike* Anna Massey, *Jackson* Larry Gilliard, *Jones*
Reg E. Cathey, *Inspector Rogers* Colin Stinton, *with* Matthew
Romero, Robert Long, Marc Aspinall.

• *Dir* Brad Anderson, *Pro* Julio Fernández, *Ex Pro* Carlos
Fernández and Antonia Nava, *Line Pro* Teresa Gefaell, *Screenplay*
Scott Kosar, *Ph* Xavi Gimenez, *Pro Des* Alain Bainée, *Ed* Luis
de La Madrid, *M* Roque Baños, *Theremin player* Lydia Kavina,
Costumes Patricia Monné and Maribel Pérez, *Sound* Briel Cabré.

Filmax Entertainment/Paramount Classics/Canal Plus-
Tartan Films.
102 mins. Spain. 2003. Rel: 18 March 2005.
Cert. 15.

Machuca ★★★★

This sincere portrait of life in Santiago, Chile in 1973 deals
with the downfall of Allende's socialist government and the
imposition of General Pinochet's military rule. It's done
through the story of two boys, the name of one of them
providing the film's title. These two become friends although
one is well off and the other is only present in the same
Catholic school because its headmaster has provided places
for the poor. As it happens, this film echoes such out-and-
out masterpieces as *Au Revoir les enfants* (1988) and *Butterfly's
Tongue* (1998). Coming later in the day it's predictable, less
overwhelming and certainly without surprises. But if my rating
seems rather generous, it reflects the probable impact of this
film on those who have not seen its illustrious predecessors.
And the historical setting is, of course, quite different.
MS

• *Gonzalo Infante* Matias Quer, *Pedro Machuca* Ariel Mateluna,
Silvana Manuela Martelli, *Maria Luisa* Aline Kuppenheim,
Roberto Ochagavia Federico Luppi, *Father McEnroe* Ernesto
Malbran, *Juana* Tamara Acosta, *Patricio Infante* Francisco Reyes,
Willi Alejandro Trejo.

• *Dir* Andres Wood, *Pro* Gerardo Herrero, Mamoun Hassan
and Andres Wood, *Assoc Pro* Nathalie Trafford, Juan Carlos
Arriagada and Patricio Pereira, *Screenplay* Wood, Hassan and
Roberto Brodsky, *Ph* Miguel J. Littin, *Pro Des* Rodrigo Bazaes,
Ed Fernando Pardo, *M* Miguel Angel Miranda and Jose Miguel
Tobar, *Costumes* Maya Mora.

Andres Wood Producciones/Tornasol Films/Mamoun
Hassan/Paraiso/Chilefilms/Canal Plus Spain/Television
Espanola-Artificial Eye.
121 mins. Chile/Spain/UK/France. 2004. Rel: 6 May 2005.
Cert. 15.

The Magic Roundabout ★★½

In the quiet backwater of the Enchanted Village, the shaggy
and gluttonous Dougal inadvertently unleashes the full power
of the evil jack-in-the-box Zeebad. Intent on world domination,
Zeebad sets about turning his opponents into ice and hunts for
the three diamonds that, once united, will give him full global
supremacy… By attempting to enthral the young of mind and
entertain a more sophisticated, drug-savvy audience, this second
attempt to film the 1965-75 TV series is a curious hybrid.
Computer-animating the original stop-motion puppetry, the
film juggles a sense of timeless innocence with a rip-roaring
parody of *The Lord of the Rings* – interspersed with drug and
film references. Thus Ian McKellen is recruited to provide a
Gandalf spin (or spring) on Zebedee, while Tom Baker fills in
for Christopher Lee as a cackling Zeebad. Toddlers will miss
most of the film's more arcane allusions and may be alarmed
by the metaphor of Zeebad as a Bush-era, environmentally
insensitive autocrat. Visually the film is quaint, but its real
success lies in the cherry-picked cast of vocal talent, with
Robbie Williams surprisingly effective as Dougal, Jim
Broadbent a perfect Brian and Joanna Lumley a scintillating
Ermintrude. Bizarre, to say the least. JC-W

• voices: *Zeebad* Tom Baker, *Brian* Jim Broadbent, *Train* Lee
Evans, *Ermintrude* Joanna Lumley, *Zebedee* Ian McKellen, *Florence*
Kylie Minogue, *Dylan* Bill Nighy, *Dougal* Robbie Williams,
Sam Ray Winstone.

• *Dir* Jean Duval, Frank Passingham and Dave Borthwick,
Pro Laurent Rodon and Pascal Rodon, *Ex Pro* François
Ivernel, Cameron McCracken, Jill Sinclair and Jake Eberts,
Screenplay Paul Bassett Davies, Tad Safran, Raoff Sanoussi and
Stéphane Sanoussi, from characters created by Serge Danot and
Martine Danot, *Ed* Mathieu Morfin, *M* Mark Thomas; Bizet,
Grieg, Richard Strauss; songs performed by Pilot, Electric
Light Orchestra, T-Rex, Kylie Minogue, Andrea Remanda
and Scaramanga X, and The Kinks, *Animation Dir* Frédéric
Bonometti, *Sound* Joseph Park Stracey.

Pathé Pictures/UK Film Council/ Pathé Renn/Pricel/

France 2 Cinéma/Canal Plus/National Lottery-Pathé.
81 mins. UK/France. 2005. Rel: 11 February 2005.
Cert. U.

Mambo Italiano ★★★

Impossible families from ethnic minorities are finding their
cinematic voice thanks to the colossal success of *My Big
Fat Greek Wedding*. This one, also adapted from a play (by
Steve Galluccio), is *My Big Fat Italian Coming Out*, being the
story of Angelo, a nice Italian boy who's had enough of his
chauvinistic paterfamilias. Angelo is gay and cannot live up
to the expectations of his parents, who are steeped in Italian
tradition and ruled by the opinion of their neighbours.
So Angelo moves out of the family home and in with his
childhood friend, Nino, a macho Italian cop who happens to
swing in his direction. Inevitably, his parents, who cannot
seem to master the orderly mambo, fly into another tarantella.
Ebullient and deftly edited, *Mambo Italiano* disguises its
theatrical roots with aplomb, a vivid musical soundtrack
ushering events along with a cinematic flourish. Stereotypes
abound, but the mickey-taking is so good-natured that one
can't help but fall into step; the audience I saw this with
lapped it up. Although the movie is rich in wit and humour
– and extremely well played – its familiar template may put
off more seasoned filmgoers. JC-W

• *Gino Barberini* Paul Sorvino, *Angelo Barberini* Luke Kirby,
Maria Barberini Ginette Reno, *Lina Paventi* Mary Walsh,
Nino Paventi Peter Miller, *Pina Lunetti* Sophie Lorain, *Anna
Barberini* Claudia Ferri, *Rosetta Pierrette* Robitaille, *Peter* Tim
Post, *Marco* Lou Vani, *with* Michel Perron, Mark Camacho,
Ellen David, Steve Galluccio.

• *Dir* Émile Gaudreault, *Pro* Denise Robert and Daniel
Louis, *Screenplay* Émile Gaudreault and Steve Galluccio,
Ph Serge Ladouceur, *Pro Des* Patricia Christie, *Ed* Richard
Comeau, *M* F.M. LeSieur; 'La gigocin' sung by Ginette Reno
and Paul Sorvino, *Costumes* Francesca Chamberland.

Cinemaginaire/Téléfilm Canada, etc-Icon.
88 mins. Canada. 2003. Rel: 1 October 2004. Cert. 15.

Ma mère ★★★

Critical assessment of a film such as this is difficult. On
the one hand we have admirable direction from newcomer
Christophe Honoré. Shooting atmospherically on Gran
Canaria, he uses natural sounds and music quite splendidly
to make us share in the bizarre world of his characters.
However, the other side of the coin is that his adaptation of
Georges Bataille's 1977 novel, while being seriously sexually
explicit rather than sensational in its approach, takes us
into a disturbingly sado-masochistic and incestuous world
as a mother (Isabelle Huppert) inducts her son (Louis Garrel
from *The Dreamers*) both indirectly and directly into a world
of sexual extremes. It's well played but offers little by way
of insight or comment on behaviour that will keep most
audiences at a distance. MS

• *Hélène* Isabelle Huppert, *Pierre* Louis Garrel, *Hansi* Emma
de Caunes, *Réa* Joana Preiss, *Loulou* Jean-Baptiste Montagut,
Marhe Dominique Reymond, *Robert* Olivier Rabourdin, *father*
Philippe Duclos.

• *Dir and Screenplay* Christophe Honoré, based on the novel
by Georges Bataille, *Pro* Paulo Branco, *Ex Pro* Marc Friedl,
Line Pro Sylvain Monod, *Ph* Hélène Louvart, *Art Dir* Laurent
Allaire, *Ed* Chantal Hymans, *Costumes* Pierre Canitrot, *Sound*
Jean-Claude Brisson.

Paulo Branco/Bernard-Henri Levy/Gemini Films/Arte
France Cinéma/Canal Plus, etc-Revolver Entertainment.
110 mins. France/Spain/Austria. 2004. Rel: 4 March 2005.
Cert. 18.

Man About Dog ★½

Northern Ireland/Republic of Ireland; the present. Mo
Chara knows all about dogs and gambling and he knows
it is an illness. His father is an inveterate gambler. But Mo
Chara has a determination to beat the odds. Unfortunately,
he's stuck with two chronic losers for friends and the game
is corrupt from the inside out. So, is Mo Chara barking
or what? Paddy Breathnach would like to think he's the
Guy Ritchie or Danny Boyle of Ireland. At least, he copies
some of the cinematic moves of the former, while Pearse
Elliott's script even paraphrases dialogue out of *Trainspotting*.
Unfortunately, Breathnach has saddled himself with a trio of
gormless stereotypes who are strapped into their templates
like squirming children in a theme park ride. If *Man About
Dog* had half the energy of a Ritchie or a Boyle, it would have
been considerably less of a dreary experience. JC-W

• *Mo Chara* Allen Leech, *Cerebral Paulsy* Tom Jordan
Murphy, *Scud Murphy* Ciaran Nolan, *J.P. McCallion* Sean
McGinley, *Fergie* Pat Shortt, *Olivia* Fionnula Flanagan, *Paddy
Rat* Maurice Henry, *with* Joe Reid, Lisa Andrews, Florrie
McDonald, Michael Collins, Jeff O'Toole, Tom Murphy.

• *Dir* Paddy Breathnach, *Pro* Simon Channing Williams and
Robert Walpole, *Ex Pro* Mark Woods, Brendan McCarthy,
Gail Egan, Jim Reeve and Steve Robbins, *Line Pro* Paula
McBreen, *Screenplay* Pearse Elliott, *Ph* Cian de Buitléar, *Pro
Des* Paki Smith, *Ed* Dermot Diskin, *M* Hugh Drumm and
Stephen Rennicks, *Costumes* Lorna Marie Mugan.

Bord Scannán na hÉireann/Irish Film Board/Visionview/
Future Films/Redbus Pictures/Element X/Potboiler
Prods/Tresure Entertainment-Redbus.
88 mins. Ireland/UK. 2004. Rel: 19 November 2004.
Cert. 15.

The Manchurian Candidate ★★★★½

Major Bennett E. Marco gives impassioned speeches on the
heroic exploits in Kuwait of his sergeant, Raymond Shaw. But
having recommended the soldier for the Congressional Medal
of Honor, Marco is beginning to have second thoughts about
Shaw's role in the Gulf. Plagued by disturbing dreams, Marco
finds that his worst fears are given credence when another
soldier from the war, Al Melvin, approaches him and shares

Liev Schreiber (right) is accepted into high office in Jonathan Demme's chilling *The Manchurian Candidate* (from UIP)

his nocturnal anxiety. Then Shaw is put in line for the vice-presidency of the US and Melvin turns up dead… Frank Sinatra films seem to lend themselves to accomplished reinterpretation. After the triumph of Steven Soderbergh's enrichment of *Ocean's Eleven* comes this proficient, wholly successful update of Sinatra's 1962 classic. Korea has been replaced by the Gulf War (1991), there is a new conflict in Indonesia and the concept of Richard Condon's 1959 novel seems as pertinent today – if not more so – than it ever was. Taking the concept of a puppet president to its logical extreme, the remake not only makes a far-fetched premise convincing but a chilling and highly charged one. With Jonathan Demme back on terrific form (after the embarrassment of *The Truth About Charlie*), the film is lent enormous credibility by Denzel Washington and in particular by Meryl Streep in a compelling display of passion, persuasion and power. JC-W

• *Major Bennett 'Ben' E. Marco* Denzel Washington, *Eleanor Prentiss Shaw* Meryl Streep, *Raymond Shaw* Liev Schreiber, *Senator Thomas Jordan* Jon Voight, *Rosie* Kimberly Elise, *Al Melvin* Jeffrey Wright, *Colonel Howard* Ted Levine, *Richard Delp* Bruno Ganz, *Jocelyn Jordan* Vera Farmiga, *with* Miguel Ferrer, Dean Stockwell, Jude Ciccolella, Simon McBurney, Obba Babatundé, Zeljko Ivanek, Paul Lazar, John Bedford Lloyd, Anthony Mackie, Robyn Hitchcock, Charles Napier, Al Franken, Pablo Schreiber, Bill Irwin, Adam LeFevre, Roger Corman, Ann Dowd, Harry Northup, Sakina Jaffrey, Robert Castle, Tracey Walter, Kenny Utt, Darrell Larson, Josephine Demme, Tom Chapin, Sidney Lumet, Anna Deavere Smith.

• *Dir* Jonathan Demme, *Pro* Demme, Scott Rudin, Ilona Herzberg and Tina Sinatra, *Ex Pro* Scott Aversano, *Screenplay*

Daniel Pyne and Dean Georgaris, *Ph* Tak Fujimoto, *Pro Des* Kristi Zea, *Ed* Carol Littleton and Craig McKay, *M* Rachel Portman; Fauré; songs performed by Wyclef Jean, Gang of Four, Big Youth, Trini, Vague Angels, Dead Kennedys, Fountains of Wayne, etc, *Costumes* Albert Wolsky, *Sound* Blake Leyh.

Paramount/Scott Rudin/Tina Sinatra-UIP.
130 mins. USA. 2004. Rel: 19 November 2004. Cert. 15.

Man of the House ★★★

Grouchy tough guy Tommy Lee Jones in a teen comedy? Something wrong, surely! Well, not too far out. The Jones boy plays it straight and raises a steady stream of good laughs as a Texas Ranger who goes undercover to protect five college cheerleaders who have witnessed the killing of an informant by a renegade FBI agent (Van Holt). With funny lines, cute and sexy pom-pom girls, bursts of exciting action spread out nicely through the movie and a game turn by lustrous Anne Archer as the teacher Jones falls for, this is loads better than expected. DW

• *Roland Sharp* Tommy Lee Jones, *Percy Stevens* Cedric the Entertainer, *Anne* Christina Milian, *Teresa* Paula Garcés, *Evie* Monica Keena, *Heather* Vanessa Ferlito, *Barb* Kelli Garner, *Prof Molly McCarthy* Anne Archer, *Eddie Zane* Brian Van Holt, *with* Ranger Holt Shea Whigham, Terry Parks, R. Lee Ermey, Paget Brewster, Shannon Marie Woodward, Liz Vassey, Curtis Armstrong, James Richard Perry.

• *Dir* Stephen Herek, *Pro* Steven Reuther, Todd Garner and Allyn Stewart, *Ex Pro* Tommy Lee Jones, Marty Ewing and

Derek Dauchy, *Screenplay* Robert Ramsey, Matthew Stone and John J. McLaughlin, from story by McLaughlin and Scott Lobdell, *Ph* Peter Menzies Jr, *Pro Des* Nelson Coates, *Ed* Chris Lebenzon and Joel Negron, *M* David Newman, *Costumes* Betsy Heimann.

Revolution Studios-Columbia TriStar.
99 mins. USA. 2005. Rel: 8 April 2005. Cert. 12A.

Man on Fire ★★★½

On average, someone is kidnapped every 60 minutes in Latin America. And of those, only 30 per cent live. It's a horrifying fact and during the opening credits of this brutal, absorbing film a man is abducted and has his ear hacked off. It's a disorientating sequence and it's unclear whether this is related to the story or just a 'taster' of life in Mexico (it's the latter). Denzel Washington plays John Creasy, a burned-out assassin who used to work for the CIA but is now just in the employ of the bottle. Visiting a friend in Mexico City, Creasy takes a temporary job as a bodyguard to a ten-year-old girl. He's hired because he's cheap; he takes the position because he gets to continue drinking. However, the girl refuses to accept him as just another hired hand. In Creasy, she sees a man waiting to be redeemed... *Man On Fire*, a remake of a 1987 Scott Glenn programmer, is a dazzling display of the filmmaking talents of Tony Scott. Aurally and visually luxuriant, it captures the smells and contradictions of Mexico City with an élan bordering on the meretricious. It is also extraordinarily manipulative, a Schwarzenegger actioner dressed up as something entirely more self-important. If you can overlook these shortcomings, though, it's one helluva ride. JC-W

• *John Creasy* Denzel Washington, *Pita Ramos* Dakota Fanning, *Rayburn* Christopher Walken, *Manzana* Giancarlo Giannini, *Lisa Ramos* Radha Mitchell, *Samuel Ramos* Marc Anthony, *Mariana* Rachel Ticotin, *Jordan* Mickey Rourke, *with* Jesus Ochoa, Angelina Pelaez, Gustavo Sanchez Parra.

• *Dir* Tony Scott, *Pro* Scott and Arnon Milchan, *Ex Pro* Lance Hool and James W. Skotchdopole, *Screenplay* Brian Helgeland, based on the novel by A.J. Quinnell, *Ph* Paul Cameron, *Pro Des* Benjamin Fernandez and Chris Seagers, *Ed* Christian Wagner, *M* Harry Gregson-Williams; Debussy, Chopin, Puccini; songs performed by Mariachi Vargas de Tecalitlan, Nine Inch Nails, Linda Ronstadt, Kinky, Toni Basil, GMS, Deakin Scott, Carlos Varela, Lisa Gerrard, etc, *Costumes* Louise Frogley.

Fox 2000/Regency Enterprises/New Regency/Scott Free-Fox.
146 mins. USA/UK. 2004. Rel: 8 October 2004. Cert. 18.

The Manson Family ★★

Staccato editing enhances the 'trippy' stylisation of *The Manson Family*, ostensibly an attempt to show the horrific events of Charlie and co from 'their point of view'. The emphasis is on the counter-culture's fascination with drug-use, free love, and a complete abandonment of any sort of personal responsibility – the very elements that create a Charles

Manson in the first place. It's too easy to dismiss Jim Van Bebber's efforts here as amateurish, however. The single tripod shots and the jumpy hand-hells all heighten the illusion of it being a documentary. Equal parts paean and apology for the Manson family, it's a provocative work certainly not suited for general viewing. It's an ugly subject told in a very ugly way. But, like the events of August 1969, it's also unforgettable. SWM

• *Charlie* Marcelo Games, *Tex* Marc Pitman, *Patty* Leslie Orr, *Sadie* Maureen Allisse, *Leslie* Amy Yates, *Bobbi* Jim VanBebber, *with* Tom Burns, Michelle Briggs, Sherri Rickman, Nate Pennington, M.M. Jones, Mark Gillespie, Jennifer Orr.

• *Dir* and *Screenplay* Jim VanBebber, *Pro* Mike King, Carl Daft and David Gregory, *Ph* King, *Ed* VanBebber and Michael Capone, *M* Superjoint Ritual, Philip Anselmo, The Disembodied, Body and Blood, The Swing Anselmo's, Necrophagia, Download, and Charles Manson, *Costumes* Sherri Rickman.

Asmodeus/Mercury Films/Blue Underground-Anchor Bay Entertainment UK.
94 mins. USA/UK. 2003. Rel: 23 July 2004. Cert. 18.

María Full of Grace ★★★★

María Alvarez is 17 and works in a Colombian flower plantation de-thorning roses. Her fingers bleed, her boss is rude and insensitive and her boyfriend admits that he doesn't love her. She sacrifices her last wage packet to pay for medicine for her sister's baby and decides to call it a day. Visiting Bogotá, she agrees to act as a 'mule' in return for $5000 – enough money to change her life for ever. All she has to do is swallow 62 thumb-sized pellets of heroin and take a plane to the States... Having established María's lot with an effective display of social realism, first-time director Joshua Marston has set things up nicely when the story kicks into high gear. Newcomer Catalina Sandino Moreno gives a credible, nicely understated performance as María, artfully balancing a natural pluck with a timidity and ingenuousness when placed in a world she knows nothing about. By turns bewitching, eye-opening and almost unbearably gripping, *María Full of Grace* exposes a little-seen underworld with a rare authority and sensitivity. JC-W

• *María Alvarez* Catalina Sandino Moreno, *Blanca* Yenny Paola Vega, *Franklin* Jhon Alex Toro, *Lucy Diaz* Guilied López, *Juana* Virgina Ariza, *Felipe* Charles Albert Patiño, *Juan* Wilson Guerrero, *Diana* Johanna Andrea Mora, *Carla* Patricia Rae, *with* Rodrigo Sánchez Borhorquez, Jaime Osorio Gómez, Juan Porras Hincapie, Orlando Tobón.

• *Dir* and *Screenplay* Joshua Marston, *Pro* Paul Mezey, *Co-Pro* Jaime Osorio Gómez, *Assoc Pro* Orlando Tobón and Rodrigo Guerrero, *Line Pro* Becky Glupczynski, *Ph* Jim Denault, *Pro Des* Monica Marulanda and Debbie de Villa, *Ed* Anne McCabe and Lee Percy, *M* Jacobo Lieberman and Leonardo Heiblum, *Costumes* Lauren Press and Sarah Beers.

HBO Films/Icon/Journeyman Pictures/Sundance
Institute-Icon.
101 mins. USA/Colombia/Ecuador. 2004.
Rel: 25 March 2005. Cert. 15.

Mayor of the Sunset Strip★★★★½

Documentary filmmaker George Hickenlooper hits all the
right notes with this poignant history of music industry mega-
sidekick and KROQ disc jockey Rodney Bingenheimer. A
veritable *Who's Who* of music giants recount how this slight,
dutchboy-coiffed enigma travelled from abandoned teen to
career-making maestro. Bingenheimer's dedication and love
for obscure sounds helped him discover and promote bands
that have become the cornerstones of half a dozen musical
genres over the past three decades. Up until now, all he's had to
show for his efforts are condescending bosses and a lifetime of
buzzing at the fringe of talented people's careers. At least, with
Mayor, Bingenheimer's contributions to modern culture are
accurately, if painfully, chronicled. SWM

• *with*: Rodney Bingenheimer, Exene Cervenka, John Doe, X,
Chris Carter, Courtney Love, Gwen Stefani, Brooke Shields,
Kim Fowley, Brian Wilson, Alice Cooper, Michael Des Barres,
Pamela Des Barres, Keanu Reeves, Deborah Harry, George
Hickenlooper, Liam Gallagher, Nancy Sinatra, Mackenzie
Phillips, Neil Young, George Wendt, Pete Townsend, Beck,
Joey Ramone, Ray Manzarek, Green Day, Rod Zombie, Noel
Ghallagher, David Bowie, Neve Campbell, Sarah Michelle
Gellar, Sonny Bono, The Mamas and the Papas, Davy Jones,
The Monkees, Jerry Lee Lewis, The Four Seasons, Mick Jagger,
The Doors, John Lennon, Linda Ronstadt, Joan Jett, David
Johansen, No Doubt, Elvis Costello, Belinda Carlisle, Phil
Spector, Sid Vicious, Johnny Rotten, Coldplay, Chris Martin,
Van Halen, David Lee Roth, Blondie, Oasis, Tori Amos, Corey
Feldman, Paul McCartney, etc.

• *Dir* and *Screenplay* George Hickenlooper, *Pro* Chris Carter,
Greg Little and Tommy Perna, *Ex Pro* Donald Zuckerman, *Co-
Pro* and *Ed* Julie Janata, *Ph* Hickenlooper, Kramer Morgenthau,
Igor Meglic and Chris Carter; *M* Anthony Marinelli.

First Look Media/Showtime/Samuel Goldwyn Films-
Tartan Films.
94 mins. USA. 2003. Rel: 11 February 2005. Cert. 15.

Mean Creek ★★½

Small-town Oregon; today. Introspective and small for his
age, Sam is tired of being picked on by the overweight school
bully, George Tooney. So his older brother, Rocky, hatches a
plan. They will pretend it's Sam's birthday, lure George on a
river trip and then humiliate him so that he'll never go near
Sam again. But on the day, George seems touched by the
invitation and has even bought Sam a birthday present. Maybe
all George needs is some companionship and understanding…
Jacob Aaron Estes exhibits an assured hand with his debut
feature, both as a painter of light and as a director of actors.
Rory Culkin, younger sibling of Kieran and Macaulay, gives
a sensitive, credible turn as the tormented Sam, although
it's Scott Mechlowicz who shows the greatest promise,

Mean Creek (from Tartan Films)

revealing a powerful stillness (and a passing resemblance
to a young Anthony Perkins). The film itself, while always
interesting, delivers less than it promises, due in part to Estes'
underdeveloped and unresolved script. The outcome should
have been deeply disturbing. Instead, it's just sad. JC-W

• *Sam* Rory Culkin, *Clyde* Ryan Kelley, *Marty* Scott
Mechlowicz, *Rocky* Trevor Morgan, *George Tooney* Josh Peck,
Millie Carly Schroeder, *Kile* Branden Williams, *Maggie Tooney*
Raissa Fleming, *Jasper* Heath Lourwood, *handsome police officer*
Hagai Shaham.

• *Dir* and *Screenplay* Jacob Aaron Estes, *Pro* Rick Rosenthal,
Susan Johnson and Hagai Shaham, *Ex Pro* Nancy Stephens,
Gigi Protzker and Deborah Del Prete, *Co-Pro* Jacob Mosler, *Ph*
Sharone Meir, *Pro Des* Greg McMickle, *Ed* Madeleine Gavin,
M tomandandy; songs performed by John Gold, Eels, Mos Def,
Five Point Plan, Lost Goat, Gretchen Lieberrum, Ethan Gold,
Death Cab for Cutie, Wilco, Orleans, and Spoon, *Costumes*
Cynthia Morrill, *Sound* Emile Razpopov.

Whitewater Films-Tartan Films.
89 mins. USA. 2004. Rel: 29 April 2005. Cert. 15.

Meet the Fockers ★★½

The spectacle of Robert De Niro, Dustin Hoffman and Barbra
Streisand goofing off in this mad pantomime is a sight to
behold. Yet whereas one Focker in the original *Meet the Parents*

Meet the muggers: Dustin Hoffman and Robert De Niro play it broad in Jay Roach's very silly *Meet the Fockers* (from UIP)

(itself a remake of a little-seen 1992 film) was enough to generate big laughs, to have a trio of Fockers is just too much. Greg Gaylord Focker is to present his liberal, laidback parents – Bernie and Roz – to his in-laws-to-be and rarely have chalk and cheddar seemed so diametrically opposed. It's a one-joke premise, but there are some major chuckles anyway, although seldom because of the over-active, overpaid stars. Jack Byrnes' one-year-old nephew (Spencer and Bradley Pickren) matches Kara and Shelby Hoffman in *Lemony Snicket* for infant scene-stealing (the child's very first word is 'ass-hooole'), while the gross-out humour is kept to a minimum (although we could've done without Ben Stiller's foreskin landing in the communal fondue). Some of the humour is predictable and too much of it over the top, reminding one that there is a thin line between the embarrassing and the excruciating. JC-W

• *Jack Byrnes* Robert De Niro, *Greg Gaylord Focker* Ben Stiller, *Bernie Focker* Dustin Hoffman, *Roz Focker* Barbra Streisand, *Dina Byrnes* Blythe Danner, *Pam Byrnes* Teri Polo, *little Jack* Spencer and Bradley Pickren, *Officer Le Flore* Tim Blake Nelson, *Kevin Rawley* Owen Wilson, *with* Alanna Ubach, Ray Santiago, Shelley Berman, Kall Rocha, Max Hoffman.

• *Dir* Jay Roach, *Pro* Roach, Jane Rosenthal and Robert De Niro, *Ex Pro* Nancy Tenenbaum and Amy Sayres, *Screenplay* Jim Herzfeld and John Hamburg, from a story by Herzfeld and Marc Hyman, based on characters created by Greg Glienna and Mary Ruth Clarke, *Ph* John Schwartzman, *Pro Des* Rusty Smith, *Ed* Jon Poll and Lee Haxall, *M* Randy Newman and Bruno Coon, *Costumes* Carol Ramsey.

Universal/DreamWorks/Tribeca/Everyman Pictures-UIP. 115 mins. USA. 2004. Rel: 28 January 2005. Cert. 12A.

Melinda and Melinda ★★

Four intellectuals sit round a table and discuss what constitutes the essence of comedy and tragedy. Al relates a story about a woman he knows called Melinda. It is a story of surprise, disappointment, infidelity and suicide and so two parallel films emerge, one quite tragic and profound, the other comical and profound. Both are about Melinda turning up out of the blue at a Manhattan dinner party... This is the best idea for a film that Woody Allen has come up with in quite a while. He's also commanded some fine performances, particularly from Radha Mitchell as the confused, bitter and fragile Melinda. But it still feels like an intellectual exercise and although there's the occasional potent insight, it's ultimately neither involving on a human level nor even very funny. JC-W

• *Ellis Moonsong* Chiwetel Ejiofor, *Hobie* Will Ferrell, *Lee* Jonny Lee Miller, *Melinda* Radha Mitchell, *Susan* Amanda Peet, *Laurel* Chloë Sevigny, *Sy* Wallace Shawn, *Walt* Steve Carell, *Billy* Daniel Sunjata, *Stacey* Vinessa Shaw, *with* David Aaron Baker, Arija Barekis, Josh Brolin, Stephanie Roth Haberle, Shalom Harlow, Geoffrey Nauffts, Zak Orth, Larry Pine, Brooke Smith, Neil Pepe, Matt Servitto, Andy Borowitz, Christina Kirk, Alyssa Pridham.

• *Dir* and *Screenplay* Woody Allen, *Pro* Letty Aronson, *Ex*

Pro Stephen Tenenbaum, *Co-Pro* Helen Robin, *Co-Ex Pro* Jack Rollins and Charles H. Joffe, *Ph* Vilmos Zsigmond, *Pro Des* Santo Loquasto, *Ed* Alisa Lepselter, *M* Stravinsky, J.S. Bach, Bartók; Duke Ellington, Erroll Garner, Dick Hyman, Barry White, *Costumes* Judy Ruskin Howell.

Fox Searchlight/Gravier Prods-Fox. 99 mins. USA. 2004. Rel: 25 March 2005. Cert. 12A.

Memories of Murder ★★★★★

One's never entirely sure where one is with this South Korean murder mystery and that is its compelling strength. Opening on a lyrical note, the film quickly switches to horror and bounces just as unexpectedly into farce. The fact is that such a major case, involving so many constabulary personnel, suspects and witnesses, is bound to run the gamut from horror to hilarity. At the time (1986) this was Korea's first multi-homicide and the local police of Gyeong-gi province were unprepared for such a historic and complex investigation. Director and co-writer Bong pulls no punches in some scenes but also brings a vivid humanity to the proceedings and constantly keeps his film out of the path of cliché. Thus, his cast of characters, while prone to predictable outbursts of violence and comic ineptitude, are ultimately rooted in a recognisable humanity and the film is all the richer for it. Credible, comic, illuminating and often quite disturbing, *Memories of Murder* is a thoroughly engrossing experience. JC-W

• *Det. Park Doo-man* Song Kang-ho, *Det. Seo Tae-yoon* Kim Sang-kyung, *Sgt. Koo Hee-bong* Byun Hee-bong, *Sgt. Shin Dong-chul* Song Jae-ho, *Det. Cho Yong-koo* Kim Rwe-ha, *Officer Kwon Kwi-ok* Koh Seo-hee, *Baek Kwang-ho, the village idiot* Park Noh-sik, *Chio Byung-soon* Ryu Tae-ho.

• *Dir* Bong Joon-ho, *Pro* Kim Moo-ryung, *Ex Pro* Lee Kang-bok and Tcha Seung-jae, *Screenplay* Bong and Shim Sung-bo, from a story by Kim Gwang-rim, *Ph* Kim Hyung-Ku, *Pro Des* Ryu Sung-hee, *Ed* Kim Sun-min, *M* Iwashiro Taro, *Costumes* Kim Yoo-sun.

CJ Entertainment/Sidus, etc-Optimum Releasing. 130 mins. South Korea. 2003. Rel: 13 August 2004. Cert. 15.

The Merchant of Venice ★★★★

Venice; 1596. Repeatedly spat upon by the Christian merchant Antonio, the Jewish moneylender Shylock contrives a devious contract when the latter turns to him to borrow 3000 ducats. Convinced that he will be able to repay the debt within three months, Antonio agrees to surrender a pound of his flesh should he forfeit… In addition to all his other talents, Shakespeare was a master at creating three-dimensional protagonists with their own point of view. It is a mark of the intelligence of Michael Radford's vivid adaptation that we care equally for the despised Shylock as we do for the confounded Antonio and his friend Bassanio. All victims of their own folly, these people are flesh-and-blood characters, registering both their flaws and their recognisable virtues. Sumptuously filmed on Luxembourg

The ancient grudge: Allan Corduner and Al Pacino in Michael Radford's resonant *The Merchant of Venice* (from Optimum Releasing)

and Venetian locations, the film is a marvellously cinematic and earthy rendition of the play, pruning the dialogue without losing its resonant poetry. Pacino's delivery of Shylock's 'Hath not a Jew eyes?' speech is moving without being melodramatic, while newcomer Lynn Collins is an outstanding Portia. FYI: This was the first production allowed to shoot inside the Doge's Palace. JC-W

• *Shylock* Al Pacino, *Antonio* Jeremy Irons, *Bassanio* Joseph Fiennes, *Portia* Lynn Collins, *Jessica* Zuleikha Robinson, *Gratiano* Kris Marshall, *Lorenzo* Charlie Cox, *Nerissa* Heather Goldenhersh, *Lancelot Gobbo* Mackenzie Crook, *Salerio* John Sessions, *Solanio* Gregor Fisher, *Old Gobbo* Ron Cook, *Tubal* Allan Corduner, *Prince of Morroco* David Harewood, *Prince of Aragon* Antonio Gil-Martinez, *with* Anton Rodgers, Al Weaver, Norbert Konne, Marc Maas.

• *Dir* and *Screenplay* Michael Radford, *Pro* Cary Brokaw, Barry Navidi, Jason Piette and Michael Lionello Cowen, *Ex Pro* Manfred Wilde, Michael Hammer, Peter James, James Simpson, Robert Jones and Alex Marshall, *Co-Pro* Nigel Goldsack, Jimmy de Brabant, Edwige Fenech, Luciano Martino and Istituto Luce, *Co-Ex Pro* Gary Hamilton, Pete Maggi and Julia Verdin, *Ph* Benoit Delhomme, *Pro Des* Bruno Rubeo, *Ed* Lucia Zucchetti, *M* Jocelyn Pook, *Costumes* Sammy Sheldon.

Movision Entertainment/Arclight Films/UK Film Council/Film Fund Luxembourg/Delux Prods/Immagine E Cinema/Dania Film/Spice Factory, etc-Optimum Releasing. 131 mins. UK/Italy. Rel: 3 December 2004. Cert. PG.

Merci Dr Rey ★★★

Owing an obvious debt to French bedroom farce, *Dr Rey* is a plot-loaded black comedy shot through with unexpected twists. Played absolutely straight by the male cast members (including, amazingly, Simon Callow), and played for high comedy by a trio of grand dames, the film is an unusual hybrid. A contemporary re-working of Molière, it trots out rent boys, a lesbian, hash brownies and a murder alongside such traditional conceits as mistaken identity, visual non-sequiturs and slapstick. An American opera diva (Wiest) is in Paris and is staying in an apartment she shares with Thomas, her 23-year-old son. She doesn't know he's homosexual and has a few secrets of her own to reveal, while Thomas becomes embroiled in murder and a fruitcake who thinks she's Vanessa Redgrave. To reveal more would be to spoil the confection, other than to say that the film is constantly intriguing if never entirely successful. Jane Birkin steals the show as Thomas' wacky confidante and there's a couple of very funny gendarmes, but the film's unevenness of tone and self-conscious camp does it no favours. JC-W

• *Elisabeth Beaumont* Dianne Wiest, *Penelope* Jane Birkin, *Thomas Beaumont* Stanislas Merhar, *Claude Sabrie* Bulle Ogier, *murderer* Karim Saleh, *Bob* Simon Callow, *police detective* Didier Flamand, *taxi driver* Roschdy Zem, *radio interviewer* Nathalie Richard, *rollerboy* Dan Herzberg, *Sybil* Jerry Hall, *herself* Vanessa Redgrave.

• *Dir* and *Screenplay* Andrew Litvack, *Pro* Ismail Merchant and Paul Bradley, *Ph* Laurent Machuel, *Pro Des* Jacques Bufnoir, *Ed* Giles Gardner, *M* Geoffrey Alexander,

Costumes Pierre-Yves Gayraud.

Merchant Ivory/East Your Soup-Parasol
Peccadillo Releasing.
96 mins. France/USA. 2003. Rel: 20 August 2004. Cert. 15.

Bull session: Joe Berlinger and Bruce Sinofsky eavesdrop on the boys from Metallica, in *Metallica: Some Kind of Monster* (from Tartan Films)

Metallica: Some Kind of Monster ★★★★

For those like myself not drawn to the heavy metal music scene, this documentary about the band Metallica may well seem at least a quarter of an hour too long (it lasts 140 minutes). But at the same time one recognises it as a classic of its kind which actually extends the boundaries of the genre. That's because this candid portrait of a band in the period from 2001 to 2003 shows the crises and problems when four musicians work together and then one leaves and another goes into rehab. No wonder the group need a therapist, and if his presence and manner lead to scenes that amuse (he's keen to assert that tensions are good because they can be creative!) the film is always sympathetic to the musicians without being heavy-handed. It's also adroitly directed and edited, even if only fans will treasure every moment. MS

• *with*: James Hetfield, Lars Ulrich, Kirk Hammett, Robert Trujillo, Zach Harmon, etc.

• *Dir* and *Pro* Joe Berlinger and Bruce Sinofsky, *Ph* Bob Richman, *Ed* Doug Abel and W. Watanabe Milmore.

@radical.media/Third Eye Motion Picture Company-Tartan Films.
140 mins. USA. 2004. Rel: 1 October 2004. Cert. 15.

Million Dollar Baby ★★★★½

The title is brutally misleading. A far more pertinent one would've been *Rope Burns*, the name of the book from which Eastwood's film is taken. There is no baby, and there is no million dollars, but there is cruelty, disillusion and death. Eastwood the actor is on commanding, charismatic form as Frankie Dunn, the grizzled owner of the Hit Pit Gym. A Yeats-reading, church-going man, Frankie has seen the dark side in the numerous years he has worked as a manager and trainer of boxers. But his over-protectiveness towards his fighters and his creed – 'Above all, protect yourself' – have held him back. Maggie Fitzgerald has little to lose when she approaches Frankie to train her, but he's not interested in 'girlies' – they're

too fragile. But then Frankie has never met anyone quite like Maggie... Dark, funny, poetic and uncompromisingly unsentimental, *Million Dollar Baby* is no *Rocky* meets *Girlfight*. This is a naturalistic drama about people of every moral hue and, with *Unforgiven* and *Mystic River*, is one of Eastwood's maturest fables yet. FYI: Production designer Henry Bumstead was 89 when he worked on this picture, his 12th collaboration with Eastwood. JC-W

• *Frankie Dunn* Clint Eastwood, *Maggie Fitzgerald* Hilary Swank, *Eddie 'Scrap-Iron' Dupris* Morgan Freeman, *Shawrelle Berry* Anthony Mackie, *Danger Barch* Jay Baruchel, *Big Willie Little* Mike Colter, *Billie 'The Blue Bear'* Lucia Rijker, *Father Horvak* Brian O'Byrne, *Earline Fitzgerald* Margo Martindale, *Mardell Fitzgerald* Riki Lindhome, *little girl in truck* Morgan Eastwood.

• *Dir* and *M* Clint Eastwood, *Pro* Eastwood, Albert S. Ruddy, Tom Rosenberg and Paul Haggis, *Ex Pro* Gary Lucchesi and Robert Lorenz, *Co-Pro* Bobby Moresco, *Screenplay* Haggis, based upon stories from *Rope Burns* by F.X. Toole, *Ph* Tom Stern, *Pro Des* Henry Bumstead, *Ed* Joel Cox, *Costumes* Deborah Hopper.

Warner/Lakeshore Entertainment/Malpaso/Ruddy Morgan-Entertainment.
132 mins. USA. 2004. Rel: 14 January 2005. Cert. 12A.

Millions ★★★★★

Children's films have either a habit of condescending to their target audience or being cynically one-dimensional. Not so *Millions*, a thematically complex yet narratively straightforward masterpiece from the director of *Trainspotting*. Imagining a world of magic in a marginally futuristic, suburban Britain, the film is blessed by finding the extraordinary in the ordinary (which children so often do) and by a child actor born to seduce the camera. Inventing a stylish new cinematic grammar with the aid of computer technology, director Boyle introduces us to the prelude to 'E-Day', when Britain is about to relinquish the pound in favour of the euro. Having just moved to a new housing estate after the death of his mother, young Damian is determined to make a good impression in his new environment. When he discovers a holdall crammed with 229,320 pound notes, he has just one week to spend the old money and sets off looking for 'the poor'... Juggling social commentary with magic realism, and buttressed by a strong storyline, *Millions* is an original and grown-up family film that is equal parts wondrous, funny, scary, thought-provoking and very moving. An instant classic. JC-W

• *Ronnie Cunningham* James Nesbitt, *Dorothy* Daisy Donovan, *Damian Cunningham* Alex Etel, *Anthony Cunningham* Lewis McGibbon, *'the poor man'* Christopher Fulford, *community policeman* Pearce Quigley, *Mum* Jane Hogarth, *himself* Leslie Phillips, *St Peter* Alun Armstrong, *St Francis* Enzo Cilenti, *a pot-smoking St Clare* Kathryn Pogson, *with* Nasser Memarzia, Harry Kirkham, Mark Chatterton, Frank Cottrell Boyce, John Nugent.

• *Dir* Danny Boyle, *Pro* Andrew Hauptman, Graham

Broadbent and Damian Jones, *Ex Pro* Francois Ivernel, Cameron McCracken, Duncan Reid and David M. Thompson, *Co-Pro* Tracey Seaward, *Screenplay* Frank Cottrell Boyce, *Ph* Anthony Dod Mantle, *Pro Des* Mark Tildesley, *Ed* Chris Gill, *M* John Murphy; songs performed by The Clash, Muse, Vangelis, S-Express, The Northwest Choir, and El Bosco, *Costumes* Susannah Buxton.

Pathé/Mission Pictures/Inside Track/UK Film Council/ BBC Films/National Lottery-Pathé.
98 mins. UK. 2004. Rel: 27 May 2005. Cert. 12A.

Milwaukee, Minnesota ★★★½

Milwaukee, Wisconsin; 2001. Albert Burroughs is different from other men. In his twenties, he still lives with his mother and knows his fish better than anyone. He can hear the fish talking under the ice and because of this faculty he has won hundreds of thousands of dollars from fishing tournaments. Then two unscrupulous outsiders – a travelling salesman and an opportunistic young woman – arrive in town. They subsequently square off against each other to take advantage of Albert's gullibility – and all that prize money... For a start, Milwaukee isn't in Minnesota, a fact that should give some indication of the offbeat nature of this film. And even as it hints at the Coens' *Fargo* and slips in a touch of *Forrest Gump* and *Rain Man* (Troy Garity, son of Jane Fonda, resembles a young Dustin Hoffman), the film is entirely its own animal. Anchored by a terrific story and fleshed out by a trio of stand-out performances from Garity, Bruce Dern and Randy Quaid (all with their own famous relatives), the movie manoeuvres its way deftly from *film noir* to something entirely more poetic. JC-W

• *Albert Burroughs* Troy Garity, *Tuey Stites* Alison Folland, *Sean McNally* Bruce Dern, *Stan Stites* Hank Harris, *Jerry James* Randy Quaid, *Edna Burroughs* Debra Monk, *Gary* Josh Brolin, *transvestite* Holly Woodlawn, *barfly* Suzanne Petri, *bartender* John Judd.

• *Dir* Allan Mindel, *Pro* Michael Brody and Jeff Kirshbaum, *Ex Pro* Frances Grill and Joseph Grill, *Co-Ex Pro* Barbara Karp, *Assoc Pro* Kim Moarefi and Helen Kallianiotes, *Screenplay* R.D. Murphy, *Ph* Bernd Heinl, *Pro Des* Dina Goldman, *Ed* David Rawlins, *M* Michael Convertino and Robert Muzingo, *Costumes* Michael Wilkinson, *Sound* Eric Marin, *Snowmaker* Dieter Sturm.

Framework Entertainment/Empire State Entertainment-Tartan Films.
95 mins. USA. 2002. Rel: 3 December 2004. Cert. 15.

The Miracle of Bern ★★½

This piece of feel-good film-making, enthusiastic rather than subtle, was a big hit in Germany. But since it is a celebration of West Germany's World Cup win over Hungary in 1954, the failure of the film to take off here is no surprise. Also included is an inept treatment of a potentially serious theme as an 11-year-old boy tries to adjust to the father he has

never known when the latter, a prisoner of war detained by the Russians, returns home and plays the disciplinarian. It's reasonably acted and father and son are portrayed by real-life father and son Peter Lohmeyer and Louis Klamroth, but it ends up as unbelievably sentimental make-believe on both the personal and sporting levels. Original title: *Das Wunder von Bern*. MS

• *Matthias Lubanski* Louis Klamroth, *Richard Lubanski* Peter Lohmeyer, *Christa Lubanski* Johanna Gastdorf, *Bruno Lubanski* Mirko Lang, *Ingrid Lubanski* Birthe Wolter, *with* Katharina Wackernagel, Lucas Gregorowicz, Peter Franke, Sascha Goepel, Knut Hartwig.

• *Dir* Sönke Wortmann, *Pro* Tom Spiess, Sönke Wortmann and Hanno Huth, *Co-Pro* Benjamin Herrmann, Stefan Gaertner and Alicia Remirez, *Screenplay* Wortmann and Rochus Hahn, *Ph* Tom Fährmann, *Pro Des* Uli Hanisch, *Ed* Ueli Christen, *M* Marcel Barsotti, *Costumes* Ursula Welter, *Sound* Dirk W. Jacob.

Little Shark Entertainment/Senator Film Produktion/ SevenPictures-Soda Pictures.
105 mins. Germany. 2003. Rel: 16 July 2004. Cert. PG.

Miss Congeniality 2: Armed and Fabulous ★½

Now a household face, field agent Gracie Hart repeatedly blows her cover on undercover stakeouts. So she can either push paper for the rest of her career or take on the offer of being the 'face of the FBI'. Ten months later and Gracie Hart has been transformed into a grating prima donna, cruising the chat show circuit and starring in book-signing photo ops. Then her good friend Cheryl – Miss United States – is kidnapped and Gracie wants in on the action... Come on Sandra, you can do better than this. At times resembling a latterday Michael Jackson and saddled with dreadful dialogue ('Do you have any idea how painful this is? They used to give an epidural for this kind of agony'), Sandra's Lucille Ball schtick has become sorrowful. Bland and brainless, *Armed and Fabulous* is like an offensive burp left over from the 1970s, with villains that sneer and a preening gay sidekick with all the best lines. JC-W

• *Gracie Hart* Sandra Bullock, *Sam Fuller* Regina King, *Jeff Foreman* Enrique Murciano, *Stan Fields* William Shatner, *Agent McDonald* Ernie Hudson, *Cheryl Frazier* Heather Burns, *Joel* Diedrich Bader, *Collins* Treat Williams, *Lou Steele* Abraham Benrubi, *Carol Fields* Eileen Brennan, *Tom Abernathy* Stephen Tobolowsky, *with* Nick Offerman, Elisabeth Röhm, Regis Philbin, Joy Philbin, Adam LeFevre, *drag queen* Dolly Parton, Megan Cavanagh, Frank Marino.

• *Dir* John Pasquin, *Pro* Marc Lawrence and Sandra Bullock, *Ex Pro* Mary McLaglen, John Kirby and Bruce Berman, *Co-Pro* Gesine Bullock-Prado, *Screenplay* Lawrence, *Ph* Peter Menzies, *Pro Des* Maher Ahmad, *Ed* Garth Craven, *M* Christophe Beck and Randy Edelman, *Costumes* Deena Appel.

Pink fuzz: Sandra Bullock and Regina King undercover in John Pasquin's sorrowful *Miss Congeniality 2: Armed and Fabulous* (from Warner)

Castle Rock/Village Roadshow/Fortis Films-Warner.
115 mins. USA. 2005. Rel: 25 March 2005.
Cert. 12A.

Mondays in the Sun ★★★½

Northern Spain; the present. When their shipyard closes due
to competition from Korea, six colleagues try to come to terms
with their unemployment. Meeting regularly at a local bar
(run by one of their own), the men discuss the injustices of the
world and then go home to the cruel reality of a future with
no guarantees... The subject is hardly a barrel of laughs, but
director León de Aranoa has brought a poignancy, compassion
and gentle humour to his disenfranchised characters which
makes it a privilege to spend time with them. And the film is
shot through with memorable, subtly delineated moments: Lino
dyeing his hair before a job interview (so that he looks suitably
younger); José's wife concealing her packed bags after a sudden
and rare moment of bonding with her husband; and Santa's
discovery of a colleague's heart-breaking poverty (after escorting
him home from the pub). The film is also elegantly unfolded,
its heartbeat never jarring or reaching for cheap sentimentality.
As social realism, it may lack the bite of, say, Ken Loach, but it
reverberates with a genuine humanity. Original title: *Los
lunes al sol.*
JC-W

• *Santa* Javier Bardem, *José* Luis Tosar, *Paulino* José Ángel
Egido, *Ana* Nieve de Medina, *Reina* Enrique Villén, *Amador*
Celso Bugallo, *Rico* Joaquín Climent, *Nata* Aida Folch, *Sergei*
Serge Riaboukine, *Angela* Laura Domínguez.

• *Dir* Fernando León de Aranoa, *Pro* Elías Querejeta and Jaume
Roures-Mediapro, *Co-Pro* Jérôme Vidal and Andrea Occhipinti,
Screenplay León de Aranoa and Ignacio del Moral, *Ph* Alfredo
Mayo, *Pro Des* Primitivo Alvaro Perez, *Ed* Nacho Ruiz Capillas,
M Lucio Godoy; Beethoven; songs performed by Charles Trenet,
and Tom Waits, *Costumes* Maiki Marín.

Sogepaq/Vía Digital/Eurimages,
etc-Feature Film Company.
113 mins. Spain/France/Italy. 2002. Rel: 27 May 2005.
Cert. 15.

Mondovino ★★★½

Although still over-long (this version lasting two and a quarter
hours has been cut down), this is a fascinating documentary
about the wine trade. Investigating the current situation in
that trade around the world but with France and Italy given
the greatest prominence, *Mondovino* shows commercially
minded conglomerates overshadowing those who care about the
individuality of the wines they produce. This we can recognise
as having a resonance that goes beyond the immediate context.
Visually this is what you might expect on TV, but many of
those featured, whether engaging or off-putting, are such
memorable individuals that they lift the film. It's certainly
not flawless but much of *Mondovino* is very appealing and
informative too. MS

• *Dir, Ph* and *Ed* Jonathan Nossiter, *Pro* Nossiter and
Emmanuel Giraud, *Ex Pro* Tommaso Vergallo, *Line Pro*
Catherine Hannoun.

Les Films de la Croisade/Goatwork Films-UGC Films UK
137 mins. France/USA. 2004. Rel: 10 December 2004.
Cert. PG.

Monster-in-Law ★½

After years without a man in her life, the remarkably
beautiful, sweet-natured Charlotte 'Charlie' Cantilini finds
her Prince Charming. Handsome, successful and unnaturally
attentive, Kevin Fields proposes to Charlie right in front of
his mother. The latter, having just lost her job as a top chat
show host, resolves to spend her new-found free time by
making Charlie's life as miserable as possible… It is perhaps
ironic that this piece of comic flotsam should open in the US
the same year as *Fun with Dick and Jane*. The latter happens
to be a remake of one of Jane Fonda's more inconsequential
comedies, but one that is nowhere near as bad as *Monster-
in-Law*. Marking Hanoi Jane's return to the cinema after an
absence of 15 years (her last film was Martin Ritt's *Stanley
& Iris*), *Monster-in-Law* is an unpleasant farce with a soft
head. Ms Fonda is the worst culprit, taking a caricature and
amplifying it a few hundred decibels, while Jennifer Lopez
is just vacuous. Thank God, then, for Elaine Stritch, who,
like the cavalry, storms in at the last minute to save the day.
Taking one look at La Fonda, she announces with a sonorous
voice, 'God, you look old!' It's the film's only truthful – and
genuinely funny – moment.
JC-W

• *Charlotte 'Charlie' Cantilini* Jennifer Lopez, *Viola Fields* Jane
Fonda, *Kevin Fields* Michael Vartan, *Ruby* Wanda Sykes, *Remy*
Adam Scott, *Fiona* Monet Mazur, *Morgan* Annie Parisse, *Kit*
Will Arnett, *Gertrude* Elaine Stritch, *with* Stephen Dunham,
Randee Heller, Mark Moses, Stephanie Turner.

• *Dir* Robert Luketic, *Pro* Paula Weinstein, Chris Bender and
JC Spink, *Ex Pro* Michael Flynn, Toby Emmerich and Richard
Brener, *Screenplay* Anya Kochoff, *Ph* Russell Carpenter, *Pro
Des* Missy Stewart, *Ed* Scott Hill and Kevin Tent, *M* David
Newman; songs performed by Etta James, Rosey, Jem,
Esthero, Nellie McKay, Rachael Yamagata, Astaire, Tegan
and Sara, Ivy, Joss Stone, Madeleine Peyroux, Magnet, Sara
Bareilles, and Dar Williams, *Costumes* Kym Barrett.

New Line Cinema/Benderspink/Spring Creek-
Entertainment.
101 mins. USA/Germany. 2005. Rel: 13 May 2005.
Cert. 12A.

Monster Man ★★

When Adam and Harley set off across country to prevent
the marriage of Adam's 'one true love' to another man, they
attract the attention of a monster truck-driving mutant
determined to add them to his collection of corpses. Make no
mistake, this is a terrible, terrible movie. It's also a *lot* of fun!
While there aren't many real scares, as a parody of the genre
(and even itself, on occasion), it revels in its own absurdity.
Eric Jungmann has real screen appeal, though Justin Urich's
Harley is so unfunny it's difficult not to end up hating the
actor as well. SWM

• *Adam* Eric Jungmann, *Harley* Justin Urich, *Sarah* Aimee
Brooks, *Brother Fred* Joe Goodrich, *monster man* Michael Bailey
Smith.

• *Dir* and *Screenplay* Michael Davis, *Pro* Yitzhak Ginsberg,
Ehud Bleiberg and Larry Ratner, *Ex Pro* Peter Block and
Moshe Peterburg, *Line Pro* Susan R. Rodgers, *Ph* Matthew
Irving, *Pro Des* Reuben A. Freed, *Ed* Kevin D. Ross, *M* John
Coda, *Costumes* Oneita Parker.

Bleiberg/Ginsberg/Lions Gate-Tartan Films.
91 mins. USA. 2003. Rel: 11 March 2005. Cert. 18

moog ★★★

It's a sign of the cinematic times that this acceptable but
totally unexceptional feature- length documentary should
obtain distribution here despite being of specialised interest.
Its subject is Bob Moog who, back in the 1960s, invented
the synthesiser named after him. This electronic instrument,
whether creating new sounds or imitating existing ones,
made its initial impact in classical music. It was then
taken up in commercials and achieved its greatest impact
in rock. The story is told by Moog himself and by his now
ageing colleagues (thus giving the film historical value).
Pop musicians such as Keith Emerson and Rick Wakeman
also appear. But, unless you treasure the contribution of the
synthesiser, this film makes a limited impact. Not many
years ago a directly comparable piece about another inventor/
instrument, *Theremin*, received a press show but significantly
never made it to our cinemas. MS

• *with:* Dr Robert A. 'Bob' Moog, Keith Emerson, Money
Mark, Mix Master Mike, Rick Wakeman, Stereolab, etc.

• *Dir, Screenplay* and *Ed* Hans Fjellestad, *Pro* Fjellestad and
Ryan Page, *Ex Pro* Gary Hustwit and Keith York, *Assoc Pro*
Adriana Trujillo, *Ph* Elia Lyssy and Daniel Kozman.

ZU33/Keyboard Magazine/KPBS Television-ICA
Projects.
70 mins. USA. 2004. Rel: 18 February 2005.
No cert.

Moolaadé ★★★★

Senegal's veteran filmmaker Ousmane Sembene is in his
eighties now but old age finds him displaying cinematic
mastery that makes everything seem direct and simple, as
it did with Visconti and is now doing with Eastwood. This
film's title refers to the protection given by the heroine to
four girls in her village community seeking to escape female
circumcision, which is still widely practised in Africa.
While thankfully eschewing scenes of surgery, this film is an
important statement on that subject but more besides. Its
story illustrates wider issues regarding the need for Africa to
embrace the modern world and to reject those traditions that
are bad. Unfortunately the last half-hour becomes drawn out
and repetitive in its message, but it remains an exceptional
film and one that shows African women in the vanguard of
change. US title: *Protection*. MS

American journey: Rodrigo De La Serna and
Gael García Bernal in Walter Salles's haunting
The Motorcycle Diaries (from Pathé)

• *Colle Ardo Gallo Sy* Fatoumata Coulibaly, *Hadjatou*
Maimouna Helene Diarra, *Amsatou* Salimata Traore, *Mercenaire*
Dominique T. Zeida, *Circumcision Elder* Mah Compaore, *Alima
Ba* Aminata Dao.

• *Dir* and *Screenplay* Ousmane Sembéne, *Ph* Dominique Gentil,
Pro Des Joseph Kpobly, *Ed* Abdellatif Raiss, *M* Boncana Maiga.

Filmi Doomirew/Direction de la Cinématographie
Nationale/Centre Cinematographique Marocain/
Cinetelefilms/Les Films de la Terre Africaine-Artificial
Eye.
124 mins. Senegal/Burkina Faso/Morocco/Tunisia/
Cameroon/Switzerland/Germany. 2004. Rel: 3 June 2005.
Cert. 15.

The Motorcycle Diaries ★★★½
Omar Sharif played him on screen in 1969 and Antonio
Banderas sung a loose interpretation of him in *Evita*, but
nobody has played Che Guevara like Gael García Bernal.
Produced by Robert Redford and drawn from the early journals
of Guevara and the biochemist Alberto Granado, this is actually
a road movie, a spirited hymn to the spirit of South America
(of 1952) punctuated by lashings of good humour and a lyrical
poignancy. It is the story of two Argentinean men, a 23-year-
old medical student (Ernesto Guevara) studying leprosy and a
29-year-old opportunist (Granado) who decide to travel round
the continent on a beat-up Norton 500 motorbike which
they christen The Mighty One. Their intent is to see the

world before they settle down to their respective lives. While
naturally episodic and often visually unprepossessing (the film
was largely shot on Super 16), *The Motorcycle Diaries* takes time
to cast its spell. It is in the second half, when the true face of
South America emerges through the stories of the indigenous
people, that the film comes into its own. At times adopting an
almost documentary-like realism – interspersed with living,
black-and-white photographs – *The Motorcycle Diaries* acquires
a poetic richness that is often disarming. JC-W

• *Ernesto 'Che' Guevara de la Serna* Gael García Bernal, *Alberto
Granado* Rodrigo De La Serna, *Chichina Ferreyra* Mía Maestro,
with Mercedes Morán, Susana Lanteri, Gustavo Bueno, Jorge
Chiarella, Igor Calvo.

• *Dir* Walter Salles, *Pro* Michael Nozik, Edgard Tenembaum
and Karen Tenkhoff, *Ex Pro* Robert Redford, Paul Webster
and Rebecca Yeldham, *Co-Pro* Daniel Burman and Diego
Dubcovsky, *Screenplay* José Rivera, *Ph* Eric Gautier, *Pro Des*
Carlos Conti, *Ed* Daniel Rezende, *M* Gustavo Santaolalla,
Costumes Beatriz Di Benedetto and Marisa Urruti.

FilmFour/South Fork Picturess/Tu Vas Voir-Pathé.
125 mins. USA/Argentina/Chile/Peru/UK/France. 2004.
Rel: 27 August 2004. Cert. 15.

Mr. and Mrs. Smith ★★
Movies don't come much dumber than this. Here, we're
expected to believe that a couple called John and Jane Smith

have been married for six years and don't know that each one of them happens to be a world-class assassin. John keeps his arsenal of state-of-the-art weaponry beneath the garden shed; Jane hides hers behind the oven. Jane also does all the cooking, which just shows how retro and superficial this supposedly high-concept conceit is. When the couple are assigned to kill each other, they don't bat an eyelid, as their marriage is a sham anyway. The trouble is, Brad Pitt and Angelina Jolie play Mr and Mrs Smith and they are both highly attractive people. The prospect of seeing them try to kill each other – and destroy their dream home in the process – is not exactly comfortable viewing. But then their characters are such cartoon ciphers, and the action sequences so preposterous, that it's hard to give a toss either way. It's a ludicrous premise, but it could've been given some wit – and some bite. Presumably, scenarist Simon Kinberg never saw *The War of the Roses*, a far more terrifying (and funny) battle of the sexes. JC-W

• *John Smith* Brad Pitt, *Jane Smith* Angelina Jolie, *Eddie* Vince Vaughn, *Benjamin Danz* Adam Brody, *Jasmine* Kerry Washington, *father* Keith David, *Martin Coleman* Chris Weitz, *Suzy Coleman* Rachael Huntley, *Gwen* Michelle Monaghan, *with* Stephanie March, Jennifer Morrison, Theresa Barrera, Perrey Reeves, Megan Gallagher, Jeff Yagher.

• *Dir* Doug Liman, *Pro* Arnon Milchan, Akiva Goldsman, Lucas Foster, Patrick Wachsberger and Eric McLeod, *Ex Pro* Erik Feig, *Co-Pro* Kim Winther, *Screenplay* Simon Kinberg, *Ph* Bojan Bazelli, *Pro Des* Jeff Mann, *Ed* Michael Tronick, *M* John Powell; Rossini; songs performed by Plastilina Mosh, Poison, Joe Strummer & The Mescaleros, Matt Hirt & Francisco Rodriguez, Ozomatli, Alana D, Magnet, Flogging Molly, Air Supply, etc, *Costumes* Michael Kaplan.

Regency Enterprises/New Regency/Summit Entertainment/Weed Road Pictures-Fox.
119 mins. USA. 2005. Rel: 10 June 2005. Cert. 15.

My Architect ★★★★

A voyage of discovery, a detective story and an appreciation of architecture, *My Architect* was deservedly nominated for an Oscar for Best Documentary. Sponsored by The New York Foundation for the Arts (and several other bodies), it is a personal, five-year journey undertaken by the documentarian Nathaniel Kahn to discover just who his father was. As it happens, Kahn's father, Louis I. Kahn, has been hailed as the most influential architect of the second half of the 20th century, an opinion supported by many of the director's interviewees. A Jewish immigrant from Estonia – and horribly disfigured from a childhood accident – Louis Kahn began his professional life as a drawing teacher and pianist for silent movies. As an architect, his career failed to take off until his fifties, when he designed a number of buildings praised for their 'geometric clarity and primitive power' as well as for their 'vigour and fundamentalism'. Others are less generous in their praise, one impartial onlooker dismissing a Kahn structure as looking like a bomb shelter. Perhaps more fascinating still is Kahn's private life, in that he maintained

three separate families and saw his only son, Nathaniel, only once a week at most. A riveting exploration, told with candour and humanity. JC-W

• *with*: Nathaniel Kahn, Louis I. Kahn, Philip Johnson, I.M. Pei, Edmund Bacon, Frank O. Gehry, Esther Kahn, Sue Ann Kahn, etc.

• *Dir* Nathaniel Kahn, *Pro* Kahn and Susan Rose Behr, *Ex Pro* Behr, Andrew S. Clayman and Darrel Friedman, *Ph* Bob Richman, *Ed* Sabine Krayenb hl, *M* Joseph Vitarelli; Beethove, Aaron Copland; songs performed by Stills-Young Band, Jefferson Airplane, Hank Williams, and The Holy Blossom Temple Singers.

The Louis Kahn Project/HBO/Climax Documentary Films-Tartan Films.
116 mins. USA. 2003. Rel: 13 August 2004. Cert PG.

My House in Umbria ★★★★

Umbria, Italy; the present. On her way by train to Milan for a shopping spree, the romance novelist Emily Delahunty makes a mental note of her fellow passengers. Then a 'timing device' derails the train, putting Emily into hospital along with a few survivors. Inviting three of the latter to convalesce at her house in Umbria, Emily revels in her new family, even if it is a somewhat damaged one. They are an elderly English general, a little American girl and a young German man – and all have lost their nearest and dearest in the blast… In the right material, Maggie Smith is an actress sublime – and seldom has a part fitted her talents so well. Adapted from the novel by William Trevor (who previously provided the narrative for *Fools of Fortune* and *Felicia's Journey*), *My House in Umbria* is an ensemble piece hinged on the indomitable Emily Delahunty. Fond of her grappa, the colourful milieu of her youth and her astrological insights, Delahunty is a character and a half, a wise old soul addicted to her own pleasures and helping others. Visually aesthetic and, beneath the social comedy, intellectually dense, *My House in Umbria* is a rare animal: a film that benefits from and complements its literary source. JC-W

• *Emily Delahunty* Maggie Smith, *Thomas Riversmith* Chris Cooper, *Quinty* Timothy Spall, *Werner* Benno Fürmann, *the General* Ronnie Barker, *Aimée* Emmy Clarke, *Inspector Girotti* Giancarlo Giannini, *Dr Innocenti* Libero de Rienzo, *Rosa Crevelli* Cecilia Dazzi, *Signora Bardini* Anna Longhi, *Phyllis* Deirdre Harrison, *Madeleine* Silvia de Santis.

• *Dir* Richard Loncraine, *Pro* Ann Wingate, *Ex Pro* Frank Doelger and Robert Allan Ackerman, *Co-Pro* Marco Valerio Pugini, *Screenplay* Hugh Whitemore, *Ph* Marco Pontecorvo, *Pro Des* Luciana Arrighi, *Ed* Humphrey Dixon, *M* Claudio Arrighi; songs performed by Sarah Vaughan, Dean Martin, Bing Crosby, Timothy Spall, Ray Charles, Cecilia Dazzi, and Andy Williams, *Costumes* Nicoletta Ercole.

HBO Films/Canine Films/Panorama Films-Momentum Pictures.

103 mins. UK/USA/Italy. 2003. Rel: 26 November 2004. Cert. 12A.

Mysterious Skin ★★

Hutchinson, Kansas/New York City; 1981-1992. In the summer of 1981, eight-year-old Brian Lackey loses five hours of his life and wakes up in the basement of his home with a nosebleed. He reckons he was abducted by aliens. Across town, little Neil McCormick falls for the Robert Redford looks of his new baseball coach and is invited back to the latter's pad for games and junk food. What happens to both boys is to inform their adolescence and to unite them 11 years later… Using mainstream actors and high-class production values, Gregg Araki pushes the boundaries of independent American cinema like few others. Bar actually showing the acts of sodomy, fellatio and masturbation, Araki makes it pretty clear what his young actors are simulating. But with his jumps from kitsch satire to sudden acts of brutal violence, he provides an uneven canvas for his dissection of America's sexually damaged youth. And by accentuating the poetic in his adaptation of Scott Heim's 1995 novel, he loses the plausible immediacy of a work like, say, *thirteen*, resulting in a somewhat stilted, distant and unpleasant cry for help. JC-W

• *Brian Lackey* Brady Corbett, *Neil McCormick* Joseph Gordon-Levitt, *Wendy Peterson* Michelle Trachtenberg, *Eric Preston* Jeff Licon, *Coach Heider* Bill Sage, *Ellen McCormick* Elisabeth Shue, *Avalyn Frieson* Mary Lynn Rajskub, *Mrs Lackey* Lisa Long, *Mr Lackey* Chris Mulkey, *young Brian* George Webster, *young Neil* Chase Ellison, *with* Richard Riehle, Billy Drago, Rachael Kraft, John Ganum.

• *Dir, Screenplay* and *Ed* Gregg Araki, *Pro* Araki, Mary Kane Skalski and Jeffrey Levy-Hinte, *Ex Pro* Wouter Barendrecht and Michael J. Werner, *Ph* Steve Gainer, *Pro Des* Devorah Herbert, *M* Harold Budd and Robin Guthrie, *Costumes* Alix Hester.

Fortissimo Films/Antidote Films/Desperate Pictures-Tartan Films.
99 mins. USA/Netherlands. 2004. Rel: 20 May 2005. Cert. 18.

My Summer of Love ★★★½

Yorkshire; the present. As her brother seeks redemption from Jesus, Mona turns to the friendly overtures of a local public schoolgirl, Tamsin. The girls could not be more different, but they discover in each other a mutual sense of rebellion and longing… Writer-director Pawel Pawlikowski makes extremely human, very real stories set in England with incredibly naff titles. *Last Resort* sounded like a Vin Diesel video reject, but was actually a forceful, uncompromising look at the asylum dilemma in contemporary Britain. *My Summer of Love* conjures up images of a Mills & Boon quickie, but is an authentic, resonant adaptation of Helen Cross' novel of the same name. Pawlikowski's strength is that he finds the truth in any given situation and has an astonishing ability to elicit nakedly honest performances from his actors. Here, he has coaxed markedly contrasting turns from two relatively inexperienced teenagers making their film debuts. Free from the ticks and mannerisms of received routine, Natalie Press and Emily Blunt are startling in that they so readily occupy the parts on paper. A character study of social contrast and sexual awakening, *My Summer of Love* rings frighteningly true while it seduces the viewer with forbidden worlds that just cannot be. JC-W

• *Mona/Lisa* Natalie Press, *Tamsin* Emily Blunt, *Phil* Paddy Considine, *Ricky* Dean Andrews, *Ricky's wife* Michelle Byrne, *Tamsin's father* Paul Antony-Barber, *Tamsin's mother* Lynette Edwards, *Sadie* Kathryn Sumner.

• *Dir* Pawel Pawlikowski, *Pro* Tanya Seghatchian and Christopher Collins, *Ex Pro* David M. Thompson, Chris Auty and Emma Hayter, *Screenplay* Pawlikowski and Michael Wynne, from the novel by Helen Cross, *Ph* Ryszard Lenczewski, *Pro Des* John Stevenson, *Ed* David Charap, *M* Alison Goldfrapp and Will Gregory; Saint-Saëns, Borodin, Mozart; songs performed by Goldfrapp, Edith Piaf, Gilberto Gil and Caetano Veloso, *Costumes* Julian Day.

BBC Films/Film Consortium/Baker Street/UK Film Council/Take Partnerships/Apocalypso-ContentFilm. 86 mins. UK. 2004. Rel: 22 October 2004. Cert. 15.

Napoleon Dynamite ★★½

Preston, Idaho; the present. It's an odd name for anybody, but when you're odd anyway it's as good as any. Napoleon Dynamite is not exactly skilled in the social graces, has developed a disconcerting bark when he speaks and still wets his bed. Yet he's verging on 17, lives with his grandmother, 32-year-old brother and a llama called Tina. In his spare moments, Napoleon sketches imaginary animals, enters milk-tasting tournaments and performs in sign-language sing-alongs. Yet does he have a talent to attract the opposite sex? As much a character study of Idaho as its socially arrested protagonist, *Napoleon Dynamite* is a prime example of *schadenfreude*. Virtually everybody on screen is weird, yet Preston native Jared Hess professes a bizarre affection for these misfits. A technically accomplished film, *Napoleon Dynamite* is a dry, piquant and often excruciating snapshot of the cultural bankruptcy of the director's own private Idaho. Admittedly a remarkable debut for one so young (Hess is just 24), the film would have been truly dynamite had a little more reality been allowed to filter through. As it is, its static tableaux and one-note quirkiness are minor pleasures that refuse to ignite. JC-W

• *Napoleon Dynamite* Jon Heder, *Uncle Rico* Jon Gries, *Kip Dynamite* Aaron Ruell, *Pedro* Efren Ramirez, *Rex Kwon Do* Diedrich Bader, *Deb* Tina Majorino, *Grandma* Sandy Martin, *Summer* Haylie Duff, *Don* Trevor Snarr, *LaFawnduh* Shondrella Avery, *with* Bracken Johnson, Carmen Brady, Ellen Dubin, Tom Lefler.

• *Dir* Jared Hess, *Pro* Jeremy Coon, Chris Wyatt and Sean C. Covel, *Ex Pro* Jory Weitz, *Screenplay* Jared Hess and Jerusha Hess, *Ph* Munn Powell, *Pro Des* Cory Lorenzen, *Ed* Coon, *M* John Swihart; songs performed by Steve Adams, Alphaville, Jamiroquai, Cyndi Lauper, Backstreet Boys, Penguin Café Orchestra, and When in Rome, *Costumes* Jerusha Hess.

Fox Searchlight/Paramount/Access Films-Fox.
95 mins. USA. 2004. Rel: 10 December 2004. Cert. PG.

Nathalie... ★★

Nathalie is a figment of the imagination. She is an invention
of the obstetrician Catherine, who is scheming to map out her
errant husband's sexuality. Having listened to his voice mail
and stumbled onto an affair, Catherine wants to know more.
Walking into a bar on a whim, she befriends a prostitute,
Marlène, and pays her to make contact with her husband
Bernard. Marlène is to be called Nathalie. However, 'Nathalie'
and Bernard take things a little further than Catherine had
hoped and by proxy Catherine herself embarks on a sexual
odyssey with her husband ... Oh, this is so typically French.
If they're not having sex, they're talking about it and there's
a lot of the latter in this cold, intellectual treatise. While the
concept is anything if not intriguing, it is processed in such a
dull, mechanical way that the characters are insulated in glass.
As Catherine, Fanny Ardant is a frigid, most unsympathetic
protagonist, shifting the audience's sympathy towards Bernard
and Marlène. The film itself is claustrophobic, defiantly uncinematic and inelegantly edited. JC-W

• *Catherine* Fanny Ardant, *Marlène* Emmanuelle Béart,
Bernard Gérard Depardieu, *François* Wladimir Yordanoff,
mother Judith Magre, *with* Rudolphe Pauly, Aurore Auteuil,
Idit Cebula.

• *Dir* Anne Fontaine, *Pro* Alain Sarde, *Ex Pro* Christine
Gozlan, *Screenplay* Fontaine, Jacques Fieschi and François-
Olivier Rousseau, based on an original script by Philippe
Blasband, *Ph* Jean-Marc Fabre, *Art Dir* Michel Barthélemy,
Ed Emmanuelle Castro, *M* Michael Nyman; Verdi; songs
performed by Amon Tobin, Pressure Drop, Koop, Leonard
Cohen, Sarah McLachlan, Joy Division, Goldfrapp, etc,
Costumes Pascaline Chevanne.

Les Films Alain Sarde/France 2 Cinéma/DD Prods/
Vertigo Films/Canal Plus-Momentum.
105 mins. France/Spain. 2003. Rel: 16 July 2004. Cert. 15.

National Treasure ★★★★

Arctic Circle/Washington DC/Philadelphia/New York City;
today. The latest in several generations of Gateses devoted to
finding the key to a historic treasure map, Benjamin Franklin
Gates stumbles across a pivotal clue which points to the back
of the Declaration of Independence. But how can a mere
fortune hunter gain access to America's most sacred – and
heavily safeguarded – document? Somehow, Gates must steal
the charter in order to preserve it, particularly as the nefarious
Ian Howe intends to swipe it for his own unscrupulous
ends... *National Treasure* has a number of strings to its bow
and for the most part plays them with engaging élan. After
a ropey start (set 'north of the Arctic Circle'), the film falls
into its stride as Nicolas Cage and his engaging cohorts
(the alluring Diane Kruger, the deftly comic Justin Bartha)
become involved in the ingenious theft of the Declaration of
Independence. Juggling gentle humour, thrilling escapes and
a genuine passion for the unsolved mysteries of history around

us, *National Treasure* is a rare beast in that it finds its pleasures
without resorting to profanity, violence or overbearing CGI
effects. And even with its plethora of public institutions,
underground catacombs and chase sequences, it has time for
some choice details (a cutaway of Diane Kruger's elevated foot
as her hostility for Cage melts away) and the odd memorable
line. JC-W

• *Benjamin Franklin Gates* Nicolas Cage, *Sadusky* Harvey
Keitel, *Patrick Gates* Jon Voight, *Abigail Chase* Diane Kruger,
Ian Howe Sean Bean, *Riley Poole* Justin Bartha, *John Adams
Gates* Christopher Plummer, *Shaw* David Dayan Fisher,
Shippen Oleg Taktarov, *with* Stewart Finlay-McLennan,
Stephen Pope, Annie Parisse, Mark Pellegrino, Don
McManus, Ron Canada, Arabella Field.

• *Dir* Jon Turteltaub, *Pro* Turteltaub and Jerry Bruckheimer,
Ex Pro Mike Stenson, Chad Oman, Christina Steinberg,
Barry Waldman, Oren Aviv and Charles Segars, *Screenplay*
Jim Kouf, Marianne Wibberley and Cormac Wibberley, from
a story by Kouf, Aviv and Segars, *Ph* Caleb Deschanel, *Pro
Des* Norris Spencer, *Ed* William Goldenberg, *M* Trevor Rabin,
Don Harper and Paul Linford; Haydn, *Costumes* Judianna
Makovsky.

Walt Disney Pictures/Jerry Bruckheimer Films/Junction
Entertainment-Buena Vista International.
130 mins. USA. 2004. Rel: 26 December 2004. Cert. PG.

New Town Original ★★★

Jason Ford's deeply committed movie set in Basildon and
made on a shoe-string budget echoes *Boston Kickout*, made
a decade ago about the limited opportunities   for young
people in Stevenage. Both films invite a warm audience
response. Even so, it has to be said that *New Town Original*
suffers from seeking to manipulate its viewers by juggling
with the material that provides its climactic scene (it doesn't
play fair) and by making too heavy demands on debut
actor Elliott Jordan to hold it all together. But, despite
my reservations, I am delighted to know that the film has
played well to young audiences responding favourably to a
movie that deals with adolescence without concentrating
on drug-taking or hooliganism. Katharine Peachey strikes
the right note as the girl whose attraction to the hero seems
to endanger him, and for a cheaply made feature the sound
quality is admirable. MS

• *Mick* Elliott Jordan, *Johnno* Nathan Thomas, *Nicki*
Katharine Peachey, *Ozzy* Richard Gooch, *Bal* Kal Aise, *Si
Naylor* Paul Mcneilly, *with* Steve Gibbs, Terry Bird, Jamie
Palmer, Jason Ford.

• *Dir* and *Screenplay* Jason Ford, *Pro* Terry Bird and Jamie
Palmer, *Ph* Fiachra Judge, *Pro Des* and *Costumes* Lisa Crawley,
Ed Emile Guertin, *M* Eudemonic.

New Town Films/Screen East-New Town Films.
88 mins. UK. 2000. Rel: 15 April 2005.
Cert. 15.

New York Minute ★★

Feuding twins Jane and Roxy Ryan head into Manhattan for the day hoping to fulfil their disparate dreams. Preppie sister Jane wants to win a college scholarship while punk wannabe Roxy plots to slip her demo tape to her favourite band. A misplaced day-planner, a stolen computer chip and a pork roll-loving dog add up to just the sort of high jinx for which both New York and pretty teens are notorious. Mary-Kate and Ashley Olsen demonstrate the ready confidence that can only come from having spent an entire life on camera. What they don't demonstrate is the talent necessary to make the transition from child media darlings to genuine actors. They are also crippled by a derivative, unoriginal and poorly conceived script that does nothing for the girls and merely invokes far better movies. SWM

• *Roxy Ryan* Mary-Kate Olsen, *Jane Ryan* Ashley Olsen, *Max Lomax* Eugene Levy, *Bennie Bang* Andy Richter, *Trey Lipton* Jared Padalecki, *Jim* Riley Smith, *Senator Anne Lipton* Andrea Martin, *with* Darrell Hammond, Alannah Ong, Bob Saget, the voice of Frank Welker (as Reinaldo).

• *Dir* Dennie Gordon, *Pro* Denise Di Novi, Robert Thorne, Mary-Kate Olsen and Ashley Olsen, *Ex Pro* Alison Greenspan, *Co-Pro* Christine A. Sacani and Jill Zimmerman, *Screenplay* Emily Fox, Adam Cooper and Bill Collage, *Ph* Greg Gardiner, *Pro Des* Michael Carlin, *Ed* Michael Jablow and Roderick Davis, *M* George S. Clinton

Warner/Dualstar Prods/Di Nova Pictures-Warner.
90 mins. USA. 2004. Rel: 30 July 2004. Cert. PG.

La niña santa

See *The Holy Girl*.

9 Songs ★

On a visit to the Antarctic, Matt reflects on the autumn he spent with Lisa, an American student in London. In between their bouts of sexual reconnaissance, they attend eight concerts together, while Matt goes to a ninth on his own… Indie rock meets *National Geographic* with a little bit of hardcore sex thrown in. This is not an entirely uninteresting idea for a movie, although it falls down on all counts. The concert footage – featuring Primal Scream, The Dandy Warhols and Franz Ferdinand – is amazingly dull, the Antarctic stuff sub-industrial and the sex, well, grainy. As it happens, this was a wonderful opportunity to make a no-holds-barred adult drama. But the unremarkable couple – with little personality or credible connection – and the love story they inhabit, lack context. Even most porn films have a semblance of a plot. JC-W

• *Matt* Kieran O'Brien, *Lisa* Margo Stilley, *with* Black Rebel Motorcycle Club, The Von Bondies, Elbow, Primal Scream, The Dandy Warhols, Super Furry Animals, Franz Ferdinand, Michael Nyman.

• *Dir* Michael Winterbottom, *Pro* Andrew Eaton, *Assoc Pro* Melissa Parmenter, *Screenplay* improvised, *Ph* Marcel Zyskind,

Ed Winterbottom and Mat Whitecross, *M* Black Rebel Motorcycle Club, The Von Bondies, Salif Keita, Elbow, Primal Scream, Melissa Parmenter, The Dandy Warhols, Goldfrapp, Super Furry Animals, Franz Ferdinand, and Michael Nyman, *Costumes* very few.

Revolution Films-Optimum Releasing.
70 mins. UK. 2004. Rel: 11 March 2005. Cert. 18.

Nobody Knows ★★★½

Many Japanese films are long and slow but rightly so. This one, however, also suffers from an even tone throughout and is a portrayal of a kind of limbo. We observe as a 12-year-old boy (award winner Yuja Yagiro) looks after his three younger siblings, burdened by a neglectful mother who eventually abandons them. This downbeat storyline derived from real life unexpectedly celebrates the togetherness of the group and those moments when ordinary childhood pleasures such as partaking in sport become possible. This mixture makes for a tale about the need for human contact that is both uplifting and tragic by turns, and the performances by the whole cast are magnificent. Sadly, however, that slow pace, maintained for every one of the film's 141 minutes, makes this something of an ordeal to sit through in spite of its qualities. MS

• *Akira* Yuya Yagira, *Kyoko* Ayu Kitaura, *Shigeru* Hiei Kimura, *Yuki* Momoko Shimizu, *Saki* Hanae Kan, *Keiko, the mother* You.

• *Dir, Pro* and *Screenplay* Kore-eda Hirokazu, *Ex Pro* Shigenobu Yutaka, *Ph* Yamazaki Yutaka, *Ed* Kore-eda Hirokazu, *M* GONTITI.

TV Man Union/Bandai Visual Co/Engine Film/c-style/Cine Qua Non-ICA Projects.
141 mins. Japan. 2004. Rel: 5 November 2004. Cert. 12A.

Notre Musique ★

'Our music,' Godard would seem to attest, is the nature of our duality and confrontation. This visual notebook of newsreel footage, Hollywood clips, interviews and Sarajevo travelogue is another typically abstruse contemplation from the now experimental filmmaker. Nothing is straightforward – his subjects are filmed in silhouette or from behind, the screen goes blank, questions are left unanswered. In short, *Notre Musique* is infuriatingly self-indulgent and wilfully incoherent. Divided into three chapters – 'Kingdom 1: Hell,' 'Kingdom 2: Purgatory' and 'Kingdom 3: Heaven' – it seems to delight in its randomness, touching on the inescapability of war, the human condition and the filmmaking process itself. JC-W

• *himself* Jean-Luc Godard, *Judith Lerner* Sarah Adler, *Olga Brodsky* Nade Dieu, *himself* Juan Goytisolo, *himself* Mahmoud Darwich, etc.

• *Dir* and *Screenplay* Jean-Luc Godard, *Pro* Alain Sarde, *Ph* Julien Hirsch and Jean-Christophe Beauvallet, Izet Kutlovac, Blaise Bauquis and Fabrice Deqeant.

Alain Sarde/Ruth Waldburger/Avventura Films/Peripheria/

France 3 Cinéma/Vega Film/Canal Plus/TSR/DFI-Optimum Releasing.
79 mins. France/Switzerland. 2004. Rel: 20 May 2005. Cert. 12A.

Ocean's Twelve ★★★½

Danny Ocean is preparing to celebrate his wedding anniversary with his wife Tess. Then Terry Benedict catches up with him. Actually, Benedict has caught up with all ten of Danny's associates-in-crime and has given them two weeks to cough up $19 million each (which will repay the money they stole from Benedict's casino vault – plus interest). If they fail to meet his deadline, Benedict will have them killed. But Danny's men are too well known in the US to carry off any major heist with impunity, so they relocate to Amsterdam, Rome, Paris... Sequels more often than not suffer from repetition and excess. *Ocean's Twelve*, a sequel of a remake, no less, suffers from both. Thus, Danny's associates are involved in another fabulous scam and there are even more locations and stars (two uncredited). Yet Soderbergh's direction is so effortlessly self-assured and his actors so sexy and confident, that you just don't want it to stop. Actually a marriage of a John Woo project called *Honor Among Thieves* and a fresh tack by Soderbergh, the ingredients fall neatly into place as the audacious plot unfolds. Eminently stylish, sophisticated and low-key, the film is distinguished by a loose narrative style that disguises a highly disciplined scenario. Even so, there are maybe too many colourful characters (the commanding Jeroen Krabbé appears in just one shot), too many seductive interiors and too many luscious locations; it's hard to keep track of the tortuous story. JC-W

• *Danny Ocean* George Clooney, *Rusty Ryan* Brad Pitt, *Linus Caldwell* Matt Damon, *Isabel Lahiri* Catherine Zeta-Jones, *Terry Benedict* Andy Garcia, *Basher Tarr* Don Cheadle, *Frank Catton* Bernie Mac, *Tess Ocean* Julia Roberts, *Virgil Malloy* Casey Affleck, *Turk Malloy* Scott Caan, *François Toulour* aka *'The Night Fox'* Vincent Cassel, *Livingston Dell* Eddie Jemison, *Saul Bloom* Carl Reiner, *Reuben Tishkoff* Elliott Gould, *Yen* Shaobo Qin, *Matsui* Robbie Coltrane, *Roman Nagel* Eddie Izzard, *Molly Starr* aka *Mrs Caldwell* Cherry Jones, *van der Woude* Jeroen Krabbé, *with* Jared Harris, Jerry Weintraub, David Lindsay, Al Faris, Candice Azzara, and (uncredited) *Gaspar Le Marque* Albert Finney, *himself* Bruce Willis.

• *Dir* Steven Soderbergh, *Pro* Jerry Weintraub, *Ex Pro* John Hardy, Susan Ekins and Bruce Berman, *Screenplay* George Nolfi, based on characters created by George Clayton Johnson and Jack Golden Russell, *Ph* Peter Andrews (aka Steven Soderbergh), *Pro Des* Philip Messina, *Ed* Stephen Mirrione, *M* David Holmes, *Costumes* Milena Canonero.

Warner/Village Roadshow Pictures/JW/Section Eight-Warner.
125 mins. USA. 2004. Rel: 4 February 2005. Cert. 12A.

Oldboy ★★★½

Chan-wook Park's Cannes prize-winner is a Korean film about a man seeking revenge after being kept a prisoner for 15 years. What event in his past accounts for his being kidnapped and incarcerated? Once free again he hopes to trace the person responsible and the way to do this is to find the answer to that question. There's a fine performance from Choi

Danny's dozen: Matt Damon, Brad Pitt and George Clooney in Steven Soderbergh's self-assured, audacious *Ocean's Twelve* (from Warner)

Min-sik (so different a presence in *Chihwaseon*) and the film has real impact. Even so, nothing can disguise the improbabilities of the plot, while the excessive violence takes it over the top and then some. Nevertheless, the film making has a quality that puts one in mind of Shakespearean or Jacobean tragedy and this could eventually become a cult classic. MS

• *Oh Dae-su* Min-sik Choi, *Lee Woo-jin* Yoo Ji-tae, *Mido* Gang Hye-jeong, *Mr Han, chief guard* Kim Byoung-ok, *No Joo-hwan* Chi Dae-han, *Park Cheol-woong* Oh Dal-sue.

• *Dir* Chan-wook Park, *Pro* Kim Dong-joo, *Ex Pro* Kim Jang-wook, *Co-Pro* Syd Lim, *Screenplay* Hwang Jo-yoon, Im Joon-hyung and Chan-wook Park, *Ph* Jung Jung-hoon, *Art Dir* Yoo Seong-hee, *Ed* Kim Sang-bum and Kim Jae-bum, *M* Shim Hyun-jung and Lee Ji-soo, *Costumes* Cho Sang-kyung, *Sound* Lee Sung-jin, *Martial Arts Dir* Yang Gil-young.

ShowEast-Tartan Films.
120 mins. South Korea. 2003. Rel: 15 October 2004.
Cert. 18.

One for the Road ★★★½
Chris Cooke's first feature was shot in Nottingham and is at heart a tragi-comedy sometimes reminiscent of the early work of Mike Leigh. Three youths charged with drunk driving are made to participate in an alcohol management course and there encounter an older rich probationer, Richard Stevens. They plan to take advantage of him but, although they adopt the language of wheeler dealers, it is apparent they are really conning themselves, for it is obvious that their plans will never succeed and save them from their drab existence. Despite good acting from all (among the youngsters it's Greg Chisholm who stands out), the effectiveness of the film's humour, central in the first half, will be a matter of taste, but the darker it gets the more telling the piece becomes. MS

• *Paul* Rupert Proctor, *Jimmy* Greg Chisholm, *Mark* Mark Devenport, *Richard Stevens* Hywel Bennett, *Liz* Julie Legrand, *with* Micaiah Dring, Jonny Phillips, Johann Myers.

• *Dir* and *Screenplay* Chris Cooke, *Pro* Kate Ogborn, *Ex Pro* Peter Carlto, Paul Trijbits and Robin Gutch, *Co-Pro* Helen Solomon and Alexander O'Neal, *Ph* N.G. Smith, *Pro Des* Jason Carlin, *Ed* Nick Fenton, *M* Steve Blackman, *Costumes* Claire Finlay.

EMMI/UK Film Council/FilmFour/National Lottery-Tartan Films.
96 mins. UK. 2003. Rel: 2 July 2004.
Cert. 18.

Ong-Bak ★★★½
When the head of a sacred Buddha is stolen from a village, it falls to local champion Ting to travel to Bangkok and retrieve the head of Ong-bak. Ting employs traditional Muay Thai, Tae Kwon Do, swordplay and gymnastics – which he learned as passive arts from the monks who raised him – to gruesome effect in his task… This is a dramatic return to more traditional martial arts films in the style of Bruce Lee. Simple in story but

enthralling with its incredible fight scenes, *Ong-Bak* utilises neither the wire-work nor CGI enhancements that have become the hallmark of modern Asian cinema. Focusing on realism, the movie was made by director Pinkaew solely to showcase Tony Jaa's amazing martial arts skills. If violence can be considered an art form, then this is indeed a masterpiece. SWM

• *Ting* Tony Jaa, *George* Petchai Wongkamlao, *Muay Lek* Pumwaree Yodkamol, *Ngek* Rungrawee Borrijindakul, *Peng* Chetwut Wacharakun, *Don* Wannakit Siriput.

• *Dir* Prachya Pinkaew, *Pro* Prachya Pinkaew and Sukanya Vongsthapat, *Ex Pro* Somsak Techaratanaprasert, *Screenplay* Suphachai Sithiamphan, *Ph* Natawut Kittikun, *Pro Des* Akhadaet Kaewchote, *Ed* Thanat Sunsin, *M* Atomix Clubbing Studio, *Martial Arts/Stunt Choreography* Phanna Rithikrai and Tony Jaa.

Sahamongkol Film/Baa-Ram Ewe-Premier Asia.
108 mins. Thailand. 2003. Rel: 13 May 2005. Cert. 18.

Only Human ★★★
Madrid; the present. Rafi is a Palestinian academic and is about to be introduced to the family of his Jewish girlfriend, Leni. In a complete sweat, he changes his shirt in the elevator and then makes love to Leni to relieve the tension. Upstairs, Leni's family – her neurotic mother, senile grandfather, devout brother, jealous sister and eccentric niece – are unprepared for an evening that is about to escalate into high melodrama… Farce is a notoriously hard genre to pull off, but the husband-and-wife team of Teresa de Pelegrí and Dominic Harari have managed to fashion a delightful conceit with credible, engaging characters. While observing such staple ingredients of the form as mistaken identities, abundant misunderstandings and even the misplacement of trousers, the film retains a sense of reality that really fuels the humour. Every family is abnormal in its own way, and any series of well-intentioned acts can backfire at a moment's notice. Even an attempt to defrost a block of frozen soup… Instantly forgettable, but sweet. Original title: *Seres queridos*. JC-W

• *Gloria Dalinsky* Norma Aleandro, *Rafi* Guillermo Toledo, *Leni Dalinsky* Marián Aguilera, *Tania Dalinsky* María Botto, *David Dalinsky* Fernando Ramallo, *Paula Dalinsky* Alba Molinero, *Dudu Dalinsky* Max Berliner, *Ernesto Dalinsky* Mario Martín.

• *Dir* and *Screenplay* Teresa de Pelegrí and Dominic Harari, *Pro* Gerardo Herrero, Javier Lopez and Blanco Mariela Besuievsky, *Ex Pro* Mariela Besuievsky, *Co-Pro* Patrick Cassavetti, Adrian Sturges, Pablo Bossi and Paulo Branco, *Assoc Pro* Robert Jones, *Ph* Danny Cohen, *Art Dir* Soledad Sesena, *Ed* Fernando Pardo, *M* Charlie Mole, *Costumes* Estibaliz Markigui.

Tornasol Films/Greenpoint Films/Patagonik Film Group/UK Film Council/Canal Plus España/National Lottery, etc-Verve Pictures.
89 mins. Spain/UK/Argentina/Portugal. 2004.
Rel: 20 May 2005. Cert. 15.

without them. Stranded in open water – out of sight of land – the couple start their wait for rescue. At times almost unbearable to watch, the film has the raw power of an aquatic *Blair Witch Project* with all hints of Hollywood artifice scraped raw. Gulp. JC-W

• *Susan* Blanchard Ryan, *Daniel* Daniel Travis, *Seth* Saul Stein, *Estelle* Estelle Lau, *Davis* Michael E. Williamson, *Linda* Cristina Zenaro.

• *Dir, Screenplay* and *Ed* Chris Kentis, *Pro* Laura Lau, *Assoc Pro* Estelle Lau, *Ph* Kentis and Laura Lau, *M* Graeme Revell and Nathan Barr, *Sound* Glenn T. Morgan.

Plunge Pictures-Redbus Film Distribution.
79 mins. USA. 2004. Rel: 9 September 2004. Cert. 15.

Open Water ★★★½

On many levels, there has never been a film like *Open Water*. For a start, this is a major release written, produced, directed, photographed and edited by a married couple, with just the wife's sister completing the intimate crew. Filmed on a DVD camera over weekends and holidays and primarily featuring two unknown actors, *Open Water* is all the more remarkable for being shot entirely on location without a single special or digital effect. Inevitably, there is a certain rawness in the acting and camera set-ups, but once the story kicks in the film takes on an extraordinary hold. Inspired by a true story, it focuses on a workaholic American couple who squeeze a one-week vacation into their busy schedules. Opting for a scuba-diving break, Daniel and Susan end up at an exotic holiday resort equipped to sample the wonders of the deep. On their first day they set off with a local diving outfit but while they are still underwater the boat returns to port

The Pacifier ★★½

A ruthless Navy SEAL is assigned to babysit a quintet of unruly kids as he hunts their house for a vital nuclear deactivator… If *Kindergarten Cop* hadn't made over $200 million, then maybe we would've been spared this automated popcorn filler. As it is, all the dirty diaper, bullied teenager and lethal toy devices are trotted out, all to the accompaniment of a possessed military orchestra. There's also a feeling of another movie having been cut out of the picture: what is the significance of the reappearing troll (which then disappears) and what happened to Carol Kane's double agent (who resurfaces unannounced in a final scene)? These brickbats aside, Vin Diesel is to be commended for playing his role straight (in contrast to Arnold's grimacing attempts

Child's play: Vin Diesel and tot in Adam Shankman's automated *The Pacifier* (from Buena Vista International)

at all-out farce), while there are a number of choice moments: not least a nicely resolved confusion over neo-Nazism and a scene in which Diesel learns a bedtime dance in order to get one of his charges to sleep. JC-W

• *Shane Wolfe* Vin Diesel, *Principal Claire Fletcher* Lauren Graham, *Julie Plummer* Faith Ford, *Zoe Plummer* Brittany Snow, *Seth Plummer* Max Thieriot, *Helga* Carol Kane, *Vice Principal Murney* Brad Garrett, *with* Chris Potter, Morgan York, Tate Donovan, Denis Akiyama, Mung-Ling Tsui, Evelyn Kaye.

• *Dir* Adam Shankman, *Pro* Roger Birnbaum, Gary Barber and Jonathan Glickman, *Ex Pro* Shankman, Jennifer Gibgot, Derek Evans, Garrett Grant and George Zakk, *Screenplay* Thomas Lennon and Robert Ben Garant, *Ph* Peter James, *Pro Des* Linda DeScenna, *Ed* Christopher Greenbury, *M* John Debney, *Costumes* Kirston Mann.

Walt Disney Pictures/Spyglass Entertainment-Buena Vista International.
95 mins. USA. 2005. Rel: 27 May 2005.
Cert. PG.

Palindromes ★★★½

Once again Todd Solondz, the director of *Welcome to the Dollhouse*, *Happiness* and *Storytelling*, has created a diversion designed to shock. On one level, *Palindromes* is a comedy about child molestation. On another, it is a decidedly un-PC polemic that challenges the innate stereotyping of conventional cinema. Aviva (yes, her name is a palindrome) is a young girl who craves to be a mother. In the film's opening scene, she is portrayed as a pudgy black girl, whose own mother is played by the decidedly blonde Ellen Barkin. Next, Aviva is white, 13 years old and impregnated in perhaps the least romantic coupling ever caught on camera. As the film progresses, Aviva changes shape and colour as she leaves home and gets a taste for casual intercourse. Along the way, Solondz introduces us to a raft of characters balanced precariously on the fringes of normality, be they dwarf, albino or boy with Down's syndrome. Solondz seems to be aiming for a strain of cheap black humour, but more likely he is poking fun at our own discomfort at accepting the disabled as figures of high comedy. Any film that questions an audience's preconceptions is to be applauded, and *Palindromes*, dodgy acting and all, is maybe more than just an intellectual exercise. JC-W

• *Joyce Victor* Ellen Barkin, *Joe/Earl/Bob* Stephen Adly Guirgis, *Steve Victor* Richard Masur, *Aviva* Jennifer Jason Leigh/Emani Sledge/Valerie Shusterov/Hannah Freiman/Rachel Corr/Will Denton/Sharon Wilkins/Shayna Levine, *Mama Sunshine* Debra Monk, *Mark Wiener* Matthew Faber, *Judah* Robert Agri/John Gemberling, *Dr Fleischer* Stephen Singer, *Peter Paul* Alexander Brickel, *Bo Sunshine* Walter Bobbie, *Dr Dan* Richard Riehle.

• *Dir* and *Screenplay* Todd Solondz, *Pro* Mike S. Ryan and Derrick Tseng, *Ph* Tom Richmond, *Pro Des* Dave Doernberg, *Ed* Mollie Goldstein and Kevin Messman, *M* Nathan Larson; songs written by Eytan, Matthew Brookshire and Curtis Moore, *Costumes* Victoria Farrell.

Celluloid Dreams/Extra Large Pictures-Tartan Films.
99 mins. USA/France. 2004. Rel: 6 May 2005.
Cert. 15.

Paparazzi ★½

When up-and-coming star Bo Laramie is hounded by four bottom-feeding paparazzi to the point of his family nearly being killed in a car chase (à la Princess Diana), he exacts revenge on each of them in turn… This is obviously the fantasy of many celebrities and several turn up in cameos (including Mel Gibson and Matthew McConaughey). What it lacks is any sort of moral centre. Yes, it's clear that some members of the paparazzi are the worst form of human garbage. However, crafting the murder of each of them in turn hardly uplifts the Bo Laramie character, especially since his entire family survives the 'final straw' accident that starts Bo's vendetta. *Pitch Black*'s Cole Hauser does credible work here but it's really only Dennis Farina's Columbo impersonation that stands out. SWM

• *Bo Laramie* Cole Hauser, *Abby Laramie* Robin Tunney, *Detective Burton* Dennis Farina, *Wendell Stokes* Daniel Baldwin, *Leonard Clark* Tom Hollander, *Kevin Rosner* Kevin Gage, *Zach Laramie* Blake Bryan, *Rex Harper* Tom Sizemore, *Emily* Andrea Baker, *Dr Kelley* Jordan Baker, *Reggie* Duane Davis, *pizza delivery guy* Chris Rock, *with* Lauren Birkell, Larry Cedar, Dennis Cockrum, Donal Gibson, Clyde Kusatsu, Fay Masterson, Brian McNamara, Tim Thomerson, Mel Gibson, Vince Vaughn, Matthew McConaughey.

• *Dir* Paul Abascal, *Pro* Mel Gibson, Bruce Davey and Stephen McEveety, *Ex Pro* Louise Rosner, *Screenplay* Forrest Smith, *Ph* Daryn Okada, *Pro Des* Robb Wilson King, *Ed* Robin Russell, *M* Brian Tyler, *Costumes* Denise Wingate, *Sound* George Simpson.

Icon/Fox-Icon.
84 mins. USA. 2004. Rel: 28 January 2005. Cert. 15.

Paradise Grove ★★

Ron Moody shines as a man approaching 80 in a North London retirement home. But this Jewish comedy is so ineptly conceived that he cannot save it. Nor will it help the career of promising newcomer Leyland O'Brien, who plays Moody's teenage grandson. The fact that the latter is half-black and half-Jewish invites insights into issues of identity in Britain's multi-cultural modern society, but they are not forthcoming. Instead we have stereotypical comic takes on old age, a totally improbable subplot about a professional assassin and a feel-good treatment of euthanasia! It's such a mess that one might declare that the biggest mystery is how the script ever got filmed, but the fact is that there's a greater mystery still: how this film, which has been on the shelf for a few years, actually came to win awards. MS

• *Izzie Goldberg* Ron Moody, *Dee Perry* Rula Lenska, *Kim Wright* Lee Blakemore, *Keith Perry* Leyland O'Brien, *Garrison Moss* Andy Lucas, *Dr Norman* John Cunningham, *Annie Libowitz* Leelo Ross, *with* Georgette Pallard, Anita Reynolds, Charles Simon.

• *Dir* and *Screenplay* Charles Harris, *Pro* David Castro, *Co-Pro* Harris, James Burke-Murphy and Michael Brooke, *Assoc Pro* Elaine Harris and Elke Hundertmark, *Ph* Miles Cook, *Pro Des* Alice Herrick, *Ed* John Hackney, *M* Roddy Skeaping, *Costumes* Leila Ransley.

Paradise Grove plc-Storyline Distribution.
93 mins. UK. 2002. Rel: 20 May 2005. Cert. 15.

Paradise is Somewhere Else ★★★½

Iran's Abdolrarsoul Golbon is a writer/director who eschews the minimalism of so many filmmakers from that country, offering instead a strong dramatic story succinctly told. Consequently, this film recalls such works as *A Time for Drunken Horses* and *The Colour of Paradise*. Its drama pivots on a 17-year-old youth living a rural existence in Eastern Iran. He hopes to escape to a better life in the Emirates but is frustrated when the circumstances of his father's death bring pressure on him. Local tradition demands that he stay and avenge this death... The director avoids any descent into melodrama but is let down by the film star looks of Jan-Mohammad Tajik, who fails to meet the considerable demands of the leading role. There is a keen sense of place and a good music score, but with a different actor the work would be far more involving. MS

• *Eidok* Yar-Mohammad Damanipour, *Gol-Mohammad* Jan-Mohammad Tajik, *mother* Fereshteh Sarabandi, *Rahman* Rasool Baharangiz, *Fereidooni* Mohammad Hamzezadeh.

• *Dir* and *Screenplay* Abdolrasool Golbon, from the screenplay The Way by Habib Fatalizadeh, *Pro* M. Hossein Haghighi, *Ph* and *Set Design* Mohammad Davoudi, *Ed* Hassan Hassandoost, *M* Saeid Ansari, *Costumes* Mohammad Davoodi, *Sound* Mohammad-Reza Delpak.

Cima Film/Farabi Cinema Foundation-Barian Entertainment.
80 mins. Iran. 2003. Rel: 23 July 2004. Cert. PG.

The Phantom of the Opera ★★★½

Paris; 1870. When the Paris Opera House is taken over by two new entrepreneurs, a shadowy figure from the building's catacombs cites some creative differences... Joel Schumacher is a proficient filmmaker but he's no Alan Parker or Baz Luhrmann. One's worst misgivings are realised from the outset as the musical starts alarmingly low-key with an uninspiring black-and-white prologue. But then the monochrome dissolves to reveal all the bustle, drama and thrill of the opera. This is one of the film's better sequences, one that highlights the fabulous costumes and art direction – indeed, this *Phantom* is anything if not a visual blow-out. Pictorially, the 17-year-old Emmy Rossum is a miracle, too, and her classically trained voice soars over her co-stars, although it's often hard to catch the gist of her words. Gerard Butler is a dashing Phantom but lacks a certain menace, while Patrick Wilson as the cocksure Raoul de Chagny is just wet. Ultimately, though, the film doesn't fly and fails to engage the emotions, resulting in a phantasmagoria of minor

delights, from the robust chords of Andrew Lloyd Webber's music to the sharply etched character turns from Minnie Driver, Simon Callow, Ciarán Hinds, et al. Incidentally, Lloyd Webber's is but one of three musicals based on the 1911 novel by Gaston Leroux, while this is the eighth film adaptation. JC-W

• *the Phantom* Gerard Butler, *Christine Daae* Emmy Rossum, *Vicompte Raoul de Chagny* Patrick Wilson, *Madame Giry* Miranda Richardson, *La Carlotta* Minnie Driver, *Gilles André* Simon Callow, *Richard Firmin* Ciarán Hinds, *Meg Giry* Jennifer Ellison, *Lefevre* James Fleet, *Piangi* Victor McGuire, *Buquet* Kevin McNally, *Reyer* Murray Melvin, *with* Imogen Bain, Miles Western, Judith Paris, Paul Brooke, Lucy Casson, Lorraine Stewart, and (uncredited) *old Raoul* James Fox.

• *Dir* Joel Schumacher, *Pro* Andrew Lloyd Webber, *Ex Pro* Austin Shaw, Paul Hitchcock, Louise Goodsill, Ralph Kamp, Jeff Abberley, Julia Blackman and Keith Cousins, *Co-Pro* Eli Richbourg, *Screenplay* Schumacher and Lloyd Webber, *Ph* John Mathieson, *Pro Des* Anthony Pratt, *Ed* Terry Rawlings, *M* Lloyd Webber; lyrics: Charles Hart and Richard Stilgoe, *Costumes* Alexandra Byrne, *Choreography* Peter Darling.

Warner/Odyssey Entertainment/Really Useful Films/
Scion Films-Entertainment.
142 mins. UK/USA. 2004. Rel: 10 December 2004. Cert. 12A.

Phone ★★★½

Inevitably, this being a psychological chiller from the Orient, *Phone* will set off ring tones comparing it to *The Ring*. However, it is nowhere near as scary but in many ways is more accomplished. Visually stylish and boasting a very strong story, it should be remembered for the quality of its performances. Not since *The Exorcist* has a horror film been so well supported by its cast. While our leading lady, Ha Ji-won, doesn't entirely convince as a hard-nosed reporter, the rest of the female ensemble is extraordinary. There is excellent work from Kim Yoo-mi as a young mother unnerved by her little daughter's erratic behaviour, a chilling turn from Choi Ji-yeon as a malevolent and sexually promiscuous schoolgirl and above all an extraordinary performance from the pre-school Eun Seo-woo (who makes Linda Blair look like a jaded drag queen). Whether playing innocently at home, knocking out the *Moonlight Sonata* on the piano or being possessed by an evil spirit, Eun Seo-woo provides an astonishing range for one so young. It is a shame, then, that the film suffers from a weak sense of place and shoddy narrative framing, rendering the middle section almost unintelligible. But then the story creeps up on you and the conclusion makes this ripe for an English-language remake. JC-W

• *Seo Ji-won* Ha Ji-won, *Gang Ho-jung* Kim Yoo-mi, *Lee Young-ju* Eun Seo-woo, *Lee Chang-hoon* Choi Woo-jae, *Park Jin-hee* Choi Ji-yeon.

• *Dir* and *Ex Pro* Ahn Byoung-ki, *Pro* Kim Young-dae, *Screenplay* Ahn Byoung-ki and Lee You-jin, *Ph* Moon Yong-

Winter magic: a rough approximation of Tom Hanks in Robert Zemeckis's technically astonishing *The Polar Express* (from Warner)

sik, *Pro Des* By Oh Seng-man, *Ed* Park Soon-deok, *M* Lee Seng-ho, *Costumes* Ahn Ji-hyun, *Sound* Lee In-kyu.

Buena Vista International Korea/Toilet Pictures-Tartan Films.
102 mins. South Korea. 2001. Rel: 27 August 2004.
Cert. 15.

Ping Pong ★★★

Derived from a Japanese manga comic, this movie by Fumihiko Sori concentrates on a sport rarely featured in movies, table tennis. But if the choice of sport is novel the story-line and the characters are anything but. There are the two life-long friends who will end up competing against each other, the coach who is past his glory days but, despite seeming pushy, has a heart of gold, and an opponent who, having been a bully as a child, is clearly identified as the villain whose defeat we are invited to relish. Unexpectedly no romantic interest is added, but the film does possess immense energy. Nevertheless, whether or not you will find it worthwhile really depends on your willingness to delight in all the clichés of sporting dramas that are served up here. MS

• *Peco* Yôsuke Kubozuka, *Smile* Arata, *China* Sam Lee Chan-Sam, *Demon* Shidô Nakamura, *Akuma* Kôji Ogawa.

• *Dir* Fumihiko Sori, *Pro* Shinji Ogawa, Sanae Suzuki and Fumio Inoue, *Ex Pro* Yasushi Shiina, *Screenplay* Kankurô Kudô, based on the comic by Taiyô Matsumoto, *Ph* Akira Sakoh, *Art Dir* Kôichi Kanekatsu, *Ed* Sôichi Ueno, *M* Mao.

Asmik Ace Entertainment/Shogakukan/Tokyo Broadcasting System/BS1/Imagica/Nippon Shuppan Hanbai-ICA Projects.
114 mins. Japan. 2002. Rel: 30 July 2004.
Cert. 12A.

The Polar Express ★★★½

At five minutes to midnight on Christmas Eve, an eight-year-old boy is lying in bed listening out for Santa Claus. Consumed by doubt, he is startled by the sound of an express train steaming to a halt outside his window. Invited to board the Arctic-bound train, the boy embarks on an extraordinary adventure… By the halfway mark *The Polar Express* looks like it's going to be sitting alongside *It's a Wonderful Life* and *Miracle On 34th Street* as a true Christmas classic. With its staggering visuals, timeless theme and building sense of anticipation, it is like nothing we have ever seen before. Utilising a brand new form of animation – 'performance capture', a process that digitalises the routine of live actors – the film takes the breath away as the eponymous express hurtles through snowy wastes towards its polar destination. And there are some staggering sequences: the rollercoaster journey of a mislaid ticket; the train's perilous slide across a frozen lake; the young hero's expedition on the roof of the train… But as soon as the locomotive arrives at the north pole and Santa's grotto turns out to be an Orwellian metropolis peopled by Yiddish elves, the crass spectre of *The Grinch* rears its nauseating head. Best not to reveal more, other than to say the film is worth catching for its initial magic and breakthrough technology. JC-W

• voices (and movements): *hero boy/boy's father/conductor/the hobo/Santa/Scrooge* Tom Hanks, *Smokey/Steamer* Michael Jeter, *girl* Nona Gaye, *know-it-all boy* Eddie Deezen, *lonely boy* Peter Scolari, *elf general* Charles Fleischer, *Sarah/mother* Leslie Zemeckis, *toothless boy* Chris Coppola, *elf lieutenant/singer* Steven Tyler.

• *Dir* Robert Zemeckis, *Pro* Zemeckis, Steve Starkey, Gary Goetzman and William Teitler, *Co-Pro* Steven Boyd, *Screenplay* Zemeckis and William Broyles Jr., from the book by Chris Van Allsburg, *Ph* Don Burgess and Robert Presley, *Pro Des* Rick Carter and Doug Chiang, *Ed* Jeremiah O'Driscoll and R.

Orlando Duenas, *M* Alan Silvestri; original songs by Silvestri and Glen Ballard; songs performed by Tom Hanks, Matthew Hall and Meagan Moore, Steven Tyler, Josh Groban, Frank Sinatra, Bing Crosby, The Andrews Sisters, Perry Como with The Fontane Sisters, Red Foley, and Kate Smith, *Sound* Randy Thom, *Visual effects* Ken Ralston and Jerome Chen.

Castle Rock/Shangri-La Entertainment/Playtone/
ImageMovers/Golden Mean-Warner.
99 mins. USA. 2004. Rel: 3 December 2004.
Cert. U.

Pooh's Heffalump Movie ★★★

After a series of mysterious events, the inhabitants of the Hundred Acre Wood decide that the Heffalumps are not only responsible, but they must be stopped (even though none of them has actually seen a Heffalump). Rabbit organises Tigger, Pooh, Piglet and Eeyore into a lynch mob that is bent on capturing the enemy. Pride is hurt, however, when they tell Roo that he is too young to join their posse… A nice idea, this, but there's hardly enough material to sustain a full-length feature and when the film drags in the middle, very young viewers may lose interest. However, for fans of Disney's take on Winnie the Pooh, this is old-fashioned family escapism of a respectable pedigree. And, as a rites of passage fable, there is a salutary warning that unfounded prejudices can result in the loss of friendship. FP

• *voices*: *Winnie the Pooh/Tigger* Jim Cummings, *Piglet* John Fielder, *Roo* Nikita Hopkins, *Kanga* Kath Soucie, *Rabbit* Ken Sansom, *Eeyore* Peter Cullen, *Mama Heffalump* Brenda Blethyn, *Lumpy* Kyle Stanger.

• *Dir* Frank Nissen, *Pro* Jessica Koplos-Miller, *Screenplay* Brian Hohfeld and Evan Spiliotopoulos, *Art Dir* Tony Pulham, *Ed* Nancy Frazen, *M* Joel McNeely; songs by Carly Simon, *Animation Dir* Don MacKinnon.

Walt Disney Pictures/DisneyToons Studio-
Buena Vista International.
67 mins. USA. 2005. Rel: 18 March 2005.
Cert. U.

The Prince & Me ★★★

There are some nice moments in *The Prince & Me* and Julia Stiles, still one of Hollywood's most promising actresses, injects some credibility into this escapist piffle. The joke is that in spite of the film's wildest leaps of fantasy, real life caught up with the fiction. Stiles plays Paige Morgan, a country girl who's studying to be a doctor at the University of Wisconsin. Determined to establish a firm footing for a life of independence, she dismisses Shakespeare as useless and is resolved not to let any old Prince Charming distract her from her studies. Prince Edvard of Denmark (England's Luke Mably) is tired of both the media spotlight and his regal responsibilities. So he decides to slum it in the American heartland because he's a sucker for loose American women. Coincidentally, Paige and Edvard end up on the same chemistry course and she takes an instant dislike to him. He's

never been rejected before but then she doesn't known he's in the direct line to the throne of Denmark… The narrative trajectory is predictable enough (albeit quite enjoyable), while the real Prince of Denmark (Crown Prince Frederick) turned fiction on its head by marrying that Australian commoner Mary Donaldson. Spooky.
JC-W

• *Paige Morgan* Julia Stiles, *Prince Edvard* Luke Mably, *Soren* Ben Miller, *King Haraald* James Fox, *Queen Rosalind* Miranda Richardson, *Amy Morgan* Alberta Watson, *Ben Morgan* John Bourgeois, *John Morgan* Zachary Knighton, *with* Steve O'Reilly, Elisabeth Waterston, Eliza Bennett, Devin Ratray, Eddie Irvine.

• *Dir* Martha Coolidge, *Pro* Mark Armin, *Ex Pro* Cami Winikoff and Robin Schorr, *Screenplay* Jack Amiel, Michael Begler and Katherine Fugate, *Ph* Alex Nepomniaschy, *Pro Des* James Spencer, *Ed* Steven Cohen, *M* Jennie Muskett; Offenbach, J.S. Bach; songs performed by Kinky, Fastball, Jessica Riddle, Ray Colcord, Junior Senior, Eve 6, Scapegoat Wax, The Cars, Joss Stone, Jennifer Stills, Forty Foot Echo, The Clumsy Lovers, etc, *Costumes* Magali Guidasci, *Royal Etiquette Coach* Václav Pavlas.

Paramount Pictures/Lions Gate/Sobini Films-Icon.
110 mins. USA/Canada. 2004. Rel: 16 July 2004.
Cert. PG.

Princesa ★★★

This is the tale of a teenage transvestite from Brazil living in Milan. This Fernando, who calls himself Fernanda, is played by Ingrid de Souza, and other characters include a male whore who becomes a victim of Aids and a transsexual who employs Fernando as a prostitute but is drawn to him. The acting is moderate, the film drawn out, but the big surprise is that what might have been played as a seriously downbeat drama of anguish leading to Fernando's decision regarding a sex change operation is portrayed instead in a highly glamorised way. Whether it's love between Fernando and one of his pick-ups or the romanticised vision of street life, this presents itself as positive, escapist fare and that makes it one of a kind. MS

• *Fernanda* aka 'Princesa' Ingrid de Souza, *Gianni* Cesare Bocci, *Karin* Lulu Pecorari, *Fabrizio* Mauro Pirovano, *Charlo* Biba Lerhue, *Fofao* Sonia Morgan.

• *Dir* Henrique Goldman, *Pro* Rebbeca O'Brien, *Ex Pro* Paolo Soravia and Angus MacDonald, *Screenplay* Goldman and Ellis Freeman, from the book by Maurizio Jannelli and Fernanda Farias de Albuquerque, *Ph* Guillermo Escalón, *Pro Des* Andrea Meló, *Ed* Kerry Kohler, *M* Giovanni Venosta, *Costumes* Nivia Sibulka.

Parallax Pictures/BIM Distribuzione/Road Movies/British Screen/BAC Films/Mango Films-Soda Pictures.
93 mins. UK/Italy/Germany/France. 2000.
Rel: 1 October 2004.
Cert. 18.

The Princess Diaries 2: The Royal Engagement ★½

It has been five years since the gawky and spectacularly shy Mia Thermopolis discovered that she was the heir apparent to the European principality of Genovia. Now she has finished college at Princeton (where else?), graduated in political science (what else?) and is ready to assume the role of queen. Then a Machiavellian schemer throws a spanner in the works by revealing that, in order to take the crown, Mia must be married. So the retiring American graduate has just 30 days to fall in love and find her appropriate Prince Charming... It's a safe bet that the target audience for this formulaic drivel has not seen most of the films that it plunders. Yet even though it's a relatively slick composite of time-worn clichés, it really does lack sparkle, chemistry and comic invention. From the predictable storyline to the inane slapstick, the film is everything that the original wasn't. Worse, the story just isn't that interesting, while the array of 'Genovian' accents (running the gamut from Cockney to American) is offensively lazy. JC-W

• *Queen Clarisse Renaldi* Julie Andrews, *Mia Thermopolis* Anne Hathaway, *Joe* Hector Elizondo, *Lilly Moscovitz* Heather Matarazzo, *Viscount Mabrey* John Rhys-Davies, *Nicholas Devereaux* Chris Pine, *Andrew Jacoby* Callum Blue, *Charlotte Kutaway* Kathleen Marshall, *Asana* Raven, *Paolo* Larry Miller, *Lord Palimore* Tom Poston, *reporter Elsie* Kim Thomson, *Helen Thermopolis* Caroline Goodall, *with* Matthew Walker, Cristi Andrews, Spencer Breslin, Barbara Marshall, Amy Edwards, Shannon Wilcox, Jane Morris, Scott Marshall, Claudia Katz, Tracy Reiner, Julie Paris, Paul Williams, Abigail Breslin, Lori Marshall, Charlee Corra Disney, Charlotte Marshall-Fricker, Sam Marshall, Lili Marshall-Fricker, Stan Lee.

• *Dir* Garry Marshall, *Pro* Debra Martin Chase, Whitney Houston and Mario Iscovich, *Ex Pro* Ellen H. Schwartz, *Screenplay* Shona Rhimes, from a story by Rhimes and Gina Wendkos, based on characters created by Meg Cabot, *Ph* Charles Minsky, *Pro Des* Albert Brenner, *Ed* Bruce Green, *M* John Debney; songs performed by Renee Olstead, Kelly Clarkson, Julie Andrews and Raven, Lillix, Pink, Avril Lavigne, Lindsay Lohan, Wilson Phillips, Norah Jones, Jesse McCartney, etc, *Costumes* Gary Jones.

Walt Disney Pictures/BrownHouse-Buena Vista International.
113 mins. USA. 2004. Rel: 15 October 2004 (in Scotland). Cert. U.

Private ★★½

Palestine; the present. Mohammad is a father of six, a schoolteacher passionate about Shakespeare, and a Palestinian. Then, one day, his house is occupied by Israeli soldiers who forbid him or any member of his family to venture upstairs in their own home. Free to leave during the day, they are locked in their living room at night... This really is an extraordinary story – and a true one, at that. Even so, with all its noble intentions and a consummate cast (with Palestinian actors playing Palestinians and Israelis playing Israelis), *Private* is dramatically underwhelming. There are a handful of scenes that make an impact – such as when Mariam describes to her little brother the human characteristics of each soldier – but the rest of the movie (shot on grubby video) borders on the mundane. Filmed in Italy. JC-W

• *Commander Ofer* Lior Miller, *Mohammad B.* Mohammad Bakri, *Private Eial* Tomer Russo, *Samiah B.* Areen Omari, *Mariam B.* Hend Ayoub, *Karem B.* Karem Emad Hassan Aly, *with* Marco Alsaying, Sarah Hamzeh, Amir Hasayen, Niv Shafir.

• *Dir* Saverio Costanzo, *Pro* Mario Gianani, *Ex Pro* Patrizia Costantini, *Screenplay* Saverio Costanzo, Sayed Qashua, Camilia Costanzo and Alessio Cremonini, *Ph* Luigi Martinucci, *Ed* Francesca Calvelli, *M* Alter Ego, *Costumes* Ludovica Amati and Einat Fadida.

Offside/Luce/Cydonia-Metrodome.
94 mins. Italy. 2004. Rel: 13 May 2005. Cert. 15.

Protection
see *Moolaadé*.

The Punisher ★★★½

There's not a lot of intellectual grit in *The Punisher*, but it's got a kick-ass attitude that makes Daredevil look like a wimp. Actually, in the hands of Ben Affleck, Daredevil looked like a wimp all on his own. Here, Tom Jane (formerly Thomas Jane) struts onto centre stage with a presence that would shrivel the skin of a lizard. He is Frank Castle, a Florida FBI agent who has decided to settle down in London with his young wife and son. But before he and his loved ones move, disgruntled gangster John Travolta sends a posse of men to the Castle farewell party and bids them all a permanent adieu. Amazingly, Castle survives and dedicates the rest of his life to punishing his aggressors... The film – adapted from the Marvel Comic – has a number of impressive set-pieces, a suitably nonchalant, sadistic villain in Will Patton (Travolta is largely wasted as Patton's boss) and a slick, sick throwaway humour. It is also gratuitously violent, in a comic-book-so-it-doesn't-really-matter sort of way, where torture and the murder of children are a matter of course. Some will find it repugnant, others will be thankful that it delivers. JC-W

• *Frank Castle/The Punisher* Tom Jane, *Howard Saint* John Travolta, *Quentin Glass* Will Patton, *Joan* Rebecca Romijn-Stamos, *Livia Saint* Laura Harring, *Frank Castle Sr* Roy Scheider, *Maria Castle* Samantha Mathis, *Dave* Ben Foster, *John Saint/Bobby Saint* James Carpinello, *Mr Bumpo* John Pinette.

• *Dir* Jonathan Hensleigh, *Pro* Avi Arad and Gale Anne Hurd, *Ex Pro* Stan Lee, Kevin Feige, John Starke, Amir Malin, Richard Saperstein, Andrew Golov, Patrick Gunn, Andreas Schmid, Christopher Roberts and Christopher Eberts, *Screenplay* Hensleigh and Michael France, *Ph* Conrad W. Hall, *Pro Des* Michael Z. Hanan, *Ed* Steven Kemper, *M* Carlo Siliotto, *Costumes* Lisa Tomczeszyn.

Lions Gate Films/Marvel Studios-Columbia.
124 mins. USA. 2004. Rel: 24 Septembr 2004. Cert 18.

Racing Stripes ★★

As the circus accidentally sets off without him in the middle of a dark and stormy night, a zebra foal is rescued by a passing farmer. Dubbed 'Stripes' by the farmer's 16-year-old daughter, the little stranger is allowed to stay on the farm, which overlooks the magnificent Turfway Park racecourse. Seduced by the sight of his racing neighbours, Stripes grows up believing that he himself is a racehorse and should have a shot at entering the Kentucky Open... It took four credited writers to come up with the story for this zebrine version of *Babe* and yet there's no on-screen credit for that 1995 classic, nor the equally plundered *Seabiscuit*, *Home On the Range*, *Fly Away Home* or *Chicken Run*. As derivative as it is predictable, *Racing Stripes* might have sparked a rush on zebrine merchandising had it aimed for charm rather than cheap laughs. The human actors are fine, but the farmyard and equestrian performers are fed some pretty duff lines. There's also an excruciating double-act from a couple of wisecracking flies who, inevitably, drag the proceedings into the dung. JC-W

• *Nolan Walsh* Bruce Greenwood, *Channing Walsh* Hayden Panettiere, *Woodzie* M. Emmet Walsh, *mailman* Caspar Poyck, *John Cooper* Gary Bullock, *Clara Dalrymple* Wendie Malick.

Running mates: Stripes and Hayden Panettiere pose in *Racing Stripes* (from Momentum Pictures)

Voices: *Stripes* Frankie Muniz, *Trenton's Pride* Joshua Jackson, *Goose* Joe Pantoliano, *Scuzz* David Spade, *Buzz* Steve Harvey, *Sandy* Mandy Moore, *Lightning* Snoop Dogg, *Clydesdale* Michael Clarke Duncan, *Tucker* Dustin Hoffman, *Franny* Whoopi Goldberg, *Sir Trenton* Fred Dalton Thompson, *young Stripes* Jansen Panettiere, *with* Jeff Foxworthy, Michael Rosenbaum.

• *Dir* Frederik Du Chau, *Pro* Andrew A. Kosove, Broderick Johnson, Ed McDonnell and Lloyd Phillips, *Ex Pro* Steven P. Wegner, *Screenplay* David F. Schmidt, from a story by Schmidt, Wegner, De Chau and Kirk DeMicco, *Ph* David Eggby, *Pro Des* Wolf Kroeger, *Ed* Tom Finan, *M* Mark Isham; Mozart, Ennio Morricone; songs performed by Smokey Robinson, David Spade, and Steve Harvey, Bryan Adams, Run DMC, and Sting, *Animation Supervisor* Alexander Williams, *Head Zebra Trainer* Steve Martin.

Alcorn Entertainment-Momentum Pictures.
102 mins. USA. 2004. Rel: 4 February 2005. Cert. U.

The Rage in Placid Lake ★★

Placid Lake may be a product of his parents' outdated hippie upbringing, but he certainly lives up to his name. Replacing animalistic rage with an intellectual detachment, Placid refuses to be an ordinary student and is abetted by his soul mate, the smart and aloof Gemma Taylor. Then, after a suicidal attempt at liberation, Placid decides to become normal, to fit in and be anything but himself... Not a sequel to 1999's *Lake Placid*, but a quirky coming-of-age story adapted from the Australian stage. To writer-director Tony McNamara's credit, the theatrical origins of his play, *The Café Latte Kid*, are invisible, but the resultant scenario is neither very cinematic nor rooted in everyday credibility. It's a jokey fable in which broadly drawn caricatures spout carefully manicured one-liners and a dry martini approach to sexual humour hopes to attain scandalous sophistication. Miranda Richardson tries hard to be funny but there's a stilted coyness afoot, typical of first features which brace themselves to shock but are afraid to tilt the humour full hog. JC-W

• *Placid Lake* Ben Lee, *Gemma Taylor* Rose Byrne, *Sylvia Lake* Miranda Richardson, *Doug Lake* Garry McDonald, *Bill Taylor* Nicholas Hammond*, young Placid* Jordan Brooking, *young Gemma* Eleeza Hooker, *Jenny* Jesse Spence, *Bull* Toby Schmitz, *Joel* Christopher Stollery, *Anton* Francis McMahon, *Jane* Saskia Smit, *girl at seminar* Claire Danes, *with* Nathaniel Dean, Stephen James King, Helen Thomson.

• *Dir* and *Screenplay* Tony McNamara, *Pro* Marian Macgowan, *Ex Pro* Bryce Menzies, Gary Phillips, Mark Vennis and Jane Smith, *Co-Pro* Louise Smith, *Ph* Ellery Ryan, *Pro Des* Roger Ford, *Ed* Lee Smith, *M* Cezary Skubiszewski; Mozart; songs by Ben Lee, and Jacket, *Costumes* Lisa Meagher.

Film Finance Corporation Australia/Showtime Australia/New South Wales Film and Television Office, etc-Guerilla Films.
89 mins. Australia/UK. 2002. Rel: 1 April 2005. Cert. 15.

Raising Helen ★★

There are a lot of wonderful things in *Raising Helen*, notably the comic calibre of the female performances. Joan Cusack can make a line like 'I'm having a banana' funny, while Helen Mirren sharpens her comic timing to a needle-point. But this doesn't save *Raising Helen* from being a sluggish, sugarcoated and frequently unbearable comedy. Helen Harris (the captivating Kate Hudson) has an ideal life: an aspiring star of the Dominique Modelling Agency, she dates male models, lives in a luxurious Manhattan apartment and has the inside track on the hottest New York clubs. Then her older sister dies and leaves her with her three children, from the precocious 15-year-old Audrey to the snot-obsessed five-year-old Sarah. Like everything else on her plate, Helen sees this as a new challenge. But her life is about to change for good… Lacking a strong narrative thrust, *Raising Helen* lurches from situation comedy to something altogether more mawkish. While it makes a few profound points about growing up, it does so with a heavy-handed shove. JC-W

• *Helen Harris* Kate Hudson, *Pastor Dan Parker* John Corbett, *Jenny Portman* Joan Cusack, *Audrey Davis* Hayden Panettiere, *Henry Davis* Spencer Breslin, *Dominique* Helen Mirren, *Mickey Massey* Hector Elizondo, *Sarah Davis* Abigail Breslin, *Lindsay Davis* Felicity Huffman, *Nilma Prasad* Sakina Jaffrey, *Ed Portman* Kevin Kilner, *with* Sean O'Bryan, Amber Valletta, Joseph Mazzello, *Amber* Paris Hilton, Sandra Taylor, Wesley Horton, Shannon Wilcox, Sunny Hawks, Jason Olive, Tracy

Reiner, Barbara Marshall, Alan Thicke, Gary Jones, Kathleen Marshall, Tom Hines, Lori Marshall, Lily Marshall-Fricker, Charlotte Marshall-Fricker.

• *Dir* Garry Marshall, *Pro* David Hoberman and Ashok Amritraj, *Ex Pro* Mario Iscovich and Ellen H. Schwartz, *Co-Pro* Todd Lieberman and Karen Stigwolt, *Screenplay* Jack Amiel and Michael Begler, from a story by Patrick J. Clifton and Beth Rigazio, *Ph* Charles Minsky, *Pro Des* Steven Jordan, *Ed* Bruce Green and Tara Timpone, *M* John Debny; songs performed by Joan Osborne, Fefe Dobson, Devo, Liz Phair, Kristyn Osborn, David Bowie, Ingram Hill, Zero 7, D4, Simon and Garfunkel, 2 Unlimited, Haylie Duff, John Hiatt, Josh Kelley, Dana Glover, Mark McGrath, Five for Fighting, etc, *Costumes* Gary Jones, *Choreography* Scott D. Grossman, *Illustrator* Harry Weinmann.

Touchstone Pictures/Beacon Pictures/Mandeville Films-Buena Vista International.
119 mins. USA. 2004. Rel: 27 August 2004. Cert. PG.

Ray ★★★★★

In the cosy, autumnal stage of his career, Ray Charles cut an avuncular figure who excelled in the fields of soul, gospel, jazz, R&B, MOR and Country. Taylor Hackford, who previously directed *The Idolmaker*, a biog of rock producer Bob Marcucci, and the documentary *Chuck Berry Hail! Hail! Rock 'n' Roll*, opens up the musician's life to reveal a victim, drug addict,

Growing up disgracefully: Kate Hudson and John Corbett in Garry Marshall's heavy-handed *Raising Helen* (from Buena Vista International)

adulterer, genius, social hero and icon. Developed in collaboration with Charles himself and his son, executive producer Ray Charles Robinson Jr, *Ray* is a colourful, stylish, moving and toe-tapping tribute to a man who fought his demons to become a genuine living legend (although, alas, he died before the film's release). Cutting back to his childhood when, aged five, he saw his younger brother drowned and, two years later, lost his sight, the film presents a series of emotive highpoints and lows as the 'blind nigger' from Florida battled prejudice and duplicity to transform the face of popular music. A stirring medley of consequential incident, groundbreaking jam sessions and a whirlwind of social history, *Ray* is a thrilling model of musical biography. And Jamie Foxx in the title role is sensational.
JC-W

• *Ray Charles Robinson* Jamie Foxx, *Della Bea Robinson* Kerry Washington, *Jeff Brown* Clifton Powell, *Joe Adams* Harry Lennix, *Gossie McKee* Terrence Dashon Howard, *Quincy Jones* Larenz Tate, *Jerry Wexler* Richard Schiff, *Margie Hendricks* Regina King, *Mary Ann Fisher* Aunjanue Ellis, *Fathead Newman* Bokeem Woodbine, *Aretha Robinson* Sharon Warren, *Ahmet Ertegun* Curtis Armstrong, *young Ray Robinson* C.J. Sanders, *Milt Shaw* David Krumholtz, *Wilbur Brassfield* Wendell Pierce, *with* Chris Thomas King, Jefferson Byrd, Rick Gomez, Denise Dowse, Warwick Davis, Patrick Bauchau, Robert Wisdom, Kurt Fuller, Kimberly Ardison, Gary Grubbs, Vernel Bagnaris.

• *Dir* Taylor Hackford, *Pro* Hackford, Stuart Benjamin, Howard Baldwin and Karen Baldwin, *Ex Pro* William J. Immerman and Jaime Rucker King, *Co-Pro* Ray Charles Robinson Jr, Alise Benjamin and Nick Morton, *Screenplay* James L. White, from a story by Hackford and White, *Ph* Pawel Edelman, *Pro Des* Stephen Altman, *Ed* Paul Hirsch, *M* Craig Armstrong, *Costumes* Sharen Davis.

Universal/Bristol Bay Productions/Anvil Films/Baldwin Entertainment-UIP.
152 mins. USA/UK. 2004. Rel: 21 January 2005. Cert. 15.

Reconstruction ★★★★
This prize-winning first feature by Denmark's Christoffer Boe is a splendidly acted and highly ambitious work in which Maria Bonnevie steals the acting honours by successfully playing two contrasted roles. The film's stylised presentation of complex material (a photographer leaves his girlfriend to take up with an author's wife, although this could be a narrative that represents the latest novel by the author himself) is as off-beat and as playful with illusion and reality as *Eternal Sunshine of the Spotless Mind*. Not all of it works (the second half turns disconcertingly surrealist at times) but at its best it's strongly poetic and emotionally intense. A film worth investigating by those who favour adventurous cinema. MS

• *Alex David* Nikolaj Lie Kaas, *Aimee Holm/Simone* Maria Bonnevie, *August Holm* Krister Henriksson, *with* Nicolas Bro, Peter Steen, Isa Dwinger, Malene Schwartz, Helle Fagralid.

• *Dir* Christoffer Boe, *Pro* Tine Grew Pfeiffer, Åke Sandgren and Lars Kjeldgaard, *Ex Pro* Rumle Hammerich, *Screenplay* Boe and Mogens Rukov, *Ph* Manuel Alberto Claro, *Art Dir* Martin de Thurah, *Ed* Mikkel E.G. Nielsen and Peter Brandt, *M* Thomas Knak, *Costumes* Gabi Humnicki, *Visual Design* Martin de Thurah.

Nordisk Film Prods/Director's Cut/TV2/Danmark/ Danish Film Institute-Soda Pictures.
92 mins. Denmark/Sweden/Germany. 2003. Rel: 12 November 2004. Cert 12A.

Breaking hearts: Carole Bouquet and Jean-Pierre Darroussin in Cédric Kahn's gripping and disturbing *Red Lights* (from Artificial Eye)

Red Lights ★★★★
For a thriller, atmosphere is everything and the 38-year-old French director Cédric Kahn (*L'Ennui, Roberto Rocco*) has created a scenario in which menace drips from every frame. With a minimal amount of music and a naturalistic *mise en scène*, Kahn sets up his tale of domestic friction with an assured hand. It's hard to imagine an actor of Jean-Pierre Darroussin's ordinariness ever taking centre stage in a Hollywood movie, but he's perfect for this ironic thriller (adapted from the Georges Simenon novel). Antoine is a timid insurance clerk stuck in a static marriage to a high-powered corporate lawyer, Hélène (Carole Bouquet). She is insensitive to her husband's insecurity and he relies on alcohol to boost his ego. On the evening they are due to set off for the south of France to visit their son and daughter in camp, Hélène is characteristically late and Antoine drinks too many beers while waiting for her. Her self-righteous indignation at his behaviour, mixed with his guilt and need for more alcoholic reinforcement, leads to a nocturnal nightmare exacerbated – and transformed – by outside forces. Gripping, disturbing and quite chilling. Original title: *Feux rouges*. JC-W

• *Antoine Dunan* Jean-Pierre Darroussin, *Hélène Dunan* Carole Bouquet, *Cristophe Montana, man on the run* Vincent Deniard, *café waitress* Charline Paul, *Inspector Levet* Jean-Pierre Gos, *with* Alain Dion, Olivier Fornara, Micky Finn.

• *Dir* Cédric Kahn, *Pro* Patrick Godeau, *Ex Pro* Françoise Galfrè, *Screenplay* Kahn, Laurence Ferreira-Barbosa and Gilles Marchand, *Ph* Patrick Blossier, *Pro Des* François Abelanet, *Ed* Yann Dedet, *M* Claude Debussy, *Costumes* Elisabeth Tavernier and Edwige Morel d'Arleux.

Tub tales: Naomi Watts and Kelly Stables in *The Ring Two* (from UIP)

Alicéléo/France 3 Cinéma/Gimages Films/Canal Plus, etc-Artificial Eye.
106 mins. France. 2003. Rel: 24 September 2004. Cert. 15.

Resident Evil: Apocalypse ★★★

A welcome sequel to 2002's $100 million hit, based on the popular video game, sees teenage boys' dream Milla Jovovich returning to Raccoon City for more kick-ass action. This time Milla teams up with Sienna Guillory and Oded Fehr to eliminate the virus that turns humans into zombies. This lurid movie is brilliantly flashy, with regular bursts of exciting action, so fans won't perhaps complain that the script's totally incoherent. And Jovovich again shows she is an action heroine to reckon with. DW

• *Alice* Milla Jovovich, *Jill Valentine* Sienna Guillory, *Carlos Olivera* Oded Fehr, *Major Kain* Thomas Kretschmann, *Angie Ashford* Sophie Vavasseur, *Sgt Peyton Wells* Raz Adoti, *Dr Ashord* Jared Harris, *LJ* Mike Epps, *with* Sandrine Holt, Matthew G. Taylor, Zack Ward, Iain Glen.

• *Dir* Alexander Witt, *Pro* Jeremy Bolt, Paul W.S. Anderson and Don Carmody, *Ex Pro* Bernd Eichinger, Robert Kulzer, Samuel Hadida and Victor Hadida, *Screenplay* Anderson, *Ph* Christian Sebaldt and Derek Rogers, *Pro Des* Paul Denham Austerberry, *Ed* Eddie Hamilton, *M* Jeff Danna, *Costumes* Mary McLeod, Sound Craig Henighan.

Screen Gems/Davis Films/Impact/Constantin Film-Columbia TriStar.
93 mins. France/Canada/UK/USA. 2004. Rel: 8 October 2004. Cert. 15.

Riding Giants ★★★

Documentary filmmaker Stacy Peralta leaves the skateboards of Dogtown behind to hit the beach and chronicle the rise of surfing from its pre-*Gidget* Zen movement to its post-*Gidget* pop phenom as an 'extreme' sport. Told through interviews with the true kings of the surf – big wave surfers who've braved Hawaii's Pahia and California's the Mavericks – Peralta lovingly focuses his lens on the most dedicated and enduring members of this cultural sub-set. Surprisingly enjoyable for the uninitiated, it transforms what could easily have been a tedious niche film into a fascinating glimpse into the lives of this small brotherhood of thrill-seekers. Proof positive that men can become obsessed with anything, even the waves breaking upon the shore. SWM

• *with*: Darrick Doerner, Laird John Hamilton, Dave Kalama.

• *Dir* Stacy Peralta, *Pro* Peralta, Agi Orsi and Jane Kachmer, *Ex Pro* Nathalie Delest, Franck Marty and Laird Hamilton, *Assoc Pro* and *Ed* Paul Crowder, *Screenplay* Peralta and Sam George, *Ph* Peter Pilafian, *M* Matter.

Forever Films/StudioCanal/Setsuna/LLC/AOP/Quicksilver-Columbia TriStar.
101 mins. France/USA. 2004. Rel: 3 December 2004. Cert. 12A.

The Ring Two ★½

After the horrific events that unfolded around Seattle two years ago, investigative reporter Rachel Keller and her son Aidan move to the sleepy backwater of Astoria, Oregon. But you can't keep a good ghost down and so the eerie spectre of the girl with the long black hair decides she doesn't need a video to scare her victims into Francis Bacon waxworks... There's this really neat moment in *The Ring Two* when the pulsating image of the girl with the long black hair appears in a still photograph on Aidan's digital camera. But that's it. For audiences still unnerved by the sight of a girl with long black hair, this redundant sequel might exert some dread, but for the rest of us it must rate as the year's most boring horror movie. Divorced from the minutiae of everyday reality, the film is like a dream that's trying very, very hard to be a nightmare. But it's so safe and 'Hollywood' that even an 11-year-old boy is forced to take a bath in his underwear. *Ring* cycle closed. *Please.* JC-W

• *Rachel Keller* Naomi Watts, *Max Rourke* Simon Baker, *Aidan Keller* David Dorfman, *Evelyn* Sissy Spacek, *Dr Emma Temple* Elizabeth Perkins, *Martin Savide* Gary Cole, *Jake* Ryan Merriman, *Emily* Emily Vancamp, *Evil Samara* Kelly Stables, *with* Kelly Overton, Daveigh Chase, Mary Joy.

• *Dir* Hideo Nakata, *Pro* Walter F. Parkes and Laurie MacDonald, *Ex Pro* Mike Macari, Roy Lee, Neil Machlis and Michele Weisler, *Screenplay* Ehren Kruger, *Ph* Gabriel Beristain, *Pro Des* Jim Bissell, *Ed* Michael N. Knue, *M* Hans Zimmer, Henning Lohner and Martin Tillman, *Costumes* Wendy Chuck, *Visual Effects* Betsy Paterson, *Make-Up* Rick Baker.

DreamWorks/Parkes/MacDonald-UIP.
109 mins. USA. 2005. Rel: 1 April 2005. Cert. 15.

Robots ★★★½

The son of a washing machine, Rodney Copperbottom dreams of greater things. Inspired by the commercials of Bigweld, a rotund inventor from Robot City, Rodney sets off for the metropolis with his flying invention made from an old coffee pot. But once there, Rodney discovers that Bigweld has been replaced by the dastardly Phineas T. Ratchet, a corporate extortionist who aims to banish spare parts so that he can push up sales of shiny and expensive upgrades... The second production from Blue Sky Studios (the animation arm of Fox which brought us *Ice Age*), *Robots* conjures up a truly phantasmagorical, retro-futuristic world, like *Metropolis* on acid. A cautionary tale of built-in obsolescence, it's a slap in the face for Microsoft (and other corporate profiteers), while providing a picturesque palette and a wealth of in-jokes and puns (both visual and verbal). And with its imaginative array of colourful automata, the film should appeal to anybody who's superimposed human emotions on an inanimate object (be it car, C-3PO or a tank engine). JC-W

• voices: *Rodney Copperbottom* Ewan McGregor, *Fender* Robin Williams, *Cappy* Halle Berry, *Phineas T. Ratchet* Greg Kinnear, *Bigweld* Mel Brooks, *Crank Casey* Drew Carey, *Madame Gasket* Jim Broadbent, *Piper Pinwheeler* Amanda Bynes, *Mrs Copperbottom* Dianne Wiest, *Aunt Fan* Jennifer Coolidge, *Herb Copperbottom* Stanley Tucci, *Tim, the gate guard* Paul Giamatti, *Loretta Geargrinder* Natasha Lyonne, *Mr Gunk* Dan Hedaya, *voice box at hardware store* James Earl Jones, *watch* Paula Abdul, *with* Terry Bradshaw, Jay Leno, Al Roker, Stephen Tobolowsky, Harland Williams, Lowell Ganz, Chris Wedge, *and UK version only:* Chris Moyles, Terry Wogan, Cat Deeley, Vernon Kay, Eamonn Holmes.

• *Dir* Chris Wedge, *Co-Dir* Carlos Saldanha, *Pro* Jerry Davis, John C. Donkin and William Joyce, *Ex Pro* Christopher Meledandri, *Screenplay* David Lindsay-Abaire, Lowell Ganz and Babaloo Mandel, from a story by Lindsay-Abaire, Ron Mita and Jim McClain, *Pro Des* William Joyce, *Ed* John Carnochan, *M* John Powell; Elgar, Rossini, Johann Strauss; songs performed by Gomez, Tom Waits, Seriogram, Fountains of Wayne, Kenny G, James Brown, Fatboy Slim, The Hit Crew, Earth Wind & Fire, WAR, Barry White, Britney

Spears, Melanie Blatt, etc, *Animation Supervisors* James Bresnahan and Michael Thurmeier, *Sound* Sean Garnhart.

Fox Animation/Blue Sky Studios-Fox.
91 mins. USA. 2005. Rel: 18 March 2005. Cert. U.

Rois et reine
see *Kings and Queen*.

Rory O'Shea Was Here
see *Inside I'm Dancing*.

Sahara ★★
Professional treasure hunter Dirk Pitt is convinced that a battleship from the American Civil War has ended up in Africa. WHO doctor Eva Rojos has stumbled across a deadly disease in Nigeria and believes that its source is in war-torn Mali. Somehow, the contrary agendas of these two bronzed, good-looking pioneers leads them both into conflict with the unscrupulous profiteer General Kazim… Juggling corporate skulduggery, Third World corruption and a hunt for a mythical hoard of treasure, *Sahara* strives to inject some Indiana Jones spice into old-fashioned cinematic territory. Unfortunately, this adaptation of Clive Cussler's 1992 novel is a rather clodhopping affair which relies too heavily on loud bangs and predictable stereotypes for its entertainment quotient, while desperately lacking wit and visual panache. JC-W

• *Dir Pitt* Matthew McConaughey, *Al Giordino* Steve Zahn, *Dr Eva Rojos* Penélope Cruz, *Massarde* Lambert Wilson, *Carl*

Penélope Cruz, Matthew McConaughey and Steve Zahn in Breck Eisner's clodhopping *Sahara* (from UIP)

Delroy Lindo, *Admiral Sandecker* William H. Macy, *General Kazim* Lennie James, *Dr Hopper* Glynn Turman, *Rudi* Rainn Wilson, *Ambassador Polidori* Patrick Malahide, *with* Paulin F. Fodouop, Jude Akuwudike, Mark Aspinall, Robert Cavanah.

• *Dir* Breck Eisner, *Pro* Howard Baldwin, Karen Baldwin, Mace Neufeld and Stephanie Austin, *Ex Pro* Matthew McConaughey, Gus Gustawes, William J. Immerman and Vicki Dee Rock, *Screenplay* Thomas Dean Donnelly, Joshua Oppenheimer, John C. Richards and James V. Hart, *Ph* Seamus McGarvey, *Pro Des* Allan Cameron, *Ed* Andrew MacRitchie, *M* Clint Mansell, *Costumes* Anna Sheppard, *Visual Effects* Mara Bryan.

Paramount/Bristol Bay Prods/Baldwin Entertainment/j.k. livin-UIP.
124 mins. UK/Spain/Germany/USA. 2005.
Rel: 8 April 2005. Cert. 12A.

Saved! ★½

The American Eagle Christian High School is dedicated to saving souls but not all its souls want to be saved. Besides, the interpretations of the Good Book are so ambiguous. Mary informs us in a predictable voice-over that 'I've been born again my whole life' and is saving herself for her marriage. However, when she discovers that her boyfriend is gay, she thinks Jesus would approve of a bit of carnal intervention. So she gets pregnant, he gets sent away to an improving school (where he falls in love with Mitch) and Mary gets left with the opprobrium of her God-loving peers… *Saved!* boasts a fertile subject and some good one-liners ('You're not born gay, you're born *again*'). It's also got a first-rate cast, but under the inexperienced direction of Brian Dannelly, every joke, beat and twist falls as flat as a communion wafer.
JC-W

• *Mary* Jena Malone, *Hilary Faye* Mandy Moore, *Roland* Macaulay Culkin, *Patrick* Patrick Fugit, *Tia* Heather Matarazzo, *Cassandra* Eva Amurri, *Dean* Chad Faust, *Veronica* Elizabeth Thai, *Pastor Skip* Martin Donovan, *Lillian* Mary-Louise Parker, *Mitch* Kett Turton, *with* Julia Arkos, Donna White, James Caldwell, and (as herself) Valerie Bertinelli.

• *Dir* Brian Dannelly, *Pro* Michael Stipe, Sandy Stern, Michael Ohoven and William Vince, *Co-Ex Pro* Kerry Rock, David Prybil, Kaye Dyal and Steven Gagnon, *Screenplay* Dannelly and Michael Urban, *Ph* Bobby Bukowski, *Ed* Pamela Martin, *M* Christophe Beck; Vivaldi; songs performed by All-Star United, Royale, Travis, Wes Cunningham, Mandy Moore and Michael Stipe, Julia Staines, Disco Pusher, Depeche Mode, Salt-N-Pepa, The Martins, The Replacements, She Boy Gub, Tag Team, etc, *Costumes* Wendy Chuck.

Single Cell Pictures/Infinity Media-Verve Pictures.
91 mins. USA. 2004. Rel: 29 October 2004. Cert. 12A.

Save the Green Planet ★★★★

A loner and social misfit, Byung-gu believes that the world is being overtaken by aliens disguised as high-ranking human officials. With the help of his dumpy girlfriend Sooni, a tightrope walker, he kidnaps Kang Man-shik, the arrogant president of the Yoojae Chemical Company. Byung-gu then subjects his prisoner to a series of bizarre tortures… 'Extraordinary' is the only way to describe Jang Jun-hwan's debut feature. A sporadically profound and disturbing examination of our planet's fragility cloaked in a bloodthirsty apocalyptic farce, *Save the Green Planet* is destined to divide viewers soundly. Those wedded to the off-kilter mentality of Kurt Vonnegut Jr should get it (comparisons can be made to the latter's *Slaughterhouse Five*), while those who prefer their entertainments neatly labelled 'drama' or 'comedy' will likely suffer overpowering nausea. Regardless of how misconceived or sick you may think this brazen original to be, you cannot deny its chutzpah, energy or style. A sly, sympathetic portrayal of a serial killer one minute, the film will switch to a Keystone Cop mentality the next, wildly juggling your standard Korean detective mystery with a sadism worthy of *The Texas Chain Saw Massacre*. Amazingly, most of this works, with a comic highlight being Inspector Chu's pathetic attempt to shoot down an angry swarm of bees (he kills two).
JC-W

• *Lee Byung-gu* Shin Ha-kyun, *Kang Man-shik* Baek Yun-shik, *Sooni* Hwang Jeong-min, *Inspector Chu* Lee Jae-yong, *Detective Kim* Lee Joo-hyun, *Det. Inspector Lee* Ki Joo-bong, *Tae Shik* Kim Dong-hyun.

• *Dir* and *Screenplay* Jang Jun-hwan, *Pro* Tcha Seung-jai and Noh Jong-yoon, *Ex Pro* Lee Kang-bok, *Ph* Houng Gyung-pyo, *Pro Des* Jang Geun-young and Kim Gyung-hee, *Ed* Park Gok-ji, *M* Lee Dong-joon, *Sound* Lee In-gyu.

CJ Entertainment/Sidus Corp/Discovery Venture Capital-Tartan Films.
116 mins. South Korea. 2003. Rel: 24 September 2004. Cert. 18.

Saw ★

The latest victims of the 'Jigsaw' killer, Adam and Dr Lawrence Gordon wake to find themselves opposite each other in a dank room chained to pipes at the ankle. Armed with a saw that will cut through flesh, but not their chains, Dr Gordon has eight hours to kill Adam or his wife and daughter's lives are forfeit… With flashbacks and red herrings aplenty, we're sent careening through this dungeon of a film. Sadly, co-writers James Wan (who also directed) and Whannell are literary cowards who fail to wring the slightest nuance from their characters or the true drama of their situation. Instead, it's one cheap 'twist' after another in this implausible paean to the turpitude of movie-going audiences. Despite this being an over-hyped mediocrity, do keep an eye on the Melbourne-bred duo who created it. There's obvious talent there. They just need to find more challenging fare. SWM

• *Dr Lawrence Gordon* Cary Elwes, *Tapp* Danny Glover, *Allison Gordon* Monica Potter, *Zep* Michael Emerson, *Jigsaw* Tobin Bell, *Adam* Leigh Whannell, *with* Ken Leung, Mackenzie Vegas, Shawnee Smith, Dina Meyer, Ned Bellamy.

• *Dir* James Wan, *Pro* Gregg Hoffman, Oren Koules and Mark Burg, *Ex Pro* Stacey Testro, *Co-Pro* Daniel Jason and Heffner and Richard H. Prince, *Screenplay* Wan and Leigh Whannell, *Ph* David Asrmstrong, *Pro Des* Julie Berghoff, *Ed* Kevin Greutert, *M* Charlie Couser, *Costumes* Jennifer Soulages.

Twisted Pictures-Entertainment.
102 mins. USA. 2004. Rel: 1 October 2004.
Cert. 18.

School for Seduction ★

Newcastle upon Tyne; the present. Various women are finding their lives – and partners – untenable just when Sophia Rosselini, a mysterious beauty from Naples, sets up a class dubbed 'School for Seduction.' Sagely, Sophia assures her nervous students that 'Seduction is not about pleasing men, it is about pleasing yourself,' adding, 'There's a little fire in every woman. Don't let it go out.' Sophia proves to be quite a success, but is she all that she's cracked up to be? Occasionally a venture surfaces that reminds one of the ineffable embarrassment of the British sex films of the 1970s. While a nostalgic glow may surround the product of Mary Millington and Fiona Richmond, their films were unforgivably bad. *School for Seduction*, which took first-time director Sue Heel five years to realise, is a sober reminder of our shameful past. Punctuated with funny music (a mandolin plays whenever Sophia makes an entrance) and blighted by muffled dialogue, the film wastes a handful of first-rate actresses in an exercise of grim predictability and obviousness. JC-W

• *Sophia Rosselini/Gillian* Kelly Brook, *Kelly* Emily Woof, *Claire Hughes* Dervla Kirwan, *Irene* Margi Clarke, *Donna* Jessica Johnson, *Craig Hughes* Neil Stuke, *Derek* Tim Healy, *Toni* Ben Porter, *Mark* Daymon Britton, *with* Jake Canuso, Sophie Dix, David Whitaker.

• *Dir* Sue Heel, *Pro* Steve Bowden, Christine Alderson and Angad Paul, *Ex Pro* Vic Bateman, Ashley Sidaway, Simon Franks and Zygi Kamasa, *Screenplay* Heel and Martin Herron, *Ph* Tony Imi, *Pro Des* Suzanne Field and Ash Wilkinson, *Ed* David Martin and Sean Barton, *M* Mark Thomas, *Costumes* Sally Plum.

Ipso Facto Films/AV Pictures/UKFS 5 LLP/Redbus Pictures-Redbus Film Distribution.
104 mins. UK. 2004. Rel: 3 December 2004.
Cert. 12A.

The Sea Inside ★★★

Ramón Sampedro has spent 28 years campaigning for the right to die with dignity. Paralysed from the neck down, he is at the total mercy of his brother, sister-in-law and nephew, who attend to his every whim. Trapped in the limited prison of his own body, Sampedro believes that his life is a right, not an obligation… It's hard for any film to live up to the hype that this has received (Golden Globe, Felix, Oscar and a slew of Goyas). And considering that this is a drama about a 55-year-old man stuck in a bed, it is remarkable. Again, Bardem reinforces his reputation as one of the finest film actors alive,

but Belén Rueda and Mabel Rivera are equally good. The film is also exquisitely crafted, its moral integrity unassailable and as a homage to the spirit of Sampedro it is exemplary. Even so, there is an intrinsic inertia in the subject matter (for once, flashbacks may have been a genuine asset) and a tastefulness that robs the drama of any gut-tugging connection with death itself. Original title: *Mar adentro*.
JC-W

• *Ramón Sampedro* Javier Bardem, *Julia* Belén Rueda, *Rosa* Lola Dueñas, *Gené* Clara Segura, *Manuela* Mabel Rivera, *José* Celso Bugallo, *Joaquín* Joan Dalmau, *Javi* Tamar Novas, *Germán* Alberto Giménez.

• *Dir, Ed* and *M* Alejandro Amenábar, *Pro* Amenábar and Fernando Bovaira, *Screenplay* Amenábar and Mateo Gil, *Ph* Javier Aguirresarobe, *Pro Des* Benjamín Fernández, *Make-up* Jo Allen.

Sogepaq/Sogecine/UGC Images/Eyescreen/Canal Plus-Entertainment.
126 mins. Spain/France/Italy. 2004.
Rel: 11 February 2005. Cert. PG.

Seed of Chucky ★★½

It's been six years since those serial-killer-possessed dolls Chucky and Tiffany were destroyed after managing to produce an heir in *Bride of Chucky*. But, when production begins on a movie about his murderous, plastic parents, Glen/Glenda ('he' has no genitalia to confirm 'his' gender, after all) heads for Hollywood to resurrect Chucky and Tiffany and rejoin his homicidal family. Much bloody mayhem ensues as Chucky rededicates himself to acquiring human hosts for the doll-trapped trio… Series writer and creator Don Mancini takes on the directing chores for this fifth outing in the *Child's Play* franchise with very mixed results. *Seed* is a parody nestled within a horror movie, but it never quite balances the two with any assurance. Counting less on tension than rapacious humour, it's perversely funny, with a sublime Meg Tilly in dual roles. Ed Wood would be so proud. SWM

• *Jennifer Tilly* Jennifer Tilly, *voice of Tiffany* Jennifer Tilly, *voice of Chucky* Brad Dourif, *voice of Glen/Glenda* Billy Boyd, *Redman* Redman, *Joan* Hannah Spearritt, *Pete Peters* John Waters, *Psychs* Keith-Lee Castle, *Stan* Steve Lawton, *Tony Gardner* Tony Gardner, *Santa* Jason Flemyng, *with* Nicholas Rowe, Rebecca Santos, Barnaby Thompson

• *Dir* and *Screenplay* Don Mancini, based on characters created by Mancini, *Pro* David Kirschner and Corey Sienega, *Ex Pro* Guy J. Louthan, *Co-Pro* Laura Moskowitz, *Ph* Vernon Layton, *Pro Des* Peter James Russell and Cristian Niculescu, *Ed* Chris Dickens, *M* Pino Donaggio, *Costumes* Oana Paunescu, *Animatronic Character/Effects* Tony Gardner, *Visual Consultant* Richard Holland.

Rogue Pictures/La Sienaga Prods-Momentum Pictures.
86 mins. USA/UK/Romania. 2004. Rel: 13 May 2005.
Cert. 15.

Strictly ballroom: Richard Gere and Jennifer Lopez in Peter Chelsom's
effortless *Shall We Dance* (from Buena Vista International)

Shaolin Soccer **S**

Shall We Dance ★★★

Chicago; today. John Clark is a successful lawyer with a loving
wife, a nice home in the suburbs and two balanced teenage
kids. But he's found himself in a rut and is ashamed to admit
to himself that he's unhappy. Then, on a bizarre whim, he
indulges himself in a secret passion – ballroom dancing
lessons… The good news is that *Shall We Dance* is nowhere near
as bad as the Americanisation of the Japanese hit *The Grudge*.
Nonetheless, it's still a packaged, glossy and rather obvious
concoction aimed to lift the hearts of American housewives the
world over. The original, directed by Masayuki Suo in 1995,
was a charming, bittersweet and believable comedy acting as a
potent commentary on contemporary Japan. Apart from casting
the most Oriental-looking stars in Hollywood (Gere and JLo),
the remake ditches the credibility of its prototype and goes for
novelty and pastiche. Gere is quite sweet as the transformed
'suit' (and cuts quite a dash on the dance floor), although Susan
Sarandon is wasted in a secondary role, in spite of a wonderful
speech about marriage ('We need a witness to our lives…'). Of
course, the music is fab, there are some amusing supporting
performances (particularly from Tucci, Jenkins and Cannon) and
the whole thing is as effortlessly arresting as a Saturday night
out at your local Wagamama. JC-W

• *John Clark* Richard Gere, *Paulina* Jennifer Lopez, *Beverly
Clark* Susan Sarandon, *Link Peterson* Stanley Tucci, *Chic* Bobby
Cannavale, *Devine* Richard Jenkins, *Bobbie* Lisa Ann Walter,

Vern Omar Benson Miller, *Miss Mitzi* Anita Gilette, *Scotty* Nick
Cannon, *Jenna Clark* Tamara Hope, *with* Mya Harrison, Stark
Sands, Ja Rule.

• *Dir* Peter Chelsom, *Pro* Simon Fields, *Ex Pro* Bob Weinstein,
Harvey Weinstein and Julie Goldstein, *Co-Ex Pro* Jennifer
Berman and Amy Israel, *Co-Pro* Mari Jo Winkler, *Assoc Pro*
Rachel Hudgins, *Screenplay* Audrey Wells, *Ph* John De Borman,
Pro Des Caroline Hanania, *Ed* Charlie Ireland, *M* Gabriel
Yared and John Altman, *Costumes* Sophie de Rakoff Carbonell,
Choreography John O'Connell.

Miramax/Simon Fields-Buena Vista International.
106 mins. USA/Canada. 2004. Rel: 18 February 2005.
Cert. 12A.

Shaolin Soccer ★★

Martial arts invade the soccer pitch in this ridiculous Hong
Kong movie. It asks us to root for a team of oddballs who
bring kung fu tactics into play when taking on rival soccer
players adept at cheating. The print imported is the so-called
'international version' courtesy of Miramax. This means that
it comes with atrocious English dubbing and presumably such
additions as the song 'Kung Fu Fighting' on the soundtrack.
Stephen Chow does have something to offer as witnessed by
his skills in directing and editing, while his screen presence in
the lead role is reminiscent of Bruce Lee. Even so, his movie

is so banal and unsophisticated that the dubbing seems appropriate, for this is an entertainment headed for the video store and an audience looking for a title that provides some silly fun best viewed at home while swilling beer. For more serious aficionados, a subtitled print was also screened. Original Mandarin title: *Shao lin ju qiu*. Aka *Siu lam juk kau*. MS

• *Sing (Brother #5)* Stephen Chow, *Mui* Vicki Zhao, *Golden Leg Fung* Man Nat Ng, *Hung* Yin Tse [as Patrick Tse Yin], *Iron Head* Yut Fei Wong, *with* Sarondar Li, Cecilia Cheung, Karen Mok.

• *Dir* Stephen Chow, *Pro* Kwok-fai Yeung, *Screenplay* Chow and Kan-Cheung Tsang, *Ph* Pak-huen Kwen and Ting Wo Kwong, *Art Dir* Kim Hung Ho, *Ed* Kit-Wai Kai, *M* Lowell Lo and Raymond Wong, *Costumes* Yim Man Choy, *Action Dir* Siu-Tung Ching.

Star Overseas/Universe Entertainment-Buena Vista International.
87 mins. Hong Kong/China/USA. 2002.
Rel: 12 November 2004. Cert. 12A.

Shark Tale ★★★

The South-Side Reef; the ocean. Oscar, a cleaner fish working at Whale Wash, is all talk. But Oscar has a smart mouth and somehow it always manages to fish him out of trouble. When he claims responsibility for the death of a shark, he becomes an overnight celebrity, complete with swish penthouse, lucrative endorsements and femme fatale. However, Don Lino,

a Great White and godfather of the Reef, intends for Oscar to sleep with the fishes… First Disney and DreamWorks locked antennae over the rival projects *A Bug's Life* and *Antz*. Now DreamWorks is in deep water with its blatant echo of *Finding Nemo* (international gross: $766m). As it happens, *Shark Tale* is more an aquatic cross between *The Godfather* and *Car Wash* with allusions to a whole bouillabaisse of film store memorabilia. With a stellar vocal cast playing on their own public personas, the film is a pandemic of piscine anthropomorphism. A product placement wonderland (Gup, Coral-Cola, Kelpy Kremes), it is at its funniest when it's just plain simple (like the sharks humming John Williams' theme tune to *Jaws*). It's sassy, funky, extravagant and skilfully calibrated entertainment. But it doesn't have charm – nor a heart. JC-W

• voices: *Oscar* Will Smith, *Don Lino* Robert De Niro, *Angie* Renée Zellweger, *Lola* Angelina Jolie, *Lenny* Jack Black, *Sykes* Martin Scorsese, *Ernie* Ziggy Marley, *Bernie* Doug E. Doug, *Frankie* Michael Imperioli, *Luca* Vincent Pastore, *Don Brizzi* Peter Falk, *with* Katie Couric, Frank Vincent, Jenifer Lewis, Sean Bishop.

• *Dir* Bibo Bergeron and Vicky Jenson, *Pro* Bill Damaschke, Janet Healy and Allison Lyon Segan, *Ex Pro* Jeffrey Kaztenberg, *Screenplay* Michael J. Wilson and Rob Letterman, *Pro Des* Daniel St Pierre, *Ed* John Venzon, *M* Hans Zimmer; songs performed by Christina Aguilera and Missy Elliott, Sean Paul and Ziggy Marley, Justin Timberlake and Timbaland, JoJo, D12, Mary J. Blige and Will Smith, Avant, Ludacris and Bobby V and Lil' Fate, India.Arie, The Pussycat Dolls,

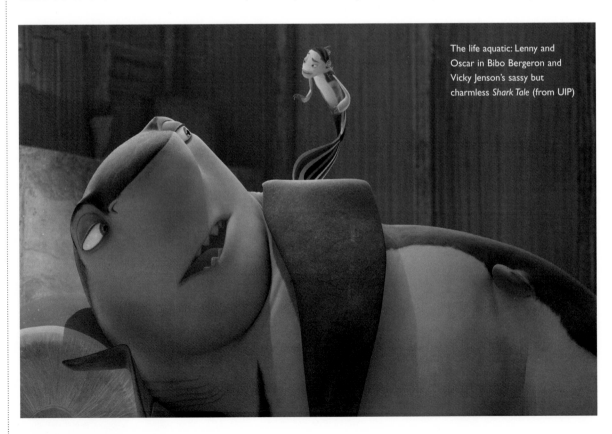

The life aquatic: Lenny and Oscar in Bibo Bergeron and Vicky Jenson's sassy but charmless *Shark Tale* (from UIP)

fan_3, Cheryl Lynn, Madness, Elvis Presley, and The Four Tops, *Sound* Wade Wilson and Mark Binder.

DreamWorks Animation-UIP.
90 mins. USA. 2004. Rel: 15 October 2004. Cert. U.

She Hate Me ★½

If you have an objection to the word 'sperm' then *She Hate Me* is best avoided. While the film explores a number of themes, its main thrust is the genetic eligibility of one John Henry 'Jack' Armstrong, a handsome, principled and urbane biotech executive. When he loses his job at a major pharmaceutical company, he is enlisted by his ex-girlfriend to supply her and a number of her lesbian associates with ovarian fertilisation. At first he resists the prospect of commitment-free sex to unusually attractive lesbians, but then he's offered $5000 a shot... *She Hate Me* is one helluva mess. A sex comedy, corporate thriller, courtroom drama and social commentary, the film meanders wildly as it embraces issues of racism, corporate greed, sexual intolerance, family values, Watergate, business ethics, Aids, organised crime and paternity, among other things. Director Spike Lee has so many bones to pick that he's landed himself in an elephant's graveyard. This aside, *She Hate Me* is bloated, sentimental, over-scored, over-directed and over-long, and at times feels like a multi-racial Carry On farce directed by Oliver Stone. There are flashbacks, montages, cartoons and even a bizarre sequence featuring Richard Nixon in a Tricky Dickie mask. Go figure.   JC-W

• *John Henry 'Jack' Armstrong* Anthony Mackie, *Fatima Goodrich* Kerry Washington, *Margo Chadwick* Ellen Barkin, *Simona Bonasera* Monica Bellucci, *Geronimo Armstrong* Jim Brown, *Song* Sarita Choudhury, *Judge Buchanan* Ossie Davis, *Chairman Church* Brian Dennehy, *Leland Powell* Woody Harrelson, *Oni* Bai Ling, *Lottie Armstrong* Lonette McKee, *Evelyn* Paula Jai Parker, *Vada Huff* Q-Tip, *Alex Guerrero* Dania Ramirez, *Don Angelo Bonasera* John Turturro, *Frank Wills* Chiwetel Ejiofor, *with* Jamel Debbouze, David Bennent, Isiah Whitlock, Joie Lee, Michael Genet, Rick Aiello, *G. Gordon Liddy* Don Harvey, *Doris* Alison Folland, Poorna.

• *Dir* Spike Lee, *Pro* Lee, Preston Holmes and Fernando Sulichin, *Screenplay* Lee and Michael Genet, *Ph* Matty Libatique, *Pro Des* Brigitte Broch, *Ed* Barry Alexander Brown, *M* Terence Blanchard, *Costumes* Donna Berwick.

40 Acres and Mule Filmworks/Rule 8 Prods/Pathé France/Kissman-Columbia TriStar.
138 mins. USA/France. 2004. Rel: 24 September 2004. Cert. 15.

Shrek 2 ★★★★★

Shrek 2 is surely the most effortlessly entertaining movie of the year, a big summer treat for kids and adults of every comic persuasion. Visually astonishing, consistently hilarious and narratively sound, it bulldozes its way to the heart and funny bone with a verve and achievement that makes one appreciate the true capacity of cinema. Every single minute is an object lesson in comic invention, relentlessly lampooning other

movies, developing fresh characters, overturning stereotypes and exploring our own place in the mythology of story-telling. A jumble of wild ideas and audacious reinvention, *Shrek 2* takes the culmination of the first movie and sends it rocketing into the reality of every newlywed's nightmare: will the in-laws approve? Of course, a fat, smelly ogre will not be every parent's idea of the perfect son-in-law, particularly with Prince Charming foot-loose and fancy-free. Thus, true love is forced once again to battle the overpowering forces of preconception, and so Shrek and Princess Fiona experience their first marital differences – just as the whole kingdom of Far Far Away conspires against them. The introduction of a wily Puss in Boots and an autocratic Fairy Godmother sweetens the brew, while the bombardment of product placement (such as the store for designer weaponry, Versarchery) will ensure a constant smile.   JC-W

• voices: *Shrek* Mike Myers, *Donkey* Eddie Murphy, *Princess Fiona* Cameron Diaz, *Queen Lillian* Julie Andrews, *King Harold* John Cleese, *Puss-in-Boots* Antonio Banderas, *Prince Charming* Rupert Everett, *Fairy Godmother* Jennifer Saunders, *with* Kelly Asbury, Cody Cameron, Conrad Vernon, Larry King, Joan Rivers, Andrew Adamson, *and (UK version only)* Jonathan Ross, Kate Thornton.

• *Dir* Andrew Adamson, Kelly Asbury and Conrad Vernon, *Pro* Aron Warner, David Lipman and John H. Williams, *Ex Pro* Jeffrey Katzenberg, *Screenplay* Adamson, Joe Stillman, J. David Stern and David N. Weiss, from a story by Adamson, based on the book by William Steig, *Pro Des* Guillaume Aretos, *Ed* Michael Andrews and Sim Evan-Jones, *M* Harry Gregson-Williams; songs performed by Counting Crows, Eddie Murphy, Jennifer Saunders, Antonio Banderas, Butterfly Boucher and David Bowie, Chic, Tom Waits, eels, Pete Yorn, Frou Frou, Joseph Arthur, Lipps, Inc., Nick Cave & The Bad Seeds, and Dashboard Confessional, *Visual Effects* Ken Bielenberg, *Supervising Animation* Raman Hui, Tim Cheung and James Baxter, *Costumes* Isis Mussenden, *Sound* Randy Thom.

DreamWorks-UIP.
92 mins. USA. 2004. Rel: 2 July 2004. Cert U.

Sideways ★★★★

Having extracted an uncharacteristically scrubbed-down performance from Jack Nicholson in *About Schmidt*, fashionable wunderkind Alexander Payne sharpens his creative scalpel on Paul Giamatti and the miserable schlemiel he plays here. Miles Raymond is an exasperatingly defeatist, negative English teacher who's placed his first novel with a small-scale publisher and is still obsessed by his ex-wife. In the week prior to the wedding of his best friend Jack, he has suggested that they enjoy a few days of relaxation and wine-tasting in California's Santa Ynex Valley. If there's one thing that brings Miles alive, it's his appetite for wine, both for its gustatory and mood-shifting qualities. In the patois of oenology, *Sideways* is a dry, sensitive yet cheeky vintage, with a wry perspective on the bourgeois values of Southern California. As always, Paul Giamatti (*Duets*, *American Splendor*) is a revelation who, with his balding pate, pot belly and hairy shoulders, is a most unlikely yet engaging leading man. There's also a delightful performance from Virginia Madsen who, as a fellow oenophile, delivers the film's greatest speech ('A bottle of wine is actually alive – it's constantly evolving and gaining complexity…'). JC-W

• *Miles Raymond* Paul Giamatti, *Jack Lopate* Thomas Haden Church, *Maya* Virginia Madsen, *Stephanie* Sandra Oh, *Miles's mother* Marylouise Burke, *Victoria* Jessica Hecht, *Cammi* Missy Doty, *Cammi's husband* MC Gainey, *Christine Erganian* Alysia Reiner, *Mrs Erganian* Shaké Toukhmanian, *Mike Erganian* Duke Moosekian, *Miles's building manager* Robert Covarrubias, *Gary the bartender* Patrick Gallagher, *Stephanie's mother* Stephanie Faracy, *wine lecturer* Peter Dennis.

• *Dir* Alexander Payne, *Pro* Michael London, *Co-Pro* George Parra, *Screenplay* Payne and Jim Taylor, from the novel by Rex Pickett, *Ph* Phedon Papamichael, *Pro Des* Jane Ann Stewart, *Ed* Kevin Tent, *M* Rolfe Kent, *Costumes* Wendy Chuck, *Editorial Cat* Lulu.

Fox Searchlight-Fox.
127 mins. USA. 2004. Rel: 28 January 2005. Cert. 15.

Sin City ★★★½

To set the tone, *Sin City* opens with a devastatingly romantic love scene. It's a bright, calm night, the moon is out and Josh Hartnett, spouting poetic Chandleresque dialogue, echoes the most intimate thoughts of a beautiful woman. The latter's eyes flash a faint green, her red dress shimmers in the moonlight, but everything else is black-and-white. And then, taking her in his arms, he shoots her. Such is the tenor of this brutal, stylised portmanteau film adapted from three stories from Frank Miller's eponymous graphic-novel series. Like *Pulp Fiction*, *Sin City* unfolds its narrative in elliptical loops, with characters straying into each other's stories. The monochromatic photography and stylised dialogue take a while to get used to, but it's a superb evocation of the comic. However, the film's overt sadism and sexism is only likely to appeal to a narrow, diehard demographic. Still, if torture, cannibalism, dismemberment, suicide, emotional cruelty and capital punishment are your cup of Earl Grey, then this is definitely for you. FYI: 'Guest' director Quentin Tarantino contributes the scene in which Clive Owen discovers that his dead passenger, played by an unrecognisable Benicio Del Toro, is still alive, in spite of the barrel of a gun embedded in his forehead. JC-W

• *Nancy Callahan* Jessica Alba, *Jackie Boy* Benicio Del Toro, *Shellie* Brittany Murphy, *Dwight* Clive Owen, *Marv* Mickey Rourke, *John Hartigan* Bruce Willis, *Kevin* Elijah Wood, *Miho* Devon Aoki, *Becky* Alexis Bledel, *Senator Roark* Powers Boothe, *Gail* Rosario Dawson, *Manute* Michael Clarke Duncan, *Lucille* Carla Gugino, *The Man* Josh Hartnett, *Cardinal Roark* Rutger Hauer, *Goldie/Wendy* Jaime King, *Bob* Michael Madsen, *Roark Jr/Yellow Bastard* Nick Stahl, *the customer* Marley Shelton, *with* Jude Ciccolella, Tommy Flanagan, Nicky Katt, *priest* Frank Miller, Lisa Marie Newmyer, Jeff Schwan, Mackenzie Vega.

• *Dir* Robert Rodriguez, Frank Miller and Quentin Tarantino, *Pro* Rodriguez, Miller and Elizabeth Avellán, *Ex Pro* Bob Weinstein and Harvey Weinstein, *Ph* and *Ed* Rodriguez, *Art Dir* Jeannette Scott and Steve Joyner, *M* Rodriguez, John Debney and Graeme Revell, *Sound* Craig Henighan.

Dimension Films/Troublemaker Studios-Buena Vista International.
124 mins. USA. 2005. Rel: 3 June 2005. Cert. 18.

Pulp friction: Jessica Alba and Bruce Willis in the stylish and sadistic *Sin City* (from Buena Vista International)

16 Years of Alcohol ★★★

This admirably ambitious but flawed first feature from writer/
director Richard Jobson is set in Edinburgh. It tells of one
man's attempts to overcome his alcoholism and his violent
tendencies that stem both from feeling disadvantaged and from
a childhood trauma when witnessing his father being unfaithful
to his mother. Kevin McKidd makes a good attempt at this
role but sometimes seems to be coming from two different
directions rather than representing contrasting sides of a single
personality. Aiming at high art, Jobson suggests influences
ranging from Terence Davies and Lynne Ramsay to Stanley
Kubrick, but his combination of realism and poetry lacks the
cohesion achieved by Tony Richardson in *A Taste of Honey*.
Splendid widescreen images blown up from digital introduce us
to Digitalscope! MS

• *Frankie Mac* Kevin McKidd, *Helen* Laura Fraser, *Mary* Susan
Lynch, *director* Jim Carter, *Jake* Ewen Bremner, *with* Elaine C.
Smith, Kate Robbins, Russell Anderson, Jim Cunningham,
John Comerford.

• *Dir* and *Screenplay* Richard Jobson, *Pro* Jobson, Hamish
McAlpine and Mark Burton, *Ex Pro* Steve McIntyre, Wouter
Barendrecht and Michael J. Werner, *Ph* John Rhodes, *Pro
Des* Adam Squires, *Ed* Ioannis Chalkiadakis, *M* Keith Atack,
Costumes Francesca Oddi, Kim Hunt and Flora Clarke.

Scottish Screen/Metro Tartan/Fortissimo/Tartan Works-
Tartan Films.
101 mins. UK/Netherlands. 2003. Rel: 30 July 2004.
Cert. 18.

Sky Captain and the World of Tomorrow ★½

Computer whiz kid and first-time director Kerry Conran is
some kind of genius. And no doubt other computer whiz kids
will recognise this. However, for all his artistic imagination
and sleight-of-hand on the mouse, Conran hasn't – yet – got
what it takes to be a great filmmaker. He has spent over six
years imagining a unique universe of retro-futurism, plucking
at aspects of science fiction, pulp fiction and World War II
melodrama and blending it into a visually remarkable film
that is part cartoon and part live-action spectacle. With his
actors working in a blue-screen vacuum, Conran has built
the majority of sets, locations, landscapes and gadgetry in
his computer. Jude Law plays Captain H. Joseph Sullivan, a
daredevil pilot who teams up with reporter and ex-flame Polly
Perkins to track down a criminal mastermind. Set prior to
the Second World War, the film grabs elements of *The Wizard
of Oz*, Indiana Jones and *Thunderbirds* and fuses them into a
universe shaped by H.G. Wells, Conan Doyle and Edgar Rice
Burroughs. While Law isn't bad as the fearless and cynical
Captain Sky, the rest of the cast falls foul of Conran's directorial
inexperience. On a thespian level, this is the worst thing that
Gwyneth Paltrow has ever done, her attempt to appear plucky
and sultry coming off as sulky and annoying, while Angelina
Jolie looks like a Muppet of Angelina Jolie. JC-W

• *Polly Perkins* Gwyneth Paltrow, *Captain H. Joseph Sullivan*
aka 'Sky Captain' Jude Law, *Franky Cook* Angelina Jolie, *Dex
Dearborn* Giovanni Ribisi, *Morris Paley* Michael Gambon,
mysterious woman Bai Ling, *Kaji* Omid Djalili, *Dr Totenkopf*
Laurence Olivier [archive footage], *with* Trevor Baxter, Julian
Curry, Stuart Milligan, William Hope.

• *Dir, Screenplay, Pro Des* and *Costumes* Kerry Conran, *Pro* Jon
Avnet, Marsha Oglesby, Sadie Frost and Jude Law, *Ex Pro*
Aurelio de Laurentiis, Raffaella de Laurentiis and Bill Haber,
Co-Pro Hester Hargett-Aupetit and Brooke Breton, *Ph* Eric
Adkins, *Pro Des* and *Costumes* Kevin Conran, *Ed* Sabrina Plisco,

Computer graphic: Jude Law and Gwyneth Paltrow in Kerry Conran's
retro-futuristic *Sky Captain and the World of Tomorrow* (from UIP)

M Edward Shearmur, *Visual Effects* Scott E. Anderson

Paramount/Brooklyn Films II/Riff Raff-Blue Flower-UIP. 106 mins. USA/UK/Italy. 2004. Rel: 1 October 2004. Cert. PG.

Somersault ★★★½

Heidi is 16 and shares a life with her mother and her mother's boyfriend Adam. When, impulsively, she kisses Adam – and is caught red-handed – she runs away from home, landing up at the ski resort of Lake Jindabyne, New South Wales. There, she uses her clumsy sexual wiles in the hope of earning work, lodging and some form of human contact... Revealing a masterful hand at painting emotional environments and coaxing naturalistic performances from her cast, writer-director Cate Shortland is a talent to watch. Her first feature-length film is a shimmering mosaic of surfaces, which are scrubbed away to reveal an interior landscape of mortal scars and bruises. Challenging our own presumptions by not showing what we think may be happening off-screen, Shortland has created a complex, percipient twilight that is both poetic and deeply affecting. Recipient of the Best Film, Director and Actress awards from the Australian Film Critics Circle. JC-W

• *Heidi* Abbie Cornish, *Joe* Sam Worthington, *Irene* Lynette Curran, *Richard* Erik Thomson, *Stuart* Nathaniel Dean, *Bianca* Hollie Andrew, *Diane* Leah Purcell, *Nicole* Olivia Pigeot, *Adam* Damian de Montemas, *Martha* Anne Louise Lambert, *with* John Sheerin, Paul Gleeson, Blake Pittman, Toby Schmitz.

• *Dir* and *Screenplay* Cate Shortland, *Pro* Anthony Anderson, *Ex Pro* Jan Chapman, *Ph* Robert Humphreys, *Pro Des* Melinda Doring, *Ed* Scott Gray, *M* Decoder Ring, *Costumes* Emily Seresin, *Sound* Sam Petty.

Film Finance Corporation Australia/New South Wales Film + Television Office/Showtime/Red Carpet-Metrodome. 105 mins. Australia. 2004. Rel: 4 March 2005. Cert. 15.

Son of the Mask ★½

A mostly annoying attempt at a live-action cartoon, *Son of the Mask* follows the god Loki's attempts to retrieve the id-freeing Mask that Jim Carrey made so famous. Reluctant dad and would-be animator Tim Avery (a clear homage to animation icon Tex Avery) manages to come across the magical mask and impregnates his wife while under its spell. Nine months later, his son is born with the same metamorphic powers the enchanted mask imbues. Contending with both his jealous dog Otis and Loki himself (a wonderfully mischievous Alan Cumming), *Son of the Mask* only misfires when it deals with Mask-related events. The dreadful CGI, poorly wrought humour and reckless plotting all fail when weighed against the poignancy of the 'real life' events surrounding a young couple starting their family. Jamie Kennedy is truly superb as an angst-ridden dad but is utterly unbearable as the Mask. SWM

• *Tim Avery* Jamie Kennedy, *Loki* Alan Cumming, *Tonya Avery* Traylor Howard, *Jorge* Kal Pen, *Daniel Moss* Steven Wright, *Odin* Bob Hoskins, *Alvey* Liam and Ryan Falconer, *Otis* Bear, *with* Ben Stein, Sandy Winton, Rebecca Massey, Magda Szubanski.

• *Dir* Lawrence Guterman, *Pro* Erica Huggins and Scott Kroopf, *Ex Pro* Beau Marks, Mike Richardson, Toby Emmerich, Kent Alterman and Michele Weiss, *Co-Pro* Stephen Jones, *Screenplay* Lance Khazei, *Ph* Greg Gardiner, *Pro Des* Leslie Dilley, *Ed* Malcolm Campbell and Debra Neil Fisher, *M* Randy Edelman; tracks perrformed by Derek McKeith, Ryan Cabrera, Chic, Neil Diamond, Dr John and the Lower 9 11, Stephen Bishop, Marissa Jaret Winokur, Paul Anka, Chubby Checker, and Jamie Kennedy, *Costumes* Mary E. Vogt, *Visual Effects Supervisor* James E. Price.

New Line Cinema/Radar Pictures/Dark Horse Entertainment-Entertainment. 94 mins. USA. 2005. Rel: 11 February 2005. Cert. PG.

Soul Plane ★

Tom Arnold's idiotic family are the only white folks on the inaugural flight of the Soul Plane piloted by a permanently stoned Snoop Dogg. I can see rows of empty seats aboard this aircraft, weighed down with an appallingly heavy cargo of endless smutty gags, miscalculated mugging and bad stereotypes. This flight is cancelled! DW

• *Mr Hunkee* Tom Arnold, *Nashawn* Kevin Hart, *Muggsy* Method Man, *Captain Mack* Snoop Dogg, *Giselle* K.D. Aubert, *Gaeman* Godfrey, *DJ* Brian Hooks, *Blanca* Sofia Vergara, *with* D.L. Hughley, Arielle Kebbel, Loni Love, Missi Pyle, Gary Anthony Williams, John Witherspoon, Stacey Travis, Terry Crews, Chris Robinson, La La, Don Wilson.

• *Dir* Jessy Terrero, *Pro* Terrero and David Scott Rubin, *Ex Pro* Bo Zenga and Paul Hall, *Screenplay* Zenga and Chuck Wilson, *Ph* Jonathan Sela, *Pro Des* Robb Buono, *Ed* Michael R. Miller, *M* The RZA, *Costumes* Shawn Burton.

MGM-Verve Pictures. 86 mins. USA. 2004. Rel: 27 August 2004. Cert. 18.

Spanglish ★★★½

John Clasky is a 'casually daring' chef and the 'stark ravingly calm' husband of Deborah Clasky, a competitive, highly strung over-achiever. John and Deborah have serious issues, problems brought to a head with the arrival of Flor Moreno, a Mexican housekeeper who quickly becomes indispensable in spite of her inability to understand a single word of English... First off, this is not an Adam Sandler movie. Adam Sandler is in it, but he isn't particularly goofy, there's no five-syllable concept and the gross-out factor is zero. This is a James L. Brooks movie, an all-American fable with laughs, tears and a whole lot of good acting. An ensemble exploration of motherhood, family disharmony and the clash of Spanish and American linguistics, *Spanglish* is weak by James L. Brooks standards but still has a lot of wonderful moments. There's

Latin spattin': Paz Vega and Téa Leoni in James L. Brooks's *Spanglish* (from Columbia TriStar)

no real dramatic momentum, more an accumulation of biting observations tempered by Sandler's good humour. Even so, this is Flor's story, the tale of a proud Mexican woman who tries to be true to herself when exposed to the chaotic materialism of a dysfunctional but comfortably appointed American family. Paz Vega is appealingly warm and passionate as Flor, Téa Leoni a small revelation as the confused and over-active Deborah and Cloris Leachman a wicked scene-stealer as Deborah's mother. JC-W

• *John Clasky* Adam Sandler, *Deborah Clasky* Téa Leoni, *Flor Moreno* Paz Vega, *Evelyn Norwich* Cloris Leachman, *Cristina Moreno* Shelbie Bruce, *Bernice Clasky* Sarah Steele, *with* Ian Hyland, Victoria Luna, Cecilia Suarez, Ricardo Molina, Thomas Haden Church, Eric Schaeffer, *narrator* Aimee Garcia.

• *Dir* and *Screenplay* James L. Brooks, *Pro* Brooks, Richard Sakai and Julie Ansell, *Ex Pro* Joan Bradshaw and Christy Haubegger, *Ph* John Seale, *Pro Des* Ida Random, *Ed* Richard Marks, *M* Hans Zimmer; songs performed by Luis Miguel, Christina Aguilera, Sweetback, and Black Eyed Peas, *Costumes* Shay Cunliffe.

Columbia/Gracie Films-Columbia TriStar.
131 mins. USA. 2004. Rel: 25 February 2005. Cert. 12A.

Spartan ★★★½

'Where's the girl?' is an oft-repeated enquiry and even acquires a comic heft as each new character barks the question. The girl is Laura Newton, the teenage daughter of the US president, who has gone missing. A remorseless, dedicated secret service agent, Robert Scott quickly takes on the case with a bright but inexperienced rookie in tow. It transpires that Laura has been taken by some shady white slavers who have no idea that she is the President's daughter… The great thing about writer-director David Mamet is that he never underestimates the intelligence of his audience. And so he provides a satisfyingly enigmatic scenario in which sudden bursts of violence take on a chilling air as the pieces of the puzzle start to fall into place. There's also a splendid claustrophobia and taut structure to the piece that ratchets up the suspense even as a few splinters of dark humour puncture the paranoia. JC-W

• *Robert Scott* Val Kilmer, *Curtis* Derek Luke, *Stoddard* William H. Macy, *Burch* Ed O'Neill, *Laura Newton* Kristen Bell, *Jackie Black* Tia Texada, *Miller* Clark Gregg, *Grace* Johnny Messner, *Swedish reporter* Sandra Lindquist, *with* Aaron Stanford, Stephen Culp, Mark Pellegrino, Saïd Taghmaoui, Lionel Mark Smith, Tony Mamet, Sophia Luke, J.J. Johnston, Natalija Nogulich, Rick Levy, Clara Mamet, Matt Malloy, Deborah Bartlett, Linda Kimbrough, Zosia Mamet, and (*uncredited*) David Paymer.

• *Dir* and *Screenplay* David Mamet, *Pro* Art Linson, Moshe Diamant, Elie Samaha and David Bergstein, *Ex Pro* Frank Huebner, Tracee Stanley and James Holt, *Co-Pro* Jan Fantl and Joseph Mehri, *Line Pro* Rick Nathanson, *Ph* Juan Ruiz Anchia, *Pro Des* Gemma Jackson, *Ed* Barbara Tulliver, *M* Mark Isham, *Costumes* Shay Cunliffe, *Ju-jitsu instructor* Renato Magno.

Franchise Pictures/Apollo Media/Apollo Promedia/Quality International/Signature Pictures-Warner.
106 mins. USA/Germany. 2003. Rel: 6 August 2004. Cert. 15.

Spider-Man 2 ★★½

After the set-up of the first film, in which the vulnerable outsider discovered that he had supernatural powers, Peter Parker has now become a hopeless loser. He loses his job as a pizza delivery boy, is about to flunk his university course in science, is on the verge of being fired as a photographer on *The Bugle* and the love of his life has fallen for another man. And yet Peter Parker is a hero, even as *The Bugle* is waging a smear campaign against Parker's alter ego, Spider-Man, and the arachnid celebrity is losing his powers… There is an interesting dichotomy in the case of the ordinary man isolated by the loneliness of a higher cause, but *Spider-Man 2* labours the point. Peter Parker has become such an outcast that he's hard to identify with, but beyond this *SM2* just recycles the old formula of the superhero genre. There is the mandatory vehicular carnage, the suppression of our hero's true identity and even an English villain. As the last-named, Dr Octopus is a formidable opponent – a scientist armed with a quartet of Inspector Gadget limbs – but even he eventually becomes a victim of one-dimensional CGI excess. JC-W

• *Spider-Man/Peter Parker* Tobey Maguire, *Mary Jane Watson* Kirsten Dunst, *Harry Osborn* James Franco, *Doc Ock/Dr Otto Octavius* Alfred Molina, *Mary Parker* Rosemary Harris, *Rosalie Octavius* Donna Murphy, *J. Jonah Jameson* J.K. Simmons, *John Jameson* Daniel Gillies, *Curt Connors* Dylan Baker, *Joseph 'Robbie' Robertson* Bill Nunn, *Louise* Vanessa Ferlito, *Mr Aziz* Assif Mandvi, *Norman Osborn* Willem Dafoe, *Ben Parker* Cliff Robertson, *with* Ted Raimi, Elizabeth Banks, Gregg Edelman, Elya Baskin, *man dodging debris* Stan Lee, Brent Briscoe, Joy Bryant, Reed Diamond, Dan Callahan, John Landis.

• *Dir* Sam Raimi, *Pro* Laura Ziskin and Avi Arad, *Ex Pro* Stan Lee, Kevin Feige and Joseph M. Caracciolo, *Screenplay* Alvin Sargent, from a story by Alfred Gough, Michael Chabon and Miles Millar, *Ph* Bill Pope, *Pro Des* Neil Spisak, *Ed* Bob Murawski, *M* Danny Elfman; Christopher Young, Schubert, J.S. Bach, Richard Wagner; songs performed by Jet, B.J. Thomas, Dashboard Confessional, Train, and Michael Bublé, *Costumes* James Acheson and Gary Jones, *Sound* Paul N.J. Ottosson, *Visual Effects* John Dykstra.

Columbia Pictures/Marvel Enterprises-Columbia TriStar. 127 mins. USA. 2004. Rel: 15 July 2004. Cert. PG.

Spivs ★★★

This ineptly written tale set in London's East End starts off as a piece about con artists who find themselves out of their depth. They face violent reprisals from smugglers when an attempted heist yields not money or goods but a cargo of illegal immigrants who promptly seize their freedom by fleeing. However, two Albanian children prefer to attach themselves to the group's leader and the film changes course by becoming a serious but sentimental study of how this man gains a heart by trying to help them. There's good support from Linda Bassett and the child players, but the only truly memorable aspect is to be found in the way that the remarkable Ken Stott in the leading role disproves the notion that an actor can only be as good as his material. MS

• *Jack Pike* Ken Stott, *Steve* Nick Moran, *Jenny* Kate Ashfield, *Goat* Dominic Monaghan, *Vee* Linda Bassett, *Nigel Blanchard* Jack Dee, *O'Brien* Paul Kaye, *Rosanna* Rita Ora, *with* Christos Zenonos, David Gant, Tamer Hassan, Roshan Seth, Elizabeth Berrington, Colin Teague, Sarah Rowe.

• *Dir* Colin Teague, *Pro* Hamish Skeggs, *Ex Pro* Michael Loveday, Andrew Loveday, Jamie Carmichael and Terry Loveday, *Screenplay* Teague and Gary Young, from a story by Michael Loveday, *Ph* Haris Zambarloukos, *Pro Des* Mike Kane, *Ed* Eddie Hamilton, *M* David Julyan, *Costumes* Glenis Foster.

Carnaby Prods-Verve Pictures. 95 mins. UK. 2003. Rel: 24 September 2004. Cert. 15.

The SpongeBob SquarePants Movie ★½

The wildly popular cartoon show makes its big-screen debut with an adventure that finds SpongeBob's boss framed for the theft of King Neptune's crown by a business rival. Loyal employee SpongeBob sets out with his best buddy Patrick to retrieve the Crown and save Mr Krab. The search takes them from his hometown of Bikini Bottom to the dreaded Shell City and beyond! Having never seen the television series, I was actually very excited to see the cult phenomenon that is SpongeBob in action. There's no denying that *SpongeBob SquarePants*' creator/writer/director Stephen Hillenburg has a unique vision and that kids seem to love it. Sadly, my generation gap must have been showing as the movie was tedious, random and, at times, nonsensical (and not in a fun way). I frequently found myself longing for the intellectual repartee of *The Teletubbies*. SWM

• voices: *SpongeBob* Tom Kenny, *Patrick Star* Bill Fagerbakke, *Mr Krabs* Clancy Brown, *Squidward* Rodger Bumpass, *Plankton* Mr Lawrence, *Dennis* Alec Baldwin, *himself* David Hasselhoff, *Mindy* Scarlett Johansson, *King Neptune* Jeffrey Tambor, *Karen (the computer wife)* Jill Talley, *Sandy* Carolyn Lawrence, *Mrs Puff* Mary Jo Catlett, *parrot* Stephen Hillenburg.

• *Dir* Stephen Hillenburg, *Pro* Hillenburg and Julia Pistor, *Ex Pro* Albie Hecht, Gina Shay and Derek Drymon, *Screenplay* and *storyboards* Hillenburg, Derek Drymon, Tim Hill, Kent Osborne, Aaron Springer and Paul Tibbitt, based on a story and the series created by Hillenburg, *Ph* Jerzy Zielinski, *Pro Des* Nick Jennings, *Ed* Lynn Hobson, *M* Gregor Nabholz, *Supervising Animation* Alan Smart, *Animation Dir* Dong Kun Won, Yu Mun Jeong, Hoon Choi, Hee Man Yang and Sang Kyun Shin, *Sound* Jeff Hutchins.

Paramount/Nickelodeon Movies/United Plankton Pictures-UIP. 87 mins. USA. 2004. Rel: 11 February 2005. Cert. U.

Stage Beauty ★★★★½

In the theatre of the 1660s, Samuel Pepys recorded in his diary that 'the prettiest woman in the whole house' was one Edward Kynaston. Trained from an early age to adopt the minutiae and mannerisms of the fairer sex, Kynaston was far more than a drag queen. Endowed with an enviable beauty and the finest bone structure, he was as comfortable in a corset as he was in the iambic pentameter of William Shakespeare. Accustomed to the admiration and adoration of both sexes, he is thoroughly thrown when he discovers that his lovestruck dresser, Maria, has been reproducing his Desdemona on the sly (at the downmarket Cockpit Tavern), an act both disloyal and illegal... Following Cromwell's 18-year closure of the British theatre, the London stage was never more exciting than in the period immediately afterwards. Not only was there a new hunger for the performing arts, but the actress was about to make her dramatic debut. Adapting his play *Compleat Female Stage Beauty* to the screen, the American playwright Jeffrey Hatcher has provided a sparkling script, vividly embodied by Richard Eyre's kinetic direction. A pulsating evocation of 1660s London, the film is distinguished by an array of outstanding performances, is a masterclass in the thrill of Shakespeare and is also very funny and sexy. JC-W

• *Edward 'Ned' Kynaston* Billy Crudup, *Maria* Claire Danes, *King Charles II* Rupert Everett, *Thomas Betterton* Tom Wilkinson, *George Villiers, Duke of Buckingham* Ben Chaplin, *Samuel Pepys* Hugh Bonneville, *Sir Charles Sedley* Richard Griffiths, *Sir Edward Hyde* Edward Fox, *Nell Gwynn* Zoë Tapper, *Sir Peter Lely* Tom Hollander, *Mistress Revels* Clare Higgins, *Lady Meresvale* Fenella Woolgar, *with* Alice Eve, Derek Hutchinson, David Westhead, Stephen Marcus.

• *Dir* Richard Eyre, *Pro* Robert De Niro, Jane Rosenthal and Hardy Justice, *Ex Pro* Eyre, Michael Kuhn, Amir Malin, Rachel Cohen and James D. Stern, *Co-Ex Pro* Jill Tandy and Malcolm Ritchie, *Co-Pro* Michael Dreyer, *Screenplay* Jeffrey Hatcher, *Ph* Andrew Dunn, *Pro Des* Jim Clay, *Ed* Tariq Anwar, *M* George Fenton, *Costumes* Tim Hatley, *Spaniel trainer* Sally Sousa.

Momentum/BBC Films/Qwerty Films/Tribeca-Momentum. 100 mins. UK/USA/Germany. 2004. Rel: 3 September 2004. Cert. 15.

Stander ★★★

Johannesburg; 1976. At the height of South African apartheid, police captain André Stander would appear to have it all: a beautiful and loving wife, a successful career and a privileged lifestyle. But the mistreatment of the blacks rankles him and, on a whim, he decides to hit back at his own community – because he can. In a startling about-turn, he robs a bank in broad daylight and then goes about investigating it. With an inside knowledge of the pitfalls of being caught, he embarks on a series of increasingly audacious robberies with breathless impunity. Soon, he becomes the most wanted man in South Africa, but can he catch himself? Unbelievable, but true. André Stander robbed 20 banks before he was caught, was then sentenced to 75 years in prison, escaped and, with two new accomplices, went on to rob another 27 banks. In spite of a grainy, stripped-down visual palette, *Stander* still feels like a Hollywood heist thriller, albeit on a smaller budget. Its main problem, though, is that André Stander never emerges as a real person, the movie-star looks of Thomas Jane further creating an illusion of make-believe. Nevertheless, it's one helluva story.

JC-W

• *André Stander* Thomas Jane, *Bekkie Stander* Deborah Kara Unger, *Alan Heyl* David Patrick O'Hara, *Patrick 'Lee' McCall* Dexter Fletcher, *General Stander* Marius Weyers, *Cor van Deventer* Ashley Taylor, *General Viljoen* At Botha, *Sergeant Smit* Lionel Newton, *Sharmiane* Melanie Merle, *Ed Janis* Sean Else, *Bekkie's father* Cor van Deventer, *Bekkie's mother* Rita van Deventer, *with* Peter Gardner, Patrick Mynhardt, Iain Paton.

• *Dir* Bronwen Hughes, *Pro* Julia Verdin, Martin F. Katz and Chris Roland, *Ex Pro* David E. Allen, Steven Markoff, Izidore Codron, Frank Hübner and Jan Fantl, *Co-Pro* Bima Stagg, *Screenplay* Hughes and Stagg, *Ph* Jess Hall, *Visual Consultant* Lester Cohen, *Ed* Robert Ivison, *M* David Holmes, Steve Hilton and The Free Association, *Costumes* Darion Hing, *Sound* Campbell Askew and James Boyle.

Seven Arts/Grosvenor Park/The Imaginarium-Momentum. 113 mins. Canada/Germany/South Africa/UK/USA. 2003. Rel: 27 May 2005. Cert. 15.

Star Wars: Episode III – Revenge of the Sith ★★★★

'Good,' pronounces Senator Palpatine, 'is a point of view.' And so the ambiguities of good and evil attest themselves in the final chapter of the second *Star Wars* trilogy. Anakin Skywalker is promoted to the Jedi council, but because of his youth is denied the title of 'Master.' His disappointment and ambition are subsequently exploited by Palpatine to cleave a wedge in the Jedi status quo. Meanwhile, Queen Amidala discovers she is pregnant by Anakin... It's been a long time coming, and as the final pieces of the narrative puzzle fall into place there is an inevitable excitement, or at least satisfaction, or maybe just relief. Technically, the film pushes the boundaries of cinema ever further, the cityscapes and planetary vistas are more fabulous and detailed than ever before and the dialogue resonates with a mythic profundity. There's a wonderful creation in the malevolent General Grievous, along with some ferocious ant-like droids, while Yoda steals the show. Yet in spite of all these wonders, there is – perhaps unavoidably – a sense of anticlimax. JC-W

• *Obi-Wan Kenobi* Ewan McGregor, *Padmé Amidala* Natalie Portman, *Anakin Skywalker* Hayden Christensen, *Supreme Chancellor Palpatine* Ian McDiarmid, *Mace Windu* Samuel L. Jackson, *voice of Yoda* Frank Oz, *Senator Bail Organa* Jimmy Smits, *C-3PO* Anthony Daniels, *Count Dooku* Christopher Lee, *Queen of Naboo* Keisha Castle-Hughes, *Commander Cody* Temuera Morrison, *Sio Bibble* Oliver Ford Davies, *Jar Jar Binks* Ahmed Best, *R2-D2* Kenny Baker, *Chewbacca* Peter Mayhew, *Owen Lars* Joel Edgerton, *with* Silas Carson, Jay Laga'Aia, Bruce Spence, Wayne Pygram, David Bowers, Rohan Nichol, Jeremy Bulloch, Amanda Lucas, Jett Lucas, Graeme Blundell, Trisha Noble, Claudia Karvan, Katie Lucas, Rena Owen, Mousy McCallum.

• *Dir, Ex Pro* and *Screenplay* George Lucas, *Pro* Rick McCallum, *Ph* David Tattersall, *Pro Des* Gavin Bocquet, *Ed* Roger Barton and Ben Burtt, *M* John Williams, *Costumes* Trisha Biggar,

Sound Ben Burtt, *Visual Effects* John Knoll and Roger Guyett, *Animation* Rob Coleman.

Lucasfilm-Fox.
140 mins. USA. 2005. Rel: 19 May 2005. Cert. 12A.

The Stepford Wives ★½

Having lost her job as the president of the EBS television network, Joanna Eberhart agrees to leave behind the cut-throat stage of Manhattan and move to the suburbs. However, the idyllic community of Stepford, Connecticut, is almost too good to be true. All the wives smile like Cheshire cats, have immaculate kitchens and appear to be sexual athletes in bed. There must be some mistake… The original concept of Ira Levin's chilling literary satire was a hard act to pull off in cinematic terms. Yet the British director Bryan Forbes did a magnificent job with his 1975 masterpiece by subtly smudging the line between reality and the feasibility of the American dream as featured in *Good Housekeeping*. Frank Oz, a dab hand at obvious slapstick, has opted for a comic approach. Thus, social commentary becomes parody and the chill factor is bunged into the microwave and electro-magnetised into submission. But even as parody – undermined by the cast's enthusiasm for winking at the camera – the film is a mess. In the intervening 29 years, robots have become increasingly commonplace, Martha Stewart has been indicted for insider trading and female emancipation has continued apace, all of which makes the entire enterprise obsolete. JC-W

Domestic engineering: Nicole Kidman in *The Stepford Wives* (from UIP)

• *Joanna Eberhart* Nicole Kidman, *Walter Kresby* Matthew Broderick, *Bobbie Markowitz* Bette Midler, *Mike Wellington* Christopher Walken, *Sarah Sunderson* Faith Hill, *Claire Wellington* Glenn Close, *Roger Bannister* Roger Bart, *Jerry Harmon* David Marshall Grant, *Dave Markowitz* Jon Lovitz, *Charmaine* Lorri Bagley, *with* Dylan Hartigan, Fallon Brooking, Matt Malloy, Andrea Anders, Mike White, Carrie Preston, Billy Bush, KaDee Strickland, Larry King.

• *Dir* Frank Oz, *Pro* Scott Rudin, Donald De Line, Edgar J. Scherick and Gabriel Grunfeld, *Ex Pro* Ron Bozman and Keri Lyn Selig, *Screenplay* Paul Rudnick, *Ph* Rob Hahn, *Pro Des* Jackson De Govia, *Ed* Jay Rabinowitz, *M* David Arnold, *Costumes* Ann Roth, *Sound* Ron Bochar, *Waltz consultants* Jennifer McCalla and Stanley McCalla.

Paramount/DreamWorks/Scott Rudin/De Line Pictures-UIP.
93 mins. USA. 2004. Rel: 30 July 2004. Cert. 12A.

The Story of the Weeping Camel ★★★★

On a number of levels, *The Story of the Weeping Camel* is extraordinary. It is the first effort by two students from Munich's film school. And it has been constructed from just ten hours of Super 16 film stock (for the documentary *Deep Blue*, over 7000 hours was shot). Nevertheless, the pupils have fashioned a genuinely absorbing tale that emerged during their short time recording the lifestyle of a group of nomadic Mongolians. The camera itself is like an invisible eye, an accepted member of this simple community that goes about its business seemingly unaware that it's participating in a movie. As the harsh weather conditions of the Gobi desert make an ordeal of preparing food and overseeing flocks of sheep and camels, a narrative of sorts evolves. A pregnant camel gives birth to a white colt over an agonising two days and then rejects it. Around this, the various members of the tribe come into focus as they cope with the hardship and ritual of surviving a very basic existence. The period could be any time in the last thousand years, but clues to the modern world assert themselves, from a grandmother's 'eyes of glass' (her spectacles) to an old radio housing six dead batteries. Enchanting. JC-W

• *Dir* and *Screenplay* Byambasuren Davaa and Luigi Falorni, *Pro* Tobias N. Siebert, *Ph* Falorni, *Ed* Anja Pohl.

Hochschule für Fernsehen und Film München-UGC Films UK.
90 mins. Germany/Mongolia. 2003. Rel: 9 July 2004. Cert. U.

Strings ★★½

When the Emperor of Hebalon cuts his own headstring, his son Hal Tara is forced to defend his father's realm from duplicitous forces within… In the wake of *Team America: World Police*, Anders Rønnow Klarlund's *Strings* arrives with an entirely different agenda. Peopled wholly by marionettes, this Danish-Swedish-Norwegian-British co-production is an odd original not without merit. While the plot itself is hard to follow – largely because of an unfamiliar universe and the unusual names – its singular world is strangely seductive. Here, the characters are only too aware that they are puppets and much is made of their lives hanging by a thread. The marionettes themselves are beautifully realised, like subjects from some forgotten corner of Norse mythology, and are exceptionally well voiced in the English version. Though their faces are full of character, it's a shame that their mouths are immobile, while the muddy video photography blurs much of the splendid production design. FYI: Ten kilometres of string was used during the production. JC-W

• voices: *Hal Tara* James McAvoy, *Zita* Catherine McCormack, *Kahro* Julian Glover, *Nezo* Derek Jacobi, *Ghrak* Ian Hart, *Jhinna* Claire Skinner, *Erito* David Harewood, *Eike* Samantha Bond, *Agra* Michael Culkin, *Talino* Andrew Kiernan, *Utay* Alex Jennings.

• *Dir* Anders Rønnow Klarlund, *Pro* Niels Bald, *Ex Pro* Peter Aalbæk Jensen, *Screenplay* Naja Marie Aidt, from a story by Aidt and Klarlund, *Ph* Kim Hattesen and Jan Weincke, *Pro Des* Sven Wichmann, *Ed* Leif Axel Kjeldsen, *M* Jørgen Lauritsen, *Sound* Hans Møller, *Visual Effects* Daniel Silwerfeldt, *Chief Puppet Builder* Joakim Zacho Weylandt.

Bald Film/Zentropa Entertainment/Nordisk Film, etc-Swipe Films.
91 mins. Denmark/UK/Sweden/Norway. 2004. Rel: 27 May 2005. Cert. PG.

Super Size Me ★★★½

Eric Schlosser wrote a stomach-curdling book called *Fast Food Nation*. In it he documented the employee exploitation of McDonald's and chronicled in detail the animal excrement that ended up in your average Big Mac. Morgan Spurlock's award-winning documentary (Best Director – Sundance) is a far jollier affair, albeit equally as worrying a proposition for the Golden Arches. Opening with a blizzard of brain-spinning facts – 46 million people visit McDonald's every day, two out of three Americans are overweight or obese – *Super Size Me* quickly gets down to its objective. Director-host Spurlock is out to record an experiment in which he eats solely at McDonald's for one month. Monitored by various medical personnel, Spurlock starts out as an extremely healthy specimen but by Day Two is already throwing up (cue an emetic close-up). *Super Size Me* is an entertaining admonition of the dangers of fast food, but it lacks the satirical edge of, say, *Bowling for Columbine*. Still, there were an amazing number of untouched tubs of popcorn at the end of the screening that I attended. Oh, and did you know that there's more sugar in a McDonald's salad than in a Big Mac? JC-W

• *with*: Morgan Spurlock, Ronald McDonald, Dr Daryl Isaacs MD (internal medicine), Dr Lisa Ganjhu DO (gastroenterologist and hepatologist), Dr Stephen Siegel MD (cardiologist), Bridget Bennett MS, RD (nutritionist), Eric Rowley (exercise physiologist).

• *Dir* and *Screenplay* Morgan Spurlock, *Pro* Spurlock and The

Con, *Ex Pro* Heather Winters and J. R. Morley, *Assoc Pro* David Pederson, *Ph* Scott Ambrozy, *Art Dir* Joe the Artist, *Ed* Stela Georgieva and Julie 'Bob' Lombardi, *M* Steve Horowitz, Michael Parrish & Folkfoot; theme by Spurlock and Doug Ray, performed by Toothpick, *Sound* Hans ten Broeke, *Animation* George Georgiev, *McPaintings/poster art* Ron English.

Roadside Attractions/Samuel Goldwyn Films/Showtime Independent/The Con/Studio-on-Hudson-Tartan Films.
99 mins. USA. 2004. Rel: 10 September 2004. Cert. 12A.

Surviving Christmas ★

Illinois; the present. With each new Christmas the suffocating embrace of materialism squeezes even more out of the original message of giving and forgiving. Ace sales rep Drew Latham ('I could sell whale steaks to Green Peace') knows all about materialism. But when his girlfriend ditches him at the tail end of December, he decides to return to the house where he grew up. He then offers the new occupants $250,000 if they will let him spend Christmas with them... The Christmas movie is a hard act to pull off and this is destined for the same Hall of Shame darkened by *Jingle All the Way* and *The Grinch* (among countless others). The scenario itself is dumb, mawkish and predictable and desperately lacks subtlety, credibility or, Heaven forbid, comic ingenuity. Only the 19-year-old Josh Zuckerman prompts the occasional smile for underplaying his despondency, while Ben Affleck lunges for another Razzie for giving the most vacant, flat and misjudged performance ever to

Junk bond: Morgan Spurlock in his own entertaining *Super Size Me* (from Tartan Films)

be rewarded by an eight-figure sum. JC-W

• *Drew Latham* Ben Affleck, *Tom Valco* James Gandolfini, *Alicia Valco* Christina Applegate, *Christine Valco* Catherine O'Hara, *Brian Valco* Josh Zuckerman, *Doo-Dah* Bill Macy, *Missy Vangilder* Jennifer Morrison, *Heinrich* Udo Kier, *Horace Vangilder* David Selby, *Letitica Vangilder* Stephanie Faracy, *Doo-Dah understudy* Sy Richardson, *with* Stephen Root, Tangie Ambrose, Tumbleweed, Kent Osborne.

• *Dir* Mike Mitchell, *Pro* Jenno Topping and Betty Thomas, *Ex Pro* Patricia Whitcher, *Assoc Pro* Erin Stam, *Screenplay* Deborah Kaplan, Harry Elfont, Jeffrey Ventimilia and Joshua Sternin, *Ph* Peter Collister and Tom Priestly Jr., *Pro Des* Caroline Hanania, *Ed* Craig McKay, *M* Randy Edelman; songs performed by Andy Williams, Ed Hartman, Chet Atkins, Ben Affleck and James Gandolfini, Lou Rawls, Lynyrd Skynyrd, The Primitives, José Feliciano, Judy Garland, The 88, Bing Crosby, etc, *Costumes* Mary Jane Fort.

DreamWorks/Tall Trees/LivePlanet-UIP.
90 mins. USA. 2004. Rel: 3 December 2004.
Cert. 12A.

Swimming Upstream ★★★½

From an autobiographical screenplay by the Australian swimming champion Anthony Fingleton, this is a classic tale of overcoming adversity. Set in 1950s Brisbane, the film stars Geoffrey Rush – oozing bitter erratic tension – as the overbearing alcoholic father who pitted his two championship-swimming sons against each other. *Neighbours* star Jesse Spencer's athletic good looks and charm light up the screen in the central role of Tony, and this is his journey navigating adolescence, the protection of his downtrodden mother – played to edgy perfection by Judy Davis – and various competitive highs and lows. But it's the retrospective study of familial abuse that cuts to the core. With the backdrop of post-war depression and the optimism of a new generation, this is an historical snapshot, and though at times it's hard to truly believe Tony's almost saintly manner in the

face of cruelty, *Swimming Upstream* captures the timeless nature of family resentment. WL

• *Harold* Geoffrey Rush, *Dora* Judy Davis, *Tony* Jesse Spencer, *John* Tim Draxl, *Billie* Deborah Kennedy, *Harold Jr* David Hoflin, *Ronald* Craig Horner, *Diane* Brittany Byrnes, *young Tony* Mitchell Delle Vergin, *young Harold Jr* Kain O'Keefee, *with* Thomas Davidson, Keera Byrnes, Mark Hembrow, Dawn Fraser.

• *Dir* Russell Mulcahy, *Pro* Howard Baldwin, Karen Baldwin and Paul Pompian, *Ex Pro* William J. Immerman, Anthony Fingleton and Andrew Mason, *Screenplay* Fingleton, *Ph* Martin McGrath, *Pro Des* Roger Ford, *Ed* Marcus D'Arcy, *M* Johnny Klimek and Reinhold Heil, *Costumes* Angus Strathie.

MGM/Crusader Entertainment-Verve Pictures.
97 mins. Australia/USA. 2002. Rel: 10 June 2005.
Cert. 12A.

Switchblade Romance ★★★★

It may be the subtitles, but there's something about a French slasher movie that has a lot more class than its blood-spattered American cousins. Here there are clear echoes of *The Texas Chain Saw Massacre*, *Halloween* and *Children of the Corn*, but there's a credibility that only the French can pull off. Recalling Jean Seberg in *A Bout de Souffle*, Cécile de France plays Marie, who is staying with her best friend's family in a remote corner of the French countryside. Marie already feels uncomfortable in such an isolated place (there aren't even any mobile phones) and she and her best friend, Alex, arrive after dark. It doesn't take long before a stranger turns up, who then methodically beheads Alex's father (using a chest of drawers) before starting on the rest of the family. Terrified and vulnerable (she's barely recovered from a self-induced orgasm), Marie listens to the butchery next door as she struggles to concoct a plan of escape. This is really unpleasant stuff, and is as suspenseful as it is gory, thanks in large part to the nonchalance of the killer, played with shambling detachment by Philippe Nahon (previously seen as the brutish butcher

Pooled resources: Jesse Spencer and Tim Draxl in Russell Mulcahy's timeless *Swimming Upstream* (from Verve Pictures)

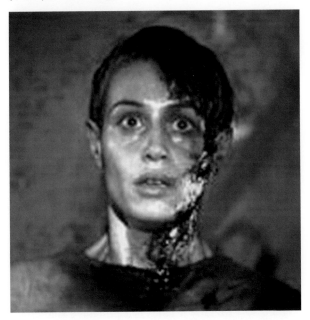

in *I Stand Alone*). If you're human, you *will* be shell-shocked. Original title: *Haute tension*; US title: *High Tension*. JC-W

• *Marie* Cécile de France, *Alex* Maïwenn, *the killer* Philippe Nahon, *Jimmy* Franck Khalfoun, *Alex's father* Andrei Finti, *Alex's mother* Oana Pellea, *Tom* Marco Claudiu Pascu, *police inspector* Jean-Claude de Goros.

• *Dir* Alexandre Aja, *Pro* Alexandre Arcady and Robert Benmussa, *Screenplay* Aja and Grégory Levasseur, *Ph* Maxime Alexandre, *Art Dir* Levasseur, *Ed* Baxter, *M* François Eudes; Muse.

Europacorp/Alexandre Films/Canal Plus/MediaPro Pictures-Optimum Releasing.
90 mins. France/Romania. 2003. Rel: 24 September 2004. Cert. 18.

Sword of Xanten ★★★½

Uli Edel's made-for-German-TV saga tells the classic story of Northern Europe's most popular epic, *Das Nibelungenlied*. It's easy to see how this thousand-year-old story could inspire Wagner's opera series as well as J.R.R. Tolkien's own *Hobbit* and subsequent *Lord of the Rings* trilogy. Benno Fürmann smoulders as the blacksmith Siegfried, whose destiny becomes entwined with the dragon Fafnir, the warrior queen Brunhild, and a cursed, magical ring. Desire, betrayal, murder and sacrifice suffuse the tale and its cast of well-worn acting veterans and brash up-and-comers are all up to the task. *T3*'s Kristanna Løken shines as Brunhild with her potent blend of strength and beauty. This is a daring production that makes the very best of its limited resources, successfully relying on the source material to bolster any minor failings. German title: *Die Nibelungen*. Aka: *Ring of the Nibelungs*. SWM

• *'Eric' Siegfried* Benno Fürmann, *Brunhild, Queen of Iceland* Kristanna Løken, *Kriemhild, Princess of Burgund* Alicia Witt, *Hagen* Julian Sands, *King Gunther* Samuel West, *Eyvind* Max Von Sydow, *Giselher* Roberrt Pattinson, *with* Mavie Hörbiger, Aletta Bezuidenhout, Sean Higgs.

• *Dir* Uli Edel, *Pro* Volker Engel, Andreas Schmid and Thoeren Konstantin, *Ex Pro* Tim Halkin and Andreas Grosch, *Screenplay* Edel, Diane Duane and Peter Morwood, *Ph* Elemér Ragályi, *Pro Des* Albrecht Konrad, *Ed* Roberto Silvi, *M* Ilan Eshkeri, *Costumes* Barbara Baum.

Tandem Communications/VIP Medienfonds 2/Channel 4/Sat.1 Television/Uncharted Territory/Castlering Pictures-Columbia TriStar.
132 mins. Germany/UK/South Africa/Italy. 2004. Rel: 19 November 2004. Cert. 12A.

Take My Eyes ★★★★

This Spanish drama by Icíar Bollain, actress turned director, is a compellingly credible study of an abused wife reluctant to admit the failure of her marriage and to leave the husband she had genuinely loved. Without offering a slavish imitation, Bollain's film evidences her admiration for the work of Ken Loach and is superbly acted, especially by Laia Marull and Luis Tosar as the couple. The subject matter may be somewhat limited but it is admirably handled, and the more so because the husband, unable to overcome his own pathological nature, is in his way as much a victim as the wife. The unfamiliar setting for this work is Toledo. Recommended. Original title: *Te doy mis ojos*. MS

• *Pilar* Laia Marull, *Antonio* Luis Tosar, *Ana* Candela Peña, *Aurora* Rosa Maria Sarda, *Rosa* Kity Manver, *therapist* Sergi Calleja, *John* Dave Mooney, *Juan* Nicolas Fernandez Luna, *Lola* Elisabet Gelabert, *Raquel* Chus Gutierrez, *Carmen* Elena Irureta.

• *Dir* Icíar Bollain, *Pro* Belén Bernuy, *Ex Pro* Santiago García de Leániz, *Screenplay* Bollain and Alicia Luna, *Ph* Carles Gusi, *Art Dir* Victor Molero, *Ed* Angel Hernandez Zoido, *M* Alberto Iglesias, *Costumes* Estíbaliz Markiegi.

La Iguana/Alta Produccion/TVE/Canal Plus-Swipe Films.
106 mins. Spain. 2003. Rel: 19 November 2004. Cert. 15.

A Tale of Two Sisters ★★

Guess what? This is another South-East Asian horror movie that's being re-packaged by Hollywood, features sexually incipient female protagonists and promotes long black hair as a scare tactic. If you've caught *The Ring*, *Dark Water*, *The Grudge* and *Phone*, then you'll know what I'm talking about. If not, then you can see the American remakes of all the aforementioned and discover a whole new world of scary big hair. Updated from an old Korean folk tale, *A Tale of Two Sisters* is a creepy story of family dysfunction which has been filmed on five previous occasions. Well, obviously something got lost in the translation. As director Kim Jee-woon lavishes exquisite attention on the smallest detail, he builds an appropriately unsettling atmosphere, although what follows is no stranger than the offhand behaviour of the two sisters. As with *The Grudge* and *Phone* there is only one really scary moment, the real problem being that it's hard to be frightened when you have no idea what's going on. JC-W

• *Eun-Joo, the stepmother* Yeom Jeong-a, *Su-Mi* Im Soo-jung, *Su-yeon* Moon Geun-young, *Mu-hyun* Kim Kab-su, *mother* Park Mi-hyun, *Sun-Kyu* Woo Gi-hong.

• *Dir* and *Screenplay* Kim Jee-woon, *Pro* Oh Ki-min and Oh Jung-wan, *Co-Pro* Kim Young, *Ph* Lee Mogae, *Pro Des* Cho Geun-hyun, *Ed* Ko Im-Pyo, *M* Lee Byeong-woo, *Costumes* Lee Byeong-woo.

iPictures/Masulpiri Pictures/b.o.m. Film-Tartan Films. 114 mins. South Korea. 2003. Rel: 13 August 2004. Cert. 15.

Tarnation ★★½

A home movie jazzed-up on a PC (utilising the computer software iMovie), *Tarnation* is a welter of domestic footage, film clips and subtitles. While at times resembling the vastly superior *Capturing the Friedmans* in its personal record of a dysfunctional family, the film – which cost $187 – is actually more like a psychedelic journal of a misspent life. Jonathan Caouette was brought up in Texas, the only son of Renee LeBlanc, a former beauty queen destroyed by two years of shock therapy. When she attempts to escape the claustrophobic grip of her parents, she takes Jonathan to Chicago and is raped in front of him. Meanwhile, the grocery store belonging to Jonathan's grandfather is burnt down. And so it goes on, a catalogue of tragedy leading to Jonathan's eventual move to New York to become an actor. At its best, *Tarnation* invents a new medium – storytelling through text and pictures. At its worst, it's a self-indulgent catharsis played out for the whole world to participate in. Incidentally, 'tarnation' is a Southern euphemism for 'damnation'. JC-W

• *with*: Jonathan Caouette, Renee LeBlanc, David Sanin Paz, Rosemary Davis, Adolph Davis, Steve Caouette.

• *Dir* and *Screenplay* Jonathan Caouette, *Pro* Caouette and Stephen Winter, *Ex Pro* Gus Van Sant and John Cameron Mitchell, *Assoc Pro* Jason Banker, *Ed* Caouette and Brian A. Kates, *M* John Califra and Max Avery Lichtenstein; songs performed by Low, Jean Wells, Glen Campbell, Iron & Wine, Cocteau Twins, Marianne Faithfull, Hex, Magnetic Fields, Mavis Staples, Dolly Parton, etc.

Tarnation Films/Wellspring Media-Optimum Releasing. 91 mins. USA. 2004. Rel: 11 February 2005. Cert. 15.

Taxi ★★

Queen Latifah teams up with US comedian Jimmy Fallon as a New York taxi driver and the cop who helps her tackle four gorgeous women Brazilian bank robbers. On the plus side of this iffy remake of a jolly 1998 French film are the admirable, effortlessly funny Latifah and the great stunts in the NY street action. Among the minuses, neither Fallon nor the script know how to raise enough laughs. DW

• *Belle Williams* Queen Latifah, *Andy Washburn* Jimmy Fallon,

Vanessa Giselle Bündchen, *Lt. Marta Robbins* Jennifer Esposito, *Washburn's mom* Ann-Margret, *Jesse* Henry Simmons, *Agent Mullins* Christian Kane, *redhead* Ana Cristina de Oliveira, *third robber* Ingrid Vandebosch, *fourth robber* Magali Amadei, with Christian Kane, Boris McGiver, Adrian Martinez, GQ, Rick Overton, Adam LeFevre.

• *Dir* Tim Story, *Pro* Luc Besson, *Ex Pro* Robert Simonds and Ira Shuman, *Co-Pro* Steve Chasman, *Ph* Vance Burberry, *Pro Des* Mayne Berke, *Ed* Stuart Levy, *M* Christophe Beck, *Costumes* Sanja Milkovic Hays.

Fox/Europacorp-Fox. 97 mins. USA/France. 2004. Rel: 19 November 2004. Cert. 12A.

Team America: World Police ★★

Team America is a fearless, high-tech police force stationed inside Mount Rushmore in South Dakota. Dedicated to fighting global terrorism, the unit calls on the acting skills of Broadway star Gary Johnston to impersonate a Muslim terrorist and infiltrate a Cairo cell. However, the real villain is North Korea's Kim Jong II who solicits the services of Alec Baldwin to facilitate an international attack 2356 times worse than 9/11… Sometimes novelty is not enough. Nor, for that matter, is unscrupulous offensiveness (in all senses of the word). Initially, there is some fun to be had in seeing marionettes demolish the centre of Paris. And, as in the Monty Python films, *Team America* gains some comic mileage from drawing attention to its limitations (such as the puppets' inability to control their finger actions). In addition, there are some refreshingly irreverent musical numbers (romantic lyric: 'I need you like Ben Affleck needs acting school'). However, once the Eiffel Tower, Great Pyramid and Panama Canal have all been torched – and the f-word flogged to death – there's not much farther one can go. JC-W

• voices: *Gary Johnston* Trey Parker, *Chris* Matt Stone, *Lisa* Kristen Miller, *Sarah* Masasa, *Joe* Trey Parker, *Spottswoode* Daran Norris, *I.N.T.E.L.L.I.G.E.N.C.E.* Phil Hendrie, *King Jong II* Trey Parker, *Hans Blix* Trey Parker, *Alec Baldwin* Maurice LaMarche, *Carson* Trey Parker, *Matt Damon* Trey Parker and Matt Stone, *Tim Robbins* Trey Parker, *Samuel L. Jackson* Fred Tatasciore, etc.

• *Dir* Trey Parker, *Pro* Parker, Scott Rudin and Matt Stone, *Screenplay* Parker, Stone and Pam Brady, *Ex Pro* Scott Aversano and Anne Garefino, *Co-Pro* Michael Polaire and Frank Agnone, *Ph* Bill Pope, *Pro Des* Jim Dultz, *Ed* Tom Vogt, *M* Harry Gregson-Williams, *Costumes* Karen Patch, *Special Effects* Joe Viskocil, *Visual Consultant* David Rockwell, *Puppet Design* Norman Tempia.

Paramount/Scott Rudin/Matt Stone-UIP. 97 mins. USA. 2004. Rel: 14 January 2005. Cert. 15.

The Terminal ★★½

It's a nice idea and there are some magical moments, but overall this is Steven Spielberg's weakest movie since *Amistad*.

String theory: The fearless protagonists of Trey Parker and Matt Stone's gleefully offensive *Team America: World Police* (from UIP)

Allegedly inspired by a true 'event' – the story of the Iranian refugee Merhan Karimi Nasseri who was stranded at Charles De Gaulle airport for years – the film is an opportunity to present a microcosm of America in a New York airport terminal. Tom Hanks plays Viktor Navorski, a tourist from the fictitious Eastern European country of Krakozhia, who finds himself stranded at JFK when his country undergoes a coup. Unable to return to Europe and legally forbidden to enter the United States, he has no choice but to wait in the International Transit Lounge. Indefinitely… After a terrific, heartbreaking start in which Navorski comes to terms with his fate, the film settles in for the long hard slog of making life interesting in a no man's land of duty free shops and fast food counters. Hanks is not ideal casting as a Balkan refugee – he is too identifiable as an all-American icon – but there are other characters that provide some colour. Unfortunately, the movie slows to a crawl at the end of its second hour and is undermined by Spielberg at his most misty-eyed.
JC-W

• *Viktor Navorski* Tom Hanks, *Amelia Jane Warren* Catherine Zeta-Jones, *Frank Dixon* Stanley Tucci, *Joe Mulroy* Chi McBride, *Enrique Cruz* Diego Luna, *Officer Ray Thurman* Barry Shabaka Henley, *Dolores Torres* Zoë Saldana, *Field Commissioner Richard Salchak* Eddie Jones, *Karl Iverson* Jude Ciccolella, *with* Corey Reynolds, Guillermo Diaz, Rini Bell, Sasha Spielberg, Benny Golson.

• *Dir* Steven Spielberg, *Pro* Walter F. Parkes and Laurie MacDonald, *Ex Pro* Andrew Niccol, Patricia Whitcher and Jason Hoffs, *Screenplay* Jeff Nathanson and Sacha Gervasi, from a story by Niccol and Gervasi, *Ph* Janusz Kaminski, *Pro Des* Alex McDowell, *Ed* Michael Kahn, *M* John Williams; Max Steiner; songs performed by Strings Unlimited, The 101 Strings Orchestra, Big Bill Broonzy, Benny Golson, and Gene Krupa, *Costumes* Mary Zophres.

DreamWorks-UIP.
128 mins. USA. 2004. Rel: 3 September 2004. Cert. 12A.

No man's land: Tom Hanks stranded in *The Terminal*, Steven
Spielberg's fascinating but schmaltzy fable (see pages 126-127)

Thirteen Conversations About One Thing ★★½

For 'conversation' think episode and for 'one thing' don't think sex. The one thing in question is the realisation and/or achievement of happiness. Or maybe the one thing is luck. Or fate. *Thirteen Conversations*, scripted by the sisters Jill and Karen Sprecher, is a stagy, melancholy contemplation of life and its meaning in a contemporary urban context. A number of stories interconnect in an elliptical narrative (à la *Pulp Fiction*) in which various New Yorkers – an attorney, college professor, insurance broker, housewife, cleaner – find their lives dramatically affected by a single event. The film doesn't always hold the interest, but is a piquant, sometimes pretentious, sporadically thought-provoking walk on the dark side, brushed with flashes of wry humour. Alan Arkin in particular – as a bitter but ultimately kind-hearted office manager – is outstanding. JC-W

• *Troy* Matthew McConaughey, *Walker* John Turturro, *Gene English* Alan Arkin, *Beatrice* Clea DuVall, *Patricia* Amy Irving, *Helen* Barbara Sukowa, *Dorrie* Tia Texada, *Dick Lacey* Frankie Faison, *with* David Connolly, Paul Austin, Rob McElhenney, Avery Glymph, Peggy Gormley, William Wise, Shawn Elliott, Alex Burns, James Murtaugh, Richard E. Council.

• *Dir* Jill Sprecher, *Pro* Beni Atoori and Gina Resnick, *Ex Pro* James Burke, Heidi Crane, Doug Mankoff, Andrew Spaulding, Sandy Stern, Michael Stipe and Peter Wetherell, *Line Pro* Stacy Plavoukos, *Screenplay* Jill Sprecher and Karen Sprecher, *Ph* Dick Pope, *Pro Des* Mark Ricker, *Ed* Stephen Mirrione, *M* Alex Wurman, *Costumes* Kasia Walicka Maimone.

Stonelock Pictures/Echo Lake Prods/Double A Films/Miracle Picture/RSUB/Self Timer/Single Cell Pictures-Arrow Films.
103 mins. USA. 2001. Rel: 17 June 2005. Cert. 15.

13 Going on 30 ★★★½

Sweets are a big thing in *13 Going on 30*, so it would be fair to draw a confectionery parallel. If film can be a candy, then this grown-up fairytale is like one of Mrs O'Malley's bitter lemons – sweet on the outside but quite tart within. Bearing a pronounced resemblance to every body-swap confection from *Vice Versa* (1988) and *Big* (1988) through to *Freaky Friday* (1977, 2004), the film addresses some heady issues via a flimsy, farcical route. Jenna Rink, 13, is desperate to belong to the in-crowd and wants breasts, sophistication and freedom. Then, when she gets her wish, she discovers she's a 30-year-old Manhattan sophisticate working for her favourite magazine, the glossy lifestyle title *Poise*. But her new alter ego appears to have lost the inner child that made her so special… Movies have a habit of sharpening dormant emotions into a heightened point and this is no exception. A dopey, formulaic conceit aimed squarely at the multiplex, *13 Going on 30* is salvaged by a very strong premise and a joyful, funny performance from Jennifer Garner. Garner radiates a Geena Davis smile with a Julia Roberts spontaneity that promises enduring stardom. This may not be in the same league as *Pretty Woman*, but it's irresistible escapism for diehard romantics.
JC-W

• *Jenna Rink* Jennifer Garner, *Matt Flamhaff* Mark Ruffalo, *Lucy Wyman* Judy Greer, *Richard Kneeland* Andy Serkis, *Bev Rink* Kathy Baker, *Alex Carlson* Samuel Ball, *with* Marcia DeBonis, Phil Reeves, Sean Marquette, Christa B. Allen, Kiersten Warren, Joe Grifasi, Mary Pat Gleason, Susan Egan, Lynn Collins.

• *Dir* Gary Winick, *Pro* Gina Matthews, Susan Arnold and Donna Arkoff Roth, *Ex Pro* Todd Garner and Dan Kolsrud, *Co-Pro* Allegra Clegg, *Assoc Pro* Desiree Van Til, *Screenplay* Josh Goldsmith and Cathy Yuspa, *Ph* Don Burgess, *Pro Des* Garreth Stover, *Ed* Susan Littenberg, *M* Theodore Shapiro; songs performed by The Go-Go's, Rick Springfield, Michael Jackson, Talking Heads, Belinda Carlisle, Madonna, Whitney Houston, Lillix, Luce, Mowo!, Vanilla Ice, Billy Joel, Liz Phair, Soft Cell, Pat Benatar, and Ingram Hill, *Costumes* Susie De Santo, *Magazine presentation consultant* Sara Ruffin.

Revolution Studios-Columbia TriStar.
97 mins. USA. 2004. Rel: 4 August 2004. Cert. 12A.

A Thousand Months ★★★½

Morocco in 1981 provides the relatively unfamiliar backcloth for Faouzi Bensaïdi's first feature. Despite French backing, it comes across as the real ethnic article. Indeed, the filmmaker has said that in producing this portrait of village life he wanted to range over the characters, giving each in turn a central focus. However, the first half is presented most effectively from the viewpoint of a seven-year-old boy whose father's absence as a jailed militant has been ascribed to other causes, and this means that the film seems to meander and lose its earlier force when other characters are emphasised instead. There's a lot of detail, both social and political, which will mystify those like myself with no knowledge of Moroccan life. But the film is welcome regardless of these problems and, shot in widescreen, its visual quality is high. MS

• *Mehdi* Fouad Labied, *Amina* Nezha Rahil, *Ahmed, the grandfather* Mohammad Majd, *Houcine* Mohamed Afifi, *the young kaïd* Abdelati Lambarki.

• *Dir* Faouzi Bensaïdi, *Pro* Laurent Lavolé, Isabelle Pragier, Bénédicte Bellocq and Souad Lamriki, *Screenplay* Bensaïdi and Emmanuelle Sardou, *Ph* Antoine Héberlé, *Art Dir* Naima Bouanani and Véronique Melery, *Ed* Sandrine Deegen.

Laurent Lavolé and Isabelle Pragier/Gloria Films/Agora Films/ZDF/ARTE/Canal Plus, etc-Optimum Releasing.
125 mins. France/Morocco/Belgium/Germany. 2003. Rel: 2 July 2004. Cert. 12A.

Three Dancing Slaves

See *Le Clan*.

Thunderbirds ★★

It's one thing to remake such TV phenomena as *Charlie's Angels*, *Mission: Impossible* and *Starsky and Hutch*, but a cheesy series featuring a cast of string puppets? *Thunderbirds*, a $60-million-plus, live-action adaptation of the cult 1965-66

'Supermarionation' show, doesn't know where to pitch its emphasis. While there is some humour to be found in the interaction between Lady Penelope and her chauffeur Parker, the film otherwise plays it pretty straight. This is a retro-futuristic romp with an eye on the *Spy Kids* market, which should just about entertain kids between the ages of four and eight. Ben Kingsley is wasted as a James Bond-ish villain bent on world domination, who uses his telekinetic powers to get his way but is hampered by two ineffectual sidekicks. So when Kingsley's The Hood strands Jeff Tracy and his fearless sons on their orbiting space station, it's up to Jeff's earthbound son Alan and young Fermat and Tin-Tin to save the day. The result is like watching a mediocre episode of a 1960s TV show, which is just not good enough for today's sophisticated young audience. JC-W

• *Jeff Tracy* Bill Paxton, *Hiram 'Brains' Hackenbacker* Anthony Edwards, *Lady Penelope Creighton-Ward* Sophia Myles, *The Hood* Ben Kingsley, *Alan Tracy* Brady Corbett, *Aloysius Parker* Ron Cook, *Fermat Hackenbacker* Soren Fulton, *Tin-Tin* Vanessa Anne Hughes, *Transom* Rose Keegan, *Mullion* Deobia Oparei, *Scott Tracy* Philip Winchester, *John Tracy* Lex Shrapnel, *Virgil Tracy* Dominic Colenso, *Gordon Tracy* Ben Torgersen, *with* Debora Weston, Lou Hirsch, Nicola Walker, Bhasker Patel.
• *Dir* Jonathan Frakes, *Pro* Tim Bevan, Eric Fellner and Mark Huffam, *Ex Pro* Debra Hayward and Liz Chasin, *Co-Pro* Joanna Burn and Chris Clark, *Screenplay* William Osborne and Michael McCullers, from a story by Osborne and Peter Hewitt, *Ph* Brendan Galvin, *Pro Des* John Beard, *Ed* Martin Walsh, *M* Hans Zimmer; 'Thunderbirds Are Go' performed by Busted, *Costumes* Marit Allen.

Universal/StudioCanal/Working Title-UIP.
87 mins. UK/USA/France. 2004. Rel: 23 July 2004. Cert. PG.

Toolbox Murders ★★

Los Angeles; the present. Nell Burrows, an out-of-work teacher, and her husband, a medical student, move into the creaky Lusman Arms apartment building. Desperately in need of repair, the 80-year-old building is privy to some pretty unnerving sounds: constant hammering, noisy love-making, shouting matches and some inexplicable screams. Nell is seriously spooked and is determined to get to the bottom of the disappearing tenants... In the wake of the *Texas Chain Saw Massacre* and *Dawn of the Dead* remakes comes this loose approximation of Dennis Donnelly's 1977 video nasty. The difference here is that scriptwriters Gierasch and Anderson haven't seen the original and that it's directed by The Master, he who helmed the first *Chain Saw*. But it's still a surprisingly conventional horror outing, with the usual sudden noises, women-in-peril and deranged, masked maniac. The film's ace card is the concept of a building hidden inside a building and the higher than average standard of acting (particularly from Angela Bettis). It's a shame, then, that the villain utilises such obvious tools (drill, nail gun, circular saw) instead of calling on the more inventive properties of a spanner, paint scraper or pair of pliers. And the victims behave even more brainlessly than they usually do in this sort of thing. JC-W

• *Nell Burrows* Angela Bettis, *Stephen Burrows* Brent Roam, *Julia Cunningham* Juliet Landau, *Chas Rooker* Rance Howard, *Luis Saucedo* Marco Rodriguez, *Ned Lundy* Adam Gierasch, *Byron McLieb* Greg Travis, *'Coffin Baby'* Chris Doyle, *with* Adam Weisman, Christina Venuti, Sara Downing.

• *Dir* Tobe Hooper, *Pro* Tony Didio, Terence S. Potter and Jacqueline Quella, *Ex Pro* Ryan Carrol, Frank Strausser, Ronnie Truss and Mark Wooding, *Assoc Pro* Adam Gierasch and Straw Weisman, *Screenplay* Jace Anderson and Adam Gierasch, *Ph* Steve Yedlin, *Pro Des* Yuda Acco, *Ed* Andrew Cohen, *M* Joseph Conlan; songs performed by Oedipus, Shithead, and Sara Downing, *Costumes* Shon LeBlanc, *Special Effects/Make-Up* Dean Jones and Starr Jones, *Original paintings* Dalia Hay-Acco.

Toolbox Films/Toolbox Murders Inc./Alpine Pictures/Scary Movies Prods-Anchor Bay Entertainment.
94 mins. USA/UK. 2003. Rel: 12 November 2004. Cert. 15.

Torremolinos 73 ★★★

Strictly speaking a co-production with Denmark but essentially Spanish in character and setting, Pablo Berger's comedy set in 1973 is very much in two sections. The engaging first half builds on the unlikely but acceptable premise of a middle-aged salesman avoiding the sack by agreeing to make educational movies (porn to you and me) featuring his wife (Candela Peña) and himself. The excellent Javier Cámara (from *Talk To Her*) brings out the comedy by underplaying beautifully, but it's erotic too. Subsequently, however, the tale sees the husband trying to make a Bergmanesque arthouse movie only to have it converted into a skin flick by the producer. Here everything becomes much sillier while simultaneously seeking to be more serious. This is the more disappointing because Cámara's performance really is a gem, but not even he can conceal how the film falls off. MS

• *Alfredo López* Javier Cámara, *Carmen García* Candela Peña, *Don Carlos* Juan Diego, *Juan Luis* Fernando Tejero, *Magnus* Mads Mikkelsen, *Vanessa* Malena Alterio, *Dennis* Thomas Bo Larson.

• *Dir* and *Screenplay* Pablo Berger, *Pro* Tomás Cimadevilla, *Co-Pro* Ghislain Barrois, Jose Herrero de Egana, Bo Ehrhardt and Lars Bredo Rahbek, *Ph* Kiko de la Rica, *Art Dir* Julio Torrecilla, *Ed* Rori Sainz de Rozas, *M* Mastretta, *Costumes* Estibaliz Markiegi.

Telespan/Estudios Picasso/Nimbus Film/Eurimages-Tartan Films.
91 mins. Spain/Denmark. 2003. Rel: 24 June 2005. Cert. 15.

Trauma ★★½

On the one hand *Trauma* is schematic, treacherous and unconvincing. On the other, it is an intriguing insight into – and perspective on – a deranged mind. It is a brave

Secrets and spies: Serge Renko in Eric Rohmer's persuasive *Triple Agent* (see page 132)

move, too, to cast Colin Firth as the key figure in this tale of delusion and murder – he is about as ordinary and sympathetic as a star can get. He plays Ben, an out-of-work painter who is recovering from a coma and the death of his wife in a car crash. Attempting to rebuild his life from scratch, Ben has moved into an old hospital that is being renovated into flats. Coincidentally, it is the very place where the music icon Lauren Parris was born, a singer murdered at the time of Ben's accident. Is there a connection? Artfully made by the director of *Resurrection Man* and the superb *My Little Eye*, *Trauma* is strong on style and detail but fails to gel when the pieces start to come together. For a start, it's hard to swallow why an attractive American blonde (Suvari) would be drawn to an unshaven, scruffy and obviously unhinged man (Firth) – 18 years her senior, to boot. Suvari plays Ben's new landlady and her design is about as incomprehensible as everything else. JC-W

• *Ben* Colin Firth, *Charlotte* Mena Suvari, *DC Jackson* Kenneth Cranham, *Elisa* Naomie Harris, *Tommy* Tommy Flanagan, *Roland* Sean Harris, *Petra* Brenda Fricker, *with* Martin Hancock, Dorothy Duffy, Dermot Murnaghan, Jamie Owen, Kirsty Young, Andrew MacLachlan, Anthony Flannagan, Liam Reilly.

• *Dir* Marc Evans, *Pro* Jonathan Cavendish and Nicky Kentish Barnes, *Ex Pro* James Mitchell, Sue Bruce-Smith, Jonathan Kelly, Kirk D'Amico, Marion Pilowsky, Donald A. Starr, Daniel J.B. Taylor, Steve Christian and David Bermingham, *Co-Pro* Lizzie Francke, *Line Pro* Bernard Bellew, *Prod Ex* Dixie Linder and Susy Liddell, *Screenplay* Richard Smith, *Ph* John Matghieson, *Pro Des* Crispian Sallis, *Ed* Marguerite Arnold, *M*

Alex Heffes and The Boilerhouse Boys, *Costumes* Ffion Elinor, *Sound* Paul Davies, *Ant wrangler* Andrew Stephenson, *Spider wrangler* Mark Amey.

BBC Films/Warner/First Choice/Isle of Man/Little Bird-Warner.
94 mins. UK/Ireland/USA. 2004. Rel: 17 September 2004. Cert. 15.

Trilogy: The Weeping Meadow ★★★½

Standing on its own but also the first part of a trilogy, this ambitious work of art sets a love story against the historical background of Greece between 1919 and 1949. With its superb visuals and with music as crucial as any Nino Rota score for Fellini, the first half of this long film finds director Theo Angelopoulos on strong form. Later, however, the drama slackens and becomes more reliant on the audience's knowledge of Greek history, while the narrative thread becomes oddly confusing at times. This falling away is disappointing, the more so because it robs the close of its full tragic power. However, those who admire Angelopoulos will certainly want to see this. MS

• *Eleni* Alexandra Aidini, *Spyros' son* Nikos Poursanidis, *Nikos, the fiddler* Yorgos Armenis, *Spyros* Vasilis Kolovos, *Cassandra* Eva Kotamanidou, *woman in coffee house* Toula Stathopoulou, *Zissis, the clarinetist* Mihalis Yannatos, *Danae* Thalia Argyriou, *teacher* Grigoris Evangelatos.

• *Dir* Theo Angelopoulos, *Pro* Angelopoulos and Fivi

Ekonomopoulos, *Ex Pro* Nikos Sekeris, *Screenplay* Angelopoulos, Tonino Guerra, Petros Markaris and Giorgio Silvagni, *Ph* Andreas Sinanos, *Art Dir* Yorgos Patsas and Kostas Dimitriadis, *Ed* Yorgos Triantafyllou, *M* Eleni Karaindrou, *Costumes* Ioulia Stavridou.

Greek Film Centre/ERT/Attika Art Prods/Canal Plus-Artificial Eye.
178 mins. Greece/France/Italy/Germany. 2004.
Rel: 21 January 2005. Cert. PG.

Triple Agent ★★★★

Scrupulously changing the names because this is a free treatment of a real-life tale and one in which the facts of the case remain uncertain, Eric Rohmer forsakes his usual territory to offer a splendidly convincing recreation of events that occurred in 1937. Set in Paris, this is a story about a married man, a Russian exile with a Greek wife, someone whose role in intelligence would seem to confirm his standing as a White Russian. Yet his activities could be a cover for someone really working for the Communists or the Nazis. A kidnapping brings matters to a head, but this is no action drama (one wouldn't expect that from Rohmer). Instead it's a wholly persuasive portrait of an era (the political detail sometimes rather formidable) and a marriage of the times when a wife could not voice her doubts and fears but had to accept whatever confidences her husband chose to share with her. There are outstandingly naturalistic performances from the two leads. MS

• *Arsinoé Vorodin* Katerina Didaskalou, *Fiodor Vorodin* Serge Renko, *Janine* Amanda Langlet, *André* Emmanuel Salinger, *Maguy* Cyrielle Clair, *Boris* Grigori Manoukov.

• *Dir* and *Screenplay* Eric Rohmer, *Pro* François Etchegaray, Jean-Michel Rey and Philippe Liégeois, *Assoc Pro* Laurent Danielou, *Ph* Diane Baratier, *Art Dir* Antoine Fontaine, *Ed* Mary Stephen, *M* Dmitri Shostakovich, *Costumes* Pierre Jean Larroque.

REZO Prods/CER/France 2 Cinéma/Canal Plus-Artificial Eye.
115 mins. France/Italy/Spain/Greece/Russia. 2003.
Rel: 29 October 2004. Cert. U.

The Triumph of Love ★★

For all its eccentricity, *The Triumph of Love* is not going to be remembered as a forgotten gem. Adapted from the 1732 play *Le Triomphe de l'amour* by Pierre de Marivaux, the film is a period comedy of deceit that attempts to be an 18th century production in cinematic clothing. Yet, shot on chilly Italian locations, it is defiantly uncinematic. The director/co-writer Clare Peploe (wife of Bernardo Bertolucci) fails to elicit convincing performances from her Oscar-winning stars (Sorvino and Kingsley) and cannot provide the cinematic flourish that the piece cries out for. Presumably cast for her height (she is 5'9"), Ms Sorvino plays a French princess disguised as a gentleman with romantic designs both on her

host and his sister. In fact, Princess Leonide lusts after their house guest, the dashing Prince Agis, whose mother and father were murdered by Leonide's parents. While singularly watchable, Sorvino cannot pull off her manly strut and bereft of the poetry of, say, Shakespeare's similarly themed *Twelfth Night*, the scenario is just daft. JC-W

• *Leonide, Princess of Sparta/Phocion/Aspasie* Mira Sorvino, *Hermocrates* Ben Kingsley, *Leontine* Fiona Shaw, *Prince Agis* Jay Rodan, *Hermidas/Corine* Rachael Stirling, *Arlequin* Ignazio Oliva, *Dimas* Luis Molteni.

• *Dir* Clare Peploe, *Pro* Bernardo Bertolucci, *Ex Pro* Massimo Cortesi, Jeremy Thomas, Thomas Schüly and Reinhard Kloos, *Screenplay* Peploe, Bertolucci and Marylin Goldin, *Ph* Fabio Cianchetti, *Pro Des* Ben Van Os, *Ed* Jacopo Quadri, *M* Jason Osborn; Mozart, Jean-Philippe Rameau, *Costumes* Metka Košak, *Dialogue coach* Carlo Ventura.

Fiction s.r.l./Recorded Picture Company/Medusa Film/Odeon Pictures-ContentFilm.
111 mins. Italy/UK/Germany. 2001.
Rel: 8 October 2004.
Cert. PG.

Tropical Malady ★★½

This two-part Thai movie is probably headed for cult status, but its strangeness, which some find atmospheric and compelling, is to my mind merely boringly obscure. The first hour has within it a sweetly done portrait of gay love between a soldier and a country youth, but the slow pace and lack of flow or incident scuppers it. In the second half the soldier pursues a naked man-beast played by the actor previously seen as the youth. Towards the close some touches of poetry do emerge, but this even slower and less eventful second section suggests *The Blair Witch Project* with all sense of menace and terror removed. The implied endorsement by society of hunting down one's fellow men while disapproving of love between males could make this an allegory about homophobia, but it is so vague that the film's meaning is anyone's guess. Original title: *Sud pralad*. MS

• *Keng* Banlop Lomnoi, *Tong* Sakda Kaewbuadee, *with* Sirivech Jareonchon, Udom Promma, Huai Deesom.

• *Dir* and *Screenplay* Apichatpong Weerasethakul, *Pro* Charles de Meaux, *Co-Pro* Paiboon Damrongchaitham, Marco Muller, Christoph Thoke, Axel Moebius and Pantham Thongsangl, *Ph* Vichit Tanapanitch, Jarin Pengpanitch and Jean-Louis Vialard, *Pro Des* Akekarat Homlaor, *Ed* Lee Chatametikool and Jacopo Quadri, *Costumes* Pilaitip Jamniam, *Sound* Akritchalerm Kalayanamitr.

Anna Sanders Films/Tifa/Downtown/Thoke + Moebius/Kick the Machine/Backup Films/RAI Cinema/Fabrica Cinema-ICA Projects.
118 mins. France/Thailand/Germany/Italy/Switzerland. 2004. Rel: 4 March 2005.
Cert. 12A.

Rumble in the jungle: Banlop Lomnoi and Sakda Kaewbuadee in Apichatpong Weerasethakul's boringly obscure *Tropical Malady* (from ICA Projects)

Tupac: Resurrection ★★★★

Love him or hate him (and there are certainly reasons for both), it's clear that when 25-year-old rapper Tupac Amaru Shakur was gunned down on Friday 13 September 1996, the world lost a formidable talent and a crucial artistic voice. MTV producer Lauren Lazin fearlessly combines a vast collection of home movies, performances, interviews, photos and news clips to create a very complete portrait of Tupac's incredible yet troubled life. It's no easy task. Still, she creates a chronicle that is as celebratory as it is cautionary. Shakur himself provides the majority of the commentary. Candid, insightful and intelligent, Tupac had a lot of things to say to the world. SWM

• *Dir* Lauren Lazin, *Pro* Lazin, Preston Holmes and Karolyn Ali, *Ex Pro* Afeni Shakur, Von Toffler and David Gale, *Ph* Jon Else, *Ed* Richard Calderon, *M* Shakur; songs performed predominantly by Tupac Shakur.

Paramount Pictures/MTV Films/Amaru Entertainment-UIP.
110 mins. USA. 2003. Rel: 2 July 2004. Cert. 15.

Turtles Can Fly ★★★

Bahman Ghobadi – director of *A Time for Drunken Horses* – felt compelled to make this film after visiting Baghdad and seeing the state of a people, crippled children among them, in a land where the earth had been mined and war was threatened. His heartfelt response is this tale of refugees and villagers, mainly children in a refugee camp in Iraqi Kurdistan (near the border between Iran and Turkey). Sadly, the plotting seems much more contrived than in the superb earlier film, the non-professional child players are not so remarkable and the location far less suited to bring out Ghobadi's poetic side. The film's bleakness is to be respected, but what can be seen as a climactic scene seems emotionally exploitative and, despite excellent intentions, one feels that the film can nowhere near match up to Ghobadi's previous effort. MS

• *Agrin* Avaz Latif, *Soran* aka *Satellite* Soran Ebrahim, *Pashow* Saddam Hossein Feysal, *with* Hiresh Feysal Rahman, Abdol Rahman Karim, Ajil Zibari.

• *Dir, Screenplay* and *Pro Des* Bahman Ghobadi, *Pro* Bahman Ghobadi, *Ex Pro* Abbas Ghazali, *Ph* Shahriar Assadi, *Ed* Moustafa Khergheposh and Hayedeh Sayifari, *M* Housein Alizadeh.

Mij Film Co.-ICA Projects.
97 mins. Iran. 2004. Rel: 7 January 2005. Cert. 15.

2046 ★★

In the year 2046 a Japanese passenger appears to be trapped

on a train staffed by androids. But maybe this is a fiction imagined by the pulp novelist Chow Mo Wan, who borrows his title from the hotel room number in which he once conducted an extramarital affair. Returning to Hong Kong in 1966, Chow attempts to re-rent the room, but is told that it is being redecorated. So he moves into 2047 and finds himself drawn to a series of female occupants next door, attractive women he woos only to jilt when they get too close to his heart. Such is the transience of love… A sequel to Wong's 2000 film *In the Mood for Love* (itself a companion piece to 1990's *Days of Being Wild*), *2046* is a maddening piece of existential introspection. Composed almost entirely of interiors and close-ups, the film is wilfully non-linear and stylised, not to say episodic, meandering and downright confusing. Four years in the making, it is a triumph of textural flamboyance – Wong paints his scenes with light, smoke, glass and neon – but it fails to connect emotionally, if only because Chow himself is such a cad and procrastinator. Some might even call *2046* pretentious. JC-W

• *Chow Mo Wan* Tony Leung, *Yang Wen-Yi* Li Gong, *Tak* Kimura Takuya, *Wang Jing Wen/wjw 1967* Faye Wong, *Bai Ling* Ziyi Zhang, *Lulu/Mimi* Carina Lau, *cc1966* Chang Chen, *Ah Ping* Siu Ping-Lam, *Mr Wang/train captain* Wang Sum, *Su Li Zhen/slz1960* Maggie Cheung, *Bird* Thongchai McIntyre, *Wang Jie Wen* Dong Jie.

• *Dir* and *Screenplay* Wong Kar-wai, *Pro* Wong, Chan Ye-cheng and Ren Zhonglun, *Ex Pro* Ren, Eric Heumann and Zhu Yongde, *Co-Pro* Jacky Pang Yee-wah and Zhuo Wu, *Line Pro* Alice Chan, *Ph* Christopher Doyle, Lai Yiu-fai and Kwan Pun-leung, *Pro Des* and *Ed* William Chang Suk-ping, *M* Peer Raben and Shigeru Umebayashi; Georges Delerue, Zbigniew Preisner; songs performed by Dean Martin, Connie Francis, Nat King Cole, and Angela Gheorghiu, *Sound* Claude Letessier, *English subtitles* Tony Rayns.

Block2 Pictures/Paradis Films/Classic SRL/Arte France Cinéma, etc-Tartan Films.
129 mins. Hong Kong/France/Italy/Germany/China. 2004. Rel: 14 January 2005. Cert. 12A.

Twin Sisters ★★½
Germany/Holland/Belgium; 1926 to the present. When both their parents succumb to early deaths, the inseparable six-year-old twins Anna and Lotte are parted to live with distant relatives. Whereas the consumptive Lotte is stationed with a rich family in Holland, Anna ends up working all hours on a small farm in Germany. Both sisters are discouraged from correspondence with each other and then the Second World War puts paid to any reconciliation, be it geographical or political… There's no denying that this is a terrific story – the film unfolds like a sprawling, page-turning novel; indeed, Tessa de Loo's original was a bestseller in both Germany and the Netherlands. Yet, even while nominated for an Oscar as Best Foreign Language Film, *Twin Sisters* doesn't really take off. There are some strong performances (particularly from Nadja Uhl), but much of the film is predictable and

the clichés keep getting in the way (a gum-chewing Yank anyone?). In addition, the colour-drained flashbacks – which make up the bulk of the film – are a tad precious, while the physical disparity between the twin siblings is downright distracting. Original title: *De Tweeling*. JC-W

• *Lotte, aged around six* Julia Koopmans, *Lotte, aged around 20* Thekla Reuten, *Lotte as a 'grand old lady'* Ellen Vogel, *Anna, aged around six* Sina Richardt, *Anna, aged around 20* Nadja Uhl, *Anna as a 'grand old lady'* Gudrun Okras, *David de Vries* Jeroen Spitzenberger, *Martin Grosalie* Roman Knizka, *with* Hans Somers, Margarita Broich, Barbara Auer.

• *Dir* Ben Sombogaart, *Pro* Anton Smit and Hanneke Niens, *Ex Pro* Madelon Veldhuizen, *Line Pro* Jani Thiltges, *Screenplay* Marieke Van Der Pol, *Ph* Piotr Kukla, *Pro Des* Michel De Graaf, *Ed* Herman P. Koerts, *M* Fons Merkies, *Costumes* Linda Bogers, *Sound* Peter Flamman.

RCV/IdtV Film/Chios Media/Samsa Film/NCRV, etc-Optimum Releasing.
137 mins. The Netherlands/Luxemburg. 2002. Rel: 6 May 2005. Cert. 12A.

Twisted ★★★
This is a formulaic, machine-tooled policier that looks good and thinks hard. Slammed by the critics in the US, it is no classic, but it connects the dots very nicely. Ashley Judd is cornering the market as the kick-ass heroine of these cat-and-mouse thrillers (cf. *Kiss the Girls*, *Double Jeopardy*, *High Crimes*) and she has a healthy relationship with the camera. Substituting Morgan Freeman with Samuel L. Jackson as her authoritative co-star, Ashley plays Jessica Shepard, a first-class cop freshly promoted to Homicide. The film starts beautifully: a series of stunningly framed shots of San Francisco are intercut with a close-up of a woman's eye. As the camera finally comes to rest, it pans down the woman's face to reveal a knife pressed hard against her throat. A minute later the woman – Jessica Shepard – has disarmed the knifeman and has him in handcuffs. However, this schmuck is not the serial killer at the film's centre. Shepard's best suspect is herself… Mechanical *Twisted* may be, but it's also slick, atmospheric and efficiently diverting. Previously known as *Blackout*. JC-W

• *Jessica Shepard* Ashley Judd, *John Mills* Samuel L. Jackson, *Mike Delmarco* Andy Garcia, *Dr Melvin Frank* David Straithairn, *Lieutenant Tong* Russell Wong, *Lisa* Camryn Manheim, *Jimmy Schmidt* Mark Pellegrino, *Dale Becker* Titus Welliver, *Ray Porter* D.W. Moffett, *Wilson Jefferson* Richard T. Jones, *Edmund Culter* Leland Orser, *with* James Oliver Bullock, William Hall, Leonard Thomas, Danny Lopez.

• *Dir* Philip Kaufman, *Pro* Arnold Kopelson, Anne Kopelson, Barry Baeres and Linne Radmin, *Ex Pro* Stephen Brown, Robyn Meisinger and Michael Flynn, *Co-Pro*, Peter Kaufman and Sherryl Clark, *Assoc Pro* Cherylanne Martin, *Screenplay* Sarah Thorp, *Ph* Peter Deming, *Pro Des* Dennis

Washington, *Ed* Peter Boyle, *M* Mark Isham, *Costumes* Ellen Mirojnick.

Paramount/Intertainment/Kopelson Entertainment-UIP. 96 mins. USA/Germany. 2004. Rel: 9 July 2004. Cert 15.

Two Brothers ★★★

Classic films about animals are a rare breed and this isn't one of them. Nevertheless, there is an uncommon privilege about staring at a couple of such noble beasts in their natural habitat. The story of two tigers separated in childhood – a sort of feline *Black Beauty* times two – the movie is another ambitious multi-national production from the director of *The Bear* and *Quest for Fire*. Filmed in the jungles of Cambodia and Thailand, *Two Brothers* is a visual feast and the interaction of the four-legged stars – courtesy of animal trainer Thierry Le Portier – is a wonder to behold. Unfortunately, the human story surrounding the beasts is wooden and amateur in the extreme. Guy Pearce plays a big game hunter who changes his stripes to pillage temples of their sacred statues. In a rare moment of decency, he feeds his favourite honey drops to a tiger cub he has orphaned, only to desert the animal when he is arrested for plunder. Luckily for us, though, Pearce takes a back seat to the antics of Kumal and Sangha (played by a total of eight tigers), who are taken into captivity and refuse to fit in. Their adventures should enchant children aged eight to 80. French title: *Deux frères*. JC-W

• *Aidan McRory* Guy Pearce, *Administrator Normandin* Jean-Claude Dreyfus, *young Raoul* Freddie Highmore, *His Excellency* Oanh Nguyen, *Mrs Normandin* Philippine Leroy-Beaulieu, *with* Moussa Maaskri, David Gant, Juliet Howland.

• *Dir* Jean-Jacques Annaud, *Pro* Annaud and Jake Eberts, *Co-Pro* Paul Rassam and Timothy Burrill, *Screenplay* Annaud and Alain Godard, from an original story by Annaud, *Ph* Jean-Marie Dreujou, *Pro Des* Pierre Queffelean, *Ed* Noëlle Boisson, *M* Stephen Warbeck, *Costumes* Pierre-Yves Gayraud.

Pathé Renn/TF1 Films/Canal Plus-Pathé. 104 mins. France/UK. 2004. Rel: 23 July 2004. Cert. U.

Uncovered: The War on Iraq ★★★

Ostensibly just another piece of anti-Bush propaganda repackaged to try and sway the 2004 US presidential election, Robert Greenwald's documentary is actually a legitimate exercise in journalism as both product and admonition of the Fourth Estate. Like all documentaries, this benefits from the gift of hindsight; it's always easy to second-guess the big decisions after they've been made. Still, despite its one-sided position, it's an insightful, even prophetic, collection of sound-bites and interviews surrounding the first genuine political quagmire of the 21st century. As both a historical record and jumping-off point for reasonable, intelligent debate, *Uncovered* is the real deal – as opposed to the sloppy, over-hyped piece of sensationalism that was *Fahrenheit 9/11*. SWM

Burning bright: Kumal and Sangha face off in Jean-Jacques Annaud's ambitious *Two Brothers* (from Pathé)

• *with*: Milt Bearden, Rand Beers, Graham Fuller, Henry Waxman, John Dean, etc.

• *Dir* and *Pro* Robert Greenwald, *Co-Pro* Kate McArdle, Devin Smith and Philippe Diaz, *Ph* various, *Ed* Kimberly Ray, *M* Brad Chiet, Jim Ervin and Mars Lasar.

Cinema Libra/MoveOn.org-Blue Dolphin.
83 mins. USA. 2004. Rel: 29 October 2004. Cert. PG.

Undertow ★★½

Georgia; the present. Hog farmer and taxidermist John Munn struggles to make a living while supporting his two sons, troubled teenager Chris and the frail, ten-year-old Tim. Then unexpected help arrives in the form of John's younger brother, Deel. But for all his expansive smiles and genial swagger, Deel appears to harbour some major grudges… The Arkansas-born filmmaker David Gordon Green has exhibited a novel take on rural America. Not for him the picture postcard views of the South, but rather a wasteland of industrial squalor positioned against a stark, untidy wilderness. After winning deserved kudos for *George Washington* and *All the Real Girls*, Green moves into genre territory with this atmospheric thriller. Again, he has fashioned an authentic picture of backwoods America, where the natives speak in fractured non-sequiturs and the countryside is potted with tumbledown shacks and abandoned vehicles. Yet Green doesn't seem sure whether he's making a thriller or an art movie. Punctuated with freeze-frames and other artificial filmic devices, the drama is constantly undermined by the director's showy technique. JC-W

• *Chris Munn* Jamie Bell, *Deel Munn* Josh Lucas, *Tim Munn* Devon Alan, *John Munn* Dermot Mulroney, *Violet* Shiri Appleby, *Lila* Kristen Stewart, *Muriel, the cashier* Leigh Hill, *with* Pat Healy, Bill McKinney, Robert Longstreet, Terry Loughlin, Eddie Rouse, Patrice Johnson, Carla Bassey.

• *Dir* David Gordon Green, *Pro* Lisa Muskat, Terrence Malick and Edward R. Pressman, *Ex Pro* John Schmidt and Alessandro Camon, *Screenplay* Green and Joe Conway, *Ph* Tim Orr, *Pro Des* Richard Wright, *Ed* Zene Baker and Steve Gonzales, *M* Philip Glass, *Costumes* Jill Newell.

United Artists/ContentFilm/Sunflower Film-Feature Film Company.
108 mins. USA. 2004. Rel: 17 June 2005. Cert. 15.

Untold Scandal ★★★

This handsome period production from Korea acknowledges as its source the much-filmed Laclos novel *Les Liaisons dangereuses*. Close to the original in plot if not in location, it shows how two kindred spirits, Jo-Won and his cousin Lady Cho, delight in sexual schemes of revenge and corruption. All versions of the tale carry a hint of double standards, since audiences are invited to relish lascivious deeds and then to endorse the comeuppance that follows. Here, however, the problems go deeper. Although hardly worthy of the '18' certificate, the film contains elements of soft porn while

playing down the crucial element of perversity, and the conclusion takes off inappropriately into high romanticism. The three leading actresses are worthy of the production values but are sold out by the misjudgments of tone. MS

• *Jo Weon* Bae Yong-jun, *Lady Jo* Lee Mi-suk, *Lady Jeong* Jeon Do-yeon, *In-ho* Jo Hyeon-jae, *Lee So-ok* Lee So-yeon.

• *Dir* E J-yong (Lee Jae-yong), *Pro* Oh Jeong-wan, *Ex Pro* Lee Kang-bok, *Co-Pro* Lee Yu-jin, *Screenplay* E J-yong, Kim Dae-woo and Kim Hyeon-jeong, adapted from *Les Liaisons dangereuses* by Choderlos de Laclos, *Ph* Kim Byeong-il, *Pro Des* Jeong Gu-ho, *Ed* Kim Yang-il and Han Seung-ryong, *M* Lee Byeong-woo, *Costumes* Kim Heui-ju.

CJ Entertainment/CJ Venture/B.O.M.-Soda Pictures.
124 mins. South Korea. 2003. Rel: 22 April 2005. Cert. 18.

Valiant ★★½

A humble wood pigeon, Valiant is determined to serve his country in the Second World War. Although very young and undersized, Valiant talks his way into the ranks of the Royal Homing Pigeon Service and embarks on a vigorous training course… Between 1943 and 1949, the PDSA bestowed its highest honour – the Dickin Medal, the animal equivalent of the Victoria Cross – to 54 creatures for 'displaying conspicuous gallantry and devotion to duty while serving with the Armed Forces or Civil Defence units.' One of those honoured was a cat, three were horses, 18 were dogs and 32 were pigeons. To honour their contribution to the war effort, this cartoon aims for a *Chicken Run* charm but comes up rather short on laughs. The animation itself is slick and efficient without being exceptional (there are some lazy short cuts), while the characters are predictable and one-dimensional. Even so, it's hard to criticise a film that is so well meaning and *Valiant* is seldom less than endearing. It's at its best when capturing the nostalgia of the British at war, prompting fond memories of John Mills and Celia Johnson maintaining a stiff upper lip. JC-W

• voices: *Valiant* Ewan McGregor, *Bugsy* Ricky Gervais, *Von Talon* Tim Curry, *Sergeant* Jim Broadbent, *Gutsy* Hugh Laurie, *Mercury* John Cleese, *Felix* John Hurt, *Lofty* Pip Torrens, *Cufflingk* Rik Mayall, *Victoria* Olivia Williams, *Big Thug* Jonathan Ross, *Charles De Girl* Sharon Horgan, *pigeon officer* Gary Chapman, *with* Brian Lonsdale, Dan Roberts, Michael Schlingmann, Sean Samuels, Annette Badland.
• *Dir* Gary Chapman, *Pro* John H. Williams, *Ex Pro* Barnaby Thompson, Ralph Kemp, Neil Braun, Robert Jones and Keith Evans, *Assoc Pro* Marci Levine, *Screenplay* Jordan Katz, George Webster and George Melrod, *Ph* John Fenner, *Pro Des* John Byrne, *Ed* Jim Stewart, *M* George Fenton, *Animation Dir* Richard Purdum.

Vanguard Animation/Ealing Studios/UK Film Council/ Odyssey Entertainment/Take Film Partnerships/Baker Street Finance/National Lottery-Entertainment.
76 mins. UK/USA. 2005. Rel: 25 March 2005. Cert. U.

Theatrical Thackeray: Reese Witherspoon as Becky Sharp in Mira Nair's *Vanity Fair* (see overleaf)

Vanity Fair ★★★

England, Belgium, India; 1802-1833. The daughter of an impecunious painter and chorus girl, Rebecca Sharp is as bright and astute as her name would suggest. Excelling at French, music and art, she leaves Miss Pinkerton's Academy resolved to conquer society... William Makepeace Thackeray's *Vanity Fair* is bit of a doorstop and, while director Nair brings a magnificent cast and visual splendour to the piece, she cannot temper it for cinematic consumption. *Vanity Fair* has miniseries written all over it and the numerous locations and characters, not to mention the time frame, demand a three-hour film at the very least. As that quintessential English heroine – the 19th century independent woman fighting class prejudice and poverty – Reese Witherspoon conducts herself extremely well, although it's a shame that a non-American could not have had the opportunity to headline such a major British production. But even as the film drags and jumps, the insight and comic acumen of Thackeray's original still glints brightly, while the period detail is simply ravishing. FYI: Becky Sharp has previously been played on screen by Helen Gardner (in 1911), Minnie Maddern Fiske (1915), Mabel Ballin (1923), Myrna Loy (1932) and Miriam Hopkins (1935). Natasha Little, who plays Jane Sheepshanks in this edition, played Becky in the 1998 miniseries.
JC-W

• *Rebecca Sharp* Reese Witherspoon, *Miss Matilda Crawley* Eileen Atkins, *Mr Osborne* Jim Broadbent, *The Marquess of Steyne* Gabriel Byrne, *Amelia Sedley* Romola Garai, *Sir Pitt Crawley* Bob Hoskins, *William Dobbin* Rhys Ifans, *Lady Southdown* Geraldine McEwan, *Rawdon Crawley* James Purefoy, *George Osborne* Jonathan Rhys Meyers, *Pitt Crawley* Douglas Hodge, *Lady Jane Sheepshanks* Natasha Little, *Joseph Sedley* Tony Maudsley, *young Becky* Angelica Mandy, *Francis Sharp* Roger Lloyd Pack, *Miss Pinkerton* Ruth Sheen, *Mrs Sedley* Deborah Findlay, *John Sedley* John Franklyn-Robbins, *Lady Crawley* Meg Wynn Owen, *Maria Osborne* Sophie Hunter, *the King* Richard McCabe, *young Georgy* Tom Sturridge, *with* Kate Fleetwood, Helen Coker, John Woodvine, Barbara Leigh-Hunt, Nicholas Jones, Sian Thomas, Trevor Cooper, Brian Pettifer, Niall O'Brien, Kelly Hunter, Camilla Rutherford, Timothy Bentinck.

• *Dir* Mira Nair, *Pro* Janette Day, Donna Gigliotti and Lydia Dean Pilcher, *Ex Pro* Howard Cohen, Pippa Cross and Jonathan Lynn, *Co-Pro* Jane Frazer, *Assoc Pro* Matthew Faulk and Mark Skeet, *Screenplay* Faulk, Skeet and Julian Fellowes, *Ph* Declan Quinn, *Pro Des* Maria Djurkovic, *Ed* Allyson C. Johnson, *M* Mychael Danna; Haydn, *Costumes* Beatrix Aruna Pasztor, *Choreography* Jill McCullough.

Focus Features/Tempesta Films/Granada Film/Inside Track-UIP.
140 mins. UK/USA. 2004. Rel: 14 January 2005. Cert. PG.

Vera Drake ★★★★

Often, the power of Mike Leigh's work is in his canny observation of the little things that ordinary people do – or do not do. Assuredly evoking North London in the autumn of 1950 – was life really that simple back then? – Leigh sketches in the lives of a group of people barely living above the poverty line but happy with their lot. Vera Drake is a determinedly contented soul, cleaning for the rich, cooking for her own husband and two grown-up children and caring for the neighbours. She also likes to help out 'women in trouble,' offers her services free and does a decent enough job with a dash of disinfectant and a syringe... Imelda Staunton was showered with awards for her work in this rich, poignant drama, but is matched by a superlative cast of peerless character actors, from Phil Davis as Vera's phlegmatic husband to Alex Kelly as the couple's painfully introverted daughter. *Vera Drake* is a pretty sombre – and often wilfully slow – drama, albeit brushed with the occasional comic elevation of a metaphorical eyebrow. However, the humanity of Leigh's *dramatis personae* and the world that they inhabit – eternally punctuated by 'a nice cup o' tea' – is simply riveting. JC-W

• *Vera Rose Drake* Imelda Staunton, *Stan Drake* Phil Davis, *Det. Inspector Webster* Peter Wight, *Frank Drake* Adrian Scarborough, *Joyce* Heather Craney, *Sid Drake* Daniel Mays, *Ethel Drake* Alex Kelly, *Susan* Sally Hawkins, *Reg* Eddie Marsan, *Lily* Ruth Sheen, *with* Helen Coker, Martin Savage, Sinead Matthews, Allan Corduner, Lesley Sharp, Nicky Henson, Jim Broadbent, Fenella Woolgar, Lesley Manville, Sandra Voe, Liz White, Elizabeth Berrington, Emma Amos, Richard Graham, Anna Keaveney, Simon Chandler, Sam Troughton, Marion Bailey, Leo Bill, Gerard Monaco, Tilly Vosburgh, Lauren Holden, Lucy Pleasence, Robert Putt, Jeffrey Wickham, Nicholas Jones, Angela Curran.

• *Dir* and *Screenplay* Mike Leigh, *Pro* Simon Channing Williams and Alain Sarde, *Ex Pro* Gail Egan, Robert Jones and Duncan Reid, *Co-Pro* Georgina Lowe, *Ph* Dick Pope, *Pro Des* Eve Stewart, *Ed* Jim Clark, *M* Andrew Dickson, *Costumes* Jacqueline Durran

Alain Sarde/UK Film Council/Inside Track/Thin Man Films/National Lottery-Momentum Pictures.
125 mins. UK/France. 2004. Rel: 7 January 2005. Cert. 12A.

A Very Long Engagement ★★★★½

France; 1917-1920. Unable to stomach the horrors of the Somme anymore, 19-year-old Manech lights a nocturnal cigarette and raises his hand above the trench line. He loses two fingers, but instead of being given compassionate leave he is court-martialled for 'self mutilation'. Thus, he and four other condemned men are pushed into the choking, ear-splitting firing line of the German artillery. Back home, his fiancée Mathilde refuses to believe that he is dead and, two years after the Great War has ended, embarks on an epic investigation into his death ... Following the beguiling enchantment of his phenomenally successful *Amélie*, Jean-Pierre Jeunet concocts a fairy tale of a much darker hue with this adaptation of Sébastien Japrisot's acclaimed novel. Adopting the same non-linear narrative as the book, Jeunet sucks the viewer into a maelstrom of horror, humour, pathos and colourful metaphor, all played out on a magnificent,

Imelda Staunton in her multi-award-winning performance as *Vera Drake* (from Momentum Pictures)

Trenchant warfare: Jérôme Kircher and Gaspard Ulliel in Jean-Pierre Jeunet's indelible *A Very Long Engagement* (from Warner)

pictorially seductive canvas. Ultimately, there is so much to assimilate – so many story strands, incidental characters, indelible images and detail – that one comes away with mental and emotional indigestion. It's a masterpiece that demands to be experienced at least twice, albeit a less satisfactory one than *Amélie*.
JC-W

• *Mathilde Donnay* Audrey Tautou, *Manech* Gaspard Ulliel, *Lt. Esperanza* Jean-Pierre Becker, *Ange Bassignano* Dominique Bettenfeld, *Benoît Notre Dame* Clovis Cornillac, *Tina Lombardi* Marion Cotillard, *Benjamin Gordes* Jean-Pierre Darroussin, *Véronique Passavant* Julie Depardieu, *Commandant Lavrouye* Jean-Claude Dreyfus, *Rouvières* André Dussollier, *Germain Pire* Ticky Holgado, *Captain Favourier* Tcheky Karyo, *Bastoche* Jérôme Kircher, *Six-Sous* Denis Lavant, *Bénédicte* Chantal Neuwirth, *Sylvain* Dominique Pinon, *postman* Jean-Paul Rouve, *L'il Louis* Michel Vuillermoz, *with* Thierry Gibault, Rufus, Michel Robin, and (uncredited) *Elodie Gordes* Jodie Foster.
• *Dir* Jean-Pierre Jeunet, *Ex Pro* Bill Gerber, *Line Pro* Jean-Lou Monthieux, *Screenplay* Jeunet and Guillaume Laurant, *Ph* Bruno Delbonnel, *Set Des* Aline Bonetto, *Ed* Herve Schneid, *M* Angelo Badalamenti; Verdi, Saint-Saëns, *Costumes* Madeline Fontaine, *Sound* Laurent Kossayan, *Digital effects* Alain Carsoux. 2003 Prods/Warner/Tapioca Films/TF1 Films/Canal Plus-Warner.
133 mins. France/USA. 2004. Rel: 21 January 2005. Cert. 15.

The Village ★★½

A close-knit community in 1897 Pennsylvania has established an uneasy truce with the inhabitants of the surrounding woods. Referred to as Those We Do Not Speak Of, the creatures are largely kept at bay by yellow flags and burning torches. Occasionally, however, they show their displeasure by skinning local dogs and daubing red paint on the villagers' doors… M. Night Shyamalan makes exceedingly interesting films, but he doesn't understand the fundamentals of suspense. Following the high profile afforded *The Sixth Sense*, *Unbreakable* and *Signs*, the buzz surrounding *The Village* was almost palpable. It's certainly a film to take home with you, but it just isn't as scary as it's made out to be. It's actually very boring and needs more subplots to sustain interest, while Those We Do Not Speak Of look as frightening as a pack of pantomime wolves. There are other weaknesses, too. Shyamalan is far too keen on arty shots for the sake of it (a distraction, particularly for a period piece), while James Newton Howard's lush symphonic score undermines the simplicity of the villagers' elemental way of life. Nonetheless, the central performance of Bryce Dallas Howard (daughter of director Ron) is the revelation of the summer. Previously known as *The Wood*. JC-W

• *Lucius Hunt* Joaquin Phoenix, *Ivy Elizabeth Walker* Bryce Dallas Howard, *Noah Percy* Adrien Brody, *Alice Hunt* Sigourney Weaver, *Edward Walker* William Hurt, *August Nicholson* Brendan Gleeson, *Mrs Clack* Cherry Jones, *Kitty Walker* Judy Greer, *Finton Coin* Michael Pitt, *Vivian Percy* Celia Weston, *Tabitha Walker* Jayne Atkinson, *with* Fran

Howard's way: Bryce Dallas Howard dazzles in M. Night Shyamalan's
otherwise undernourished *The Village* (from Buena Vista International)

Kranz, Jesse Eisenberg, Frank Collison, Charlie Hofheimer, Liz Stauber, M. Night Shyamalan.

• *Dir* and *Screenplay* M. Night Shyamalan, *Pro* Shyamalan, Scott Rudin and Sam Mercer, *Ph* Roger Deakins, *Pro Des* Tom Foden, *Ed* Christopher Tellefsen, *M* James Newton Howard, *Costumes* Ann Roth, *Sound* Steve Boeddeker and Frank Eulner, *Creature design* Crash McCreery.

Touchstone Pictures/Blinding Edge Pictures/Scott Rudin-Buena Vista International.
107 mins. USA. 2004. Rel: 20 August 2004. Cert. 12A.

Vodka Lemon ★★★

Since the Russians left in 1990, the inhabitants of a remote Kurdish village have had to sacrifice a modicum of comfort for their freedom. There's not a lot to do here, other than to sit outside in the snow and smoke and drink and think. Hamal, a 60-year-old widower, is finding it hard to make ends meet. Unable to survive on his miserly pension, he sells what few belongings he has left – a wardrobe, a Russian television set, his military uniform… Composed of a series of virtually wordless tableaux, *Vodka Lemon* is a poetic hymn to the plight of the Kurdish people. Directed with affection and wry humour by the Paris-based Kurd Hiner Saleem, the film suffers from a certain stasis but is a visually striking venture rich with offbeat observation. To reach a wider audience, it would have benefited from a spark of ebullience, but its understated humour and bleak atmosphere still exude a pathos that is quite haunting. JC-W

• *Hamo* Romen Avinian, *Nina* Lala Sarkissian, *Dilovan* Ivan Franek, *Giano* Zaal Karielachvili, *Zine* Ruzan Mesropyan.

• *Dir* Hiner Saleem, *Ex Pro* Michel Loro, *Ph* Christophe Pollock, *Ed* Dora Mantzorou, *M* Michel Korb.

Dulcine Films/Arte France Cinema/Sintra/Amka Films/ Paradise/Cine-FactoMetrodome.
89 mins. France/Switzerland/Armenia/Italy. 2003. Rel: 24 September 2004. Cert PG.

Walking Tall ★★★

When the original, ultra-violent *Walking Tall* came out in 1973, who would have thought that it would spawn two sequels, a TV movie, a TV series and now a remake? 'Inspired by a true story,' this calculating vehicle for the 6'5" wrestler The Rock bears little resemblance to reality, but is as buff and lean as its hulking star. At a trim 74 minutes (minus credits), the film wastes no time with narrative (or human) flab and delivers the goods in clean, broad strokes. Our hero is Chris Vaughn, a US Special Forces' veteran who returns home to connect with his grass roots. But things have changed in the sleepy Washington town of Chris' youth, the mill has closed and a gambling joint has become the community's main source of income. The latter is run by Jay Hamilton, a silky operator with the police in his back pocket. Of course, Chris intends to change all this and all he needs is a big stick and

a whole lotta attitude… With its bone-crunching violence, scantily clad babes and fortune cookie moralising, *Walking Tall* is an efficient piece of testosterone-fuelled escapism. Tag it *Rambo* with diction. JC-W

• *Chris Vaughn* Dwayne 'The Rock' Johnson, *Ray Templeton* Johnny Knoxville, *Jay Hamilton* Neal McDonough, *Michelle Vaughn* Kristen Wilson, *Deni* Ashley Scott, *Pete Vaughn* Khleo Thomas, *Chris Vaughn Sr.* John Beasley, *Connie Vaughn* Barbara Tarbuck, *Sheriff Stan Watkins* Michael Bowen, *Booth* Kevin Durand.

• *Dir* Kevin Bray, *Pro* Jim Burke, Lucas Foster, Paul Schiff, Ashok Amritraj and David Hoberman, *Ex Pro* Keith Samples and Vince McMahon, *Co-Pro* Bill Bannerman, *Screenplay* David Klass, Channing Gibson, David Levien, and Brian Koppelman, based on a screenplay by Mort Briskin, *Ph* Glen MacPherson, *Pro Des* Brent Thomas, *Ed* George Bowers and Robert Ivison, *M* Graeme Revell, *Costumes* Gersha Phillips.

MGM/A Hyde Park Entertainment/Mandeville Films/ Burke/Samples/Foster Prods/WWE Films-Fox.
87 mins. USA. 2004. Rel: 9 July 2004. Cert 15.

Wall ★★★★

This feature-length documentary about the wall cutting off the West bank from Jerusalem is all the better for being made by an Arab Jew (born in Morocco, Simone Bitton regards herself as a citizen of both Israel and France). This results in a document that has no political bias but is presented as a statement about the inhumanity of the wall that keeps neighbours apart and fosters division without achieving any reduction in hostilities. Slow at the start, the film soon settles down to become a compelling testament from those on both sides of the wall. Indeed, we are made to feel that we are experiencing the situation for ourselves as though we were physically present. The film's sense of location and space also gives it a kind of poetry within this harsh setting. Original title: *Mur*. MS

• *Dir* and *Screenplay* Simone Bitton, *Ex Pro* Thierry Lenouvel, *Ph* Jacques Bouquin, *Ed* Catherine Poitevin-Meyer and Jean-Michel Perez.

Ciné-Sud Promotion/Arna Prods-Artificial Eye.
99 mins. France/Israel/USA. 2004. Rel: 3 December 2004. Cert 12A.

A Way of Life ★★

Contemporary Wales provides the setting for this desperately sincere but totally depressing portrait of a racially prejudiced single mother living in poverty. Director Amma Asante, a black woman who grew up in Streatham, is concerned about the social conditions she depicts and anguished by the racial violence which occurs at the film's climax. But, while her players are not without talent, the film is mainly peopled by utterly repulsive characters, some of the plot details seem contrived and the director's emphasis on colours that will show bleak lives against pretty backgrounds is nothing more than a self-conscious, self-defeating device. The intentions behind the film are undoubtedly good, but it is, alas, quite impossible to recommend it. MS

• *Leigh-Anne Williams* Stephanie James, *Gavin Williams* Nathan Jones, *Robbie Matthews* Gary Sheppeard, *Stephen Rajan* Dean Wong, *Julie Osman* Sara Gregory, *Hassan Osman* Oliver Haden, *Annette Lewis* Brenda Blethyn, *Rebecca Williams* Eli Williams and Darcy Williams, *with* Lynsey Richards, Victoria Pugh, Philip Howe, Lindsey Williams.

• *Dir* and *Screenplay* Amma Asante, *Pro* Charlie Hanson, Patrick Cassavetti and Peter Edwards, *Ex Pro* Paul Trijbits and Tristan Whalley, *Line Pro* Meinir Stoutt, *Ph* Ian Wilson, *Pro Des* Hayden Pearce, *Ed* Steve Singleton and Clare Douglas, *M* David Gray, *Costumes* Susie Lewis.

UK Film Council/Arts Council of Wales/ITV Wales/
Portman Film/AWOL Films-Verve Pictures.
90 mins. UK. 2004. Rel: 12 November 2004.
Cert. 15.

The Wedding Date ★★½

Although a successful professional woman, New Yorker Kat Ellis has a problem with self-esteem. So when she's invited to attend the wedding of her younger sister in England, she hires a dashing male escort to pose as her other half. Besides, she's determined to make her ex-boyfriend jealous, particularly as the groom's best man… This star vehicle for Debra Messing is trying very hard to be *My Best Friend's Wedding* with a dash of *Four Weddings*… gentrification. They've even imported Dermot Mulroney from the former and found some lovely English countryside to summon up memories of the latter. While there are a smattering of good lines ('Mom, this is *so* not the time to be yourself') and a scene-stealing turn from Sarah Parish as Kat's forthright girlfriend, the film fails to find its stride or generate the requisite sparkle. Originally known as *Something Borrowed* (a much better title). JC-W

• *Kat Ellis* Debra Messing, *Nick Mercer* Dermot Mulroney, *Amy Ellis* Amy Adams, *Edward Fletcher-Wooten* Jack Davenport, *TJ* Sarah Parish, *Jeffrey* Jeremy Sheffield, *Victor Ellis* Peter Egan, *Bunny Ellis* Holland Taylor, *Woody* Jolyon James, *with* Kerry Shale, Danielle Lewis, Helen Lindsay, John Sackville, Anna Sands.

• *Dir* Clare Kilner, *Pro* Nathalie Marciano, Michelle Chydzik Sowa, Jessica Bendinger and Paul Brooks, *Ex Pro* Norm Waitt, Scott Niemeyer, Steve Robbins and Jim Reeve, *Line Pro* Mairi Bett, *Screenplay* Dana Fox, from the Elizabeth Young novel *Asking for Trouble*, *Ph* Oliver Curtis, *Pro Des* Tom Burton, *Ed* Mary Finlay, *M* Debbie Wiseman; songs performed by The Corrs, Texas, Air Supply, The Chiffons, KC & The Sunshine Band, Amy Ward, James Brown, Maroon 5, and Michael Bublé, *Costumes* Louise Page.

Universal Pictures/Gold Circle Films/26 Films/Visionview-Entertainment.
88 mins. UK/USA. 2004. Rel: 22 April 2005.
Cert. 12A.

We Don't Live Here Anymore ★★★

Washington state; the present. Two university teachers and their respective wives find that their tightly knit camaraderie overflows into musical beds as their lives start to break up… The short story writer Andre Dubus' *Killings* was used as the basis for Todd Field's *In the Bedroom* and director John Curran has drawn on the author's rich psychological palette to provide the emotional meat for this grown-up tale of marriage, lust, deception and adultery. Showcasing his confident command of the visual derived from his years directing commercials and music videos, Curran presents a film of pictorial beauty, artfully weaving together the parallel lives of his protagonists. He has also elicited first-rate performances from his actors, who manage to make bookish lines like 'Even adultery has morality to it' sound half credible. There are plenty of prickly truths here, but Curran's overriding style tends to distance the viewer from the broiling emotions heaving beneath the surface. Ultimately, then, *We Don't Live Here Anymore* impresses more than it actually engages the emotions. JC-W

• *Jack Linden* Mark Ruffalo, *Terry Linden* Laura Dern, *Hanks Evans* Peter Krause, *Edith Evans* Naomi Watts, *Sean Linden* Sam Charles, *Natasha Linden* Haili Page, *Sharon Evans* Jennifer Bishop, *with* Jennifer Mawhinney, Amber Rothwell, Meg Roe.

• *Dir* John Curran, *Pro* Harvey Kahn, Naomi Watts and Jonas Goodman, *Ex Pro* Larry Gross, Ruth Epstein and Mark Ruffalo, *Screenplay* Larry Gross, *Ph* Maryse Alberti, *Pro Des* Tony Devenyi, *Ed* Alexandre de Franceschi, *M* Michael Convertino, *Costumes* Katia Stano.

Warner Independent Pictures/Front Street Pictures-Redbus Film Distribution.
98 mins. USA/Canada. 2004. Rel: 17 June 2005.
Cert. 15.

What the Bleep Do We Know? ★★★

'The real trick of life is not to be "in the know" but to be "in the mystery",' counsels one talking head. Another argues that 'There is no "out there" out there.' And yet another explains that every second our brains filter 2000 pieces of information out of the 400 billion or so that bombard us. And so the insights trickle on, as delivered by an array of scientists, physicists, psychiatrists, professors, theologians and hierophants. Variously passionate and/or composed, the talking heads are for the most part articulate and good value. But then this attempt to make quantum physics accessible to a mass audiences loses the plot. It's like Mel Brooks unleashed on Stephen Hawking, with Marlee Matlin as a fictitious photographer thrown down a metaphysical rabbit hole and joined by some singing quarks. This is not so much popular science as artless spiritualism run riot. Yet, for all its absurdity, it is a true original and should get the hoi-polloi thinking – which is a better prospect than *The Ring 3*. US title: *What the #$*! Do We Know!?* JC-W

• *Amanda* Marlee Matlin, *Jennifer* Elaine Hendrix, *Frank* Barry Newman, *Reggie* Robert Bailey Jr, *with* Armin Shimerman, John Ross Bowie, Larry Brandenburg, Prof. David Albert, Dr Joseph Dispenza, Prof Amit Goswami, Prof Andrew B. Newberg, Prof.

Candace Pert, etc.

• *Dir* and *Screenplay* William Arntz, Betsy Chasse and Mark Vicente, *Pro* Arntz and Chasse, *Ph* Mark Vicente and David Bridges, *Pro Des* Nava, *Ed* Jonathan Shaw, *M* Jonathan Shaw and Brent Pendleton, *Costumes* Ron Leamon, *Sound* George Nemzer.

Captured Light Industries/Lord of the Wind Films-Revolver Entertainment.
108 mins. USA. 2004. Rel: 20 May 2005. Cert. 12A.

When the Last Sword is Drawn ★★

Kyoto, Japan; near the end of the Edo period. Kanichiro Yoshimura is not like other samurai. He is money-grabbing, sanctimonious and almost buffoonishly modest. Yet he can wield his sword like few others. Hajime Saito, a fellow samurai, takes a great dislike to Yoshimura and decides to kill him. It is a task that proves more difficult than he could have imagined… In the wake of *Zatoichi* and *Kill Bill*, any samurai epic is going to be hard put to appear exciting. This diligent adaptation of the award-winning novel by **Jiro Asada** has 'worthy' written all over it and, in spite of a few picturesque scenes and interesting characters, it is a real endurance test. At times painfully slow and repetitive, it just refuses to end and milks every poetic nuance to death. Nevertheless, Kîchi Nakai is outstanding as Yoshimura. JC-W

• *Kanichiro Yoshimura* Kîchi Nakai, *Hajime Saito* Koichi Sato, *Nui* Miki Nakatani, *Shizu* Yui Natsukawa, *Jiroemon Ono* Yuji Miyake, *Chiaki Ono* Takehiro Murata.
• *Dir* Yojiro Takita, *Pro* Hideshi Miyajima and Nozomu Enoki, *Screenplay* Takeshi Nakajima, based on the story *Mibu gishi den* by Jiro Asada, *Ph* Takeshi Hamada, *Art Dir* Kyoko Heya, *Ed* Isao Tomita and Nobuko Tomita, *M* Joe Hisaishi.

Shochiku-Tartan Films.
137 mins. Japan. 2003. Rel: 17 December 2004. Cert. 15.

White Chicks ★★★

Two on-the-edge FBI agents are given one last chance to prove themselves by guarding a pair of kidnapping targets during a holiday weekend in the Hamptons. A car accident *en route* causes the Wilson sisters to sequester themselves in a hotel (they each have a single, nearly microscopic cut on their faces). Donning layers of latex and body paint, the black agents assume the roles of the rich white chicks to foil the bad guys… Avoiding just about every cliché one would expect (or dread) from either aspect of this story – eg, blacks impersonating whites or cross-dressing men – *White Chicks* is a slyly wrought social commentary that lampoons many aspects of American culture. It's so much more than the broad comedy you'd expect from the Wayans men and delivers on levels both subtle and gross. Marlon and Shawn Wayans are uncanny in their roles – far beyond the elaborate make-up. Each has grown into a very nuanced actor, especially under the guiding hand of their directing brother Keenen

Ivory Wayans. SWM

• *Kevin Copeland* Shawn Wayans, *Marcus Copeland* Marlon Wayans, *Heather Vandergeld* Jaime King, *Section Chief Elliot Gordon* Frankie Faison, *Agent Jake Harper* Lochlyn Munro, *Warren Vandergeld* John Heard, *Karen* Busy Philipps, *Latrell Spencer* Terry Crews, *Megan Vandergeld* Brittany Daniel, *Agent Vincent Gomez* Eddie Velez, *Tori* Jessica Cauffiel, *Brittany Wilson* Maitland Ward, *Tiffany Wilson* Anne Dudek, *Denise Porter* Rochelle Aytes, *Lisa* Jennifer Carpenter, *Gina Copeland* Faune Chambers.

• *Dir* Keenen Ivory Wayans, *Pro* Keenen Ivory Wayans, Shawn Wayans, Marlon Wayans, Rick Alvarez and Lee R. Mayes, *Screenplay* Keenen Ivory Wayans, Shawn Wayans, Marlon Wayans, Andy McElfresh, Michael Anthony Snowden and Xavier Cook, from a story by Keenen Ivory Wayans, Shawn Wayans, Marlon Wayans, *Ph* Steven Bernstein, *Pro Des* Paul J. Peters, *Ed* Jeffrey Stephen Gourson and Stuart Pappe, *M* Teddy Castellucci, *Costumes* Jori Woodman.

Revolution Studios/Wayans Bros-Columbia TriStar.
108 mins. USA. 2004. Rel: 15 October 2004. Cert. 12A.

White Noise ★★

When Jonathan Rivers' wife dies in what appears to be an accident, he becomes obsessed with an electronic phenomenon that allows him to communicate with the dead. Receiving premonitions via his VCR, his life slowly unravels until he pays the ultimate price for interfering with three violent ghosts… Electronic Voice Phenomena (EVP) is a fascinating and genuinely terrifying field of study first embarked upon by Thomas Edison in 1928, whereby he truly believed that the voices of the dead could be recorded. Lending absolute credibility to this topic is Michael Keaton's flawless performance as the desperate, grieving widow. Geoffrey Sax directs with stylish panache but Niall Johnson's sloppy, careless script is as disappointing as they come. What starts as a slick, psychological thriller chronicling an Everyman's immersion into the paranormal languidly degenerates into a hackneyed piece of dreary nonsense. SWM

• *Jonathan Rivers* Michael Keaton, *Anna Rivers* Chandra West, *Sarah Tate* Deborah Kara Unger, *Raymond Price* Ian McNeice, *Jane* Sarah Strange, *Mike Rivers* Nicholas Elia, *Detective Smits* Mike Dopud, *with* Marsha Regis, Amber Rothwell, Suzanne Ristic.

• *Dir* Geoffrey Sax, *Pro* Brooks and Shawn Williamson, *Ex Pro* Simon Brooks, Stephen Hegyes, Scott Niemeyer and Norm Witt, *Screenplay* Niall Johnson, *Ph* Chris Seager, *Pro Des* Michael S. Bolton, *Ed* Nick Arthurs, *M* Claude Foisy, *Costumes* Karen Matthews.

Universal/Gold Circle Films/White Noise UK/Brightlight Pictures/Endgame Entertainment- Entertainment.
98 mins. UK/Canada/USA. 2004. Rel: 7 January 2005. Cert. 15.

Wicker Park ★★

It's not really fair to judge a Hollywood remake against the prototype, as most cinemagoers will not have seen the original. However, when a masterpiece is botched up so damn badly, one can't help but draw comparisons. In this instance, *Wicker Park* is a translation of Gilles Mimouni's astonishingly stylish and achingly romantic *L'Appartement* (1996). The myriad plot strands are adhered to quite closely here, but the whole timbre of the film is wrong. Whereas the first was a stylish carousel of romantic manoeuvres and red herrings, the remake is a film of surfaces that dazzle but do not engage. Part of the problem is the casting of Josh Hartnett, a pretty but unconvincing actor who cannot convey the romantic desperation of his character. Instead of hanging on to his coattails as he races across Chicago to pursue his elusive love, one is left thinking what a jerk he is to miss his plane to China and to lie to his prospective fiancé. The film's phoniness is aggravated by false snow, superimposed breath, coy lovemaking and even a fake pigeon, not to mention the MTV direction of Scottish director Paul McGuigan. Only Diane Kruger, as the elusive love interest, displays any real class or conviction.
JC-W

• *Matthew* Josh Hartnett, *Alex* Rose Byrne, *Luke* Matthew Lillard, *Lisa* Diane Kruger, *Daniel* Christopher Cousins, *Rebecca* Jessica Paré, *with* Vlasta Vrana, Amy Sobol, Ted Whittall, Joanna Noyes, Ye Lu, Christian Paul, Gillian Ferrabee.

• *Dir* Paul McGuigan, *Pro* Andre Lamal, Marcus Viscidi, Tom Rosenberg and Gary Lucchesi, *Ex Pro* Georges Benayoun, Gilles Mimouni, Henry Winterstern and Harley Tannebaum, *Screenplay* Brandon Boyce, *Ph* Peter Sova, *Pro Des* Richard Bridgland, *Ed* Andrew Hulme, *M* Cliff Martinez, *Costumes* Odette Gadoury, *Sound* Douglas Murray.

MGM/Lakeshore Entertainment-Momentum Pictures.
114 mins. USA. 2004. Rel: 10 September 2004.
Cert. 12A.

Wild Side ★★★½

A film about outsiders, this drama from Sébastien Lifshitz was co-written by its leading player Stéphanie Michelini, who echoes her own life by playing a transsexual and naming the character Stéphanie. However, the story, set both in Paris and in northern France, also features a Russian immigrant and an Arab youth who, like Stéphanie, turn to prostitution in order to survive. Sexually explicit, the film is matter-of-fact about prostitution – like Godard's *Vivre Sa Vie* – but tender and caring in portraying the *ménage-à-trois* at its centre. Either the back stories or the plot development would have gained from more detailed elaboration but the sympathetic tone is amplified by the beautiful photography of Agnès Godard and the sensitive music score by Jocelyn Pook. There's also a poetic quality that helps to avoid both melodrama and sensationalism.
MS

• *Stéphanie* Stéphanie Michelini, *Mikhail* Edouard Nikitine, *Djamel* Yasmine Belmadi, *mother* Josiane Stoleru, *Caroline* Perrine Stevenard.

• *Dir* Sebastien Lifshitz, *Pro* Gilles Sandoz, *Screenplay* Lifshitz and Stéphane Bouquet, *Ph* Agnès Godard, *Art Dir* Roseanna Sacco Colas and Véronique Mellery, *Ed* Stephanie Mahet, *M* Joceyln Pook, *Costumes* Elizabeth Mehu.

Maia Films/YC Aligator Film/Zephyr Films/Arte France Cinema/AB3/Canal Plus/Cine Cinema/CNC France/CNC Belgium-Peccadillo Pictures.
94 mins. France/Belgium/UK. 2004.
Rel: 15 April 2005.
Cert. 18.

William Shakespeare's The Merchant of Venice
see *The Merchant of Venice*.

Wimbledon ★★★

No doubt tennis aficionados will laugh at the liberties taken with the sport here, but for mere mortals *Wimbledon* is a seductive take on a game little explored by the cinema. And so we have sprained ankles, on-court tantrums, lesbian players and plenty of 'rain stopped play'. Paul Bettany is Peter Colt, a British has-been in his thirties who has decided to make this his last tournament. Once rated 11th in the world, Colt has now slipped to 119th and his confidence along with it. Ensconced in a small room at the Dorchester Hotel, he accidentally bumps into star seed Lizzie Bradbury and somehow a connection is made. In spite of the strict rules of celibacy during the championship, Peter and Lizzie find a little surplus energy and Peter's game takes off on an unexpected trajectory… In his first romantic comedy lead, Paul Bettany cuts a likeable figure and there's sparky repartee to stoke his performance. There's also a calculated gloss and predictability to the film that robs it of any real suspense or romantic traction. Cute, but no *Notting Hill*.
JC-W

• *Lizzie Bradbury* Kirsten Dunst, *Peter Colt* Paul Bettany, *Dennis Bradbury* Sam Neill, *Ron Roth* Jon Favreau, *Dieter Prohl* Nicolaj Coster-Waldau, *Augusta Colt* Eleanor Bron, *Edward Colt* Bernard Hill, *Carl Colt* James McAvoy, *Ian Frazier* Robert Lindsay, *Jake Hammond* Austin Nichols, *Mrs Kenwood* Celia Imrie, *with* John McEnroe, Chris Evert, Mary Carillo, John Barrett, Jeremy Child, Penny Ryder, Annabel Leventon, Amanda Walker, Barry Jackson, Peter Cartwright, Eve Pearce, Jesse Loncraine, Danny Baker, Chris Moyles.

• *Dir* Richard Loncraine, *Pro* Tim Bevan, Eric Fellner, Liza Chasin and Mary Richards, *Ex Pro* Debra Hayward and David Livingstone, *Screenplay* Adam Brooks, Jennifer Flackett and Mark Levin, *Ph* Darius Khondji, *Pro Des* Brian Morris, *Ed* Humphrey Dixon, *M* Edward Shearmur; songs performed by RJD2, OK Go, Spoon, David Gray, Sugababes, Craig Armstrong, Avril Lavigne, and Groove Armada, *Costumes* Louise Stjernsward, *Tennis consultant* Pat Cash.

Universal/StudioCanal/Working Title-UIP.

THE NEW ROMANTIC COMEDY
FROM THE MAKERS OF
NOTTING HILL,
BRIDGET JONES
& LOVE ACTUALLY

KIRSTEN   PAUL
DUNST   BETTANY

WIMBLEDON
NOTHING BEATS PLAYING ON GRASS

UNIVERSAL PICTURES and STUDIOCANAL present a WORKING TITLE production a RICHARD LONCRAINE film KIRSTEN DUNST PAUL BETTANY
"WIMBLEDON" SAM NEILL JON FAVREAU music by KLAUS BADELT costume designer LOUISE ST JERNSWARD editor HUMPHREY DIXON production designer BRIAN MORRIS
director of photography DARIUS KHONDJI afc asc executive producers DEBRA HAYWARD DAVID LIVINGSTONE produced by TIM BEVAN ERIC FELLNER
LIZA CHASIN MARY RICHARDS written by ADAM BROOKS and JENNIFER FLACKETT & MARK LEVIN directed by RICHARD LONCRAINE

www.uip.co.uk   www.wimbledonthemovie.com

AT CINEMAS EVERYWHERE SEPTEMBER 24, 2004

98 mins. UK/USA/France. 2004. Rel: 24 September 2004. Cert. 12A.

Without a Paddle ★½

Now in their thirties, three childhood friends are reunited to embark on a canoe trip in the Oregon wilderness. Then they find themselves up shit creek... Funny title. And an ironic one, considering that what is the nucleus of an interesting idea is cut loose from its moorings and allowed to drift downstream. The toothless monotony isn't helped by the unsympathetic nature of the main protagonists, while the film hasn't even the courage of its own tasteless convictions. It's a shame, too, that the villains are so unthreatening, while a cameo by Burt Reynolds merely serves as a sad footnote and a poignant homage to *Deliverance*. Imagine it – *Deliverance* with laughs. Now that would be something. JC-W

• *Dr Dan Mott* Seth Green, *Jerry Conlaine* Matthew Lillard, *Tom Marshall* Dax Shepard, *Elwood* Ethan Suplee, *Del Knox* Burt Reynolds, *Dennis* Abraham Benrubi, *Flower* Rachel Blanchard, *Butterfly* Christina Moore, *with* Bart the Bear, Anthony Starr, Nadine Bernecker, Bonnie Somerville, Ray Baker.

• *Dir* Steven Brill, *Pro* Donald De Line, *Ex Pro* Richard Vane, Andrew Haas and Wendy Japhet, *Screenplay* Jay Leggett and Mitch Rouse, from a story by Fred Wolf, Harris Goldberg and Tom Nursall, *Ph* Jonathan Brown, *Pro Des* Perry Andelin,

Ed Debra Neil-Fisher and Peck Prior, *M* Christophe Beck, *Costumes* Ngila Dickson.

Paramount/De Line Pictures-UIP.
99 mins. USA. 2004. Rel: 26 December 2004. Cert. 12A.

The Woodsman ★★★★½

In the words of one character, Walter Rossworth is 'damaged goods'. On parole after 12 years in prison, Walter has to find his own feet but is systematically shunned by society, even by his own family. His parole officer reminds him that he is a monster and as he wrestles with his own guilt, he finds that his only release is in his old, terrible impulses... Wading courageously into dark waters rarely broached by the cinema (give or take *Happiness* and *Re-Inventing Eddie*), *The Woodsman* questions our own demons with an uncompromising insight. Kevin Bacon, in a fearless career move, plays the Woodsman of the title, a carpenter-turned-lumber worker whose history of hanging out in wooded parks carries a heavy emotional price. The power of the film rests in its refusal to offer any neat or easy solutions, while exploring the complexity of Bacon's character without judgment or sensationalism. It's also an extremely well-made piece, the ambient music and subtle camera moves enhancing the action rather than distracting from it. Bacon is extraordinary, but so is his wife Kyra Sedgwick, and together their sex scenes display an uncommon charge and understatement. It's tempting to say that only a woman (Nicole Kassell) could have made a film of

The monster within: Kevin Bacon in Nicole Kassell's intelligent and riveting *The Woodsman* (from Tartan Films)

such intrepidity and sensitivity. JC-W

• *Walter Rossworth* Kevin Bacon, *Vickie* Kyra Sedgwick, *Sgt Lucas* Mos Def, *Carlos* Benjamin Bratt, *Bob* David Alan Grier, *Mary-Kay* Eve, *Candy* Kevin Rice, *Rosen* Michael Shannon, *Robin* Hannah Pilkes, *with* Carlos Leon, Jessica Nagle, Aunt Dot.

• *Dir* Nicole Kassell, *Ex Pro* Damon Dash, Kevin Bacon, Brook Lenfest and Dawn Lenfest, *Co-Pro* Lisa Cortés and Dave Robinson, *Line Pro* Valerie Hoffman, *Assoc Pro* Candice Williams and Simone Sheffield, *Screenplay* Kassell and Steven Fechter, *Ph* Xavier Pérez Grobet, *Pro Des* Stephen Beatrice, *Ed* Brian A. Kates and Lisa Fruchtman, *M* Nathan Larson, *Costumes* Frank L. Fleming.

Dash Films/Lee Daniels Entertainment-Tartan Films. 87 mins. USA. 2004. Rel: 25 February 2005. Cert. 15.

Would I Lie To You? ★★

This feeble Jewish comedy set in Paris reminds one of Francis Veber's *The Closet*. This time, however, it's not a straight man seeking to pass as gay but a goy who, to get work in a business in the garment district – and to ingratiate himself as a possible son-in-law to his new boss – pretends to be Jewish. It's a promising notion unimaginatively developed. If it never builds effectively as farce, it fails equally on the level of romantic comedy by incorporating moments of violence, some perpetrated by our hero, who thereby forfeits all our sympathy. Not appalling but misjudged and decidedly banal. MS

• *Eddie Vuibert* Richard Anconina, *Victor* Richard Bohringer, *Sandra Benzakem* Amira Casar, *Dov Mimram* Vincent Elbaz,

Karine Aure Atika, *Rafi* Élie Kakou, *Serge Benamou* José Garcia.

• *Dir* Thomas Gilou, *Pro* Aïssa Djabri, Farid Lahouassa and Manuel Munz, *Screenplay* Munz and Gérard Bitton, *Ph* Jean Jacques Bouhon, *Art Dir* Olivier Raoux, *Ed* Nathalie Hubert, *M* Gérard Presgurvic.

Vertigo Prods/France 2 Cinéma/M6 Films/Orly Films/Canal Plus-Arrow Films. 100 mins. France. 1997. Rel: 5 November 2004. Cert. 15.

xXx 2: The Next Level ★★★½

Darius Stone doesn't do subtle. Correction. Inmate 3655 doesn't do subtle. An ex-Navy SEAL and a Special Forces sniper, 3655 was sent down for 20 years for disobeying orders and punching a general's lights out. Now he's the best bet the National Security Agency has to disarm a plot to sabotage the Presidency. He can get himself out of prison, but to stop World War IV he'll need some serious hardware and all the junk food he can eat... If you adored *xXx* (2002), then you'll eat this up with a spoon. Adopting the same comic-book vibe, junk dialogue and spectacular effects, the film is a mind-blowing combination of chutzpah, verve and calculating commercialism. Replacing the Neanderthal Vin Diesel, Ice Cube gives attitude a bad name – but is all the funnier for playing his role straight. Again, the film blows it near the end – the digitally tuned stunts are a bit naff – but the popcorn crowd will whoop for joy. US title: *xXx: State of the Union.* JC-W

• *Darius Stone/Inmate 3655* Ice Cube, *Augustus Gibbons* Samuel L. Jackson, *Secretary of Defence George Deckert* Willem Dafoe,

Nona Gaye, daughter of Marvin, stars opposite Ice Cube in Lee
Tamahori's mind-blowing *xXx 2: The Next Level* (from Columbia TriStar)

Agent Kyle Steele Scott Speedman, *President Sanford* Peter
Strauss, *Zeke* Xzibit, *Toby Lee Shavers* Michael Roof, *Charlie
Mayweather* Sunny Mabrey, *Lola* Nona Gaye, *with* Rich
Bryant, Mary Castro, John G. Connolly, Brian David, Ramon
De Ocampo, Matt Gerald, Thom Gossom Jr, Eli Harris,
Bryan Holly, Charles Howerton, Kevin Jaskela,
Chris J. Johnson.

• *Dir* Lee Tamahori, *Pro* Neal H. Moritz and Arne L.
Schmidt, *Ex Pro* Todd Garner, Rob Cohen and Derek Dauchy,
Screenplay Simon Kinberg, *Ph* David Tattersall, *Pro Des* Gavin
Bocquet, *Ed* Mark Goldblatt, Steven Rosenblum and Todd
E. Miller, *M* Marco Beltrami, *Costumes* Sanja Milkovic Hays,
Special Effects John Frazier.

Revolution Studios/Original Films-Columbia TriStar.
100 mins. USA. 2005. Rel: 29 April 2005.
Cert. 12A.

The Yes Men ★★★½

Youthful audiences especially may relish the almost
undergraduate fun inherent in this documentary's record
of how two iconoclastic rebels set up bogus websites and
passed themselves off as representatives of the World Trade
Organisation. They did this as a means of protesting about
the WTO's treatment of third world countries. The duo,
Andy Bichlbaum and Mike Bonanno, dubbed themselves the
Yes Men and hoaxed audiences who accepted then as genuine
members of the WTO. In following their increasingly
outrageous activities, the film itself is a bit juvenile and self-
congratulatory; the balance between seriousness and fun was
more adept in the superior *Super Size Me*. Nevertheless, it's all
quite enjoyable. MS

• *with*: Andy Bichlbaum, Mike Bonanno, Michael Moore,
Marco Deseriis, Laura Nix.

At the sign of the black horse: The equine star of
Simon Wincer's *The Young Black Stallion* (from Buena
Vista International)

• *Dir, Pro, Ph* and *Sound* Chris Smith, Dan Ollman, Sarah Price, *Assoc Pro* Doug Ruschhaupt and Randy Russell, *Ed* Ollman.

Bluemark Prods/Yes Men Films-Tartan Films.
81 mins. USA. 2004. Rel: 15 February 2005.
Cert. 15.

The Young Black Stallion ★★

1946; North Africa. The ten-year-old daughter of an affluent horse breeder, Neera barely escapes with her life when a caravan is attacked by bandits. Alone in the desert, she befriends a wild black stallion that she manages to mount and ride back home. There, she discovers that bandits have taken all her family's horses and that her parents have fled in terror. Only her grandfather remains and he thinks the stallion is a figment of her imagination... Adapted from the novel by Walter and Steve Farley (written as a prequel to Walter Farley's novel *The Black Stallion*, filmed in 1979), *The Young Black Stallion* is a misguided attempt to harness a dramatic narrative to the IMAX format. Not only has the story been condensed to a ludicrous simplicity (to accommodate the enormous cost of filming with widescreen cameras), but the concept itself hardly merits such specialist photography. What is left, then, is a corny and predictable tale in which a photogenic ten-year-old is expected to carry the brunt of a film in which pertinent issues of race, religion and gender are blatantly ignored. The Namibian and South African locations are very pretty, though. JC-W

• *Ben Ishak* Richard Romanus, *Neera* Biana G. Tamimi, *Aden* Patrick Elyas, *Rhamon* Gerard Rudolf, *Mansoor* Ali Al Ameri, *with* Andries Rossouw, Emma Deetlefs, Silke Bezuidenhout, Bill Lawrence.

• *Dir* Simon Wincer, *Pro* Fred Roos and Frank Marshall, *Ex Pro* Jeanne Rosenberg and Kathleen Kennedy, *Assoc Pro* Patricia Churchill, *Screenplay* Rosenberg, *Ph* Reed Smoot, *Pro Des* Paul Peters, *Ed* Bud Smith and Terry Blythe, *M* William Ross, *Costumes* Jo Katsaras, *Equine advisor* Corky Randall.

Walt Disney Prods/Moonlighting Films/Abracadabra Prods-Buena Vista International.
45 mins. USA. 2003.
Rel: 23 July 2004.
Cert. U.

You're My Hero ★★★

Seville, 1975. Aged 12, Ramón (Manuel Lozano) is still young enough to treat an Indian from a Western movie as his imaginary confidant, but he is brought face to face with reality just before the Franco regime draws to a close. It's not just bullying at school that he encounters but pressure to be an informant. The victim is a sympathetic teacher who is staunchly anti-Fascist... Although sometimes glib and unconvincing, the film means well and is no disgrace. Nevertheless, it's entirely overshadowed by the 1998 masterpiece *Butterfly's Tongue*, also featuring Lozano as a child and with a teacher as the other main figure. Depicting the

approach of the Spanish Civil War, the earlier film had such depth, power and insight that this seems relatively superficial by comparison.
MS

• *Ramón* Manuel Lozano, *Fr Mateo* Toni Cantó, *David* Félix López, *Nube de Agua* Antonio Dechent, *Paloma* Carmen Navarro, *Don Félix* Juan Fernandez, *Rafa* Alfonso Mena, *Ortega* Pablo Acosta.

• *Dir* Antonio Cuadri, *Pro* Cuadri, Philippe Parser and Juan C. Orihuela, *Ex Pro* Joxé Portela and Antonio Jimenez Filpo, *Screenplay* Cuadri, Miguel Angel Perez and Carlos Asorey, *Ph* Alex Catalan, *Art Dir* Luis Manuel Carmona, *Ed* Mercedes Cantero, *M* Carita Boronska, *Costumes* Lucía Navarro.

Manufacturas Audiovisuales/Caligari Films/Canal Sur Television/Canal Plus-Parasol Peccadillo Releasing.
103 mins. Spain. 2003. Rel: 3 September 2004.
Cert. 15.

Yu-Gi-Oh! The Movie: Pyramid of Light ★

In this kids' feature-length fantasy adventure based on the Japanese animated TV series and a popular playground card game, little Yugi gets embroiled with an awakened ancient evil force and duels with opponents in the game, which involves invoking monsters and then trumping them with better ones. Feebly animated and written, director Hatsuki Tsuji's unfathomable, no-thrills English-dubbed item will get the thumbs down from its target audience of canny ten-year-old boys).
DW

• voices: *Yugi Moto/Yami Yugi* Dan Green, *Seto Kaiba* Eric Stuart, *with* Scottie Ray, Wayne Grayson, John Campbell, Amy Birnbaum, Tara Jayne, Maddie Blaustein, Darren Dunstan, Ben Baron, Mike Pollock, Andrew Paull, Ed Paul, Lisa Ortiz, Marc Thompson, Sebastian Arcelus.

• *Dir* Hatsuki Tsuji, *Animation Dir* Nak Soo Choi, Hee Nam Cho and Koung Tae Kim, *Pro* Noriko Kobayashi, Naoki Sasada, Lloyd Goldfine, Katia Milani and Michael Pecoriello, *Ex Pro* Hideyuki Nagai, Tamizo Suzuki, Hideki Yamashita, Alfred R. Kahn and Norman J. Grossfeld, *Assoc Pro* Shane Guenego and Chris Guido, *Screenplay* Matthew Drdek, Lloyd Goldfine, Norman J. Grossfeld and Michael Pecioriello, based on characters created by Kazuki Takahashi and Studio Dice, from a story by Junki Takegami and Masahiro Hikokubo, *Ph* Hiroaki Edamitsu, Duk Gyu Choi, Tae Hee Heo and Kang Ok Kim, *Ed* Masao Nakagawa, *M* Elik Alvarez, John Angier, Joel Douek, Ralph Schuckett, Wayne Sharpe, Freddy Sheinfeld and Gil Talmi.

Studio Dice/TV Tokyo/4Kids Entertainment/ NAS/Dong Woo Animation-Warner.
89 mins. Japan/USA/South Korea. 2004.
Rel: 13 August 2004.
Cert. PG.

DVD Premieres

A selection of films released direct to DVD in the UK between July 2004 and June 2005.

by Daniel O'Brien

ALEX & EMMA

This comedy spin on *The French Lieutenant's Woman* never takes off. Alex (Luke Wilson) is a struggling writer with serious gambling debts. If he doesn't finish his novel in 30 days, Cuban loan sharks will finish him. He hires Emma (Kate Hudson), a straight-talking stenographer whose suggestions make the book a lot better. As the novel progresses, Alex and Emma become the two main characters. Director Rob Reiner has lost the sureness of touch that made *This Is Spinal Tap* an instant classic.
With: Chino XL, Lobo Sebastian, Sophie Marceau, Rob Reiner.
Warner Home Video. July 2004. Cert 12.

ALL ABOUT YOU

This affable romantic comedy suggests that not all African Americans are afflicted by drugs, crime and social breakdown.
Written and directed by Christine Swanson.
With: Renee Goldsberry, Terron Brooks, Debbie Allen, LisaRaye.
Ventura International. February 2005. Cert PG.

AZUMI

In medieval Japan, elite assassins hunt down the feuding warlords who threaten to destroy the country. Samurai epics get the *Young Guns* treatment in this comic-book fantasy, with a driving rock score and pin-up leads. Heroine Aya Ueto is a major pop star in Japan.
Directed by Ryuhei Kitamura.
With: Shun Oguri, Hiroki Narimiya, Kenji Kohashi.
Optimum Releasing. August 2004. Cert 18.

BANG-RAJAN

This impressive, if flawed, Thai epic outclasses recent Hollywood examples of the genre. Set in 1765, *Bang-Rajan* tells the true story of heroic villagers, who held off Burmese invaders despite overwhelming odds. While the characters are from stock, director Thanit Jitnukul keeps the story

moving and the battles ferocious. The title refers to the village itself, which becomes a rallying point for Thai refugees. Opting to stand and fight, the defenders of Bang-Rajan remain national heroes.
With: Jaran Ngamdge, Winai Kraibutr, Bongkot Khongmalai.
Premier Asia. February 2005. Cert 15.

BATTLE ROYALE II: REQUIEM

Kenji Fukasaku's gory, provocative *Battle Royale* (2000) was a worthy finale to the veteran director's career. This ambitious sequel falls short for a number of reasons. Fukasaku died shortly after starting the film and most of it was directed by his son, Kenta Fukasaku. After an audacious opening sequence – an obvious reference to 9/11 – *Battle Royale II* is sombre, hysterical, heavy-handed and trite. The satire and black humour of the original are barely in evidence. The anti-US sentiment is both crude and ironic, given the obvious lifts from *Saving Private Ryan* and *Butch Cassidy and the Sundance Kid*. A re-edited version of the film, *Battle Royale II: Revenge*, is generally regarded as superior, with more character development and improved special effects. This edition is scheduled for a UK release in late 2005.
With: Tatsuya Fujiwara, Ai Maeda, Shugo Oshinari, 'Beat' Takeshi Kitano (cameo), Shinichi 'Sonny' Chiba (cameo).
Tartan Video. August 2004. Cert 18.

BEYOND THE LIMITS

A German horror movie, filmed in English, with a US setting. Directed by Olaf Ittenbach, *Beyond the Limits* is an ultra-gory variation on the compendium horrors once popularised by Amicus. When a female reporter investigates America's oldest cemetery, the creepy caretaker tells her the stories of its two most infamous residents, a drug-dealing gangster and a medieval inquisitor. While Ittenbach has a flair for

gory set-pieces, the script and acting are less impressive. The 'twist' ending is very familiar.
With: Kimberly Liebe, Hank Stone, Darren Shahlari.
Anchor Bay UK. April 2005. Cert 18.

THE BIG BOUNCE

Elmore Leonard disowned this second screen adaptation of his debut novel (though the 1969 version, with Ryan O'Neal, is even worse). Owen Wilson plays a con artist on the loose in Hawaii, where he's ensnared in a $200,000 scam. Director George Armitage shows none of the wit that distinguished *Grosse Pointe Blank* (1997). Co-star Morgan Freeman is wasted as an elderly judge. Wilson's ruffled charm counts for little without a decent script. The film was probably toned down during post-production, especially the language. At times, the actors' lip movements don't match the dialogue.
With: Sara Foster, Butch Helemano, Charlie Sheen, Vinnie Jones, Willie Nelson.
Warner Home Video. September 2004. Cert 12.

BLESSED

A bland rip-off of *Rosemary's Baby*, *The Omen* and every movie featuring spooky twins. Heather Graham and James Purefoy play a couple desperate for a baby. Offered free treatment by a mysterious fertility clinic, Graham finds herself impregnated with the Devil's DNA. The Devil has DNA? In this instance, two Antichrists for the price of one isn't much of a bargain.
With: Stella Stevens, Andy Serkis and David Hemmings (his last film).
Directed by Simon Fellows.
High Fliers. April 2005. Cert 15.

BLIND HORIZON

Val Kilmer stars as an amnesiac drifter, shot and left for dead in the New Mexico desert. Haunted by flashbacks, he becomes convinced there's a plot to assassinate the president. Directed by Michael Haussman, this atmospheric, convoluted thriller plays fair by the audience.

With: Neve Campbell, Sam Shepard, Faye Dunaway.

High Fliers. January 2005. Cert 15.

BLUE RITA

This 1977 Jesús Franco effort won't win many converts for the cult Spanish filmmaker. Blue Rita (Martine Flety) runs a popular Paris nightclub and brothel. She also works as a freelance interrogator for criminal gangs. Suspects are given 'love liquid', which sends them into an uncontrollable sexual frenzy. Supposedly, Franco was aiming for comic-book visuals and kitsch eroticism. As with many of the director's films, he seems to lose interest along the way.

Anchor Bay UK. November 2004. Cert 18.

THE BONE SNATCHER

This British-Canadian-South African co-production is an effective variation on *Alien*. Geological surveyors disappear in the Namib Desert while looking for diamonds. The search party soon discovers why, running into the Sandmother, a demonic creature with a taste for human bones. The standard plot is enlivened by atmospheric locations and some decent special effects. Filmed in Namibia and Cape Town.

With: Scott Bairstow, Rachel Shelley, Warrick Grier, Adrienne Pearce.

Directed by Jason Wulfsohn.

Anchor Bay UK. July 2004. Cert 18.

BREAKING ALL THE RULES

Hot from *Collateral* and *Ray*, Oscar-winner Jamie Foxx looks set to join Hollywood's A-list, but he needs stronger vehicles than this underwhelming romantic comedy. Dumped by his fiancée, a depressed journalist writes a break-up handbook for men. When it becomes a bestseller, he finds his friendships and integrity sorely tested. Written and directed by Daniel Taplitz, *Breaking All the Rules* runs strictly to formula, with just a handful of laughs. Original title: *Breakin' All the Rules*.

With: Gabrielle Union, Morris Chestnut, Peter MacNichol.

Columbia-TriStar. October 2004. Cert 12.

THE CARD PLAYER

A subdued thriller from Dario Argento, master of the *giallo* shocker. There's a serial killer on the loose in Rome. Kidnapping young women, he challenges the police to deadly games of internet poker. If they win, the victim goes free. If he wins, the police have to watch the woman die via video link-up. When a British tourist is snatched, Irish cop Liam Cunningham is brought onto the case. *The Card Player* attempts to move beyond Argento's regular fan-base, appealing to a wider audience. Toning down the gore, the director emphasises mood and atmosphere. Unfortunately, his trademark visual flair and outlandish set-pieces are also absent. Boasting competent performances and a coherent plot – by Argento's standards – *The Card Player*'s only real crime is being unremarkable.

With: Stefania Rocca, Claudio Santamari, Fiore Argento (the director's eldest daughter).

Arrow Films/Fremantle Home Entertainment. November 2004. Cert 15.

CHAMPION

A biopic of Korean boxer Kim Deuk Gu (Yoo Oh Sung), who escaped an impoverished background to become a champion fighter throughout South East Asia. Directed by Kyung Taek Kwak, *Champion* is an inspirational against-the-odds tale, blending elements of *Rocky* and the less upbeat *Raging Bull*. The high-adrenaline fight scenes are complemented by in-depth characterisation and strong performances. In 1982, on the brink of international fame, Kim went up against Ray 'Boom Boom' Mancini in a showcase bout at Caesar's Palace, Las Vegas. Having wowed the crowd over 14 rounds, Kim looked set to become a superstar. Sadly, real life doesn't always give the underdog a fair break.

With: Chae Min Seo.

Premier Asia. July 2004. Cert 15.

CHASING LIBERTY

In this flat romantic comedy, the US President's daughter goes AWOL in Europe, looking for a normal life. Star Mandy Moore should have looked for a better movie.

Directed by Andy Cadiff.

With: Stark Sands, Tony Jayawardena, Jeremy Piven, Annabella Sciorra.

Warner Home Video. December 2004. Cert 12.

THE CLEARING

The powerhouse casting of Robert Redford, Helen Mirren and Willem Dafoe lifts this kidnap drama a notch above the ordinary. Based on real events, the plot has a wealthy businessman (Redford) abducted by an embittered former employee (Dafoe). Emphasising character over suspense, *The Clearing* benefits from strong performances, particularly Mirren as Redford's estranged wife. The heart of the film is their crumbling marriage, worn down by years of routine, apathy and lies. On the surface, Redford's character embodies the great American success story: the self-made millionaire with an adoring wife and family. Dafoe's kidnapper is the ultimate loser, blaming his failure on everyone but himself. In truth, both men have lost their way in life. Unfortunately, the supporting characters are largely redundant, dragging the film into perfunctory soap opera.

Directed by Pieter Jan Brugge.

Twentieth Century Fox. February 2005. Cert 12.

CONTROL

Psychopathic killer Lee Ray Oliver (Ray Liotta) waits on Death Row for his date with the needle. He's offered a reprieve if he'll test a new drug that suppresses the urge to kill. While the treatment is successful, Lee has problems dealing with his violent past. Tormented by guilt and remorse, he suffers terrible flashbacks. Director Tim Hunter, who made the unsettling *River's Edge* (1986), creates an intriguing drama. Ray Liotta is surprisingly sympathetic as Lee, desperate to atone for unforgivable crimes. The various plots twists are unsurprising and the final 'revelation' feels like a cheat. Set in the US, *Control* was filmed in Sofia, Bulgaria, rendering some of the background detail unconvincing.

With: Willem Dafoe, Michelle Rodriguez, Stephen Rea.

High Fliers. March 2005. Cert 15.

CORONADO

Raiders of the Lost Ark meets *Romancing the Stone* in the fictional Central American country of Coronado. Our American heroine searches for her kidnapped fiancé, tangling with a ruthless dictator – is there any other kind? – and joining the revolution. Sold on its special effects, *Coronado* borrows ideas from dozens of better movies. The end result barely registers on the brain. Note: The DVD release of *Coronado* is noticeably cropped from its original 2.35:1 scope format.

Directed by Claudio Faeh.

With: Kristin Dattilo, John Rhys Davies, Clayton Rohner.

DEJ Productions. February 2005. Cert PG.

CRUEL INTENTIONS 3

Amoral college roommates get their kicks seducing and dumping naïve girls. Plotting to ensnare the 'coldest' student in college, they recruit a female friend assigned to look after her. However, things are not what they seem. *Cruel Intentions 2* was stitched together from two episodes of the aborted TV series. This second 'sequel' has no such excuse for its formula plotting and perfunctory execution.
Directed by Scott Ziehl.
With: Kerr Smith, Kristina Anapau, Nathan Wetherington, Ashley Elizabeth.
Columbia-TriStar. July 2004. Cert 15.

CUTTHROAT ALLEY

Something is rotten in LA South Central. Gang members are being stalked and slashed by a psycho killer. The pitch must have seemed irresistible: *Boyz N the Hood* meets *Scream*. The execution – so to speak – is less inspired.
Written and directed by Timothy Wayne Folsome.
With: Mack 10, Bizzy Bone.
MIA. January 2005. Cert 15.

DEAD BIRDS

During the American Civil War, a gang of thieves hides out in an abandoned plantation house. Unfortunately, they're not alone. This above-average horror movie benefits from its unusual setting, creepy atmosphere and solid performances.
Directed by Alex Turner.
With: Henry Thomas, Nicki Aycox, Isaiah Washington, Michael Shannon.
Columbia-TriStar. May 2005. Cert 15.

DEATH DUEL

This 1977 Shaw Brothers epic was written and directed by Chor Yuen, a specialist in swordplay movies. Derek Yee stars as Ah Chi, an unbeaten master swordsman. Weary of the constant challenges, Ah fakes his death to start a new life with his mistress. However, an old enemy stages a confrontation with the one swordsman who could defeat him. *Death Duel* is an entertaining effort, boasting Shaw's usual lavish production values. By Shaw standards, there are relatively few fight scenes. Cast for his looks, Yee isn't the best screen fighter, being obviously doubled for some shots.
With: Lo Lieh, Ti Lung, David Chiang (Yee's older brother).
Momentum Asia. May 2005. Cert 15.

DIRTY DANCING 2

This unrelated follow-up to the 1987 hit works well enough on its own terms. While the original traded on 1960s nostalgia, the sequel is set in 1950s Cuba. An all-American family takes a vacation in Havana on the eve of the revolution. The teenage daughter falls for a hotel busboy, experiencing the thrill of dirty dancing. Needless to say, her straightlaced parents don't approve. You get the picture. *Dirty Dancing* star Patrick Swayze makes a cameo appearance as a dance instructor. Filmed in Puerto Rico, for obvious reasons. Original title: *Dirty Dancing: Havana Nights*.
Directed by Guy Ferland.
With: Diego Luna, Romola Garai, Sela Ward, John Slattery.
Buena Vista Home Entertainment. November 2004. Cert PG.

EVICTED

Faced with eviction, two Los Angeles slackers decide to trash their apartment in a 24-hour binge of booze, drugs and general debauchery. Presumably, this shapeless, aimless mess was intended as a counterculture classic. Unfortunately, writer-director-star Michael Tierney has nothing new to say about the scene, and little concept of what constitutes entertainment. Veteran character actor Lawrence Tierney, the director's uncle, plays a supporting role. Shannon Elizabeth, who dominates the DVD artwork, has only a few scenes.
With: Terence Tierney (the director's brother), Alvis Le Gate, Terry Camilleri.
MIA. March 2005. Cert 18.

FRANKENFISH

There's something nasty lurking in the Louisiana bayou. Could it be a genetically modified killer fish? An enjoyable schlock horror that revels in its absurdities.
Directed by Mark A. Z. Dippe.
With: Tory Kittles, K. D. Aubert, China Chow, Matthew Rauch.
Columbia-TriStar. February 2005. Cert 15.

GHETTO DAWG

An effective LA thriller set in the world of illegal dogfights. When a young car thief (J-King) tries to go straight, the local gang boss makes it clear he'll never escape. Realising he's no better off than the dogs, he hatches a daring plan that puts his life on the line. While the parallel between the pit bull tournaments and LA's gangland is hardly subtle, *Ghetto Dawg* delivers the goods. Co-star Drena De Niro is Robert De Niro's stepdaughter.
Directed by Brian Averill.
With: Gianna Palminteri, Russ Russo.
MIA. June 2005. Cert 15.

GHOST LAKE

An upstate New York town is flooded to create an artificial lake. Unfortunately, a number of the residents are drowned. One hundred years later, their restless spirits return for vengeance. While the premise is sound, this horror movie is inept in every department.
Written and directed by Jay Woeffel.
With: Tatum Adair, Timothy Prindle, Gregory Lee Kenyon, Azure Sky Decker.
Third Millennium. December 2004. Cert 15.

GINGER SNAPS: UNLEASHED

A disappointing sequel to the cult Canadian horror *Ginger Snaps* (2000). Surviving sister Bridget (Emily Perkins) is slowly transforming into a werewolf. Mistaken for a drug addict, she's confined to a psychiatric institution for disturbed young women. *Ginger Snaps* worked because the sisters' relationship gave a heart to the familiar horror elements. While *Unleashed* avoids rehashing the original, the sequel is filled with loose ends and wrong turns. Director Brett Sullivan, who edited the first film, conjures some efficient set-pieces but no dark undercurrents. As *Unleashed* progresses, Bridget is sidelined in favour of Ghost (Tatiana Maslany), a creepy woman-child who lives in a dangerous fantasy world. The late-lamented Ginger (Katherine Isabelle) makes a few appearances, either as a ghost or a figment of Bridget's tortured mind (is there a difference?)
With: Brendan Fletcher, Janet Kidder.
Mosaic Movies. October 2004. Cert 18.

GINGER SNAPS BACK: THE BEGINNING

Filmed back-to-back with *Ginger Snaps: Unleashed*, this curious prequel relocates Ginger (Katherine Isabelle) and Bridget (Emily Perkins) to an 1815 trading fort besieged by werewolves. Harbouring a dark secret, their problems intensify when Ginger is bitten and starts to transform. Distinguished by its desolate winter landscape, *Ginger Snaps Back* falls short in other departments. Ginger and Bridget are too modern in their speech and attitudes,

Ginger Snaps: Unleashed (see page 153)

jarring with the period setting. The leads seem subdued, failing to recapture the chemistry of the original film. Director Grant Harvey, who shot second unit on *Ginger Snaps*, has problems maintaining the pace and tension. A heavy dose of Native American mysticism fails to mask the plot holes. While the werewolf scenes are OK, the film works best as a parable on male fear and loathing of women.
With: Nathaniel Arcand, Hugh Dillon.
Mosaic Movies. January 2005. Cert 18.

HATCHETMAN

A poor *Scream* clone, with LA strippers stalked by a masked killer. Postmodern irony is conspicuous by its absence. The strip club setting provides the pretext for plentiful T&A. Our heroine is a would-be lawyer who strips to finance her studies. Telling social comment? Not really. Abel Ferrara did it better with *Fear City* (1984), which at least had the courage of its dubious convictions.
Written and directed by Robert Tiffi.
With: Chris Moir, Jon Briddell, Mia Zottoli.
MIA. February 2005. Cert 15.

THE HEROIC ONES

A 1970 Shaw Brothers epic, directed by the legendary Chang Cheh. During the Tang Dynasty, a Mongol king sends his favourite sons to defeat rebel forces. Unfortunately, there's treachery at work. Boasting impressive battle scenes, *The Heroic Ones* is a strong vehicle for Shaw stars David Chiang and Ti Lung. That said, newcomers to the Shaw style may find the film studio-bound and overly theatrical.
Momentum Asia. February 2005. Cert 18.

HOUSE OF THE DEAD

Teenagers land on an island inhabited by zombies. Based on a hit video game, *House of the Dead* rips off numerous zombie movies to little effect.
Directed by Uwe Boll.
With: Jonathan Cherry, Tyron Leitso, Clint Howard, Ona Grauer, Jurgen Prochnow.
Redbus. October 2004. Cert 15.

HUMAN LANTERNS

Shaw Brothers responded to the 1980s Hong Kong horror boom with this grisly combination of martial arts and

extreme gore. Shaw regular Lo Lieh plays a demented craftsman, who turns his enemies' loved ones into the title objects. Director Chung Sun handles the material with obvious relish. Note: While this UK release has more gore and violence than the Hong Kong DVD, it's missing some of the skin-stripping footage. This is down to the distributor rather than the BBFC, which passed the film uncut. A forthcoming US release is reported to be complete.
With: Tanny Tien Ni, Wing Lau, Yuen Wah.
Momentum Asia. May 2005. Cert 18.

I ACCUSE

A powerful Canadian TV movie on a familiar theme: an abused woman's lonely fight for justice. Estella Warren stars as a blue-collar single mother, convinced she was drugged and raped by her respected doctor (John Hannah). When he protests his innocence, backed up by DNA evidence, the local community turns its back on her. Rather than give up, she looks for a way to prove the doctor's guilt. *I Accuse* makes the valid – if depressing – point that social prejudice can harm a victim as much as

the actual crime. Ex-model Warren gives a strong performance, light years away from her vapid turn in *Planet of the Apes*.
Directed by John Ketcham.
With: John Kapelos.
High Fliers. October 2004. Cert 15.

THE I INSIDE

An intriguing blend of amnesia drama and time travel fantasy. Unfortunately, the film loses its way – much like the protagonist – and the ending is predictable.
Directed by Roland Suso Richter.
With: Ryan Philippe, Sarah Polley, Piper Perabo, Stephen Rea.
Pathe Distribution. March 2005. Cert 15.

INTO THE SUN

Steven Seagal keeps turning them out, with surprisingly watchable results. US agent Travis Hunter investigates the murder of a Japanese government official. He discovers that a Yakuza boss has recruited Chinese triads for all-out gang warfare. Only Hunter can stop the carnage, largely by killing all the bad guys. While the mid-section drags, *Into the Sun* delivers on the action front, featuring a lot of gory swordplay. The soundtrack draws from Seagal's album 'Songs from the Crystal Cave'.
Directed by Mink.
With: Matthew Davis, Takao Osawa, William Atherton, Ken Lo (Jackie Chan's bodyguard).
Sony Pictures Home Entertainment. April 2005. Cert 18.

THE KEEPER

An unhinged cop (Dennis Hopper) kidnaps a dancer (Asia Argento) for her own 'protection'. This psychological thriller has little new to offer. Hopper can do the twitchy psycho bit in his sleep and Argento needs better scripts to sustain her US career.
Directed by Paul Lynch.
With: Helen Shaver, Lochlyn Munro.
Momentum. December 2004. Cert 15.

THE LAST SHOT

A would be filmmaker (Matthew Broderick) is recruited by an FBI agent (Alec Baldwin) for an elaborate Mafia sting operation. Set in the mid-1980s, *The Last Shot* aims for the absurdist black humour of *Catch-22*. Though by no means a classic, the end result is both inventive and amusing. What happens when an undercover agent prefers his assumed identity to his real life?
Written and directed by Jeff Nathanson.
With: Toni Collette, Calista Flockhart, Ray

Liotta, Buck Henry (who scripted the 1970 film of *Catch-22*).
Buena Vista. June 2005. Cert 15.

LD50: LETHAL DOSE

Animal rights activists try to rescue a colleague from a sinister laboratory. Directed by Simon De Selva, this British science fiction-thriller aims to be another *28 Days Later*. While the scares are minimal, *LD50* has a few tense moments.
With: Katherine Towne, Tom Hardy, Melanie Brown (the artist formerly known as Scary Spice).
Buena Vista. February 2005. Cert 15.

LEXIE

A former music producer attempts a comeback, falling for a beautiful singer-dancer. Can their love endure in a business riven with corruption and organised crime? Director Fred Williamson, a veteran blaxploitation star, has been turning out this kind of fare for 30 years. Offering a sour view of LA's music scene, *Lexie* is nothing new.
With: Ice-T, Cindy Herron, Gary Busey, Fred Williamson.
MIA. June 2005. Cert 15

THE LOCALS

Two friends on a weekend jaunt meet a pair of attractive women who invite them to a party. Forced off a country road, they end up in a strange town where the locals are not friendly. This New Zealand horror movie deserves points for effort, though many of the ingredients seem over-familiar. Working on a low budget, writer-director Greg Page handles the initial mystery more successfully than the plot twists.
With: John Barker, Dwayne Cameron, Kate Elliott, Aidee Walker, Paul Glover, Greg Page.
Mosaic Movies. October 2004. Cert 15.

LOVE DON'T COST A THING

A high school loser bribes a popular cheerleader to be his girlfriend for two weeks. Needless to say, things don't work out as they expected. A remake of the superior *Can't Buy Me Love* (1987), this stale romantic comedy wastes an interesting premise. Most of the blame lies with writer-director Troy Beyer, who inflicted the dreadful *BAPS* on the world.
With: Nick Cannon, Christina Milian, Jordan Burg, Jackie Benoit.
Warner Home Video. July 2004. Cert 15.

LOVE LETTERS OF A PORTUGUESE NUN

Back in 1979, Jesús Franco's nunsploitation movie was rejected outright by the BBFC. Fans praise the film for its 'arthouse' visuals and potent attack on the hypocrisies of the Catholic Church. Most viewers will feel the film revels in scenes of teenage girls being tortured and sexually abused. Unimpressed by Franco's moral message, the BBFC have cut over six minutes from this release.
With: 'Susan Hemingway' (rn Maria Rosalia Coutinho), William Berger, Ana Zanatti, Anton Diffring.
Anchor Bay UK. July 2004. Cert 18.

MADHOUSE

A young intern discovers dark secrets at a psychiatric hospital. A decent thriller with enough twists to keep the viewer interested.
Directed by William Butler.
With: Joshua Leonard, Jordan Ladd, Natasha Lyonne, Lance Henriksen.
Redbus. December 2004. Cert 15.

THE MAGNIFICENT TRIO

This 1966 Shaw Brothers epic was a vehicle for Jimmy Wang Yu, Hong Kong's first action superstar. Wang Yu plays a soldier who helps villagers defeat a corrupt magistrate. Directed by Chang Cheh, *The Magnificent Trio* features strong action scenes and high production values. Any political subtext is played down: it's amoral individuals who exploit the poor, not the system itself.
With: Lo Lieh, Yuen Woo Ping.
Momentum Asia. May 2005. Cert 12.

MIRACLE

Ice hockey fans should check out this biopic of Herb Brooks (Kurt Russell), the player-turned-coach who led the US team to victory at the 1980 Olympics. A notorious hard-ass, Brooks bullied, cajoled and inspired a squad of college kids into beating the professional USSR team. The Cold War backdrop gives the film an extra edge. Probably the best ice hockey movie since *Slap Shot*.
Directed by Gavin O'Connor.
With: Patricia Clarkson, Noah Emmerich, Sean McCann.
Buena Vista. February 2005. Cert PG.

MISSION WITHOUT PERMISSION

A remake of the hit Danish film *Klatretosen* (2002), this enjoyable variation on *Spy Kids*

also borrows from *Ocean's 11* and *Mission Impossible*. A 12-year-old girl (Kristen Stewart) plans a bank heist to finance a life-saving operation for her father, who has been injured in a mountaineering accident. Fortunately, her mother designed the bank's hi-tech security system. Strong on action, *Mission Without Permission* could do with more humour. While some may object to the crime-does-pay message, this is not a film to be taken seriously. Original title: *Catch That Kid*.
Directed by Bart Freundlich
With: Jennifer Beals, Sam Robards, Michael Des Barres.
Twentieth Century-Fox. October 2004. Cert PG.

MR 3000

In this baseball comedy-drama, an arrogant star player (Bernie Mac) emerges from retirement to get his 3000th strike. A selfish egomaniac, he gradually learns the value of humility and team spirit. Strong performances lift a formulaic script.
Directed by Charles Stone III.
With: Angela Bassett, Michael Rispoli, Paul Sorvino, Chris Noth.
Buena Vista. February 2005. Cert 12.

NATURAL CITY

A South Korean spin on *Blade Runner*. In 2080 Seoul, a cop assigned to eliminate violent cyborgs, falls for a beautiful female android. Sound familiar? Impressive visuals balance a thin plot and sketchy characters.
Written and directed by Min Byung Chun.
With: Yu Ji Tae, Lee Jae Un, Seo Rin.
Optimum Home Entertainment. August 2004. Cert 15.

NEVER DIE ALONE

A drug kingpin provokes gang warfare when he returns to his home turf. Told in flashback, *Never Die Alone* is an effective spin on an old story.
Directed by Ernest Dickerson.
With: DMX, Michael Ealy, Drew Sidora, Robby Robinson, David Arquette.
Twentieth Century Fox. January 2005. Cert 18.

NO GOOD DEED

Samuel L. Jackson is Jack Friar, a cultured detective who plays the cello. When a neighbour asks him to find her missing daughter, he's abducted by an eccentric criminal gang. Despite the impressive cast, this offbeat drama, loosely based on the Dashiell Hammett story 'The House on Turk Street', is sunk by a weak script and

overheated direction.
Directed by Bob Rafelson.
With: Milla Jovovich, Stellan Skarsgård, Joss Ackland.
Momentum Pictures. July 2004. Cert 15.

NORA'S HAIR SALON

This indie variation on *Barbershop* offers the usual collection of ethnic stereotypes and a handful of laughs. While Nora (Jennifer Lewis) is upstaged by her employees and clients, she gets the big dramatic scene towards the end. Cameos from Bobby Brown and Whitney Houston don't help much.
Directed by Jerry LaMothe.
With: Tatyana Ali, Kristian Bernard, Brandi Burnside.
DEJ Productions. September 2004. Cert 15.

OUT OF REACH

Steven Seagal is Billy Ray Lancing, an ex-secret agent employed in an animal shelter (no, really). When his East European penpal disappears, he discovers that her foster programme is a front for a human trafficking ring. It's kick-ass time! This middling Seagal effort clearly suffered post-production problems. In some scenes, the star is dubbed by another actor. Could it be that Seagal was less than impressed with the movie? Filmed in Poland.
Directed by Leong Po Chih.
With: Ida Nowakowska, Agnieszka Wagner, Matt Schulze, Nick Brimble.
Columbia-TriStar. August 2004. Cert 15.

PASSIONADA

The lives and loves of a Portuguese family in New Bedford, Massachusetts. When a widowed mother refuses to go on dates, her daughter schemes to find her a 'perfect' man, enlisting a roguish gambler with plans of his own. For all the plots and counter-plots, *Passionada* is a bland romantic comedy. Apparently, the depiction of Portuguese language and culture is wildly inaccurate (even the title isn't Portuguese).
Directed by Dan Ireland.
With: Jason Isaacs, Sofia Milos, Emmy Rossum, Theresa Russell, Seymour Cassel.
Columbia-TriStar. November 2004. Cert PG.

THE PERFECT HUSBAND

A California woman disappears, eight months pregnant. When a body is found, her husband is charged with murder. Based on the case of Laci and Scott Peterson, this formula TV movie restages real-life events with indecent haste; it was made before the

latter's trial even began. Former Superman Dean Cain gives a solid performance as Scott, the cheating husband who was anything but perfect. Original title: *The Perfect Husband: The Laci Peterson Story*.
Directed by Roger Young.
With: G.W. Bailey, Sarah Brown, Meredith Lieber, Dee Wallace Stone.
Columbia-TriStar. November 2004. Cert 15.

PERFECT STRANGERS

Filmed in New Zealand, this psychological drama depicts the deadly consequences of a kidnapping. Well acted by Sam Neill and Rachael Blake, the film also benefits from its island location and unpredictable twists. If nothing else, *Perfect Strangers* is an awful warning against one-night stands.
Written and directed by Gaylene Preston.
With: Joel Tobeck, Robyn Malcolm.
High Fliers. May 2005.
Cert 15.

PURSUED

In this dreary techno-thriller, a corporate head-hunter (Christian Slater) turns stalker when his target proves unresponsive. Slater has done the grinning psycho bit before – think Jack Nicholson on a bad day – and it doesn't improve with repetition.
Directed by Kristoffer Tabori.
With: Gil Bellows, Conchita Campbell, Michael Clarke Duncan, Estella Warren.
DEJ Productions. June 2005.
Cert 15.

RAISE YOUR VOICE

Another mediocre vehicle for Hilary Duff. A small-town girl spends an eventful summer at a Los Angeles high school for the performing arts. An attempt at depth – Duff is haunted by her brother's recent death – doesn't work.
Directed by Sean McNamara.
With: Oliver James, David Keith, Dana Davis, Rebecca De Mornay.
Momentum. May 2005. Cert PG.

REDEMPTION

A biopic of Stan 'Tookie' Williams (Jamie Foxx), the LA Crips gang leader who renounced his old life. Imprisoned for murder, Williams became an anti-violence campaigner, children's author and Nobel Peace Prize nominee. As with many biopics, basis in fact doesn't guarantee credibility. Generally well made, *Redemption* sometimes has the feel of inspirational soap opera, though Foxx gives Williams' transformation a dramatic force lacking in the script.

Original title: *Redemption: The Stan Tookie Williams Story*. Note: Stan Williams is still on Death Row in San Quentin Prison.
Directed by Vondie Curtis-Hall.
With: Lynn Whitfield, Lee Thompson Young, CCH Pounder.
High Fliers. April 2005. Cert 15.

REESEVILLE

An atmospheric murder mystery, set in America's rural Mid-West. Favouring character over suspense, the film suffers from a patchy script. *Star Wars* actor Mark Hamill is effective in a supporting role.
Written and directed by Christian Otjen.
With: Brad Hunt, Majandra Delfino, Brian Wimmer, Missy Crider.
Warner Home Video. February 2005. Cert 15.

RETURN TO THE BATCAVE: THE MISADVENTURES OF ADAM AND BURT

This engaging oddity pays homage to the 1960s *Batman* TV show. When the Batmobile is stolen, original stars Adam West and Burt Ward go in hot pursuit. En route, they recall their experiences on the television series, good and bad. Part nostalgia trip, part parody, *Return to the Batcave* is surprisingly successful. West and Ward gamely send up their characters and their own offscreen images. The supporting cast includes *Batman* guest stars Lee Meriwether, Julie Newmar and Frank Gorshin. That's two Catwomen and a Riddler. Fans of *Batman Begins* will probably be baffled.
Directed by Paul A. Kaufman.
Anchor Bay UK. June 2005. Cert 12.

ROMASANTA: THE WEREWOLF HUNT

The true story of Manuel Romasanta (Julian Sands), a 19th century mass murderer. Brought to justice, Romasanta escaped execution by claiming to be a werewolf. Despite the subtitle, this Spanish production has no supernatural element. Sands is effectively creepy as the charming, charismatic Romasanta, who murdered numerous women and children. Not bad, as period serial killer movies go.
Directed by Francisco Plaza.
With: Elsa Pataky, John Sharian, Gary Piquer.
Mosaic. August 2004. Cert 15.

SEVENTEEN AGAIN

Rejuvenated by a miracle formula, a divorced elderly couple realise they still love life and each other. This half-arsed feel-good fantasy is a flimsy vehicle for TV twins Tia and Tamera Mowry.
Directed by Jeff Byrd.
With: Mark Taylor, Tahj Mowry, Robert Hooks.
Contender Entertainment. July 2004. Cert 12.

SHADE

LA poker hustlers run into trouble with the Mob. A sharply scripted ensemble piece with strong performances all round. Sylvester Stallone and Melanie Griffith show what they can do with decent material.
Written and directed by Damian Nieman.
With: Stuart Townsend, Gabriel Byrne, Hal Holbrook, Thandie Newton, Jamie Foxx, Michael Dorn.
DEJ Productions. July 2004. Cert 15.

SHADOW OF FEAR

An accidental killing leads to blackmail, adultery, betrayal and worse. Another thriller involving a secret society that operates outside the law. Despite a strong cast, the end result is contrived and confusing.
Directed by Rich Cowan.
With: James Spader, Matt Davis, Aidan Quinn, Peter Coyote, Alice Krige, Robin Tunney.
DEJ Productions. February 2005. Cert 12.

SHAOLIN VERSUS THE EVIL DEAD

An enjoyable throwback to the Hong Kong kung fu horror-comedies of the 1980s. Shaw Brothers legend Gordon Liu Chia Hui stars as a Shaolin monk battling the forces of darkness. Highlights include an exploding mini-demon. Unfortunately, the film ends very abruptly, building to a climax that doesn't arrive. Apparently, *Shaolin versus the Evil Dead* was split into two films, à la *Kill Bill*, which also features Gordon Liu. Hopefully, part two will appear in the near future.
Directed by Douglas Kung.
MIA. March 2005. Cert 15.

SHUT UP AND KISS ME

Set in Miami, this romantic comedy goes downhill after a reasonable start.
Directed by Gary Brockette.
With: Brad Rowe, Christopher Barnes, Krista Allen, Kristin Richardson, Burt Young.
Lighthouse. March 2005. Cert 15.

SNIPER 3

Tom Berenger returns in this second sequel to *Sniper* (1992), set in Vietnam. Hired to eliminate a terrorist suspect, our sharp-shooting hero realises things aren't what they seem. Director P.J. Pesce, who made the enjoyable *From Dusk Till Dawn 3*, delivers a solid 'B' action movie. That said, the feeling persists that Berenger deserves better. Filmed in Thailand.
With: Byron Mann, John Doman, Denis Arndt, Troy Wimbush.
Columbia-TriStar. December 2004. Cert 15.

SORCERESS I & II

Two movies for the price of one isn't necessarily good value. *Sorceress* (1995) is above-average sexploitation with black magic trimmings (like anyone cares). While bad witch Julie Strain knows the score, good witch Linda Blair plays the film for serious drama. *The Exorcist* this isn't. The dreadful *Sorceress II* (1996), with Strain, centres on a pagan cosmetics firm.
Directed by Jim Wynorski and Richard Styles.
With: Eddie Albert, Michael Parks, William Marshall (*Sorceress*), Sandahl Bergman, Greg Wrangler, Julie K. Smith (*Sorceress II*).
Anchor Bay UK. November 2004. Cert 18.

SPIRITUAL BOXER

Lau Kar Leung, Shaw Brothers' leading action director, made his directing debut with this 1975 martial arts comedy. In rural China, a con man promotes the bogus art of 'spiritual boxing', supposedly endowing a fighter with supernatural strength. Eventually he sees the light, helping villagers defeat the local crime boss. Atypical of Lau's later films, *Spiritual Boxer* is worth a look.
With: Wang Yu (not Jimmy Wang Yu), Chan Koon Tai, Ti Lung.
Momentum Asia. February 2005. Cert 12.

SUSPECT ZERO

In this intriguing, if contrived, thriller, a serial killer is hunting down other serial killers. The FBI agent on his tail has the gift of 'remote viewing', enabling him to visualise events happening elsewhere. The long-gestating script passed through various hands, including those of Ben Affleck and Paul Schrader, but the numerous plot holes are countered by Ben Kingsley's haunting performance.
Directed by E. Elias Merhige.
With: Aaron Eckhart, Carrie-Anne Moss, Harry Lennix.

Sony Pictures Home Entertainment. May 2005. Cert 15.

THE TESSERACT

Loosely based on Alex Garland's novel, this is a flawed yet fascinating film. Various oddball characters descend on a rundown Bangkok hotel, their interweaving stories of drugs, murder and dreams linked by a thieving bellboy. The fragmented style will either intrigue or infuriate most viewers. Many rate this as superior to *The Beach* (2000), another Garland adaptation set in Thailand. A tesseract, incidentally, is the four-dimensional equivalent of a cube.
Directed by Oxide Pang Chun.
With: Jonathan Rhys-Meyers, Saskia Reeves, Alexander Rendel, Carlo Nanni.
Momentum Asia. February 2005. Cert 15.

THE THIRD WHEEL

A shy young man (Luke Wilson) on a hot date knocks over a homeless person and can't get rid of him. Another romantic comedy sunk by irritating characters and a weak script. Luke Wilson seems to lack brother Owen's instinct for picking the right projects. Executive produced by Ben Affleck and Matt Damon, who make cameo appearances.
Directed by Jordan Brady.
With: Denise Richards, Jay Lacopo (who also scripted).
Buena Vista. October 2004. Cert 12.

UNSTOPPABLE

A disturbed war veteran (Wesley Snipes) is injected with an experimental mind control drug. Plagued by hallucinations, he must find the antidote before his brain fries. An intriguing premise develops into a routine action movie. Fans of Snipes' *Blade* series may enjoy it.
Directed by David Carson.
With: Jacqueline Obradors, Stuart Wilson, Kim Coates, David Schofield.
Columbia-TriStar. January 2005. Cert 15

VLAD

Students in the Carpathian mountains revive Vlad Tepes (Francesco Quinn, son of Anthony), the inspiration for Count Dracula. Filmed on authentic Romanian locations, *Vlad* is a curious hybrid. Tepes is depicted as a tortured spirit rather than a vampire, an interesting idea that doesn't go anywhere.
Written and directed by Michael D. Sellers.
With: Billy Zane, Paul Popowich, Kam Heskin, Brad Dourif.
Prism Leisure Corporation. February 2005. Cert 15.

WARRIORS OF HEAVEN AND EARTH

A sweeping Chinese epic, set in a visually stunning Gobi Desert. Two Japanese soldiers – one sent to kill the other – call a temporary truce to defend a Buddhist monk and his treasure from bandits. Can their fragile alliance hold until they reach safety? This release has been cut by seven seconds, removing shots of alleged animal cruelty.
Written and directed by He Ping.
With: Wen Jiang, Kiichi Nakai, Xueqi Wang, Vicky Zhao.
Columbia-TriStar. December 2004. Cert 15.

WELCOME TO MOOSEPORT

A former US president (Gene Hackman) decides to run for mayor in his hometown of Mooseport, Maine. His opponent is a hardware store owner (Ray Romano). This mediocre comedy was intended to launch TV star Romano (*Everybody Loves Raymond*) on the big screen. Romano is hopelessly outclassed by Hackman, who wrings some laughs from a weak script.
Directed by Donald Petrie.
With: Marcia Gay Harden, Maura Tierney, Fred Savage, Rip Torn.
Twentieth Century-Fox. September 2004. Cert PG.

WILD THINGS 3

Two ruthless young women chase a $4 million inheritance. This second 'sequel' is a tame, witless retread of the 1998 movie. Original title: *Wild Things: Diamonds in the Rough*.
Directed by Jay Lowi.
With: Sarah Laine, Sandra McCoy, Linden Ashby, Ron Melendez.
Columbia-TriStar. May 2005. Cert 15.

THE GENERAL

In spite of the historical significance of this remarkable DVD, its release appeared to slip under the radar. Such is the regard in which Buster Keaton seems to be held today: a near-invisible figure relegated to second-banana status behind Chaplin and Laurel & Hardy. Yet Keaton's *The General* (1926), which has all but vanished from public consciousness, is often cited as one of the ten greatest films of all time. It is easy to see why, and this painstakingly restored print – with every single frame digitally cleaned, corrected and stabilised – is a technological miracle.

Keaton, the vaudevillian who became a consummate screen clown and filmmaker, wrote his own material and performed his own stunts, risking his life daily for an immortal moment of cinema. *The General*, his most ambitious project, is said to be the most authentic film ever made about the American Civil War – which goes to show just how meticulous Keaton was about every detail.

Amazingly, it is based on a true story – about a train conductor, William Fuller, who foiled an attempt by Union soldiers to capture the Southern locomotive 'The General' – and still has the power to enthral and astound today: without a single special effect or cliché. The numerous DVD extras include a moving introduction by Orson Welles and candid footage of Keaton in his grumpy, autumnal years. JC-W

With: Buster Keaton, Marion Mack, Glen Cavender.
Cinema Club. April 2005. Cert U.

Faces of the Year

Eva Birthistle

Emily Blunt

EVA BIRTHISTLE

Born: 1974 in Dublin, Ireland.
In a nutshell: An Irish blonde with porcelain skin, Eva Birthistle is a real head-turner. You could imagine her at the pub or on the farm but, if male, you would still herald her with a wolf whistle. She passed almost unnoticed as Deborah in Conor McPherson's surreal, surprising *Saltwater* but when chosen by Ken Loach to star in *Ae Fond Kiss* she was a revelation. As a Catholic music teacher who falls for a Glaswegian Pakistani, she was believable, vulnerable and driven – and walked off with the London Film Critics' award for Best British Actress. A few more good directors like Loach and she'll be a star. That's pronounced Bur-thistle, by the way.
Other films: *Red Rum* (2000), *Borstal Boy*, *Mystics*, *Timbuktu*.
Major TV: *The American* (2001), *Bloody Sunday* (released theatrically),

Sunday, *Trust*, *The Baby War*.
Next up: The comedy *Save Angel Hope* in which she plays a con artist masquerading as Angel Hope, a sexy Mother Teresa.
On Hollywood: 'It's not my goal to go, "Oh my God, I have to make it! I have to be Charlize Theron!" If they come a-knocking, I'll open the door and go, "C'mon in, have a cup of tea." But just as long as I keep working, that's fine.'

EMILY BLUNT

Born: appears to be her secret…
In a nutshell: Emily Blunt's materialisation on a white charger in the low-budget hit *My Summer of Love* is up there with Ursula Andress and Bo Derek's eye-catching arrivals in *Dr. No* and *10*. With her finely chiselled bone structure and luxuriant hair, Blunt was a vision to behold. Yet this wasn't merely

a comely decoration for a piece of multiplex flotsam, but a young actress who all but dominates a convincingly resonant and critically applauded film.
Major TV: *Boudica* (2003), *Henry VIII* (as Catherine Howard), *Poirot: Death On the Nile* and *Empire*.
Next up: Ann Turner's Australian drama *Irresistible*, with Susan Sarandon and Sam Neill, Gillies MacKinnon's adaptation of Paul Gallico's *The Snow Goose*, with Olivier Martinez and Billy Connolly, and *Who Killed Norma Barnes?*, an update of Dostoyevsky's *The Idiot* set in contemporary Brighton, directed by Malcolm McKay and co-starring Ralph Fiennes and Emily Mortimer.

JAMIE FOXX

Born: 13 December 1967 in Terrell, Texas.
Real name: Eric Morlon Bishop.
In a nutshell: Without doubt, this was

Jamie Foxx

TOPHER GRACE

Born: 12 July 1978 in New York, New York.

Real name: Christopher Grace.

In a nutshell: Topher Grace was playing Pseudolus in a high-school production of *A Funny Thing Happened on the Way to the Forum* when he was spotted by TV producers Bonnie Turner and Terry Turner. They cast him in the nostalgic TV comedy *That '70s Show* – as awkward teenager Eric Forman – and the series took off. From there he played a preppy drug user in Steven Soderbergh's *Traffic* (who lures Michael Douglas' daughter into cocaine and heroin) and was Julia Stiles' swain in *Mona Lisa Smile*. But it was his comic timing and deadpan delivery in *Win a Date with Tad Hamilton!* that made the difference. In *In Good Company* he proved up to the task, playing Dennis Quaid's boss, nemesis and potential son-in-law with a humour and empathy that lifted the part out of the drawer marked 'stock villain'.

Other movies: *Ocean's Eleven* (as himself), the romantic fantasy *P.S.* with Laura Linney and Gabriel Byrne, and *Ocean's Twelve* (as himself).

Next up: The villain in *Spider-Man 3*.

He said it: 'I hate these guys who've done five movies, like 25-years-old, but they want to write, direct, have a production company. I just want to learn. I am very open about being green.'

the year of Jamie Foxx. On the poster of Michael Mann's *Collateral* he shared equal billing with Tom Cruise and went on to snare an Oscar nomination for the film, while winning the Best Actor statuette for his uncanny, exhilarating performance as Ray Charles. *Collateral* went on to gross $217,715,551 worldwide, while *Ray* clocked up $123,479,282. Since then he has provided some much-needed comic relief in the adrenaline-powered *Stealth* and took the Ricardo Tubbs role in the big-screen adaptation of *Miami Vice* opposite Colin Farrell.

Other films: *Toys* (1992), *The Truth About Cats & Dogs*, *The Great White Hype*, *Booty Call*, *The Players Club*, *Held Up*, *Any Given Sunday*, *Bait*, *Ali*, *Shade*, *Redemption: The Stan Tookie Williams Story* (as Williams), *Breakin' All the Rules*

(2004).

Major TV: *In Living Color* (1990), *The Jamie Foxx Show* (1996).

Next up: The male lead in the long-awaited film version of the smash Broadway musical *Dreamgirls* and the starring role in Michael Mann's legal drama *Damage Control*.

He said it: 'C.C.H. Pounder taught me one thing. She said, "Characters are like putting on a coat. You put the coat on while you work, you take the coat off after it's over." You need that freshness. I know people who stay in character, and it's the worst thing in the world. I like to go do it, flip it on like a light switch and then flip it off. Then, when we come back in the next morning I flip it back on. That's what keeps things fresh for me.'

JOSH LUCAS

Born: 20 June 1971 in Arkansas, USA.

Real name: Joshua Maurer.

In a nutshell: Josh Lucas has been circling Hollywood like a camouflaged buzzard. Occasionally, he will dip out of the ether and make his presence known and will then fly back into the clouds. His list of credits is impressive – if not downright prodigious – and yet household stardom has eluded him. High-profile projects have included *A Beautiful Mind*, *Sweet Home Alabama* and *Hulk*. His co-stars have numbered Sean Penn, Val Kilmer and Michael Caine – and as long ago as 1996 he had a starring role in the British film *True Blue*. But this looks like being his year for breakout stardom. With his muscular frame, crystalline blue eyes and passing

Topher Grace

Josh Lucas

performance as a war photographer in *In My Father's Den* is a picture of restrained emotion, his eyes giving away more than his dialogue. He's also got a great face, a visage that, at the actor's will, can seem ordinary, intimidating or utterly disarming.

Significant other: The actress Keeley Hawes (who played Zoe Reynolds in *Spooks*).

Other films: *Maybe Baby* (2000), *Enigma*, *The Reckoning* (aka *Morality Play*).

Major TV: *Wuthering Heights* (1998), *Warriors*, *Perfect Strangers*, *The Way We Live Now*, *The Project*, *Spooks* (as Tom Quinn).

He said it: 'If you love acting, then to be able to work is such a treat. And it all happened with alarming ease, really. Well, not ease, but you feel guilty if it feels like you're winging it.'

resemblance to Paul Newman, Lucas has the makings of a major, major star. He can do funny (cf. *Sweet Home Alabama*), he can do menacing (check out this year's *Undertow*) and he can do romantic (see *An Unfinished Life*, with JLo).

Past love: Salma Hayek.

Other films: *Alive* (1993), *Father Hood*, *Stephen King's Thinner*, *Minotaur*, *The Definite Maybe*, *Harvest*, *Restless*, *You Can Count On Me*, *American Psycho*, *Drop Back Ten*, *The Dancer*, *The Weight of Water*, *The Deep End*, *When Strangers Appear*, *Session 9*, *Coastlines*, *Four Reasons*, *Secondhand Lions*, *Wonderland*, *Undertow*, *Around the Bend*.

Next up: The sports drama *Glory Road* (in which he plays real-life basketball coach Don Haskins) and the lead in Wolfgang Petersen's star-studded *Poseidon*.

He said it: 'I just feel like I really want to be someone who literally disappears in the role. I want to be so strong as an actor that people wouldn't say, "Oh, that's Ben Affleck".'

MATTHEW MACFADYEN

Born: 1974 in Great Yarmouth, Norfolk.

In a nutshell: Matthew MacFadyen made himself known with his starring role in *Spooks*, the mega-hyped TV series set inside the world of MI5. However, the year 2005 should see him become a household name thanks to two movies, the intelligent, atmospheric New Zealand thriller *In My Father's Den* and the accomplished, sumptuous new film version of *Pride and Prejudice*. In the latter

he plays Mr Darcy, a role that didn't do Colin Firth any harm back in 1995. And MacFadyen can brood very well. His

Matthew MacFadyen

James McAvoy

Eva Mendes

JAMES MCAVOY

Born: 1979 in Scotstoun, Glasgow.
In a nutshell: Besides all his sterling TV work (see below), McAvoy pretty much outshone the all-star cast of *Bright Young Things*, in which he played the scheming but tragic gossip columnist Simon Balcairn. Then within the space of three weeks he turned up in two such eye-catching, stunningly divergent roles, he had critics scrambling for their superlatives. In the first, *Wimbledon*, he delivered a performance of comic precision as the carefree, cocky Carl Colt, who bets against his own brother (Paul Bettany) winning any games at the eponymous championship. Then, in *Inside I'm Dancing* – a criminally overlooked film – he played the rebellious, plain-speaking Rory O'Shea who is paralysed with Duchenne muscular dystrophy. That he could turn a bicycle into a comic tool in the former and act only from the neck up in the latter established McAvoy as a star of thrilling potential.
Significant other: The actress Anne-Marie Duff (from TV's *Shameless*).
Other films: *The Near Room* (1995), *Regeneration*, *Swimming Pool* (aka *Der Tod feiert mit*), *Bollywood Queen*, *Strings* (voice only).
Next up: The role of Mr Tumnus in *The Chronicles of Narnia: The Lion, The Witch and the Wardrobe*, the lead in Kevin Macdonald's Ugandan drama *The Last King of Scotland* (with Forest Whitaker as Idi Amin) and the biographical drama *Burns*, with Gerard Butler and Julia Stiles (with McAvoy as Robert Ainslie).
Major TV: *Lorna Doone*, *Band of Brothers*, *White Teeth*, *Children of Dune*, *State of Play*, *Early Doors*, *Shameless*.

EVA MENDES

Born: 5 March 1974 in Houston, Texas, USA.
In a nutshell: Eva Mendes smoulders. She's not afraid to play hard, mean even, and she almost toppled the boat in *Hitch* (did her character *deserve* Will Smith?). But it's refreshing to find an actress who puts her balls before her peroxide hair and can stand up to the likes of Denzel Washington (twice) and Antonio Banderas. With her Latino steel and the commercial success of *Hitch* – not to mention a lucrative Revlon contract

Cillian Murphy

Sophie Okonedo

– Mendes is really hitting her stride.
Other films: *A Night at the Roxbury*
(1998), *My Brother the Pig*, *Urban Legends:
Final Cut*, *Exit Wounds*, *Training Day*, *All
About the Benjamins*, *2 Fast 2 Furious*, *Once
Upon a Time in Mexico*, *Out of Time*, *Stuck
On You*, *Trust the Man*, *The Wendell
Baker Story*.
Next up: The female lead in the long-
awaited comic-strip thriller *Ghost Rider*,
playing Roxanne Simpson to Nicolas
Cage's Johnny Blaze.
Rumoured lover: Matt Damon.
She said it: 'I'm feeling more and more
like an actress now, which is good. But
I'm no Cate Blanchett.'

CILLIAN MURPHY

Born: 25 May 1976 in Douglas,
Cork, Ireland.
In a nutshell: With his understated
manner, camera-friendly features,
impossibly translucent eyes and a knack
for being picked by world-class directors,
Cillian Murphy is a force to be reckoned
with. After his starring role in *Disco Pigs*
– as Pig, a passionate, poetry-spouting
Romeo – he landed the lead in Danny
Boyle's post-apocalyptic *28 Days Later*,
a slow-burning cult hit. Anthony
Minghella then cast him as a rapist in
Cold Mountain before he snared the role
of The Scarecrow in Christopher Nolan's
triumphant *Batman Begins*, providing an
exercise in genuinely chilling evil.
Other films: *The Tale of Sweety Barrett*
(1998), *Sunburn*, *The Trench*, *Filleann an
Feall*, *On the Edge*, *How Harry Became
a Tree*, *Zonad*, *interMission*, *Girl With a
Pearl Earring*, *Red-Eye*.
Next up: The lead in Neil Jordan's
Breakfast on Pluto, Danny Boyle's sci-fi
thriller *Sunshine* and Ken Loach's *The
Wind That Shakes the Barley*.
He said it: 'I can't be the next Colin
Farrell because we're all individuals. It's
just journalism. But we've had a laugh
about it.'

SOPHIE OKONEDO

Born: 1 January 1969 in London,
England, UK.
In a nutshell: When North-East
London's Sophie Okonedo landed the
female lead in the mega-hit *Ace Ventura:*

Paz Vega

When Nature Calls, hardly anyone noticed. Jim Carrey all but consumed the film. Okonedo, who is of Nigerian-Jewish stock, struggled on in small film parts and distinguished herself on the English stage – at the RSC, the National and her favourite creative arena, London's Royal Court Theatre. Then she was cast as Tatiana, the long-suffering wife of the heroic hotel manager Paul Rusesabagina in *Hotel Rwanda*. The part landed her global accolades and an Oscar nomination as Best Actress. Visiting a stately home at the time, Okonedo was escorted from the building after receiving news of the nomination. The excitement was too much.

Other films: *Young Soul Rebels* (1991), Michael Winterbottom's *Go Now*, *The Jackal*, *This Year's Love*, *Mad Cows*, *Peaches*, *Dirty Pretty Things*, *Cross My Heart*, *Aeon Flux*.

Next up: Menno Meyjes' dramatic comedy *The Martian Child*, with John Cusack, and the British spy romp *Stormbreaker*.

Major TV: *The Governor* (1995), *Staying Alive*, *Deep Secrets*, *In Defence*, *Never Never*, *Sweet Revenge*, *Dead Casual*, *Clocking Off*, *Alibi*, *Whose Baby?*, *Born with Two Mothers*.

She said it: 'I don't mind falling flat on my face so long as I feel I'm open to the possibility of something extraordinary happening.'

PAZ VEGA

Born: 2 January 1976 in Seville, Spain.
Real name: Paz Campos Trigo.
In a nutshell: With her generous curves and Latino mien, Paz Vega fits the description of 'bombshell' very well. She's been in some very risqué Spanish movies, and with Julio Medem's *Sex and Lucía*, Pedro Almodóvar's *Talk to Her* and Emilio Martinez-Lazaro's *The Other Side of the Bed*, she has more subtitled hits

to her name than most of her European contemporaries. Look at her in *Carmen* and you'll see what all the fuss is about. She positively burns up the celluloid. And with an Adam Sandler comedy – *Spanglish* on her résumé, Paz has Hollywood on high alert.
Significant other: Orson Salazar.
Other films: *Perdón, perdón* (1998), *Zapping*, *Sobreviviré*, *Nadie conoce a nadie* (aka *Nobody Knows Anybody*), *El Chico en la puerta* (*Wrinkle Movie*), *Sólo mía*, *Novo*,

Di que sí.
Next up: The family drama *December Boys*, with Daniel Radcliffe, and *Fade to Black*, a post-war thriller with Danny Huston and Christopher Walken.
She said it: 'I'm Spanish and I'm very proud of that. My base is in Spain. It is possible to go to Hollywood by plane – and I sleep on the plane very well.'

Film World Diary
July 2004 – June 2005

JULY 2004

Dennis Quaid ties the knot with Kimberley Buffington, a Texan estate agent, in Montana • **Johnny Depp** buys a 45-acre island in the Bahamas for £2 million • Following her private wedding last month to the actor and sometime waiter Chris Backus – 14 years her junior – **Mira Sorvino**, 36, is at the centre of a second, more elaborate ceremony on the Italian island of Capri. The actress is adorned in a white satin number designed for her by Giorgio Armani • **Whoopi Goldberg** is fired as the spokeswoman of Slim-Fast after making lewd puns in public on the name of President Bush • *Spider-Man 2* smashes all opening-day box-office records with a $40.5m take in its first 24 hours • *Dodgeball: A True Underdog Story* grosses $100m in the US • Lovebirds **Jake Gyllenhaal** and **Kirsten Dunst** call it a day • **Laura Dern** and her fiancé, the musician **Ben Harper**, announce that they are expecting a baby by the end of the year. The couple already have one son, Ellery Walker, who will turn three next month • **Minnie Driver** signs a £1 million recording contract with EMI. Her debut single, *Everything I've Got In My Pocket* – which the actress wrote herself – is to be released in September • *Fahrenheit 9/11* grosses $100m in the US, the first documentary to do so – by a long shot.

AUGUST 2004

The Bourne Supremacy grosses $100m in the US – in two weeks • *The Village* grosses $100m in the US • **Nicolas Cage**, 40, ties the knot for the third time, marrying the sushi waitress Alice Kim, who is 21 years his junior. The actor's previous wives were **Patricia Arquette** and **Lisa Marie Presley** • **Diane Lane** marries the actor **Josh Brolin**, son of **James Brolin** and stepson of **Barbra Streisand**. Ms Lane was previously married to **Christopher Lambert** and Brolin was previously engaged to **Minnie Driver** • **Danny Glover** is arrested while protesting at the Sudanese embassy in Washington DC over the situation in Darfur • **Sandra Bullock** pulls out of the romantic comedy *Prime* just two weeks before production is due to start. The actress, who was to co-star with **Meryl Streep**, cited concerns over the script. • Following the death of his wife, **Mark Pellington** pulls out as director of the **Harrison Ford/ Paul Bettany** action-thriller *The Wrong Element*. He is replaced by **Richard Loncraine**, who previously directed Bettany in *Wimbledon*.

SEPTEMBER 2004

Macaulay Culkin is arrested in Oklahoma for possession of marijuana and other drugs. Held by police after the car in which he was travelling was stopped for speeding, the 24-year-old actor was released on $4,000 bail • **Michael Eisner**, Chairman and CEO of the Walt Disney Company, shocks the film community by announcing that he'll leave the company when his contract expires in September 2006 • During a press conference at the Venice Film Festival, **Lauren Bacall** causes a storm when she condemns a journalist for referring to her co-star **Nicole Kidman** as 'a legend'. The 80-year-old icon snaps, 'She's a beginner, she can't be a legend – you have to be older.' But 24 hours later in Deauville, France, Bacall turns up at another conference with Kidman, who plays her daughter in *Birth*, in tow. Bacall enthuses, 'Not only do I admire Nicole as an actress – for she is a *great* actress – but we have been great friends since we met a few years ago.' Still, the Hollywood legend refused to bestow legendary status on her friend • **Mike Leigh**'s *Vera Drake* wins the coveted Golden Lion for Best Film at the Venice Film Festival. **Imelda Staunton**, who plays Vera Drake, is named Best Actress • **Uma Thurman**

replaces **Sandra Bullock** in the troubled romantic comedy *Prime* ● The non-profit organisation, The Columbus Citizens Foundation, which celebrates Italian-American culture, is up in arms at the portrayal of their kind as voracious marine fish in *Shark Tale*. In a written complaint, the film was condemned for putting such words as 'capeesh,' 'consigliere' and 'maronne' into the mouths of sharks ● Sony buys MGM/United Artists for around the $5 billion mark, including an assumption of debt ● According to the *Daily Mirror*, **Halle Berry** wrote to the agony aunt of the *Los Angeles*

Sentinel, saying: 'This thing with *Catwoman* is really affecting me. I wish the world viewed me as any other woman that makes mistakes when it comes to life, men and decisions in general … Feel free to print my name, because I'm not ashamed.' The aunt, **Deanna Michaud**, suggested professional counselling, although she may not know that Halle's mother was a psychiatric nurse ● **Billy Bob Thornton**, 49, announces that he and his girlfriend, **Connie Angland**, 39, are the proud parents of a six-pound, one-and-a-half ounce girl they're calling Bella. Thornton already has three children from two of his five

previous marriages ● **Justin Timberlake** allegedly cancels plans to wed **Cameron Diaz** because his mother disapproves of the liaison ● **Kevin Costner** marries the handbag designer **Christine Baumgartner** at his ranch outside Aspen, Colorado. As the couple exchange their vows by a stream, celebrity guests **Tim Allen** and **Don Johnson** look on ● Six of the eight films featured at the top of the US box-office charts top-bill women, with **Julianne Moore** leading the pack in *The Forgotten*. **Bette Davis** and **Joan Crawford** would be proud.

OCTOBER 2004

Sir **Sean Connery** pulls out of **Brett Ratner**'s *Josiah's Canon*. The actor cites a commitment to his memoirs as his reason for jumping ship, although insiders say Connery is becoming increasingly disillusioned with contemporary Hollywood ● *Collateral* grosses $100m in the US ● *Shark Tale* grosses $100m in the US ● Apparently **Orlando Bloom** proposes to **Kate Bosworth** and

she gives him the green light. Word has it that they are hoping for a June wedding ● The Ontario-born **Jim Carrey** takes up American citizenship ● **Billy Bob Thornton** gets his star on the Hollywood Walk of Fame ● **Angelina Jolie** embarks on the adoption process for a second son. Allegedly, Angelina has already set her sights on a Russian boy called Gleb. However, the

paperwork could take up to six months before the actress and Gleb are officially united ● **Jennifer Garner** takes **Ben Affleck** home to meet her folks. So, it's serious then… ● **Jim Sheridan**, the Oscar-nominated writer-director of *My Left Foot* and *In the Name of the Father*, signs up to direct **50 Cent** in *Locked and Loaded*. Are we missing something?

NOVEMBER 2004

The Incredibles smashes box-office records as it nabs $70.3 million in its opening weekend. It's the best opening in Disney's history, even beating *Finding Nemo*, which ended up being the top-grossing release of 2003 ● **Cameron Diaz** is photographed in a scrimmage with two shutterbugs as she leaves the Chateau Marmont hotel with **Justin Timberlake**. The photographers press charges and both Cameron and Justin are subpoenaed ● At the Irish Film and TV Awards in Dublin, **Pierce Brosnan** says that several actors are qualified to step into the tux of James Bond but 'I'll give it to **Colin Farrell**. He'll eat the head off them all.' However, Farrell

laughs at the idea of playing 007 and gives a resounding negative. Instead, he's negotiating to star opposite **Jamie Foxx** in a redux of NBC TV's *Miami Vice*. He would play Sonny Crockett, the detective character that made **Don Johnson** a household name in the 1980s. Foxx – who's tipped for an Oscar for his uncanny portrayal of *Ray* Charles, would play Ricardo Tubbs ● **Billy Zane** and **Kelly Brook** are spotted holding hands in a Los Angeles jewellery store. The tabloids make their predictable assumptions ● **Penélope Cruz** reveals in a Mexican newspaper that she and **Matthew McConaughey** – her co-star in *Sahara* – are officially a

couple ● **Claudia Schiffer** and her husband, director-producer **Matthew Vaughan**, welcome the birth of a baby girl, their second child together ● **Mira Sorvino**, 37, and her husband Chris Backus, 23, are the proud parents of a baby girl ● *The Incredibles* grosses $100m in the US, suffocating Warner Bros.' ambitious *The Polar Express*. The latter launches the new animation system of 'performance capture' in which the actors' performance in the studio is processed into a computer to make it look cartoon-like ● *The Grudge* grosses $100m in the US ● **Robert De Niro** and wife Grace Hightower reaffirm their wedding vows in front of a star-studded crowd * **Kate Bosworth** reveals that she is moving to London to be closer to her boyfriend of two years, **Orlando Bloom** * *The Incredibles* grosses $200m in the US – in under three weeks * **Julia Roberts** gives birth to twins, a son, Phinnaeus Walter, and a daughter, Hazel Patricia.

DECEMBER 2004

Bruce Willis gives ex-wife **Demi Moore** a private jet as an early Christmas present. The aircraft, which cost Willis £10 million, includes an on-board hair salon ● *National Treasure* grosses $100 million in the US, marking the first hit for Nicolas Cage in 13 movies ● After insolent reviews and a rickety start at the box-office, *The Polar Express* gathers steam and grosses $100m at the US box-office ● **Zach Braff** (*Garden State*) and **Mandy Moore** (*Saved!*) are spotted at the Chateau Marmont with 'their faces buried in each other's necks,' according to a spy ● **Liv Tyler** and her husband Royston Langdon become the proud parents of a baby boy, Milo William. That makes the Aerosmith rocker **Steven Tyler**, 56, a grandpa ● **Jude Law** gives his girlfriend **Sienna Miller** a most unusual Christmas present: a £20,000 platinum and gold engagement ring. The couple met while filming *Alfie* ● **Richard Attenborough** loses his granddaughter, Lucy, 14, his daughter Jane, and her mother-in-law in the tsunami that takes the lives of an estimated 273,800 people on the rim of the Indian Ocean on Boxing Day.

JANUARY 2005

Meet the Fockers grosses $100m in the US ● **Sandra Bullock** donates $1,000,000 to the American Red Cross to support the tsunami fund ● **Julia Roberts** buys 32 acres of prime real estate in Taos, New Mexico, adjacent to 80 acres that she already owns. Interestingly, the property is sold to her by Secretary of Defence **Donald Rumsfeld** ● The 17-year-old son of **Chris Cooper** dies of natural causes. The boy, Jesse, was born with cerebral palsy ● **Tom Cruise** displays his charitable side when, stopping to purchase an ice cream at a Diary Queen in Lexington, Virginia, he drops $6,000 into a donation box set up to raise funds for the medical costs of a local child injured in a go-carting accident ● **Brad Pitt** and **Jennifer Aniston** announce that their marriage is over after Jen reportedly catches Brad in the midst of an 'intimate' phone call with **Angelina Jolie**, his co-star from *Mr and Mrs Smith* ● *Lemony Snicket's A Series of Unfortunate*

Right: Jennifer Aniston and Brad Pitt at the Emmy Awards in September 2004

Angelina Jolie at the
Los Angeles premiere
of *Mr. and Mrs. Smith*
in June 2005

Events grosses $100m in the US ● *Meet the Fockers* grosses $200m in the US. Interestingly, the first new film to grab the number one spot in 2004 was *Along Came Polly*, also starring **Ben Stiller** ● **Nicole Kidman** discovers surveillance equipment installed outside her Sydney mansion ● After going steady for more than two years, **Orlando Bloom** and **Kate Bosworth** decide to go their separate ways. 'It was a mutual decision,' their publicist elucidates ● On a BA flight to London, **Lara Flynn Boyle** lets the free alcohol go to her head. Having divested herself of her clothes, she tries to get into the bed of a male passenger before being escorted back to her own seat. Later on the same flight she flashes her breasts at airline staff while walking to the loo.

FEBRUARY 2005

Tara Reid agrees to get married on **Ellen DeGeneres**' TV chat show if the latter's media campaign to find Tara a suitor proves successful. The actress, whose film credits include *Cruel Intentions*, *American Pie* and *Josie and the Pussycats*, says she's looking for 'a nice guy. Nice, funny, good sense of humour, cute – obviously. Just a good guy.' Tara was previously engaged to the MTV veejay **Carson Daly** ● According to *Variety*, **Pierce Brosnan** is demanding $40m to play James Bond a fifth time. However, the amount is hotly denied by sources close to the production, while Sony has expressed interest in **Clive Owen** playing the new 007 ● *Hitch* grosses $100m in the US in just over two weeks * Shocked by the negative depiction of Kim Jong II in *Team America: World Police*, the North Korean embassy in Prague approaches the Czech Ministry of Foreign Affairs to ban the film in the Central European republic. However, the Czech Ministry informs the embassy that it's not really their business.

MARCH 2005

Director **Emir Kusturica** finds himself entangled in a row involving a pigeon. In his latest film *Life is a Miracle* there is a shot of a cat pouncing on a pigeon that has upset the British censor. The BBFC argues that the two-second shot contravenes the 1937 Cinematograph Films (Animals) Act, which forbids cruelty against animals for the purpose of cinema. Kusturica, unable to appreciate the controversy, tells the *Guardian* newspaper that 'I am not cutting my film for this jerk [the censor]. What is the problem with you English? You killed millions of Indians and Africans, and yet you go nuts about the circumstances of the death of a single Serbian pigeon. I am touched you hold the lives of Serbian birds so dear, but you are crazy.' Eventually, the 'jerk' and the director come to a compromise and the film is released uncut ● **Katie Holmes** and **Chris Klein** call off their engagement. Klein wooed his former fiancée with a $500,000 diamond engagement ring back in December 2003 ● **Sandra Bullock** gets her star on the Hollywood Walk of Fame ● At the ShoWest convention in Las Vegas to plug their new movie, *Mr and Mrs Smith*, **Brad Pitt** and **Angelina Jolie** could not appear less romantic. With his hand tucked into his pocket and Angelina standing at a respectable distance, the stars refuse to give the paparazzi anything to fuel their print cartridges. Pitt's estranged wife – **Jennifer Aniston** – turns up just a few hours later to accept her honour as Female Star of the Year. **Matt Damon**, Pitt's co-star in *Ocean's Twelve*, is named Male Star of the Year. 'It's got to be tough,' notes Damon. 'Brad is as nice and as regular a guy as there is, but attention follows him everywhere' ● *The Aviator* grosses $100m in the US – after 14 weeks on release ● **Robert Blake** is acquitted of murdering his wife ● Martial arts star **Yuen Qiu**, most recently seen as the pitiless, chain-smoking landlady in *Kung Fu Hustle*, is arrested in an underground mah-jong parlour and fined for illegal gambling. An unidentified source explained that the star 'knows she did something wrong.' She pleads guilty and is fined $510 ● **Ben Affleck** reveals that he will be making his directorial debut with *Gone, Baby, Gone*, for Touchstone Pictures at Disney ● **Alicia Keys** will play her first dramatic role in a movie in *Compositions in Black and White* for Sony Pictures ● **Christian Bale** and his wife Sandra 'Sibi' Blazic are the proud parents of a baby girl ● **Bob** and **Harvey Weinstein** leave Miramax – the company they co-founded 25 years ago – and join Argo, in which they share a minority stake with **Robert De Niro**.

APRIL 2005

Robots grosses $100m in the US • *Meet the Fockers* grosses $500m worldwide • **Joaquin Phoenix** voluntarily checks into an undisclosed rehabilitation centre to combat 'alcohol abuse problems'. The actor's publicist says that by going public Phoenix hoped to set an example for others who needed to get help. His

brother, **River Phoenix**, died of a drug overdose in 1993 • **Vincent Pastore** – who plays Big Pussy in HBO's *The Sopranos* – is charged with assaulting his girlfriend, Lisa Regina. Allegedly, he punched her in the head and then threw her out of his car by the hair. Pastore is well known for his hulking presence

in such films as *GoodFellas*, *Carlito's Way* and *Mickey Blue Eyes* • *Hitch* grosses $300m worldwide • Word leaks out that **Ben Affleck** and **Jennifer Garner** are engaged, although the couple have made no official announcement • **Beyoncé Knowles** is set to star in the film adaptation of the Broadway

Third time lucky? Tom Cruise with his future bride, Katie Holmes, in June 2005

musical *Dreamgirls* ● **Brad Pitt** visits Ethiopia and South Africa as a celebrity ambassador for DATA, a campaign set up by **Bono** to promote Aids awareness. However, while there he and **Angelina Jolie** are photographed playing on a beach together with Angelina's son, Maddox ● *The Pacifier* grosses $100m in the US ● New Yorker **Woody Allen**, who has famously refused to work outside the Big Apple for almost all his films (a notable exception being *Everyone Says I Love You*) completed *Match Point* in August of last year, which was shot entirely in London. Now Woody announces that his next picture – as yet untitled – will also be filmed in the Big Smoke, again utilising a British cast and crew ● After being photographed canoodling on the fly, **Tom** Cruise and Katie Holmes go public with their affections moments before Cruise picks up his Lifetime Achievement award at the David di Donatello ceremony in Rome, the Italian equivalent of the Oscars. Holmes, who plays Rachel Dawes in *Batman Begins*, was previously engaged to the actor **Chris Klein**.

MAY 2005

On her second day in London to make a film, *Last Holiday*, **Alicia Witt** samples a beer garden in Notting Hill Gate. However, the actress is rushed to hospital when a cat falls out of a window and lands on her head, claws first ● **Renée Zellweger** marries country singer **Kenny Chesney** on the Virgin island of St John, Chesney's home. The couple met in January at a tsunami relief benefit ● It's official: **Jennifer Garner** is pregnant and **Ben Affleck** is the father ● **Cate Blanchett** borrows a private jet to whisk her one-year-old son to London to visit a top burns specialist. The actress was filming the drama *Babel* in Morocco when her son, Roman, was burned in an accident ● **Macaulay Culkin** testifies in court that he was never the victim of molestation at the hands of **Michael Jackson**. However, he admits that he slept in Jackson's bed, but added that he used to fall asleep all over Jackson's Neverland ranch ● *Star Wars*: Episode III *Revenge of the Sith* smashes box-office records, grossing an unprecedented $50m on its opening day in the US. However, its $108.5m weekend gross falls shy of the almighty $115.8m racked up by *Spider-Man 2* in 2004 ● *Star Wars*: Episode III *Revenge of the Sith* grosses $144.7 million in its first five days across the world (excluding the US), eclipsing the previous record set by *The Lord of the Rings: The Return of the King* ● In its first week, *Star Wars*: Episode III *Revenge of the Sith* scores $191.4m at the US box-office ● **Rupert Everett** receives a reputed £1,000,000 advance from Time Warner for the rights to his self-penned autobiography. It's a huge sum for an actor not on the A-list, although Everett has the inside track on **Princess Margaret**, **Paula Yates** and **Madonna** and started out as a male prostitute. Could make interesting reading ● **Lindsay Lohan** suffers cuts and bruises when her car is rammed by a pursuing photographer. She reveals that 'I was so shaken up, but I was still nice 'cause I was like, "I understand it's your job. But you don't have to ram into me next time. I'll give you a picture."'

JUNE 2005

Million Dollar Baby grosses $100m at the US box-office ● *Madagascar* grosses $100m at the US box-office ● *The Longest Yard* grosses $100m at the US box-office ● **Corin Redgrave** suffers a heart attack while campaigning for the rights of travellers in Basildon, Essex. The actor is resuscitated by specially trained police officers ● **Tom Cruise** displays an uncharacteristic side of his nature when, on **Oprah Winfrey**'s TV chat show, he jumps on a sofa, wrestles with his hostess, punches the air and shouts, 'I'm in love, I'm in love.' Apparently, the behaviour so worries executives at Paramount that they consider pulling the plug on *Mission: Impossible III* ● Following the enormous success of his impersonation of **Paul Michael Glaser** in *Starsky and Hutch*, **Ben Stiller** is up for the film version of the semi-cult TV series *The Persuaders!*. Stiller will play **Tony Curtis** and **Steve Coogan** will be **Roger Moore** ● An employee of the Mercer Hotel in SoHo, New York, requires stitches after being hit in the face by a phone thrown by **Russell Crowe**. Crowe, enraged that he couldn't place a call to his wife in Australia, is arrested and charged with second-degree assault and third-degree criminal possession of a 'weapon' ● After eight years of dating, **Alicia Silverstone** ties the knot with boyfriend Christopher Jarecki, lead singer of the neo-punk band S.T.U.N. The couple exchange their vows barefoot beside Lake Tahoe ● **Tom Cruise** proposes to **Katie Holmes** on the Eiffel Tower ● *Mr. and Mrs. Smith* grosses $100m in the US – in just over a week ● In a brief respite from the Tom-Katie show, the tabloids home in on photographs of **Jennifer Aniston** and **Vince Vaughn** getting down and intimate.

Movie Quotations of the Year

Alexander the Great, expressing the unwelcome debt he feels towards his mother: 'It's a high ransom she charges for lodging nine months in her womb.' Colin Farrell in *Alexander*

Liz, opening a bottle of the green stuff: 'You know what they say. Absinthe makes the heart grow fonder.' Susan Sarandon in *Alfie*

Brian Fantana, in a rare moment of confidentiality: 'I loved a woman once. She was Brazilian. Or Chinese. Something weird.' Paul Rudd in *Anchorman: The Legend of Ron Burgundy*

Gangster kingpin Marion Bishop: 'Marcus is still alive. I find this unacceptable.' Laurence Fishburne in *Assault on Precinct 13*

Rachel Dawes: 'Justice is about harmony; revenge is about you making you feel better.' Katie Holmes in *Batman Begins*

Henri Ducard: 'To conquer fear you must become fear – and what men fear most is what they cannot see.' Liam Neeson in *Batman Begins*

Carmine Falcone, to corrupt cop: 'Don't burden yourself with the secrets of scary people.' Tom Wilkinson in *Batman Begins*

Bruce Wayne to Alfred, his butler: 'Keep the guests happy until I arrive. Tell them that joke you know.' Christian Bale to Michael Caine in *Batman Begins*

Alfred to Bruce Wayne: 'Why do we fall? So we can learn how to pick ourselves up.' Michael Caine to Christian Bale in *Batman Begins*

Henri Ducard: 'Gentlemen, time to spread the word. And the word is panic.' Liam Neeson in *Batman Begins*
Batman, to Rachel Dawes: 'It's not what I am underneath, it's what I do that defines me.' Christian Bale in *Batman Begins*

Movie star Jack Wyatt, getting amorous with co-star Isabel Bigelow: 'Let's make love in a petting zoo!' Will Ferrell to Nicole Kidman in *Bewitched*

A muddled Aunt Martha: 'It looks like Thursday's gone missing with last October.' Zoë Wanamaker in *Five Children and It*

Coach Gary Gaines, giving his high school football team a pep talk before the Big Game: 'Being perfect is not about that scoreboard out there. It's not about winning. It's about you and your relationship with yourself, your family and your friends. Being perfect is about being able to look your friends in the eye and know that you didn't let them down because you told them the truth. And that truth is you did everything you could. There wasn't one more thing you could've done. Can you live in that moment as best you can, with clear eyes, and love in your heart, with joy in your heart? If you can do that gentleman – you're perfect.' Billy Bob Thornton in *Friday Night Lights*

Advice from date doctor Alex 'Hitch' Hitchens: 'Begin each day as if it was on purpose.' Will Smith in *Hitch*

Alex 'Hitch' Hitchens: 'Any guy can sweep any girl off her feet, he just needs the right broom.' Will Smith in *Hitch*

Vance's pick-up line to Sara Melas: 'I couldn't help but notice, you look an awful lot like my next girlfriend.' Jeffrey Donovan in *Hitch*

Hitch, making a toast: 'Never lie, steal, cheat, or drink. But if you must lie, lie in the arms of the one you love. If you must steal, steal away from bad company. If you must cheat, cheat death. And if you must drink, drink in the moments that take your breath away.' Will Smith in *Hitch*

A desperate Albert Brennaman, who's taking his unrequited love of Allegra Cole very seriously: 'I've waited my whole life to feel this miserable.' Kevin James to Will Smith in *Hitch*

Carlton Morrow to his little brother Bobby: 'We'll find you a woman in the sixth grade. A woman with a little experience.' Ryan Donowho to Andrew Chalmers in *A Home at the End of the World*

Dan Foreman, on the phone to his daughter's new boyfriend: 'I want you to know that if you ever give my daughter an alcoholic beverage or a joint, I shall hunt you down and neuter you.' Dennis Quaid in *In Good Company*

Alex Foreman, who's embarking on a university course in creative writing: 'I'm cursed with a functional family.' Scarlett Johansson in *In Good Company*

Mortie: 'My wife got a promotion. I'm hoping she'll raise my allowance.' David Paymer in *In Good Company*

A grateful Carter Duryea, to Dan Foreman: 'Nobody took the time to give me a hard time before.' Topher Grace in *In Good Company*

Penguin, surveying the windswept wasteland of Antarctica for the first time: 'Well, this sucks.' From *Madagascar*

An elderly Michael Jesperson, explaining to his grown-up daughter about his new love: 'Maybe I needed 70 years of life to be ready for a woman like Ellen.' Hector Elias in *Me and You and Everyone We Know*

Jane Smith, to marriage counsellor: 'There's this huge space between us and it keeps filling up with everything we don't say to each other.' Angelina Jolie, being serious, in *Mr. and Mrs. Smith*

Detective Sadusky, snapping at his tongue-tied assistant: 'This is not a day for 'um…'.' Harvey Keitel in *National Treasure*

Beverly Clark, emphasising one virtue of marriage: 'We need a witness to our lives. There's a billion people on the planet … I mean, what does any one life really mean? But in a marriage, you're promising to care about everything. The good things, the bad things, the terrible things, the mundane things … all of it, all of the time, every day. You're saying, "Your life will not go unnoticed because I will notice it. Your life will not go un-witnessed because I will be your witness".' Susan Sarandon in *Shall We Dance*

Maya, using her love of wine as foreplay: 'I like to think about the life of wine – how it's a living thing. I like to think about what was going on the year the grapes were growing, how the sun was shining that summer. I think about all those people who tended and picked the grapes … I love how wine continues to evolve, how every time I open a bottle it's going to taste different than if I had opened it on any other day. Because a bottle of wine is actually alive; it's constantly evolving and gaining complexity. And it tastes so fucking good.' Virginia Madsen in *Sideways*

Yoda: 'The fear of loss is a path to the Dark Side.' Frank Oz in *Star Wars: Episode III Revenge of the Sith*

Yoda: 'Train yourself to let go of everything you fear to lose.' Frank Oz

in *Star Wars: Episode III Revenge of the Sith*

Supreme Chancellor Palpatine: 'Good is a point of view.' Ian McDiarmid in *Star Wars: Episode III Revenge of the Sith*

Yoda: 'Destroy the Sith we must.' Frank Oz in *Star Wars: Episode III Revenge of the Sith*

Ray Ferrier to his son and daughter: 'We're leaving this house in 60 seconds.' Tom Cruise in *War of the Worlds*

Ray Ferrier, trying to explain the killing machine to his kids: 'It came from someplace else.' Robbie: 'What? From Europe?' Tom Cruise and Justin Chatwin in *War of the Worlds*

An unsettled Ogilvy: 'This is not a war, any more than a war between men and maggots. This is an extermination.' Tim Robbins in *War of the Worlds*

An unsettled Ogilvy: 'I'm dead-set on living.' Tim Robbins in *War of the Worlds*

Kat, introducing her mother to her new 'date': 'Mom, this is *so* not the time to be yourself.' Debra Messing to Holland Taylor in *The Wedding Date*

T.J., having just seen Nick Mercer for the first time: 'Oh God – I think I just came.' Sarah Parish in *The Wedding Date*

Kat, to male escort Nick Mercer: 'Getting your phone number was harder than getting into college.' Debra Messing to Dermot Mulroney in *The Wedding Date*

Kat, to Nick: 'I've been spilling my guts all weekend and I don't know anything about you.' Nick: 'I'm allergic to fabric softener, and I majored in comparative literature at Brown. I hate anchovies and I think I'd miss you even if we'd never met.' Dermot Mulroney in *The Wedding Date*

T.J. to Kat and Nick: 'The only thing you have in common is that you both secretly lust after me.' Sarah Parish in *The Wedding Date*

Nick, to Kat, after their first argument has died down: 'I'd rather fight with you than make love to anybody else.' Dermot Mulroney in *The Wedding Date*

Walter's therapist Rosen, on the virtues of recapitulation: 'By going round in circles, sometimes we find things we have missed the first time round.' Michael Shannon in *The Woodsman*

Prison escapee Darius Stone, explaining his premature release from the slammer: 'They let me out early for bad behaviour.' Ice Cube in *xXx 2: The Next Level*

Off-screen – or, what four celebrities said without the aid of a scriptwriter

'I can't remember how many hours a year a person uses being in their car in LA, but it's, like, a lot of time.' An informative **Kate Bosworth**

'When I go to a big dinner party, the first thing I do is try to sneak off to the kitchen to see if I can take over the dishwashing. There are few things I enjoy as much as washing dishes.' An accommodating **Willem Dafoe**

'With my sunglasses on, I'm Jack Nicholson. Without them, I'm fat and 60.' **Jack Nicholson**

'In some way I failed to communicate his [Alexander's] story properly. I still think it's a beautiful movie, but Alexander deserved better than I gave him.' Director **Oliver Stone**, apologising for his critically eviscerated *Alexander*

And a couple of choice lines from the critics…

'About as lively and funny as a busy day down at the crematorium … Depression seeps out of the screen like carbon monoxide.' Peter Bradshaw reviewing *Fat Slags* in the *Guardian*

'*Alexander* is full of brilliant highlights, and they're all in Colin Farrell's hair.' Wesley Morris reviewing *Alexander* in the *Boston Globe*

Soundtracks

This year the veteran composer **John Williams** secured his 43rd Oscar nomination. So, not a lot has changed then. Has it? While Williams was short-listed for his music to *Harry Potter and the Prisoner of Azkaban*, it was at least his best work for the HP franchise. And it was the supremely talented **Jan A.P. Kaczmarek** from Poland who walked away with the statuette – for his enchanting score to *Finding Neverland*. But then **John Debney** was also nominated, for *The Passion of the Christ*, although this was probably because Mel Gibson's film was exotic and a lot of voters had seen it. As it happens, Debney's music was full of clichés and had the usual compliment of trembling violins, choruses of wailing fishwives and that old movie staple, the duduk (you'd be surprised how often the duduk creeps into these things). With the recent fondness for historical epics, one might have hoped for something more inspirational, but **James Horner**'s *Troy*, **Harry Gregson-Williams**' *Kingdom of Heaven* and even **Vangelis**' *Alexander* were all much of a muchness.

However, after the drought of decent film music last year, the 2004-2005 period was a decided improvement. Surprisingly, one of the best scores of the year came from the creative well of **Mick Jagger** and **Dave A. Stewart**, who worked wonders with the sonic landscape of *Alfie*, otherwise a mediocre film. There were others, too: the classic collaboration of **Hans Zimmer** and **James Newton Howard** on *Batman Begins*, a spot-on pastiche from **Mark Mothersbaugh** for Wes Anderson's *The Life Aquatic with Steve Zissou* and another

resonant musical banquet from **Mychael Danna**, who added much spice to Mira Nair's *Vanity Fair*. Otherwise, the year's finest soundtracks were musicals, compilations or works from lesser-known composers. Of the last named, the most promising figures were the British **Richard G. Mitchell** (*A Good Woman*), **Nigel Hess** (*Ladies in Lavender*), **John Murphy** (*Millions*) and in particular **Alex Heffes**, whose subtle, delicate score to *Dear Frankie* is something really special.

As usual, the other best soundtracks were from abroad and included *The Motorcycle Diaries*, *House of Flying Daggers*, *A Very Long Engagement*, *The Chorus* and *2046*. But, if you were to put an AK47 against my head, I'd have to say that my favourite soundtracks of the year (at least, those I played most often) were *Ray*, *De-Lovely* and *Pride & Prejudice*, the latter a sumptuous, exquisite composition from the Italian **Dario Marianelli**.

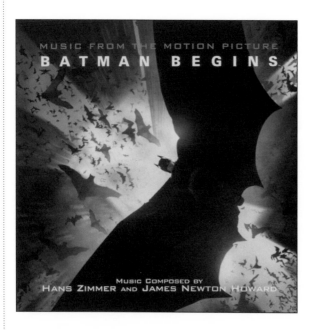

Alexander

After a hiatus of 12 years (not counting his score for the little-seen Greek film *Kavafis*, 1996), Vangelis returns to the international stage with a score that seems to emulate the new fashion for pre-historical epics. That is, there are a whole lot of drums, celestial choirs and bleating horns. One just expected a little bit more, something a tad original, from the man who brought us *Chariots of Fire* and *Blade Runner*. Having said that, there are a handful of striking tracks, notably the slight but unreal 'Bagoa's Dance', the stirring, bellicose 'The Drums of Guagamela' and the rousing anthem 'Eternal Alexander.' Still, this is not enough to applaud a return to form for the Greek master.

Alfie

With **Dave A. Stewart** and **Mick Jagger** cooking up a funky, atmospheric score – right up there with *The Graduate* and *Pat Garrett and Billy the Kid* as one of the great pop soundtracks of all time – this is an instant classic.
Stand-out tracks include the Jagger songs 'Let's Make It Up' and 'Blind Leading the Blind', while teen sensation Joss Stone obliterates memories of Cilla Black with the title song.

Batman Begins

For a thumping, full-blown Gothic score to the new, all-profound Batman redux you couldn't do much better than this. A joint effort by two of Hollywood's most accomplished composers, Hans Zimmer and James Newton Howard, it is Gilbert and Sullivan in hell, without the lyrics. Accompanied by blasts of bat-propelled flutter, the whole thing is so orgiastically momentous that you can't help but get sucked into the holy vortex.

Beyond the Sea

Kevin Spacey is a resourceful entertainer but he outdoes himself with this rousing biog of crooner Bobby Darin. Silkily embodying the professional ease of his idol, Spacey is an uncanny doppelgänger, bringing a seductive, velvet design to some great, stirring standards. Of course, if you don't like Bobby Darin…

Bridget Jones: The Edge of Reason

Beneath the same old same old – Kylie, Barry White, Minnie Riperton, 10cc – there are a number of noteworthy tracks crammed onto this 20-track CD. Largely cover-driven, the covers are at least more interesting than hearing Carly Simon declaring 'Nobody Does it Better' for the 1,111th time. Amy Winehouse brings exquisite agony to 'Will You Still Love Me Tomorrow' and Mary J. Blige rewrites 'Sorry Seems To Be the Hardest Word' with conviction. More Blige and less bilge would've been nice.

The Chorus

This is a consummate combination of a rich incidental score (composed by **Bruno Coulais** and the film's director, **Christophe Barratier**) with original songs performed by the young, euphonious cast of what is really a wonderful film. There's also some of the original (French) dialogue, which completes a perfect memento of a glorious musical experience. Heaven on a disc.

Dear Frankie

This is a small miracle in that it is a delightful composition that lightly touches the heart without wringing the tear ducts dry. In fact, one of the many reasons that the film works so well is because it isn't swamped by music. Composer **Alex Heffes** (*Touching the Void*) has a real ear for the subtle melody, at his best when he's coaxing a gentle smile out of the piano. The brief extract from Arvo Pärt's 'Spiegel im Spiegel' is unnecessary, but hearing Jack McElhone as Frankie (writing to his 'da') is an additional delight.

The Definitive Blues Brothers Collection

Despite John Belushi's early demise, the music of the Blues Brothers has never really gone away. From the jazzy 'Soul Man' at university gigs to 'Everybody Needs Somebody to Love' at many a wedding reception, the legacy lives on. Whether you think of this two-disc collection of 35 fun tracks as nostalgia or as classic rocking blues, it is unquestionably great party music.

De-Lovely

Sublime is really the only way to describe this compilation. They don't make 'em like they used to, but they sure know how to jazz up an old standard – and here a generous dollop of the cream of today's songsters pay polished tribute to **Cole Porter**. The lyrics still resonate and amuse and Kevin Kline, Sheryl Crow, Alanis Morissette, Elvis Costello, Diana Krall, Natalie Cole, Mick Hucknall and even Cole Porter himself really do them justice.

Finding Neverland

An appropriately magical work from the great Polish composer Jan A.P. Kaczmarek, this won the Oscar for Best Original Music. Kaczmarek, who's written beautiful scores for the likes of *Washington Square*, *Aimée & Jaguar* and *Unfaithful*, has picked a simple melody here and by guiding it through various musical transformations, provides a strong emotive thrust to this wonderful film. The playful piano recitals are deftly performed by Leszek Mozdzer.

Garden State

A truly hip, mellow and agreeable collection of songs; as Natalie Portman says in the movie, 'You gotta hear these songs, they will change your life, I promise you.' All good stuff, from Coldplay, The Shins, Nick Drake, Cary Brothers, Simon & Garfunkel, Iron and Wine, and Bonnie Somerville. One to keep in the glove compartment.

A Good Woman

The film was not much cop, but beyond its artistic and dramatic failings the soundtrack – composed by **Richard G. Mitchell** – positively soars. Buttressed with operatic highlights and choice period songs, the score wafts around like vivid flurries of sunshine and bonhomie. Definitely one to put on when one's spirits are low.

The Hitchhiker's Guide to the Galaxy

With 33 tracks, this ambitious soundtrack does provide considerable pleasure, which is more than can be said for the film. It's quite a resourceful, enterprising work from **Joby Talbot**, while the comic notes actually work better on CD than in the film (music should not have to force an audience to laugh – something's either funny or it isn't).

Hotel Rwanda

Evocative collection of African hymns, including such legends as South Africa's Yvonne Chaka Chaka and Uganda's Bernard Kabanda. It's a pity, then, that the flagship song, the Golden Globe-nominated *Million Voices* - performed by Wyclef Jean against a tide of children's voices – is such a banal, sentimental ballad.

House of Flying Daggers

Epic, elegiac, exotic, mysterious, dreamy and thrilling, this is one of the year's most outstanding soundtracks. Its strength is that it doesn't fall back on a single motif, but unveils a panoramic spectacle of dramatic sounds and melodies, from frenetic percussion to the sweetness of the bamboo flute. Japan's Shigeru Umebayashi, who also scored Wong Kar-wai's *2046*, puts it all together.

Ladies in Lavender

It's unfair on other soundtracks to have a violinist as a leading character and even more unfair to have the immortal Joshua Bell fiddling his strings. And this is euphonious stuff, penned by the English composer Nigel Hess, with a dash of Debussy and Paganini for good measure. But there's also some fine piano, performed by Hess himself, along with sprightly contributions from Simon Mulligan.

Layer Cake

This is not in the same league as Guy Ritchie's opening double salvo, but there's some good stuff here. Lisa Gerrard and Ilan Eshkeri's electronic score is certainly moody and compelling and there's a mesmerising track from Craig Armstrong, as well as top work from Duran Duran ('Ordinary World'), Joe Cocker and Starsailor. On the debit side, there's Kylie Minogue going on about how 'I just can't get you out of my head... la la la la la la la la' and none of the cheeky chat that made *Lock, Stock...* and *Snatch* so endearing.

Lemony Snicket's A Series of Unfortunate Events

A playful alloy of the sinister and the childlike, this earned **Thomas Newman** his seventh Oscar nomination. Setting the mood with the cynically twisted 'The Bad Beginning' (in which a child's giggle and jolly chorus is cut short by a scratched stylus), the score unfolds into a gallimaufry of magical, frenetic and menacing sounds.

The Life Aquatic with Steve Zissou

What the film misses in comic tone, its soundtrack more than makes up for. With rough and ready covers of Bowie performed in Portuguese by the idiosyncratic Seu Jorge, the album is on a winning streak. But there is also a rich, off-centre and jokey score from **Mark Mothersbaugh** and some choice cuts from Joan Baez, The Zombies, Scott Walker and, yes, David Bowie.

Madagascar

A rather jaunty soundtrack, this, and one that scored in the US album charts. Besides a sprightly, tongue-in-cheek score by the ever resourceful and prolific **Hans Zimmer**, there's Earth, Wind & Fire's 'Boogie Wonderland' and The Bee Gees' 'Stayin' Alive.' There are also extended versions of *Hawaii Five-0*, *Chariots of Fire* and *Born Free*, used as comic cues in the movie. Fun, fun, fun.

The Merchant of Venice

Depending on one's mood, this is either a depressing, monotonous drone or a spiritually pure crystallisation of 16th century Venice. **Jocelyn Pook**'s authentic score (utilising the cornet, dulcimer, hurdy-gurdy, krumhorn, serpent and theorbo) certainly serves Michael Radford's film well, but for an accompaniment to what is classed as one of Shakespeare's comedies, it is relentlessly dour in the listening. The 17-year-old soprano Hayley Westenra supplies the exquisite 'Bridal Ballad'.

Millions

John Murphy, best known for scoring *Lock, Stock...* and *Snatch*, really does know how to summon up the magic in his music. Just listening to Murphy's ethereal score to this undervalued gem sends shivers of awe and expectation down the spine. Whether utilising piano, string section, xylophone or choir, Murphy turns pure notes into aural rhapsody. In addition there's Muse, Feeder, The Clash and a soaring, magical anthem from Bosco – 'Nirvana' - that cements the essence of the film.

The Motorcycle Diaries

Strong on Spanish guitar and pulsating with Latin beats, this musical diary of Che Guevara is a flavoursome tour of the South American continent. Suffused with passion, pathos and even profundity, this is another resonant score from the Argentinean producer/songwriter **Gustavo Santaolalla**. And all this spiced with songs from María Esther Zamora, Dámasco Pérez Prado and Jorge Drexler.

The Notebook

Lush as an Ewok's armpit, this really knows how to coat the listener in a lachrymose film of glucose. In other words, it's a good old-fashioned wallow in all things romantic, along with bursts of choice period cuts courtesy of Billie Holiday, Duke Ellington, Glenn Miller, Jimmy Durante... **Aaron Zigman** pulls the strings.

The Phantom of the Opera

Handsome, epic two-CD deluxe gift box, with Andrew Lloyd Webber's towering score spread over two hours of music, song, connecting dialogue and that ghastly new ballad ('Learn to be Lonely') thrown away by Minnie Driver. A really handsome effort, a keepsake that does the film more than justice.

The Polar Express

A heady combination of the banal, crass and uplifting, this tribute to all things magical and Christmassy reflects all the virtues and pitfalls of the film. The new songs are best skipped over (save for the simplistic but effective *Believe*), while the soaring music of Alan Silvestri can grab you by the heart (if you're in the right mood). And then there's all that wonderfully kitsch stuff from Bing, Perry and Sinatra.

Pride & Prejudice

Following on from his striking scores to *The Warrior* and *I Capture the Castle*, **Dario Marianelli** outdoes himself with this exquisite hymn to Jane Austen. With the legendary Jean Yves-Thibaudet banging out some delightful melodies on piano, the English Chamber Orchestra captures the heady, romantic rush of Marianelli's music with aplomb. Mournful, touching, profound and quite irresistible.

Raging Bull

Brought out to coincide with the 25th anniversary DVD release of Martin Scorsese's 1980 film, this 37-track two-CD set is a small miracle. As usual, Scorsese manages to define an era without plumping for the obvious, so that for every 'Whispering Grass' and 'Blue Velvet' he has a little gem you won't have heard before (such as Ella Fitzgerald & The Ink Spots' 'Cow-Cow Boogie'). There's also De Niro doing his Jake LaMotta schtick, adding to the atmosphere of a splendid document of a genuine classic.

Ray

Seventeen tracks of pure gold as 'the Genius' gets down to boogie. Running the gamut from soul and gospel to jazz and pop, the album even includes live cuts from the star's own private archive. And that's where the album really comes into its own. A fitting tribute to the Master.

Team America: World Police

There's a substantial line between wit and the incorrigible. While the lyrics on this audacious

musical satire prompt the occasional chuckle ('I need you like Ben Affleck needs acting school'), it's the muscular audacity of **Harry Gregson-Williams'** military braggadocio and po-faced love ballads that secure a more permanent smile. An absolute hoot.

2046

As much a character in the film as its love-worn protagonists, this sensual storm of changeable sound sweeps the listener into a hallucinogenic dream. A sensually Western experience, the film's bluesy, soulful airs are the musings of Japan's **Shigeru Umebayashi**. On top of this, director Wong Kar-wai has blended in snippets of other film music, opera, Nat King Cole and a haunting ballad from Connie Francis. A heady cocktail. Interestingly, the accompanying booklet contains nary a word.

Two Brothers

An unexpected pleasure from the Southampton-born composer

Stephen Warbeck, this melodic rhapsody is every bit as rich and sumptuous as the visuals it accompanies. Running the gamut from the majestic and sweeping to the playful and contemplative, it is quite as beguiling as the tiger cubs it escorts.

Vanity Fair

Drawing on his characteristic range of the resonant, dramatic and mystical, **Mychael Danna** is the perfect choice to infuse this typically English story with a dash of the Eastern. Director Mira Nair previously engaged Danna's services for her *Karma Sutra* and *Monsoon Wedding*, and here they collaborate again on introducing the exotic. Better still, though, are the simple pieces on piano, augmented by Custer LaRue's haunting voice (standing in the for the larynges of Reese Witherspoon).

Awards and Festivals

Leonardo DiCaprio and Gwen Stefani in Martin Scorsese's multi-Oscar-winning *The Aviator*

The 77th American Academy of Motion Picture Arts and Sciences Awards ('The Oscars') and Nominations for 2004, 27

February 2005
• **Best Film**: *Million Dollar Baby*.
Nominations: *The Aviator*; *Finding Neverland*; *Ray*; *Sideways*.
• **Best Director**: Clint Eastwood, for *Million Dollar Baby*.
Nominations: Taylor Hackford, for *Ray*; Mike Leigh, for *Vera Drake*; Alexander Payne, for *Sideways*; Martin Scorsese, for *The Aviator*.
• **Best Actor**: Jamie Foxx, for *Ray*.
Nominations: Don Cheadle, for *Hotel Rwanda*; Johnny Depp, for *Finding Neverland*; Leonardo DiCaprio, for *The Aviator*; Clint Eastwood, for *Million Dollar Baby*.
• **Best Actress**: Hilary Swank, for *Million Dollar Baby*.
Nominations: Annette Bening, for *Being Julia*; Catalina Sandino Moreno, for *María Full of Grace*; Imelda Staunton, for *Vera*

Drake; Kate Winslet, for *Eternal Sunshine of the Spotless Mind*.
• **Best Supporting Actor**: Morgan Freeman, for *Million Dollar Baby*.
Nominations: Alan Alda, for *The Aviator*; Thomas Haden Church, for *Sideways*; Jamie Foxx, for *Collateral*; Clive Owen, for *Closer*.
• **Best Supporting Actress**: Cate Blanchett, for *The Aviator*.
Nominations: Laura Linney, for *Kinsey*; Virginia Madsen, for *Sideways*; Sophie Okonedo, for *Hotel Rwanda*; Natalie Portman, for *Closer*.
• **Best Animated Feature**: *The Incredibles*.
Nominations: *Shark Tale*; *Shrek 2*.
• **Best Original Screenplay**:
Charlie Kaufman, for *Eternal Sunshine of the Spotless Mind*.
Nominations: John Logan, for *The Aviator*; Terry George, for *Hotel Rwanda*; Brad Bird, for *The Incredibles*; Mike Leigh, for *Vera Drake*.
• **Best Screenplay Adaptation**: Alexander Payne and Jim Taylor, for *Sideways*.
Nominations: Richard Linklater, Julie Delpy and Ethan Hawke for *Before Sunset*; David Magee, for *Finding Neverland*; Paul

Haggis, for *Million Dollar Baby*; José Rivera, for *The Motorcycle Diaries*.
• **Best Cinematography**: Robert Richardson, for *The Aviator*.
Nominations: Zhao Xiaoding, for *House of Flying Daggers*; Caleb Deschanel, for *The Passion of the Christ*; John Mathieson, for *The Phantom of the Opera*; Bruno Delbonnel, for *A Very Long Engagement*.
• **Best Editing**: Thelma Schoonmaker, for *The Aviator*. Nominations: Jim Miller and Paul Rubell, for *Collateral*; Matt Chesse, for *Finding Neverland*; Joel Cox, for *Million Dollar Baby*; Paul Hirsch, for *Ray*.
• **Best Original Score**: Jan A.P. Kaczmarek, for *Finding Neverland*.
Nominations: John Debney, for *The Passion of the Christ*; James Newton Howard, for *The Village*; Thomas Newman, for *Lemony Snicket's A Series of Unfortunate Events*; John Williams, for *Harry Potter and the Prisoner of Azkaban*.
• **Best Original Song**: 'Al otro lado del río' (On the Other Side of the River), by Jorge Drexler, from *The Motorcycle Diaries*. Nominations: 'Accidentally in Love' by

Left: Jamie Foxx in his Oscar-winning performance as *Ray* Charles

Right: The BAFTA-winning Clive Owen in *Closer*

Adam Duritz, Charles Gillingham, Jim Bogios, David Immergluck, Matthew Mallery and David Bryson (music) and Duritz and Daniel Vickrey (lyrics), from *Shrek 2*; 'Believe' by Glen Ballard and Alan Silvestri, from *The Polar Express*; 'Learn To Be Lonely' by Andrew Lloyd Webber (music) and Charles Hart (lyrics), from *The Phantom of the Opera*; 'Look to Your Path' by Bruno Coulais (music) and Christophe Barratier (lyrics), from *The Chorus*.
• **Best Art Direction**: Dante Ferretti (art), Francesca Lo Schiavo (set), for *The Aviator*.
Nominations: Gemma Jackson (art), Trisha Edward (set), for *Finding Neverland*; Rick Heinrichs (art), Cheryl A. Carasik (set), for *Lemony Snicket's A Series of Unfortunate Events*; Anthony Pratt (art), Celia Bobak (set), for *The Phantom of the Opera*; Aline Bonetto, for *A Very Long Engagement*.
• **Best Costume Design**: Sandy Powell, for *The Aviator*.
Nominations: Alexandra Byrne, for *Finding Neverland*; Colleen Atwood, for *Lemony Snicket's A Series of Unfortunate Events*; Sharen Davis, for *Ray*; Bob Ringwood, for *Troy*.
• **Best Sound Editing**: Michael Silvers, for *The Incredibles*.
Nominations: *The Polar Express*; *Spider-Man 2*.

• **Best Sound Mixing**: Scott Millan, Greg Orloff, Bob Beemer and Steve Cantamessa, for *Ray*.
Nominations: *The Aviator*; *The Incredibles*; *The Polar Express*; *Spider-Man 2*.
• **Best Make-Up**: Valli O'Reilly and Bill Corso, for *Lemony Snicket's A Series of Unfortunate Events*.
Nominations: *The Passion of the Christ*; *The Sea Inside*.
• **Best Visual Effects**: John Dykstra, Scott Stokdyk, Anthony LaMolinara and John Frazier, for *Spider-Man 2*.
Nominations: *Harry Potter and the Prisoner of Azkaban*; *I, Robot*.
• **Best Animated Short Film**: *Ryan*, by Chris Landreth.
Nominations: *Birthday Boy*; *Gopher Broke*; *Guard Dog*; *Lorenzo*.
• **Best Live Action Short Film**: *Wasp*, by Andrea Arnold.
Nominations: *Everything in This Country Must*; *Little Terrorist*; *7:35 in the Morning*; *Two Cars, One Night*.
• **Best Documentary Feature**: *Born Into Brothels: Calcutta's Red Light Kid*, by Ross Kauffman and Zana Briski.
Nominations: *The Story of the Weeping Camel*; *Super Size Me*; *Tupac: Resurrection*; *Twist of Faith*.

• **Best Documentary Short**: *Mighty Times: The Children's March*, by Robert Hudson and Bobby Houston.
Nominations: *Autism is a World*; *The Children of Leningradsky*; *Hardwood*; *Sister Rose's Passion*.
• **Best Foreign Language Film**: *The Sea Inside* (Spain/France/Italy).
Nominations: *As It Is In Heaven* (Sweden); *The Chorus* (France); *Downfall* (Germany); *Yesterday* (South Africa).
• **Honorary Award**: Sidney Lumet.

Australian Film Critics' Circle Awards: Sydney, 7 November 2004

• **Best Film**: *Somersault*.
• **Best Actor**: Colin Friels, for *Tom White*.
• **Best Actress**: Abbie Cornish, for *Somersault*.
• **Best Supporting Actor**: Dan Spielman, for *Tom White*.
• **Best Supporting Actress**: Lynette Curran, for *Somersault*.
• **Best Director**: Cate Shortland, for *Somersault*.
• **Best Original Screenplay**: Daniel Keene, for *Tom White*.
• **Best Screenplay Adaptation**: Rolf De Heer, for *The Old Man Who Told Love Stories*.
• **Best Cinematography**: Robert Humphreys, for *Somersault*.
• **Best Editing**: Ken Sallows, for *Tom White*.
• **Best Music**: David Hobson, Josh Abrahams and Lisa Gerrard, for *One Perfect Day*.
Acknowledgement of Emerging Talent: Sejong Park, writer-director of *Birthday Boy*.
• **Best Foreign Language Film**: *The Barbarian Invasions* (Canada).
• **Best Foreign Film - English Language**: *Lost In Translation* (USA).
• **Best Feature Documentary**: *The Men Who Would Conquer China*.
• **Best Documentary** (under 60 minutes): *Mr Patterns*.
• **Best Short Film**: *Birthday Boy*, written and directed by Sejong Park.

The 55th Berlin International Film Festival: 19 February 2005

• **Golden Bear for Best Film**: *Carmen in Khayelitsha* (South Africa).
• **Silver Bear, Jury Grand Prize**: *Peacock* (China).
• **Silver Bear for Best Director**: Marc Rothemund, for *Sophie Scholl – The Final Days* (Germany).
• **Silver Bear, Best Actor**: Lou Taylor Pucci, for *Thumbsucker* (USA).
• **Silver Bear, Best Actress**: Julia Jentsch, for *Sophie Scholl – The Final Days*.
• **Blue Angel Prize**: *Paradise Now* (France/Germany/Netherlands).
• **Alfred Bauer Prize**: *The Wayward Cloud* (Taiwan/China/France).
• **Silver Bear for Individual Artistic Contribution**: Tsai Ming Liang, for *The Wayward Cloud*.
• **Gold Bear for Best Short Film**: *Milk* (UK).
Jury Prize (Silver Bear) for Short Films: *The Intervention* (USA) and *Jam Sessions* (Poland).
• **Wolfgang Staudte Award**: *Before the Flood* (China).
• **Caligari Film Prize**: *Oxhide* (China).

NETPAC Prize: *This Charming Girl* (South Korea).
• **CICAE** (international confederation of arthouse cinema):
Panorama: *Ultranova* (Belgium/France).
Forum: *Odessa Odessa ...* (Israel/France).
Special Mentions: *Starlit High Noon* (Japan) and *Berlin Stories* (Germany).
• **Gay Teddy Bear Award, Best Feature**: *A Year Without Love* (Argentina).
• **Gay Teddy Bear Award, Best Documentary**: *Feline Masquerade* (Switzerland).
• **Gay Teddy Bear Award, Best Short**: *The Intervention* (USA).
• **Peace Film Prize**: *Turtles Can Fly* (Iran/Iraq).
• **Ecumenical Jury Prize**: *Sophie Scholl – The Final Days*.
• **FIPRESCI (International Critics Assn.) Prizes: In Competition**: *The Wayward Cloud* (China,)
Panorama: *Massacre* (Germany/Lebanon/Switzerland/France).
Forum: *Oxhide*.
• **Panorama Audience Award**:
Feature: *Live and Become* (France/Belgium/Israel).
Short: *Hi Maya* (Switzerland).

• **Amnesty International Film Prize**: *Paradise Now*.

The 2004 British Academy of Film and Television Arts Awards ('BAFTAs'): Odeon Leicester Square, London, 12 February 2005

• **Best Film**: *The Aviator*.
• **Orange Audience Award**: *Harry Potter and the Prisoner of Azkaban*.
• **David Lean Award for Best Direction**: Mike Leigh, for *Vera Drake*.
• **Best Actor**: Jamie Foxx, for *Ray*.
• **Best Actress**: Imelda Staunton, for *Vera Drake*.
• **Best Supporting Actor**: Clive Owen, for *Closer*.
• **Best Supporting Actress**: Cate Blanchett, for *The Aviator*.
• **Best Original Screenplay**: Charlie Kaufman, for *Eternal Sunshine of the Spotless Mind*.
• **Best Adapted Screenplay**: Alexander Payne and Jim Taylor, for *Sideways*.
• **Best Cinematography**: Dion Beebe and Paul Cameron, for *Collateral*.
• **Best Production Design**: Dante

Ferretti, for *The Aviator*.
• **Best Editing**: Valdís Óskarsdóttir,
for *Eternal Sunshine of the Spotless Mind*.
Anthony Asquith Award for Best Music:
Gustavo Santaolalla, for *The Motorcycle
Diaries*.
• **Best Costumes**: Jacqueline Durran,
for *Vera Drake*.
• **Best Sound**: Steve Cantamessa,
Scott Millan, Greg Orloff and Bob Beemer,
for *Ray*.
• **Best Special Visual Effects**: Karen E
Goulekas, Neil Corbould, Greg Strause and
Remo Balcells, for *The Day After Tomorrow*.
• **Best Make Up/Hair**: Morag Ross,
Kathryn Blondell and Siân Grigg,
for *The Aviator*.
• **Best Short Film**: *The Banker*, by Kelly
Broad and Hattie Dalton.
• **Best Animated Short**: *Birthday Boy*,
by Andrew Gregory and Sejong Park.
• **Michael Balcon Award for
contribution to British Cinema**:
Angela Allen.
• **Alexander Korda Award for Best
British Film**: *My Summer of Love*.
• **Best Foreign Language Film**: *The
Motorcycle Diaries* (USA/Argentina/Chile/
Peru/UK/France).
• **Carl Foreman Award for the Most** •
Promising Newcomer: Amma Asante,
director-writer, for *A Way of Life*.
• **BAFTA Fellowship**: John Barry.

British Independent Film Awards of 2004: Hammersmith Palais, London, 30 November 2004

• **Best British Independent Film**:
Vera Drake.
• **Best Director**: Mike Leigh,
for *Vera Drake*.
• **Best Actor**: Phil Davis, for *Vera Drake*.
• **Best Actress**: Imelda Staunton, for
Vera Drake.
• **Best Supporting Performance**:
Eddie Marsan, for *Vera Drake*.
• **Most Promising Newcomer**: Ashley
Walters, for *Bullet Boy*.
• **Best Screenplay**: Simon Pegg and Edgar
Wright, for *Shaun of the Dead*.
• **Douglas Hickox Award (Debut
Director)**: John Crowley, for *interMission*.
• **Technical Achievement**: Mike Eley,
cinematography, for *Touching the Void*.
• **Best Achievement in Production**:
Vera Drake.
• **Best Foreign Film**: *Old Boy*

(South Korea).
• **Best Documentary**: *Touching the Void*.
The Raindance Award: *The Barn*.
• **Best British Short Film**: *School of Life*.

The 25th Canadian Film Awards ('Genies'): Metro Toronto Convention Centre, 21 March 2005

• **Best Film**: *Les Triplettes de Belleville*
(*The Triplets Of Belleville*), by Paul Cadieux.
• **Best Director**: Francis Leclerc, for
Mémoires affectives (*Looking for Alexander*).
• **Best Actor**: Roy Dupuis, for *Mémoires
affectives*.
• **Best Actress**: Pascale Bussières, for *Ma
vie en cinémascope*.
• **Best Supporting Actor**: Jean Lapointe,
for *Le Dernier tunnel* (*The Last Tunnel*).
• **Best Supporting Actress**: Jennifer
Jason Leigh, for *Childstar*.
• **Best Original Screenplay**: Francis
Leclerc and Marcel Beaulieu, for *Mémoires
affectives*.
• **Best Adapted Screenplay**: Luc Dionne
and Sylvain Guy, for *Monica la mitraille*
(*Machine Gun Molly*).
• **Best Cinematography**: Paul Sarossy,
for *Head in the Clouds*.
• **Best Editing**: Dominique Fortin,
for *Head in the Clouds*.
• **Best Art Direction/Production Design**:
Jean-Baptiste Tard, for *Nouvelle-France*.
• **Best Music**: Terry Frewer, for *Head in
the Clouds*.
• **Best Original Song**: 'Pantaloon in Black'
by Ron Proulx and Jacob Tierney, from
Twist.
• **Best Costumes**: Mario Davignon, for
Head in the Clouds.
• **Best Sound Editing**: Craig Henighan,
Steve Baine, Stephen Barden, Tony Lewis,
Jill Purdy and Nathan Robitaille, for
Resident Evil: Apocalypse.
• **Best Overall Sound**: Dominique
Chartrand, Gavin Fernandes and Pierre
Paquet, for *Le Dernier Tunnel*.
• **Claude Jutra Award for Best First
Feature**: *La Peau Blanche*, by Daniel Roby.
• **Best Feature-Length Documentary**:
The Corporation, by Mark Achbar, Jennifer
Abbott and Bart Simpson.
• **Best Animated Short**: *Ryan*, by Chris
Landreth, Steven Hoban, Marcy Page and
Mark Smith.
• **Best Live-Action Short**: *Capacité 11
Personnes*, by Gaël d'Ynglemare and

Yves Fortin.
• **The Golden Reel Award for Best
Box-Office Performance**: *Resident
Evil: Apocalypse,* produced by Paul W.S.
Anderson, Jeremy Bolt and Don Carmody.
Host: Andrea Martin

The 58th Cannes Film Festival Awards: 11-22 May 2005

• **Palme d'Or for Best Film**: *L'Enfant*
(*The Child*) (Belgium), by Jean-Pierre and
Luc Dardenne.
• **Grand Prix du Jury**: *Broken Flowers*
(France/USA), directed by Jim Jarmusch.
• **Best Actor**: Tommy Lee Jones for *The
Three Burials of Melquiades Estrada* (USA).
• **Best Actress**: Hanna Laslo, for *Free Zone*
(Israel/Belgium).
• **Best Director**: Michael Haneke, for
Caché (*Hidden*) (France/Austria/Germany/
Italy).
• **Best Screenplay**: Guillermo Arriaga,
for *The Three Burials of Melquiades Estrada*.
Palme d'Or for Best Short: *Podorozhini*
(*Wayfarers*) (Ukraine), by Igor Strembitsky.
• **Jury Prize for Best Short**: *Clara*
(Australia), by Van Sowerwine.
• **Prix du Jury (Fiction)**: *Shanghai Dreams*
(China), by Wang Xiaoshuai.
• **Camera d'Or** (for first feature): *Sulanga
Enu Pinisa* (*The Forsaken Land*) (Sri Lanka),
by Vimukthi Jayasundara, tying with *Me
and You and Everyone We Know* (USA), by
Miranda July.
• *Prix Un Certain Regard*: *The Death
of Domnului Lazarescu*, by Cristi Puiu
(Romania).
• *Prix de L'Intimité*: *Filmman*, by Alain
Cavalier (France).
• *Prix de L'Espoir*: *Delwende*, by S. Pierre
Yameogo (Burkina Faso).
Jury: Emir Kusturica (president); Fatih
Akin, Javier Bardem, Nandita Das, Salma
Hayek, Benoit Jacquot, Toni Morrison,
Agnes Varda, John Woo

49th David Di Donatello Academy Awards ('The Davids'): Rome, 29 April 2005

• **Best Film**: *The Consequences of Love*,
by Paolo Sorrentino.
• **Best Director**: Paolo Sorrentino,
for *The Consequences of Love*.
• **Best Debut Director**: Saverio Costanzo,
for *Private*.

• **Best Screenplay**: Paolo Sorrentino, for *The Consequences of Love*.
• **Best Producer**: Rosario Rinaldo, for *A Children's Story*.
• **Best Actor**: Toni Servillo, for *The Consequences of Love*.
• **Best Actress**: Barbara Bobulova, for *Sacred Heart*.
• **Best Supporting Actress**: Margherita Buy, for *Manual of Love*.
• **Best Supporting Actor**: Carlo Verdone, for *Manual of Love*.
• **Best Cinematography**: Luca Bigazzi, for *The Consequences of Love*.
• **Best Music**: Riz Ortolani, for *But When Do the Girls Get Here?*
• **Best Original Song**: 'Christmas in Love' from *Christmas in Love*.
• **Best Set Design**: Andrea Crisanti, for *Sacred Heart*.
• **Best Costume Design**: Daniela Ciancio, for *The Remains of Nothing*.
• **Best Editing**: Claudio Cutry, for *A Children's Story*.
• **Best Sound**: Alessandro Zanon, for *The Keys to the House*.
• **Best European Union Film**: *The Sea Within* (Spain/France/Italy), by Alejandro Amenabar.
• **Best Foreign Film**: *Million Dollar Baby*, by Clint Eastwood.
• **Lifetime Achievement Award**: Tom Cruise.
Hosts: Mike Bongiorno and Luisa Corna.

Director Mike Leigh on the set of the award-winning *Vera Drake*.

The 18th European Film Awards ('the Felixes'): Barcelona, 11 December 2004

• **Best European Film**: *Gegen die Wand* (*Head-On*) (Germany), by Fatih Akin.
• **Best Director**: Alejandro Amenábar, for *Mar dentro* (*The Sea Inside*) (Spain/France/Italy).
• **Best Actor**: Javier Bardem, for *The Sea Inside*.
• **Best Actress**: Imelda Staunton, for *Vera Drake* (UK/France).
• **Best Screenplay**: Agnès Jaoui & Jean-Pierre Bacri, for *Comme une image* (*Look at Me*) (France).
• **Best Cinematography**: Eduardo Serra, for *Girl with a Pearl Earring* (UK).
• **Best Music**: Bruno Coulais, for *Les Choristes* (*The Chorus*) (France).
• **Best Short Film**: *J'attendrai le suivant*, by Philippe Orreindy (France).
• **Discovery of the Year** (Fassbinder Award): Andrea & Antonio Frazzi, for

Certi bambini (*Stolen Childhood*) (Italy).
• **Best Documentary**: *Darwin's Nightmare*, by Hubert Sauper (France/Austria/Belgium).
• **Achievement in World Cinema**: Liv Ullmann (actress and director), Norway.
• **Critics Award** (Prix Fipresci): *Trilogia – To Livadi Pou Dakrizi* (*Trilogy – The Weeping Meadow*), by Theo Angelopoulos (Greece).
• **Best Non-European Film**: *2046*, by Wong Kar-Wai (France/China).
• **Lifetime Achievement Award**: Carlos Saura.
• **People Awards**:
• **Best Actor**: Daniel Brühl, for *Was nützt die Liebe in Gedanken* (*Love in Thoughts*) (Germany).
• **Best Actress**: Penélope Cruz, for *Non ti muovere* (*Don't Move*) (Italy).
• **Best Director**: Fatih Akin, for *Head-On*.

The 30th French Academy ('Cesar') Awards: Paris, 28 February 2005

• **Best Film**: *L'Esquive*.
• **Best Director**: Abdellatif Kechiche, for *L'Esquive*.
• **Best Actor**: Mathieu Amalric, for *Rois et reine* (*Kings and Queen*).
• **Best Actress**: Yolande Moreau, for *Quand la mer monte...*
• **Best Supporting Actor**: Clovis

Cornillac, for *Mensonges et trahisons et plus si affinité...*
• **Best Supporting Actress**: Marion Cotillard, for *A Very Long Engagement*.
• **Most Promising Young Actor**: Gaspard Ulliel, for *A Very Long Engagement*.
• **Most Promising Young Actress**: Sara Forestier, for *L'Esquive*.
• **Best First Film**: *Quand la mer monte...*, by Gilles Porte and Yolande Moreau.
• **Best Original Screenplay**: Abdellatif Kechiche and Ghalya Lacroix, for *L'Esquive*.
• **Best Cinematography**: Bruno Delbonnel, for *A Very Long Engagement*.
• **Best Production Design**: Aline Bonetto, for *A Very Long Engagement*.
• **Best Editing**: Noëlle Boisson, for *Two Brothers*.
• **Best Music**: Bruno Coulais, for *Les Choristes* (*The Chorus*).
• **Best Costumes**: Madeline Fontaine, for *A Very Long Engagement*.
• **Best Sound**: Daniel Sobrino, Nicolas Cantin and Nicolas Naegelen, for *Les Choristes* (*The Chorus*).
• **Best Short**: *Cousines*, by Lyes Salem.
• **Best European Film**: *Ae Fond Kiss* (UK/Italy/Germany/Spain/France), tied with *Life is a Miracle* (France/Serbia/Montenegro).
• **Best Foreign Film**: *Lost in Translation* (USA/Japan).
• **Honoary Cesars**: Will Smith and Jacques Dutronc.

The 25th Golden Raspberries ('The Razzies'): Ivar Theatre, Hollywood, California, 26 February 2005

- Worst Film: *Catwoman*.
- Worst Actor: George W. Bush, for *Fahrenheit 9/11*.
- Worst Actress: Halle Berry, for *Catwoman*.
- Worst Screen Couple: George W. Bush and either Condoleeza Rice or his pet goat, in *Fahrenheit 9/11*.
- Worst Supporting Actor: Donald Rumsfeld, for *Fahrenheit 9/11*.
- Worst Supporting Actress: Britney Spears, for *Fahrenheit 9/11*.
- Worst Director: Pitof, for *Catwoman*.
- Worst Screenplay: Theresa Rebeck, John Brancato, Michael Ferris and John Rogers, for *Catwoman*.
- Worst Remake or Sequel: *Scooby Doo 2: Monsters Unleashed*.

The 62nd Hollywood Foreign Press Association ('Golden Globes') Awards: 16 January 2005

- Best Picture – Drama: *The Aviator*.
- Best Picture – Musical or Comedy: *Sideways*.

- Best Actor – Drama: Leonardo DiCaprio, for *The Aviator*.
- Best Actress – Drama: Hilary Swank, for *Million Dollar Baby*.
- Best Actor – Musical or Comedy: Jamie Foxx, for *Ray*.
- Best Actress – Musical or Comedy: Annette Bening, for *Being Julia*.
- Best Supporting Actor: Clive Owen, for *Closer*.
- Best Supporting Actress: Natalie Portman, for *Closer*.
- Best Director: Clint Eastwood, for *Million Dollar Baby*.
- Best Screenplay: Alexander Payne and Jim Taylor, for *Sideways*.
- Best Original Score: Howard Shore, for *The Aviator*.
- Best Original Song: 'Old Habits Die Hard' from *Alfie*, by Mick Jagger and David A. Stewart.
- Best Foreign Language Film: *The Sea Inside* (Spain/France/Italy).

The 25th London Film Critics Circle Awards: The Dorchester, London, 9 February 2005

- Best Film: *Sideways*.
- Best Actor: Jamie Foxx, for *Ray*.
- Best Actress: Imelda Staunton, for *Vera Drake*.
- Best Director: Martin Scorsese,

---

for *The Aviator*.
- Best Screenwriter: Charlie Kaufman, for *Eternal Sunshine of the Spotless Mind*.
- Attenborough Award for Best British Film: *Vera Drake*.
- Best British Director: Mike Leigh, for *Vera Drake*.
- Best British Actor: Daniel Craig, for *Enduring Love*.
- Best British Actress: Eva Birthistle, for *Ae Fond Kiss*, tying with Kate Winslet, for *Eternal Sunshine of the Spotless Mind*.
- Best British Supporting Actor: Phil Davis, for *Vera Drake*.
- Best British Supporting Actress: Romola Garai, for *Inside I'm Dancing*.
- Best British Screenwriter: Mike Leigh, for *Vera Drake*.
- Best British Newcomer: Natalie Press (actress, *My Summer of Love*).
- Best Foreign Language Film: *The Motorcycle Diaries* (USA/Argentina/Chile/Peru/UK/France).

The 30th Los Angeles Film Critics' Association Awards: Los Angeles, 12 December 2004

- Best Picture: *Sideways*.
- Best Actor: Liam Neeson, for *Kinsey*.
- Best Actress: Imelda Staunton,

Sandra Oh, Thomas Haden Church, Virginia Madsen and Paul Giamatti in *Sideways*, which was voted best film by the Hollywood Foreign Press Association, the London Film Critics Circle and the LA and New York Critics' Circles

for *Vera Drake*.
- **Best Supporting Actor:**
Thomas Haden Church, for *Sideways*.
- **Best Supporting Actress:** Virginia
Madsen, for *Sideways*.
- **Best Director:** Alexander Payne,
for *Sideways*.
- **Best Screenplay:** Alexander Payne
and Jim Taylor, for *Sideways*.
- **Best Cinematography:** Dion Beebe
and Paul Cameron, for *Collateral*.
- **Best Music:** Michael Giacchino,
for *The Incredibles*.
- **Best Production Design:**
Dante Ferretti, for *The Aviator*.
- **New Generation Award:** Joshua
Marston (director) and Catalina Sandino
Moreno (lead actress), for *María Full
of Grace*.
- **Best Animation:** Brad Bird,
for *The Incredibles*.
- **Best Foreign-Language Film:**
House of Flying Daggers, by Zhang Yimou
(Hong Kong/China).
- **Best Documentary:** *Born into Brothels*,
by Ross Kauffman and Zana Briski.
- **Douglas Edward Independent
Experimental Film & Video Award:**
Star Spangled to Death, by Ken Jacobs.
- **Special citation:** Richard Schickel and
Brian Jamieson and his supporting staff at
Warner Bros.

The 13th MTV Movie Awards:
6 June 2005, Shrine Auditorium,
Los Angeles

- **Best Movie:** *Napoleon Dynamite*.

- **Best Male Performance:** Leonardo
DiCaprio, for *The Aviator*.
- **Best Female Performance:**
Lindsay Lohan, for *Mean Girls*.
- **Best Comedic Performance:**
Dustin Hoffman, for *Meet the Fockers*.
- **Best On-Screen Team:** Lindsay Lohan,
Rachel McAdams, Lacey Chabert and
Amanda Seyfried, for *Mean Girls*.
- **Best Breakthrough Male Performance:**
Jon Heder, for *Napoleon Dynamite*.
- **Best Breakthrough Female
Performance:** Rachel McAdams,
for *Mean Girls*.
- **Best Frightened Performance:**
Dakota Fanning, in *Hide and Seek*.
- **Best Villain:** Ben Stiller, for *Dodgeball:
A True Underdog Story*.
- **Best Action Sequence:** The destruction
of Los Angeles in *The Day After Tomorrow*.
- **Best Fight:** between Uma Thurman and
Darryl Hannah in *Kill Bill Vol. 2*.
- **Best Kiss:** Rachel McAdams and
Ryan Gosling, in *The Notebook*.
- **Best Musical Performance:**
Jon Heder (for his 'election dance'),
in *Napoleon Dynamite*.
- **Generation Award:** Tom Cruise.

The 96th National Board of
Review Awards: 1 December 2004
(presented on 11 January 2005)

- **Best Film:** *Finding Neverland*.
- **Best Director:** Michael Mann,
for *Collateral*.
- **Best Actor:** Jamie Foxx, for *Ray*.
Best Actress: Annette Bening, for

Being Julia.
- **Best Supporting Actor:** Thomas Haden
Church, for *Sideways*.
- **Best Supporting Actress:** Laura Linney,
for *Kinsey*.
- **Best Foreign Film:** *The Sea Inside*
(Spain/France/Italy).
- **Best Documentary:** *Born into Brothels*,
by Ross Kauffman and Zana Briski.
- **Best Animated Feature:** *The Incredibles*.
- **Best Original Screenplay:** Alexander
Payne and Jim Taylor, for *Sideways*.
- **Best Screenplay Adaptation:**
Charlie Kaufman, for *Eternal Sunshine
of the Spotless Mind*.
- **Best Production Design/Art Direction:**
House of Flying Daggers (Hong Kong/China).
- **Best Music:** Jan A. P. Kaczmarek, for
Finding Neverland.
- **Special Achievement Award in
Filmmaking:** Clint Eastwood, for
producing, directing, acting in and
scoring *Million Dollar Baby*.
- **Best Ensemble Performance:**
Julia Roberts, Jude Law, Natalie Portman
and Clive Owen, for *Closer*.
- **Best Breakthrough Actor:** Topher
Grace, for *In Good Company* and *P.S.*
- **Best Breakthrough Actress:** Emmy
Rossum, for *The Phantom of the Opera*.
- **Directorial Debut:** Zach Braff, for
Garden State.
- **Producers Award:** Jerry Bruckheimer.
**William K. Everson Award for Film
History:** Richard Schickel.
- **Billy Wilder Award for Excellence
in Directing:** Milos Forman.
- **Career Achievement:** Jeff Bridges.
- **Career Achievement in**

The Incredibles, voted best animated feature by the American
Academy of Motion Picture Arts and Sciences

Hero cinematographer Christopher Doyle received an award from the New York Film Critics Circle

Cinematography: Caleb Deschanel.
• **Freedom of Expression Award:** *Fahrenheit 9/11*, *The Passion of the Christ*, *Conspiracy of Silence*.

2004 New York Film Critics Circle Awards: 13 December 2004 (presented on 9 January 2005)

Best Picture: *Sideways*.
Best Actor: Paul Giamatti, for *Sideways*.
• **Best Actress:** Imelda Staunton, for *Vera Drake*.
• **Best Supporting Actor:** Clive Owen, for *Closer*.
• **Best Supporting Actress:** Virginia Madsen, for *Sideways*.
• **Best Director:** Clint Eastwood, for *Million Dollar Baby*.
• **Best Screenplay:** Alexander Payne and Jim Taylor, for *Sideways*.
• **Best Cinematographer:** Christopher Doyle, for *Hero*.
• **Best Foreign Film:** *Bad Education* (Spain).
• **Best Non-Fiction Film:** *Fahrenheit 9/11*.
• **Best Animated Film:** *The Incredibles*.
• **Best First Film:** *María Full of Grace*.

• **Special Award:** Milestone Films received a special award in honor of 15 years of restoring classic films.

Sundance Film Festival: Park City and Salt Lake City, Utah, 30 January 2005

• **Grand Jury Prize** (best feature): *Forty Shades of Blue*, by Ira Sachs.
• **Grand Jury Prize** (best documentary): *Why We Fight*, by Eugene Jarecki.
• **Best Performance:** Amy Adams, for *Junebug*, and Lou Pucci, for *Thumbsucker*.
• **Best Direction:** Noah Baumbach, for *The Squid and the Whale*.
• **Best Direction** (best documentary): Jeff Feuerzeig, for *The Devil and Daniel Johnston*.
• **Best Cinematography:** Amelia Vincent, for *Hustle and Flow*.
• **Best Cinematography** (documentary): Gary Griffin, for *The Education of Shelby Knox*.
• **World Cinema Grand Jury Prize** (best feature): *The Hero* (Angola), by Zeze Gamboa.
• **World Cinema Grand Jury Prize** (best documentary): *Shape of the Moon*

(Netherlands), by Leonard Retel Helmrich.
• **Audience Award** (best feature): *Hustle and Flow*, by Craig Brewer.
• **Audience Award** (best documentary): *Murderball*, by Henry Alex Rubin and Dana Adam Shapiro.
• **Audience World Cinema** (best feature): *Brothers* (Denmark), by Susanne Bier.
• **Audience World Cinema** (best documentary): *Shake Hands with the Devil: The Journey of Roméo Dallaire* (Canada), by Peter Raymont.
• **Waldo Salt Screenwriting Award:** Noah Baumbach, for *The Squid and the Whale*.
• **Special Jury Award:** Rian Johnson, for *Brick*.
• **Special Jury Award for Originality of Vision:** Miranda July, for *Me and You and Everyone We Know*.
• **Special Jury Award** (documentary): *After Innocence*, by Jessica Sanders.
• **Special Jury Award** (editing/ documentary): Geoffrey Richman and Conor O'Neill, for *Murderball*.
• **World Cinema, Special Jury Award** (best feature): *Live-In Maid* (Argentina/ Spain), by Jorge Gaggero.
• **World Cinema, Special Jury Award**

(best documentary): *The Liberace of Baghdad* (UK), by Sean McAllister; and *Wall* (France/Israel), by Simon Bitton.

• **Short Filmmaking Award:** *Family Portrait*, by Patricia Riggen.

• **Short Filmmaking Award** (international): *Wasp* (UK), by Andrea Arnold.

• **Short Filmmaking** (special mention): *Bullets in the Hood: A Bed-Stuy Story*, by Terrence Fisher and Daniel Howard.

• **Short Filmmaking** (honorable mention): *One Weekend a Month*, by Eric Escobar; *Ryan*, by Chris Landreth; *Small Town Secrets*, by Katherine Leggett; *Tama Tu* (New Zealand), by Taika Waititi; *Victoria Para Chino*, by Cary Fukunaga.

The 61st Venice International Film Festival: 1 September-11 September 2005

• **Golden Lion for Best Film:** *Vera Drake* (UK/France), by Mike Leigh.

Special Jury Grand Prize: *Mar adentro* (aka *The Sea Inside*) (Spain/France/Italy), by Alejandro Amenábar.

• **Best Director:** Kim Ki-duk,

for *Bin jip* (South Korea).

• **Best Actor:** Javier Bardem, for *Mar adentro*.

• **Best Actress:** Imelda Staunton, for *Vera Drake*.

• **Luigi De Laurentiis Award for Best First Feature:** *Le grand voyage* (France/Morocco), by Ismaël Ferroukhi.

• **Marcello Mastroianni Award for Emerging Actor or Actress:** Marco Luisi and Tommaso Ramenghi, for Guido Chiesa's *Lavorare con lentezza – Radio Alice 100.6 Mhz* (aka *Radio Alice*) (Italy).

• **Osella Award for Technical Contribution:** *Hauru no ugoku shiro* (aka *Howl's Moving Castle*) (Japan), by Hayao Miyazaki.

• **Special Mention, Lion of the Future Award:** *Saimir* (Italy), by Francesco Munzi.

• *Venice Horizons Prize: Les petits fils* (France),

by Ilan Duran Cohen.

• *Venice Horizons Special Mention: Vento di terra* (aka *Wind from the Earth*) (Italy), by Vincenzo Marra.

• **Venice Digital Award**: *20 angosht* (aka *20 Fingers*) (Iran), by Mania Akbari. *Venice Digital Special Mention: La vita è breve ma la giornata è lunghissima* (*Life is Short, But the Day is Superlong*) (Italy), by Lucio Pellegrini and Gianni Zanasi.

• **Leone d'Argento Citroën Corto Cortissimo:** *Signe d'appartenence*, by Kamel Cherif.

• **Special Mention:** *The Carpenter and His Clumsy Wife*, by Peter Foott.

• *UIP Award for the Best European Short Film: Goodbye*, by Steve Hudson.

Vera Drake: winner of the Golden Lion at Venice

In Memoriam

EDDIE ALBERT

Born: 22 April 1906 in Rock Island, Illinois.

Died: 26 May 2005 of pneumonia in Pacific Palisades, California.

Real name: Edward Albert Heimberger.

Job description: TV star, leading environmentalist and Oscar-nominated actor. Although forever associated with the role of Oliver Wendell Douglas, the lawyer-turned-farmer in the much-loved TV sitcom *Green Acres* (1965-1971), Albert led a rich and varied career in and out of the limelight. The son of German immigrants, he started out in a variety of professions, including trapeze artist (in a Mexican circus), cinema usher and radio announcer. He made his film debut in *Brother Rat* (1938) – alongside an unknown Ronald Reagan – and during the Second World War was awarded the Bronze Star for rescuing scores of wounded Marines under heavy fire. After the war, he gained some controversy for producing the sex-educational films *Human Beings* and *Human Growth* – aimed at school children – and then settled into an astonishingly durable acting career. After parts in *You're In the Navy Now* (1951) and *Carrie* (1952) – among many others – he was nominated for an Oscar for the comic role of a paparazzo in William Wyler's *Roman Holiday* (1953). He also received some kudos for his performance as an unhinged, cowardly captain in Robert Aldrich's anti-war *Attack!* (1956) and clocked up notable parts in *Oklahoma!*, *Teahouse of the August Moon* and *The Sun Also Rises*. He received a second Oscar nomination for *The Heartbreak Kid* (1972) and made further impressions in *McQ*, *The Longest Yard* and *The Big Picture*. He was also an influential defender of physical fitness and organic foods, fought publicly against the use of DDT and lived to see Earth Day annually celebrated on his birthday, in his honour. His son is the actor Edward Albert (*Butterflies Are Free*, *Guarding Tess*).

ANNE BANCROFT

Born: 17 September 1931 in The Bronx, New York.

Died: 6 June 2005 of cancer, in Mount Sinai Hospital, New York.

Real name: Anna Maria Luisa Italiano.

Job description: Oscar-winning actress. In spite of a career spanning 53 years, Anne Bancroft is primarily remembered for two roles. After a lacklustre series of films in which she played second fiddle to the likes of Cornel Wilde, David Wayne, Van Heflin and Anthony Quinn, she made her stage debut in 1958 in William Gibson's *Two for the Seesaw*, creating the part of Gittel Mosca and winning the Tony for her pains. She also originated the role of Annie Sullivan in Gibson's *The Miracle Worker* (1959) and won another Tony as well as the New York Drama Critics' Award. While Shirley MacLaine played Gittel in Robert Wise's film version of the former, Bancroft got to play Sullivan in Arthur Penn's big-screen adaptation of *The Miracle Worker* (1962). According to the critic David Thomson, she 'so dramatised the struggle between liberty and discipline that she probably helped reveal Penn's own talent to himself.' The part won her an Oscar – beating out Bette Davis and Katharine Hepburn

– as well as a BAFTA, and established her as one of America's leading dramatic actresses. She confirmed the honour with her outstanding turn in Jack Clayton's *The Pumpkin Eater* (1964) – as an English housewife facing a mid-life crisis – and was duly bestowed with an Oscar nomination. She then starred opposite Sidney Poitier as a suicide case in Sydney Pollack's *The Slender Thread* (1965) and joined Margaret Leighton and Flora Robson for John Ford's vapid *Seven Women* (1966). However, her next performance was iconic. In Mike Nichols' *The Graduate* (1967) she played the cynical and seductive Mrs Robinson, received yet another Oscar nomination and was immortalised in the legendary Simon and Garfunkel song 'Mrs Robinson'. Inevitably, the rest was downhill, albeit sparked by the occasional gemstone. Of the latter, we can be thankful for *Young Winston* (as Lady Randolph Churchill), *The Turning Point* (another Oscar nomination), *The Elephant Man* (as Dame Madge Kendal), *Agnes of God* (Oscar-nominated again), *84 Charing Cross Road* (as the writer Helene Hanff), *Torch Song Trilogy*, Jodie Foster's *Home for the Holidays* and as the voice of the Queen in the splendid computer-animated cartoon *Antz*. She also directed one film, the unsatisfactory *Fatso* (1980), and married the director and comic Mel Brooks in 1964, forming one of the most durable romantic partnerships in Hollywood.

ELMER BERNSTEIN

Born: 14 April 1922 in New York, New York.

Died: 18 August 2004 after a long illness, at his home in Ojah, California.

Job description: Composer. One of the most popular, prolific and versatile film composers of his generation, Elmer Bernstein will forever be remembered for his scores to *The Magnificent Seven* (which was

immortalised by promoting the dubious merits of Marlboro cigarettes) and *The Great Escape* (which was rehashed for the 2000 claymation hit *Chicken Run*). Trained as a concert pianist, Bernstein (no relation to Leonard) began his career working alongside Glenn Miller and his Army Air Corps Band for Armed Forces Radio. His military experience led to his composition of a radio drama that in turn led to his first film, the football programmer *Saturday's Hero* (1951). Four years later Bernstein won his first Oscar nomination for his memorable jazz accompaniment to Otto Preminger's *The Man With the Golden Arm*, which was followed by Cecil B. DeMille's *The Ten Commandments* (when he replaced the recently deceased Victor Young). Bernstein followed this with *The Sweet Smell of Success*, *The Magnificent Seven*, *Summer and Smoke*, *To Kill a Mockingbird*, *Return of the Seven*, *Hawaii* and *Thoroughly Modern Millie*, winning his only Oscar for the last named. He changed tack dramatically for his comic score to *National Lampoon's Animal House* and found himself typecast as a comedy composer, animating the likes of *Airplane!*, *The Blues Brothers* and *Ghostbusters*. In his autumnal years he was approached by Martin Scorsese to adapt Bernard Herrmann's 1962 music for *Cape Fear* for the 1991 remake and worked for Scorsese again on *The Age of Innocence*, which secured him his penultimate Oscar nomination. He was nominated again in 2003 – aged 80 – for his pastiche of Herrmann and the like for Todd Haynes' 1950s' homage *Far From Heaven*.

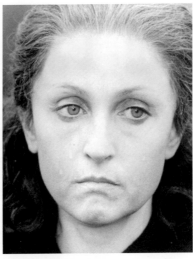

LAURA BETTI

Born: 1 May 1934 in the northern Italian city of Bologna.
Died: 31 July 2004 of a heart attack in Rome.
Real name: Laura Trombetti.
Job description: Character actress. Starting out a jazz singer, Betti made her acting debut in Fellini's *La Dolce Vita* (1960) and established close associations with Pier Paolo Pasolini and Bernardo Bertolucci, appearing in the latter's *Last Tango in Paris, 1900* and *La Luna*. For Pasolini she made seven films, including *Oedipus Rex*, *Theorem* and *The Canterbury Tales*. She and Pasolini became close friends and in 2001 she wrote and directed a documentary about him, *Pier Paolo Pasolini e la ragione di un sogno*.

ED BISHOP

Born: 11 June 1932 in Brooklyn, New York.

Died: 8 June 2005 in England, from a viral infection.
Real name: George Victor Bishop.
Job description: Character actor. Best known for his starring role as Commander Ed Straker in the 26 episodes of Gerry Anderson's *UFO* TV series (1971-72), Bishop also appeared in many feature films. He notched up parts in Stanley Kubrick's *Lolita* and *2001: A Space Odyssey* and appeared uncredited in the James Bond films *You Only Live Twice* and *Diamonds Are Forever*.

JOHN BOX

Born: 27 January 1920 in Hampstead, London.
Died: 7 March 2005 in Leatherhead, Surrey.
Job description: Oscar-winning production designer – aka The Magician. Having trained as an architect, Box found little work in post-war Britain and, inspired by the designs for David Lean's *Great Expectations*, tried his hand at the film business. He worked uncredited on *The Importance of Being Earnest* and was art director on Ronald Neame's *The Million Pound Note* and José Ferrer's *The Cockleshell Heroes*. However, it was as art director of *The Inn of the Sixth Happiness* (1958) that he made his mark, recreating a Chinese walled city in Snowdonia, Wales. He won his first Oscar as production designer for Lean's *Lawrence of Arabia* (1962), contributing to one of the cinema's most memorable moments – when Omar Sharif rides into view out of the desert heat. Box insisted on painting the path of the camel white, bordered with black pebbles. 'No one noticed it,' Lean recalled, 'but I'm quite sure that it helped contribute to the impact of the sequence.' If nothing else, Box was quite ingenious and recreated an icy Russia in sunny Spain for *Doctor Zhivago* (1965), winning his second Oscar. His own favourite film was *A Man for All Seasons* (1966), although he won further Oscars for *Oliver!* (1968) and *Nicholas and Alexandra* (1971). His later credits included *The Great Gatsby* (1974), *Rollerball* (1975), David Lean's *A Passage to India* (1984) and *First Knight* (1995).

MARLON BRANDO

Born: 3 April 1924 in Omaha,

Nebraska.

Died: 1 July 2004 of lung failure in Los Angeles.

Job description: Oscar-winning actor. An icon of Brando's stature is bound to inspire wild hearsay. He was rumoured to be taking up Irish citizenship, he was thought to be sharing accommodation with Jack Nicholson, he was possibly the father of Courtney Love. The truth is that almost single-handedly Brando transformed the face of contemporary acting. By mumbling his way through his early roles, he brought a new naturalism to the cinema and his dress code of white T-shirt and leather jacket fashioned a sartorial statement still dominant today. Yet as soon as Brando became aware of his position at the forefront of a new acting style, he changed tack, taking on a wide diversity of projects, from playing Marc Antony in Shakespeare's *Julius Caesar* (1953) to the toe-tapping musical *Guys and Dolls* (1955) and the part of a Japanese interpreter in *Teahouse of the August Moon* (1956). The son of a salesman and an alcoholic actress, Brando was born in Omaha and, after a stint digging ditches, switched to the theatre, studying in New York under Stella Adler and with the Actor's Studio. It was his stage performance as Stanley Kowalski in Tennessee Williams' *A Streetcar Named Desire* (1947) that made his name, his potent combination of passion, inarticulate delivery and matinée idol looks sealing his reputation as a force to be reckoned with. Three years later he was starring in his first movie

– Stanley Kramer's *The Men* (1950) – and he followed this with a slew of high-profile projects culminating with *On the Waterfront* (1954), for which he won the Oscar. His declaration in that film – 'I coulda had class, I coulda been a contender' – has been much mimicked since. In the 1960s his career petered out somewhat and he only made six films in the 1970s, but the few he made were iconic. He received a second Oscar for *The Godfather* (1972), but turned it down in protest at Hollywood's treatment of American Indians. Next, he was electric as a grieving, amoral widower in *Last Tango in Paris* (1973), a film that did for sex and butter what Brando had done for acting two decades earlier. Then, for *Superman* (1978), he received $3 million for ten minutes' screen time, making him, pro rata, the highest paid actor in history. It was downhill from there and his last years were mired in tragedy. In 1990 his eldest son, Christian, was convicted of manslaughter after shooting dead the boyfriend of his half-sister, Cheyenne Brando. Their father was forced to borrow heavily in order to finance his son's defence and then Cheyenne hanged herself a year before Christian's release. Meanwhile, Brando had ballooned to a grotesque size, subsisting chiefly on ice cream and frankfurters. Then, at the time of his death, he was on government aid living in a one-room bungalow and in debt to the tune of almost $20 million. His other notable films include *A Streetcar Named Desire* (1951), *Viva Zapata!* (1952), *The Wild One* (1953), *The Young Lions* (1958), *Mutiny on the Bounty* (1962), *The Missouri Breaks* (1976), *Apocalypse Now* (1979), *A Dry White Season* (1989), *The Freshman* (1990) and *The Score* (2001).

J.D. CANNON

Born: 24 April 1922 in Salmon, Idaho.
Died: 20 May 2005 in Hudson, New York.
Job description: Character actor. Although best known for his recurring role as Chief of Detectives Peter B. Clifford in TV's *McCloud* (1970-77), J.D. Cannon was a regular face in film. His big-screen credits include *Cool Hand Luke* (1967), *Lawman*, *Scorpio*, *Raise the Titanic* and *Death Wish II*, although he was even more prolific on the small screen.

MICHEL COLOMBIER

Born: 23 May 1939 in Lyon, France.
Died: 14 November 2004 of cancer, in Santa Monica, California.
Job description: Film composer. Classically trained and an accomplished pianist and conductor, Colombier began his career as a recording artist. As a composer, he started out in his native France working for the likes of Claude Lelouch, Marcel Carné and Vittorio De Sica before moving to the United States in his capacity as musical director for Petula Clark. Known for his versatility and speed, Colombier composed over one hundred scores for film and television, including *Against All Odds*, *Purple Rain*, *White Nights*, *Ruthless People*, *The Golden Child*, *New Jack City*, *Posse* and Guy Ritchie's *Swept Away*.

GEORGE PAN COSMATOS

Born: 4 January 1941 in Florence, Italy.
Died: 19 April 2005 in Victoria, Canada, of lung cancer.
Job description: Flamboyant, cigar-smoking filmmaker who was happiest directing all-star casts.
Raised in Egypt and Cyprus, Cosmatos started out as an assistant on *Exodus* (1960), had an uncredited role in *Zorba the Greek* (1964) and wrote for the prestigious film magazine *Sight and Sound*. As a director, he was generally dismissed by the critics but had a knack for attracting major stars. He produced his first film, *The Beloved* (1970), with Raquel Welch, and went on to also direct *Massacre in Rome* (1973) with Richard Burton, *The Cassandra Crossing* (1976) with Sophia Loren, Burt Lancaster and Richard Harris, *Escape to Athena* (1979) with Roger Moore and David Niven, *Of Unknown Origin* (1983), *Rambo: First Blood Part II* (1985, by far his biggest success), *Cobra* (1986) with Sylvester Stallone, *Leviathan* (1989), *Tombstone* (1993) with Kurt Russell and Val Kilmer, and *Shadow Conspiracy* (1997) with Charlie Sheen and Donald Sutherland.

RODNEY DANGERFIELD

Born: 22 November 1921 in Babylon, New York.
Died: 4 October 2004 after heart surgery

in Los Angeles.

Real name: Jacob Cohen.

Job description: Bug-eyed stand-up comic who segued into movies.

Rodney Dangerfield went from Jacob Cohen to Jack Roy in the nightclub scene of the 1940s, turned to business in the 1950s and then returned to stand-up comedy in the 1960s (as Rodney Dangerfield). His first film, *The Projectionist* (1971), was barely released and it was to be nine years before he was noticed on the big screen, as the boorish Al Czervik in *Caddyshack*. He was 59. He had the lead in *Easy Money* (1983) and *Back to School* (1986), both of which were savaged by the critics, but a section of the US public took to them. He was notable as Juliette Lewis' monstrous father in Oliver Stone's *Natural Born Killers* and became the first entertainer to have his own website. Other films included the disastrous *Meet Wally Sparks* (1997) and *Little Nicky* (2000), in the latter playing Lucifer. He married Joyce Indig twice (and divorced her twice), finally marrying a florist 31 years his junior.

OSSIE DAVIS

Born: 18 December 1917 in Cogdell, Georgia, USA.

Died: 4 February 2005 in Miami, Florida, of natural causes.

Real name: Raiford Chatman Davis, known as 'Ossie' ever since the county clerk registered him as such when he misinterpreted Mrs Davis' pronunciation of the initials 'R.C.'

Job description: Character actor, writer, director, producer and human rights activist.

As an actor, Ossie Davis' colourful personality and innate dignity brightened scores of movies, including *The Cardinal* (1963), *The Hill, A Man Called Adam, The Scalphunters, Slaves, Let's Do It Again, Harry and Son, Do the Right Thing, Jungle Fever, Malcolm X, Grumpy Old Men, The Client, Get On the Bus, I'm Not Rappaport, Dinosaur* (voice only), *Bubba Ho-Tep* and *She Hate Me* (2004). He was married to the cherished actress Ruby Dee for more than 56 years and in 2001 was honoured with a lifetime achievement award by the Screen Actors Guild. His humanitarian works prompted SAG president Melissa Gilbert to note that his 'impact on America can be seen not only in his rich body of creative works, but equally so as a passionate advocate for social justice and human dignity.' Indeed, such was his position in humanitarian causes that he spoke at the funerals of both Martin Luther King and Malcolm X.

PHILIPPE de BROCA

Born: 15 March 1933 in Paris.

Died: 26 November 2004 of cancer, in Paris.

Job description: Director of lively action-comedies.

Having studied photography at the Ecole Louis Lumière, Philippe de Broca served as a cameraman for the armed forces in Africa, where he shot a number of documentaries. As an assistant director, he collaborated with Claude Chabrol and François Truffaut, working on the latter's *The 400 Blows*, but he later declared that the New Wave bored him. To prove this, he made his directorial debut on *The Love Game* (1960), a charming romp with Jean-Pierre Cassel, which he followed with two more effervescent Cassel vehicles. He had a huge hit with the ebullient *Cartouche* (1962), starring Jean-Paul Belmondo, which allowed him to crank up the budget for a series of action-comedies leading to the international success of *That Man from Rio* (1964), also with Belmondo. *Chinese Adventures in China* (1965) was another triumph, revealing de Broca's penchant for a dizzy combination of sophistication, wild stunts and exotic

locations. Ironically perhaps, the director made *King of Hearts* the same year, a Franco-British co-production starring Alan Bates as a Scotsman who stumbles across a town in France inhabited entirely by escapees from a lunatic asylum. Although a disappointment in France, the film went on to become a cult favourite at American universities and is now de Broca's most famous film in the States. In France, he returned to commercial favour with *Devil by the Tail* (1968), a picturesque farce with Yves Montand and Jean Rochefort, and had another huge hit with *Dear Detective* (1977), which spawned a sequel and an American TV movie. Then there was the popular *The African* (1982), with Philippe Noiret and Catherine Deneuve, and perhaps his finest film, the robust, swashbuckling and earthy *Le Bossu* (aka *On Guard!*) (1997), with Daniel Auteuil as the impertinent swordsman Lagardere. His last film was the children's costumer, *Viper in the Fist* (2004).

SANDRA DEE

Born: 23 April 1942 in Bayonne, New Jersey.

Died: 20 February 2005 in Thousand Oaks, California, from complications with kidney disease.

Real name: Alexandria Zuck.

Job description: Virginal sex goddess of the early 1960s.

A sunny blonde, Sandra Dee found fame in modelling and on TV while still in high school. However, she was taken seriously as Lana Turner's daughter in

Douglas Sirk's *Imitation of Life* (1959), was a hit as Troy Donahue's sweetheart in *A Summer Place* and had the title role in *Gidget* (later made into two separate TV series). She found further success in *Tammy Tell Me True* (1961) and *Tammy and the Doctor* (1963), and became a media staple when she married the crooner Bobby Darin (1960-67). Even though her career eventually descended to *Doctor, You've Got To Be Kidding!* (1967) and *The Dunwich Horror* (1970), she was made famous again by the immortal lyrics from *Grease*: 'Look at me, I'm Sandra Dee, lousy with virginity.' She was played by Kate Bosworth in Kevin Spacey's *Beyond the Sea* (2004).

BADJA DJOLA

Born: 9 April 1948 in Brooklyn, New York.
Died: 8 January 2005 of a heart attack, in Los Angeles.
Job description: Colourful character actor, not to mention dancer, drummer, historian, musician, playwright and poet. With his hypnotic eyes and commanding demeanour, Djola brightened many a dud movie. His major credits include *Penitentiary* (1980), *The Serpent and the Rainbow* (1988), *Mississippi Burning*, *A Rage in Harlem*, *The Waterdance* and *Heaven's Prisoners*.

FRED EBB

Born: 8 April 1932 in New York, New York.
Died: 11 September 2004 of a heart attack, in New York, New York.
Job description: Lyricist, TV producer. With his partner, the composer John Kander, Fred Ebb was responsible for some of the best-loved musicals of the 20th century, including *Chicago*, *Cabaret* and *Woman of the Year* – not to mention a Frank Sinatra standard called 'New York, New York'. After earning a master's degree in English literature at Columbia University, Ebb started out writing revues, collaborating with Jerry Herman on the Broadway musical *From A to Z* (1960). Meeting Kander in 1962, he and his new partner penned the songs 'My Coloring Book' and 'I Don't Care Much' for Barbra Streisand, but it was to be Liza Minnelli who became the

duo's guiding light. In 1965, Ebb and Kander made their Broadway debut with *Flora, the Red Menace*, a musical that won Minnelli her first Tony award. Although *Flora* ran for only 87 performances, Ebb and Kander were invited to write the score for *Cabaret*, a show which did a little better, winning seven Tonys and a big-screen adaptation, for which they wrote the new songs 'Money, Money' and 'Mein Herr'. The film version notched up eight Oscars, including one for Ms Minnelli and another for Original Song Score. On his own, Ebb produced the TV special *Liza with a Z* for Minnelli and *Ol' Blue Eyes is Back* for Sinatra – the former production winning both an Emmy and a Grammy. With Kander, he wrote three more Broadway musicals, *The Happy Time*, *Zorba* and *Girls*, before they hit pay dirt with *Chicago* (1975), which originally ran for 923 performances and spawned an Oscar-winning movie (2002) for which they contributed the original, Oscar-nominated number 'I Move On'. The duo also penned some songs for the Streisand musical *Funny Lady* (1975) and, for Minnelli, the films *A Matter of Time* and *New York, New York* as well as the Broadway shows *The Act* (1977) and *The Rink* (1984). In between these, they managed to slip in a musical for Lauren Bacall, *Woman of the Year*, and the multi-Tony winning *Kiss of the Spider Woman*. In 1997 they collaborated on their last Broadway musical together, *Steel Pier*, which was nominated for 11 Tonys, and in 2001 they produced their final show, *The Visit*, which starred Chita Rivera and played in Chicago. At the time of Ebb's death, the pair were still working, preparing the groundwork for two new productions, the murder-mystery *Curtains* and a musical adaptation of Thornton Wilder's *The Skin of Our Teeth*.

DANA ELCAR

Born: 10 October 1927 in Ferndale, Michigan.
Died: 6 June 2005 in Ventura, California.
Job description: Character actor. The son of Danish immigrants, Dana Elcar was most famous on television, playing the resourceful Peter Thornton in ABC TV's *MacGyver* (1986-1992). Nonetheless, he was also a familiar face

in films, appearing in *Fail Safe* (1964), *The Boston Strangler*, *Pendulum*, *Soldier Blue*, *A Gunfight*, *The Sting*, *W.C. Fields and Me*, *The Champ*, *Buddy Buddy* and *All Of Me* (1984). Elcar was also the founder of two theatre companies, The L.A. Actor's Theater and the Santa Paula Theater Center.

SUZANNE FLON

Born: 28 January 1918 in Le-Kremlin-Bicêtre, Val-de-Marne, Île-de-France, France.
Died: 15 June 2005 in Paris, of complications from gastroenteritis.
Job description: Star of the French screen and stage.
Starting out in showbusiness as secretary to Edith Piaf, Suzanne Flon went on to carve out a long-lasting career, beginning with *Capitaine Blomet* in 1947. She was voted best actress at the 1961 Venice Film Festival for *Thou Shalt Not Kill* (*Tu ne tueras point*) and won two Cesar awards, for *One Deadly Summer* (*L' Été meurtrier*) (1983) and *The Dragon* (*La Vouivre*) (1989). In 2003 she appeared in Claude Chabrol's *The Flower of Evil* and had just completed a role in Danièle Thompson's *Fauteuils d'orchestre* before her death.

JERRY GOLDSMITH

Born: 10 February 1929 in Los Angeles.
Died: 21 July 2004 after an extended battle with cancer, at his home in Beverly Hills.
Job description: Composer.
One of the biggest names in film music, Jerry Goldsmith won an Oscar for his seminal, chilling score to *The Omen* and was bestowed with a further 17 nominations. He was also a five-time Emmy winner and took home seven Grammy and nine Golden Globe nominations. A writer of prodigious output, Goldsmith scored the themes to such TV series as *Dr Kildare*, *The Man from U.N.C.L.E.*, *The Waltons*, *Barnaby Jones* and *Police Story* as well as such films as *Lonely Are the Brave* (1962), *Freud*, *Seven Days in May*, *Lilies of the Field*, *A Patch of Blue*, *The Blue Max*, *The Sand Pebbles*, *Planet of the Apes* (1968), *Patton*, *Papillon*, *Chinatown*, *The Wind and the Lion*, *The Boys from Brazil*, *Alien*, *Star Trek – The Motion Picture*,

Poltergeist, Under Fire, Gremlins, Hoosiers, Basic Instinct and *L.A. Confidential*. In all, he scored more than 170 movies and has handed the baton on to his son, the composer Joel Goldsmith. But, like so many greats, Jerry Goldsmith had the ignominy of ending his career with a turkey, the ludicrously hyperactive *Looney Tunes: Back in Action* (2003).

FRANK GORSHIN

Born: 5 April 1933 in Pittsburgh, Pennsylvania.
Died: 17 May 2005 in Burbank, California, from complications with lung cancer, emphysema and pneumonia.
Job description: Celebrated impressionist and The Riddler in TV's *Batman*.
While working as a cinema usher, Gorshin picked up a knack for impersonating the stars on screen and at 17 was mimicking the likes of James Cagney and Cary Grant in a nightclub act. After entertaining the troops in Korea, he embarked on a cinema career, making his film debut in *The Proud and Profane* (1956), with William Holden and Deborah Kerr. Other films included *Bells are Ringing* (in which he aped Marlon Brando), *Where the Boys Are* and *Ring of Fire*, before he landed the role of The Riddler in the *Batman* TV series (1966), repeating his performance in the film. Later big-screen appearances included roles in *The Meteor Man*, Terry Gilliam's *12 Monkeys* and the avant-garde *Twilight of the Ice Nymphs* (1997).

JULIUS W. HARRIS

Born: 17 August 1923 in Philadelphia, Pennsylvania.
Died: 17 October 2004 of heart failure, at the Motion Picture and Television Fund home in Los Angeles.
Job description: Character actor.
A powerful, charismatic presence, Harris will be best remembered for his role as the demonic Tee Hee in the 1973 James Bond film *Live and Let Die*. However, he also made quite an impression in *Superfly, Trouble Man, Black Caesar, Hell Up in Harlem, The Taking of Pelham 1-2-3, Let's Do It Again* and *Looking for Mr Goodbar*. In 1976 he played President Idi Amin in *Victory at Entebbe* – to Anthony Hopkins'

Yitzhak Rabin – and on television appeared in *Kojak, The Incredible Hulk, St Elsewhere* and *ER*.

DEBRA HILL

Born: 11 October 1950 in Haddonfield, New Jersey.
Died: 7 March 2005 of cancer in Los Angeles.
Job description: Writer-producer specialising in horror films.
After working as a second unit director, Debra Hill met John Carpenter and together they scripted *Halloween*, which Hill produced for $320,000. The film went on to gross $60m worldwide and cemented the Carpenter-Hill partnership. They also collaborated on *Halloween II, Halloween: Resurrection, Halloween 5* and *Halloween: The Curse of Michael Myers* as well as *The Fog* and *Escape from New York*. Post-*Halloween*, Hill teamed up with producer Lynda Obst to form Hill/Obst Productions, which spawned Terry Gilliam's *The Fisher King*, after which she produced short films for Walt Disney's theme parks. She also produced such pictures as David Cronenberg's *The Dead Zone* and *Attack of the 50 ft. Woman*. She was working on her directorial debut, *Tales Not Told*, when she died.

RUTH HUSSEY

Born: 30 October 1917 in Providence, Rhode Island.
Died: 19 April 2005 of complications from an appendectomy, in Newbury Park, California.
Real name: Ruth Carol O'Rourke.
Job description: Oscar-nominated actress.
A fashion commentator on the radio, Ruth Hussey was picked up as a contract player by MGM. In 1940, she landed the female lead in *Northwest Passage* – opposite Spencer Tracy – but will be best remembered for her role as James Stewart's brassy girlfriend Elizabeth Imbrie in George Cukor's immortal *The Philadelphia Story*. For the latter, she was nominated for an Academy Award as best supporting actress. Her other notable films included *The Uninvited* (1944), *The Great Gatsby* (1949) and *The Facts of Life* (1960), with Bop Hope.

HOWARD KEEL

Born: 13 April 1917 in Gillespie, Illinois.
Died: 7 November 2004 of colon cancer, in Palm Desert, California.
Real name: Harry Clifford Leek.
Job description: Singer, stage performer, movie actor, dancer and TV soap star.
After a brief career as a singing waiter, Howard Keel broke into musicals playing Curly in a touring production of *Oklahoma!* He then landed the part in London, changing his surname from Leek to Keel. While in England, he made his film debut in *The Small Voice* (1948), a tense kidnap drama with Valerie Hobson, and then returned to America to star in the film version of *Annie Get Your Gun* (1950) opposite Betty Hutton. With his powerful baritone and commanding presence, Keel was an overnight success and went on to star in a slew of film musicals, including *Show Boat* (1951, as Gaylord Ravenal), *Calamity Jane* (1953, as Wild Bill Hickok), *Kiss Me Kate* (1953), *Rose Marie* (1954), *Kismet* (1955, as 'The Poet') and his favourite, *Seven Brides for Seven Brothers* (1954, as Adam Pontipee). As the big Hollywood musical was phased out, Keel resorted to non-singing roles in such films as *The Day of the Triffids* (1963), *Waco* (1966) and *The War Wagon* (1967) and continued singing in touring productions of *Man of La Mancha, South Pacific, Annie Get Your Gun* and *Seven Brides*. At the age of 66, he found a second lease of fame when he was cast as Clayton Farlow in TV's *Dallas* (1981-1991), prompting him to remark, 'I couldn't believe it – I was suddenly a

star, known to more people than
ever before.'

GRAHAM KENNEDY

Born: 15 February 1934 in St. Kilda,
Melbourne, Victoria, Australia.
Died: 25 May 2005 in Bowral, New
South Wales, Australia, of pneumonia.
Job description: Ribald TV host and
character actor.

After years of success on radio and
television, Graham Kennedy capitalised
on the New Wave of Australian cinema,
appearing in *Don's Party* (1976), *The Odd
Angry Shot, The Club, The Killing Fields,
Les Patterson Saves the World* and *Travelling
North* (1987).

JANET LEIGH

Born: 6 July 1927 in Merced, California.
Died: 3 October 2004 in Beverly Hills,
California.
Real name: Jeannette Helen Morrison.
Job description: Actress.
Janet Leigh never won an Oscar but she
was a fixture in the Hollywood pantheon,
if only because her third husband was
Tony Curtis and together they produced
Jamie Lee Curtis. Leigh broke into the
movies young (after being discovered by
Norma Shearer) and featured as a chaste
appendage to such stars as Van Johnson,
Walter Pidgeon, Van Heflin, Glenn Ford
and Robert Mitchum before hooking up
with Curtis in 1951. Together they were
the new 'it' couple and appeared in seven
movies together, starting with *Houdini*
(1953). She was good in *The Naked Spur*

(1953), *Pete Kelly's Blues* (1955) and
Orson Welles' *Touch of Evil* (1958) but
will forever be remembered for the classic
shower scene in Alfred Hitchcock's *Psycho*
(1960). The sequence took seven days
to film and Leigh swore that she never
had a shower again, although she was
not averse to signing shower curtains
for charity. Other notable films included
John Frankenheimer's *The Manchurian
Candidate* (1962) and *An American Dream*
(1966), and she teamed up with Jamie
Lee in *The Fog* (1980) and *Halloween
H20: 20 Years Later* (1998). She is
survived by her fourth husband, the
writer-director Robert Brandt.

ROBERT LEWIN

Born: 1920 in New York City.
Died: 28 August 2004 in Santa Monica,
California, of lung cancer.
Job description: Screenwriter.
Oscar-nominated for his very first
screenplay, *The Bold and the Brave* (1956),
Lewin went on to write scripts for TV,
notably for *Rawhide, The Fugitive, I Spy,
Gunsmoke, Mission: Impossible, Hawaii
Five-0, Cannon* and *Kung Fu.* He also
served as supervising producer of *Star
Trek: The Next Generation,* among others.

BRUCE MALMUTH

Born: 4 February 1934 in Brooklyn,
New York.
Died: 29 June 2005 in Los Angeles,
of cancer.
Job description: Film director and
sometime actor.
Making his name as a director of
commercials, Malmuth made his feature
film debut with *Nighthawks* (1981),
starring Sylvester Stallone, and went on
to direct *Where Are the Children?* (1986),
with Jill Clayburgh, and *Hard to Kill*
(1990), starring Steven Seagal. He
also worked on the Emmy-winning
documentary *A Boy's Dream.*

VIRGINIA MAYO

Born: 30 November 1920 in St Louis,
Missouri.
Died: 17 January 2005 of pneumonia
and heart failure, in Thousand Oaks,
California.
Real name: Virginia Clara Jones.

Job description: Dancer and actress
with a bright, peaches-and-cream aspect.
A ballet dancer at the age of 17, Virginia
Jones switched careers to play straight
girl to a performing horse in vaudeville.
The horse was actually two chaps known
as the Mayo brothers, so the dancer-
actress became known as Virginia 'Mayo'.
Four years after that she moved on to
the nightclub circuit and then danced
her way into the movies as a chorus girl,
appearing in the likes of *Follies Girl,
Rosie O'Grady* and *Hello Frisco, Hello* (all
1943). Samuel Goldwyn caught her act
and signed her up, first as decoration
in the Danny Kaye musical *Up in Arms*
and then as the female lead opposite Bob
Hope in *The Princess and the Pirate* (both
1944). She became a favoured pin-up
of the US forces and was reunited with
Danny Kaye in *Wonderman* (1945), *The
Kid from Brooklyn* (1946), *The Secret Life
of Walter Mitty* (1947) and *A Song is
Born* (1948). She tackled serious drama
in the Oscar-winning *The Best Years
of Our Lives* (1946), as the inconstant
wife of Dana Andrews, and went on to
tackle a wide range of genres, including
melodrama (*Flaxy Martin*), Western
(*Colorado Territory* with Joel McCrea),
gangster film (*White Heat* with James
Cagney) – all 1949 – and swashbuckler
(*The Flame and the Arrow*, 1950 – with
Burt Lancaster). She had top billing in
Victor Saville's *The Silver Chalice* (1954),
but it was her younger co-stars, Paul
Newman and Natalie Wood, who got
all the attention. As the studio system
declined, Mayo faded along with it, and,
refusing to appear in the lesser medium

of TV, turned to the stage. Periodically, she still popped up on screen, her last film being the critically reviled thriller *The Man Next Door* (1997). Such was her beauty that the Sultan of Morocco once remarked that she was 'tangible proof for the existence of God.' She was married to the sunny leading man Michael O'Shea from 1947 until his death in 1973.

ISMAIL MERCHANT

Born: 25 December 1936 in Bombay, India.
Died: 25 May 2005 in London following surgery for abdominal ulcers.
Real name: Noormohamed Abdul Rehman.
Job description: The mercantile half of Merchant Ivory.
A man of enormous charm and keen business acumen, Merchant, in collaboration with director James Ivory and the German-born screenwriter Ruth Prawer Jhabvala, set up the Merchant Ivory enterprise in 1961. With Merchant, Ivory and Jhabvala equally involved in the budgeting, casting process and selection of locations, Merchant Ivory produced a steady stream of reasonably priced yet critically revered films that attracted major stars and proved to be a huge boost to the British cinema. Although the director Alan Parker famously dismissed their work as 'the Laura Ashley school of filmmaking,' the company won six Oscars and produced almost 50 films. Said to possess the 'cheek of the devil and the charm of an angel,' Merchant

also directed *In Custody* (1993), *The Proprietor* (1996), *Cotton Mary* (1999) and *The Mystic Masseur* (2001), and at the time of his death was preparing to helm *The Goddess*, a musical fantasy with Tina Turner. He also produced a cookbook, *Ismail Merchant's Indian Cuisine*.

RUSS MEYER

Born: 21 March 1923 in San Leandro, California.
Died: 18 September 2004 in the Hollywood Hills from complications with pneumonia.
Real name: Russell Albion Meyer.
Nickname: King Leer.
Job description: Film director, producer, editor, screenwriter and mammary-monger.
Since he was given a movie camera by his mother, Russ Meyer was passionate about film. He was also passionate about large-breasted women and after a stint as a combat photographer in the Second World War, he worked his way through shooting industrial films to being industrial in the sex market. After working on such Hollywood productions as *Guys and Dolls* and *Giant*, he directed his first 'nudie', *The Immoral Mr Teas*, in 1959, investing $12,000 of his own. The result grossed more than one million in the US alone. Amazingly, it circumvented protestations from the clergy, was passed uncut and changed the face of adult cinema. 'The public was waiting for something new,' Meyer revealed. 'I think they were becoming disenchanted with the so-called European sex films. Once this goddam picture caught on, it was booked all over the country.' Meyer was different from other adult directors in that he cared about his production values, had the skill to implement them (even on a four-day shooting schedule) and exhibited a sly sense of humour. Above all he was totally unpretentious. His subsequent features included *Wild Gals of the Naked West* (1962), *Europe in the Raw* (1963), *Faster Pussycat! Kill! Kill!* (1966), *Cherry, Harry and Raquel* (1969) and *Vixen!* (1968). In 1969 Twentieth Century-Fox signed him up to direct *Beneath the Valley of the Ultravixens* (1970), his biggest success. However, he despised the studio machine and, after the failure of *The Seven Minutes*

(1971), went back to distributing his own independent productions, such as *Supervixens* (1974), *Up!* (1976) and *Beneath the Valley of the Ultravixens* (1979). But by now hardcore had taken hold, a genre he abhorred, and while he talked of making the ultimate sexual epic, his milieu had become outdated and his energy sapped. He was married six times, among his wives the amply endowed actress Edy Williams.

ARTHUR MILLER

Born: 17 October 1915 in New York, New York.
Died: 10 February 2005 from complications with cancer and pneumonia, in Roxbury, Connecticut.
Job description: Playwright and screenwriter.
Considered one of the three greatest American playwrights of the 20th century (alongside Eugene O'Neill and Tennessee Williams), Miller inevitably dabbled in the cinema. Besides marrying the Hollywood icon Marilyn Monroe (a union that lasted five years, 1956-1961), Miller penned the screenplays *The Story of GI Joe* (1945), *The Misfits* (1960, which starred Monroe, Clark Gable and Montgomery Clift), *Everybody Wins* (1990) and *The Crucible* (1996). His plays *All My Sons*, *Death of a Salesman*, *The Crucible*, *A View From the Bridge* and *The Price* were all translated to the screen. Meanwhile, his daughter, Rebecca Miller, is proving to be a talented filmmaker, having directed the raw, funny and perceptive *Personal Velocity* (2002) and *The Ballad of Jack and Rose* (2005).

JOHN MILLS

Born: 22 February 1908 in Felixstowe, Suffolk, England.
Died: 23 April 2005 in Denham, Buckinghamshire.
Real Name: Lewis Ernest Watts Mills.
Job description: Oscar-winning actor.
In the 1940s, John Mills embodied the heart and soul of the ordinary, brave, honest, self-effacing Englishman, generally in uniform. The son of a headmaster, he was drawn to the world of showbusiness by the success of his sister, Annette Mills. Starting as a chorus boy, he came to prominence on stage

when cast by Noël Coward in the latter's musical spectacular *Cavalcade* (1931). A year later Mills made his film debut in *The Midshipmaid*, with Jessie Matthews, and popped up in a string of forgettable quickies before playing a soldier in *Royal Cavalcade* and a sailor in *Forever England* (both 1935). The latter won Mills some good reviews, which in turn led to successful stage parts. He was an RAF pilot in *Cottage to Let* (1941) but it was his turn as a sailor in Noël Coward and David Lean's intensely moving *In Which We Serve* (1942) that really upped his ante. The film also saw the debut of his daughter Juliet, who was just 11 weeks old at the time. The war also brought *Waterloo Road*, Lean's *This Happy Breed* (from the play by Coward) and another unforgettable classic, Anthony Asquith's *The Way to the Stars* (1945), which established Mills as Britain's biggest attraction after James Mason. He played the grown-up Pip in David Lean's legendary *Great Expectations* (1946) and gave one of his best performances in the title role of Ealing's *Scott of the Antarctic* (1948). He was a producer of *The History of Mr Polly* (1949) – also playing Alfred Polly to outstanding reviews – and was then reunited with Lean on *Hobson's Choice* (1953), in which he gave his favourite performance. He was a POW in Guy Hamilton's *The Colditz Story* (1954), a submarine commander in *Above Us the Waves* (1955), a major in *I Was Monty's Double* and a lance corporal in *Dunkirk* (both 1958). He was a captain in another classic, J. Lee Thompson's *Ice Cold in Alex*, was then paired with his 12-year-old daughter Hayley in Thompson's

Tiger Bay (1959), and teamed up with Alec Guinness in the well-received *Tunes of Glory* (1960). In 1965 he made his only picture as a director, *Sky West and Crooked*, which was co-written by his wife and starred his daughter Hayley – but it was a decided flop. His key role in his friend Richard Attenborough's *Oh! What a Lovely War* was a latterday boost, but nothing compared to his transformation into a mute village idiot in Lean's *Ryan's Daughter* (1970), for which he received an Oscar. In his later years his most notable films included Attenborough's *Young Winston* (1972) and *Gandhi* (1982), plus the apocalyptic Raymond Briggs cartoon *When the Wind Blows* (1986), in which he supplied the voice of Jim. Ever the good sport, he was still acting in his mid-nineties and played a cocaine-sniffing partygoer in Stephen Fry's *Bright Young Things* (2003) – even though he was completely blind. He was married initially to the actress Aileen Raymond (mother of Ian Ogilvy) but in 1941 wed the novelist and playwright Mary Hayley Bell. He published his autobiography, *Up in the Clouds, Gentlemen Please*, in 1981.

DAN O'HERLIHY

Born: 1 May 1919 in Wexford, Ireland.
Died: 17 February 2005 in Malibu, California, after a long illness.
Job description: Oscar-nominated actor.
After a considerable stint at the Abbey Theatre in Dublin, O'Herlihy made his film debut in Carol Reed's *Odd Man Out* (1947) and a year later was designing sets and costumes for Orson Welles' *Macbeth*. He also played Macduff in the latter and stayed on in America, notching up credits in *Kidnapped* (starring as Alan Breck), *Imitation of Life*, *The Cabinet of Caligari* (as Caligari), *Fail Safe* and *100 Rifles*. He was nominated for an Oscar for playing Crusoe in Luis Buñuel's *The Adventures of Robinson Crusoe* (1952), played Marshal Michel Ney in *Waterloo* (1970), was Franklin D. Roosevelt in *MacArthur* (1977) and also appeared in *Halloween III: Season of the Witch*, *The Last Starfighter*, *RoboCop* and John Huston's *The Dead* (1987).

JERRY ORBACH

Born: 20 October 1935 in the Bronx,

New York.
Died: 29 December 2004 of prostate cancer in Manhattan.
Job description: Broadway star and movie character actor.
Orbach studied singing with Mazel Schweppe and acting with Lee Strasberg and made his Broadway debut in *The Threepenny Opera* (1957). He originated the role of El Gallo and Narrator in *The Fantasticks* (1960) and in 1969 won the Tony award for *Promises, Promises*. He also starred in *Chicago* and *42nd Street*. On screen, he cut a distinctive, often threatening figure, playing cops or gangsters, his credits including *Cop Hater* (1958), *Mad Dog Coll*, *The Gang That Couldn't Shoot Straight* (co-starring Robert De Niro), *Prince of the City*, *F/X*, *Dirty Dancing*, *Someone to Watch Over Me*, *Crimes and Misdemeanors*, *Last Exit to Brooklyn*, *Beauty and the Beast* (as the voice of Lumiere, the singing candelabra), *Straight Talk* and *Universal Soldier*. In 1992 he played Det. Lennie Briscoe in NBC TV's hugely popular *Law & Order* and stayed with the show for 12 seasons, then resurrected Briscoe in the spin-off, *Trial by Jury*.

DANIEL PETRIE Sr

Born: 26 November 1920 in Glace Blay, Nova Scotia.
Died: 22 August 2004 of cancer, in Los Angeles.
Job description: Director.
Best known to the public as a director, Petrie was deeply involved in the industry and held a number of positions

on the national board of the Directors Guild of America. In return, the DGA nominated him 11 times, bestowing the award on him for the TV productions *Eleanor and Franklin, Eleanor and Franklin: The White House Years* and *The Dollmaker*. Petrie's feature film credits included *A Raisin in the Sun* (1961), *The Neptune Factor, Buster and Billie, Lifeguard, The Betsy, Resurrection, Fort Apache The Bronx, Square Dance* and *Cocoon: The Return*. His son, Donald Petrie, is also a director (*Mystic Pizza, Grumpy Old Men, Miss Congeniality*), while Daniel Petrie Jr is the president of the Writers Guild of America.

OTTO PLASCHKES

Born: 13 September 1929 in Vienna.
Died: 14 February 2005 in London, of a heart attack.
Job description: Producer, active promoter of British cinema in the 1960s and teacher at the National Film School. Arriving in England in 1939 through the kindertransport, Plaschkes grew up in Salisbury and began working as a runner at Ealing Studios. By 1962 he was a production assistant on *Lawrence of Arabia* and went on to produce such films as *Georgy Girl* (1966) and *The Bofors Gun* before becoming an executive producer for the American Film Theater. Under the latter banner he was responsible for *The Homecoming, Galileo, Butley* and *In Celebration*, although his most commercially successful film was the American *Hopscotch* (1980), starring Walter Matthau and Glenda Jackson.

TONY RANDALL

Born: 26 February 1920 in Tulsa, Oklahoma.
Died: 17 May 2004 in his sleep after a long illness, in New York.
Real name: Leonard Rosenberg.
Job description: Actor.
Tony Randall excelled at comedy on the stage, on film, on radio and in the theatre. After majoring in speech and drama at Northwestern University, he made his theatrical debut in 1941 in *A Circle of Chalk*, and was a stand-out in the 1955 Broadway triumph *Inherit the Wind*. He made his film debut in *Oh, Men! Oh, Women!* (1957, with Ginger Rogers and David Niven) and moved on to star in the successful *Will Success Spoil Rock Hunter?*, reprising his stage role. He was then best friend to Doris Day and Rock Hudson in *Pillow Talk* (1959), *Lover Come Back* (1961) and *Send Me No Flowers* (1964), establishing his niche as the fastidious side act. He was very much the star of the TV hit *The Odd Couple* (1970-1975), playing the pernickety Felix Unger to Jack Klugman's slovenly Oscar Madison, and when, in 1975, he finally won the Emmy – after the show had been cancelled – he quipped, 'I'm so happy I won. Now if I only had a job.' He won more praise for the NBC sitcom *Love, Sydney* (1981-83) and played himself in Martin Scorsese's *The King of Comedy* (1983). He was on Broadway in *M. Butterfly* (1989) and then founded the National Actors Theater in New York, a lifelong dream. His other films included *The Mating Game* (1959), *Let's Make Love* (1960) with Marilyn Monroe, *7 Faces of Dr Lao* (1964), *Fluffy* (1965), *The Alphabet Murders* (1965, as Hercule Poirot), *Our Man in Marrakesh* (1966), *Everything You Always Wanted to Know About Sex* (1972), *Fatal Instinct* (1993) and *Down With Love* (2003).

CHRISTOPHER REEVE

Born: 25 September 1952 in New York City.
Died: 10 October 2004 in Bedford, New York, from heart failure related to an infection from a pressure sore.
Job description: Actor, disability campaigner and lobbyist for the legalisation of stem cell research.
A Juilliard-trained stage actor and

daytime TV hunk (he played the callous bigamist Ben Harper for three years on CBS TV's *Love of Life*), Reeve became a household name when he landed the title role in the Salkinds' *Superman* (1978). He brought enormous charm to the task and certainly had the physical attributes, a physicality that restricted his chances in more dramatically challenging parts. He did try, though, and took serious roles in James Ivory's *The Bostonians* (1984) and *The Remains of the Day* (1993), even appearing on the West End stage in Michael Redgrave's adaptation of *The Aspern Papers* in 1984. However, after making a small fortune with *Superman II* (1981), *III* (1983) and *IV: The Quest for Peace* (1987), he floundered in such films as *Somewhere in Time* (1980), *Monsignor* (1982) and *The Aviator* (1985). Then, after starring in the run-of-the-mill *Village of the Damned* and *Above Suspicion* (both 1995), he was thrown from his horse while competing in a three-day event in Virginia and was paralysed from the neck down. At first suicidal, Reeve rallied himself (largely due to the ministrations of his wife, Dana) and was convinced that, by the age of 50, he would walk again. Wheelchair-bound, he toured the US raising awareness of disability issues and even returned to acting, narrating various TV productions and playing the James Stewart part in a remake of *Rear Window* (1998). He never did walk again but made enormous strides in promoting medical research into the condition of paraplegics everywhere.

SERGE REGGIANI

Born: 2 May 1922 in Reggio Nell'Emilia, northern Italy.
Died: 22 July 2004 of a heart attack, in Paris.
Job description: Actor, singer.
A hairdresser, actor and singer, Reggiani worked for the likes of Carné, Ophuls, Melville, Visconti and Sautet in a distinguished career that spanned 60 years. Among his more notable films were Ophuls' *La Ronde* (1950), Jacques Becker's *Casque d'or* (1951), Martin Ritt's *Paris Blues*, Visconti's *The Leopard* and Aki Kaurismaki's *I Hired a Contract Killer* (1991).

MICHAEL RELPH

Born: 16 February 1915 in Broadstone, Dorset, England.
Died: 30 September 2004 in Selsey, West Sussex.
Job description: Film producer, production designer, director and screenwriter.
A major cog in the wheel of Ealing Studios, Relph was the last of a dynasty in the British cinema. The son of the actor George Relph, Michael started out as a stage designer in the West End theatre and as a trainee art director for Gaumont-British. In 1942 he joined Ealing, where he designed the Tommy Trinder-James Mason wartime melodrama *The Bells Go Down* before becoming associate producer in 1946 with *The Captive Heart*. His other producing credits include *Kind Hearts and Coronets*, *The Blue Lamp*, *The Gentle Gunman*, *The Ship That Died of Shame*, *The Smallest Show on Earth*, *The League of Gentlemen*, *Victim*, *Woman of Straw*, *The Assassination Bureau* and *The Man Who Haunted Himself* (1970). With Basil Dearden, he co-directed *I Believe In You* (1952), *The Gentle Gunman*, *The Square Ring* and *The Ship That Died of Shame*, and made his solo directorial debut with Ealing's very last comedy, *Davy* (1957), starring Harry Secombe and George Relph. He also directed *Rockets Galore* (1958 – a sequel to *Whiskey Galore*) and *Desert Mice* (1959). In 1971 he became chairman of the Film Production Association of Great Britain and a year later chairman of the British Film Institute's production board.

After his tenure at the BFI, he returned to producing, developing such movies as *Scum* (1979), *An Unsuitable Job for a Woman* (1982) and *Heavenly Pursuits* (1986).

PAT ROACH

Born: 19 May 1937 in Birmingham, England.
Died: 17 July 2004 of cancer, in Birmingham, England.
Job description: Actor.
While best known for his role as Brian 'Bomber' Busbridge in TV's *Auf Wiedersehen, Pet*, Pat Roach had the distinction of playing a different character in all three Indiana Jones films and working for Stanley Kubrick twice, in *A Clockwork Orange* and *Barry Lyndon*. He also popped up in *Never Say Never Again*, *Willow*, *Conan the Destroyer* and *Robin Hood: Prince of Thieves* (as a Celtic chieftain), his towering 6'4" frame invariably making a solid impression.

EUGENE ROCHE

Born: 22 September 1928 in Boston, Massachusetts.
Died: 28 July 2004 of a heart attack, in Encino, California.
Job description: Character actor.
A plump, amiable character actor, Roche was perhaps better known on television (with recurring roles in *Webster*, *All in the Family*, *Magnum P.I.*, *Soap* and *Perfect Strangers*), although he made an impact in such movies as *Slaughterhouse Five*, *The Late Show* and *Foul Play*. He left behind nine children.

PATSY ROWLANDS

Born: 19 January 1934 in Palmers Green, London.
Died: 22 January 2005 of breast cancer, in Hove, East Sussex.
Job description: Comedy actress and singer.
Although Patsy Rowlands made a number of big-screen appearances, in such major productions as *A Kind of Loving*, *Tom Jones* and *Tess*, she is best remembered for her work in the Carry On films, appearing in nine in all, from *Carry On Again Doctor* in 1969 (as Miss Fosdick) to *Carry On Behind* in 1975 (as

Linda Upmore). She was more often seen on TV (in the likes of *The Dick Emery Show*, *The Les Dawson Show* and as Betty Lewis in *Bless This House*). She was also a regular in London's West End theatre and appeared in the musicals *Into the Woods* (as Jack's mother) and the Sam Mendes production of *Oliver!*

PEGGY RYAN

Born: 28 August 1924 in Long Beach, California.
Died: 30 October 2004 in Las Vegas, from complications following two strokes.
Real name: Margaret O'Rene Ryan.
Job description: Dancing dynamo.
A professional dancer from the age of three (in her parents' vaudeville act), Peggy Ryan will be best remembered for the films in which danced alongside Donald O'Connor, in *When Johnny Comes Marching Home* (1942), *Mister Big* (1943), *This is the Life* and *Chip Off the Old Block* (both 1944). Over two decades later she found new fame on TV as Jenny Sherman, secretary to Jack Lord's Steve McGarett in *Hawaii Five-0* (1969-76).

MARIA SCHELL

Born: 15 January 1926 in Vienna, Austria.
Died: 26 April 2005 of pneumonia, in Kaernten, Austria.
Real name: Margarete Schell.
Job description: Celebrated Swiss star of 1950s German cinema.
Discovered at 16, Maria Schell was

launched into the limelight as the star of the popular *The Angel With the Trumpet* (1948), which two years later was remade in an English version, also starring Schell. In the 1950s she was the toast of Germany and in 1954 won the best actress prize at Cannes for *The Last Bridge*. In Hollywood she played Grushenka in *The Brothers Karamazov* (1958), opposite Yul Brynner, and was a blind Swiss immigrant befriended by Gary Cooper in *The Hanging Tree* (1959). She was also in the British *The Heart of the Matter* (1953), with Trevor Howard, and after retirement in the 1960s emerged to take supporting roles in *The Odessa File* (1974) and *Superman: The Movie* (1978). She was the subject of the documentary *My Sister Maria* (2002), directed by her brother, the actor-filmmaker Maximilian Schell.

SIMONE SIMON

Born: 23 April 1910 in Béthune, Pas-de-Calais, France.
Died: 22 February 2005 in Paris, of natural causes.
Job description: French pin-up and Hollywood import.
Something of a Gallic stunner, Simone made her initial imprint on the catwalk before becoming a star in such local films as *Le Chanteur inconnu* (1931), Jean Renoir's *La Bête humaine* and Max Ophuls' *La Ronde*. In spite of her difficulty with the English language, Darryl F. Zanuck exported her to America where she starred in *Cat People* (1942), *Curse of the Cat People*, *The Devil*

and Daniel Webster and *Johnny Doesn't Live Here Anymore* (co-starring a young Robert Mitchum). In 1975 she made her last film, appearing as a madam in Michel Deville's *La Femme en bleu*.

LANE SMITH

Born: 29 April 1936 in Memphis, Tennessee.
Died: 13 June 2005 from Lou Gehrig's disease, in Northridge, California.
Job description: Character actor.
Adept at playing slimy figures of authority, Smith notched up appearances in *Rooster Cogburn* (1975), *Network*, *Between the Lines*, *Blue Collar*, *Over the Edge*, *Honeysuckle Rose*, *Resurrection*, *Prince of the City*, *Frances*, *Places in the Heart*, *Air America*, *My Cousin Vinny*, *The Mighty Ducks*, *The Distinguished Gentleman* and *The Legend of Bagger Vance*. He was best known, however, for his Golden Globe-nominated impersonation of Richard Nixon in the 1989 docudrama *The Final Days*.

CARRIE SNODGRESS

Born: 27 October 1946, in Barrington, Illinois.
Died: 1 April 2004 in Los Angeles, of heart and liver failure.
Job description: Oscar-nominated actress and common-law wife of Neil Young.
After receiving a master's degree from Chicago's Goodman Theater School, Snodgress (who was often mis-credited as

Snodgrass) found roles in such TV series as *The Virginian*, *The Outsider* and *Marcus Welby, M.D.* However, after an uncredited appearance in *Easy Rider* (1969), she landed the lead in Frank Perry's *Diary of a Mad Housewife* (1970) and was nominated for an Academy Award. She played Tina Balser, the bullied missus of the title, who takes a lover (Frank Langella) only to discover that he is no better than her husband. She also starred opposite James Caan in *Rabbit Run* and then abandoned acting to focus on her relationship with Neil Young and to bring up their son, Zeke, who suffered from cerebral palsy. Later roles included *A Night in Heaven* (1983), *Pale Rider*, opposite Clint Eastwood, *Blueberry Hill*, *The Ballad of Little Jo*, *8 Seconds*, *Blue Sky*, *White Man's Burden*, *Wild Things* and *Bartleby*. Her career may have turned out very differently had she landed the role of Adrian Balboa in *Rocky*, for which she was originally earmarked.

JOHN VERNON

Born: 24 February 1932 in Zehner, Saskatchewan, Canada.
Died: 8 February 2005 in Van Nuys, California, after recently suffering a heart attack.
Real name: Adolphus Raymondus Vernon Agopsowicz.
Job description: Character actor.
With his resounding voice, icy eyes and lived-in face, Vernon was destined to be typecast as men you wouldn't trust with your dog. Among his considerable film credits, his appearances in the following stand out: *1984* (1956, as the voice of Big Brother), *Point Blank*, *Topaz*, *Dirty Harry*, *The Outlaw Josey Wales*, *National Lampoon's Animal House* (as Dean Wormer) and *Airplane II: The Sequel*. His last film was *Warrior Angels* (2002).

JACQUES VILLERET

Born: 6 February 1951 in Loches, Indre-et-Loire, France.
Died: 28 January 2005 of an internal haemorrhage, in Evreux, Eure, France.
Job description: Tubby stage and film actor particularly adept at playing buffoons.
After attending the drama conservatory in Paris (in the same class as Nathalie

Baye, Richard Berry and André Dussollier), Jacques Villeret forged a career as a stand-up comic and character actor in films, winning the Cesar award for Best Supporting Actor in Claude Lelouch's *Robert et Robert* (1978). Then in 1993 he landed the central role of François Pignon in Francis Veber's phenomenally successful farce *Le Dîner de cons* (aka *The Dinner Game*), which he played for 900 performances. The subsequent film (1998) was an international success, leading to such notable productions as *Mookie*, *The Children of the Marshland*, *Les Acteurs*, *Strange Gardens*, *Malabar Princess* and *Viper in the Fist*. Over all, Villeret appeared in more than 60 movies.

KAY WALSH

Born: 27 August 1911 in London, England.
Died: 16 April 2005 in London.
Job description: Occasional screenwriter and Cockney favourite of the 1930s and 1940s.
A former dancer and chorus girl, Kay Walsh cornered the market in Cockneys, whether playing the black sheep in David Lean's immortal classic *This Happy Breed* (1944), the tragic, cheerful Nancy in Lean's *Oliver Twist* (1948) or the blackmailer in Hitchcock's *Stage Fright* (1949). She met Lean in 1936, when he was still an editor, and married him in November 1940. Together, they scripted *Great Expectations* (1946) – in collaboration with Ronald Neame, Anthony Havelock-Allan and Cecil

McGivern – but their marriage was a turbulent affair and they divorced in 1949. She made her screen debut in *Get Your Man* (1934) – in the lead – and went on to appear opposite some of Britain's greatest leading men. She starred opposite George Formby in *Keep Fit* (1937) and *I See Ice* (1938), appeared with Alec Guinness in *Oliver Twist*, *Last Holiday* (1950), *The Horse's Mouth* (1958), *Tunes of Glory* (1960) and *Scrooge* (1970), and was a regular co-star of John Mills, who died just seven days after her. Her last film was Delbert Mann's *Night Crossing* (1981) – in which she played the mother of Jane Alexander – and she retired shortly afterwards. She had also contributed dialogue to Anthony Asquith and Leslie Howard's *Pygmalion* (1938) and wrote some of her own material for *Oliver Twist*, but in both instances she remained uncredited. 'I loved the cinema but had no dreams to be an actress,' she said. 'I didn't think I would be good enough. I really wanted to be a writer.'

RUTH WARWICK

Born: 29 June 1915 in St Joseph, Missouri.
Died: 15 January 2005 in New York, of complications with pneumonia.
Job description: Film and TV actress.
Ruth Warwick, like the director and co-star of her first film, *Citizen Kane* (1941), started at the top and worked her way down. However, in 1970 she earned herself an enduring place in the heart of the American public with her role as the socially aware Phoebe Tyler in the long-running soap *All My Children* (1970-2005). After a brief career as a singer on radio, she made her film debut as Emily Norton Kane, the first wife of *Citizen Kane*. Other films included *Journey Into Fear* (1942), also with Orson Welles (as Joseph Cotten's wife), *The Corsican Brothers*, *China Sky*, *Song of the South* (as Bobby Driscoll's mother), *Driftwood* and *Let's Dance* (1950). On Broadway, she appeared with Debbie Reynolds in a revival of *Irene* (1973) and starred opposite Jackie Gleason in *Take Me Along*. She published her autobiography, *The Confessions of Phoebe Tyler*, in 1980 and in May 2004 received a Lifetime Achievement Emmy.

ONNA WHITE

Born: 24 March 1922 in Inverness, Nova Scotia, Canada.
Died: 8 April 2005 in West Hollywood, Los Angeles, of natural causes.
Job description: Oscar-winning choreographer.
Starting out as a dancer, White assisted Michael Kidd on the choreography of *Guys and Dolls*, then established herself as a solo choreographer with *Carmen Jones*. Later, she orchestrated both the Broadway and film versions of *The Music Man*, *Mame* and *1776* and in 1969 was given a special Oscar for her work on *Oliver!* Other film credits include *Bye Bye Birdie*, *The Great Waltz* and *Pete's Dragon*.

PAUL WINFIELD

Born: 22 May 1940 in Los Angeles.
Died: 7 March 2004 in Los Angeles, of a heart attack.
Job Description: Emmy-winning and Oscar-nominated actor.
Although Paul Winfield found his best parts on the stage and the small screen, he notched up a formidable amount of cinematic credits. After an unbilled performance as a garbage collector in *Who's Minding the Mint?* (1967), he landed a regular role on the NBC sitcom *Julia* (1968-70), playing the boyfriend of Diahann Carroll's eponymous Julia Baker. Then in 1972 he was cast as the noble sharecropper Nathan Lee Morgan in Martin Ritt's *Sounder* and was nominated for an Oscar as best actor. He was also Emmy-nominated for playing Martin Luther King in the 1978 miniseries *King*

and for *Roots: The Next Generation* (1979). He finally won TV's highest honour in 1992 for playing Judge Harold Nance in *Picket Fences*. His most notable big-screen credits included *Gordon's War* (1973, as Gordon Hudson), *Conrack*, *The Greatest*, *Star Trek II: The Wrath of Khan*, *White Dog*, *The Terminator*, *Presumed Innocent*, *Cliffhanger* and *Mars Attacks!* Ironically, his last role was in a TV remake of *Sounder* (2003).

Ladd and Edward G. Robinson. Her last acting role was in the 1980 TV movie *Gideon's Trumpet*, with Henry Fonda. She also wrote a play and a discerning memoir, *On the Other Hand*, and received a standing ovation at the 1998 Oscars. In her posthumous honour, the lights of the Empire State Building were dimmed for a quarter of an hour.

more or less remained typecast as the co-operative girl-next-door. She was notable in William Wyler's *The Best Years of Our Lives* (1946) and then turned a corner in Raoul Walsh's tough, suspenseful Western *Pursued* (1947), as the wife of a tormented Robert Mitchum. In later years she emerged as a fine character actress, but failed to find vehicles worthy of her ability. However, she had good roles in *Enchantment* (with David Niven), *The Men* (with Marlon Brando) and was memorable as an elderly ballroom dancer in James Ivory's *Roseland* (1977). Her last film was Francis Ford Coppola's *The Rainmaker*, in which she had a nice little role as Matt Damon's landlady. She married the playwright Robert Anderson twice.

FAY WRAY

Born: 15 September 1907 on a farm in Alberta, Canada.
Died: 8 August 2004 at her apartment in Manhattan.
Real name: Vina F. Wray.
Job description: Actress.
A beauty to the ultimate beast, Fay Wray will forever be associated with her role as Ann Darrow in the 1933 *King Kong*. Before that, she was a staple in Hal Roach comedies and Universal Westerns until whisked to stardom by Erich von Stroheim for *The Wedding March* (1928). Five years later she was paid $10,000 to scream her heart out in the grip of a six foot long arm. 'I'd stand on the floor,' she recalled, 'and they would bring this thing down and cinch it round my waist, then pull me up in the air. Every time I moved, one of his fingers would loosen, so it would look like I was trying to get away. Actually, I was trying not to slip through his hand.' The screaming continued – notably in *Mystery of the Wax Museum* (1933) – and endured right up to *Hell on Frisco Bay* (1955), with Alan

TERESA WRIGHT

Born: 27 October 1918 in Manhattan, New York.
Died: 6 March 2005 in New Haven, Connecticut, of a heart attack.
Real name: Muriel Teresa Wright.
Job description: Oscar-winning actress.
Blessed with a lovely complexion of innocence, Teresa Wright was a natural for the cinema screen. After a stint in the theatre, she was signed up by Sam Goldwyn when he caught her on Broadway in a performance of *Life with Father*. She then landed an Oscar nomination for her very first film, *The Little Foxes* (1941), playing Bette Davis' daughter and prompting *Photoplay* to gush, 'the public has snapped at sweet, unspoiled Teresa like a shipwrecked sailor at a T-bone steak.' The following year she was Oscar-nominated for her second and third performances, in *Mrs Miniver* and *The Pride of the Yankees*, winning the statuette for the former, as Greer Garson's winsome daughter-in-law. She landed the lead – and top billing – in Hitchcock's *Shadow of a Doubt* (1943), in which she was besotted with her schizophrenic uncle (Joseph Cotten), and

Index